D1131532

SMALL GROUP
RESEARCH

Joseph E. McGrath
University of Illinois

Irwin Altman
Naval Medical Research Institute
Bethesda, Maryland

SMALL GROUP

RESEARCH

A Synthesis and Critique of the Field

HOLT, RINEHART AND WINSTON, INC.

New York • Chicago • San Francisco • Toronto • London

Preface

This is a work about small group research, but it is not a report of a small group experiment or a small group field study in the usual sense. It does not present new empirical data to be added to the extraordinary fund of knowledge now being accumulated in the small group field. On the contrary, the research program that led to this volume started with the assumption that we already had accumulated an enormous pool of facts about small group behavior and that the time had come to organize this knowledge so that we could see what we did know and what we did not know about small groups. Thus, this volume summarizes an attempt to build a classification system for organizing and synthesizing small group research information, describes results (in the form of a compilation of reference materials) of application of that classification system to small group studies, and presents some insights and impressions gained about small group research, small group researchers, and the small group research "culture."

The research program began in 1957 and was supported by the Behavioral Sciences Division of the Air Force Office of Scientific Research. During the first year of the program, a pilot study was conducted to build a classification system for the categorization of a limited area of small group research. Following this preliminary work, a broader classification system was developed to evaluate the research information contained in small group studies. Next, the system was applied to a sample of over 250 small group studies, which generated a pool of approximately 12,000 empirical relationships. During the final phase of the program analyses were conducted to evaluate the usefulness of the classification system as a device for synthesis of research information and the substantial body of research information that had been accumulated was compiled in several alternative forms. One major purpose of this book is to make available these compilations of research information to members of the small group research community and to others who have an interest in the field. The reference materials appear as Part III of the book.

As the program progressed it became apparent that the small group field is more than a mere compilation of research information; it has a social psychology of its own. We felt we were gaining some access to this culture because of the breadth of the work and the resulting opportunities for contact with researchers. The experience led to some subjective impressions about the field—its findings, its methodology, its *modus operandi*—that the authors felt should be conveyed to others for their consideration. Thus, a second purpose of the book is to present the series of perspectives about *substantive, methodological,* and *institutional* characteristics of the field that is contained in Part II, Chapters 5, 6, 7, and 8. These perspectives go beyond the literal facts of the reference materials of the book. They are interpretations and extrapolations, both from the material in the studies reviewed and from the authors' own experience as members of the small group research community. Although such impressions are personal views, they are impressions that may stimulate others to view the field and their own work from a slightly different perspective.

It also became apparent that this program was dealing with a very difficult and philosophically complex problem—the classification of scientific knowledge and scientific information. At the time the program began, the scientific community was far less sensitized to the need for information-processing sciences than it is today. While the authors' work was in progress, however, the classification and synthesis of information in science came to be seen as a critical problem in many fields, especially in the natural sciences—and, to a lesser extent, in the social sciences. In this sense the authors joined others in becoming, to use E. G. Boring's phrase, the "agents of history." In retrospect, our approach to the problem of classification of research information in the small group field may represent a clumsy attempt to do the job. In the course of this endeavor, however, a number of general problems inherent in classification of knowledge became apparent. Necessarily, solutions or techniques for handling those problems were adopted. Others may profit from these choices through adoption or avoidance. Therefore, a third purpose of this book is to present the research program as a case history in the classification and synthesis of scientific knowledge—an area that will assume more and more importance in the coming years. The description of the classification system, its development, and its results is presented in Part I of the book.

Thus, the book deals with three aims in reverse order. Part I of the book is the case history of the research program. Part II is a presentation of some perspectives on the small group field. It contains a discussion of substantive generalizations that seem to be of importance in the body of the material compiled, a discussion of methodological problems and possibilities, and a discussion of the sociocultural setting of the small group research field, which has an impact on how research is done and what ensues from it. Part III contains compilations of reference materials generated in the program: an extensive presentation of specific research relationships tested in the sample of approximately 250 studies that were reviewed, a set of systematic annotations of those studies, and a broadly comprehensive bibliography of research in the small group field up to 1962.

If the research contribution of this program even remotely approaches the accumulated debts to colleagues during the research program, then the work will have been successful. The largest debt is to Dr. Charles E. Hutchinson, to whom this book is dedicated. Dr. Hutchinson is a courageous and patient man, as well as a scientist with a great deal of wisdom. He is courageous, among other reasons, because he sponsored two researchers who possessed a total of four post-Ph.D. years of experience between them at the start and who had the wild idea of integrating a vast body of research information. We hope that we have succeeded to an extent worthy of his courage. He is a patient man because he accepted the blind alleys we entered, helped redirect us, and continually provided encouragement at times when our own expansive hopes had faltered. In a phrase, Charles E. Hutchinson was a good mentor.

This program has capitalized on the work of many scientists—the most apparent being the work of Clyde Coombs on the nature of data. The comments and suggestions of many colleagues, particularly those who attended the Air Force Office of Scientific Research conferences at the University of New Mexico in 1957 and 1958, are of special note. In addition, the authors owe a great deal to the small group of conferees who met after the pilot phase of the program in 1957, commented on the work, and provided guidance for subsequent stages of the research: Dr. Edgar Borgatta, Dr. Jerry Kidd, Dr. Theodore Newcomb, Thornton B. Roby, and Dr. John Thibaut. We also wish to thank Dr. Barry Indik and Dr. Philip Runkle for their careful and critical reviews of this manuscript.

The authors had a varied research staff through the years. Each member of the group brought a freshness to the program that the authors hope is reflected in the product. Special thanks go to the coders and research assistants, Janet Griner, Sally Messick, Catherine Pendleton, and especially Anita Terauds. These women ably managed a split allegiance to their families and to the research program. As research assistants they faithfully and diligently pored through the many studies of the review sample. Mrs. Anita Terauds deserves a special thanks for her role in the preparation of the bibliography, in the annotation of studies, and in the preparation of the catalogue of relationships. Her loyalty over the past several years would be difficult to match.

The program began under the auspices of Psychological Research Associates, Inc., of Arlington, Virginia. Most of the research in the program was conducted during the authors' stay at Human Sciences Research, Inc., also at Arlington, from 1957 to 1960. To our colleagues at HSR, the authors owe thanks for stimulation and encouragement.

As is the case with most authors, our wives, Gloria and Marion, played a very important role in the research program. Their management of their husbands' alternate periods of mania and depression was admirable. Their tolerance of continued shoptalk about the work in the most inappropriate situations and their assistance in the hard and tedious tasks of proofreading, typing, and preparation of the final manuscript are instances of extraordinary devotion.

Finally, to all those unsung heroes—secretaries, librarians, printers, and others, of whom there were too many to mention by name—the authors offer their thanks.

As one final acknowledgment the authors give credit to themselves, not so much for the product itself, but for their ability to complete this manuscript while separated by a distance of some 800 miles during the past three years.

<table>
<tr><td>Urbana, Illinois</td><td>J. E. M.</td></tr>
<tr><td>Annandale, Virginia</td><td>I. A.</td></tr>
</table>

January 1966

Contents

PART 1 ·

Classification of Small Group Research Information: A Case Study

Introduction

HISTORICAL PERSPECTIVE

The history of small group research parallels that of social psychology and certain areas of sociology. Although roots can be traced to Greek philosophers, to thinkers of the Renaissance, and to Western European scholars of the sixteenth, seventeenth, and early eighteenth centuries, modern social psychology and its offspring, small group research, may be said to have begun in the waning years of the nineteenth century. These were years when men such as Tarde and LeBon in France were concerned with the "pathological" group—the mob or crowd. The German sociologist Simmel and Cooley, Mead, and Ross in America were investigating the nature of social interaction processes, the two-person dyad as the basic social unit, the family as a primary group, and similar problems. These and later periods have been described in detail by Allport (1954).

The formative years of social psychology, and indirectly of small group research, were turbulent. This was a time when scholars stood at extreme poles with respect to fundamentals such as the origin of man's social behavior, with environmentalist-behaviorists (e.g., Watson) at one extreme and the innate-inborn adherents (e.g., McDougall) at the other. The concern of the times was a search for basic assumptions and primitive terms, much as the concern of the book of Genesis, in its early pages, is a search for answers to questions about man's origins and his basic nature.

The turmoil ended in the early 1920's, when scholars withdrew from the problems and questions that they had posed earlier, with the objective-behaviorist-environmentalist school scoring more victories than the opposition. The social psychologist and small group researcher retreated to the laboratory no longer swept up in grand philosophical issues, but concerned rather with developing rigorous methodology and with studying narrow, delimited aspects of man's social behavior. It was in this period, typified by the work of F. H. Allport on social facilitation, that the methodological seeds of the years to come were sewn. A new norm was established in the decade of the 1920's, not with regard to substance, but with regard to methodology.

The 1930's saw the small group researcher, swept along by the field as a whole, emerging out of the laboratory and beginning to deal with broader problems, problems perhaps stimulated by the great depression. As the agents of history, researchers began to study mass movements, lynchings, prejudice,

3

rumor flow, and a host of phenomena relevant to the extra laboratory secular world. The well-known Hawthorne Western Electric Studies (Roethlisberger & Dickson, 1939) demonstrated the importance of social-psychological dynamics operating in small groups in the real world.

Perhaps most important, the development of the group dynamics movement, under the leadership of Kurt Lewin, signified the tenor of the years to come—for it was not only the germination of theory in small group research that made the work of Lewin significant but also the tackling of problems (frustration of goal achievement, leadership styles, attitude change, and so on) in an experimental fashion. The marriage of theoretically based ideas, real-world problems, and experimental methodology had not occurred before in small group research.

With the coming of World War II, the 1940's became the muscle-flexing years for social psychology and small group research. Research expanded on two fronts: methodological development and the accumulation of empirical knowledge in several areas, the most noteworthy perhaps being leadership. There was little contribution to theory in these years, possibly because such efforts during times of crisis are considered luxuries. But by this time social-psychological research and small group research had become legitimized; it was now deemed a respectable area of study, and students flocked to its centers and took their vows.

The results in the 1950's and into the 1960's have been interesting. There has been a research boom in the United States which has not been dampened in the slightest by occasional reversals in the nation's economy. The research production curve has kept mounting, at an enormous rate. Theory was minimal throughout most of the 1950's and has continued to be so to the present. But there have been rumblings of the future with respect to theory. Festinger's work on uniformity pressures in small groups (Festinger, 1950; Festinger, Schachter, & Back 1950), Thibaut and Kelley's (1959) cost-reward theory of group phenomena, and the theoretical analyses of leadership compiled by Petrullo and Bass (1961) represent some of the major attempts to contribute to theory.

Because of the unabated race toward more empirical knowledge and the comparative absence of integrating theory, the question of what we should try to find out about small group phenomena began to be asked in the middle 1950's by many people. Some developed answers reflected in reviews of the literature of the field. Perhaps the first was a *Psychological Bulletin* article by Mary Roseborough (1953) which summarized experimental studies of small group behavior. This article was followed by Kelley and Thibaut (1954) and by Riecken and Homans (1954) in the *Handbook of Social Psychology*, a two-volume work that in itself was a symptom of the need for organization of knowledge in social psychology. At about the same time, Cartwright and Zander (1953) and Hare, Borgatta, and Bales (1954) edited volumes that were collections of research publications from other sources. These collections were organized to reflect the dominant approaches, methodology, and findings in the field as a whole and in delimited sections. The Hare, Borgatta, and Bales volume included a fairly comprehensive bibliography with short abstracts of the bibliographic entries.

These works were primarily reference sources, however. They were not intended to induce theory, or to evaluate existing theory; they served as a summarization. But while the research continued as profusely and diffusely as ever, the tone of the integrators and literature reviewers changed somewhat. Thibaut and Kelley (1959) offered a theoretical analysis of small group phenomena which not only involved the integration of a large amount of prior work, but also proposed areas of work which derived from this theory. Except in the work of Lewin and Festinger, such an approach had been infrequent. From another tack, Golembiewski (1962) sought to tie small group research together and produced a philosophical-methodological critique of the field along with an integration of many research findings. From a third direction both Argyle (1957) and Hare (1962) published books which reviewed a vast amount of the literature of the field, organized around selected variables that have been studied frequently.

THE RESEARCH PROGRAM

It was in this cultural milieu that the present research program was begun. We too felt the need for a summing up. We hoped to do more than description and cataloging. We wanted an approach that would allow identification of gaps in knowledge, have predictive value regarding future research, contribute toward inductive theory, and absorb new concepts and new findings as they appeared. Thus, the authors found themselves concerned equally with two problems: (1) the problem of developing a method and philosophy for classifying scientific knowledge, on the one hand; and (2) the problem of organizing the substantive findings of the small group field, on the other. This dual concern is reflected in the organization of this volume, in which Part I focuses on the classification system—its rationale, application, and evaluation—and Parts II and III focus on the small group field as a whole. Thus, the authors see this work not only as an investigation within the stream of concern about integration of small group knowledge, but also as a pioneering effort within a much smaller stream of concern for the problem of how to organize scientific knowledge.

To be more specific, the authors see their work and this volume as having three purposes. The first is to summarize the state of knowledge in the small group field by providing a set of reference materials based on review of a sample of 250 small group research studies. This intent is similar to that of prior efforts, but here the material is based largely on a broad sample of empirical studies and is organized in a systematic, encyclopedic fashion. The second purpose is to provide a broader perspective on the field via an integration and interpretation of many empirical findings. This perspective will include substantive generalizations and gaps in knowledge, methodological aspects of the field, and some comments on the social psychology of small group research. The third aim is to present a case study in the classification of social science knowledge. The problem of organization of knowledge will be with us in the future, whether we are small group researchers or otherwise, and we need to begin developing effective methods for organizing such knowledge. The authors believe that their work contributes to this problem area, if not by way of positive direction, then at least by way of pointing to errors to be avoided.

PLAN OF THE BOOK

The various sections to follow are arranged in a way to make them most usable to the reader; they do not reflect the chronological steps involved in the research program.

Part I contains a description, discussion, and evaluation of the classification system used to describe and integrate small group research information. This part provides most of the material applying to the third purpose of the volume, that of presenting a case study of a systematic attempt to integrate a field of knowledge. In these pages, the authors discuss the general problem of their research program—the problem of the rapidly accumulating fund of scientific knowledge and attempts at organizing such knowledge. In addition, the authors' classification system is described in detail. The authors' intent was to develop a formal, operationally based method for description of variables of the small group field. More specifically, the authors argued that a more useful classification of existing knowledge in the small group field could be achieved through the development of a set of categories or a metalanguage that would reflect the operational or formal nature of small group variables and thereby avoid many pitfalls of a substantive, "content-type" classification. The approach can best be described as one that defines variables in terms of operational definitions or that describes variables in terms of a series of properties of data. The approach discussed in Part I is novel in several other respects. For one, it is a logically exhaustive system; i.e., it is not restricted to past variables studied in the small group field, but rather is capable of including in the classification space a very large number of variables—some of which may not have been studied as yet. In this sense, the system is analogous to the type developed by Mendeleev in chemistry, where the classification hypothesized chemical elements that, at the time of development of the system, had not as yet been empirically discovered.

Part I also describes the application of the system to a sample of nearly 250 studies selected from a bibliography of over 2,000 entries. Here an attempt was made to present information relevant to the usefulness of the system and to its validity as a classificatory device. The classification system was planned to contain a built-in, theoretically based idea for testing its usefulness—the principle of operational concordance. To preview, the principle of operational concordance states that the more similar two variables are in terms of operational definition (which is the basis of variable definition in the present classification approach), the greater the probability is that the two variables will be statistically related at any given significance level. The extent to which this basic principle was upheld served as one form of check on the usefulness of the authors' system, both as a descriptive device and as a predictive device. As Part I describes, the validity of the classification system was generally upheld. However, the value of the classification system as a descriptive device was only partly successful. It became apparent that the authors had been less than totally successful in several areas; e.g., the authors had not identified *all* relevant properties of data, and needed to fall back on substantive, content descriptions of variables in order to make the body of information gathered readily communicable.

Part I ends with a modification of the original classification system and with a discussion of its potentialities for further application to the small group field and the potentialities of the approach for the integration of knowledge in other fields.

Part II is entitled "Perspectives on the Small Group Field." The plan for Part II changed quite often as the research program progressed. Originally, it was to be called "The Integration of Small Group Research" and was to include only a description of the empirically established facts and gaps of the field. Although this material is still included, Part II goes beyond the question of factual citation. As we came to know the small group field through an intensive analysis of its studies and through repeated discussions and conferences with its students, we came to feel that we had gained insights that were not carried in statements of empirical facts alone. We felt that we had learned some things about the social psychology of small group research and about the cultural milieu in which small group researchers functioned, and that these insights might prove useful to students, users, and patrons of the field. Thus, Part II was expanded.

Chapter 5 presents an actuarial description of the field to deal with the questions "Who are small group researchers, and where and how do they do their research?" Chapter 6 is a discussion of some substantive generalizations about the field which derive, to a large extent, from the data of the review sample of 250 studies. Following this discussion, in Chapter 7 the methodology of the small group field is considered from the point of view of major problems and prospects for their resolution. Finally, Chapter 8, is a discussion of the culture of small group research from the point of view of its recent history and its relation to the larger societies of which it is a part (e.g., the university society and that of the government). This chapter also considers the implications of several changing roles of the small group researcher as an artist, as an actor in social affairs, and as a businessman.

Part III of the book contains reference materials. It satisfies the first of the three aims of the program listed earlier—namely that of making available to the small group research community an organized compilation of reference materials. This portion of the book was generated throughout the program, from initial stages through final days. Embodying the hard facts that were culled from the 250 studies of the review sample, the material should be extremely useful to the small group reseacher as he reviews the literature, identifies problems worthy of investigation, and designs his studies. Part III is organized into three sections. (1) The first is a catalogue of empirical relationships organized around 31 major variables of the small group field. The 31 variables are described in terms of their operational definitions, the studies in which they appear, the frequency with which they appear, and the extent and nature of their association with other variables in the review sample. (2) The second section contains annotations of the 250 studies of the review sample. The same information is presented in the preceding section, but now it is organized around individual studies. (3) The third section is a bibliography of approximately 3,000 items of research in the small group field. It contains a general bibliography of roughly 2,100 studies, from which the 250 reviewed in the study were sampled, plus a supplementary list of studies through the latter part of 1962.

This book should have several potential uses and appeals for different readers. Its most obvious use, as a straight reference source, is most visible in Part III, containing the reference materials. According to his particular interest, the reader can enter this part through individual variables, through individual studies, or through bibliographic entries. For those who are relatively new to the field or who are interested in a more general analysis and evaluation of the small group field, Part II, "Perspectives on the Small Group Field," is perhaps the most useful point of entry. In this section, the reader can obtain some broad-brush treatments of the small group field. Having familiarized himself with the field at a fairly general level, he can then make use of the more detailed reference material of Part III as a basis for further analysis of individual areas. For those who wish to obtain a fuller understanding of the logic of organization of the reference material, Part I, which describes the classification system, is critical. Part I can be viewed as a case history of an attempt to take complex behavioral-science knowledge, translate it into a metalanguage, and reproduce the results in an integrated, systematized form. Thus the authors see Part I as useful to those small group researchers, and to psychologists in general, who are interested in the problem of integration of scientific knowledge.

1 The Problem and Its Background

"Research on small groups has gotten out of hand! The rate of production of small group research studies has increased tremendously in recent decades. At the same time, the rate at which empirical results have been adequately digested and integrated into theoretical formulations has not kept pace. If we continue to generate studies at even the present rate, without a major 'leap forward' in terms of integrative theory, we shall drown in our own data."

Thus did the authors believe in 1957, when the research program on which this book is based was begun. And for good reason! In the two preceding decades, hundreds upon hundreds of small group research studies had been conducted and reported, and the rate of their production was increasing rapidly. At the same time, there had been a very limited effort to develop broad theory and/or to integrate findings from various studies into a systematic, detailed body of knowledge. Instead, there had transpired a mass production of small-scale, more-or-less unrelated experiments with small groups of varying types (most often, *ad hoc* laboratory groups), resulting not in a systematic body of knowledge but in an accumulation of unrelated bits of evidence.

What was seriously needed, the authors reasoned, was a major effort toward a systematic integration of the many existing bits of evidence gleaned from all this small group research, in order to clarify two basic questions: (1) "What is *already known* (at a reasonable level of confidence) about small group behavior?" and (2) "What questions still need to be researched?" If such an effort could lead to an effective integration of existing knowledge, the result could provide the basis for the induction of empirical generalizations from existing evidence, and for subsequent development and testing of deductive theory.

RELATED EFFORTS AT SMALL GROUP INTEGRATION

To be sure, at the time the research program began there had been several recent attempts to compile small group research findings. A number of additional compilations or summaries of the field have subsequently appeared. Some of these were noted in the discussion of history in the Introduction. They have tended to be of several types:

1. Collections of readings, which have contained key studies in each of a number of problem areas (Hare et al., 1954; Cartwright & Zander, 1960)

2. Bibliographic materials, often with extensive classifications (Raven, 1959 a and b; Hare et al., 1954)

3. Summaries of notable findings organized around more-or-less arbitrarily selected substantive concepts with no attempt at exhaustiveness even within the selected topical areas (Argyle, 1957; Hare, 1962; Roseborough, 1953; Kelley & Thibaut, 1954; Riecken & Homans, 1954; and the integrative chapters of Cartwright & Zander, 1960)

4. Development of substantive theory and summarizations of research related to the concepts of that theory (Thibaut & Kelley, 1959)

Although each of these approaches has made a valuable contribution to the integration of knowledge within the small group field, none has seemed wholly adequate in itself. One difficulty has been that these approaches for the most part have maintained the verbal-conceptual distinctions and terms used by each investigator and thus have tended to perpetuate rather than reduce the already notable semantic chaos of the field. Another problem has been that although the approaches have usually developed a set of substantive categories in terms of which existing knowledge has been organized, these have tended to be lists of unrelated, nominal categories rather than formal classification systems whose categories are mutually exclusive, collectively exhaustive, and conceptually related to one another. Thus, it has not always been possible to relate results of one topical area to those of another. A third problem has been that these approaches have tended to be noncomprehensive in two senses: (1) they have seldom dealt with *negative* as well as positive results of research—i.e., they usually have not compiled evidence about statistically nonsignificant relationships; and (2) the classifications used have seldom been capable of subsuming *all* variables that have been (or *might* be) studied within the problem area of concern. Thus, although useful, the classifications have not met the need for a complete systematization of existing evidence in a common and generic language applicable to future findings as well as to those of the past.

The propositional inventory approach, as exemplified by March and Simon (1958) in the field of organization research, seems to the authors to offer a more systematic method of integrating a body of scientific knowledge. Employed by Sullivan (1963) in relation to political science and by Mann (1959) in a portion of the small group field, this approach develops a systematic codification of variables and relationships within a field of study, translates concepts into a common language, and thus makes it possible to tie together related findings from different studies. The method used in the present research is more closely related to the propositional inventory approach than to other forms of small group compilations.

GENERAL APPROACH OF THE RESEARCH PROGRAM

Essentially, the authors' aim was to develop a method for classifying *all* variables which had been or were likely to be studied in small group research, and for compiling evidence on the relationships that obtained between each pair of variables. This aim meant that the authors needed to have a classification system which would provide a common, generic language for codifying all variables of the small group research field in such a way that each one could be related to every other within a complex classification space. Furthermore, this aim implied the need for a "strong" classification system, one whose categories would be distinct and mutually exclusive yet conceptually related, and collectively exhaustive in the sense that they could handle a wide range of types of variables including those that had not as yet been studied.

The authors' general aim also seemed to imply the need for classification on some basis other than that of the verbal labels that researchers had used to designate the variables of their studies—e.g., "cohesiveness," "conformity," "introversion." Substantively based classification seemed undesirable for several reasons. First, various investigators had often used the *same* verbal label for variables that are operationally and conceptually distinct; consider the many meanings of "cohesiveness," as noted by Gross and Martin (1952). At the same time, different researchers sometimes had used *different* verbal labels for variables that are operationally and conceptually similar; see Newcomb's (1953; 1961) use of interpersonal "attraction" and Fiedler's (Fiedler, Hutchins & Dodge, 1959) use of interpersonal "esteem." Hence, a classification of variables that merely reflected the verbal labels used by researchers in the field would hardly have led to a heuristically valuable integration.

The use of substantive classification terms seemed unprofitable for other reasons as well. In the authors' observation, substantive classifications tended to be lists or sets of nominal categories which were unrelated to one another. They also tended to be "open-ended" systems, which had to be continually modified by addition of new categories whenever they were applied to classify new concepts. The kind of general system for which the authors aimed needed to be based on a logically "closed" and internally "tight" or highly interrelated set of classification distinctions.

As an alternative to developing a substantively based classification, the authors chose to develop an operationally based classification system. That is, instead of being grouped or distinguished on the basis of verbal labels or conceptual definitions, variables were classified in terms of properties of the *data* by means of which they had been measured.

Use of an operational basis for classification was one of the distinctive features of the research program. It made possible the translation of variables used in different studies into a common language which was independent of the verbal and conceptual idiosyncrasies of the researchers who had conducted the studies. Furthermore, it facilitated the development of a logically closed and internally tight classification system in which all variables could be placed in relation to one another. Some other advantages of an operation-based classification system—and some disadvantages—will become apparent as the authors describe the classification system and its application in subsequent chapters.

Another distinguishing feature of the present approach to classification is that the system contains a set of highly interrelated classification categories and postulates a built-in principle for relating the categories to one another. Consequently, the system offers two further advantages not normally present in classifications based on sets of nominal categories. First, it offers a mechanism for partial validation of the system by testing whether or not the postulated principle for ordering categories does in fact order the empirical data of the field. Procedures and results of this validation step are presented in Chapter 3. Second, to the extent that the ordering principle holds, the classification system offers the further advantage of being a *predictive* device as well as a merely descriptive system for organizing research information. That is, if the empirical evidence is orderly in the manner postulated by the system, then users would be able to anticipate, or predict, outcomes for portions of the small group field for which empirical evidence is not yet available. Further discussion of the predictive applications of the classification system will be delayed until Chapter 4, after the system itself has been described and results of its validation presented.

CHRONOLOGY OF THE RESEARCH PROGRAM

We turn now to a brief chronology of the research program, to give a temporal perspective which may make succeeding chapters easier to follow. The program began with a pilot study to test the feasibility and utility of a general approach to the classification of small group research literature. The pilot study (McGrath, 1957) produced the following major results:

1. The development of a classification system that categorized small group research studies into nine interrelated classes on the basis of their form or logical structure, rather than their content

2. The development of a detailed classification system for analysis of research information from one of these formal categories—namely, studies of small group performance effectiveness

3. Application of the classification system to compile information from a sample of 61 studies in the small group performance effectiveness category

4. The compilation of a 1,279-item working bibliography, classified in terms of the nine formal study categories

After completion of the pilot phase of the program, a working conference, composed of several experienced small group researchers and members of the research team, was held to evaluate the program and to consider various alternative directions for continuation.[1] Results of the conference discussions led to the decision to attempt to broaden the system so as to enable classification of research information from all types of small group studies. This decision meant that major emphasis in the program would be placed on the development of a broadened system, with its application to a limited though more representative sample of small group studies, rather than work more intensively and thoroughly within a single subarea (such as studies of group performance effectiveness).

---

[1] The authors wish to acknowledge a great debt to the participants in that conference: Dr. Edgar Borgatta, Dr. Jerry Kidd, Dr. Charles Hutchinson, Dr. T. M. Newcomb, Dr. T. B. Roby, and Dr. John Thibaut. Their astute criticism of the pilot study and their helpful guidance as to subsequent directions aided the research program substantially.

In the second phase of the program, therefore, the system for classification of research information was extended and refined; procedures for training coders to apply that system were developed, the working bibliography was extended to make it as comprehensive as possible, and a sample of studies to which the system could be applied was selected. Then, after a trial use of the extended system on 21 studies (Altman & McGrath, 1959), the classification system was applied to a general sample of approximately 200 small group studies and a special supplemental sample of 50 studies. Sampling procedures, coder training and reliability, and related matters are discussed in the last section of Chapter 2 following a description of the classification system itself.

When the sample of studies had been coded, the authors then conducted data analyses to test the utility of the classification system as a device for ordering research information on small groups. Results of this validation step are described in Chapter 3. Subsequent modifications in the classification system, intended to make it simpler and more communicable, and an over-all evaluation of the program are presented in Chapter 4. The three major products of the research are presented as reference materials in Part III of this book; they include the systematic compilation of research information contained in the 250 studies that were reviewed, the systematic annotations of each of the 250 studies, and the extensive bibliography of small group research.

2 The Classification System

This chapter describes the classification system developed by the authors for integration of small group research. The first section of the chapter presents the underlying rationale and the terms of the system.[1] The second section of the chapter describes procedures for application of the system to a large sample of small group studies.

UNITS OF ANALYSIS

The unit of research information of the classification approach is assumed to be the statement of results of a statistical test that examines the relationship between two variables. Each such statement has three parts: (1) a *resultant variable* whose variation is to be accounted for; (2) an *agent variable* which is presumed or predicted to account for all or some of the variation in the resultant variable; and (3) a *relational term*, in the form of the results of a statistical test of significance, ordinarily a statement of the probability of the variables being associated. The classification system is designed to describe the operational data properties of the variables of a relationship and to describe the nature and form of the association between variables.

Each variable that serves as Agent or Resultant variable in a relationship statement is operationally defined in terms of responses or measures on one or more data items. A data item is a specific single response or judgment. The basic terms of the classification system have to do with the operational characteristics of the data items that underlie a given variable.

BASIC PARAMETERS OF DATA

The heart of any classification system is the set of dimensions or terms of classification and the categories or "magnitudes" that can occur on each dimension. For purposes of the present study, items of data are classified in terms of six fundamental properties—here termed the *parameters of data*—which are

---

[1] Although this section should enable the reader to understand the system and to apply it, a more detailed coder manual is presented in Altman and McGrath (1959). It is too lengthy to reproduce here.

operational rather than substantive in nature. It is assumed that every item of data takes one and only one "value" or category on each of the six parameters, and that the six parameters together provide an exhaustive classification of data items. Thus, each item of data is classified by specifying its category on each data parameter. Each combination of categories on the six parameters defines a class of data items. Following are the parameters of the classification system.

PARAMETER 1: OBJECT. The object of a data item is the level of reference of the entity to which that response or judgment refers. For example, if a data item deals with a characteristic of a group member, then it is at the individual (Member) level of reference. If the judgment or response deals with the group as an entity, then its object is at the Group level of reference. When the level of reference of the data item is an entity external to the group it is classified as Surround.

When the object of the data is a group member, a distinction is necessary when a member responds about himself as object (Member-Self) and when he responds about some other member of the group (Member-Other). For surround objects, it is necessary to differentiate between individual, group, and nonhuman aspects.

Thus, major categories for the Object parameter are Member (self, other), Group, and Surround (individual, group, nonhuman object).

PARAMETER 2: MODE. The mode of a data item is the type of object characteristic that is being judged. A data item may be a State or an Action property of the object. State property describes one aspect of the object, as an entity, and provides a summary up to a specified point in time. Thus, a state property is cumulative in time. Examples are biographical, attitudinal, and personality properties of individuals and groups.

An action is a dynamic property of an object. Action items depict an event that occurs during a temporal interval. Thus, actions are noncumulative in time. Examples are group or member performances, communications, and interactions.

The difference between state and action is roughly analogous to the biologist's distinction between the nerve (state) and the nerve impulse (action) or between organ structure (state) and organ function (action); or the grammarian's distinction between the verb *to be* (state) and the verb *to do* (action).

PARAMETER 3: TASK.[2] Task parameter refers to the type of judgment that is made about the object. If the judgment has to do with the amount of a characteristic possessed by the object, it is classified as Descriptive. If the judgment has to do with the degree to which the object departs from a standard or ideal value or level on a characteristic, it is classified as Evaluative.

Description involves placement of some object on a stimulus or attribute continuum. Examples are individual and group biographical data, certain personality data, and group structural properties.

---

[2] The task parameter is identical to Coombs' (1952) distinction between Task A and Task B. The distinction between relative and irrelative judgments (parameter 4) is also borrowed from Coomb's theory of data.

Evaluation involves a statement of the difference or discrepancy between the amount of an attribute possessed by an object and the amount of that attribute judged to be "desirable." Thus, evaluation involves placement of both the object and a standard on a stimulus continuum, and a comparison of those two values. The result of this comparison of object and standard is the placement of the object on a continuum that may be conceived of as a preference continuum rather than a stimulus continuum. Evaluation, then, involves a statement of the discrepancy of the object from the standard of the judge on the attribute in question. Examples are attitude data, sociometric choice data, and performance effectiveness data.

For evaluative judgments, the preference continuum can be *monotonic* or *nonmonotonic* with respect to the attribute continuum. There is a monotonic relationship between preference and attribute continua when the standard is at one end of the attribute continuum. (A maximum or a minimum is desirable.) When the standard is not at one extreme of the attribute continuum, an object can deviate from the desired value in one of two ways—it can possess either "too much" or "too little" of the attribute. As the object deviates from the standard in either direction, the preferability is reduced. Such a situation yields a nonmonotonic relationship between the attribute continuum and the preference continuum. (The monotone-nonmonotone distinction is applicable only to *irrelative* evaluations on parameter 4.)

PARAMETER 4: RELATIVENESS.[3] The Relativeness parameter classifies the absolute or comparative basis of the response. If a data item represents an absolute judgment about a characteristic of an object, it is classified as Irrelative. If it represents a comparison of an object with one or more other objects, it is classified as Relative.

PARAMETER 5: SOURCE. The Source of a data item refers to the person or instrument making the response or judgment. In small group research investigations, a number of gross categories of source are applicable. In some cases, a person who is part of the group (Member) may serve as data source. In other cases, data may be provided by the group or its representative (Group), by the individual conducting the experiment (Investigator), by an individual who is *not* a group member but is acting for the investigator (Investigator Surrogate, such as raters, judges, etc.), or by an objective recording device (Investigator Instrument). In short the categories of the Source parameter are Member, Group, External (investigator, investigator surrogate, instrument).

PARAMETER 6: VIEWPOINT. The Viewpoint parameter is the frame of reference from which the source makes the judgment which constitutes a data item. When a member is source, he may judge an object from his own frame of reference (Member-Self, or Subjective), from another member's viewpoint (Member-Other, Projective), from the viewpoint of the referent

---

[3] The Relative-Irrelative parameter was originally included in the classification system and is discussed here and in Chapter 3 for the sake of historical accuracy. However, application of the classification system resulted in the coding of 90 percent of all variables into one of the two categories of this parameter. Hence, it does not provide any effective discrimination of these empirical data, and so was not used in analysis of these data.

group (Group, Projective), or from the viewpoint of a person or group external to the referent group (Surround, Projective). If a member or the investigator attempts to respond from an impersonal frame of reference, the data item is classified as Objective.

There are certain restrictions on the categories of the Viewpoint parameter. For example, when an investigator or investigator-surrogate acts as source, only the objective category of the Viewpoint parameter can apply. When the group acts as source and judges itself as object, both object and viewpoint categories are considered "group." When a member is judging another member as object, he may take either of two projective viewpoints: member A as source may judge member B as object from member B's point of view, or he may judge member B from another person's (member C's) viewpoint.

At this point it may be useful to give an illustrative example to show how the classification parameters are applied to the codification of variables. Let us assume that an investigator wants to find out whether liking for the group is a determinant of the interactive behavior of members of a small discussion group. Liking for the group is measured by means of a questionnaire which asks each member of each group to express his attitudes toward the group as a whole, on each of a series of questions.

Assume further that each group engages in a discussion which the investigator observes and records. For our purposes, let us suppose that the investigator records only the number of times that each member participates in the discussion, and obtains a measure of over-all activity per subject by summing the total number of times each member spoke. Thus, interactive behavior (the resultant variable) is operationally defined as the number of times each group member participated in the group discussion. Attraction for the group (agent variable) is operationally defined as the responses or "score" on an instrument designed to tap attitudes of members toward the group. By correlating these two scores, the investigator will obtain a statement of statistical covariation among these two indexes, which are presumed to be representative of the variables: "attraction for the group" and "member participation."

Let us now return to the parameters of data and code the variables of this hypothetical relationship:

1. *Object:* "What entity is being observed or judged?" In the index of attraction for the group, the *group* as an entity is the object of judgment; whereas in the participation index the individual group *member* is the judged object.

2. *Mode:* "What is it about the object that is being recorded?" In the group attraction index, the group is being judged as a *static* entity; whereas in the participation index, the judgment is of a behavior or *action* of the member object.

3. *Task:* "In what terms is the respondent judging the object?" Group attraction data are *evaluations* of the group by the member, whereas participation data are *descriptions* of member actions.

4. *Relativeness:* "Is the judgment a comparative one, such as a rank order, or an absolute one, such as a single-stimulus type?" In both examples cited, the judgments made were of an *irrelative* type.

5. *Source:* "Who is providing the response or judgment about the object ?" Individual *members* are the source of the group attraction data, whereas the *investigator* records member participation.

6. *Viewpoint:* "From whose point of view does the source make his judgments or responses ?" Individual members judge the group's attractiveness from their own *(subjective)* viewpoint, whereas the investigator attempts to record participation from an *objective* viewpoint.

Thus, the six operational parameters of data answer the questions for each item of data: who (Source) responds in what form (Task and Relative-Irrelative) about what kind of property (Mode) of what entity (Object) from what or whose frame of reference (Viewpoint). In the illustration, the measure of group attraction is classified as "*member evaluates* (on an *irrelative* basis) a *static* characteristic of the *group* from his *subjective* frame of reference." The measure of member participation is classified as "*investigator describes* (from an *irrelative* point of view) an *action* characteristic of group *members* from an *objective* frame of reference."

CLASSES OF VARIABLES AND INDEXING OPERATIONS

Each data item is classified in one and only one of the categories of each of the six basic parameters. Thus, the parameters define a set of related classes, each of which is characterized by a specific combination of categories. The number of data classes is the product of the number of categories of the six parameters.

A variable may be composed of a single data item or a combination of several data items. Variables that are made up of one data item, or of a number of data items of the same data class, are termed *Simple* variables. There are as many classes of Simple variables as there are data classes. Variables that are made up of data items from two or more data classes are termed *Complex* variables. Although there are a huge number of potential classes of Complex variables, relatively few of them have actually been employed in the sample of studies reviewed in this program.

Empirical indexes of variables are formed from combination of data items via one or more arithmetic *indexing operations.*[4] Indexing operations may be performed to combine items of the same data class or of different data classes.

The definition of an index, and the operational meaning of the variable it represents, is a function of the data items that compose the index and of the types of indexing operations that are performed to combine those data items.

---

[4] This discussion of indexing operations is included for the sake of logical completeness and historical accuracy. Results of application of the system indicated that most indexes in small group research were based on data items of a single data class combined by summation into what the authors termed *simple variables.* Complex variables were both infrequent and widely variable; hence there was not a sufficient number of replications of any one complex variable class for useful summarizations. Thus, indexing operations were of little heuristic value for integration.

Two indexes of variables may be composed of the same items of data but be "different" in terms of the type and sequence of indexing operations performed.

There are two basic types of indexing operations for combining data items: summation (Σ) and discrepancy (Δ) operations. Summation includes those arithmetic operations that have as their logical basis the addition of units and that yield a representative or total estimate (e.g., frequency of occurrence, measures of central tendency). Discrepancy operations are those procedures that yield comparisons among items (e.g., subtraction, estimates of scatter).

When data items are *summed*, the resulting index refers to a characteristic of the *individual data items* upon which the summing operation was carried out. When data items are combined by some *discrepancy* operation, the resulting index refers to a characteristic of the *combination* of those individual items. For example:

1. If the investigator *adds* a single member's responses to a number of similar items, the resulting "scale score" is an estimate of the difficulty of the *average item* in the scale. If the investigator computes a *variance* among the member's responses, the resulting index relates to the *heterogeneity* of the scale items; i.e., the index refers to a relationship among items, rather than to items per se.

2. If the investigator *sums* the responses of many members to a single item, the resulting index is an estimate of the *average member* response to the item or the average difficulty or preferability of the item. If the investigator computes a *variance* among the members' responses to a single item, the index refers to the *heterogeneity* of member responses and thus has a group referent; i.e., the index refers to a relationship among members.

Thus, the conceptual referent of the resulting index is partly determined by whether the data were combined by a summing or a discrepancy procedure. This distinction plays an important part in determining the mappings from classes of data items to classes of variable indexes, particularly with respect to the Object parameter. The type and sequence of indexing operations, as well as the classes of data involved, determine the meaning of the resulting index.

In the illustration used in the previous section, the agent index, group attraction, was coded as follows: a member (Source) evaluating (Task) on an irrelative basis, the state (Mode) of the group (Object) from a subjective frame of reference (Viewpoint). With respect to indexing operations, we may say that the investigator *summed* data items with respect to the Mode parameter, because he computed a total score on a series of attitude items for each group member. Each item of the questionnaire may be considered as an item of data dealing with a particular aspect of the state of the referent group. The total questionnaire, then, represents judgments by the same data source about a number of related aspects of group state.

For the resultant index, we coded member participation as a description on an irrelative basis of member action by the investigator from an objective point of view. In indexing, the investigator determined each member's participation score by totaling the number of times he participated in the discussion; the investigator *summed* data items with respect to the Mode parameter (member actions).

Let us consider the implications of additional types of indexing that could have been performed with respect to the agent and resultant components of our hypothetical relationship, focusing on the member participation example. By summing data items with respect to the Mode parameter (member actions), we obtained a score that described each member's participation in the discussion. If we then summed data items with respect to the Object (member) parameter, we would have obtained an *average member participation score*. Note that the result of these indexing operations would not be a group index, but an average individual measure. However, if we had combined member scores by a discrepancy operation such as a standard deviation, instead of by the summing operation, we would have obtained a measure of the distribution of participation in the group. Such a measure of the relative homogeneity of the group with respect to participation would have a *group* referent.

This section of the chapter has discussed two basic indexing operations by means of which items of data are combined to yield indexes of variables: summation and discrepancy. The specification of indexing operations supplements the classification of data items in terms of the parameters of data. Taken together, indexing and data item classification provide the basis for examining empirical covariation of agent and resultant variables. In the following section, the classification of the relational term in empirical relationships is discussed. Then we discuss the way in which relationship information which has been classified in terms of data items, indexing operations, and relational terms can be brought together to provide an integrated picture of small group research information.

CLASSIFICATION OF THE RELATIONAL TERM

Agent and resultant variable indexes are linked together by a relational term, which may express the presence, direction, degree, and form of empirical covariation between them. Relational terms assessing the covariation between two indexes are usually in the form of a statement of results of a specific statistical test. The classification system deals with three aspects of such relational statements: the type of statistical test used, the direction and degree of association between the two indexes as indicated by the statistical test, and a statement of the statistical probability that the obtained relationship is merely a chance relationship.

Type of Statistical Test

There are a large number of specific statistical tests that can be applied to assess the covariation between indexes within the small group area. Each of these has different requirements for its use and/or different assumptions about the nature of the data to which it is applied. For the most part, statistical tests can be subdivided into two general classes: tests of association, correlation, or covariation between continuous or discrete indexes; and tests of difference between two or more subsamples of the data. The former include correlation coefficients and certain forms of Chi-square tests. The latter include t-tests, F-tests associated with analyses of variance, and similar tests of difference.

Degree, Direction, and Form of Association

From the point of view of the present study, the major import of these two classes of statistics is that tests of association frequently provide estimates of the degree, direction, and form of a relationship, as well as an estimate of the probability that such a relationship exists. On the other hand, tests of difference usually only express direction and presence of a relationship; they do not provide estimates of the degree or form of relationships. Tests of association, therefore, usually provide more research information than do tests of difference.

Statistical Probability of Association

Some statement of the probability that the obtained relationship could have arisen by chance usually accompanies each statement of results of a statistical test. Most often, the investigator uses a preset level of probability—usually a highly conservative level—which he takes as an arbitrary cutoff point. He considers findings that do not reach the cutoff point as not statistically significant and those that do reach or exceed it as statistically significant.

The use of probability of significance of the relational term as a basis of classification of empirical relationships has two advantages for the present system. First, it is applicable to all relational terms, whether based on tests of association or tests of difference. Second, it takes into account variations in the number of cases upon which a test is based, because probability statements are usually referred to a (theoretical) probability distribution relative to the number of cases. Because the number of cases used in studies of small groups varies widely, the use of the probability form of the relational term provides a means for legitimate comparison among them. Therefore, the probability statement provides the major basis of classification of relational terms in the present study, although estimates of the degree of association (proportion of variance accounted for) were recorded when that information was given or could be computed from the study report.

CLASSIFICATION OF RELATIONSHIPS

All variables that are based on data items having the same combination of categories on the data parameters belong to the same variable class, Vi. All members of a variable class Vi are alike from the point of view of this classification system, however different they may be in "substantive" terms. Furthermore, they all bear the same relationship to any variable that is a member of the class Vj. Hence, a statistical test of relationship (Rij) between a variable of the class Vi and a variable of the class Vj is considered as a test of the relationship between those two *classes*. Given that there are a number of specific instances of tests of relationship between variables of class Vi and variables of class Vj, then the proportion of those tests that achieve a given level of statistical significance is an index of the probability of relationship (at that level) for any member of the relationship class Rij. The proportion of relationships of a class Rij that achieve a given significance level is termed the "*batting average*" for the relation class Rij (at that significance level). It is considered an estimate of the probability that any given variable Vi will be related to a given variable Vj.

The Concordance Principle

It is assumed that two variables that are classified alike in all respects are identical within the frame of reference of the classification system. Further, it is assumed that the more parameters there are on which two variables are classified alike, the more similar are those two variables to one another. One index of the degree of similarity between any two variables is a simple count of the number of parameters on which those two variables have the same classification category. This index is termed the *Concordance level* of the relationship between those two variables.[5]

Thus, it is possible to order all relationship classes Rij into one of seven levels of Concordance: those in which the two variables are alike on all six parameters, those in which the two variables are alike on five of the six parameters, and so forth, down to those whose variables are dissimilar on all six parameters.

The basic *predictive hypothesis* of the classification system is that the more two variables are alike (that is, the higher their level of Concordance), the greater the chances are that they will be significantly related to one another at any fixed significance level. Thus, the authors predicted a positive association between the Concordance level and the "batting average" of the relationship classes in the small group field.

The ordering of relationships according to the concordance principle can also be viewed in terms of an integrative matrix. Each resultant variable forms a column of the matrix, each agent variable forms a row of the matrix, and each measure of statistical relationship between a pair of variables is an entry in the cell defined by those variables. Because the classification of a variable as agent or resultant refers to its functional use in a particular relationship, each variable identified in the small group literature is listed as both a row and a column of the matrix. Each cell of the matrix thus defines a *class of potential relationships* within the small group domain.

Such a matrix yields several classes of information without further manipulation. The entries in a particular column summarize the kinds of agent variables which do and do not predict the resultant variable defined by the column. Similarly the entries along a row summarize the predictive usefulness of a particular agent variable with respect to various resultant variables.

The number of entries within a given cell indicates how *often* given classes of variables have been related to one another. Concurrence of results within a cell indicates verification of a given empirical relationship and can provide the basis for formulation of an empirical generalization. Conflicting entries within a cell indicate the need for more incisive tests of relationships defined by that cell and for examination of the study conditions within which the conflicting findings were obtained. The entries in the cells along the diagonal of the matrix represent tests of the definition of similarity of classes of variables—the extent to which variables of the same class covary highly.

---

[5] The Index of Concordance level for relationships that are not the Simple type is somewhat more complex than here described. However, results for Simple relationship classes and for all relationship classes were so parallel (see Chapter 3) that further analyses focused solely on the former. Furthermore, several more complex indexes of Concordance, including a priori weighting methods, did not appreciably alter the Concordance/"batting average" function; hence, the simple counting measure was used.

The concept of concordance is both a logical premise by means of which the rows and column of the relationship matrix can be ordered and a hypothesis that could be empirically tested within the framework of the present study. To the extent that the principle of operational concordance provides a logical ordering of relationships, which jibes with their empirical ordering in terms of frequency of significance, it both validates the logic of the integrative framework and provides a basis for generation of predictive hypotheses as to the probable significance of untested relationships within the small group domain. The test of the validity of the concordance principle is discussed in the following chapter.

It should be noted that the authors' classification system is a special case of Guttman's facet analysis (Guttman, 1959; Foa, 1958). Data parameters correspond to facets, categories of the parameters correspond to categories of facets, and the concordance principle corresponds to the principle of contiguity. The authors were not aware of the relationship between their system and facet analysis until after the basic system had been developed. Furthermore, although the authors' classification system has the same logical structure as facet analysis, it does not approach the mathematical rigor of Guttman's formulation. For both of these reasons, the authors did not employ the terminology of facet analysis here, although it would be generally appropriate.

SUMMARY

This chapter has thus far presented a detailed discussion of the major concepts of the classification system developed in the research program. The classification system has as its unit of analysis the empirical research relationship and is developed at three levels: data items, indexes of variables, and relationships. It is assumed that data items can be described in terms of a set of six fundamental properties or parameters. Each combination of categories on these parameters defines a class of data items. Items of data are combined arithmetically by either summation or discrepancy procedures to yield indexes of variables. Indexes may include similar or different classes of data. Relationships between variables are then determined by classification of statistical tests of covariation.

When all relationships have been classified, a master matrix of relationships is generated. The rows and columns of the matrix are agent and resultant variables. Cell entries indicate results of statistical tests of relationships. Empty cells indicate gaps in research knowledge; cells with high incidence of statistically significant relationships indicate well-established empirical findings. A proper ordering of the matrix, which can be accomplished on logical and empirical bases, will permit statements of empirical generalizations and specification of research needs.

The last section of this chapter will describe procedures by which the classification system was applied to code a large sample of small group research studies. This presentation will include discussion of procedures for sampling studies, coder-training procedures, checks on the reliability of coding, and methods used for processing the resulting data. Chapter 3 describes results of the attempt to validate the classification system by testing the postulated principle of concordance.

APPLICATION OF THE CLASSIFICATION SYSTEM

Sampling

A working bibliography developed in the pilot study was extended to make it as complete as possible. This extended bibliography, consisting of over 2,000 titles, constituted the basic population of studies from which the authors sampled.[6] The authors drew several samples of studies from the population by entering at random into a list alphabetized by senior author and selecting every seventh title. Each sample drawn in this manner varied in size from 50 to 100 titles. Two departures were made from this procedure. First, any selected study that proved upon examination to be a discursive or wholly theoretical piece which did not present original empirical data was passed over. Second, any selected study that utilized factor analysis was passed over in favor of the next study in sequence. The authors reluctantly omitted the few factor analytic studies drawn in the sample (about 1 percent) because the authors felt that, although the classification system would handle the zero-order correlations as any other correlation, it did not adequately handle the higher order concepts of factor analysis such as factor loadings, factor scores, and so on. This inadequacy, representing a conceptual limitation of the classification system, introduced a systematic, though probably slight, bias in the sample.

From the outset, the authors planned to apply the system to as large a sample of studies as their resources would permit. Several steps were taken in an effort to assess the adequacy of the sample size. For the first 70 studies coded, the number of *new* variable classes tapped by each successive set of seven studies was plotted. This plotting yielded a negatively accelerated curve, indicating that the point of "diminishing returns" per study, in terms of the addition of new variable classes, was already being approached. The authors projected the obtained decelerating curve as a prediction, then plotted the next 70 studies in the same manner. Results showed a remarkable correspondence to the projected curve and indicated that the rate of generation of new variable classes was essentially asymptotic by the time 100 studies had been coded. As a further check, the sets of seven studies were put into a new, random sequence, and the occurrence of new variable classes was replotted. This check confirmed the decelerating form of the curve, indicating that the curve form was not a function of accidental inclusion of many studies especially rich in a variety of variables within the first sets coded. On the basis of these results, it was decided that extension of the sample to approximately 200 studies should provide a set of data that would include most or all of the variable classes that had been used with relatively high frequency in small group studies.

In addition to the general sample of 200 studies, the authors decided to code a special supplementary sample of studies dealing with group and member performance effectiveness. One main product of the pilot study phase of the program had been the integration of research information from a sample of

---

[6] The basic bibliography presented in Terauds, Altman, and McGrath (1960) appears as Part III, Section C of this book. It has been updated with an Addenda so that the population of studies from which a sample was chosen remains intact as the basic bibliography.

61 studies dealing with group performance effectiveness. Because this special class of studies seemed of particular relevance for both theoretical and applied efforts in the small group field, the main bibliography was screened (by title where possible, by abstract where necessary) and a number of group and member performance effectiveness studies were identified which had not been included in the general sample. From these, about 50 were randomly selected and constituted a special supplementary sample.

It should be noted that, although the authors coded *all* relationships in studies of the general sample, for the special sample only those relationships involving performance effectiveness were coded (with the qualification that a record of the total number of relationships and variables in each study was made, as indicated in the study annotations). Thus the compilation of research information (Part III, Section A) is unduly weighted in the direction of over-inclusion of relationships involving measures of group and member performance effectiveness.

Coders were trained to record all relationships in the studies reviewed, including those relationships for which no statistical tests were reported. When possible, results for untested relationships were inferred. For example, when the investigator used several groups and reported a nonsignificant difference between the two most-extreme group means, it was assumed that differences between all other pairs of means were also nonsignificant.

In all 250 studies, 12,000 relationships were coded. Of these, over 9,000 reported results of tests of statistical significance. In addition, more than 75 percent of all relationships had variables which were simple variables—i.e., were composed of data items of a single data class. Although the classification system permits the occurrence of over 2,400 different variable classes of the simple type, a total of 40 variable classes accounted for more than half the Simple relationships in the sample. Further "demographic" characteristics of the sample of relationships are discussed in Chapter 5.

Coding

The authors were responsible for development of the classification system and coded a number of studies as "check coders," but the primary coding task was carried out by several research assistants who had undergraduate training in social psychology and statistics and who received extensive training in the classification system and its application. As each coder was brought into the program, he received instruction in the system both verbally and through a coder-training manual, which contained detailed instructions and illustrations for all aspects of the coding task (Altman & McGrath, 1959). Then the new coder applied the system to several studies which had already been coded by the authors, and these results were used as the basis for extensive training critiques. This process was repeated with additional studies until the new coder was able to perform all coding tasks with high reliability—i.e., to code reliably against the criterion of codings by the authors.

In the early stages of the program, samples of studies were coded by two coders independently to check reliability. Results have been reported in detail in Altman and McGrath (1959). Reliability of coding of most types of information was adequate. Results of these analyses were used to modify coder-training procedures for those types of information for which initial reliability had been weak. Spot checks of reliability throughout the production coding effort were made to insure continuity in coder orientations.

Many kinds of information about the study and its results were coded in addition to the basic categorization of data items, indexing operations, and relational terms. For example, for each study coders recorded institutional affiliation of the author; type of monetary support, if any; type of study setting and research design; number, size and constancy of groups; procedures used for sampling and assigning cases to conditions; and other features of study methodology. Some of these data are discussed in Chapter 5. Coders also recorded the substantive labels that investigators assigned to the variables of their studies. These were subsequently used to supplement the operational classification of variables, as discussed in Chapter 4.

Data-Processing Procedures

A specially designed card was used to code all information about a study as a whole (including total number of relationships and number of different variables contained in it) and a separate coding card was used for each relationship in that study. Each item of information recorded on the study card was converted into a set of numerical coding categories, and the information was subsequently punched onto IBM cards for machine processing. This information was tabulated over studies and results are summarized in Chapter 5. This information also supplied the basis for development of the set of study annotations which are presented in Part III, Section B.

The basic information of the relationship cards was also transformed into a set of numerical codes and punched on cards for machine processing. For example, for the Mode parameter of each variable, the state category was punched 1, the action category was punched 2. (These numbers have nominal rather than quantitative status.) Thus, the parameter coding of each variable appeared as a six-digit number, denoting the classification category for each of the six data parameters. The card layout had space for punching the parameter code (up to three different data item classes) and the indexing operations (up to a sequence of three indexing operations) for each of the two variables of the relationship, plus space for coding information about the relational term and the significance level of the relationship.

Relationship cards were processed by aggregating all relationships of a given class. Processing involved use of a complex sorting procedure on all six data parameters and indexing operations simultaneously. The number of relationships of each class was tallied, along with the proportion of those relationships that were significant ($p \leq .05$).[7] These tabulations provided the basic data for the compilation of small group research information in Part III, Section A.

---

[7] The probability level $p \leq .05$ was arbitrarily selected as a criterion of significance for all analyses. It would be possible to repeat analyses for any other chosen significance level, although most studies report results only with respect to a chosen p value (usually .01 or .05) rather than reporting exact p values. Hence, the use of alternative p values (except possibly the value $p \leq .01$) would necessitate omitting many relationships from the analysis.

Machine analysis was also used on the relationship cards to compute and record various indexes of concordance for each relationship, in order to provide data for testing the concordance principle of the classification system (Chapter 3). The simplest of these analyses was a count of the number of data parameters on which the two variables of the relationship were coded as having the same category. When applied to relationships in which both variables were based on a single data class, this concordance index could vary from zero (no classification similarities between the two variables) to six (the two variables were classified the same on all six parameters). When applied to relationships in which one or both of the variables contained two or more data classes, the concordance index was computed in a somewhat more complex manner.

Several more-complex concordance measures were also developed. One of these included a count of differences in indexing operations as well as in data parameter codings. Another included an a priori weighting for concordance on certain parameters (concordance on Object, Source, and Task parameters was given extra weight). A third attempted to give additional weight to differences on certain categories of the parameters. (For example, two variables with self and other-member as object, respectively, were assumed to be *less different* than two variables with self and surround as objects, respectively.) Subsequent analyses of differences in proportion of significance in relation to degree of concordance, however, indicated that none of these more-complex measures of concordance added appreciably to the "ordering power" obtained with the basic concordance measure based on a simple count of number of parameter coding similarities. Hence, these less-parsimonious concordance indexes will not be discussed further. Results of the analyses of concordance indexes are presented and discussed next, in Chapter 3.

3 A Validation of the Classification System

One major advantage inherent in the kind of classification system used here is that it contains a hypothesized ordering principle which allows for an empirical test of the usefulness or "validity" of the system itself. The ordering principle, which derives from the logic of the classification system, is expressed as the principle of concordance. This principle postulates that the more similar two variables are to one another, in terms of their operational properties, the greater the probability is that they will be significantly related to one another at any given level of statistical reliability.

The principle of concordance is a direct derivation of the logical structure of the classification system in the same sense that the contiguity principle derives from the logical structure of facet analysis (Guttman, 1959): namely, things (variables) that are classified alike in all respects within a given classification system *are alike* from the point of view of that system. Hence, those things should *act* alike, empirically. A test of whether or not they *do* act alike, empirically, is a test of the adequacy of the classification system. This same basic logic underlies much of the work on reliability and validity of measurement—e.g., the multitrait, multimethod analysis of Campbell and Fiske (1959).

In the present study, we evaluated the concordance principle by testing the hypothesis that the proportion of significant relationships within a relationship class (the "batting average" of that class) varies directly with the degree of concordance of that relationship class (i.e., the number of operational parameters that are the same for the two variables defining the relationship class). The test of this hypothesis represents a test of the validity of the present classification system, both as a descriptive device for providing a parsimonious and heuristic organization of small group research information, and as a predictive device for anticipating results of as-yet-untested relationships and for formulating useful empirical generalizations. The remainder of this chapter presents a description of the procedures, results, and implications of the validation analysis.[1]

RESULTS

The concordance hypothesis was tested by the following procedures. All relationships in the approximately 250 small group studies of the review sample were assigned to one of seven levels of concordance. A concordance

---

[1] Much of the material in this chapter also appears in McGrath (1963).

level of 6 was assigned to all relationships in which the two related variables had the same classification on all six parameters. A concordance level of 5 was assigned to relationships in which the two variables were classified alike on five but different on one parameter. The minimum concordance score, O, was assigned to relationships in which the two variables were dissimilar on all six parameters.

Then, the proportion of statistically significant relationships within each concordance level was computed. A significance level of $p \leq .05$ was used for all analyses. These proportions, or "batting averages," were compared for different levels of concordance.

Concordance Level Versus "Batting Average"

Table 1 and Figure 1 show results for all relationship classes and for those relationship classes in which both variables are Simple in their data item composition. It is not appropriate to apply standard statistical tests to assess the degree of association between concordance level and "batting average," because these data do not meet the requirement of experimental independence of cases. Nevertheless, the data appear to depart markedly from the "flat line" that would be expected if only a chance association existed between concordance level and "batting average." For the maximum concordance level, 53 percent of all relationships and 56 percent of all simple-type relationships were significant at the .05 level; whereas for minimum concordance, only 26 percent of all relationships and 28 percent of all simple-type relationships achieved that significance level. Other analyses used more complex measures of concordance, including an a priori weighting of parameters and categories, and a concordance

TABLE 1

ASSOCIATION BETWEEN CONCORDANCE LEVEL AND "BATTING AVERAGE"

Con-cordance Levels[a]	All Relationship Classes			Simple Relationship Classes		
	Significant Relationships	Total Relationships	"Batting Average"[b]	Significant Relationships	Total Relationships	"Batting Average"[b]
0	13	49	26%	12	44	28%
1	256	834	31	242	762	32
2	592	1909	31	515	1618	32
3	576	1635	35	504	1403	36
4	578	1995	29	492	1599	31
5	607	1541	39	510	1222	42
6	600	1135	53	538	969	56
		9098			7617	

[a] Concordance level equals number of parameters on which the two variables of the relationship have similar classification.

[b] "Batting average" equals proportion of relationships at a given concordance level that are significant at or beyond the .05 level.

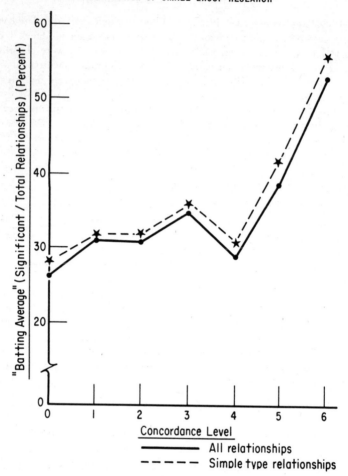

FIG. 1.   Association between concordance level and "batting average"

measure that took into account number and type of indexing operations. All of these yielded essentially the same results as obtained using the simple counting measure of concordance. These findings were taken to indicate at least tentative support for the concordance hypothesis.

Contributions of Individual Parameters

We next examined the separate contributions of each of the six parameters to the over-all association between concordance level and "batting average." Table 2 and Figure 2 show results for all simple relationship classes and for 44 major relationship classes.[2] The Relativeness parameter was omitted from

---

[2] Major relationship classes were those that contained at least 25 instances and that occurred in at least three different studies. The 44 major relationship classes included over 3,000 relationships.

further analysis because over 90 percent of all variables were classified in one of its two categories.

TABLE 2

ASSOCIATION BETWEEN CONCORDANCE ON
INDIVIDUAL PARAMETERS AND "BATTING AVERAGE"

| Parameters[b] | Major Relationship Classes[a] | | All Simple Type Relationships |
	Number of Classes	"Batting Average"	"Batting Average"
Object			
Concordance	23	50%	48%
Nonconcordance	21	32	30
Mode			
Concordance	21	48	42
Nonconcordance	23	39	33
Task			
Concordance	22	43	37
Nonconcordance	22	42	36
Source			
Concordance	24	49	39
Nonconcordance	20	34	33
Viewpoint			
Concordance	24	48	40
Nonconcordance	20	34	33
Total	44	43	37

[a] Major relationship classes are those which have at least 25 relationships and which appear in at least three studies.
[b] The Relativeness parameter was omitted from the analysis because over 90% of all relationships were classified into one if its two categories.

The Object parameter was clearly the strongest single contributor to the concordance–"batting average" relationship, although Mode, Source and Viewpoint parameters also appeared to have made substantial contributions. The Task parameter, however, did not contribute to the over-all relationship. Furthermore, examination of the data showed that the Source and Viewpoint parameters, although conceptually distinct, were almost entirely redundant in their data. Therefore, it was concluded that three parameters had made major contributions to the association between concordance and "batting average"— namely, the Object and Mode parameters and Source-Viewpoint considered as a joint parameter.

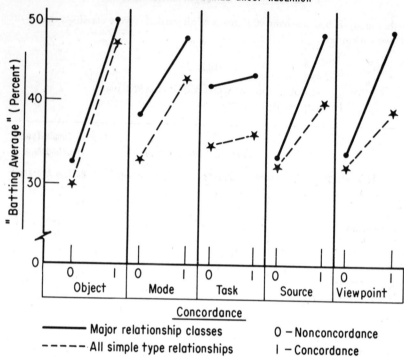

FIG. 2. Association between concordance on individual parameters and "batting average"

TABLE 3

ASSOCIATION BETWEEN "BATTING AVERAGE"
AND CONCORDANCE ON TWO AND ON THREE PARAMETERS
FOR MAJOR RELATIONSHIP CLASSES

Level of Concordance	"Batting Averages" for Two-Parameter Combinations		
	Object & Mode	Object & Source	Mode & Source
Concordance on both parameters	57%	51%	54%
Concordance on one parameter	40	44	42
Nonconcordance on both parameters	32	28	32

Level of Concordance	"Batting Averages" for Three-Parameter Combinations
Concordance on all three parameters	57%
Concordance on two of the three parameters	46
Concordance on one of the three parameters	37
Nonconcordance on all three parameters	26

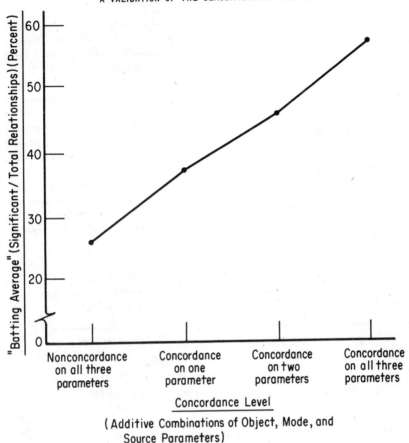

FIG. 3. Association between "batting average" and concordance on object, mode, and source for major relationship classes

Additive Combinations of Two and Three Parameters

Concordance levels were then compared to "batting average" for pairs, and for all three of the effective parameters—Object, Mode, and Source (Table 3 and Figure 3). The concordance–"batting average" relationship for the additive combination of Object, Mode, and Source was almost perfectly linear, with a slope equaling that obtained when all six parameters were taken into account. Relationships concordant on all three parameters had a "batting average" of 57 percent, whereas those that were not concordant on any of the three parameters had a "batting average" of only 26 percent.

Lexicographic Combination of Parameters

The possibility of nonadditive combinations of the three parameters was next considered. A "batting average" was computed for each of the eight combinations of concordance and nonconcordance for the three effective parameters. These were then arranged in terms of combinations of the Mode and Source parameters for Object concordance and Object nonconcordance separately (Table 4 and Figure 4). The data indicates that, although the Object parameter was clearly the most-effective single parameter, the Mode and Source parameters appeared to have different effects for Object concordant and Object nonconcordant relationships. Specifically, concordance or nonconcordance on the Mode parameter was related to "batting average" for Object concordant relationships, but not for those relationships in which there was nonconcordance of Object. Conversely, concordance on the Source parameter seemed to make a difference in "batting average" for relationships with nonconcordant Objects, but not for relationships with concordant Objects.

These findings suggest that the three parameters combine in a lexicographic (Coombs, 1952) rather than an additive fashion. The Object parameter is dominant. The Mode and Source parameters are secondary parameters, the former operating only when there is Object concordance and the latter operating

TABLE 4

ASSOCIATION BETWEEN "BATTING AVERAGE" AND CONCORDANCE ON MODE AND SOURCE PARAMETERS FOR OBJECT CONCORDANT AND OBJECT NONCONCORDANT RELATIONSHIPS

	Object Concordance		
	Source		
Mode	Source Concordance	Source Nonconcordance	Total
Mode concordance	57%	56%	57%
Mode nonconcordance	45	43	45
Total	51	47	50

	Object Nonconcordance		
	Source		
Mode	Source Concordance	Source Nonconcordance	Total
Mode concordance	38%	31%	33%
Mode nonconcordance	41	26	32
Total	40	28	32

Concordance Combination	Lexicographic Combination "Batting Average"
Object concordance and mode concordance	57%
Object concordance and mode nonconcordance	45
Object nonconcordance and source concordance	40
Object nonconcordance and source nonconcordance	28

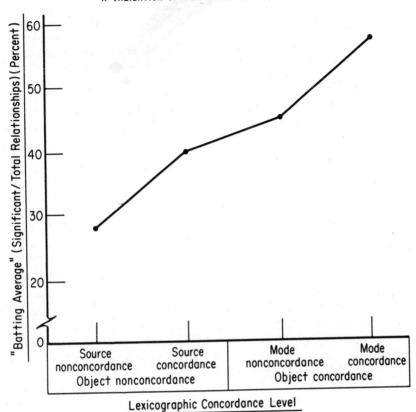

FIG. 4.   Association between concordance and "batting averages" for the lexico-graphic combination of object, mode, and source parameters

only when there is Object nonconcordance. Thus, substantially all the pre-dictability of the concordance hypothesis appears to be subsumed in three basic distinctions:

1. Do the variables being related have the same or different levels of reference? (Object concordance or nonconcordance)

2. If the same in level of reference, then do both refer to states or actions, or is one a state variable while the other is an action variable? (Mode concordance or nonconcordance, given Object concordance)

3. If different on level of reference, then are data on both variables from the same or different sources? (Source concordance or nonconcordance, given Object nonconcordance)

Analysis by Categories

Some analyses were also conducted to determine whether specific categories of the various parameters made a difference in "batting average" over and above the effect of level of concordance. This question could not be fully explored, even with the rather voluminous data of the study. However, there was some indication that relationships between two variables at the group level of reference were more likely to be significant than relationships between two variables at the member level of reference (56 percent versus 48 percent). The direction of this difference was consistent for Mode concordant and Mode nonconcordant relationships. Although this difference is relatively small, it tends to confirm results found in the pilot study (McGrath, 1957), that relationships between two measures at the group level of reference are more likely to be significant than relationships between measures at the individual level.

DISCUSSION

Summary of Results

The concordance principle appears to be generally supported, although the nature of the data does not permit a firm statistical test of the hypothesis. Results strongly suggest that the proportion of relationships found to be statistically significant (at a given significance level) is associated with the degree of concordance of the two classes of variables whose relationships are being examined. Thus, the parameters of the classification system appear to be, at least to some extent, valid. Application of the classification system permits ordering of research relationships into classes on the basis of level of concordance, and these classes show a parallel order in terms of "batting average."

However, not all of the distinctions included in the classification system contributed to this differentiation. The discriminability of the system comes, for the most part, from classification on Object, Mode, and the Source-Viewpoint parameters. Results also suggest that a nonadditive, lexicographic combination of the parameters may be more efficient than an additive combination. Specifically, the Object parameter appears to be dominant, whereas the Mode and Source-Viewpoint parameters are effective only within certain conditions of Object concordance.

Finally, there is some indication that relationships between variables at the group level of reference are more often significant than relationships between variables at the level of individual group members. This finding, though not definitive, is consistent with earlier results.

Relation of Finding to Other Research

It was noted earlier that the conceptual approach of this research is essentially a form of facet analysis as developed by Guttman (1959). Parameters of data correspond to facets, and the principle of concordance corresponds to the contiguity principle of Guttman's facet theory. The present classification system is far less sophisticated, mathematically, than facet analysis. Furthermore, the purposes for which the two methodologies were developed are quite different. Nevertheless, the results obtained in this study are in close correspondence with results reported by Foa (1958) utilizing facet analysis.

The findings are also in accord with results obtained in substantive research programs by Bales (1960) and Borgatta (1960). Both researchers have reported consistent patterns of relationship among self-report judgments of individual characteristics and among observer judgments of group interaction. At the same time, both programs failed to find consistent patterns by which the two sets of data could be related to one another. The present authors' findings are also in accord with results reported by Fiedler and co-workers (Fiedler, Dodge, Jones, & Hutchins, 1958) in studies of interpersonal perception and adjustment. A series of self-report measures were intercorrelated, and a series of peer ratings also were intercorrelated, but there were few correlations between these two sets of data. In each case, the data for which intercorrelation patterns were obtained had concordant Objects and Modes, whereas the sets of data that failed to show systematic patterns of relationship had nonconcordant Objects, Sources, and/or Modes.

The apparent convergence of findings from studies carried out by a number of investigators working from diverse points of view lends support to the results of this study and their interpretation.

Interpretation of Results

Results are most directly interpretable in terms similar to the "general systems theory" approach (Miller, 1955; Von Bertalanffy, 1955). The three main levels of reference defined by the Object parameter can be considered different system levels. With the group taken as the basic point of reference, they represent subsystem (individual member), system (group), and supra-system (external environment). Concepts within each of these system levels tend to be interdependent, as reflected by the relatively high "batting average" for relationships between variables at the same level. The different system levels appear to be relatively independent, however, as reflected by the relatively low "batting average" for relationships between variables at different levels.

Results for the Mode parameter (state versus action) further suggest that there may be two relatively distinct sets of phenomena within each system level, one structural and one dynamic. The structural phenomena within a given system level seem highly interdependent, and so do the dynamic phenomena within each system level, as reflected by the high "batting average" for relationships with Mode concordance and Object concordance. However, that the degree of relatedness is less between structural and dynamic phenomena, even at the same system level, is reflected by the lower "batting average" for relationships with Object concordance and Mode nonconcordance.

This interpretation suggests that research information from the small group field can perhaps best be treated as six separate systems of information: a structural and a dynamic system at the individual level, comparable systems of group structure and group dynamics, and systems of structural and dynamic phenomena external to the group. The six systems are represented in Figure 5.

There appears to be a body of relatively well established relationships within each of these six systems, as reflected by the relatively high "batting averages" for relationships with concordance of both Mode and Object. However, the small group field is still weak in establishing relationships between the six systems, even between the structural and dynamic systems at the same level of reference. This weakness is perhaps to be expected for a relatively young field, and may be indicative of a "normal" pattern and rate of progress in the development of a scientific area.

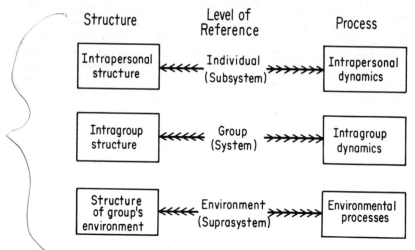

FIG. 5.   Diagram of the six "systems of information" within small group research studies

The relatively high "batting average" obtained for intrasystem relationships implies that existing research information on small groups can be systematized as a guide for future small group research. A catalogue of the relatively well established relationships within each system of information can be developed by a careful examination of the relationship classes that showed relatively high "batting averages" and by consideration of content-based subclasses within each of these relationship classes. The reference material in Part III, Section A provides such a catalogue.

The relatively low "batting averages" obtained for cross-system relationships may have any of several meanings. They may mean that the separate systems are relatively independent, empirically, and that we must ultimately develop separate "sciences" for each. Conversely, they may be viewed as part of a normal pattern of development for a relatively young scientific area. Formulation of sound hypotheses may inevitably proceed from "close" to more "distant" relationships. If this is the case, then our findings merely reflect the relatively early stage of development of the field. Related to this possibility is the notion that intersystem relationships vary in their strength as a function of the distance between systems. For example, it may be predicted that a higher number of relationships will occur between intrapersonal system variables and intrapersonal dynamics than between intrapersonal dynamics and intragroup structure. Effects in the latter case may be mediated by or interact with intervening system variables. Thus, as we shall see in Part II, confusing relationships probably exist between variables such as individual personality characteristics and group performance, because of the conceptual distance between the variables and the need to understand the set of intervening processes that probably occur and alter the precise nature of the effects. It may be best to conceive of the six systems not as categorically differing from each other, but as blending into each other, with variables in each having varying degrees of closeness (in operational terms) to variables of other systems. Thus, the intra-personal structure variable "ability" is probably conceptually closer to the intrapersonal dynamics variable "member task performance" than it is to "manifestation of disruptive behavior." Predictions of intersystem relationships will evidently vary as a function of the properties of the individual variables being studied.

In any case, there is need for continued effort to try to relate phenomena from the different systems. Relationship classes involving cross-system relation-ships should be examined to identify particular content subclasses with relatively high "batting averages." These may offer important clues to the basic principles by which different systems can be related to one another. Perhaps in the search for consistently significant cross-system relationships, we should relax the criterion of statistical significance or of consistency (the "batting average" that is to be considered high). Such a shift in the relative risks of Type One and Type Two errors would prevent the grossness of the classification system and the early stages of development of the field from obscuring important though marginal evidence about cross-system relationships. This problem is considered again in Chapter 4, as we discuss some of the limitations and contributions of the research program.

4 Evaluation, Modifications, and Implications of the Classification System

SOME LIMITATIONS OF THE CLASSIFICATION SYSTEM

It is obvious from the preceding chapter that the classification system was generally successful and that the fundamental concepts are of substantial value. It is equally obvious that the system still needs a great deal of refinement. The concordance principle does in fact hold, but that principle, as applied within the classification system, only accounts for a relatively small proportion of the "total variability" in the research information contained in the sample of studies reviewed.

For the small group field, the foregoing classification system seems to have been imperfect in several general ways. For one, it contained some parameters that apparently did not make any difference for these data. The Task parameter, with categories of description and evaluation, showed no relationship with "batting average" as a function of concordance or nonconcordance. In addition the Source and Viewpoint parameters empirically tended to have related categories, in effect yielding a single parameter. Of course, these problems are not intrinsically serious, because they can be handled by collapsing dimensions.

Another problem of the system is that it has insufficient inclusiveness and lack of refinement of many categories, so that a great deal of the variability remains unsystematized. For example, it is likely that the state–action distinction on the Mode parameter was not sufficiently sensitive to handle the range of states and actions that occur in small group research. This difficulty is most clearly reflected in the variable class "general structural properties of the group," listed later in Table 5, wherein a number of rather disparate types of variables (such as group size, communication nets, and group composition) are grouped together.

Several other ways in which the classification system was limited have become apparent in retrospect. It did not adequately treat statistical interactions of variables and multivariate relationships in general. It was necessary, in fact, to totally exclude factor analytic studies, as noted before. This limitation is more a conceptual flaw than a practical one, given the present body of data, for the total number of multivariate relationships contained in the sample of studies was quite small. Nevertheless, the inability to handle multivariate relationships adequately is a serious conceptual limitation, for the classification system was intended to be quite general in its applicability.

The classification system also did not provide a sufficiently refined means for treating *levels* of variables manipulated at two or more qualitative values — e.g., studies of different leadership styles, studies of different methods of critique, and studies of different forms of feedback. Often, the levels of such variables included in a given study have only a nominal scale relation to one another; seldom do they have more than an order relation. Furthermore, there is often little comparability between "high" and "low" levels of a given variable as used in different studies—and the system did not contain a yardstick for cross-comparing intensity levels of manipulated variables. Thus, "high" and "low" cohesion levels were not comparable across studies.

The classification system was particularly inadequate in dealing with the *time* dimension, partly as a consequence of the existing state of the small group field. Each of several kinds of temporal factors enters into the complex of considerations that affect small group behavior: (1) time in the sense of the history of the group, prior to the onset of the study; (2) time with respect to intervals between premeasures and postmeasures; (3) time in the sense of developmental changes in the group; and (4) temporal fluctuations, cycles, or phase characteristics of group activity. The classification system did not treat any of these temporal aspects adequately.

USES AND IMPLICATIONS

In spite of these limitations, the classification system seems to be a major step forward in the task of integration of small group research information. For one thing, its use has revealed that the broad domain of small group research may actually be composed of six relatively distinct, internally interdependent "systems" of information—based on level of reference and mode—that are *conceptually* but not necessarily empirically related to one another. Furthermore, results give at least general support to the concordance principle which implies that the classification system has some value as a predictive basis for future research.

The authors can foresee a number of ways in which results of this program can be of heuristic value. First, of course, is the direct use as reference materials of the program's products: a compilation of a body of research information, a set of study annotations that are systematic and parallel in form, and an extensive bibliography of the literature of the field. Presentation of these reference materials to make them widely accessible to small group researchers is of course one of the purposes of this volume. The reference materials, as already noted, constitute Part III of the book.

The data contained in the reference materials, particularly the compilation of research relationships (Part III, Section A), also provide a fruitful base for development of empirical generalizations about small groups. Some of the more apparent generalizations are stated in Chapter 6. The interested student of the field can undoubtedly induce still others, and improve those we have stated, by careful study of the reference materials given here and of other small group research evidence. In our opinion, one major criterion of the value of this research program is the extent to which it stimulates and facilitates the development of such inductively based "theory of the middle range."

Beyond these direct and immediate uses, results of the program can also serve some important functions with respect to the conduct of future small group research. First of all, the possible predictive uses of the classification system, with the principle of concordance, have already been suggested. If it is true that the probability of obtaining a significant relationship between two variables is a function of the degree of similarity of those variables on certain operational properties (level of reference, mode, source), then it follows that we can predict, and with some degree of accuracy, whether or not a given relationship is likely to obtain, once we have decided upon data collection procedures. This proposition, to the extent that it holds, has far-reaching implications, indeed. The most apparent—and ultimately most trivial—is that it provides a Machiavellian researcher (or an aspiring MA candidate!) with a basis for maximizing the odds that his study will yield statistically significant results. A much more important implication is that we can use the concordance principle to help guide study design, by suggesting what kinds of variables need special attention for experimental control, which variables are probably worthy of systematic manipulation and study, what kinds of conditions are most likely to show substantial effects, and what operational mappings of a given conceptual variable are most appropriate in a given study.

The classification system and its concordance principle may also offer a new perspective regarding significance testing and Type One and Type Two errors. The data suggest that a within-system relationship (Object concordance and Mode concordance) is fairly likely to be significant, whereas a cross-system relationship, especially if the variables involved also differ in Source, is far less likely to be significant. How, then, should we view a research study that tests, say, the relationship between a particular member trait and group task performance effectiveness? (Actually, much work in the field of leadership research does just this—e.g., Fiedler, 1961.) The two variables differ in Object (member and group, respectively), in Mode (state and action, respectively), and in Source (self-report and objective, respectively). This relationship class has minimum concordance, hence is generally unlikely to result in a significant relationship. If a student proposed to base his dissertation on the test of such an hypothesis, we might be justified in discouraging him, or at least in acquainting him with the actuarial "facts of life" involved. On the other hand, when such a relationship is tested, found to be significant, and replicated in successive studies (e.g., Fiedler, 1961), then perhaps we ought to view that substantive relationship as a very notable "fact" indeed. Moreover, it may be useful to adjust our criterion of significance (in advance, of course) in terms of the degree of concordance of the relationship to be tested, so that we stand a better chance of finding the "real," but attenuated, relationships between distant classes of variables. (We do this, implicitly, in the reverse direction, when we interpret reliability coefficients. No one would rejoice in obtaining a test-retest correlation coefficient of .30, even if that coefficient was statistically significant beyond the .001 level. We *expect* a higher level of association for the correlation of a variable "with itself.") We would not agree with Campbell and Stanley's (1963) contention that we must be more fearful of the "false positive" than of the "false negative," at least in regard to cross-system relationships in the small group area. The "false positives" will ultimately fall by the wayside when they fail to hold up upon replication. The "false negatives" are less likely to be replicated, because they appear to be unprofitable avenues of investigation.

The classification system and results of its present application also can provide a *diagnostic* guide for programing research in the small group area. For example, the data clearly point up certain relationship classes that have been tested many, many times with consistently negative results (e.g., relationships between measures of authoritarian attitudes and measures of group task effectiveness). We should avoid pouring additional resources into such areas, unless the endeavor involves some new approach that offers promise of success in spite of past findings. On the other hand, the data also show many relationship classes that have not been examined at all within the studies reviewed. These represent gaps in the body of knowledge, hence areas toward which future research can profitably be directed. Identification of the major gaps, or understudied areas, in the small group field and assessment of the theoretical relevance of research in those areas is another potential application of results of this program.

The advantage of the classification system as a common language for small group research should also be noted. In the light of results, it would seem that some of the parameters of the classification system—notably Object, Source, and Mode—could well serve as reference axes for small group studies, if only to aid communication about operational definitions in the field. On the other hand, the nonsubstantive nature of the basic classification concepts also gives rise to some communication problems. These are noted in the next section of this chapter, along with a discussion of how the classification system was modified to simplify presentation of the reference materials and to make them more communicable to other researchers in the small group field.

Finally, it should be pointed out that certain aspects of the classification system have application for classification of scientific knowledge beyond the area of small group research. The basic approach is quite general, with potential applicability to many fields of study. Many of the specific concepts and categories also have broader applicability. For example, the value of classification in formal or operational terms, rather than in terms of fairly loose, verbal, substantive concepts, certainly has proven useful in areas within the physical sciences. Also, changes in labeling of some of the categories, such as member, group, and surround, to more general labels such as "subsystem," "system," and "suprasystem" would make them applicable to many fields in which the system concept is useful. Certainly, many of the problems encountered in this program represent basic dilemmas in the classification of scientific knowledge. Indeed, one important function of this research program has been to serve as a pioneering case study in the emerging science (or technology) of classification of scientific knowledge.

MODIFICATIONS OF THE CLASSIFICATION SYSTEM

Two considerations led us to modify certain specifics of the classification system. The first and most important consideration derived from the validation analyses and subsequent indications of the differential importance of certain parameters for the body of data compiled. It seemed desirable to modify the system to highlight the Object, Mode, Source-Viewpoint parameters in describing small group research knowledge. Second, it became clear that any program designed to integrate a mass of verbal material must somehow compromise between elegance of the structure of the classification system on the one hand, and communicability of its results to potential users on the other. Up to this point in the program emphasis had been on development of a strong, formal classification system, while recognizing that this development was done at some cost in communicability. For example, one of the earlier products of the research program was a catalogue of major variables and relationships in the small group field (Altman & Terauds, 1960). This catalogue was produced before completion of the validation study and therefore utilized all of the distinctions of the classification system, leading to a very complex catalogue of information. Furthermore, the operational language used in the classification system was unfamiliar, hence hard to follow for most small group reseachers used to dealing in substantive language. Thus, it seemed highly desirable to modify the classification system to make the reference materials more communicable.

With these considerations in mind, the authors set forth a classification of variables that retained the essential fabric of the generic classification system in a more communicable form. The result of this effort is shown in Table 5. It can be seen that the six major classes of variables listed in the table reflect differences on the three important parameters. The Object parameter contribution is reflected in the distinction between member and group levels of reference; the Mode parameter role is shown by the distinctions between properties of members and groups as entities or states (e.g., personality, task capabilities, group structure) and members and groups as behaving objects (e.g., measures of performance, discussion behavior). The Source-Viewpoint parameter is represented by the differential classification of subjective measures (perceptions) and objective measures of member and group performance. A final modification of the system, as a descriptive device, was the incorporation of some content terminology, but now containing definitional meaning that attached to operational properties of the data on which it had been based. In a sense, then, for purposes of integration, the authors completed a full cycle from translation of data of the field into a new language, evaluation of that translation, and translation back to a more communicable language, now based on more-standardized terms.

Definitions of each of the variable classes shown in Table 5, along with references to studies in which each occurs and a compilation of research information relevant to each of them, are presented in Part III, Section A. This set of 31 substantive classes of variables is also used as the basis for information presented in the study annotations of Part III, Section B.

TABLE 5

LIST OF VARIABLE CLASSES OF THE CLASSIFICATION SYSTEM

Substantive Classes	Operational Classes
100 Properties of group members	
110 Biographical characteristics of members	Member state
120 Personality characteristics of members	Member state
130 Abilities of members	
131 General abilities of members	Member state
132 Task abilities of members	Member state
140 Attitudes of members	
141 Attitudes toward the task	Surround state
142 Attitudes toward the situation	Surround state
143 Attitudes toward nongroup persons and other groups	Surround state
144 Attitudes toward issues, concepts, ideologies	Surround state
150 Positions of members in the group	
151 Social position in the group	Member state
152 Task or physical position in the group	Member state
200 Properties of the group	
220 Group capabilities	
221 Group abilities	Group state
222 Group training and experience	Member and Group state
230 Interpersonal relations in the group	Member and Group state
240 General structural properties of the group	Group state
300 Conditions imposed on the group	
310 Social conditions	
311 Influence and conformity pressures	Group state
312 Induced social conditions	Group state
320 Task and operating conditions	
321 Stimulus properties of the task	Surround state
322 Feedback and reinforcement conditions	Member and Group state
323 Induced task conditions	Group state
400 Interaction process	
410 Content of interaction	Member and Group action
420 Patterns of interaction	Member and Group action
430 Outcomes of interaction	Member and Group action
500 Subjective measures of member and group performance	
510 Perceptions of task performance of self and others	Member action
520 Perceptions of social behavior of self and others	Member action

TABLE 5 *(continued)*

Substantive Classes	Operational Classes
600 Objective measures of member and group performance	
610 Leadership performance	Member action
620 Task performance of members	
621 Member task performance in experimental settings	Member action
622 Member task performance in operational settings: global measures	Member action
623 Member task performance in operational settings: specific measures	Member action
630 Task performance of groups	
631 Group task performance in experimental settings	Group action
632 Group task performance in operational settings: global measures	Group action
633 Group task performance in operational settings: specific measures	Group action

PART 2 ·

Perspectives on the Small Group Field

5 Descriptive Characteristics of the Small Group Field

This chapter contains an "actuarial" description of the small group field. It considers who small group researchers are, where they conduct their research, who supports it, and how broadly and intensively their studies cover the variables of the field. The description is based on an extrapolation from fairly objective information contained in the approximately 250 studies of the review sample. The chapter is a prelude to discussions of substantive, methodological, and institutional aspects of the field in the next three chapters, respectively.

RATE OF PRODUCTION

Examination of the small group field from a purely descriptive viewpoint reveals some interesting properties. Figure 6 shows a cumulative distribution over time (1910–1959) of small group research studies in the main bibliography (Part III, Section C) and in the sample of 250 studies reviewed in this program. The most striking feature of these data is the sharp rise during the 1950's. The field has grown, roughly, *tenfold* in the last decade! There is no apparent reason to expect this rate of growth to diminish.

It should be noted, however, that the data distort the recent production rate of the field somewhat. The bibliography probably does not cover the earliest decades as comprehensively as the later ones. Moreover, during the later years, a given research study (i.e., a given body of empirical data) often appears in several forms: as a technical report, as a journal article, as a conference presentation, and as a chapter in a volume of readings. This duplication tends to increase the bibliographic entries, though not the empirical data of the field. Even discounting these distortions, though, the basic point regarding the enormous growth rate of the field still holds.

LOCATION AND SUPPORT

Figure 7 shows the institutional affiliation of authors of studies in the review sample and the source of supporting funds, if any. An overwhelming proportion of studies (over 75 percent) was done by researchers affiliated with academic institutions. Most studies (over 80 percent) acknowledged some financial support, with the bulk of the support coming from governmental sources,

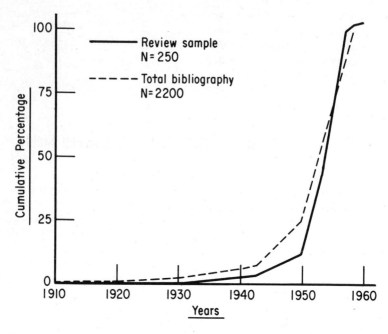

FIG. 6. Cumulative percentage of small group research studies for the period 1910–1959

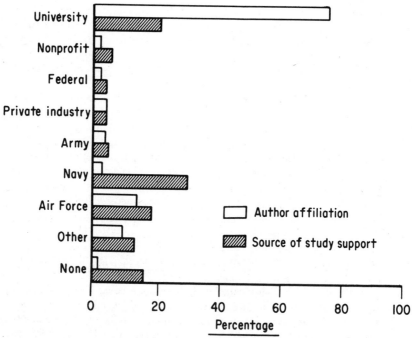

FIG. 7. Author affiliation and source of support of small group studies

predominantly parts of the defense establishment. Over 50 percent of all studies were supported by Navy, Air Force, or Army funds, with these services contributing in decreasing order. It is probable that the use of military and other governmental funds to support small group research has become more common during the later decades of the time period covered. It is also interesting to note that the armed services differed in the extent to which they supported "in-house," as opposed to "extramural," research programs. The Air Force maintained a balance between inside and extramural research, whereas the Navy predominantly supported extramural programs, mostly in university settings. The Army supported relatively little small group research during this period.

RESEARCH SETTINGS

Over half of the studies in our sample (about 55 percent) were done in laboratory settings. Another 30 percent were conducted in field-experimental settings, in which some realism was introduced but considerable "laboratory-type" control was maintained. Few studies (less than 5 percent) were done in natural settings. The preponderance of laboratory studies is not surprising in view of the preponderance of university affiliation of small group researchers. The dominant use of laboratory settings probably stems from many sources, including the desire for methodological rigor by way of precision and control and the availability of laboratory facilities and subjects in university settings. It is probably also influenced by a strong norm, derived from our historical tradition, which views the laboratory method as the quintessence of science, regardless of the substantive problem involved.

BREADTH OF STUDIES

Figure 8 shows the distribution of the number of relationships per study for the review sample. Most studies presented fewer than 50 tests of relationships (median 25, mean 62), with relatively few (less than 20 percent) having 100 or more empirical relationships. These data are underestimates, however for two reasons. First, the authors systematically omitted factor analytic studies, as noted in Part I; these constituted around 1 percent of the field. Second, it is likely that investigators examined many relationships that never appeared in reports; thus, negative results are probably underestimated. Nevertheless, these results suggest that small group studies tend to be relatively "small" in the number of pieces of empirical information that they generate, or at least in the number that they communicate to their readers. One reason for the relatively small number of relationships per study, as reported, is probably the scarcity of publication space and the consequent emphasis on brevity. This emphasis has the effect, of course, of screening out negative results and of predisposing researchers either (1) to do "little," but neat, studies or (2) to subdivide comprehensive studies into several smaller ones, published separately, with much of the comprehensiveness vanishing in the translation. Another

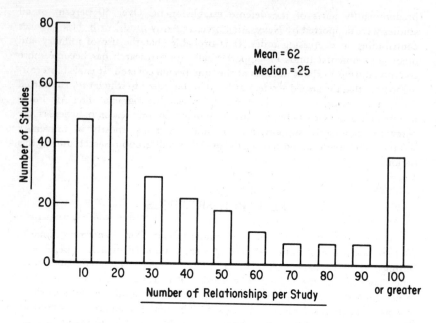

FIG. 8.   Frequency distribution of relationships among studies of the review sample

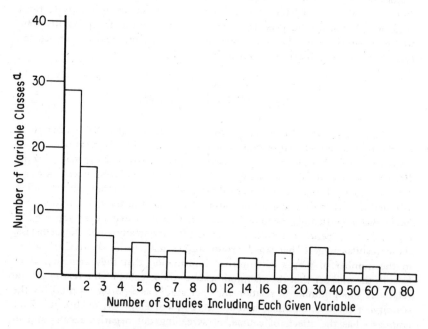

FIG. 9.   Occurrence of variable classes across small group studies

[a] There was a total of 92 different, unique variable classes in the review sample.

reason for the limited scope of many small group studies is, of course, the high
cost in time and resources for data analysis. This problem should diminish
greatly as we come to use computor technology more widely.

DISTRIBUTION OF VARIABLE CLASSES

Figure 9 shows the distribution of variable classes over the studies of the
sample. Note that the authors are here using the term *variable class* as employed
in the original classification system; that is, a variable class is defined as a unique
set of values on the six data parameters (see Part I). Hence the authors refer to
the large set of *operational* variable classes, *not* to the revised set of 31 *substantive*
variable classes.

Nearly one third of the variable classes appeared in only a single study,
and over two thirds appeared in seven or fewer studies. Note that each operational variable class can contain many different substantive variables. Even at
this fairly gross level of classification, however, there was very little replication
in the use of variables. Examination of individual substantive variables would
probably show that when the same variable was used in two or more studies it
was usually by the same investigator or his associates. Hence, variables of the
small group field tend to be idiosyncratic or unique to specific researchers.
Furthermore, variables of a given (operational) class were likely to be related
in the 250 studies only to variables of a few other classes (median about 4). Thus,
variables tend to be limited, in users and in usage.

SUMMARY

These analyses present a quite interesting picture of the "modal" small
group study. The typical study is done by an academic, with supporting funds
from some military service, using the laboratories (and sophomores!) of his
university. It involves a relatively small number of variables, covering a limited
operational and substantive range. The study is done more or less in isolation
from other small group research endeavors, in the sense that it seldom attempts
to replicate the findings, variables, or studies of others. It is done at a fairly
rapid pace and is often reported in several different forms, usually in successively
condensed versions.

Let us extend this modal picture further, going beyond these data somewhat, in terms of some general impressions gained from the review of many
small group studies. The typical study report is likely to give only a passing
glance at the research of others and a halfhearted swipe at theoretical formulation of the problem or the hypotheses. However, it usually spells out data
collection and data analysis procedures in considerable detail, exhibiting much
sophistication and methodological rigor.

Then it presents results, carefully limiting statistical conclusions only to
those justified by a purist interpretation of statistical inference. In a subsequent
section, results are discussed—often in terms that go far beyond the data and
imply much stronger and less equivocal results than were obtained. Unfortunately, it is usually the speculations of the discussion section rather than the

stringent conclusions of the results section that get cited in subsequent reviews of the study. The study often notes that a more detailed presentation of these and related data appears elsewhere, in an unpublished thesis or in a technical report. Finally, the need for further research—which replicates these findings and explores these variables further—is strongly urged. However, as pointed out before, this urging is seldom heeded, even by the urger.

This is of course an overgeneralization, even as a description of a typical or modal study; it is a composite picture of a number of features, each of which occurs with high frequency, but presented as if all of these occur together in many studies. It is certainly true that some small group studies do build carefully on past theory and findings—just as it is true that many studies do not appear rigorous in methodology. The point, here, is that lack of rigor in method is not a very general problem in small group research, whereas lack of theoretical emphasis, lack of ties with other work, and lack of replication all are very general problems of the field.

As noted at the outset, this chapter is a prelude to the three succeeding chapters, which attempt to draw generalizations about substantive, methodological, and institutional aspects of the small group research field, respectively. In reading Chapter 6, in which the authors draw some substantive generalizations from the data reviewed in this program, the reader should have in mind the descriptive picture provided here, as a frame of reference for assessing the "meaning" of those substantive generalizations. In Chapter 7, which discusses methodological problems in the small group field, the authors will bring to the foreground some of the features of small group studies alluded to in the present chapter (e.g., lack of replication, lack of breadth of studies, de-emphasis of theory) and try to trace their methodological consequences for small group research. Chapter 8 is a discussion of the small group field as a subculture within several broader cultures (e.g., the university, the professional community) and of certain cultural forces that operate on and affect the conduct of research in the small group field. That chapter will try to show how many of the methodological problems and present limitations of the small group field, some of which have been noted in the present chapter, arise and/or are nourished by existing cultural norms in the small group field.

6 Generalizations from Small Group Research Data

This section presents some generalizations about small group phenomena based on analysis of empirical relationships contained in the studies of the review sample. The reader should recall that the intent is not to abstract and summarize the data contained in the catalog of relationships (Part III, Section A) but rather to interpret and extend beyond those data so as to provide a perspective on the state of knowledge in the small group field.

The discussion here will parallel the organization of variables described in Chapter 4 of Part I and in the introduction to the catalogue of relationships (Part III, Section A). Relationships that involve properties of group members— e.g., biographical characteristics, personality characteristics, abilities, and attitudes—will be discussed first. Next, generalizations about properties at the group level—e.g., group capabilities and training, interpersonal relations, and general structural properties—will be presented. The discussion then turns to an analysis of member and group task performance in a variety of settings.

CHARACTERISTICS OF GROUP MEMBERS

Member Abilities and Experience

It may appear trite to say that a consistent, positive relationship exists between the capabilities and skills of group members and their performance. However, that this apparently simple relationship is not quite so simple is suggested by the data of the review sample. It seems clear, as common sense will suggest, that member characteristics such as intelligence, aptitudes, and specific abilities have a direct and positive impact on performance, when we are dealing with *objective* measures of such capabilities. However, there is a much more ambiguous relationship between estimates of members' capabilities based on *self-reports* (either by the subject, by his peers, or by his superiors) and individual performance. Thus, use of subjective estimates of member capabilities does not lead to clear predictions of member performance. It is probable that part of the reason for the lack of a stronger relationship between subjective estimates of abilities and individual performance is the operation of a halo factor. This factor is indicated by the generally high intercorrelation between various estimates of individual task abilities and general abilities made by group members about each other.

Of equal importance is the general finding that the abilities of individual members, even in terms of objective measures, are not necessarily useful predictors of group task performance, although such measures do seem to exhibit consistent, positive relationships with member performance. Thus, it may not be possible to predict the performance of a group, as a group, from knowledge of individual abilities however measured. The differential relationship of member abilities to individual versus group performance certainly highlights the old question of whether individuals *summate* to form a group or whether the characteristics of individual members combine in some nonadditive but otherwise unknown way. Although the present data are only suggestive on this question, the way in which member capabilities are or are not transformed into effective group outputs seems an interesting area needing further study.

It is also interesting to note that there is a very consistent and positive relationship between member abilities and manifestation of leadership performance, as judged by observers or superiors. What is especially striking about this relationship is that it holds when one uses either objective or subjective (peer) measures of abilities as predictors of leadership performance. Most of these strong relationships occur for relationships between judgments of leadership potential and measures of leadership performance, suggesting that a characteristic such as leadership potential is a fairly visible, though global, property of the individual. Recall that there was no such relationship between peer estimates of ability and task performance.

To recapitulate: research on group member abilities does not fully support the adage that the more capabilities members possess, the better group performance will be. It seems clear that *member* performance is enhanced by high *member* capabilities, but this does not seem to be the case, generally, with respect to group performance. Moreover, even the member capability versus member performance relationship applies only where we are dealing with objective measures of member capabilities; when peers make subjective judgments of capabilities, the relationship is much less clear-cut. Apparently, members are not good judges of one another's capabilities, except with respect to judgments of leadership potential.

This discrepancy between the predictive value of peer ratings of ability versus peer ratings of leadership potential also holds for relationships with various aspects of interaction process. For example, there are very weak relationships between group members' perceptions of one another's skills and objective ratings of morale, cooperation, and various other indexes of interaction process. On the other hand, people rated high on leadership potential are also seen by others as exhibiting more power and receiving deference from others, which, in turn, is related to the effectiveness of their leadership performances (as determined by both objective and subjective measures). It would seem that leadership antecedents, behavioral manifestations of leadership, and leadership effectiveness may all be visible to group members and be empirically related to one another.

Personality and Biographical Characteristics of Members

Surprising as it may seem, biographical and personality characteristics have not been studied very extensively in the small group literature, at least within the sample of studies reviewed. For those cases in which such variables have been studied, there do not seem to be any pervasive or general propositions that emerge. Clichés to the effect that the more stable the person is, the better he is as a leader or the more effective he is as a task performer are substantiated to some extent, but by no means are they firmly established conclusions. Actually very few data are available about the role of personality characteristics of members on various group phenomena. We suspect, however, that it would not be wholly profitable to pursue research in this area from the point of view of *individual* personality characteristics. Rather, such properties should be studied with respect to the composition of the group. It is probably not the presence or absence of member anxiety per se, for example, but rather the *pattern* of anxiety among group members that makes a difference for groups. In any case the influence of member personal characteristics on group functioning is an area worthy of further study.

Member Attitudes

One generally clear proposition is that favorable member attitudes toward the group task and toward the situation seem to be partly a consequence of high social or task status in the group, job autonomy, cooperative group conditions, and induced perceptions of task success. These relationships suggest that attitudes toward the task and toward the situation are associated with or reflect an over-all personal success in the situation. It is very interesting to note, however, that there is no indication that such attitudes enhance the individual's performance on the task or bear any definitive relationship to the quality of interpersonal relations in the group. The results on which this statement are based are very scattered, so it would perhaps be more accurate to say that we know very little about the impact of attitudes toward the task and the situation on member and group performance, or on interpersonal relations in the group. These would certainly be interesting and important areas for research.

Authoritarian Attitudes

One of the most popular variables in small group research is authoritarian attitudes. A distinction should be made between authoritarian attitudes of one or more members of the group, as measured by the F-scale or a similar instrument, and authoritarian role behavior by a leader who is deliberating implementing an experimental condition, as in the classic Lewin, Lippitt, and White (1939) study. For authoritarian attitudes, there has been a decided lack of consistent relationship with other variables. It should be noted that authoritarian attitudes have shown high *negative* relationships with sociometric choices as friend or as leader, and positive relationships with striving for high status and with several types of interaction behavior. However, in general, authoritarian attitudes show very little relationship to most interaction behaviors and inconsistent relationships with performance on tasks of various types. In short, the picture is at best quite sporadic. Thus, one of our most frequently studied variables has yielded extremely confusing and/or negative results.

Positions of Members in the Group

A general proposition that can be induced from the accumulated data is that group members who have high social or task status in the group are likely to have high power and use it, and to react favorably to the group.

Specifically, in comparison with low-status members, those with high status are likely to be seen as having high tasks skills; to more frequently exhibit diagnosing behavior, action initiation, information giving, and attempts to lead; to perceive themselves as having high influence and high authority, and as delegating responsibility; to exhibit leadership behavior in leaderless situations; to have higher task satisfaction and involvement; and to perceive the group as doing well on its task. Although these general propositions may seem obvious when viewed superficially, it should be recognized that it is not conceptually necessary that those with high status have high power. The fact that this relationship appears to be consistent bears on the fundamental nature of interpersonal relations in small groups. Furthermore, the fact that high-status persons are more involved in the group's task and perceive group success is by no means a necessary empirical outcome. Its consistency implies that status is not only related to power, but also to the individual's commitment to the group and his motivation toward group achievement.

With respect to task performance, it is interesting to note that there is very little relationship between the task performance of individual members and their social or task position in the group. Although the absence of a positive relationship is based on a fairly small number of cases, it does suggest that an understanding of an individual's performance cannot be gained solely from knowledge of his position in the group. This type of relationship requires more study, as does the relationship between the position of members in the group and the performance of the group as a whole. It would seem important to an understanding of group behavior in general, and group performance in particular, to know how various task or social positions that members occupy contribute to over-all group performance. There have been a large number of communication-net studies, but none of these to our knowledge examines the relative contributions of different positions in the group to over-all group performance. They study the effect of differences in network pattern on group performance but do not investigate the contribution of individual positions within that network pattern. It might be predicted that the more central a member's position in the group, either in the physical or functional sense, the greater would be his contribution to the total amount of variance with respect to group performance. Examination of this type of relationship would enable identification of the critical locations within the group network. This is a neglected and important area of research in the small group field.

CHARACTERISTICS OF THE GROUP

Group Capabilities and Experience

The adage "practice makes perfect" seems to be fairly well substantiated by small group research. The more task training and experience groups and group members have, the better they perform as individuals and groups. This generalization holds for *ad hoc* laboratory groups and for operational (e.g., military) task groups. However, if we attempt to predict performance from knowledge of group abilities, the situation is much less clear. Results of the very limited data on this issue suggest that knowledge of group capabilities alone is not sufficient to predict level of group performance. It is likely that group capabilities set an upper limit on performance potential of the group, which is achieved to the extent that the group and its members have the opportunity to practice and to gain experience as individuals and as a team. This probability is discussed in more detail in the section on member and group performance later in this chapter.

There has been very little research concerned with the way in which group properties (such as capabilities and level of training) achieve their impact on group performance. Small group researchers ordinarily select such input variables and relate them to output variables involving performance, final satisfaction with the situation, ultimate interpersonal attraction among members, and so on. Little attempt is made to study *how* various input variables produce their ultimate effect, in terms of intermediate processes and events. For example, granting a positive relationship between group training and group performance, how is such a relationship mediated? Do more-highly trained groups generate necessary information more readily; is it transmitted to others more efficiently; is there less redundancy in analysis and synthesis of information? In short, we have here a fairly well-established general proposition but we do not clearly understand why the general proposition holds, in terms of the dynamics of group functioning. This is a very noticeable gap in small group research.

Group Size

Variation in group size, including the difference between working alone and working with others, has been much studied in group research. Unfortunately, variations in size have ranged widely but not necessarily systematically. The review sample included studies using groups with up to 50 members. Results of different studies pertain to different ranges of group size. Nevertheless, a few apparently consistent relationships have been accrued. Relatively small group size is likely to be accompanied by the following:

1. Less perceived need for guidance and for a definite leader but less perceived competence and ability of the group as a whole
2. Fewer expressed ideas and less change in attitudes or other responses by members
3. Less-frequent perceptions of the leader as exhibiting coordinating behavior, clarifying rules, or wisely delegating authority
4. Greater perception of group task success

Although the general proposition that the smaller the group, the more effective its performance is often substantiated, the situation is very ambiguous. There are cases where the proposition holds but also cases where it does not, and it is very difficult to identify the factors that contribute to this difference. From study to study, different types of tasks are used, members differ in personal characteristics, and group sizes range from 2–3 persons to 30–50—not to mention social facilitation situations where people work alone but in the presence of others. A comprehensive and systematic exploration of the effects of a broad range of differences in group size, for a range of member, group, and task characteristics, is definitely needed. Thomas and Fink (1963) reviewed 31 studies on the effects of group size and reached essentially the same conclusions with repect to the need for more systematic research.

The Composition of Groups

Historically one of the main arguments for the study of groups has been that groups are not mere summations of individuals but a different system level, with properties arising from the pattern of member characteristics in interaction with the situation. In spite of this much-honored credo, there is very little research on group composition, and what little there is gives an unclear picture of the role of composition. The range of variables that are potentially important for group composition is very broad—interests, values, personality characteristics, biographical properties, abilities, and so on. Moreover, hypotheses about directions of effect have little theoretical underpinning, and are often little more than formalizations of such contradictory premises as "birds of a feather flock together," "opposites attract," or "one bad apple ruins the barrel." For some variables, it is likely that need complementarity (some members high on a given property, some low on the property) is required for good group performance or adequate interpersonal relationships. For other variables, it may be important that all group members exhibit a high (or low) amount of the property. The authors' review produced only a handful of studies on the composition question, and the literature in general reflects a similar paucity of research. Clearly, considerably more energy needs to be expended on group composition problems. This problem is discussed again in Chapter 7.

INTERPERSONAL RELATIONS IN THE GROUP

Interpersonal attraction among members of a group seems to be consistently and positively associated with, and perhaps derived from, member perceptions of their own and each other's status, power, and attitudes. For example, perceptions of others' task-related abilities and others' social and task status bear a positive relationship to liking others. This finding suggests that one of the bases of interpersonal attraction may be identification with those in favored positions or with those who possess desirable task- and situation-related characteristics. The phenomenon also appears to be two-way, for those who are liked by others (and who are in the favored positions or have the desired skills) are also highly attracted to their group. It might be hypothesized that this cycle is self-supporting, with members being attracted to those in favored positions or with relevant skills, who in consequence are more strongly attracted to the group. However, it is also likely that such a mutuality occurs only in groups where the members have consensually adopted a goal to pursue and in transient groups such as we find in a laboratory situation. In real groups, where motivations and aims are more complex, it is not likely that the simple picture presented here applies.

To pursue this question further, it appears that *mutuality* of perceptions, with respect to the situation or task and to each other, is associated with member attraction to one another and to the group. People are attracted to those who they think like them, who they think have the same task orientations as they do, who they are told like them (via any of a host of induced congeniality manipulations), who they are told to cooperate with rather than compete with, and so forth.

The bases of interpersonal attraction seem fairly clear. What implications for group functioning do variations in intermember and member-group attraction have? One of the results of high member attraction toward one another or toward the group is an increased communication rate. People communicate with those they like, and in doing so they show less aggressiveness and defensiveness, fewer communication difficulties, and more attentiveness to others. Furthermore, positive interpersonal relations in the group are also associated with member perceptions that other members and the group as a whole are performing well on the task. Thus, at this juncture, the picture indicates that group members are attracted to others who are in desired positions or who have desired skills, and these favored persons likewise are attracted to the group; that individuals like those who like them, are attracted to cooperative conditions, and see congenial groups and their members as doing well on their jobs.

Unfortunately, the sequence ends at this point. The relationship between interpersonal attraction per se and performance is quite unclear. Although there have been few direct tests of this relationship, what data do exist suggest an equivocal relationship. High member congeniality, cooperativeness, mutuality of liking, and other similar indicators of high cohesion do not appear to bear a universally positive relationship to performance. This problem will be discussed more fully in a presentation of factors associated with performance.

In summary, the over-all picture suggests that interpersonal attractions, interpersonal communication, and perceptions of task success may vary interdependently, so that a manipulation of any one of them will lead to correlated changes in the other two. Successful induction of greater interpersonal attraction produces greater communication and increased perceptions of group task success. Similarly, successful manipulation of perceptions of group success produces greater interpersonal attraction and communication. Finally, it is possible that increasing the amount of communication among group members will lead to more favorable perceptions of other members and of the group's performance effectiveness, although the latter point is not established in the present body of research information. In these terms, we can suggest that attraction, perceived task success, and communication constitute an *interdependent system of variables*. We can further suggest that certain other variables—e.g., cooperative conditions, job autonomy, and high member status—are associated with or are determinants of this system.

LEADERSHIP

A distinction is made here between measures of the effectiveness of performance of a leader *as a leader* and measures of the effectiveness of performance of the group he leads. This distinction is analogous to that of Hemphill (1961) between successful leadership and effective leadership. The former is discussed here, whereas the latter is discussed under group task performance effectiveness.

Most of the research information about leadership performance comes from studies of leaderless group situations, although some also comes from studies using superiors' ratings of leadership performance in operational settings. Effective leadership behavior seems to be a function of a number of characteristics and conditions:

1. Individual personality characteristics such as extroversion, assertiveness, and social maturity, but not a host of other, seemingly similar, characteristics
2. Education, but not age or other biographical characteristics
3. Intelligence, general ability, and task ability
4. High group status
5. Training in leader techniques

In turn, groups with effective leaders tended to be characterized by good work relations with other groups, care of equipment, orderliness, and a range of indexes of morale. As to behavior, effective leaders tended to be characterized by a high frequency of problem proposing, information seeking, and ego-involvement, in addition to the actions used to define their leadership effectiveness. However, they were not distinguishable from nonleaders, or ineffective leaders, on a number of other behavioral indexes.

Thus, there seems to be a fairly clear picture of who will emerge as leader, or be an effective leader; in essence, the member with highest status, skills, and training. There is a far less clear picture of just what behaviors characterize an effective leader or distinguish leaders from nonleaders. Notably, also, there were no data in the sample on the task effectiveness of groups that had such leaders, nor on what kind of effect, if any, the presence of a good leader had on task performance of group members. These latter classes of relationship reside at the core of group research and represent an uncharted area to which much attention should be given in the future.

TASK PERFORMANCE OF GROUP MEMBERS

The impact of several classes of variables on the performance effectiveness of group members and the group as a whole has already been noted. Therefore, this section and the next will be somewhat redundant, to insure coverage of key points and to expand on central issues where appropriate. Generally, the discussion to follow focuses on the performance of groups or their members, where performance is defined in terms of relatively objective measures, including ratings by supervisors. It should be noted that much of the discussion involves a synthesis of data gathered in many different settings—from highly artificial laboratory environments to real teams operating in industrial or military situations. In addition, the measures of performance effectiveness employed in small group research vary from very global judgments to measures of molecular aspects of performance in narrowly defined temporal spaces.

The Role of Member Characteristics

Research results support some common-sense suppositions about the impact of member-level properties on individual task performance in groups. For example, the higher a person's general abilities or intelligence and the greater his task aptitude, the better is his performance in a group. Moreover, there is a positive relationship between job performance and actual job knowledge, training, and experience. Thus, if we are aiming to increase the performance of individuals in a group situation we should select bright people who have relevant aptitudes and knowledge of the job, and who are trained and possess experience. Although not seemingly profound findings, they do lend objective credence to institutional wisdom; and they also contrast somewhat with the factors that enhance group performance, to be discussed later.

It appears that personal-social factors, such as member personalities, attitudes, and subjective perceptions, do not have consistently clear-cut relationships to individual performance. In some situations, such personal variables are important correlates of performance, but not in other cases. Interestingly, this ambiguity, if further research continues to yield such results, may suggest re-examination of the extreme "human relations" approach to management which has been in vogue in recent years. Some possible reasons for the confusing role of these more "romantic" variables are discussed in the next section. In any case, we can predict member performance in group situations more consistently from knowledge of intelligence and job-related characteristics than from personal-social properties. Further, as discussed earlier, member estimates of one another's performance capabilities do not relate very well to actual (objectively measured) performance.

The Role of Environmental Factors

In examining the role of "outside" influences on individual performance we again obtain some expected findings. Individual autonomy seems to have a positive effect on performance. In addition, feelings of participation in decision making about various aspects of the job (whether it actually takes place or not) and feedback in the form of reward and knowledge of performance enhance member performance. Moreover, imposing the requirement to make a (task-relevant) decision upon individuals affects their performance favorably. Thus, freedom, a sense of involvement, the requirement to act, and feedback all enhance member performance. This generalization is certainly compatible with common-sense notions, substantiated by a scientific approach to behavior.

TASK PERFORMANCE OF THE GROUP

The Role of Member Characteristics

When we examine factors that bear on over-all group performance rather than individual member performance, some interesting findings appear. Results suggest that *member* intellectual and task-relevant abilities (e.g., mechanical aptitude) are not consistently good predictors of group performance;

individual job experience is. Thus, merely having intelligent, high-potential people in a group does not necessarily produce an effective team.

The data also suggest that personality and attitudinal characteristics are not consistently related to group performance, except that the absence of extreme personality characteristics enhances group functioning. In addition, subjective perceptions of various types (e.g., personal skill estimates or estimates of the skills of others) are not always associated with good group performance.

The Role of Group Characteristics

Results at the group level appear to tie in with the preceding discussions. Experience as a group (working together for a period of time) has a positive relationship with group performance, as does relatively small size of the group. However, favorable interpersonal relations in the group (e.g., high cohesion, high morale) show unclear effects, although the trend is for high morale and cohesion to be accompanied by better performance. Such results are compatible with those for individual member performance, where job-related factors have a definite impact on productivity whereas the more "romantic," social-personal variables play a less precise role.

The Role of Environmental Factors

Outside influences play a similar role for group and individual productivity, with reward and punishment, rather than explanation and illustration alone, tending to enhance performance. In addition, there are differential effects of types of feedback on group performance (e.g., structured critiques have a more enhancing effect than completely unstructured ones). Further, several work conditions (such as efficient routing of necessary information or direct and rapid access to information) have a positive effect on group performance. Clarity of role definition (i.e., jobs each person is to do and relationships between various jobs) also aids group performance.

THE ROLE OF PERSONALITY AND SOCIAL FACTORS ON PERFORMANCE

As indicated, results are equivocal regarding the effects of personal-social factors on individual and group performance; this equivocation is somewhat in contrast to the attention such variables have received by researchers and consumers. How can we account for such findings and what potential role do the variables play?

It may be that the confused results are due to a methodological problem. For example, in aptitude and ability measurement, psychologists have well-developed tools whereas in the measurement of personality, attitudes, and group cohesion our measurement technology is less advanced.

On the other hand, consider the role of these variables from a conceptual point of view. When we speak of abilities and experience as determinants of performance, we are usually presuming that the more of the characteristic the better, and this usually is true. However, for personal-social variables this monotonic principle may not apply; rather, we may be in a realm where either *too much or too little* of a characteristic interferes with performance, with some optimum, in-between point enhancing performance. Schutz (1959) has posited such nonmonotonic effects for interpersonal needs.

Another hypothesis related to the role of these variables is that they are *mobilizers* of individual and group productivity potential. Perhaps individual and group abilities and experience tend to set limits within which the group can function just as intelligence may have limits set by heredity. In the same way that the environment may only exert an influence within the fixed bounds of intellectual capacity, so may it be that social-personal variables can enhance group performance only within limits set by abilities, training, and experience. Thus, if sufficient ability and experience are present, then favorable interpersonal relations will allow the group to achieve its potential. If they are not present to a sufficient degree, then the member or group may not perform up to its performance potential. Steiner and Rajaratnam (1961) have presented a model of group productivity that builds upon this basic premise.

Without attempting to resolve the possibilities raised here, we may say that personal-social variables cannot be simply viewed within the common-sense adage that "the happy, well-adjusted worker is the good worker."

There are, of course, many gaps to be filled with respect to research on performance effectiveness of individuals and groups. Some of these have already been pointed out in earlier pages. By way of summary, however, let us consider two especially salient areas that seriously warrant attention: (1) We need a better understanding of the sequential linkages that begin with inputs in the form of member, group, and task characteristics, that become *manifested in* intermediate interactive processes, and that culminate in a performance output. Too little attention has been given to systematically establishing the links in this complex chain. What has been done is to explore relationships between initial inputs and final outputs, with insufficient attention to the ways in which input characteristics enhance or hamper final output via intermediate processes. (2) We need a more sensitive appreciation of the parameters and properties of different types of performance. It is oversimplifying to group all types of performance under a single heading. There must be a better appreciation of what the varieties of performance are and a better appreciation of differences in performance across situations and tasks. Behavior does not occur in a vacuum; it results from an interaction of behavior, situation, and task. The question of task analysis is discussed in the following chapter in more detail. Here it is raised only in connection with the need for a better understanding of the dependent variables of member and group task performance effectiveness.

The preceding presentation has not tried to make all of the substantive generalizations that are possible from the fund of small group information contained in the catalogue of relationships in Part III, Section A. The authors have treated areas which they considered interesting and important, and for which they had some appreciation beyond the bare facts of the collected data. Several areas, which legitimately fall within the small group field, have been omitted for any of several reasons: because there were no easily describable themes; because the data on them appeared segmented and fragmentary;

or contrariwise, because the data covered so much as to be worthy of analysis beyond the present limited scope. Some good examples of the latter are the areas of conformity and of interpersonal perception. Both are vast topics, as indicated by the recent appearance of several books on each. In addition, these terms have come to include so many different classes of phenomena that it appears no longer fruitful to attempt to place all relevant research under one unitary umbrella of a general label such as "conformity" or "interpersonal perception."

No doubt each reader has an interest in some variable or class of variables that was only summarily covered in the preceding pages or was totally neglected. For this limitation, we apologize, reiterating our aim to provide a broad perspective, not an intensive analysis. For those who wish further information on a given variable or cluster of variables, the reference materials of Part III contain materials for more detailed consideration.

7 Methodology of Small Group Research: Problems and Prospects

The extensive and intensive review of small group research studies has given us a fairly rare opportunity to view the field from an "institutional" perspective, in addition to our usual perspective as practitioners of small group research. Several features of the field which are striking from this broad perspective are far less obvious from the narrower perspective of a single investigator pursuing his own line of inquiry. Some of these seem to have important consequences—both favorable and unfavorable—for research on small groups. This and the following chapter will attempt to describe these salient features and some of their consequences. The present chapter will focus on some general and specific features of research methodology in the small group field and try to indicate major problems and possibilities. In Chapter 8 we will go on to regard the small group field in terms of some important cultural forces that seem to be operating on the researcher and that help shape the form and substance of his research. The two chapters are related in that many of the methodological problems described in the present chapter arise, in part, because of the social-cultural forces at work in the small group field.

The first section of the chapter discusses some very general characteristics of small group research and the kinds of methodological difficulties to which they give rise. The second section deals with several more specific problems and weaknesses in methodology which seem to have retarded progress in the field. The chapter ends with a discussion of the need for more theory, both "small" and "large," and a plea for greater emphasis on theory in the small group field.

SOME GENERAL METHODOLOGICAL PROBLEMS

There are several striking features about research in the small group field, viewed in the collective, that have implications for methodology. One is the tremendous empirical vigor of the field, as indicated by the number of studies and the rate of their production. In the last three decades at least 2,500 small group studies have been conducted and reported, and the rate of production appears to be accelerating (see Chapter 5). A second striking feature of small group research is that studies vary widely in rigor and methodological sophistication all the way from case studies, almost anecdotal in form, to highly complex programs of experimentation on extensive samples of groups. There is also variation in research settings, as indicated in Chapter 5, although most studies are done in the laboratory and relatively few are carried out in naturalistic settings.

Another noticeable feature of small group research en masse is the tremendous diversity of terms, concepts, and operations which are used and the relative lack of replication. Replication of studies is practically nonexistent in the field. In the hundreds of studies reviewed throughout this program, the authors found only one instance of a near replication: studies of the interrelations among group cohesiveness, pressures to conform, and productivity by Schachter, Ellerton, McBride, and Gregory (1951) and by Berkowitz, (1957). Even that pair of studies differed in several crucial features (e.g., age, intelligence, and sex composition of groups and certain task details). Furthermore, there is relatively little replication in the use of variables across studies and in tests of specific relationships, as pointed out in Chapter 5. Nearly one third of the variable classes used in the sample of approximately 250 studies appeared in only a single study of the sample, and nearly two thirds appeared in seven or fewer studies. It should be emphasized that each variable class, as defined by the six *operational* parameters, includes a wide range of possible *substantive* variables; thus the frequency of replication of variables at the substantive level is considerably less than the foregoing figures suggest.

In fact, at the substantive level, the small group field seems to be shot through with idiosyncratic concepts and labels used only by one investigator and a few of his disciples. Frequently, the same term is applied to label operationally different concepts; at the same time, different terms are often used by different researchers to label what appears to be the same concept. Clearly, we do not yet have a common, shared language in the small group field; and the presence of a shared language is a prerequisite for the successful accumulation of knowledge. (Some cultural influences within the small group field that may be partly responsible for such diversity of labels are discussed in Chapter 8.) These general issues, along with other features of the small group field, give rise to several methodological problems or needs. Three such needs are discussed next.

The Need for Cumulation of Knowledge

The diverse and idiosyncratic nature of our terms, coupled with the vigorous production of empirical studies of varied methodological quality, provides a context for denoting what is perhaps a major dilemma of the small group field: though we have a very high volume of research activity, we have not had a rapid growth of a body of knowledge, because we are not gaining empirical evidence in a form which permits us to integrate it cumulatively with prior evidence. We cannot readily tie one set of findings to another, simply because there is no broad, shared frame of reference in terms of which they can be related. The existence of a systematic and cumulating body of empirical knowledge is one necessary condition, if not a definitional requisite, for the existence of a science. Regardless of the fact that most small group researchers have learned to conduct their single, separate investigations with extremely sophisticated and rigorous methods, the field as a whole is still prescientific in regard to the accumulation of knowledge.

Three more specific needs underlie this need for systematic accumulation of knowledge; their fulfillment would advance the field greatly. The first is the need for more replication of studies. Replication is at least as essential for the small group field as it is in the physical sciences. The failure of a given finding to be reproduced, upon replication, is an essential (and pretty efficient) means for screening out "false positives" which, as Campbell and Stanley (1963) have pointed out, are likely to be exceedingly numerous in a field geared to relatively "weak" alpha levels for its significance tests.

A problem arises, however, because although frequent replication of studies is very valuable for the field as a whole, it is an unrewarded and potentially dangerous pursuit from the point of view of the individual researcher. Not only is there lack of a strong norm for replication; there is a rather strong norm against it. Replicating someone else's study is often not viewed as a sufficient contribution to the field to be a worthy endeavor for even a master's level thesis, let alone a doctoral dissertation or a publishable article. (Other ramifications of the importance of "publishability" and "distinctiveness of product" are discussed in Chapter 8.) From the institutional viewpoint, the authors would strongly support the contrary position, viewing a replication—or a failure to replicate—as a highly valuable contribution and urging the small group research community to develop a strong norm *for*, rather than against, the conduct of studies to replicate empirical findings.

A second methodological need, directly related to the difficulties in accumulation of knowledge that the authors have been discussing, is the need for more terminological rigor—even standardization. The inherent complexity and embryonic stage of development of the small group field (and, indeed, of all the social sciences) probably requires continued use of concepts defined in somewhat loose, verbal-discursive terms. However, it may be that the need to use verbal, rather than more-rigorous, symbol systems has been an invitation to select and use terms for maximum distinctiveness and attention value rather than for maximum semantic rigor. While the authors hold with Lewis Carroll's Humpty Dumpty that we can indeed make words mean whatever we want to, we also argue that our science will progress much faster and more efficiently to the extent that we curb our appetites for distinctiveness of terms and develop stronger appetites for standardization. By standardization of terms, in this context, we simply mean that for each concept or variable in the field, we ought to call a spade a spade; we ought to all agree to call it that in all its uses; and we ought to all agree not to call the same variable by some other label nor to call some other variable by that label. We do not hold a brief for any particular set of terms; but are only arguing for a shared use of terms. We would naturally urge, of course, that distinction between variables be specified in operational terms, as well as (or instead of) in verbal-discursive, substantive terms.

Of course, if variables are going to be defined in terms of operations, we must then find some way to prevent the generation of a literally infinite number of variables, each defined in terms of different sets of data collection operations. This problem points up a third need, related to the problem of accumulations of knowledge—namely, greater concern with the task of construct validation. Nowhere does Campbell and Fiske's (1959) multitrait multimethod analysis, with its mandate that we establish both convergent and divergent validity for our concepts, pose a more relevant challenge (or threat!) than for investigators in the small group field. Small group research is characterized by very agile and cavalier "mappings" of equivalence (on a priori grounds and often mainly on the basis of similar verbal labels) between different operational forms of manipulated variables, of response variables, of tasks. As with replication studies, there seems to be a norm against studies that establish the empirical similarities and differences (convergences and divergences) of sets of operations. Because of such norms, the conduct of construct validation studies, however institutionally valuable, are dysfunctional for the individual researcher. Here, too, the authors urge a shift in norms and a subsequent increase in commitment of our limited resources for validation of constructs in the small group field.

If major progress can be achieved in these three areas—more replication of studies, more standardization and sharing of terms, and more effort toward empirical validation of constructs—we would be well on the way toward solving the dilemma of having much "information," but little accumulated "knowledge." This achievement would hasten us along the road toward becoming a science, institutionally, in terms of having a systematic body of knowledge, as well as being scientific, individually, in terms of rigor and sophistication of procedure. There may be some opposition, however, between what is good for the field, institutionally, and what is efficacious for the individual researcher in the field, in the light of the forces playing upon him. We have indicated this opposition of individual and institutional viewpoints along the way and will discuss some further aspects of it in Chapter 8.

The Need for Programed Diversity of Research Settings

It was noted earlier that a large proportion of small group research studies are done in laboratory settings and relatively few in naturalistic or field settings. There are several good reasons for emphasis on laboratory settings in a relatively young field where real-life settings are apt to be very complex. The laboratory offers much by way of precision of measurement, control of conditions, and opportunity for manipulation of theoretically lucrative variables. There are some serious limitations inherent in the laboratory method in social science, however, and these cast doubt on the wisdom of using it to the exclusion of other research strategies (cf. Festinger & Katz, 1953; McGrath, 1964). The most notable limitation is the relatively artificial nature of the laboratory setting for the study of human social behavior and the relatively limited ability to generalize from findings of the laboratory to social phenomena in real-life situations. We all presume that the ultimate goal of our research is to gain understanding about real social phenomena. (The authors are not referring to the resolution of applied problems, but to broad understanding of human behavior, as distinct from evidence about behavior under highly special conditions.) If so, then exclusive use of the laboratory as the research setting for studies of small group phenomena runs a substantial risk that, though we succeed in each individual inquiry, we may fail in over-all aim. By highly disproportionate use of laboratory settings alone, we may gain much information about behavior in the laboratory, but we may neglect the bridge from laboratory to real-life settings.

It is perhaps belaboring a point with which all would agree to say that there is a need for programmatic research that utilizes a range of research strategies or settings and that builds from study of actual social phenomena by way of theory, to controlled experimentation, and back to actual situations for validation of laboratory findings. Although this is a part of our generally accepted credo or research philosophy, it is a part that is seldom exemplified in practice in small group research. There are notable exceptions to this general statement; e.g., the excellent programmatic work of Festinger and associates on communication in groups (Festinger, 1950, 1954, 1957; Festinger, Schachter, & Back, 1950; Festinger, Riecken, & Schachter, 1956). But these are fairly rare exceptions. Most research on small groups is not discernably programmatic. Nor does it manifest deliberate, conscious choice of research strategy. Rather, choice of method in most small group research studies seems to derive either from repeated use of a given research strategy because of a personal preference for a particular paradigm or research style, or from an opportunistic use of an available situation by whatever research strategy is most easily utilized. Both of these are perfectly *human* modes of behavior, and ones of which the present authors have most assuredly been guilty on many occasions; but they are not very scientifically useful ways of behaving over the long run.

Here, as with the problems raised previously about replication and construct validation studies, we are faced with a duality of aim and efficacy. It is institutionally essential that research on small groups be programmatic, in both substance and method. At the same time, it is often impossible for the individual small group researcher to pursue his work on a programmatic basis. Usually, the individual researcher does the best possible job of whatever research activity he is in a position to pursue. By this statement the authors refer to the use of sophisticated and rigorous methodology in design, data collection, and data analysis. Thus, as a field, small group research excels in methodology at the study level; at the same time, we seem to be floundering, methodologically, at the programmatic and institutional level.

The Need for Multivariate Approaches

Just as there is a need for more systematic and comprehensive efforts regarding replication of studies, selection of terms, construct validation of operations, and choice of research strategies, there is also a need for use of data collection and analysis methods that fit the complex, multivariate nature of the phenomena of the small group field. Nearly all would subscribe to the statement that small groups represent complex systems influenced by a multiplex of interdependent variables. But like our belief in programmatic study, our premise of interdependence of multiple variables is usually ignored in the practice of small group research. Most studies of small groups deal with a highly restricted set of variables and relate them to each other two at a time. (It must be noted here that factor analytic studies are an exception to this general statement; however, our experience indicates that they represent only about 1 percent of small group studies.)

The primary reason that small group researchers continue to preach multivariate interdependence but practice single-variable analysis is that we do not yet have adequate analytic and statistical tools and concepts to do otherwise.

Factor analysis is, indeed, becoming more widely used—for good or ill—with the advent of efficient computer programs for extracting and rotating factors. In small group studies, however, factor analysis is more often used as an instrumental step (e.g., to "purify" a lengthy questionnaire) than as a central methodology (e.g., to identify the factorial structure of a population of groups), although there are several notable examples of the latter use (Hemphill & Westie, 1950; Cattell, Saunders, & Stice, 1953; Borgatta, 1955). Recent advances in multivariate methodology, such as three-way factor analysis (Tucker, 1963) and multivariate analysis of variance (Bock, 1963), offer promise as methods for multidimensional analysis of data from small group research. The use of computers, to simulate small groups and/or organizations, also offers a means for assessing the effects of the simultaneous operation of many variables, at each of many combinations of values—assuming, of course, that one can program adequately many of the simpler relationships involved on the basis of current empirical data and theory. Such methodological advances as these, if utilized by small group researchers, may make it possible for research practice to approach the multivariate nature of the phenomena.

SOME SPECIFIC METHODOLOGICAL PROBLEMS

Besides the broad methodological problems described in the previous section, there are a number of more specific methodological problems in the small group field. Many of these are, in effect, methodological gaps or parts of the small group research "space" that remain more or less virgin territory. Each of these will be treated briefly; there is little to say about a gap except that it exists and should be plugged.

Time

One of the major operational parameters used in the classification system— and one which is apparently of consequence, empirically—is the mode distinction between state and action, or structure and process. This distinction is essentially in the temporal dimension; structure implies a static temporal referent, process implies movement or change through time. We need to develop better formal conceptualizations of structure and process and of how they articulate with one another. We also need better methods for measurement of change—or its equivalent, time 1–time 2 differences.

Beyond this need, we must recognize that time represents a fundamental dimension, or reference axis, in any metalanguage for small group research, and that a better methodology for dealing with temporal considerations is necessary. Temporal relationships of at least three kinds are of concern in small group research: (1) temporal aspects of the group's prestudy history; (2) directional changes in the group through time—"between-session" patterns of group development; and (3) phasic, cyclical, or sequential fluctuations in group activity through time—"within-session" patterns of group process. The first of these temporal aspects has received little attention, perhaps because we so frequently use newly formed, experimentally created groups, with "no" past history, in laboratory studies of small groups. One major justification for creating and using "zero history" groups is that we can trace group development through time. Yet such longitudinal studies of small groups are quite rare, and most of them are essentially case studies of one or two groups (e.g., Newcomb, 1961; Festinger, Riecken, & Schachter, 1956; Sherif, Harvey, White, Hood, & Sherif, 1961). The third temporal aspect—phases in group process —has received some attention (e.g., Bales & Strodtbeck, 1951; Heinecke & Bales, 1953; Landsberger, 1955; Schutz, 1959), but the over-all subject area has barely been tapped.

By ignoring one or more of these three aspects of temporal considerations, we implicitly make some tenuous assumptions that may seriously affect our progress, particularly with respect to comparing among studies. For example, if we ignore the temporal aspects of a group's activity we implicitly assume that all groups are at the same stage of development. This is a weak assumption; yet if we are to achieve comparability among studies and the ability to pool information in an accumulative fashion, we must have some appreciation of the developmental stage at which a group is functioning. Related to the foregoing is another implicit assumption—namely, that experimental manipulations operate all at once, with no temporal delay or lag. In using laboratory situations, we often implicitly make the assumption that effects of manipulations by instruction, general environmental conditions, and so forth will occur in a very short period and that the lag of impacts will happen equally for all groups. Pilot work is directed toward testing this assumption, but too often we feel secure once any type of difference in the expected direction is obtained and spend too little time tracing such effects over time and observing them develop. For example, it may be that instructions to "be cohesive" do produce differential interaction process as compared with instructions to "not be cohesive" in the short one-hour laboratory experiment, but perhaps the presence of confusion among results of different studies may be attributable to the fact that the impact of the same variable was observed at different stages of group development.

There are probably several reasons for lack of attention to these aspects of the time dimension. Study of process is conceptually difficult and complex. Longitudinal or long-term studies are expensive. Methodology for measuring process and change is still crude. In our judgment, however, investigation of aspects of the time dimension is absolutely crucial for understanding small group phenomena. Hence, we urge a far greater commitment of resources to this problem in spite of the barriers to progress.

Group Interaction

Closely related to the problem of temporal analysis is the need for more attention to analysis of the behavior of groups—their interaction—as opposed to the products or outcomes of that behavior. Typically, we assume that various "inputs" to the group—members, group structure, task conditions—have effects or outcomes that are mediated via interactive behavior. Yet relatively few studies of small groups attempt to measure their intervening, interactive behavior directly; most small group researchers are apparently content to measure and relate "input" and "output" variables and then to make inferences about the intervening processes accounting for obtained relationships.

There is a great need for better methods of observing, recording, and analyzing group interaction and for more studies that utilize such methods. There are many technical problems still unresolved for present interaction systems. The proper unit of observation for interaction remains a problem. Almost all existing interaction-recording systems deal with monadic units (acts of an individual group member), whereas there are strong conceptual reasons for preferring dyadic or polyadic units (interacts of two or more group members). There are few clear ground rules for choosing between structural units (e.g., spoken sentences), functional units (e.g., meaningful or codable inputs), and temporal units (e.g., 10-second intervals), and few for decoding the most meaningful or useful unit within any one of those forms. The problem of use of "live" versus taped versus written transcript is unsolved and largely unstudied. Choices among them seem to be made on the basis of comprehensiveness of the recording system, reliability, and training costs.

There also remains a substantial problem in selecting an appropriate frame of reference for coding. This problem includes that of what kinds of distinctions to make (content, function, structure); what depth or inference level to use (manifest content, motivational inference, etc.); and how structured the set of categories should be (nominal, ordinal and unidimensional, multidimensional, etc.).

From the point of view of small group research as a field, there seems to be a need for a general or multipurpose interaction-recording system. The Bales (1950) system, probably the most general-purpose one now extant, is not equipped to deal adequately with nonverbal actions and seems to be useful primarily for those group situations where a problem-solving orientation is appropriate. There appears to be no generally used system that reflects power relations or influence relations among group members, nor is there a good system for treating the flow of positive and negative affect in interaction. Most interaction systems also fail to deal adequately with the time dimension.

On the other hand, interaction systems should derive from theory. They should reflect the purposes and hypotheses of the study. Hence, in any specific case, it may not be possible or even advisable to construct a generic system. Rather, it may be more useful to tailor an interaction-recording system to the particular content and design of a given study. This tailoring will, of course, greatly limit generality of findings, but it may be the best we can hope for until we have a general theory of groups.

One of the effects of the many difficulties associated with charting and studying interactions through time and relating group behaviors to one another is that we seem to have gravitated more and more toward becoming a science of the independent variable. It seems as if much effort is being expended, as it should be, on careful delineation of the independent (usually manipulated) variable in individual studies. On the other hand, there seems to be an equivalent neglect of intensive concern with the dependent variable, not so much with respect to sensitivity of measurement as with respect to numbers of measures in a given study and relationships between dependent variables—both sequential and simultaneous. In spite of the difficulties inherent in such work, the authors urge a greater focus on the dependent, behavioral side of small group studies.

Task

There is clearly a need for a broader and deeper consideration of the small group task. Most individual group studies are conducted with a single, unique task, often tailored for the particular study. In the task area, small group researchers have exhibited far more ingenuity than rigor. Very few studies have generated findings relevant to a range of types of tasks. Those which have utilized different tasks (e.g., Carter, Haythorn, & Howell, 1950; Carter, Haythorn, Shriver, & Lanzetta, 1951; Haythorn, 1953) have not related task differences to any firm conceptual schema. Several small group researchers (e.g., Roby & Lanzetta, 1958; Shaw, 1963) have urged more effort in clarifying and elaborating the task domain in small group studies. The authors add their voices to that chorus.

Task is an artificial construct. What is "task" and what is "group" tend to shade together in many specific instances (e.g., actions toward organizing a division of labor in the group). It is probably useful to conceptualize *all* groups as having tasks—hence equating tasks with "shared goals." In this view, the task of a group such as a family may be entirely that of maintaining the group's existence and well-being.

Task can also be defined to include all factors impinging on the group and its members whose origins are not properly attributable to members or to the group. This kind of definition tends to equate task and environmental effects, as the total situation.

The task domain can be dealt with in any of three ways: (1) by concern with task qua task, which asks "What pattern of stimuli is impinging on the group ?"; (2) by concern with task as behavior requirement, which asks the normative question "What responses *should* the group emit, given the stimulus conditions, if it is to attain some criterion of task success ?"; (3) by concern with task as behavior, which asks the descriptive question "What responses *do* the group emit, given the stimulus conditions ?" It can be argued that, as psychologists, we do not care about the first (the stimulus properties of the task, as such). The second approach is useful but requires imposition of normative judgments about group purpose and goals and optimal states and actions in relation to those goals. The third approach permits comprehensive description of group activity and subsequent induction of possible patterns, likely patterns, and effective patterns of activity. This approach makes the description of tasks identical with the description of group behavior or interaction, and as such may not always focus our observations sharply enough.

Most listings of task characteristics include two or all three of these levels, but do not always distinguish among them. Roby and Lanzetta (1958) have dealt with task qua task considerations and with behavior requirements or demands. Shaw (1963) is developing a set of dimensions that will provide gross descriptions of group tasks. These include dimensions dealing with behavior requirements, dimensions dealing with member perceptions, dimensions dealing with how performance is scored, and dimensions descriptive of elicited behavior. Many or all of these distinctions may be very useful ones. It is certainly the case, though, that we will progress more rapidly on the problem if we distinguish between these conceptually distinct aspects of the group-task situation.

Group Composition

One of the most striking aspects of the data reviewed here is the lack of attention to problems of group composition. Relatively few studies of composition exist. Most of these are studies of the relationship between some group member property (summed over members, or averaged) on some group output. Historically one of the major justifications for research at the group level, rather than research at the level of individuals in groups, has been the argument that groups are not a simple summation of member properties. Yet it is a rare study, indeed, that deals with nonadditive patterns of relationship among member characteristics. Exceptions include Haythorn, Couch, Haefner, Langhan, and Carter, (1956 a and b) on homogeneity-heterogeneity of attitudes, Cohen (1956) on homogeneity–heterogeneity of defenses, and Schutz (1959) on compatibility–incompatibility of interpersonal needs.

There are many potentially meaningful patterns of relation among members on any given characteristic—including conjunctive and disjunctive combinations—as well as many member characteristics where composition effects are worthy of study. Far more effort is needed here because the area offers a major route for articulating our body of knowledge across system levels, from member to group.

The gaps and problem areas discussed here—time, task, interaction, and composition—exist in part because we do not yet have an adequate theory to guide research on small groups or to provide an integrating framework for its results. This underlying problem of lack of theory is the topic of discussion in the final section of this chapter.

THE NEED FOR THEORY

The greatest need in the small group research field is for more and better theory. By theory, here, the authors simply mean systematic attempts to formulate sets of principles, postulates, and hypotheses about relationships among the variables of the field which can then be tested empirically. By theory the authors do not mean the formulation of verbal explanations or rationalizations as to why the data came out as they did in a completed study. Although such explanatory efforts are often useful, leading to important insights, they are not theory development in the present context. Theory, as used here, also does not mean the formulation of a descriptive model of the problem—whether that description be in the form of mathematical, verbal, diagrammatic, or computer-terminology symbols. These are often very useful frameworks, which offer new ways to conceptualize phenomena of the field; but they, too, are not theory as we here intend to use the word. To be theory, the formulation must hypothesize specific outcomes under specified conditions, in terms that make it possible to test the prediction, and must anchor the hypothesis in a broader context of postulates and assumptions.

Having excluded ex post facto explanations and descriptive models from theory, the authors feel justified in stating that relatively little theory underlies research in the small group field. More accurately, we may say that most studies involve little in the way of explicit formulation of theory. There are notable exceptions, of course. Deutsch's (1949) formulation regarding cooperation and competition, Thibaut and Kelley's (1959) theoretical formulations (primarily for the dyad), Homans' (1958) theory of exchange, Festinger's (1950) and Newcomb's (1961) formulations on communication and attraction in groups, French's (1956) theory of power, and Schutz's (1959) theory of interpersonal needs offer excellent examples of theory in the small group area. But the great preponderance of research in this field is done (or at least, is reported) with little more theory than a casual comment that it is based on the concepts of Lewin, Freud, Mead, or Festinger. The present lack of emphasis on theory has historical roots, as noted in the introductory chapter, being in part the aftermath of the empirical rebellion against an earlier ethos that stressed the armchair rather than the laboratory. Nevertheless, a theoryless science is as out of balance as a science without an empirical base, and a return of the scales to a more-equal valuation of theory and data seems long overdue. In our judgment, the small group research field has too much data and too little theory; adding further data to the existing, unrelated mountain of bits of information will not help progress toward a science of small groups, and may actually hinder such progress. After all, Brahe's many careful observations about positions of the planets did not achieve their full significance until Kepler's theoretical integration of those data.

The lack of emphasis on theory, like the other problems raised in this chapter, does not arise because of the stupidity or recalcitrance of small group researchers. Let us make our position clear in that regard! We consider ourselves full-fledged, card-carrying small group researchers. We view ourselves as more-or-less typical researchers in the field, as to volume, rigor, and sophistication of our own research. Where we seem to be critical of the small group field, it should be obvious that we do not mean to blame the researchers of the field, individually, for those weaknesses. Rather, we are pointing to limitations which, if made explicit, may be overcome or at least guarded against in future small group research, including our own.

The lack of emphasis on theory, like the other methodological problems raised in this chapter, is fostered by certain cultural factors and norms that are operative in the small group research community. Because it may well be necessary to change those sociocultural norms before we can correct the methodological weaknesses of the small group field, we will try in the next chapter to describe the small group field as a subculture and to identify some of the normative forces that play a part in shaping research in the field.

8 The Culture of the Small Group Research Field

Since completing this intellectual journey through the small group field—and we have traveled quite broadly and made quite extensive observations—we have become acutely aware that there is more to a field of science than data and reports. Specifically, we have been impressed by the realization that small group research, or rather the set of people who do that research, represents a distinctive community or subculture, and that various cultural forces or norms operate within that community and affect the behavior of its members. Furthermore, as noted in Chapter 7, certain oppositions between the perspective of the individual researcher and institutional perspectives of the field in the aggregate can be discussed. These oppositions arise or are nourished by the normative forces in the small group community. Hence, we need to examine the characteristics of the small group culture, in order to appreciate *why* the field has some of the methodological problems that it has.

This chapter is presented with some trepidation, because its intent may easily be misunderstood and its message readily misinterpreted. Our purpose in writing this chapter has to do with a felt responsibility to our colleagues in the small group area. We have chosen to direct a major portion of our careers and we received substantial support from others in the conduct of the enterprise reported in this volume. The endeavor gave us an opportunity to view the small group field from an institutional rather than a narrowly personal viewpoint. What we have seen from that institutional perspective has been of great value to us, personally and professionally, and may be of value to others. Because of the opportunity given to us in conducting this program, along with our own individual research activities, we probably have a broader and more detailed view of this particular subarea than the average colleague of our vintage. In a sense, we owe it to our colleagues to share that experience, insofar as it may be helpful to them.

Therefore, we will attempt to describe some salient aspects of the history and current culture of the small group field and some of the effects of cultural processes on the changing roles of the small group research scientist. The cultural forces that are to be discussed are neither good nor bad in themselves, but they are *real* forces, influencing our collective work. And they have consequences—both good and bad—upon the progress of scientific inquiry in the small group field.

It should be noted that the small group field shares some of its history and much of its current cultural context with other areas of social psychology, and with the parent disciplines of psychology, sociology, and anthropology. It is likely that to a greater or lesser degree these fields reflect at least some of the consequences of history and culture that will be discussed here. Let us emphasize, however, that the present endeavor has been limited to the small group field and that we wish the present chapter to be similarly limited in its reference. We do not wish to extend what is said here to other substantive fields, or to compare small group research to related fields in terms of these historical and cultural forces and their consequences. The reader, of course, may do so at his own risk.

It should also be noted that we are here attempting to describe the small group culture as it now exists without raising questions as to etiology of the historical and cultural forces or the underlying causal relations among them and current trends and problems. It may be true that we will not describe (or even suspect) the full complexity of many of the factors and consequences that are discussed. We willingly accept this limitation, in the hope that what is presented in this chapter will stimulate others to pursue such questions further, for the benefit of all in the small group research field.

HISTORICAL ROOTS OF THE
CURRENT SMALL GROUP CULTURE

The relatively short history of small group research and of social psychology as a whole has been turbulent and dynamic. The early, stormy years from 1900 to the 1920's contained grand theorizing about man's social nature and its "true" essence. The 1920's focused on methodology. The 1930's emphasized national problems such as leadership and prejudice, and contained the broad theorizing of Kurt Lewin. The postwar 1940's were times of application and amplification. We entered the 1950's with vigor and increased resources, scurrying to conduct research on matters learned about during the war or temporarily held in abeyance because of the war. That decade saw a research boom which has continued into the 1960's.

But research in current boom times is different from past research in several ways. For one thing, there is little theory, and none comparable in breadth and sweep to the early formulations of MacDougall or the field theory of Lewin. What little theory has been propounded in recent years is narrow, dealing only with delimited aspects of group phenomena. Moreover, many of the more recent theories—such as those of Festinger (1950, 1954), Festinger et al., (1950), French (1956), Heider (1958), Newcomb (1953), Thibaut and Kelley (1959)—have been essentially extensions or applications of some of Lewin's basic notions.

The current times also seem to have a certain air of intellectual staleness, which contrasts with the intellectual excitement of the Lewinian era of the 1930's, the pre-1920 era of broad theory, and the turbulent war years of the 1940's, and is closely akin to the austere, methodologically oriented years of the 1920's. In a recent review of the field, Steiner (1964) seemed to sense a similar intellectual blandness. He said, in part, "Although research has proceeded at an accelerated pace, the past three years have been a peaceful era in the development of group dynamics. There have been few attempts to challenge the legitimacy of the group concept, to outlaw the use of molar terms, or to force a sovereign theory upon those who investigate collective behavior. ... The prevailing mood of small group research has been one of peaceful harmony. ... Whether this penchant for laissez-faire acceptance of diversity is a healthy sign of maturity, or a foreboding indicative of pathological apathy, remains to be seen." (Pp. 421–423.)

The staleness does not have to do with the cleverness of experimental procedures, for they are often truly ingenious. Nor does it have to do with the potential value of the ideas investigated. Rather, it has to do with more intangible qualities related to the presence of intellectual controversy, the sense of purpose and fervor, and the intellectual breadth of concepts.

The staleness appears, in one respect, in the absence of missionarylike zeal among researchers. There is little sense, nowadays, of "I'm on the trail of something big!" as there was in the days of Lewin, Hull, Tolman, and their contemporaries. The modern small group researcher has set his intellectual sights quite low. He often selects a limited range of variables, methods, and instruments, and then runs them into the ground. He is not, emotionally, on the trail of something big. Furthermore, our students do not seem imbued with the zeal of disciples, setting out into the world to test and spread a set of intellectually challenging ideas.

Associated with this lack of zeal (though not lack of vigor) is an absence of intellectual controversy. Small group researchers do not often enough disagree with one another in the public forum of journals—certainly not at the level of controversy of the Hull-Tolman-Guthrie debates about learning or the sharp criticisms of the nonpredictive, nontestable nature of Lewin's field theory. It is not that there is nothing to argue about, for there is knowledge, or at least extensive empirical information. Nor can this lack of controversy be credited to the much publicized trends toward conformity in all aspects of our current society. Rather, the problem seems to arise because research in the small group field is so segmented—in the form of idiosyncratic variables, tasks, and measures peculiar to individual investigators—that no one has a common base from which to argue.

Furthermore, argument and controversy in science presuppose alternative theories. But for the most part, there are no alternative theoretical approaches to understanding of the same phenomena about which to argue! Much of current theorizing is balance theory in origin; and most of that is stated at such a high level of abstraction that people can hardly disagree with one another. There are very few cases where alternative theories deal with the same phenomena at a level of detail that will permit argument!

Thus, we utter a plea for theory, as large and encompassing as can be evolved; for a sense of involvement and missionarylike zeal; and for more of the lifeblood of science—intellectual controversy. At the present stage of our history, all of these are minimal or absent. What occupies our energies now are methods, individual variables, task situations, and other accouterments which are more important for distinguishing us as unique researchers than they are for increasing our understanding of small group processes.

And what makes this situation of crucial importance is that the culture of the small group field is perpetuating these stultifying conditions by transmitting them to its young in the form of norms *valuing* smallness of concept, efficiency of effort, noncontroversality of approach, and uniqueness of area of jurisdiction. Let us now turn to an examination of certain aspects of the small group culture which seems to serve to perpetuate and foster the set of conditions just described.

SOME CULTURAL NORMS OF THE SMALL GROUP FIELD

The small group researcher has at least two large and important reference groups whose norms and values affect his work. First, he is usually a member of a university (or an equivalent organization) and does his research within that organizational setting. Second, he usually has a number of ties and allegiances to various portions of a broader, extrauniversity community of researchers and research-related agencies in his own and allied fields. Each of these groups has its own values and norms, and the small group researcher is subject to their influence. In this section, we will consider some of the more salient norms of the two reference groups, in turn, and try to trace their effects—good and bad—on the small group researcher and his research.

Norms of the University Community

The university as a community has many traditions, norms, and ideals, but the two most important ones for present purposes are epitomized in the phrases "publish or perish" and "money is power." The first of these refers to the idea that the worth of the scientist—as reflected in salary, rank, job offers, colleague assessments, not to mention self-esteem—is to be reckoned in terms of the number of publications he has generated.

Parenthetically, we might note that, at a most general level, the "publish or perish" norm is but one instance of a class of merit or achievement criteria that pervade our entire national culture. Men in many areas of business must produce (or sell), else they perish; students must get grades or get out; athletic coaches must win or be replaced. Indeed, the prime criterion for evaluating success of social scientists in nonacademic settings—"sell, and please the client, or die"—though different in form is no less demanding and restrictive than the publish-or-perish criterion of the academic.

Although all of us have probably criticized the publish-or-perish norm in informal discussions, we probably also recognize that there are many sound reasons for its existence as a criterion for academic success. Various alternative criteria—sheer seniority, administrative skill, personal charm—would certainly court far worse problems. Even the criterion of teaching excellence, intrinsic to the university setting, proves to be nearly impossible to assess without either violating the crucial norm of academic freedom or making success in the academic world contingent on popularity with (rather than stimulation of) the student body.

Actually, most persons in the field probably accept the basic value of the publication norm as a criterion. When we quarrel with the norm, it is on grounds of inequities in its application. How shall we judge quality as well as quantity of publications? How shall we evaluate *place* of publication (i.e., relative prestige of journals) and *form* of publication (e.g., the number of journal articles one book is worth, and the number of technical reports not editorially reviewed by colleagues one article is worth—if technical reports are counted at all)? How shall we take into account the nature of the published material (e.g., theory as opposed to experiment)? It is upon such questions of complexity of application that our complaints and criticisms usually center, rather than upon the use of a publication criterion per se.

But whatever the difficulties in its implementation, we nearly all live under the publish-or-perish dictum (or its industrial equivalent), and recognize and accept it to some degree. And this norm has some important consequences, both good and bad, for our research. On the positive side, the importance of publishing in acceptable journal sources has led to a sharp competition among authors that results in anywhere from 50 percent to 70 percent rejection of submitted manuscripts for the more highly reputed journals. One effect of this sharpened competition has been an increased methodological rigor in studies that results in better design and more foresight in planning and conducting research, more thorough and sophisticated analyses of data, and, to forestall the editorial consultant's ax, better anticipation of and sensitivity to criticism. These are substantial benefits.

The publish-or-perish norm also has some negative consequences. These take varied forms. One negative effect of the emphasis on number of publications is that few researchers nowadays seem to conduct research *without* the intent to end with something that is publishable. As a problem is weighed, as colleagues are consulted, as data are gathered and analyzed, there lurk not only the questions of substance, theory, method, but also the issue of whether a publication is in the offing. Another negative effect is the frequent exploitation of a single piece of work. In our review, it became apparent that a single piece of work often appeared in several places, in at best a slightly modified form. The typical history goes something like this. The author publishes a technical report stemming from a contract or grant. This is usually a voluminous report with a great deal of data and many analyses, some of which do not support the hypotheses tested. Thereafter, or simultaneously, the author presents a paper at one or more professional society meetings or at a topical conference. Then the study appears in a professional journal, this time considerably shortened, with the positive results highlighted and an appearance of smooth conduct and precise results. The piece may turn up still a third time, perhaps modified in title and condensed in form but more or less intact, within a collection of articles published in book form. In this manner, it is possible to inflate a publication list four- or fivefold. Thus, one important consequence of the "publish or perish" norm is a highly competitive interest by researchers in publishing their work *to satisfy that norm*, as well as to communicate contributions to the field.

The second salient norm of the university community is summarized in the cliché "money is power." In many university communities, especially the larger ones, the person who can point to funds he has obtained wields influence. (This, of course, has historically been the case for alumni, for endowing sources, etc. But it is only recently that the members of the university faculty themselves have and can use such influence.)

The man who brings in the bacon gains leverage in several tangible and intangible ways. For one, he can command facilities worthy of his dollar volume, and the associated accouterments of secretaries, office equipment, and so on. More important, he will have more access to students to help with his research, and the students he acquires as apprentices will often be the better ones. Moreover, he will probably recruit or attract students interested in the type of work he is conducting and thereby may gradually change the shape of a whole curriculum. And then "money goes to money." If he is successful (i.e., publishes a great deal), he will probably attract more money from sponsoring agencies. Thus, the cycle of influence, facility acquisition, student recruitment, and curriculum influence will be perpetuated and intensified.

Like the emphasis on publication volume, the emphasis on the researcher's acquisition of funds has both advanced small group research in many ways and has posed some potentially serious negative features. On the positive side, for example, the existence of funds has enabled, and will enable in coming years, more large-scale research than has been possible in the past. Better facilities for effective observation, recording, data reduction, and data analysis have come into being. Without such facilities and equipment, small group research would certainly be greatly hampered. Several additional positive features of the availability of funds for support of small group research will be discussed later within the context of the norms arising from the general professional community.

However, like the drive for publication, the drive for funds and the accompanying status, power, and opportunity may also become functionally autonomous, with the original intent of using the new dollars for important and dedicated research gradually receding into the background.

Norms of the Broader Professional Community

The university researcher no longer works in an ivory tower, isolated from the world, as he was formerly thought to do. During the last two decades, the social scientist has become intimately involved with the outside world, because of the war and his research role in it, because of community interest in social science research, and because of the acknowledged contribution that social science can potentially make to the social problems besetting our modern world. For these and other reasons, the small group researcher nowadays is exposed to a wide range of stimulation from the community at large, and this stimulation surely affects the nature of the research which he undertakes. One major aspect of this broadened community is the availability of financial support for social science research from a variety of governmental agencies and foundations.

Research is expensive. Ordinarily, the individual researcher does not have sufficient personal funds to buy tape recorders and other equipment, to pay for computer facilities or for teams of interviewers. Much of the research currently being done could not be done at all were it not for the availability of supporting funds.

But as the researcher seeks out financial support for his research via oral and written communications with various potential patrons, he quickly learns that a whole new set of skills must be acquired. The research must be justified to a larger organization, beyond the scientist-administrator who will serve as sponsor and monitor. Even for most basic research programs, the research to be supported must have some long-range applicability to real-world problems that fall within the charter of the sponsoring agency. The researcher must learn to assist in this justification effort.

Thus he learns how to highlight the relevance of his research to a particular body of real-world phenomena, and he learns how to project a long-range program so as to insure continuity of support. (Often, to do this, he must describe his plans far beyond his thinking.) Frequently, it may be necessary to alter certain aspects of the original research idea, plan, or design, so as to make its contribution to the program of the supporting organization more visible and actual.

He also must learn to plan budgets and keep track of expenditures, and to work skillfully within a labyrinth of governmental, corporate, and/or university regulations on when and how funds may be expended, so that he can keep his research program progressing smoothly. He must learn to prepare progress reports, substantive and administrative, to account for the current status of his work and to justify what he has done, how he has spent his money, and why he may need to alter his original plans.

Thus, the small group researcher must gain a variety of skills, out of necessity, if he is to gain support for the research he wishes to do. He must learn to converse with laymen-administrators in complex negotiations, to anticipate the needs of potential sponsors, to give briefings and otherwise sell himself and his work to other than his academic colleagues, to plan and manage a budget efficiently, and to spend funds wisely.

He also learns that his sponsoring patron, as well as the university, places value on publications, for the former also has few means to evaluate the "worth" of the research and even fewer bases to justify it to budget-managers and upper echelons of management. Although the scientist-administrator-sponsor often makes use of advisory panels of well-known scientists, he (and his advisors!) often rely on quantity of publications in accepted professional journals to help them select the recipients of their limited funds. Thus, the publish-or-perish norm is part and parcel of the broader community as well as of the university. And the process is self-feeding: the more publications, the greater the opportunity for further support; the greater the support, the greater the influence, the greater the facilities, and the more access to top students, hence the more potential publications and funds; ad infinitum.

Thus, the broader community to which he attends has required the small group researcher to develop new skills and to view his work not only from the perspective of his own interests but from the viewpoint of a larger community which will provide funds for support of his research. This set of requirements also has some positive effects. The need to view one's work from the point of view of a broader framework of problems may help one select problems to study when equally interesting alternatives exist—and multiple alternatives always exist. Moreover, the broadened range of contact frequently stimulates new areas of research and interest which would not otherwise have been pursued. Along more practical lines, much good research could never have been done at all without the assurance of adequate levels of support over reasonable lengths of time via extrauniversity support. In addition, the existence of research funds helps immeasurably in the training of students.

Thus, there are favorable and unfavorable consequences of the requirements of the broader professional community, just as there are favorable and unfavorable effects of the norms of the university community, and current small group research is of necessity conducted within the context of all of these effects. We do not pretend to have completely described the milieu within which the modern small group researcher functions. Up to this point the authors have only highlighted some main themes of the cultures within which the researcher lives. These themes are that research publications are critical to survival, that position is also partly a function of ability to obtain supporting funds, and that a larger community requires the acquisition of new, nonresearch skills and requires the scientist to view research from a broader perspective than that of his own personal interests.

We now will try to trace the consequences of these norms and pressures on the conduct of small group research and its outcome. First, briefly, we will describe how the norms pose a serious dilemma for the individual researcher, in terms of the methodological problems of the field that were discussed at length in the preceding chapter. Then, the final section will discuss the effects of the norms on the changing roles of the small group researcher.

Some Methodological Consequences of the Norms

In the preceding chapter the authors pointed out several crucial methodological problems which beset the small group field, and suggested that there is an opposition between the needs of the field, institutionally viewed, and the aims and interests of the individual researcher. We can now follow up that suggestion in more specific terms. One major reason that there has been practically no replication of studies in the small group field is that replications are often not felt to be worthy of prime publication space and are seldom seen as justifying renewal of a grant. The same basic reason applies to the lack of construct validation studies; they are endeavors with high risk (i.e., the construct may well not "validate") and low payoff potential (i.e., they have dubious publishability and dubious value in attracting further funds). The near-chaotic profusion of idiosyncratic terms and the widespread use of highly personalized variables, tasks, and procedural gimmicks may also stem in part from the need for the individual researcher to make himself and his research distinctive, so that his products will fare well in the market places of publication and funds. Even the seeming narrowness of small group studies and their limited reference to theory and to other relevant research may arise in part because of the pressure to present the terse, condensed, empirically oriented manuscripts that are competitive for scarce space in the journals with high prestige.

Thus, we are posed with a serious dilemma. We insisted in the preceding chapter that the field of small group research must have more replication of studies and findings, more construct validation efforts, more standardization in terms and operations, more comprehensive research, more concern with tying research to other research, more development of theory. Yet, in the present context, it is apparent that the individual researcher in the small group field cannot afford to pursue his research in a manner that would achieve these aims. To do so would minimize his ability to accrue publications, funds, and associated status and power. Hence, in the long run, he would reduce his opportunity to do research at all!

The solution to this basic dilemma is not apparent, unless the underlying norms of the university and professional communities can be altered. We do not suggest that we cease valuing publications or money; rather, we urge a change that places increased value on the *kinds of research activities that will maximally advance the field*, rather than the individual's career.

CHANGING ROLES OF THE SMALL GROUP RESEARCHER

In addition to the direct effects on small group research methodology, these norms and requirements (and of course many others as well) have gradually changed the expectations and behavior of the small group researcher with respect to at least four of his important roles: as a creative-artist and scientist; as an educator; as a force for social action; and as an administrator-manager. We now turn to a description of these roles and recent changes in them.

Before beginning, we again point out that this is *not* an exposé, an attack on the field, or a plea for return to the good old days. All influences on the small group researcher—from university, from sponsors, from the secular nature of the times—have multiple effects, some good and some regrettable. The point here is neither to criticize nor to praise, but to try to describe the forces at work in our culture and specify their effects, so that we may bootstrap ourselves in whichever directions we deem desirable.

The Small Group Researcher as Creative Artist-Scientist

Given latitude and freedom, the scientist is an artist in that he will conduct research stemming from his own personal feelings, impressions, and insights. Of course, the scientist proceeds quite differently from the artist; he applies a specific set of procedures and criteria (the scientific method) to confirm or refute his hypotheses, intuitions, and hunches. But basically, the hunches are subjective in origin. This statement is not meant to be profound, but only to indicate that science is personal in some respects and that the scientist projects himself as a person into his work at certain points. And we value this personal aspect of science positively, for this is how creative concepts are forged and new directions charted.

However, it is our impression that as the cultural trends described earlier have become more pervasive, the creative spur that *can* characterize research is rapidly being lost in the small group field. Instead of being creative, inspired artist-scientists, we are tending to become (and to breed) "commercial technicians" who apply energy and resources to the production of products (publications and renewed grants) rather than to the production of stimulating ideas.

In many ways, the cultures of which we are part (the university and the larger professional community) foster a set of values and norms that seem to lead toward a tendency to commercialize our research. As indicated previously, strong norms support the accumulation of a publication list as long as possible and the development of a power position closely tied with financial resources. As one corollary, there has been a tendency for rigor and methodological sophistication to increase. The demands placed on journals are so heavy, and there is so much competition, that evaluation of methodological rigor has become a major means for screening out unsuitable work. Such criteria of value may mean that the *substance* of the research becomes less important than its method. Besides, idea-generation takes time and is not always productive in the sense of leading to publications. Thus, more and more focus has been placed on procedures, and less on substance. The dual nature of science seems at present to be greatly out of balance, elevating rigor of procedures to the detriment of creativity of substantive ideas. This lack of balance is both good and bad—good for the obvious reason that our armamentarium for dealing with ideas is steadily growing, but bad in the sense that it increases ideational sterility. Perhaps this last is one of the factors involved in the absence of controversy in small group research. The focus on methods has led researchers to a position in which substance is often in the background. Thus, paradoxically, our concern with requirements of the commercial market has led to an emphasis on procedure rather than substance, for it is method, not concepts, that we are selling.

As another result of the cultural trends discussed earlier, we see scientists searching for ways to generate research studies more rapidly and efficiently so they can get their product in the public's view. This production speedup is accomplished by any of several means, all of which can be labeled as the search for and development of gimmicks. One form that such gimmicks take is the development of a unique procedure, piece of equipment, or task. A researcher can then employ the procedure, task, or piece of equipment over and over, introducing new variables or slight modifications of old variables, and thereby generate a host of studies rather quickly. Another means for rapid production of studies and publications is to take an atheoretical point of departure, select and study a given variable and, so to speak, drive it into the ground. Both the methodological gimmick and the personal-variable approaches have been used extensively in the small group field. One result is a host of isolated pockets of research, conducted by individual investigators, with little compatability, linkage, similarity, or overlap. (The data in our review markedly reflect this trend, as noted in Chapters 5, 6, and 7.)

It is as if each researcher is seeking a means for making himself and his work unique in the field, for gaining an identifiable and visible research style and "sales territory." We are tempted to label this process "marginal differentiation of product," or "territoriality." Often, the researcher then assembles around him a group who help him pursue his "commercial line." They, in turn, seek out individuality within his narrow framework; and so the process goes. One result of this differentiation of product is very little communication among diverse researchers, and thus little to argue about, synthesize, or cumulate. Each scientist is so busy setting up his own area of jurisdiction and distinction that there is no time for, or interest in, cross-fertilization and cross-communication with others in the field.

A constricted set of attitudes and values often characterizes the "commercial-artist" tone of modern small group research. This constriction takes the form of a deliberate attempt on the part of the researcher to search out an area: (1) that is small, narrow, easy to manage; (2) that no one else has tapped; (3) that is a sure bet for significant results; and (4) that will be financially supported by someone. The emphasis is on theoretically and creatively barren aspects of the phenomena, because any other emphasis would have low probability of payoff.

It is as if we deal with our phenomena in reverse fashion. Instead of focusing on problems and then asking about methods, techniques, uniqueness, we ask the latter questions first. This reversal has led to considerable stultification and narrowness, in our opinion, although it also can and has led to a great quantity of competently conducted research.

We utter a simple plea for the future, namely: to allow back into the formative stages of research the forces of intuition, allegiance to problems, and projection of the researcher's subjective insights. Then let methodological rigor enter into testing and evaluating the ideas. Every researcher should be exposed at least once to the adventure of an idea generated and studied from the perspective of his own personal frame of reference—whether it ultimately leads to a publication or not. We have obviously overstated the case, but still hold fast to the basic point: namely, that many cultural forces are tending to make the small group researcher more and more a technician rather than an artist-scientist.

The Small Group Researcher as an Educator

The majority of small group researchers are affiliated with universities and spend some portion of their time in teaching and/or supervising the research training of graduate students. Thus, deliberately or unaware, they are socializing agents who inculcate the values and attitudes of the culture, as well as the facts and techniques, into the next generation of researchers. And it is often the values here described that are most prominent in the socialization of our scientists.

The student learns the economic and survival value of publication, and only secondarily its value for communication and criticism. He also learns the value of "territoriality," in which it makes sense to carve out a distinctive area and become well known for knowledge in that area alone. He learns to appreciate the importance of methodology, for it is through knowledge and skill in methods that one can generate a large number of studies quickly and efficiently. He learns the techniques of "grantsmanship" (which will be discussed later) as he observes his mentor deal with research administrators and laymen.

Now, all this is not wicked, for the student of today is being prepared for the world in which he must learn to survive and, let us hope, to thrive. He is developing skills that the student of yesteryear had little exposure to (or need for)—administration, planning, and management of long-range research programs; supervision of teams of researchers; and communication with lay persons on whom he may come to depend heavily. Unfortunately, the negative implications of this aspect of the changing role and values of the scientist are some-what intangible and less visible. Some of these have already been alluded to: a decline in concern for large-scope, high-risk theoretical areas; lack of contro-versy (because all must live with one another); the exploitation of students to accomplish one's own research rather than to guide their development along lines compatible with the students' interests and needs; the elimination from the research process of personal-subjective creative flair. It is such negative values as these that are perpetuated in the culture, as students learn and practice the role behaviors exhibited by their mentors.

We have not meant to portray the situation as hopeless, for it is not. As our professional lives and responsibilities expand, as they have been doing, certain of our older values must necessarily compete with newer ones, and it is good that they do so, for the sake of growth and potential progress. However, it does not necessarily follow that newer values cannot live side by side with, or incor-porate, more traditional and fundamental ones. Regardless of the times, science must have scholarliness, freedom for pursuit of highly experimental ideas, and, to some extent, isolation from the demands of the real world in an explicit sense. In addition, there must be controversy among scientists, for this is the anvil on which valid ideas are forged. These less-tangible values seem to be in the background nowadays, as we educate our young graduate students. In the fore are the more-visible, practical, and immediately rewarding require-ments of the times. The short-run implications of the changing role of the small group researcher as an educator may not appear very weighty; but the longer-run effects can be insidious.

The Small Group Researcher as a Social-Action Force

Though affiliated with universities, the small group researcher has become involved in studies closely applicable to many secular issues, often assists in foundation and government planning activities, and has frequent contacts with extrauniversity scientists and laymen. This expanding range of involve-ments is due to many factors—the war, the acknowledged contribution that social scientists can make to such problems, the availability of support for such research, and the increased confidence of the social scientist in his ability really to contribute to such problems. Although we have no data on the point, it is also likely that the biographical origins of the small group researcher have led him in directions involving social action research. It is probable that many researchers in this field are second- and third-generation Americans, who are middle class in socioeconomic background, and who are members of ethnic-minority groups. If so, it can easily be seen how research topics associated with social-action issues could capture their interest. Witness the types of subject matter in which small group researchers have become involved that are directly relevant to secular matters: interpersonal conflict, interpersonal influence and persuasion, civil defense, intercultural communication, prejudice, military crew effectiveness, mental health activities, community-planning, team-training methods, and so on.

Aside from the fact that research may help shed new information on social problems and thereby contribute to their solution, we see many other gains relevant to the research process itself. New research areas can be stimulated by social problems. New methods may have to be developed to tackle new problems. The researcher may become interested in extending and validating laboratory-derived concepts in more realistic situations. The need to communicate with non professionals may sharpen the scientist's view regarding salient features of his work.

However, many of these potential virtues are not realized. When the small group researcher comes to work on a problem such as searching for means to improve weapons systems or to facilitate international communication, two things can and often seem to happen. First, he tends to become an applied researcher, in the sense of solving a specific and delimited problem. Applied research ordinarily does not involve the development of new concepts or even new information, but rather the extension or application of existing ideas and information. Applied research is not bad, but such studies are often cloaked under the banner of basic research, when in fact they ordinarily are not, and they seldom produce the same types of findings as would more loosely defined and less-restricted studies. Here, the question is not one of which kind of research is right or best; it is a question of allocation of our resources among basic and applied pursuits.

A second outcome, and a more subtle and potentially dangerous one, is that as a scientist works on a social-action problem for a group that believes in the value of a certain outcome, he too may gradually tend to come to believe in the correctness of that side of the issue to which his sponsoring group is committed. Thus, by a very subtle process he often comes to take sides in issues of a secular nature. This secularization, too, is not, in and of itself, serious, except insofar as it tends to affect a researcher's objectivity as a scientist. Nevertheless, one effect of the changing norms and values of the small group research field has been to make the scientists of that field a very important social-action force and to threaten their objectivity in dealing with certain subject matters relevant to social issues.

The Small Group Researcher as a Businessman-Manager

To this point we have described the changing role of the small group researcher as an artist, educator, and social-action force. Now we turn to a relatively new role of the scientist, that of businessman. In some respects the discussion will be redundant, but this is necessary to round out and present a complete portrait of the small group researcher.

As a businessman, the researcher's products are publications—a fact that has already been dwelt upon at length. His raw materials are funds obtained from supporting agencies of various types (largely portions of the defense establishment). This fact too, has been introduced, with respect to the skills he must learn and techniques he must use—skills and techniques that might be summed up under the labels of "grantsmanship" and "empire building."

"Grantsmanship" is the "game" of learning where sources of funds are, establishing contacts with those sources, preparing proposals that indicate interest and ability to manage the problem, and so forth. To play grantsmanship successfully in the big leagues sometimes requires knowledge of accounting, logistics, taxation, corporate financing, public relations, personnel administration, and many other nonresearch areas.

Because grantsmanship is a self-feeding phenomenon (the more grant money one has, the easier it is to get more grants) and because the culture places value on dollars, grantsmanship is often accompanied by "empire building." Empire building is the accumulation by the researcher of titles, facilities, students, support personnel—or in more delicate terms, the development of a "program of research." Empire building takes a variety of forms including establishment of institutes and centers of research, the conduct of workshops, symposia, conferences, and the like. In a somewhat more subtle form, the small group researcher-businessman may establish a virtual "monopoly" by assuming quasiproprietary rights on concepts, methods, and gimmicks—a technique alluded to earlier as "marginal differentiation of product" or "territoriality." Thus, he comes (and deliberately so, in many cases!) to be identified with a given product; and all who wish to make use of that product, especially students, provide a "commission" or "royalty," usually in the form of coauthorship.

One implication of grantsmanship and empire building is that the productive and successful researcher often finds himself "kicked upstairs"—elevated to an administrative position. Often to his dismay, he finds himself weighed down by the administrative duties that the empire requires for its survival, with layer upon layer between himself and the actual conduct of research. He gradually becomes akin to middle management, anxious to return to the research production line, but ever drawn upward by the burdens of administration and the lure of further success.

The small group researcher is a businessman in some other respects, too. These involve consulting activity and job hopping. As he partakes of grantsmanship and empire building, with their associated titles, publications, and travels, his contacts in the research world ever widen. If he has competence as a researcher and communicator (and some degree of personal charm), private research organizations, government agencies, and even other researchers not only come to view his name on a proposal as an asset, but also come to see him as one who can help them on a problem. Therefore they seek him out as a consultant on a temporary, paid basis. This can become a pleasant and profitable activity. It allows one to meet new people, locate new sources of funds, and become exposed to new areas of subject matter.

As a correlate of such consulting activity, empire building, and grantsmanship, the horizons of the researcher are broadened considerably, not only with regard to research matters, but also with respect to job opportunities other than the one currently held. As he travels, writes, and communicates with others, he discovers that many seek his services: other universities, private research agencies, and government agencies. The job market is ripe, and what makes it even more attractive is that, like the traveling medicine shows of the early West, the modern researcher can pick up his grant or contract and take it with him wherever he goes. The culture has bred and accepted large-scale geographic mobility.

Unfortunately, such moves do cost the researcher time. Because the move is often to another university, his research can theoretically continue more or less unabated, but he must first train new graduate-student apprentices. Moreover, he must learn how to function in the new department and university, often at the expense of a considerable investment of hours in executive-administrative functions. When a large number of the potentially most creative scientists of a field expend a major part of their time and energies engaging in these activities—pursuing grants, building empires, consulting, playing the job market—the resultant effect can be disastrous. Not only does the field lose many potentially creative hours from its leading contributors but it also tends to develop a value pattern that is antithetical to creativity and scholarly endeavor and to transmit that value pattern to its young students and future colleagues. It is such *institutional* consequences for the field, rather than the consequences for the individual scientist, with which we are here concerned.

The authors hope the fervor with which mobility, grantsmanship, and consulting activities are conducted eventually slows down, for ultimately they are all only in the service of better research, not ends in themselves. Yet at present there seems to be a certain degree of functional autonomy about the flurry of activity devoted to such ends, as opposed to the pursuit of new knowledge.

A Capstone Thought

It is likely that we are in a period of history where the utility of social science to the real world, the middle-class background of our researchers, the availability of funds for research, the population explosion at universities, and a multiplicity of other factors have all come together to establish in this generation of researchers a new pattern of values and norms, which we here choose to call the *entrepreneurial ethic*. The underlying values of this ethic stress quantity at the expense of quality in research, rigor of method at the expense of the creative-theoretical aspects of science, research funds at the expense of research ideas. The influence of this ethic tends to change the researcher, in his role as scientist, from a creative artist to a commercial artist-technician. It downgrades his role as an educator and leads him to transmit procedural, rather than inspirational, values to his students. It has increased the salience of his role as social-action force, with many concomitant gains but with a serious threat to his scientific objectivity. Finally, it has created for the researcher a new role: that of businessman-manager of research enterprises, which leads him to expend much of his energy in creating and managing research opportunities rather than in conducting exciting and challenging research.

Together, these values and role changes issuing from the entrepreneurial ethic say to the researcher as creative artist, "Paint what sells. Paint for the highest bidder. Paint as fast and as furiously as you can. Believe in what you paint. Get a good sales force and an efficient home office behind you."

As with all value patterns, the entrepreneurial ethic both spurs the researcher on to greater things and detracts from his pursuit of greater things. So it is, we believe, with small group research in the 1960's. How the scales of vice and virtue balance at the present time is a matter for each of us to judge for himself; it is not really a crucial matter. What is crucial, for ourselves and for future generations of researchers, is that we try to estimate where the scales now lie, and try to move them, deliberately, in directions that we value as worthwhile. We hope to have aided in this assessment process by identifying some of the potential sources of imbalance, as we subjectively see them, in the modern culture of the small group research field.

EPILOGUE

The task of presenting this work describing the small group field from a variety of perspectives is now complete. The remainder of this volume presents many of the empirical facts of the field in the form of reference materials that we hope will be of value to the small group research community. In this review, a great deal of subject matter has been covered, and from widely disparate points of view. From all this, several themes stand out as especially worthy of emphasis:

Small group researchers must try to develop theory and integrating concepts to a greater extent than has occurred to date.

Intellectual controversy and subjectivity must be allowed to enter into our research, as stimulants.

Methodological scope must be broadened beyond the confines of the laboratory, and we badly need some standardization in concepts, terms, and operations.

The concern with synthesis of knowledge must continue and broaden, if we are to keep pace with the outpouring of empirical data and prevent it from being aimless, though well meant and well executed.

Some traditional values of research—scholarliness, intellectual adventure, willingness to make mistakes—must be revitalized and elevated at least to the status of some newer values such as accrual of publications for the sake of economic and social survival, pursuit of grants for the sake of building research empires, and so on.

We must recognize that the laissez-faire pursuit of individual interests may work no better in a scientific field than it does in the political-economic domain of a complex social system; and, indeed, that the pursuit of many individualistic, narrow interests and of diversity for its own sake has led us to some serious inadequacies in the field as a whole, while providing us with no mechanisms by which they can readily be overcome.

Finally, we must recognize that as "agents of history," we can alter the present status and future course of the small group field, and set it upon any course which we collectively and distributively deem worthwhile.

References

Allport, G. W. The historical background of modern social psychology. In G. Lindzey (Ed.), *Handbook of social psychology*. Reading, Mass.: Addison-Wesley, 1954. Pp. 3–56.

Altman, I., Jenkins, J. P., & McGrath, J. E. *The translation of small group research information for computer analysis.* Arlington, Va.: Human Sciences Research, Inc., October 1959. (AFOSR TN 59-1194, ASTIA AD No. 230 241)

Altman, I., & McGrath, J. E. *A conceptual framework for the integration of small group research information.* Arlington, Va.: Human Sciences Research, Inc., February 1959. (AFOSR TN 59-252, ASTIA AD No. 212 252)

Altman, I., Pendleton, Catherine A., & Terauds, Anita *Annotations of small group research studies.* Arlington, Va.: Human Sciences Research, Inc., October 1960. (AFOSR TN 60-1208, ASTIA AD No. 248 440)

Altman, I., & Terauds, Anita *Major variables of the small group field.* Arlington, Va.: Human Sciences Research, Inc., November 1960. (AFOSR TN 60-1207, ASTIA AD No. 250 740)

Argyle, M. *The scientific study of social behavior.* New York: Philosophical Library, 1957.

Bales, R. F. *Interaction process analysis: a method for the study of small groups.* Reading, Mass.: Addison-Wesley, 1950.

Bales, R. F. Psychological determinants of interpersonal behavior. Paper read at Pers. Interaction Conf., Cornell University, June, 1960.

Bales, R. F., & Strodtbeck, F. L. Phases in group problem solving. *J. abnorm. soc. Psychol.*, 1951, *46*, 485–495.

Berkowitz, L. Liking for the group and the perceived merit of the group's behavior. *J. abnorm. soc. Psychol.* 1957, *54*, 353–357.

Bock, R. D. Multivariate analysis of variance of repeated measures. In C. W. Harris (Ed.), *Problems in measuring change.* Madison, Wis: University of Wisconsin Press, 1963. Pp. 85-103.

Borgatta, E. F. Analysis of social interaction: actual, role playing and projective. *J abnorm. soc. Psychol.*, 1955, *51*, 394–405.

Borgatta, E. F. A systematic study of interaction process scores, peer and self-assessments, personality and other variables. Paper read at Pers. Interaction Conf., Cornell University, June, 1960.

Campbell, D. T., & Fiske, D. W. Convergent and discriminant validation by the multitrait-multimethod matrix. *Psychol. Bull.*, 1959, *56*, 81–105.

Campbell, D. T., & Stanley, J. C. Experimental and quasi-experimental design for research on teaching. In N. L. Gage (Ed.), *Handbook of research on teaching*. Skokie, Ill.: Rand McNally, 1963. Pp. 171–246.

Carter, L. F., Haythorn, W., & Howell, M. A further investigation of the criteria of leadership. *J. abnorm. soc. Psychol.*, 1950, *45*, 350–358.

Carter, L. F., Haythorn, W., Shriver, B., & Lanzetta, J. The behavior of leaders and other group members. *J. abnorm. soc. Psychol.*, 1951, *46*, 589–595.

Cartwright, D., & Zander, A. (Eds.) *Group dynamics* (2nd ed.) New York: Harper & Row, 1960.

Cattell, R. B., & Wispe, L. G. The dimensions of syntality in small groups. *Hum. Relat.*, 1953, *6*, 331–356.

Cohen, A. R. Experimental effects of ego-defense preference on interpersonal relations. *J. abnorm. soc. Psychol.*, 1956, *52*, 19–27.

Coombs, C. A theory of psychological scaling. *Univer. Michigan, Engng Res. Inst. Bull. No. 34.* Ann Arbor: University of Michigan Press, 1952.

Deutsch, M. A theory of cooperation and competition. *Hum. Relat.*, 1949, *2*, 129–152.

Festinger, L. Informal social communication. *Psychol. Rev.*, 1950, *57*, 271–292.

Festinger, L. Theory of social comparison process. *Hum. Relat.*, 1954, *7*, 117–140.

Festinger, L. *A theory of cognitive dissonance*. New York: Harper & Row, 1957.

Festinger, L., & Katz, D. *Research methods in the behavioral sciences*. New York: Holt, Rinehart and Winston, 1953.

Festinger, L., Riecken, H. W. Jr. & Schachter, S. *When prophecy fails*. Minneapolis: University of Minnesota Press, 1956.

Festinger, L., Schachter, S. & Back, K. *Social pressures in informal groups: a study of human factors in housing*. New York: Harper & Row, 1950.

Fiedler, F. E. Leadership and leadership effectiveness traits: a reconceptualization of the leadership trait problem In L. Petrullo & B. Bass (Eds.), *Leadership and interpersonal behavior*. New York: Holt, Rinehart and Winston, 1961. Pp. 167–186.

Fiedler, F. E., Dodge, J. S., Jones, R. E., & Hutchins, E. B. Inter-relations among measures of personality adjustment in nonclinical populations. *J. abnorm. soc. Psychol.*, 1958, *56*, 345–351.

Fiedler, F. E., Hutchins, E. B. & Dodge. J. S. Quasi-therapeutic relations in small college and military groups. *Psychol. Monogr.*, 1959, *73* (3), 1–28 (Whole No. 473).

Foa, U. G. The contiguity principle in the structure of interpersonal relations *Hum. Relat.*, 1958, *11*, 229–238.

French, J. R. P., Jr. A formal theory of social power. *Psychol. Rev.*, 1956, *63*, 181–194.

Golembiewski, R. *The small group: an analysis of research concepts and operations*. Chicago: University of Chicago Press, 1962.

Gross, N., & Martin, W. E. On group cohesiveness. *Amer J. Sociol.*, 1952, *57*, 546–554.

Guetzkow, H., Alger, C. F., Brody, R. A., Noel, R. C., & Snyder, R. C. *Simulation in international relations: Developments for research and teaching.* Englewood Cliffs, N. T.: Prentice Hall, 1963.

Guttman, L. A structural theory for intergroup beliefs and actions. *Amer. Sociol. Rev.*, 1959, *24* (3), 318-328.

Hare, A. P. *Handbook of small group research.* New York: The Free Press of Glencoe, 1962.

Hare, A. P., Borgatta, E., & Bales, R. F. *Small groups: studies in social interaction.* New York: Knopf, 1954.

Haythorn, W. The influence of individual members on the characteristics of small groups. *J. abnorm. soc. Psychol.*, 1953, *48*, 276-284.

Haythorn, W., Couch, A., Haefner, D., Langhan, P., & Carter, L. The behavior of authoritarian and equalitarian personalities in groups. *Hum. Relat.*, 1956, *9*, 57-74. (a)

Haythorn, W., Couch, A., Haefner, D., Langhan, P., & Carter, L. The effects of varying combinations of authoritarian and equalitarian leaders and followers. *J. abnorm. soc. Psychol.*, 1956, *53*, 210-219. (b)

Heider, F. *The psychology of interpersonal relations.* New York: Wiley, 1958.

Heinecke, C., & Bales, R. F. Developmental trends in the structure of small groups. *Sociometry*, 1953, *16*, 7-38.

Hemphill, J. K. Why people attempt to lead. In L. Petrullo & B. M. Bass (Eds.), *Leadership and interpersonal behavior.* New York: Holt, Rinehart and Winston, 1961. Pp. 201-215.

Hemphill, J. K., & Westie, C. M. The measurement of group dimensions. *J. Psychol.*, 1950, *29*, 325-242.

Homans, G. C. Social behavior as exchange. *Amer. J. Sociol.*, 1958, *63*, 597-607.

Kelley, H. H., & Thibaut, J. W. Experimental studies of group problem solving process. In G. Lindzey (Ed.), *Handbook of social psychology.* Reading, Mass.: Addison-Wesley, 1954. Pp. 735-786.

Landsberger, H. A. Interaction process analysis of the mediation of labor-management disputes. *J. abnorm. soc. Psychol.*, 1955, *51*, 552-558.

Lewin, K., Lippitt, R., & White, R. K. Patterns of aggressive behavior in experimentally created "social climates." *J. soc. Psychol.*, 1939, *10*, 271-299.

McGrath, J. E. *A framework for integration of small group research studies: A pilot study.* Arlington, Va.: Psychological Research Associates, Inc., October 1957. (*PRA Rep. No.* 57-20, AFOSR TN 57-87, ASTIA AD No. 136 680)

McGrath, J. E. *A summary of small group research studies.* Arlington, Va.: Human Sciences Research, Inc., June, 1962. (AFOSR Document No. 2709)

McGrath, J. E. Systems of information in small group research studies. *Hum. Relat.*, 1963, *16*, 263-277.

McGrath, J. E. Toward a "theory of method" for research on organizations. In W. W. Cooper, N. J. Leavitt, & M. W. Shelly (Eds.), *New perspectives in organization research.* New York: Wiley, 1964. Pp. 533-556.

Mann, R. D.   A review of the relationships between personality and performance in small groups. *Psychol. Bull.*, 1959, *56*, 241–270.

March, J. G., & Simon, H. A.   *Organizations.* New York: Wiley, 1958.

Miller, J. G. Toward a general theory for the behavioral sciences. *Amer.
Psychologist,* 1955, *10*, 523. (Abstract)

Newcomb, T. M.   An approach to the study of communicative acts. *Psychol.
Rev.,* 1953, *60*, 393–404.

Newcomb, T. M.   *The acquaintance process.* New York: Holt, Rinehart and
Winston, 1961.

Petrullo, L., & Bass, B. (Eds.)   *Leadership and interpersonal behavior.* New
York: Holt, Rinehart and Winston, 1961.

Raven, B. H.   *A bibliography of publications relating to the small group.* Los
Angeles: University of California, Department of Psychology, November,
1959. (Tech. Rep. No. 1, Contract Nonr 253(54) (NR 171-350)) (a)

Raven, B. H.   *Index to bibliography of publications relating to the small group.*
Los Angeles: University of California, Department of Psychology,
November, 1959. (Tech. Rep. No. 1, Suppl. No. 3, Contract Nonr
253(54) (NR 171-350)) (b)

Riecken, H., & Homans, G.   Psychological aspects of social structure. In
G. Lindzey (Ed.), *Handbook of social psychology.* Reading, Mass.:
Addison-Wesley, 1954. Pp. 786–833.

Roby, T. B., & Lanzetta, J. T.   Considerations in the analysis of group tasks.
Psychol. Bull., 1958, *55* (2), 88–101.

Roethlisberger, F. J., & Dickson, W. J.   *Management and the worker—an
account of a research program conducted by the Western Electric Company,
Hawthorne works.* Cambridge, Mass.: Harvard University Press, 1939.

Roseborough, Mary E.   Experimental studies of small groups. *Psychol. Bull.,*
1953, *50*, 275–303.

Schachter, S., Ellerton, N., McBride, D., & Gregory, D.   An experimental
study of cohesiveness and productivity. *Hum. Relat.,* 1951, *4*, 229–238.

Schutz, W. C.   *FIRO: a three-dimensional theory of interpersonal behavior.* New
York: Holt, Rinehart and Winston, 1959.

Shaw, M. E.   *Scaling group tasks: a method for dimensional analysis.* Gainesville,
Fla.: University of Florida, 1963. (Tech. Rep. No. 1, Contract Nonr
500(11) (NR 170-266))

Sherif, M., Harvey, O. V., White, B. V., Hood, W. R., & Sherif, C. W.   *Intergroup conflict and cooperation: The robber's cave experiment.* Norman,
Okla.: University of Oklahoma Press, 1961.

Steiner, I. D.   Group dynamics. In P. Farnsworth (Ed.), *Annual review of
psychology.* Palto Alto, Calif.: Annual Reviews, Inc., 1964. Pp. 421–446.

Steiner, I. D., & Rajaratnam, N.   A model for the comparison of individual
and group performance scores. *Behav. Sci.,* 1961, *6*, 142–147.

Sullivan, D. H.   Towards an inventory of major explanatory propositions in
current international relations textbooks. Unpublished doctoral dissertation, Northwestern Univer., 1963.

Terauds, Anita, Altman, I., & McGrath, J. E.   A bibliography of small
group research. Arlington, Va.: Human Sciences Research, Inc., April
1960. (AFOSR TN 60-365, ASTIA AD No. 237-304)

Thibaut, J., & Kelley, H. H.   *The social psychology of groups.* New York: Wiley, 1959.

Thomas, E. J., & Fink, C. F.   Effects of group size. *Psychol. Bull.*, 1963, *60*, 371–385.

Tucker, L. R.   Implications of factor analysis of 3-way matrices for measurement of change. In C. W. Harris (Ed.), *Problems in measuring change.* Madison, Wis.: University of Wisconsin Press, 1963. Pp. 122–137.

Von Bertalanffy, L.   General system theory. *Main Currents in Modern Thought*, 1955, *11*, 77.

PART 3 ·

Catalogue of Relationships, Annotations,
and Bibliography with Addenda

SECTION A

Catalogue of Relationships between Variables

INTRODUCTION

This section presents a detailed compilation of the research information that has been abstracted from a sample of nearly 250 small group studies. It is organized in terms of 31 variable classes, as listed in the following Table of Variable Classes and discussed in earlier parts of the book. Material for each of the variable classes is presented in four parts:

1. A definition of the variable class and examples of operational measures used in studies in the review sample.

2. Certain summary information about the variable class (e.g., number of studies in which the variable appeared, total number of tests for relationships, over-all proportion of significant relationships). Following is a list of reference numbers indicating the studies that contained variables of the class. The reference numbers refer to the general bibliography in Part III, Section C.

3. An overview or summary of the relationship history of the variable of concern, with emphasis on the variables to which it was strongly related and the variables to which it was weakly related. In addition, relationship gaps are presented—that is, variables for which there were no tests for association in the review sample.

4. A detailed statement of the extent of association between the given variable class and those other classes of variables with which association was tested. Statements of relationships between specific variables are included where possible.

This form of presentation contains a certain amount of redundancy, because the relationship between each pair of variable classes is presented twice. Thus, the reader can obtain full information about any one variable class without cross referencing.

The variable classes are identified by numbers, as shown in the accompanying Table of Variable Classes. Associative strength between variables is indicated by a ratio—e.g., (25/32)—specifying the number of relationships between the two variables significant at the .05 level of significance or better, relative to the total number of times the two variables were associated. Strengths of association between variables are described as shown in the Table of Terminology for Describing Relationship Strength.

TABLE OF VARIABLE CLASSES

Substantive Classes	Operational Classes
100 Properties of group members	
110 Biographical characteristics of members	Member state
120 Personality characteristics of members	Member state
130 Abilities of members	
131 General abilities of members	Member state
132 Task abilities of members	Member state
140 Attitudes of members	
141 Attitudes toward the task	Surround state
142 Attitudes toward the situation	Surround state
143 Attitudes toward nongroup persons and other groups	Surround state
144 Attitudes toward issues, concepts, ideologies	Surround state
150 Positions of members in the group	
151 Social position in the group	Member state
152 Task or physical position in the group	Member state
200 Properties of the group	
220 Group capabilities	
221 Group abilities	Group state
222 Group training and experience	Member and Group state
230 Interpersonal relations in the group	Member and Group state
240 General structural properties of the group	Group state
300 Conditions imposed on the group	
310 Social conditions	
311 Influence and conformity pressures	Group state
312 Induced social conditions	Group state
320 Task and operating conditions	
321 Stimulus properties of the task	Surround state
322 Feedback and reinforcement conditions	Member and Group state
323 Induced task conditions	Group state
400 Interaction process	
410 Content of interaction	Member and Group action
420 Patterns of interaction	Member and Group action
430 Outcomes of interaction	Member and Group action
500 Subjective measures of member and group performance	
510 Perceptions of task performance of self and others	Member action
520 Perceptions of social behavior of self and others	Member action
600 Objective measures of member and group performance	
610 Leadership performance	Member action

Substantive Classes	Operational Classes
620 Task performance of members	
621 Member task performance in experimental settings	Member action
622 Member task performance in operational settings: global measures	Member action
623 Member task performance in operational settings: specific measures	Member action
630 Task performance of groups	
631 Group task performance in experimental settings	Group action
632 Group task performance in operational settings: global measures	Group action
633 Group task performance in operational settings: specific measures	Group action

TABLE OF TERMINOLOGY FOR DESCRIBING RELATIONSHIP STRENGTH

Proportion of Significant Relationships (percent)	Descriptive Terminology
60 or more	Highly related
40–60	Moderately related
30–40	Somewhat related
15–30	Slightly related
Less than 15	Not related

110. BIOGRAPHICAL CHARACTERISTICS OF MEMBERS

Definition

"Biographical characteristics of members" includes such variables as sex, age, education, marital status, race, religious affiliation, geographical region of birth and/or upbringing, weight, and height. Nearly all of these measures were obtained via self-report.

References

Variables of this class were used in a total of 32 studies in the sample and were tested for relationships to seven other variable classes, in a total of 132 associations, of which 35 (27%) were significant. Reference numbers of studies are 110, 132, 133, 136, 308, 315, 344, 351, 566, 756, 757, 766, 767, 856, 999, 1054, 1098, 1099, 1195, 1252, 1325, 1333, 1401, 1450, 1505, 1751, 1841, 1895, 1976, 2008, 2046, 2076.

Summary of Major Relationships

In the sample of studies reviewed, this variable was highly or moderately related to only one of seven other variables—attitudes toward the task (141).

"Biographical characteristics of members" was somewhat, slightly, or not related to several measures of member and group task performance (610) (621) (623) (633). It also showed no relationship with perceptions by members of task performance of self and others (510).

There were no cases of tests for association between biographical characteristics and a number of member characteristics: e.g., attitudes toward the situation and toward nongroup persons and other groups (142) (143), position in the group (151) (152), personality characteristics (120), and abilities (131) (132). Of course, one would not expect tests of relationship between biographical characteristics and many of the above, because several would also normally be used as independent variables. There were also no cases of tests for association between biographical characteristics and various properties of the group (240) (221) (222) and interpersonal relations in the group (230). In addition, as expected, member biographical characteristics were not compared with respect to various conditions imposed upon the group (311) (312) (321) (322) (323).

Finally, this variable class was not examined with respect to associations with content, patterns, and outcomes of member interaction (410) (420) (430) nor with several measures of group performance effectiveness (631) (632).

Index of Relationships

140) Attitudes of members as related to biographical characteristics of members

141. Attitudes toward the task. Moderately related (6/15)

In one study, women were consistently more satisfied with work conditions than were men (5/6), but there was no such relationship in another study (1/9).

144. Attitudes toward issues, concepts, ideologies. Somewhat related (8/21)

Upperclassmen were more similar to their faculty advisors in personal values than were underclassmen (2/3). In another setting, individuals who were only children, who had more education, or who were Jewish were more influential in changing others' opinions (3/3). Several other biographical characteristics were only slightly related to influence on others or susceptibility to influence by others (3/12).

510) Perceptions of task performance of self and others as related to biographical characteristics of members. Not related (0/8)

For example, sex was not related to perceived similarity of own answers to those of others or to working hard.

610) Leadership performance as related to biographical characteristics of members. Somewhat related (8/23)

Those with higher education had higher leaderless group discussion scores (6/6), but age and leadership in leaderless group discussions were not related (0/9). Biographical characteristics were only slightly related to leadership in operational settings (2/8).

620) Task performance of members as related to biographical characteristics of members

621. Member task performance in experimental settings. Slightly related (13/51)

In one study, men performed consistently better than did women (9/10). Other results did not provide a clear-cut pattern (4/41)

623. Member task performance in operational settings: specific measures. Not related (0/7)

633. Group task performance in operational settings: specific measures. Not related (0/7)

Measures such as age and education were not related to performance of industrial work groups or military squads.

120. PERSONALITY CHARACTERISTICS OF MEMBERS

Definition

"Personality characteristics of members" contains scores from a number of standard personality measures—MMPI, Bernreuter Personality Inventory, Taylor Anxiety Scale, Guilford-Zimmerman Temperament Survey, and so on. It also includes self-ratings and peer ratings of such traits as self-reliance and insecurity, and measures from projective tests such as the Rorschach and Blacky Pictures tests.

References

Variables of this class were used in a total of 52 studies in the sample and were tested for relationships to 13 other variable classes, in a total of 207 associations, of which 57 (28%) were significant. Reference numbers of studies are 11, 136, 254, 319, 384, 417, 418, 512, 660, 663, 695, 728, 766, 794, 856, 862, 919, 927, 1033, 1054, 1074, 1128, 1134, 1145, 1195, 1276, 1333, 1356, 1390, 1420, 1428, 1450, 1451, 1471, 1472, 1557, 1558, 1607, 1650, 1751, 1793, 1832, 1926, 1930, 1939, 1963, 1968, 1979, 2004, 2046, 2054, 2104.

Summary of Major Relationships

"Personality characteristics of members" was highly or moderately related to 5 of 13 other variable classes. These included group level variables such as general structural properties (240), group training and experience (222), and group task performance in operational settings: specific measures (633). In addition, personality characteristics were moderately related to leadership performance (610) and member task performance in operational settings: global measures (622).

There were only slight relationships or no relationships between personality characteristics and member variables such as attitudes toward the task (141) and social position in the group (151). In addition, personality characteristics were not related or only slightly related to interpersonal relations in the group (230) and processes such as content of interaction (410) and outcomes of interaction (430). Finally, personality characteristics were not related to individual task performance in experimental settings (621) or to induced social conditions imposed on the group (312).

In the sample reviewed, there were no tests for relationship between personality characteristics and member level variables such as biographical characteristics (110), abilities (131) (132), several member attitudes (142) (143) (144), and task or physical position of members in the group (152). In addition, there were no tests for relationships with such various conditions imposed upon the group as influence and conformity pressures (311) and various task and operating conditions (321) (322) (323). Further, there were no relationships tested for subjective measures of member and group performance (510) (520) and certain objective measures of member and group task performance (623) (631).

Index of Relationships

140) Attitudes of members as related to personality characteristics of members

    141. Attitudes toward the task. Not related (1/7)

        Characteristics such as personal submissiveness were not related to ratings of task desirability.

150) Positions of members in the group as related to personality characteristics of members

    151. Social position in the group. Slightly related (12/50)

        Leaders of task groups (e.g., fire team captains) exhibited personality characteristics different from those exhibited by other group members; however, no such relationship was found for nontask groups.

220) Group capabilities as related to personality characteristics of members

    222. Group training and experience. Highly related (2/2)

        Groups trained in discussion procedures showed less change in defensiveness than did untrained groups.

230) Interpersonal relations in the group as related to personality characteristics of members. Not related (0/4)

        Personality measures such as Rorschach anxiety-adjustment scores were not related to measures of personal attraction among members.

240) General structural properties of the group as related to personality characteristics of members. Moderately related (1/2)

        Dyads who used projection as a common defense mechanism showed less achievement motivation than did dyads who used dissimilar defenses or common defenses other than projection.

310) Social conditions as related to personality characteristics of members

    312. Induced social conditions. Not related (0/5)

        Such measures as perceived threat were not related to anxiety, relaxation, and so on.

410) Content of interaction as related to personality characteristics of members. Slightly related (2/10)

        Personality adjustment measures tended not to be consistently related to irrelevant communications, job questions, and so on.

430) Outcomes of interaction as related to personality characteristics of members. Slightly related (6/36)

        For example, observed group competitiveness and adaptability tended not to be related to such personality characteristics of members as emotional stability and maturity.

610) Leadership performance as related to personality characteristics of members. Moderately related (12/24)

        There was a high relationship between scores on such personality measures as extroversion, assertiveness, and social maturity when they were associated with leaderless group discussion behavior (10/14). However, there was slight relationship between other traits, such as seriousness and general activity, and leaderless group discussion behavior (2/10).

620) Task performance of members as related to personality characteristics of members

    621. Member task performance in experimental settings. Not related (2/14)

    622. Member task performance in operational settings: global measures. Moderately related (4/8)

Better over-all personal ratings were positively related to ratings of leadership in industrial work situations (3/3) but only slightly related to ratings of leadership performance in military field situations (1/5).

630) Task performance of groups as related to personality characteristics of members

    632. Group task performance in operational settings: global measures. Somewhat related (12/38)

The less members exhibited extreme personality characteristics, the more effective was their group's performance (7/12). Members who rated themselves high on physical prowess and self-reliance belonged to groups rated high on over-all military field problem effectiveness (5/8).

    633. Group task performance in operational settings: specific measures. Moderately related (3/7)

Supervisors rated high in interviews on traits such as reasonableness and democratic behavior had high-producing work sections (3/3), but no such relationship was found for ratings of other, similar characteristics (0/4).

131. GENERAL ABILITIES OF MEMBERS

Definition

"General abilities of members" includes such objective measures of ability as AGCT scores, California Mental Maturity Test scores, ACE Psychological Examination scores, and records of academic and/or military-training course grades or class rankings. Also included are peer ratings of athletic ability, intelligence, expertness in music, leadership potential, and so on.

References

Variables of this class were used in a total of 31 studies in the sample and were tested for relationships to ten variable classes, in a total of 230 associations, of which 119 (52%) were significant. Reference numbers of studies are 1, 1a, 125, 132, 133, 272, 450, 715, 728, 767, 794, 856, 1054, 1074, 1098, 1195, 1227, 1242, 1333, 1354, 1401, 1522, 1552, 1751, 1781, 1782, 1785, 1963, 1976, 2046, 2054.

Summary of Major Relationships

"General abilities of members" was highly or moderately related to seven of ten variable classes studied. These strong relationships included member characteristics such as other general abilities (131) and task abilities (132). In addition, various member measures such as leadership performance (610) member task performance in experimental settings (621), and member task performance in operational settings: specific measures (623) were strongly related to general abilities of members. This variable class was also moderately related to induced task conditions (323) and to member perceptions of social behavior of self and others (520).

General abilities of members were slightly or not related to patterns of interaction (420) and to group task performance in operational settings (632) (633).

In the sample reviewed there was no occurrence of tests for relationships between general abilities of members and various other member level variables such as personality characteristics (120), biographical characteristics (110), member attitudes (141) (142) (143) (144), and position of members in the group (151) (152). In addition, there were no tests for relationship with various properties of the group such as general structural properties (240), interpersonal relations in the group (230), and group capabilities (220). Also, there were no tested relationships with certain task and operating conditions (321) (322) or various social conditions imposed upon the group (311) (312). Finally, except for the cases cited, there were no tested relationships with subjective measures of member and group performance (510) and measures of group task performance (631) (632).

Index of Relationships

130) Abilities of members as related to general abilities of members

132. 131. General abilities of members. Moderately related within variable class (16/27)

There were consistently high interrelationships among measures such as word-analogy scores, vocabulary skills, verbal and mathematical skills, and scholastic grades (5/5). There were moderate interrelationships among perceptions of other members' abilities, such as expertness in music, skill in sports, and so on (11/22).

132. Task abilities of members. Highly related (10/15)

The higher a person's intelligence, the more frequently he was rated by others as being a leader, as having power, and so on.

320) Task and operating conditions as related to general abilities of members

323. Induced task conditions. Moderately related (19/45)

Confederates who deliberately performed poorly on the task were rated lower on general motivation and dependability after their role playing than before (15/17). However, type of judgment set (ratings from an "administrative" as opposed to a "research" set) was not related to ratings of member general abilities (3/25).

420) Patterns of interaction as related to general abilities of members. Slightly related (1/4)

>There was no clear-cut pattern of results.

520) Perceptions of social behavior of self and others as related to general abilities of members. Moderately related (2/4)

>Members who behaved impulsively were rated by peers as being more independent from adults but not different in amount of group power they held, as compared with that of less-impulsive members.

610) Leadership performance as related to general abilities of members. Highly related (30/50)

>Group members with high general intelligence exhibited high emergent-leader behavior in leaderless group discussions (6/7). Peer ratings of a number of general abilities were related to leaderless group discussion behavior, but a number of similar abilities were not (16/26). In an operational setting, the higher a leader's problem-solving ability and word fluency, the higher he was rated on leadership abilities by supervisors; however, this relationship held for some departments but not others (8/17).

620) Task performance of members as related to general abilities of members

>621. Member task performance in experimental settings. Highly related (28/46)

>>The higher members' school grades and intelligence, the better members performed on maze-learning tasks (15/15). Intelligence was also highly and positively related to performance on two types of intellectual problems, especially for older members (11/16). However, there was no relation between intelligence and skill in perceptual tasks such as estimating number of objects (0/4). Human relations role-playing performance was moderately related to athletic ability (2/4).

>623. Member task performance in operational settings: specific measures. Moderately related (12/29)

>>The role-playing competence of Air Force officers was highly and positively related to member ratings of intelligence, energy, and so on (8/8), but not related to such similar peer ratings as adaptability and orderliness, (0/12).

630) Task performance of groups as related to general abilities of members

>632. Group task performance in operational settings: global measures. Not related (1/10)

>>For example, satisfaction with leader tended not to be related to such measures as production rate, simulated air crew task performance, and so on.

>633. Group task performance in operational settings: specific measures. Not related (1/10)

>>For example, member intelligence was not related to group performance on air crew tasks and Army field problems.

132. TASK ABILITIES OF MEMBERS

Definition

"Task abilities of members" includes objective measures such as achievement tests, job knowledge tests, training school grades, and tests of retention of material. It also includes self-ratings and peer ratings of member task abilities— ratings of own or others' skills, knowledge, leadership ability, and so on.

References

Variables of this class were used in a total of 26 studies in the sample and were tested for relationships to 20 variable classes, in a total of 1022 associations, of which 282 (28%) were significant. Reference numbers of studies are 132, 133, 136, 361, 438, 439, 450, 473, 512, 642, 678, 698, 715, 728, 766, 856, 984, 1046, 1195, 1333, 1585, 1684, 1751, 1979, 2000, 2054.

Summary of Major Relationships

This variable was highly or moderately related to 11 of 20 variable classes. There was a strong relationship to other member characteristics, such as general abilities (131) and other task abilities (132). This variable class was also strongly associated with attitudes toward the situation (142) and attitudes toward issues, concepts, ideologies (144). In addition, task abilities showed strong relationships with members' social position in the group (151) and interpersonal relationships in the group (230). The variable was also highly associated with several group level variables, such as training and experience (222) and induced task conditions (323). Finally, members' task abilities showed a high relationship with leadership performance (610), members' task performance in experimental settings (621), and patterns of interaction (420).

Member task abilities had little relationship to attitudes toward the task (141) and attitudes toward nongroup members and other groups (143). It also showed little relationship with certain measures of task performance: e.g., member performance in operational settings: global and specific measures (622) (623), group task performance: global and specific measures (632) (633), or patterns and outcomes of interaction (410) (430).

No tests for relationship between member task abilities and personality characteristics (120), biographical characteristics (110), and members' task or physical position in the group (152) occurred in the review sample. There were also no tests for relationship between task abilities of members and various subjective measures of member and group performance (510) (520).

Index of Relationships

130) Abilities of members as related to task abilities of members

    131. General abilities of members. Highly related (10/15)

        The higher a person's intelligence, the more frequently he was rated by others as being a leader, as having power, and so on.

132. Task abilities of members. Moderately related within variable class (83/164)

Perceptions of other-member task abilities, such as leadership ability and combat attitudes, were moderately related to one another (73/144). Members rated by others as being leaders and as having various relevant task skills were rated higher by superiors on task proficiency and were higher on examination scores (8/9). However, objective measures of task ability, such as OCS grades and faculty ratings of leadership ability, were only slightly related to one another (2/11).

140) Attitudes of members as related to task abilities of members

141. Attitudes toward the task. Not related (0/6)

Member satisfaction with the group leader's ability did not affect feelings of task involvement.

142. Attitudes toward the situation. Moderately related (9/16)

Members rating themselves high on power over others were rated by others as having power (6/6). There was a less clear-cut but moderate relationship between perceptions of supervisor-imposed discipline and ratings of supervisor competence (3/6). Feelings of belongingness to the group were not related to attitudes toward the leader (0/4).

143. Attitudes toward nongroup persons and other groups. Slightly related with no clear-cut pattern (4/15)

144. Attitudes toward issues, concepts, ideologies. Moderately related (4/9)

The lower the authoritarian attitudes of a member, the more frequently he was chosen as a leader (2/2). In a different setting, the extent of perceived deviations of own views from the endorsed views was not related to the desire to have a supportive communication partner (0/4).

150) Positions of members in the group as related to task abilities of members

151. Social position in the group. Highly related (6/6)

The higher a member's military rank, the more frequently he was chosen as having high task skills.

220) Group capabilities as related to task abilities of members

222. Group training and experience. Moderately related (2/4)

After a military-training period, group members expressed greater confidence in one another and rated one another higher in task proficiency. However, there was no increase in morale or in willingness to go to combat with group members.

230) Interpersonal relations in the group as related to task abilities of members. Highly related (20/21)

For example, perceptions of other members' general task interests consistently related to personal attraction to members.

240) General structural properties of the group as related to task abilities of members. Slightly related (12/59)

> Groups with a change in leader had members who changed their attitudes toward their leader more than did members of groups without such changes (5/6). Judgments of leader skills were not related to variations in group size (less than or more than 30 members) (7/53).

320) Task and operating conditions as related to task abilities of members

> 323. Induced task conditions. Highly related (14/19)

>> Confederates who deliberately performed poorly were rated low on task competence by others in the group (8/8). Members of industrial work groups who were allowed some degree of autonomy in their jobs were more satisfied with their supervisors and more strongly changed attitudes in the positive direction (2/4) than did members of less-autonomous groups (0/3). In another setting, members rewarded for group performance changed more strongly in ratings of a poorly performing confederate's task competence than did members who were rewarded on an individual basis (3/3).

410) Content of interaction as related to task abilities of members. Slightly related (1/6)

> For example, perceptions of other members' task abilities were not consistently related to such discussion behavior measures as giving suggestions and asking opinions.

420) Patterns of interaction as related to task abilities of members. Highly related (4/6)

> Members who were more active in discussions learned and retained more knowledge of the topic than did less-active members.

430) Outcomes of interaction as related to task abilities of members. Slightly related (32/108)

> The more highly members were rated by others on power, the more they were observed as influencing others directly and indirectly, as receiving deferent behavior from others, and so on (27/44). However, confidence in own abilities was not related to active vs. passive discussion role, nor were objective measures of supervisory ability related to observed carefulness (1/8). Perceptions of other members' task skills were only slightly related to group discussion morale, cooperativeness, cohesiveness (2/11). Perceived crew member proficiency was not related to air crew coordination (0/30).

610) Leadership performance as related to task abilities of members. Moderately related (23/47)

> Leadership nominations by friends were highly related to observed measures of leadership behavior (5/7). There was a generally high and positive relationship between ratings of supervisory or leadership potential and performance in leaderless group discussions (11/18), but the relationship was only moderate between the same variables in an Army setting (6/15).

620) Task performance of members as related to task abilities of members

    621. Member task performance in experimental settings. Highly related (4/5)

    Over-all grades in Air Force ground school were positively related to grades on a specific written examination.

    622. Member task performance in operational settings: global measures. Slightly related (17/74)

    There was a high and positive relationship between an Army squad leader's knowledge of military problems and his rated performance on an actual field test (3/3), but slight relationship between Air Force ground school grades and superiors' ratings of combat performance (2/8). Perceived task abilities of self and others were only slightly related to measures such as flight proficiency (12/63).

    623. Member task performance in operational settings: specific measures. Slightly related (2/8)

630) Task performance of groups as related to task abilities of members

    632. Group task performance in operational settings: global measures. Slightly related (4/21)

    For example, satisfaction with leader tended not to be related to such measures as production rate, simulated air crew task performance, and so on.

    633. Group task performance in operational settings: specific measures. Not related (31/410)

    For example, measures of production line effectiveness and performance on simulated air crew tasks were only slightly related to member judgments of competence and confidence in superiors (7/37). Moreover, such objective measures of task ability as ground school grades were not related to measures of performance on simulated air crew tasks (24/373).

141. ATTITUDES TOWARD THE TASK

Definition

"Attitudes toward the task" includes questionnaire and interview ratings of satisfaction with the job and its surrounding conditions, attitudes toward the material, attitudes toward the testing procedures, and so on.

References

Variables of this class were used in a total of 32 studies in the sample and were tested for relationships to eight variable classes, in a total of 119 associations, of which 44 (37%) were significant. Reference numbers of studies are 182, 184, 201, 398, 417, 418, 439, 462, 697, 715, 777, 806, 941, 979, 1033a, 1054, 1139, 1252, 1382, 1450, 1451, 1522, 1716, 1716a, 1756, 1780, 1884, 1968, 2004, 2029, 2058, 2104.

Summary of Major Relationships

"Member attitudes toward the task" was highly or moderately related to four of eight variable classes. These strong relationships included other measures of member attitudes toward the task (141), task or physical position in the group (152), and induced task conditions (323). In addition, certain biographical characteristics (110) were moderately related to attitudes toward the task.

Various member characteristics such as personality (120) and task abilities (132) were not related to member attitudes toward the task. Group level variables such as general structural properties of the group (240) and group task performance in operational settings: specific measures (633) were only slightly or not related to member attitudes toward the task.

There were no cases of tests for relationship between attitudes toward the task and various other member attitudes (142) (143) (144) or to members' social position in the group (151). A series of group characteristics such as abilities (221), training and experience (222), and interpersonal relations (230) were not tested. With the exception of the case cited, there were also no tested relationships with such various operating conditions imposed upon the group as influence and conformity pressures (311), induced social conditions (312), stimulus properties of the task (321), and feedback and reinforcement conditions (322). There were no relationships with a series of interaction process variable classes (410) (420) (430) or various subjective measures of member and group performance (510) (520). Finally, there were no tested relationships with several objective measures of member and group performance, including leadership (610), member task performance (621) (622) (623), and group task performance (631) (632).

Index of Relationships

110) Biographical characteristics of members as related to attitudes toward the task. Moderately related (6/15)

> In one study, women were more satisfied with work conditions than were men (5/6), but there was no such relationship in another study (1/9).

120) Personality characteristics of members as related to attitudes toward the task. Not related (1/7)

> Characteristics such as personal submissiveness were not related to ratings of task desirability.

130) Abilities of members as related to attitudes toward the task

132. Task abilities of members. Not related (0/6)

> Member satisfaction with the group leader's abilities did not affect feelings of task involvement.

140) Attitudes of members as related to attitudes toward the task

141. Attitudes toward the task. Highly related within variable class (11/12)

> Job satisfaction, job enjoyment, and job opportunities tended to intercorrelate.

150) Positions of members in the group as related to attitudes toward the task

    152. Task or physical position in the group. Moderately related (12/27)

        Members in more central positions in a group's communication net showed higher satisfaction than did those in peripheral positions (8/13) but did not differ from members in intermediate positions (0/3). However, centrally located members did not see their positions as having any more status than peripheral members (1/5).

240) General structural properties of the group as related to attitudes toward the task. Slightly related (1/6)

        Homogeneity in personality characteristics was only slightly related to task satisfaction.

320) Task and operating conditions as related to attitudes toward the task

    323. Induced task conditions. Moderately related (12/24)

        Members who were given some degree of job autonomy and members whose task status was improved (by the experimenter) were more satisfied with their jobs than were members not so manipulated (7/10). However, instructions regarding task desirability were only slightly related to perceptions of task desirability (1/6).

        Groups under perceived success conditions saw the task as more difficult and had more consensus on that judgment than did groups under failure conditions (3/4). However, perceived probability of goal achievement was not related to task satisfaction (0/2).

630) Task performance of groups as related to attitudes toward the task

    633. Group task performance in operational settings: specific measures. Not related (1/22)

142. ATTITUDES TOWARD THE SITUATION

Definition

    "Attitudes toward the situation" includes questionnaire and rating scale responses regarding general and specific feelings about situational conditions. Examples are feelings of ease, of freedom to express opinion, of being under pressure, and of organizational identification.

References

    Variables of this class were used in a total of 24 studies in the sample and were tested for relationships to 10 other variable classes, in a total of 102 associations, of which 41 (40%) were significant. Reference numbers of studies are 136, 144, 201, 398, 418, 439, 526, 663, 678, 695, 806, 984, 1054, 1075, 1252, 1325, 1382, 1451, 1607, 1756, 1780, 1914, 1976, 2091.

Summary of Major Relationships

Member attitudes toward the situation were highly or moderately related to 4 of 10 other variable classes. These strongly related variables included task abilities of members (132), induced task conditions (323), and content and outcomes of interaction (410) (430).

Attitudes toward the situation were either not related or only slightly related to interpersonal relations in the group (230), member task performance in experimental settings and operational settings: global measures (621) (622), and group task performance in operational settings: specific measures (633).

There were no cases of tested relationships in the review sample between attitudes toward the situation and a series of member characteristics such as personality characteristics (120), biographical characteristics (110), various member attitudes (141) (142) (143) (144), positions of members in the group (151) (152), and group capabilities (221) (222). There were no tested relationships with such operating conditions imposed upon the group as influence and conformity pressures (311), stimulus properties of the task (321), and feedback and reinforcement conditions (322), or with subjective measures of member and group performance (510) (520). Also, there were no tested relationships with leadership performance variables (610) and some other objective measures of member and group task performance (623) (631) (632).

Index of Relationships

130) Abilities of members as related to attitudes toward the situation

132. Task abilities of members. Moderately related (9/16)

Members rating themselves high on power over others were rated by others as having power (6/6). There was a less clear-cut but moderate relationship between perceptions of supervisor-imposed discipline and ratings of supervisor competence (3/6). There was no relationship between feelings of belongingness and attitudes toward the leader (0/4).

230) Interpersonal relations in the group as related to attitudes toward the situation. Slightly related (1/4)

240) General structural properties of the group as related to attitudes toward the situation. Somewhat related (2/6)

Members of dyads who used projection as a common defense mechanism tended to be more insecure than were dyads who used dissimilar defenses or common defenses other than projection. However, such groups did not differ on other attitudes toward the situation.

310) Social conditions as related to attitudes toward the situation

312. Induced social conditions. Somewhat related (8/23)

In a moderate relationship, members of cooperative groups felt less desire to excel personally, more influence of other members, more obligation to the group, more desire for respect from other members, more desire to achieve as a group, more desire to excel other groups, and more desire to please the experimenter than did members of competitive groups. However, these results occurred differentially as a function of tasks (8/15).

320) Task and operating conditions as related to attitudes toward the situation

323. Induced task conditions. Highly related (2/2)

Members of groups operating under success conditions saw less discrepancy between their own and other members' opinions (2/2).

410) Content of interaction as related to attitudes toward the situation. Moderately related (5/9)

Members who saw themselves as having more power were observed as attempting to influence others more; however, between-group variations tended to make results less than clear-cut.

430) Outcomes of interaction as related to attitudes toward the situation. Moderately related (7/12)

Groups whose members perceived consensus of group opinion were judged to be more orderly (3/4); no other systematic pattern of results was identified.

620. Task performance of members as related to attitudes toward the situation

621. Member task performance in experimental settings. Slightly related (2/8)

Problem-solving performance tended not to be consistently related to variables such as attitudes toward problem solving.

622. Member task performance in operational settings: global measures. Slightly related (4/16)

Men with feelings of well-being in the Air Force and a sense of safety in flying were rated higher by superiors on combat performance. No other results were clear-cut.

630) Task performance of groups as related to attitudes toward the situation

633. Group task performance in operational settings: specific measures. Slightly related (1/6)

Such measures as perceived social distance between self and subordinates tended not to be related to group production time.

143. ATTITUDES TOWARD NONGROUP PERSONS AND OTHER GROUPS

Definition

"Attitudes toward nongroup persons and other groups" is a combination of several kinds of variables, each of which has a relatively small frequency. The class includes questionnaire and rating scale measures of attitudes toward supraordinate groups or persons. Examples are attitudes toward an industrial company, military company, squadron, armed force, profession, and so on.

In addition, attitudes toward hypothetical outside persons (for example, most- and least-preferred co-workers) and real and hypothetical outside groups (such as ethnic minority groups) are also included.

References

Variables of this class were used in a total of 16 studies in the sample and were tested for relationships to six other variable classes, in a total of 119 associations, of which 40 (34%) were significant. Reference numbers of studies are 83, 433, 439, 450, 678, 766, 777, 806, 972, 979, 1054, 1333, 1382, 1522, 1793, 1914.

Summary of Major Relationships

"Attitudes toward nongroup persons and other groups" was highly or moderately related to two of six other variable classes. The strongly related classes were stimulus properties of the task (321) and induced task conditions (323).

This variable class was either not related or only slightly related to member task abilities (132) and to measures of group task performance in operational settings: specific measures (633).

There were no cases of tested relationships between attitudes toward nongroup persons and other groups and various member properties such as personality characteristics (120), biographical characteristics (110), other member attitudes (141) (142) (143) (144), and member position in the group (151) (152). The variable was not tested for relationships to group properties such as structural factors (240) and group capabilities (221) (222), nor to several operating conditions imposed upon the group such as social conditions (311) (312) and feedback and reinforcement conditions (322). It was also not studied for relationship to various interaction process measures (410) (420) (430) and to subjective measures of member and group performance (510) (520). Finally, attitudes toward nongroup persons and other groups were not tested against various objective measures of member performance such as leadership (610) and member and group task performance (621) (622) (623) (631).

Index of Relationships

130) Abilities of members as related to attitudes toward nongroup persons and other groups

132. Task abilities of members. Slightly related (4/15)

There was no clear-cut pattern of results.

230) Interpersonal relations in the group as related to attitudes toward nongroup persons and other groups. Somewhat related (2/6)

There was no clear-cut pattern of results.

320) Task and operating conditions as related to attitudes toward nongroup persons and other groups

321. Stimulus properties of the task. Moderately related (7/16)

In a moderate relationship, change in attitudes toward minority groups was an interactive function of exposure to films and discussions, initial attitudes, and short- and long-range testing times (6/11). In another study, exposure to discussion was only slightly related to change in attitudes toward minority groups (1/5).

323. Induced task conditions. Highly related (5/6)

Groups were more satisfied with their companies after introduction of experimental conditions, regardless of type of manipulation.

630) Task performance of groups as related to attitudes toward nongroup persons and other groups

632. Group task performance in operational settings: global measures. Somewhat related (3/8)

Army squad members who exhibited favorable attitudes and adjustment to the Army were members of squads rated high on over-all performance (3/4). However, there was no relationship between satisfaction with the Air Force or with an industrial organization and ratings of crew or group performance (0/4).

633. Group task performance in operational settings: specific measures. Slightly related (19/68)

The less similarity of traits that the leader attributed to a hypothetical most- and least-preferred co-worker, the more effective was team performance for basketball teams, surveying teams, air crews (on simulated air crew tasks), and tank teams (on tank training problems). However, these variables interacted with sociometric patterns: namely, the relationship here described held only when the leader had positive sociometric relationships with others in the crew (9/12). In another study, attraction toward an industrial company or the Navy was not related either to factory production work time or military task proficiency (1/10).

144. ATTITUDES TOWARD ISSUES, CONCEPTS, IDEOLOGIES

Definition

"Attitudes toward issues, concepts, ideologies" includes attitude scale measures of authoritarianism, of attitudes on mental health, of personal values, of attitudes on the importance of issues used in the study, and so on. It also has pattern measures of attitudes (disagreement between individual and group viewpoint, change in private opinions, differences between initial private and later public attitude) for a whole range of topics from wire tapping to taste.

References

Variables of this class were used in a total of 29 studies in the sample and were tested for relationships to 18 variable classes, in a total of 375 associations, of which 105 (28%) were significant. Reference numbers of studies are 111,

122, 136, 298, 351, 450, 484, 526, 693, 806, 814, 837, 867, 868, 1046, 1134, 1227, 1242, 1325, 1333, 1354, 1450, 1505, 1552, 1666, 1742, 1755, 2004, 2104.

Summary of Major Relationships

This variable class was highly or moderately related to 9 of 18 variable classes. There were strong relationships to member characteristics such as task abilities (132) and other attitudes toward issues, concepts, ideologies (144). Strong relationships also occurred for interpersonal relations in the group (230) and such conditions imposed upon the group as influence and conformity pressures (311) and induced task conditions (323). Significant relationships also occurred with certain objective measures of member task performance (621) (623) and certain measures of interaction pattern (420).

There were only slight relationships or no relationships between attitudes toward issues, concepts, and ideologies and several group level variables such as group training and experience (222), group task performance in operational settings: specific measures (633), and general structural properties of the group (240). There was also little relationship between this variable class and various interaction measures, such as content and outcomes of interaction (410) (430), as well as measures of member task performance in operational settings: global measures (622).

There were no instances of tests for relationship between attitudes toward issues, concepts, ideologies and a number of member level variables, such as personality characteristics (120), other types of attitudes (141) (142) (143), and task or physical position of members in the group (152). In addition, this variable class was not related to several measures of group task performance (631) (632) or subjective measures of performance (510) (520).

Index of Relationships

110) Biographical characteristics of members as related to attitudes toward issues, concepts, ideologies. Somewhat related (8/21)

> Upperclassmen were more similar to their faculty advisors in personal values than were underclassmen (2/3). In another setting, individuals with more education, who were only children, or who were Jewish were more influential in changing others' opinions (3/3). Several other biographical variables were only slightly related to influence on others or susceptibility to influence by others (3/12).

130) Abilities of members as related to attitudes toward issues, concepts, ideologies

132. Task abilities of members. Moderately related (4/9)

> The lower the authoritarian attitudes of a member, the more frequently he was chosen as a leader (2/2). In a different setting, the extent of perceived deviation of own views from the endorsed views was not related to the desire to the desire to have a supportive communication partner (0/4).

140) Attitudes of members as related to attitudes toward issues, concepts, ideologies

    144. Attitudes toward issues, concepts, ideologies. Highly related within variable class (18/28)

        Measures such as authoritarianism and personal values were consistently interrelated.

150) Positions of members in the group as related to attitudes toward issues, concepts, ideologies

    151. Social position in the group. Highly related (4/4)

        Those who desired and attained membership in a high-status group showed more authoritarian attitudes and less long-term reduction in these attitudes than did persons who did not desire and attain such membership.

220) Group capabilities as related to attitudes toward issues, concepts, ideologies

    222. Group training and experience. Not related (1/9)

230) Interpersonal relations in the group as related to attitudes toward issues, concepts, ideologies. Moderately related (5/12)

        For example, authoritarians tended to be less liked by their fellow members than were nonauthoritarians (5/9).

240) General structural properties of the group as related to attitudes toward issues, concepts, ideologies. Slightly related (2/11)

        For example, individuals did not differ from two- or three-man groups in general attitudes or changes in attitudes toward topic importance.

310) Social conditions as related to attitudes toward issues, concepts, ideologies

    311. Influence and conformity pressures. Highly related (1/1)

        Members under high pressure toward opinion uniformity changed personal opinions more often than did those under low pressure (1/1).

    312. Induced social conditions. Somewhat related (4/12)

        There was no clear-cut pattern of results.

320) Task and operating conditions as related to attitudes toward issues, concepts, ideologies

    321. Stimulus properties of the task. Slightly related (8/34)

        There was slight relationship between change in nationalistic and internationalistic attitudes as a function of discussion–no discussion conditions (5/20). But in another setting, although there was prior difference in opinion or opinion heterogeneity about mental health concepts (0/6), those exposed to films or films and discussion showed more positive change than did those not exposed (3/4).

323. Induced task conditions. Highly related (2/3)

Among members believing that all in the group had equal skills, the majorities changed opinions less but varied more in judgments of topic importance than did the minorities (2/3).

410) Content of interaction as related to attitudes toward issues, concepts, ideologies. Slightly related (22/131)

High-authoritarian group leaders were less secure, sensitive, and equalitarian in their discussion behavior; they made fewer diagnoses, sanction-seeking proposals, initial acts, and positive acts; they led less, were less agreeable, clarified less, asked for opinions less, and were more withdrawn than were equalitarian leaders.

420) Patterns of interaction as related to attitudes toward issues, concepts, ideologies. Moderately related (3/5)

There was no clear-cut pattern of results.

430) Outcomes of interaction as related to attitudes toward issues, concepts, ideologies. Slightly related (15/66)

Authoritarians seemed to exhibit less-intelligent discussion behavior (5/8), although such attitudes were not related to adaptability, sensitivity, and social abilities shown during discussions (2/14). Authoritarian attitudes were only slightly related to observed discussion behavior measures such as equal participation, friendliness, clique formation, group motivation, competence, and communication effectiveness (6/34).

620) Task performance of members as related to attitudes toward issues, concepts, ideologies

621. Member task performance in experimental settings. Highly related (4/6)

Members with low authoritarian attitudes performed better on a maze task.

622. Member task performance in operational settings: global measures. Not related (1/12)

For example, authoritarian attitudes were not related to job performance.

623. Member task performance in operational settings: specific measures. Moderately related (3/5)

There was no clear-cut pattern of results.

630) Task performance of groups as related to attitudes toward issues, concepts, ideologies

633. Group task performance in operational settings: specific measures. Not related (0/6)

For example, authoritarian attitudes were not related to drill proficiency and cleanliness.

151. SOCIAL POSITION IN THE GROUP

Definition

"Social position in the group" includes both self-reports by members on group rank or status (such as military rank, job title, salary) and experimenter designations (such as assigned leader, assigned status in group).

References

Variables of this class were used in a total of 29 studies in the sample and were tested for relationships to 12 other variable classes, in a total of 234 associations, of which 99 (42%) were significant. Reference numbers of studies are 32, 272, 319, 361, 362, 418, 450, 608, 608a, 678, 715, 766, 767, 1059, 1195, 1195a, 1428, 1471, 1650, 1742, 1751, 1760, 1871, 1874, 1895, 1914, 1961, 2046, 2091.

Summary of Major Relationships

Member social position in the group was highly or moderately related to 7 of 12 other variable classes, including member characteristics such as task abilities (132); attitudes toward issues, concepts, ideologies (144); and subjective perceptions of task and social behavior of self and others (510) (520). Strong relationships also occurred for leadership performance (610) and interpersonal relations in the group (230). Finally, interaction process measures such as outcomes of interaction (430) were strongly related to social position in the group.

Member social position showed only slight or no relationship to personality characteristics of members (120), patterns of interaction (420), and member task performance in operational settings: global and specific measures (622) (623).

There were no instances of tested relationships between member social position and a host of other member characteristics such as biographical properties (110), various member attitudes (141) (142) (143), and positions of members in the group (151) (152). There were also no cases of tested relationships with group properties such as structural characteristics (240) and group capabilities (221) (222), or with various conditions imposed upon the group (311) (312) (321) (322) (323). Finally, there was no study of relationships with various measures of group task performance (631) (632) (633) or with member task performance in experimental settings (621).

Index of Relationships

120) Personality characteristics of members as related to social position in the group. Slightly related (12/50)

Leaders of task groups (e.g., fire team captains) exhibited personality characteristics different from those exhibited by other group members; however, no such relationship was found for nontask groups.

130) Abilities of members as related to social position in the group

132. Task abilities of members. Highly related (6/6)

The higher a member's military rank, the more frequently he was chosen as having high task skills.

140) Attitudes of members as related to social position in the group

144. Attitudes toward issues, concepts, ideologies. Highly related (4/4)

Those who desired and attained membership in a high-status group showed more authoritarian attitudes and less long-term reduction in these attitudes than did those who did not desire and attain such membership.

230) Interpersonal relations in the group as related to social position in the group. Moderately related (10/19)

Attitudes toward the group: The higher a member's military rank, the more he was attracted to his air crew (5/6). In addition, those achieving a higher status (from the experimenter) had more-positive feelings about their groups (2/3).

Attitudes toward other members: The higher a member's military rank, the more frequently he was chosen as a desirable personal friend or companion (5/6). There was only a slight relationship between personal attractiveness of confederates and of other group members (1/6).

410) Content of interaction as related to social position in the group. Somewhat related (26/82)

Appointed leaders of discussion groups more often diagnosed situations, initiated action, gave information, and desired action than did other members (12/13). Remaining results showed slight relationship and no particular pattern (14/69).

420) Patterns of interaction as related to social position in the group. Slightly related (2/10)

There was no clear-cut pattern of results.

430) Outcomes of interaction as related to social position in the group. Moderately related (2/4)

Those with high assigned importance in the group attempted to lead others more often than did those with low assigned importance (2/2).

510) Perceptions of task performance of self and others as related to social position in the group. Moderately related (10/19)

Own task performance: The higher the member's salary and position in the group, the more perceived authority he felt he had and the more he delegated responsibility (4/6).

Other-member task performance: Position in group as confederate or naïve member was only slightly related to perception of performance effectiveness of others (2/8).

Group task performance: The higher the rank of an air crew member, the higher he rated air crew performance adequacy (4/5).

520) Perceptions of social behavior of self and others as related to social position in the group. Highly related (20/32)

> *Own social behavior:* The higher a member's status in an air crew, the more he reported attempting to influence others (5/5).

> *Other-member social behavior:* The higher a member's rank in the group, the more others indicated they worked with him (10/16), although there was some ambiguity of results because of between-group variations. Perception of social behavior of other members was only slightly related to social position in the group (2/8).

610) Leadership performance as related to social position in the group. Highly related (6/6)

> Members with higher group rank exhibited more leadership behavior in leaderless group discussions.

620) Task performance of members as related to social position in the group

> 622. Member task performance in operational settings: global measures. Slightly related (1/4)

> For example, time spent in the Army tended not to be related to over-all member performance.

> 623. Member task performance in operational settings: specific measures. Not related (0/7)

152. TASK OR PHYSICAL POSITION IN THE GROUP

Definition

"Task or physical position in the group" is composed of experimenter-designated variables, including member's centrality or independence in communication nets, his job position, his seating position vis-à-vis other members, and so on.

References

Variables of this class were used in a total of 24 studies in the sample and were tested for relationships to four other variable classes, in a total of 82 associations, of which 30 (37%) were significant. Reference numbers of studies are 128, 144, 252, 424, 450, 462, 693, 697, 767, 869, 927, 941, 999, 1139, 1567, 1598, 1716, 1716a, 1781, 1796, 1810, 1945, 1961, 1968.

Summary of Major Relationships

"Task or physical position in the group" was highly or moderately related to two out of four other variable classes—attitudes toward the task (141) and patterns of interaction (420).

Leadership performance (610) and member task performance in experimental settings (621) showed no relationship.

There were no instances of tests for relationship between this variable class and member biographical or personal characteristics (110) (120), abilities, (131) (132), several attitudes (142) (143) (144), and positions in the groups (151) (152). In addition, there were no tests for relationship with properties of the group (221) (222) (230) (240), certain measures of interaction process (410) (430), various objective and subjective measures of member task performance (510) (520) (622) (623), and measures of group task performance (631) (632) (633).

Index of Relationships

140) Attitudes of members as related to task or physical position in the group

141. Attitudes toward the task. Moderately related (12/27)

Members in more central positions in a group's communication net showed higher task satisfaction than did those in extreme positions (8/13), but did not differ from members in intermediate positions (0/3). However, centrally located members did not see their positions as having more status than peripheral members (1/5).

420) Patterns of interaction as related to task or physical position in the group. Highly related (15/19)

The more centrally located were members in a group's communication net, the more heavily they became involved in the transmission of messages (11/15).

610) Leadership performance as related to task or physical position in the group. Not related (3/23)

For example, leaderless group discussion behavior was not related to seating positions in the group.

620) Task performance of members as related to task or physical position in the group

621. Member task performance in experimental settings. Not related (0/13)

Performance measures such as symbol identification were not related to centrality of position in the communication net.

221. GROUP ABILITIES

Definition

"Group abilities" includes member, observer, and supervisor ratings of group abilities such as performance potentiality, flexibility, crew compatibility in combat, teamwork, motivation, and value to squadron.

References

Variables of this class were used in a total of 5 studies in the sample and were tested for relationships to four other variable classes, in a total of 40 associations, of which 30 (75%) were significant. Reference numbers of studies are 439, 606a, 887, 1756, 1939.

Summary of Major Relationships

Group abilities were moderately or highly related to three of four other variables. These strongly related variables were general structural properties of the group (240), outcomes of interaction (430), and group task performance in operational settings: specific measures (633).

The variable class with which group abilities were only slightly related was group task performance in operational settings: global measures (632).

In the sample reviewed, group abilities were not studied for relationships with a host of member variables, such as personality (120), biographical characteristics (110), member abilities (131) (132), member attitudes (141) (142) (143) (144), and the position of members in the group (151) (152). The variable class was not tested for association with several group level variables such as group capabilities (221) (222), interpersonal relations in the group (230), and conditions imposed on the group (311) (312) (321) (322) (323). In addition, there were no cases of tested relationships between group abilities and content and patterns of interaction process (410) (420) and subjective measures of member and group performance (510) (520). Finally, group abilities were not tested against measures of leadership performance (610) or member task performance (621) (622) (623).

Index of Relationships

240) General structural properties of the group as related to group abilities. Highly related (10/10)

> In groups ranging in size from two to seven, the larger groups were rated by their members as having greater need for guidance and for a definite leader, and were viewed by members as having more competence and ability than was the case in the smaller groups.

430) Outcomes of interaction as related to group abilities. Highly related (11/11)

> Air crews judged high on over-all value to their squadron were rated high on working with other crews, aircraft handling, military bearing, and so on (5/5). Air crews rated high on degree of consideration shown among members were also rated high on working with other crews, military bearing, aircraft handling, and so on (6/6).

630) Task performance of groups as related to group abilities

632. Group task performance in operational settings: global measures. Slightly related (1/5)

> Air crew problem-solving test performance was not related to ratings of over-all group training performance adequacy.

633. Group task performance in operational settings: specific measures. Moderately related (8/14)

> The higher that air crews were rated on over-all value to their squadron (by superiors), the greater was the number of missions they completed and the greater their performance effectiveness on a series of simulated air crew tasks (7/8). However, perceptions of task-related abilities of groups were only slightly related to group performance on aircraft manufacturing tasks, surveying tasks, and so on (1/6).

222. GROUP TRAINING AND EXPERIENCE

Definition

"Group training and experience" covers self-reports by members of time in combat, time in job, and so on, as well as experimenter designations of such variables as stage of training, amount of training or practice, and testing or stimulus sequence.

References

Variables in this class were used in a total of 43 studies in the sample and were tested for relationships to 12 other variable classes, in a total of 225 associations, of which 99 (44%) were significant. Reference numbers of studies are 1a, 95, 144, 351, 404, 433, 462, 470, 593, 642, 715, 807, 837, 941, 1033, 1033a, 1122, 1134, 1151, 1249, 1249a, 1354, 1467, 1471, 1557, 1572, 1574, 1575, 1586, 1602, 1641, 1684, 1701, 1704, 1707, 1716, 1716a, 1755, 1756, 1782, 1998, 1999, 2008.

Summary of Major Relationships

Of the 12 other variable classes with which "group training and experience" was tested for association, 8 yielded high or moderate relationships. These included member properties such as personality (120), task abilities (132), and interpersonal relations in the group (230). It is interesting to note that group training and experience was strongly related to all measures of group task performance (631) (632) (633) and to member task performance in experimental settings (621), as well as to patterns of interaction (420).

There were only slight or no relationships between this variable and leadership performance (610), outcomes of interaction (430), perceptions of task performance of self and others (510), and attitudes toward issues, concepts, ideologies (144).

There were no cases of tested relationships in the review sample between group training and experience and a number of member properties such as biographical characteristics (110), general abilities (131), certain member attitudes (141) (142) (143), and positions in the group (151) (152). There were also no instances of tests for relationship between group training and experience and conditions imposed upon the group (311) (312) (321) (322) (323); this gap is to be expected because all these types of variables would normally be independent variables. Interestingly, there were no cases of tested relationship between group training and experience and content of interaction (410) or between group training and some measures of member performance effectiveness (622) (623).

Index of Relationships

120) Personality characteristics of members as related to group training and experience. Highly related (2/2)

Groups trained in discussion procedures showed less change in defensiveness than did untrained groups.

130) Abilities of members as related to group training and experience

    132. Task abilities of members. Moderately related (2/4)

        After a military-training period, group members expressed greater confidence in one another and rated one another higher in task proficiency. However, there was no increase in morale or in willingness to go to combat with group members.

140) Attitudes of members as related to group training and experience

    144. Attitudes toward issues, concepts, ideologies. Not related (1/9)

230) Interpersonal relations in the group as related to group training and experience. Moderately related (4/8)

        More experience with a military crew resulted in *less* member attraction to the group (2/3), whereas more experience with a laboratory group produced *more* positive feelings (1/1).

420) Patterns of interaction as related to group training and experience. Highly related (4/4)

430) Outcomes of interaction as related to group training and experience. Not related (3/30)

510) Perceptions of task performance of self and others as related to group training and experience. Slightly related (8/44)

        Other-member task performance: Measures such as (pre-experimental) flying experience were not related to perceptions of leader supervisory behavior or to crew agreements on ratings of other members (2/29). Also, there was slight relationship between leader training in human relations techniques and higher ratings by subordinates on human relations behavior (1/5).

        Group task performance: Another set of results, although unclear, suggested that members of groups in a success condition saw their groups as performing better than did members of failure groups as the task series progressed (5/10).

610) Leadership performance as related to group training and experience. Slightly related (4/18)

        Leaders with training in leader techniques were rated higher on permissiveness, frankness, regulation of discussion participation, and effective resolution of conflicts than were leaders without such training.

        However, trained and untrained leaders did not differ on several similar measures.

620) Task performance of members as related to group training and experience

    621. Member task performance in experimental settings. Highly related (33/46)

        Members exposed to direct training had higher performance ratings than did those members trained by a more-passive method (3/3). In another setting, there was slight relationship between performance improvement and experience (1/4). However, the greater the training on maze, switch adjustment, and similar motor tasks, or the later the period of testing, the better was the performance (28/35).

630) Task performance of groups as related to group training and experience

631. Group task performance in experimental settings. Moderately related (15/26)

Group performance improved over successive stages of practice in symbolic-motor tasks (8/8). With symbolic tasks, all groups showed learning and greater performance proficiency over time (4/4). Sequence of experimental conditions was only slightly related to performance (3/14).

632. Group task performance in operational settings: global measures. Highly related (9/11)

Length of time in job was highly related to group effectiveness (4/5). Crews with more flying experience were rated by supervisors as being more proficient (5/6).

633. Group task performance in operational settings: specific measures. Highly related (14/23)

Group performance improved over successive stages of practice (9/13). Crew aircraft-flying experience was positively related to performance on simulated air crew tasks, but not on other tasks (5/10).

230. INTERPERSONAL RELATIONS IN THE GROUP

Definition

"Interpersonal relations in the group" includes sociometric choices and ratings of absolute or differential liking of other group members, preference for them as social companions, roommates, confidants, and so on. It also contains ratings of liking for the group as a whole, willingness to work with this group again, morale, satisfaction with group, pride in group, pleasantness of group, and similar attitudes.

References

Variables of this class were used in a total of 82 studies in the sample and were tested for relationships to 15 variable classes, in a total of 336 associations, of which 145 (43%) were significant. Reference numbers of studies are 32, 83, 111, 182, 285, 298, 308, 404, 417, 438, 439, 450, 484, 496, 512, 526, 542, 566, 593, 606a, 660, 678, 766, 767, 777, 778, 806, 811, 849, 856, 862, 887, 944, 949, 972, 979, 984, 999, 1033, 1033a, 1054, 1075, 1077, 1151, 1195, 1276, 1305, 1325, 1382, 1420, 1471, 1505, 1522, 1528, 1552, 1564, 1567, 1598, 1639, 1641, 1650, 1707, 1716, 1716a, 1755, 1780, 1785, 1793, 1810, 1832, 1871, 1895, 1914, 1926, 1933, 1945, 1976, 2046, 2076, 2091, 2104, 2108.

Summary of Major Relationships

Of 15 variable classes to which it was tested for association, "interpersonal relations in the group" was highly or moderately related to 8. These included member properties such as task abilities (132), attitudes toward issues, concepts, ideologies (144), and social position in the group (151). In addition, the variable was strongly related to induced social conditions (312) and induced task conditions (323). Finally, this class was strongly related to group training and experience (222) and patterns of interaction (420).

Interpersonal relations in the group was only slightly or not related to personality characteristics of members (120), member attitudes toward the situation and toward nongroup persons and other groups (142) (143), and outcomes of interaction (430).

There were no cases of tests for relationship of interpersonal relations in the group with a number of member level variables, such as biographical characteristics (110), general abilities (131), and task or physical position in the group (152). In addition, interpersonal relations in the group were not studied with respect to association with certain conditions imposed on the group (311) (322). Interestingly, the variable was not tested for relationships to a series of objective measures of member and group performance (610) (621) (622) (623) (631) (632) or subjective measures of member and group effectiveness (510) (520).

Index of Relationships

120) Personality characteristics of members as related to interpersonal relations in the group. Not related (0/4)

> Personality measures such as Rorschach anxiety-adjustment scores were not related to measures of personal attraction among members.

130) Abilities of members as related to interpersonal relations in the group

132. Task abilities of members. Highly related (20/21)

> For example, perceptions of other member's general task interests consistently related to personal attraction to members.

140) Attitudes of members as related to interpersonal relations in the group

142. Attitudes toward the situation. Slightly related (1/4)

143. Attitudes toward nongroup persons and other groups. Somewhat related (2/6)

> There was no clear-cut pattern of results.

144. Attitudes toward issues, concepts, ideologies. Moderately related (5/12)

> For example, authoritarians tended to be less liked by their fellow members than were nonauthoritarians (5/9).

150) Positions of members in the group as related to interpersonal relations in the group

151. Social position in the group. Moderately related (10/19)

The higher a member's military rank, the more frequently he was chosen as a desirable personal friend or companion (5/6), and the more he was attracted to his air crew (2/2).

There was only a slight relationship between personal attractiveness of confederates and of other group members (1/6). Those achieving a higher status (from the experimenter) had more positive feelings about their groups (2/3).

220) Group capabilities as related to interpersonal relations in the group

222. Group training and experience. Moderately related (4/8)

More experience with a military group resulted in *less* attraction to the group (2/3), whereas more experience with a laboratory group produced *more* positive feelings (1/1).

230) Interpersonal relations in the group as related to interpersonal relations in the group. Moderately related within variable class (4/10)

Measures of personal attraction among members were fairly consistently related.

240) General structural properties of the group as related to interpersonal relations in the group. Somewhat related (32/92)

Dyads who used projection as a common defense mechanism were more negative about their groups (4/4) than were dyads who used dissimilar defenses or common defenses other than projection (0/3). Dyads using projection as a common defense also showed more negativism toward their partner than did members of dissimilar groups or dyads whose members used other defense mechanisms in common (6/9). Unspecified between-group differences were also highly related to attraction to the group (3/5). The more dissimilar were dyads in marital status, birthplace of parents, outside sources of income, and college attendance, the more mutually attracted they were (7/8). The more similar were dyads in military background and intentions, the greater their mutual attraction (6/10). However, results with triads and quartets yielded no consistent differences between similar and dissimilar groups (4/50).

310) Social conditions as related to interpersonal relations in the group

312. Induced social conditions. Highly related (24/30)

Members who felt themselves to be personally compatible, congenial, and accepted by others consistently rated others as being personally attractive to them (7/7).

The more members perceived themselves as accepted by others, congenial with others, etc., via experimental instructions, the more they reported feelings of group attraction (16/21). In addition, in a moderate relationship, members of groups instructed to work under cooperative arrangements were more attracted to their groups than were members of competitive groups (1/2).

320) Task and operating conditions as related to interpersonal relations in the group

    321. Stimulus properties of the task. Somewhat related (4/13)

       There was no clear-cut pattern of results.

    323. Induced task conditions. Moderately related (6/15)

       Confederates who purposely performed poorly on the task were not personally liked less after their poor performance than they were before (1/11).

       Members of groups who perceived themselves to be successful were more attracted to their groups than to failure groups (2/2). Members of groups instructed about the high probability of goal achievement were less attracted to their groups than were less likely goal achievers, but actual goal attainment did not affect feelings toward the groups (1/2).

420) Patterns of interaction as related to interpersonal relations in the group. Highly related (23/34)

       Members communicated more with those they liked or disliked than with those toward whom they were personally indifferent (8/8). In another setting personal attraction measures were positively and highly related to such indexes of discussion participation as amount of participation and amount of member interaction (11/15). Sociometric choices and measures such as Rorschach reaction time and number of responses were somewhat related (4/11).

430) Outcomes of interaction as related to interpersonal relations in the group. Not related (0/34)

       Such measures as crew coordination and attrition from the group were not related to personal attraction among members.

630) Task performance of groups as related to interpersonal relations

    633. Group task performance in operational settings: specific measures. Somewhat related (10/34)

       On a factory production task, group members who were more personally attracted to one another performed more effectively (4/4), but this finding did not hold for members of military task groups (3/19). Group attraction was only slightly related to clerical or manufacturing productivity (2/9).

240. GENERAL STRUCTURAL PROPERTIES OF THE GROUP

Definition

"General structural properties of the group" includes variables such as group size (including individual vs. group), communication nets, unity and permanency of group, and indexes of homogeneity–heterogeneity of group members with respect to certain characteristics (age, sex, personality traits, and task skills). It also includes a number of tests of significance of differences among individual groups (for example, among air crews or between different training classes) in which no conceptual basis for the obtained differences is indicated.

References

Variables of this class were used in a total of 67 studies in the sample and were tested for relationships to 16 other variable classes, in a total of 590 associations, of which 229 (39%) were significant. Reference numbers of studies are 1, 1a, 40, 83, 101, 111, 144, 212, 344, 351, 411, 417, 462, 464, 496, 542, 576, 642, 663, 693, 740, 758, 778, 789, 794, 806, 814, 856, 868, 874, 887, 919, 941, 968, 972, 979, 1046, 1085, 1097, 1098, 1099, 1199, 1210, 1243, 1252, 1276, 1294, 1325, 1333, 1486, 1558, 1574, 1598, 1603, 1607, 1666, 1701, 1707, 1756, 1895, 1920, 1930, 1933, 1945, 1961, 1996, 1999.

Summary of Major Relationships

Of the total of 16 other classes against which this variable was tested for relationship, 8 showed high or moderate associations. The only member level variable strongly related to general structural properties of the group was personality characteristics (120), although group abilities showed a high relationship (221). One interaction process measure—outcomes of interaction (430)—and perceptions of social behavior of self and others (520) also showed strong relationships with this variable class, as did a number of objective measures of member and group performance (621) (623) (631) (633).

Slight or no relationship occurred between group structural properties and several member characteristics—e.g., task abilities of members (132) and certain member attitudes (141) (144). In addition, patterns of interaction (420) showed slight relationship. A number of other variables also showed equivocal relationships.

There were no cases of tests for relationships between group structural properties and member attitudes toward nongroup persons and other groups (143), positions of members in the group (151) (152), and measures of leadership and certain task performances (610) (622) (632).

Index of Relationships

120) Personality characteristics of members as related to general structural properties of the group. Moderately related (1/2)

> Groups homogeneous in use of projection as a defense mechanism showed less achievement motivation than did groups similar in use of other defenses or dissimilar in defenses.

130) Abilities of members as related to general structural properties of the group

132. Task abilities of members. Slightly related (12/59)

> Groups with a change in leader had members who changed their attitudes more toward their leader than did members of groups without such changes (5/6).

Judgments of leader skill were not related to variations in group size (less than or more than 30 members) (7/53).

140) Attitudes of members as related to general structural properties of the group

141. Attitudes toward the task. Slightly related (1/6)

Homogeneity in personality characteristics was only slightly related to task satisfaction.

142. Attitudes toward the situation. Somewhat related (2/6)

Members of dyads who used projection as a common defense mechanism tended to be more insecure than were dyads who used dissimilar defenses or common defenses other than projection. However, such groups did not differ in other attitudes toward the situation.

144. Attitudes toward issues, concepts, ideologies. Slightly related (2/11)

For example, individuals did not differ from two- or three-man groups in general attitudes or changes in attitudes toward topic importance.

220) Group capabilities as related to general structural properties of the group

221. Group abilities. Highly related (10/10)

In groups ranging in size from two to seven, the larger groups were rated by their members as having greater need for guidance and for a definite leader, and were viewed by members as having more competence and ability than was the case in the smaller groups.

230) Interpersonal relations in the group as related to general structural properties of the group. Somewhat related (32/92)

Attitudes toward other members: Dyads who used projection as a common defense mechanism showed more negativism toward their partners than did dyads using dissimilar defenses or common defenses other than projection (6/9). In another setting, the more dissimilar were dyads in marital status, birthplace of parents, outside sources of income, and college attendance, the more mutually attracted they were (7/8); whereas the more similar they were in military background and intentions, the greater was their mutual attraction (6/10). However, results with triads and quartets yielded no consistent difference between similar and dissimilar groups (4/50).

Attitudes toward the group: Dyads using projection as a common defense mechanism were more negative about their groups (4/4) than were dyads dissimilar in defenses or using other defenses in common (0/4). There also were unclear between-group differences in attraction to the group (3/6).

410) Content of interaction as related to general structural properties of the group. Somewhat related (15/48)

Two- and three-man groups expressed more ideas and showed more changes in responses than did individuals, although two- and three-man groups did not differ from one another (4/5) in these respects.

Groups with an emergent leader had members with higher leadership behavior in discussions than did groups without an emergent leader (5/7), but the leadership behavior of designated leaders was not different from that of other group members (0/4).

In another setting, differences in group permanency were only slightly related to differences in discussion behavior of members or groups (6/32).

420) Patterns of interaction as related to general structural properties of the group. Slightly related (5/22)

For example, size and type of communication net tended not to be consistently related to amount of communication, degree of aggressiveness in interaction, friendliness, and so on.

430) Outcomes of interaction as related to general structural properties of the group. Moderately related (21/41)

Members with equal power were more likely to form coalitions, members with lower power were more likely to initiate coalitions, and members with high power relative to that of another member were more likely to be involved in coalitions with disproportionate distribution of rewards (10/18).

Groups homogeneous in authoritarian attitudes were rated as more productive and more effective in communicating than were less-homogeneous groups after a period of experience (2/2). Relationships between ratings of competence and definiteness of leadership were only moderate (3/6), and there was slight relationship with member competency, sensitivity in discussion, and so on (2/8).

In a frustrating situation, organized groups showed more we-feeling, frustration, and mutual encouragement than did unorganized groups (4/6).

510) Perceptions of task performance of self and others as related to general structural properties of the group. Somewhat related (32/94)

Members of heterogeneous groups more often saw others as more qualified than themselves (2/3). In other setting, dyads using projection as a common defense more often saw their partners as less successful (2/3) and saw their groups as performing more poorly than did dyads with dissimilar defenses or with other defenses in common (3/4).

In another study, the smaller the group (ranging from 2 to 4 members), the more did members see it as performing effectively (4/4). Leaders of groups larger than 30 were more often rated as coordinating activities well, giving clearer rules to members, having greater achievement effort, having greater physical courage, and making wise delegation of authority (7/26). Members of groups smaller than 30 more frequently indicated "don't know" or "inapplicable" to a whole series of items about the leader (10/26). There was no relationship between largeness or smallness of groups and ratings of behavior "occasionally exhibited" by leaders (2/26).

520) Perceptions of social behavior of self and others as related to general structural properties of the groups. Highly related (3/4)

Organized groups exhibited more fear in a threatening situation than did unorganized groups (1/1). Members of dyads using projection as a common defense mechanism attempted to influence each other more than did dissimilar dyads or dyads using other defenses in common (2/2).

620) Task performance of members as related to general structural properties of the group

621. Member task performance in experimental settings. Moderately related (27/68)

Statistically derived measures of "group" judgment were more accurate than were "individual" judgments, especially for unfamiliar materials (3/3). Working alone, as contrasted with working in the presence of others, was but slightly related to motor performance (2/11). Arithmetic performance did not differ for individuals working alone or in groups. There were significant differences due to age, sex, and race of members although in an unclear pattern. The over-all relationship was moderate (15/27).

Performance did not differ for various communication nets, except that Y nets were better than circle nets (4/4).

623. Member task performance in operational settings: specific measures. Highly related (16/26)

There was a negative relationship between group size (ranging from 10 to 50) and performance effectiveness in one situation (8/9) but only a slight negative relationship in a different situation (1/5).

630) Task performance of groups as related to general structural properties of the group

631. Group task performance in experimental settings. Moderately related (25/62)

Members working alone performed better on a maze task than did those working in groups (3/3). Similar results held for "extreme errors" in another situation (2/2), although there were generally no differences between individual and group performance (1/3). On symbolic tasks, members in groups performed better than did members working alone, although less so on arithmetic and verbal problems (8/14).

In another setting, differences in performance were slightly related to differences in types of communication nets (9/35), with circle nets better than wheel nets on complex symbolic problems (5/5) but not on simple problems (0/5).

633. Group task performance in operational settings: specific measures. Highly related (25/39)

Small groups were more efficient than were larger groups when groups ranged in size from 10 to 50 members (5/5).

Unspecified differences among groups such as individual differences among air crews and training classes, as well as mission differences, were moderately related to differences in group performance (20/34).

311. INFLUENCE AND CONFORMITY PRESSURES

Definition

"Influence and conformity pressures" includes induced conditions having to do with pressures toward uniformity of opinion or response. Examples are use of confederates giving wrong answers and falsification of feedback about group opinion.

References

Variables of this class were used in a total of 11 studies in the sample and were tested for relationships to six other variable classes, in a total of 60 associations, of which 21 (35%) were significant. Reference numbers of studies are 53, 693, 1085, 1236, 1244, 1356, 1390, 1641, 1793, 1930, 2029.

Summary of Major Relationships

This variable was highly or moderately related to two of six other variable classes. High associations occurred with attitudes toward issues, concepts, ideologies (144) and member task performance in experimental settings (621).

There were only slight relationships with perceptions of social behavior of self and others (520) and group task performance in experimental settings (631).

No tests for relationship occurred in the review sample between influence and conformity pressures and a host of member properties such as personality characteristics (120), biographical characteristics (110), abilities (131) (132), several attitudes (141) (142) (143), and positions in the group (151) (152). In addition, there were no tested relationships with group structural properties (240), group capabilities (221) (222), and interpersonal relations in the group (230). Also, there were no tested relationships with two of the interaction process measures (410) (430) or with perceptions of task performance of self and others (510). Finally, there were no cases of tested relationships between influence and conformity pressures and leadership (610), certain measures of member task performance (622) (623), and certain measures of group task performance (632) (633).

Index of Relationships

140) Attitudes of members as related to influence and conformity pressures

    144. Attitudes toward issues, concepts, ideologies. Highly related (1/1).

       Members under high pressure toward opinion uniformity changed personal opinions more than did those under low pressure (1/1).

310) Social conditions as related to influence and conformity pressures

312. Induced social conditions. Somewhat related (4/11)

> Members who saw themselves as not personally accepted by others conformed more to group perceptual judgments (2/2). However, in a different setting, members differing in both perceived acceptance and attraction were only slightly different in conformity behavior (2/9).

420) Patterns of interaction as related to influence and conformity pressures. Somewhat related (9/25)

> In general, there was no relationship between level of participation and judgment change in an advocated direction (2/15); but those persons exposed to pressures changed more than did those not exposed to pressures (6/6).

520) Perceptions of social behavior of self and others as related to influence and conformity pressures. Slightly related (1/6)

> Perceptions of own social behavior, such as attempted influence, were only slightly related to group pressure (1/4).

620) Task performance of members as related to influence and conformity pressures

621. Member task performance in experimental settings. Highly related (2/2)

> Members working under continuous influence pressures showed more conformity than did members working under no such pressures.

630) Task performance of groups as related to influence and conformity pressures

631. Group task performance in experimental settings. Slightly related (4/15)

> Groups exposed to a unanimous, incorrect majority more often erred in their performance in the direction of the majority than did groups not exposed to such pressures (3/3); the generality of this finding was shown by the fact that it was not related to differences between several types of groups (0/9).

312. INDUCED SOCIAL CONDITIONS

Definition

"Induced social conditions" primarily includes social perceptions and conditions induced by experimenter instructions, falsification of feedback, and behavior of an experimenter-confederate, together with perceptions of congeniality, compatibility with other members, own and others' relative status, threat from various sources and of various degrees, and teammate indifference. This class also contains experimental manipulations of leadership style (by a leader who is an experimenter-confederate) such as authoritarian vs. democratic leadership and instructions to cooperate or to compete.

References

Variables of this class were used in a total of 30 studies in the sample and were tested for relationships to 13 other variable classes, in a total of 384 associations, of which 128 (33%) were significant. Reference numbers of studies are 144, 189, 526, 542, 566, 593, 695, 756, 757, 904, 968, 984, 1075, 1077, 1128, 1129, 1227, 1315, 1390, 1467, 1471, 1472, 1528, 1586, 1641, 1761, 1764, 2008, 2101, 2108.

Summary of Major Relationships

This variable class was highly or moderately related to 2 of 13 other variable classes—namely, interpersonal relations in the group (230) and group task performance in experimental settings (631).

There was no relationship or only a slight one with personality characteristics (120), content of interaction (410), and member perceptions of task and social performance of self and others (510) (520). In addition, there were no relationships with member task performance in experimental settings (621) and group task performance in operational settings: specific measures (633). It is interesting that there was a series of equivocal relationships between induced social conditions and several measures of member attitudes (142) (144) and certain interaction process measures (420) (430).

In the review sample there was no occurrence of tested relationships between induced social conditions and biographical characteristics (110), various member abilities (131) (132), and member positions in the group (151) (152). It is likely that this is the case because induced social conditions and the cited other variable classes are usually independent, often-manipulated variables. This likelihood also accounts for the absence of tested relationships between induced social conditions and various group properties (221) (222) (240) and certain conditions imposed upon the group (321) (322) (323). There was also an absence of tests for relationship with various measures of performance such as leadership (610), two classes of member performance (622) (623), and one class of group performance measures (632).

Index of Relationships

120) Personality characteristics of members as related to induced social conditions. Not related (0/5)

> For example, anxiety and relaxation were not related to degree of perceived threat.

140) Attitudes of members as related to induced social conditions

142. Attitudes toward the situation. Somewhat related (8/23)

> Cooperative groups had less desire to personally excel and felt more influenced by others than did competitive groups. Cooperative groups also felt more motivation to achieve, to please the experimenter, and to excel other groups, but, as these results held only for some tasks, the over-all relationship was moderate. Members of cooperative

groups also felt more obligated to their groups and more desire for respect from others, but these results held only for some tasks, so that over-all the variables were only somewhat related (8/15).

144. Attitudes toward issues, concepts, ideologies. Somewhat related (4/12)

There was no clear-cut pattern of results.

230) Interpersonal relations in the group as related to induced social conditions. Highly related (24/30)

Attitudes toward other members: Members who felt themselves to be personally compatible, congenial, or accepted by others consistently rated others as being personally attractive to them (7/7).

Attitudes toward the group: In a moderate relationship, members of groups working under cooperative instructions were more attracted to their groups than were those under competitive instructions (1/2). A high relationship between cooperative instructions and group attraction prevailed for members who felt compatible with one another (via experimental instructions) (16/21).

310) Social conditions as related to induced social conditions

311. Influence and conformity pressures. Somewhat related (4/11)

Members who saw themselves as not personally accepted by others conformed more to group perceptual judgments (2/2). However, in a different setting, members differing in both perceived acceptance and attraction were only slightly different in conformity behavior (2/9).

410) Content of interaction as related to induced social conditions. Slightly related (17/84)

Inductions such as threat conditions were not related to discussion behavior measures such as agreement, tension, and opinion giving (5/61). Members of groups in cooperative conditions showed less criticism, aggression, defensiveness, and blocking behavior on human relations tasks than did members of competitive groups (6/6), but there were no differences on puzzle tasks (0/6). Competitive groups had more members working simultaneously than did cooperative groups (5/5).

420) Patterns of interaction as related to induced social conditions. Somewhat related (15/47)

Social support received from confederates was positively and highly related to length of speeches (for stable personalities only) and to low response latency (6/8). Such support was also positively related to increased group activity and negatively related to time needed to complete the task for stable personalities (3/3); but, there was no relationship for unstable personalities (0/2). In another setting, perceived member compatibility was only slightly related to amount of communication (1/5).

430) Outcomes of interaction as related to induced social conditions. Somewhat related (18/59)

> Cooperative groups were rated as more coordinated, orderly, and effective in communication than were competitive groups (8/8); members of cooperative groups also worked together more and were more attentive (5/8).
>
> Groups working under no-threat conditions were rated higher on efficiency and adaptability than were threatened groups (2/2), although such differences only occur for certain sources and targets of threat (0/4). In other settings, perceived threat was not related to such measures as group goal orientation, conflict, and cohesiveness (0/21). Other results did not show a clear-cut pattern.

510) Perceptions of task performance of self and others as related to induced social conditions. Slightly related (12/45)

> Groups anticipating membership changes and working under cooperative sets rated other members' performance high (4/4), whereas perception of own task behavior was not related to knowledge of membership changes, etc. (0/4).
>
> Those working under cooperative rather than competitive sets saw more group cooperation, assistance from others, and so on (4/6). Those perceiving congeniality with co-workers estimated co-workers' performance to be good (3/4). In other settings, however, source, amount, and target of threat were not related to member judgments of such measures as group goal orientation, conflict, and cohesiveness (1/27).

520) Perceptions of social behavior of self and others as related to induced social conditions. Not related (1/7)

> For example, perceptions of own aggressive behavior tended not to be related to conditions such as induced threat.

620) Task performance of members as related to induced social conditions

> 621. Member task performance in experimental settings. Not related (3/31)
>
> > Members of democratically led groups made more correct responses and fewer errors early in performance on a maze task than did members of authoritarian-led groups, but did not differ in performance later in the task series (3/7). In other settings, conditions such as cooperation–competition did not relate to differences in performance, knowledge of audience did not relate to recall, and so on (0/24).

630) Task performance of groups as related to induced social conditions

> 631. Group task performance in experimental settings. Highly related (23/31)
>
> > Leaders instructed to behave in an authoritarian fashion had groups who performed better than did nonauthoritarian-led groups (9/9). However, in another setting, variations by a confederate in social reinforcement of others or in authoritarian–democratic behavior

were only somewhat related to group performance effectiveness (4/11). Cooperative groups performed more adequately than did competitive groups (7/8).

633. Group task performance in operational settings: specific measures. Not related (1/14)

Authoritarian vs. democratic leadership was not related to performance on a simulated military task.

321. STIMULUS PROPERTIES OF THE TASK

Definition

"Stimulus properties of the task" includes experimental variations in nature and difficulty of task or stimulus materials. These variations include differences of subject matter, familiarity of objects, clarity of stimulus, nature of stimulus, and relevancy of task information.

References

Variables of this class were used in a total of 41 studies in the sample and were tested for relationships to seven other variable classes, in a total of 153 associations, of which 64 (42%) were significant. Reference numbers of studies are 53, 144, 254, 351, 428, 856, 909, 1005, 1046, 1098, 1210, 1244, 1249a, 1252, 1345, 1354, 1390, 1401, 1456, 1572, 1574, 1575, 1603, 1701, 1705, 1707, 1751, 1755, 1756, 1764, 1782, 1785, 1832, 1884, 1920, 1930, 1933, 1940, 1996, 2008, 2029.

Summary of Major Relationships

"Stimulus properties of the task" was highly or moderately related to five of seven other variable classes. These high or moderate relationships occurred with a variety of classes—attitudes toward nongroup persons and other groups (143), outcomes of interaction (430), perceptions of social behavior of self and others (520), member task performance in experimental settings (621), and group task performance in experimental settings (631).

The variable was only slightly related to attitudes toward issues, concepts, ideologies (144).

There were no instances of tests for relationship in the review sample between stimulus properties of the task and various member properties such as personality characteristics (120), biographical characteristics (110), abilities (131) (132), certain member attitudes (141) (142), and positions in the group (151) (152). In addition, there were no cases of tested relationships with group level variables such as general structural properties (240) and group capabilities (221) (222). Moreover, there were no tested relationships with other operating conditions imposed upon the group (311) (312) (322) (323). Because this variable is usually independent and often manipulated, one would not expect occurrences of tests for relationships with many other ordinarily independent variables, such as operating conditions. Finally, there were no cases of tested relationships with certain interaction process measures (410) (420) and with several objective measures of member and group performance (610) (622) (623) (632) (633).

Index of Relationships

140) Attitudes of members as related to stimulus properties of the task

143. Attitudes toward nongroup persons and other groups. Moderately related (7/16)

In a moderate relationship, change in attitudes toward minority groups was an interactive function of exposure to films and discussions, initial attitudes, and short- and long-range testing times (6/11). In another study, exposure to discussion was only slightly related to change in attitudes toward minority groups (1/5).

144. Attitudes toward issues, concepts, ideologies. Slightly related (8/34)

There was slight relation between change in nationalistic and internationalistic attitudes as a function of discussion–no discussion conditions (5/20). But in another setting, although there was no prior difference in opinion or opinion heterogeneity about mental health concepts (0/6), those exposed to films or films and discussion showed more positive change than did those not exposed (3/4).

230) Interpersonal relations in the group as related to stimulus properties of the task. Somewhat related (4/13)

There was no clear-cut pattern of results.

430) Outcomes of interaction as related to stimulus properties of the task. Moderately related (19/45)

Those exposed to a frustrating situation showed more cooperation and less conflict if they were strong friends (6/6), but both weak and strong friends showed negative and destructive behavior under frustration (10/10). There was no relationship between different types of play situations and various types of play behavior (social, social parallel, emotionality) (0/15). Degree of voluntariness of participation in a discussion was not related to subsequent volunteering behavior (0/4).

520) Perceptions of social behavior of self and others as related to stimulus properties of the task. Highly related (4/4)

There were more reported transmissions of rumors in an ambiguous situation than there were in a clearly defined situation.

620) Task performance of members as related to stimulus properties of the task

621. Member task performance in experimental settings. Moderately related (15/28)

In a moderate relationship, group problem solving was more effective if preceded by a discussion (2/4). In another setting, the greater the clarity of the stimulus, the more accurate and less variable were member judgments (6/6). In another setting, however, there was only a moderate relationship between accuracy and differences in materials (e.g., familiar vs. unfamiliar, social science vs. natural science, and so on) (7/17).

630) Task performance of groups as related to stimulus properties of the task

631. Group task performance in experimental settings. Moderately related (7/13)

The greater the discrepancy between the standard stimulus and the stimulus being judged, the greater was the performance error (7/9). However, time and phase aspects of the task were not related to group performance (0/4).

322. FEEDBACK AND REINFORCEMENT CONDITIONS

Definition

"Feedback and reinforcement conditions" includes experimental manipulations of reinforcement (such as continuous negative or positive reinforcement) and of knowledge of results (such as variations in methods of critique and feedback of own or of partner's performance error data).

References

Variables of this class were used in a total of 18 studies in the sample and were tested for relationships to six other variable classes, in a total of 69 associations, of which 20 (29%) were significant. Reference numbers of studies are 807, 972, 1033, 1059, 1086, 1236, 1451, 1472, 1528, 1557, 1585, 1602, 1705, 1716, 1716a, 1780, 1919, 1940.

Summary of Major Relationships

Of the six other variable classes with which "feedback and reinforcement conditions" was tested for relationship, only two yielded high or moderate associations. These were member task performance in experimental settings (621) and group task performance in operational settings: specific measures (633).

The variable showed no relationships with all measures of interaction process (410) (420) (430).

There were no tests for relationships with group member properties—personality characteristics (120), biographical characteristics (110), member abilities (131) (132), member attitudes (141) (142) (143) (144), and member positions in the group (151) (152). In addition, no instances of tested relationships occurred with the various properties of the group—structure (240), capabilities (221) (222), and interpersonal relations (230). Moreover, there were no tested relationships, as would be expected, with other conditions imposed upon the group (311) (312) (321) (323). Interestingly, there were no tests of relationships with various subjective measures of member and group performance (510) (520), with leadership performance (610), or with three measures of member and group task performance (622) (623) (631).

Index of Relationships

410) Content of interaction as related to feedback and reinforcement conditions. Not related (0/4)

> For example, the nature of intragroup communication was not affected by feedback about performance success.

420) Patterns of interaction as related to feedback and reinforcement conditions. Not related (1/11)

> For example, amount of praise or criticism by Air Force instructors was not related to measures of group discussion behavior.

430) Outcomes of interaction as related to feedback and reinforcement conditions. Not related (2/19)

> For example, praise or criticism by an Air Force instructor was not related to crew orderliness or similar group characteristics.

620) Task performance of members as related to feedback and reinforcement conditions

621. Member task performance in experimental settings. Moderately related (5/12)

> Members working under positive reinforcement made fewer yielding (conforming) errors than did members working under negative reinforcement (2/2). In another setting, members performed better when feedback was their own error data (3/4), but in another study there was no relationship between difference in performance as a function of whether feedback was own or a combination of own and partner data (0/6).

630) Task performance of groups as related to feedback and reinforcement conditions

632. Group task performance in operational settings: global measures. Somewhat related (2/6)

> The more personal criticism instructors gave crews about performance and the more they praised their crews, the better was the group performance (2/2), although frequency of explanations, illustrations, and so on did not relate to crew performance (0/4).

633. Group task performance in operational settings: specific measures. Moderately related (10/17)

> Different critique methods produced some differences in performance of groups on later tasks. For example, expert critiques were better than unstructured crew-centered critiques and self-critiques, but were not better than structured methods (3/4). Self-critique procedures were less effective than were expert critiques but were not different from any of the other methods (1/3). An unstructured technique was poorer than an expert or structured procedure but was not different from self- and noncritique methods (2/4). Structured methods were better than unstructured ones, but no different from other procedures (1/4).

323. INDUCED TASK CONDITIONS

Definition

"Induced task conditions" primarily includes task perceptions and conditions induced by experimental instructions. For example, the class includes variations in perceived success or probability of success, perceived distribution of rewards, task vs. ego-oriented sets, motivation and task desirability, requirement to reach a decision, and opportunity for mobility.

References

Variables of this class were used in a total of 41 studies in the sample and were tested for relationships to 15 other variable classes, in a total of 250 associations, of which 117 (47%) were significant. Reference numbers of studies are 171, 384, 418, 512, 695, 927, 979, 984, 1005, 1033a, 1074, 1085, 1139, 1242, 1249, 1316, 1382, 1450, 1456, 1572, 1574, 1575, 1607, 1639, 1684, 1701, 1704, 1705, 1780, 1781, 1782, 1832, 1914, 1919, 1920, 1926, 1968, 1998, 2008, 2076.

Summary of Major Relationships

Of the 15 other variable classes with which "induced task conditions" was tested for relationship, 14 showed high or moderate associations. These included general and task abilities of members (131) (132) and the series of member attitudes (141) (142) (143) (144). In addition, the variable was highly or moderately related to all interaction process measures (410) (420) (430) and to interpersonal relationships in the group (230). Finally, this variable class was highly or moderately related to several measures of member and group task performance effectiveness (621) (623) (631) (633).

The only variable class with which induced task conditions showed a slight relationship was perceptions of task performance of self and others (510).

The relationship between induced task conditions and several member level variables such as personality characteristics (120), biographical characteristics (110), and member position in the group (151) (152) was not examined in the review sample. This omission is to be expected because such variables are ordinarily independent and manipulated variables. As would also be expected, there were no tests for relationship with various other operating conditions imposed upon the group (311) (312) (321) (322). Interestingly, there were no cases of tested relationship with measures of leadership performance (610) or certain member and group performance effectiveness measures (622) (632).

Index of Relationships

130) Abilities of members as related to induced task conditions

    131. General abilities of members. Moderately related (19/45)

        Confederates who deliberately performed poorly on the task were rated lower on general motivation and dependability after their role playing than before (15/17). However, there was no relationship between the type of judgment set (an "administrative" as opposed to a "research" set) and obtained ratings of member general abilities (3/25).

132. Task abilities of members. Highly related (14/19)

Confederates who deliberately performed poorly on the task were rated low on task competence by others in the group (8/8). Members of industrial work groups who were allowed some degree of autonomy in their jobs were more satisfied with their supervisors and more strongly changed attitudes in the positive direction (2/4) than did members of less-autonomous groups (0/3). In another setting, members rewarded for group performance changed more strongly in ratings of a poorly performing confederate's task competence than did members who were rewarded on an individual basis (3/3).

140) Attitudes of members as related to induced task conditions

141. Attitudes toward the task. Moderately related (12/24)

Members who were given some degree of job autonomy and members whose task status was improved (by the experimenter) were more satisfied with their jobs than were members not so manipulated (7/10). However, instructions regarding task desirability were only slightly related to perceptions of task desirability (1/6). Groups under perceived success conditions saw their tasks as more difficult and had more consensus on that judgment than did groups under failure conditions (3/4). However, perceived probability of goal achievement was not related to task satisfaction (0/2).

142. Attitudes toward the situation. Highly related (2/2)

Members of groups operating under success conditions saw less discrepancy between their own and other members' opinions (2/2).

143. Attitudes toward nongroup persons and other groups. Highly related (5/6)

Groups were more satisfied with their companies after introduction of experimental conditions than before, regardless of type of manipulation.

144. Attitudes toward issues, concepts, ideologies. Highly related (2/3)

Among members believing that all in the group had equal skills, the majorities changed opinions less but varied more in judgments of topic importance than did the minorities (2/3).

230) Interpersonal relations in the group as related to induced task conditions. Moderately related (6/15)

Attitudes toward other members: Confederates who performed poorly were not personally liked less after their poor performance than before it (1/11).

Attitudes toward the group: Members of groups who perceived themselves to be successful were more attracted to their groups than to failure groups (2/2). Members of groups instructed about the high probability of goal achievement were less attracted to their groups than were less likely goal achievers, but actual goal attainment did not affect feelings for the group (1/2).

410) Content of interaction as related to induced task conditions. Highly related (8/11)

> Members in disadvantageous but potentially upward-mobile positions within the over-all group sent fewer irrelevant communications to others, conjectured more about the desired job, were less critical of higher-status members, and exhibited less-cohesive communications about their own group.

420. Patterns of interaction as related to induced task conditions. Moderately related (8/18)

> Members in disadvantageous but potentially upward-mobile positions within the over-all group communicated more with those in high-status positions than with other low-status members (3/4). In another setting, members operating under ego-oriented instructions showed no different decision times than did those operating under task-oriented instructions (2/9). Conditions of induced motivation were moderately related to amount of communication, but without a clear-cut pattern (2/5).

430) Outcomes of interaction as related to induced task conditions. Moderately related (5/10)

> Members operating under high-motivation conditions exhibited higher motivation (3/3). In another setting, requirements to reach a decision about volunteering, or the publicness of that decision, were only slightly related to volunteering or other positive responses (1/5).

510) Perceptions of task performance of self and others as related to induced task conditions. Slightly related (12/65)

> *Other-member performance:* Members operating under success conditions did not rate other members' performances higher, as compared to groups in failure conditions (0/4). In another study, members allowed some autonomy of decision were more satisfied with their superior's job performance (3/4) than were members in a hierarchal decision-making situation (1/3).

> *Group task performance:* Members of groups operating under perceived success saw their groups more as a vehicle to goal attainment than did members of failure groups (3/3). Results also suggested that perceived success was associated with higher ratings of group performance effectiveness than was a failure condition (15/51).

620) Task performance of members as related to induced task conditions

620. Member task performance in experimental settings. Moderately related (3/5)

> In a moderate relationship, problem-solving performance was more effective if groups were required to reach a decision than if they were not (1/2).

623. Member task performance in operational settings: specific measures. Highly related (7/7)

Employees operating under general conditions of decision autonomy had better job performance than did those working under a more hierarchal arrangement.

630) Task performance of groups as related to induced task conditions

631. Group task performance in experimental settings. Highly related (9/13)

Groups receiving confirmation of expected actions by the experimenter were better performers than were those whose expectations about procedures were contradicted (5/6).

A systematic distribution of information in communication nets, rather than a random distribution among members, aided effectiveness especially for the comcon (each communicating to each) net (3/4). There was no such difference for degree of knowledge about the information distribution (0/2).

633. Group task performance in operational settings: specific measures. Highly related (5/7)

Groups with immediate access to relevant information performed better than did those with difficult access to task-related information (2/2). In another study, however, dispersion and directness of information availability was only moderately related to group performance (2/4).

410. CONTENT OF INTERACTION

Definition

"Content of interaction" covers indexes of the substantive nature of group interaction, including such aspects as goal setting, information giving, agreeing, opinion giving, and asking for suggestions.

References

Variables of this class were used in a total of 27 studies in the sample and were tested for relationships to 15 variable classes, in a total of 584 associations, of which 171 (29%) were significant. Reference numbers of studies are 182, 212, 252, 272, 362, 418, 424, 462, 512, 526, 693, 949, 1005, 1122, 1128, 1145, 1195, 1195a, 1244, 1345, 1558, 1639, 1755, 1841, 1914, 1939, 1945.

Summary of Major Relationships

"Content of interaction" was highly or moderately related to 6 of 15 variable classes, including certain measures of interaction process (410) (420). In addition, content of interaction was highly or moderately related to leadership performance (610), member task performance in experimental settings,

(621), member attitudes toward the situation (142), and induced task conditions (323).

There were only slight or no relationships with member properties such as personality characteristics (120), task abilities (132), and attitudes toward issues, concepts, ideologies (144). There was only slight relationship with induced social conditions (312) and no relationship with feedback and reinforcement conditions (322). Equivocal relationships occurred between this variable and several group level variables—e.g., group structural properties (240) and two measures of group task performance (631) (632).

Although occasional examples occurred, there were very few instances of tested relationships with a number of member properties such as biographical characteristics (110), general abilities (131), certain attitudes (141) (143), and task or physical position in the group (152). In addition, there were few cases of tested relationships with various group properties such as group capabilities (221) (222) and interpersonal relations in the group (230). Finally, there were no investigated relationships between interaction content and subjective measures of member and group performance (510) (520) or with certain measures of member task performance (622) (623).

Index of Relationships

120) Personality characteristics of members as related to content of interaction. Slightly related (2/10)

> Personality adjustment measures tended not to be consistently related to irrelevant communications, job questions, and so on.

130) Abilities of members as related to content of interaction

132. Task abilities of members. Slightly related (1/6)
> For example, perceptions of other member's task abilities were not consistently related to such discussion behavior measures as giving suggestions and asking opinions.

140) Attitudes of members as related to content of interaction

142. Attitudes toward the situation. Moderately related (5/9)
> Members who saw themselves as having more power were observed as attempting to influence others more; however, between-group variations tended to make results less than clear-cut.

144. Attitudes toward issues, concepts, ideologies. Slightly related (22/131)
> Leaders with high authoritarian attitudes were less secure, submissive, sensitive, and equalitarian in their discussion behavior. They made fewer sanction-seeking proposals, initial acts, positive acts, and diagnoses, and led less than did those with lower authoritarian scores. They also were less agreeable, diagnosed and clarified less, asked less often for expressions of opinion, were more withdrawn and inattentive than were equalitarian leaders.

150) Positions of members in the group as related to content of interaction

151. Social position in the group. Somewhat related (26/82)

Appointed leaders of discussion groups more often diagnosed situations, initiated action, gave information, and desired action than did other members (12/13). Remaining results showed slight relationship (14/69).

240) General structural properties of the group as related to content of interaction. Somewhat related (15/48)

Group size: Two- and three-man groups expressed more ideas and showed more change in responses than did individuals, although two- and three-man groups did not differ from one another in those respects (4/5).

Other structural properties: Groups with an emergent leader had members with higher leadership behavior in discussions than did groups without an emergent leader (5/7), but the leadership behavior of designated leaders was not different from that of others in the group (0/4). In another setting, differences in group permanency were only slightly related to differences in discussion behavior of members or group (6/32).

310) Social conditions as related to content of interaction

312. Induced social conditions. Slightly related (17/84)

Group members operating under cooperative conditions exhibited less criticism, aggression, defensiveness, and blocking behavior than did group members working under competitive conditions for a human relations task (6/6) but not for a puzzle task (0/6). On the other hand, more members worked simultaneously in competitive groups than in cooperative groups (5/5). Various threat conditions were not related to discussion behavior measures such as agreement, tension, and opinion giving (5/61).

320) Task and operating conditions as related to content of interaction

322. Feedback and reinforcement conditions. Not related (0/4)

For example, the nature of intragroup communication was not affected by feedback about performance success.

323. Induced task conditions. Highly related (8/11)

Members in disadvantageous but potentially upward-mobile positions within the over-all group sent fewer irrelevant communications to others, conjectured more about the desired job, were less critical of higher-status members, and exhibited less-cohesive communications about their own group.

410) Content of interaction as related to content of interaction. Moderately related within variable class (15/32)

420) Patterns of interaction as related to content of interaction. Moderately related (5/9)

Active discussion participants elicited more orientation comments, questions, and negative comments than did more-passive members (3/3) but did not differ in positiveness of responses, suggestions, and opinions (0/3).

610) Leadership performance as related to content of interaction. Moderately related (8/15)

> Emergent leaders were higher on problem proposing, information seeking, and ego involvement and lower on development giving than were other members (4/4). Leaders did not differ from members on goal setting, information giving, opposing, supporting, and other categories (0/7).

620) Task performance of members as related to content of interaction

> 621. Member task performance in experimental settings. Moderately related (4/8)
>
> There was no clear-cut pattern of results.

630) Task performance of groups as related to content of interaction

> 631. Group task performance in experimental settings. Somewhat related (11/29)
>
> There was no clear-cut pattern of results. Successfully performing groups seemed to exhibit fewer disagreements, less hostility, and more support among members than did less-successful groups. Also, when more-successful groups produced stories about hypothetical groups, the stories contained more satisfactory outcomes, orderliness, harmony, and so on.

> 632. Group task performance in operational settings: global measures. Somewhat related (32/106)
>
> When crews rated as more effective in combat produced stories about hypothetical groups, the stories contained more perceptions of satisfactory outcomes, orderly functioning, friendship, productivity, agreement, and so on.

420. PATTERNS OF INTERACTION

Definition

"Patterns of interaction" includes indexes of the formal properties of the interaction process. Such indexes include number of communications (over-all, by a particular member, or between a particular pair of members), length of time spent talking, time for making a decision, number of simultaneous conversations, and number of participating members.

References

Variables of this class were used in a total of 32 studies in the sample and were tested for relationships to 16 variable classes, in a total of 275 associations, of which 157 (57%) were significant. Reference numbers of studies are 40, 81, 122, 144, 171, 418, 484, 526, 593, 693, 715, 740, 777, 869, 904, 919, 972, 984, 1139, 1195, 1354, 1471, 1701, 1707, 1755, 1761, 1796, 1841, 1914, 1945, 2101, 2108.

Summary of Major Relationships

"Patterns of interaction in the group" was highly or moderately related to 8 of 16 variable classes. The high and moderate relationships included a series of member level variable classes such as task abilities (132), attitudes toward issues, concepts, ideologies (144), and task or physical position in the group (152). At the group level, there were high relationships with group training and experience (222). In addition, moderate relationships occurred with one operating condition imposed upon the group, induced task conditions (323). As would be expected, there were moderate or high relationships or interrelationships with certain measures of interaction process (410) (420) and with interpersonal relations within the group (230).

Only slight relationships occurred with certain member properties such as general abilities (131) and social position in the group (151), and with general structural properties of the group (240). There were no strong relationships with a series of operating conditions imposed upon the group such as induced social conditions (312), influence and conformity pressures (311), and feedback and reinforcement conditions (322). Finally, there was no relationship with some measures of member and group task performance (621) (633).

There were no cases of tested relationships between interaction patterns and member properties such as personality characteristics (120), biographical characteristics (110), several attitudes (141) (142) (143), and subjective measures of member and group behavior (510) (520). In addition, there were no tested relationships in the review sample between patterns of interaction and leadership performance (610) and most task performance measures of members and groups (622) (623) (631) (632).

Index of Relationships

130) Abilities of members as related to patterns of interaction

 131. General abilities of members. Slightly related (1/4)

  There was no clear-cut pattern of results.

 132. Task abilities of members. Highly related (4/6)

  Members who were more active in discussions learned and retained more knowledge of the topic than did less-active members.

140) Attitudes of members as related to patterns of interaction

 144. Attitudes toward issues, concepts, ideologies. Moderately related (3/5)

  There was no clear-cut pattern of results.

150) Positions of members in the group as related to patterns of interaction

 151. Social position in the group. Slightly related (2/10)

  There was no clear-cut pattern of results.

 152. Task or physical position in the group. Highly related (15/19)

  The more-centrally located were members in a group's communication net, the more heavily they became involved in the transmission of messages (11/15)

220) Group capabilities as related to patterns of interaction

    222. Group training and experience. Highly related (4/4)

230) Interpersonal relations in the group as related to patterns of interaction. Highly related (23/34)

> Members communicated more with those whom they liked or disliked than with those toward whom they were personally indifferent (8/8). In another setting, personal attraction measures were highly and positively related to such various indexes of discussion participation as amount of participation and amount of member interaction (11/15). Sociometric choices and measures such as Rorschach reaction time and number of responses were somewhat related (4/11).

240) General structural properties of the group as related to patterns of interaction. Slightly related (5/22)

> For example, size and type of communication net tended not to be consistently related to amount of communication, degree of aggressiveness in interaction, friendliness, and so on.

310) Social conditions as related to patterns of interaction

    311. Influence and conformity pressures. Somewhat related (9/25)

> In general, there was no relationship between level of participation and judgment change in an advocated direction (2/15); but those exposed to pressures changed more than did those not exposed to pressures (6/6).

    312. Induced social conditions. Somewhat related (15/47)

> Social support received from confederates was positively and highly related to length of speeches (for stable personalities only) and to low response latency (6/8). Such support was also positively related to group activity and negatively related to time needed to complete the task for stable personalities (3/3); but there was no relationship for unstable personalities (0/2). In another setting, perceived member compatibility was only slightly related to amount of communication (1/5).

320) Task and operating conditions as related to patterns of interaction

    322. Feedback and reinforcement conditions. Not related (1/11)

> For example, amount of praise or criticism by Air Force instructors was not related to measures of group discussion behavior.

    323. Induced task conditions. Moderately related (8/18)

> Members in disadvantageous but potentially upward-mobile positions within the over-all group communicated more with those in high-status positions than with other low-status members (3/4). In another setting, members under ego-oriented instructions did not differ in decision times from members under task-oriented instructions (2/9). Conditions of induced motivation were moderately related to amount of communication, but without a clear-cut pattern (2/5).

410) Content of interaction as related to patterns of interaction. Moderately related (5/9)

>Active discussion participants elicited more orientation comments, questions, and negative comments than did more-passive members (3/3) but did not differ in positiveness of responses, suggestions, and opinions (0/3).

420) Patterns of interaction as related to patterns of interaction. Highly related within variable class (64/67)

>For example, members ranking high as initiators of discussion ranked high as recipients of communications from others.

620) Task performance of members as related to patterns of interaction

621. Member task performance in experimental settings. Not related (0/5)

>For example, various measures of speech quality, articulation, and so on were not related to rate of verbal participation.

630) Task performance of groups as related to patterns of interaction

633. Group task performance in operational settings: specific measures. Not related (0/4)

430. OUTCOMES OF INTERACTION

Definition

"Outcomes of interaction" contains the member and group behaviors that are not direct indexes of task performance effectiveness, as observed by the experimenter or others outside the group. This variable class includes measures of task vs. interpersonal focus of activity, employee turnover, copying of other members' behavior, adaptability or flexibility of group, formation of cliques or coalitions, exhibition of we-feeling, coordination, care of aircraft, cleanliness, and communication effectiveness. The foregoing are essentially global indexes of interaction and/or of its results.

References

Variables of this class were used in a total of 69 studies in the sample and were tested for relationships to 18 variable classes, in a total of 561 associations, of which 193 (34%) were significant. Reference numbers of studies are 40, 53, 111, 122, 132, 189, 285, 298, 315, 428, 438, 462, 512, 542, 606a, 621, 663, 693, 715, 790, 806, 849, 862, 867, 868, 949, 972, 984, 1005, 1054, 1074, 1075, 1077, 1085, 1086, 1122, 1128, 1134, 1151, 1195, 1195a, 1236, 1244, 1249, 1249a, 1266, 1316, 1356, 1382, 1390, 1401, 1456, 1528, 1564, 1607, 1751, 1756, 1760, 1785, 1793, 1919, 1930, 1976, 1996, 1998, 2029, 2076, 2101, 2108.

Summary of Major Relationships

Of the 18 variable classes to which "outcomes of interaction" was tested for relationships, 9 showed high or moderate associations. These included member characteristics such as attitudes toward the situation (142) and social position in the group (151). At the group level, general structural properties of the group (240) and group abilities (221) were strongly related to outcomes of interaction. Two conditions imposed upon the group also showed high or moderate relationships with this variable class—stimulus properties of the task (321) and induced task conditions (323). Finally, leadership performance (610), one measure of group task performance (633), and measures of outcomes of interaction (430) showed high to moderate associations with outcomes of interaction.

No, slight, or equivocal relationships occurred with member level variables such as personality characteristics (120), task abilities of members (132), and attitudes toward issues, concepts, ideologies (144). In addition, there were no strong relationships with two measures of member task performance (621) (623), interpersonal relationships in the group (230), group training and experience (222), and feedback and reinforcement conditions (322).

There were no instances of tested relationships between outcomes of interaction and several member characteristics—biography (110), certain attitudes (141) (143), and general abilities (131). There were also no cases of tested relationships with influence and conformity pressures (311), two measures of interaction process (410) (420), and subjective measures of member and group performance (510) (520). Finally, certain objective measures of member and group performance (622) (631) (632) were not studied with respect to their association with outcomes of interaction.

Index of Relationships

120) Personality characteristics of members as related to outcomes of interaction. Slightly related (6/36)

> For example, personal characteristics such as maturity and emotional stability tended not to be related to group competitiveness, adaptability, and so on.

130) Abilities of members as related to outcomes of interaction

132. Task abilities of members. Slightly related (32/108)

> The more highly members were rated by others on power, the more they were observed as influencing others directly and indirectly, as receiving deferent behavior from others, and so on (27/44). However, confidence in own abilities was not related to active vs. passive discussion role, nor were objective measures of supervisory ability related to observed carefulness (1/8). Perceptions of other members' task skills were only slightly related to group discussion morale, cooperativeness, cohesiveness (2/11). Perceived crew member proficiency was not related to air crew coordination (0/30).

140) Attitudes of members as related to outcomes of interaction

142. Attitudes toward the situation. Moderately related (7/12)

> Groups whose members perceived consensus of group opinion were judged to be more orderly (3/4); no other systematic pattern of results was identified.

144. Attitudes toward issues, concepts, ideologies. Slightly related (15/66)

Authoritarians seemed to exhibit less-intelligent discussion behavior (5/8), although such attitudes were not related to adaptability, sensitivity, and social abilities shown during discussions (2/14). Authoritarian attitudes were only slightly related to observed discussion behavior measures such as equal participation, friendliness, clique formation, group motivation, competence, and communication effectiveness (6/34).

150) Positions of members in the group as related to outcomes of interaction

151. Social position in the group. Moderately related (2/4)

Those with high assigned importance in the group attempted to lead others more often than did those with low assigned importance (2/2).

220) Group capabilities as related to outcomes of interaction

221. Group abilities. Highly related (11/11)

Air crews judged high on over-all value to their squadron were rated high on working with other crews, aircraft handling, military bearing, and so on (5/5). Air crews rated high on degree of consideration shown among members were also rated high on working with other crews, aircraft handling, military bearing, and so on (6/6).

222. Group training and experience. Not related (3/30)

230) Interpersonal relations in the group as related to outcomes of interaction. Not related (0/34)

Such measures as crew coordination and attrition from the group were not related to personal attraction among members.

240) General structural properties of the group as related to outcomes of interaction. Moderately related (21/41)

Homogeneity of member characteristics: Members with equal power were more likely to form coalitions, members with lower power were more likely to initiate coalitions, and members with high power relative to that of another member were more likely to be involved in coalitions with disproportionate distribution of rewards (10/18). Groups homogeneous in authoritarian attitudes were rated as more productive and more effective in communicating than were less-homogeneous groups after a period of experience (2/2). Relationships between ratings of competence and definiteness of leadership were only moderate (3/6), and there was slight relationship with member competency, sensitivity in discussion, and so on (2/8).

Other structural properties: In a frustrating situation, organized groups showed more we-feeling, frustration, and mutual encouragement than did unorganized groups (4/6).

310) Social conditions as related to outcomes of interaction

312. Induced social conditions. Somewhat related (18/59)

Cooperative groups were rated as more coordinated, orderly, and effective in communication than were competitive groups (8/8); members of cooperative groups also worked together more and were more attentive (5/8).

Groups working under no-threat conditions were rated higher on efficiency and adaptability than were threatened groups (2/2), although such differences only occur for certain sources and targets of threat (0/4). In other settings, perceived threat was not related to such measures as group goal orientation, conflict, and cohesiveness (0/21). Other results did not show a clear-cut pattern.

320) Task and operating conditions as related to outcomes of interaction

321. Stimulus properties of the task. Moderately related (19/45)

Those exposed to a frustrating situation showed more cooperation and less conflict if they were strong friends (6/6), but both weak and strong friends showed negative and destructive behavior under frustration (10/10). There was no relationship between different types of play situations and various types of play behavior (social, social parallel, emotionality) (0/15). Degree of voluntariness of participation in a discussion was not related to subsequent volunteering behavior (0/4).

322. Feedback and reinforcement conditions. Not related (2/19)

For example, praise or criticism by an Air Force instructor was not related to crew orderliness or similar observed group characteristics.

323. Induced task conditions. Moderately related (5/10)

Members operating under high-motivation conditions exhibited higher motivation (3/3). In another setting, requirements to reach a decision about volunteering, or the publicness of that decision, were only slightly related to member volunteering or other positive responses (1/5).

430) Outcomes of interaction as related to outcomes of interaction. Highly related within variable class (28/30)

There was high reliability for measures of direct or indirect influence and a high relationship between degree of consensus in arriving at a decision about volunteering and the number of volunteering or positive responses (6/6). There were also high interrelations for measures of air crew ability to work with other crews, to work with superiors, to care for aircraft, and so on (22/24).

610) Leadership performance as related to outcomes of interaction. Highly related (5/5)

Crew leaders rated high on combat performance by superiors had crews rated high on work relationships with other crews, care of aircraft, military bearing, and so on.

620) Task performance of members as related to outcomes of interaction

621. Member task performance in experimental settings. Somewhat related (4/12)

There was a high and positive relationship between degree of disclosure of personal identity and yielding to group judgment (2/3). In another setting, members shifted more toward a correct majority opinion than toward an incorrect one and showed more opinion shift when initial opinions were split than when they were either unanimously correct or incorrect (2/2). In a third setting, there was no relationship between positiveness of group leader behavior and quality of group member's speech behavior (0/6).

623. Member task performance in operational settings: specific measures. Not related (1/14)

For example, factory production was not related to absenteeism.

630) Task performance of groups as related to outcomes of interaction

633. Group task performance in operational settings: specific measures. Moderately related (14/25)

For example, crew performance in training and in combat tended to be related to crew performance in discussion tasks on use of manpower for such measures as effective coordination, control flexibility, and so on.

510. PERCEPTIONS OF TASK PERFORMANCE OF SELF AND OTHERS

Definition

"Perceptions of task performance of self and others" deals with member perceptions of own and other members' task-related behavior and task effectiveness. It includes indexes such as adequacy of group performance, perceived group task progress, quality of product, general job behavior, control, enforcement of rules, group morale, and consideration shown to others. Ratings of own task behavior, such as own influence, own difficulty in communicating with others, own structuring and organizing activities, own consideration of others, and coherence of own arguments are also included.

References

Variables of this class were used in a total of 72 studies in the sample and were tested for relationships to 10 variable classes, in a total of 490 associations, of which 155 (32%) were significant. Reference numbers of studies are 53, 144, 171, 182, 189, 201, 308, 319, 361, 398, 404, 417, 418, 433, 438, 439, 473, 484, 512, 566, 593, 693, 697, 758, 790, 806, 814, 837, 862, 867, 877, 904, 909, 941, 972, 979, 984, 1005, 1054, 1128, 1139, 1236, 1244, 1356, 1451, 1471, 1522, 1528, 1552, 1557, 1567, 1607, 1650, 1716, 1716a, 1755, 1760, 1780, 1810, 1841, 1871, 1926, 1945, 1961, 1976, 2029, 2046, 2054. 2058, 2091, 2104, 2108.

Summary of Major Relationships

"Perceptions of task performance of self and others" was highly or moderately related to 4 of 10 variable classes. High or moderate associations occurred with member social position in the group (151) and, as would be expected, with other measures of perception of task performance (510). Interestingly, perceptual judgments of performance were highly or moderately related to objective measures of member task performance in experimental settings (621) and to group task performance in operational settings: global measures (632).

No relationship occurred between the variable under consideration and biographical characteristics (110). In addition, there were no strong relationships with group training and experience (222) and certain operating conditions imposed upon the group—induced social conditions (312) and induced task conditions (323). Finally, there was slight relationship between this variable class and group task performance in operational settings: specific measures (633).

There were no cases of tested relationships between this variable and a large number of member properties such as personality characteristics (120), member abilities (131) (132), and member attitudes (141) (142) (143) (144). There were also no cases of tests for relationships between this variable class and interpersonal relations in the group (230). Moreover, the studies reviewed did not investigate the impact of three general operating conditions imposed upon the group: stimulus properties of the task (321), feedback and reinforcement conditions (322), and influence and conformity pressures (311) on member perceptions of performance.

Index of Relationships

110) Biographical characteristics of members as related to perceptions of task performance of self and others. Not related (0/8)

> For example, sex was not related to perceived similarity of own answers to those of others or to working hard.

150) Positions of members in the group as related to perceptions of task performance of self and others

> 151. Social position in the group. Moderately related (10/19)
>
> The higher the member's salary and position in the group, the more perceived authority he felt he had and the more he delegated responsibility (4/6).
> Position in group as confederate or naïve member was only slightly related to perception of performance effectiveness of others (2/8).
> The higher the rank of an air crew member, the higher he rated air crew performance adequacy (4/5).

220) Group capabilities as related to perceptions of task performance of self and others

> 222. Group training and experience. Slightly related (8/44)
>
> Measures such as (pre-experimental) flying experience were not related to perceptions of leader supervisory behavior or to crew agreements on ratings of other member (2/29). Also, there was slight

relationship between leader training in human relations techniques and higher ratings by subordinates on human relations behavior (1/5). Another set of results, although unclear, suggested that members of groups in a success condition saw their groups as performing better than did members of failure groups as the task series progressed (5/10).

240) General structural properties of the group as related to perceptions of task performance of self and others. Somewhat related (32/94)

> *Size of group:* The smaller the group (ranging from 2 to 4 members), the more did members see it as performing effectively (4/4). Leaders of groups larger than 30 were more often rated as coordinating activities well, giving clearer rules to members, having greater achievement effort, having greater physical courage, and making wise delegation of authority (7/26). Members of groups smaller than 30 more frequently indicated "don't know" or "inapplicable" to a whole series of items about the leader (10/26). There was no relationship between largeness and smallness of groups and ratings of behavior "occasionally exhibited" by leaders (2/26).

> *Homogeneity of member characteristics:* Members of heterogeneous groups more often saw others as more qualified than themselves (2/3). In another setting, dyads using projection as a common defense more often saw their partners as less successful (2/3) and saw their groups as performing more poorly than did dyads with dissimilar defenses or with other defenses in common (3/4).

310) Social conditions as related to perceptions of task performance of self and others

> 312. Induced social conditions. Slightly related (12/45)

> > Groups anticipating membership changes and working under cooperative sets rated other members' performance high (4/4), whereas perception of own task behavior was not related to knowledge of membership changes, etc. (0/4). Those perceiving congeniality with co-workers estimated co-workers' performance to be good (3/4).
> > Those working under cooperative rather than competitive sets saw more group cooperation, assistance from others, and so on (4/6). In other settings, however, source, amount, and target of threat were not related to member judgments of such measures as group goal orientation, conflict, and cohesiveness (1/27).

320) Task and operating conditions as related to perceptions of task performance of self and others

> 323. Induced task conditions. Slightly related (12/65)

> > Members operating under success conditions did not rate other members' performances higher, as compared with rating within groups in a failure condition (0/4). In another study, members allowed some autonomy of decision were more satisfied with their superior's job performance (3/4) than were members in a hierarchal decision-making situation (1/3).

Members of groups operating under perceived success saw their groups more as a vehicle to goal attainment than did members of failure groups (3/3). Results also suggested that perceived success was associated with higher ratings of group performance effectiveness than was a failure condition (15/51).

510) Perceptions of task performance of self and others as related to perceptions of task performance of self and others. Highly related within variable class (27/40)

There was high reliability of judgment of leader supervisory behavior, crew member judgments of air crew task activities, and so on.

620) Task performance of members as related to perceptions of task performance of self and others

621. Member task performance in experimental settings. Highly related (18/29)

The higher the rating of own performance, the better was the actual performance (3/3). There was a less-clear pattern for relationships between estimates of own performance and yielding to an incorrect majority (5/8) and between level of aspiration and actual performance (10/18), although the latter tended to be highly related early and late in the task series if not in intermediate stages.

630) Task performance of groups as related to perceptions of task performance of self and others

632. Group task performance in operational settings: global measures. Moderately related (16/36)

Perceptions of own task performance were highly related to group performance measures such as forestry management effectiveness (3/3). However, perceptions of performance effectiveness of other members were only slightly related to effectiveness of air crews and forestry management groups (3/12).

Air crew members' agreement on certain task procedures was positively associated with crew proficiency ranking, but this finding did not hold with respect to other procedures (10/21).

633. Group task performance in operational settings: specific measures. Slightly related (20/110)

Reports of own work procedures were not related to group production work time (1/13). Perceptions of other members' performances were not related to performance on military tasks (1/48) and were only somewhat related to work group productivity in industrial tasks (7/20). However, member ratings of leaders on ability to make judgments, on ability to organize and enforce safety rules, on general organizing ability, on maintenance of adequate communication channels, and on conference practice and behavior consistency were positively related to group performance on air crew tasks and factory production tasks. However, other similar measures did not relate to group performance (11/29).

520. PERCEPTIONS OF SOCIAL BEHAVIOR
OF SELF AND OTHERS

Definition

"Perceptions of social behavior of self and others" is similar to variable 510, but it includes perceptions of social, rather than task, behavior and effectiveness. It consists of such indexes as perceived agreement or disagreement with others, exhibited aggression and dominance, avoidance of job unpleasantness, others' efforts to impress, leaders' personal familiarity with subordinates, human relations behavior, and pleasantness. It also includes perceptions of the social behavior of the group.

References

Variables of this class were used in a total of 44 studies in the sample and were tested for relationships to 10 other variable classes, in a total of 132 associations, of which 44 (33%) were significant. Reference numbers of studies are 212, 319, 404, 411, 438, 484, 496, 512, 526, 566, 593, 606, 606a, 608, 608a, 663, 715, 806, 814, 877, 941, 944, 984, 1054, 1128, 1151, 1195, 1227, 1244, 1356, 1471, 1472, 1528, 1552, 1666, 1701, 1716, 1716a, 1793, 1871, 1914, 2046, 2058, 2101.

Summary of Major Relationships

Perceptions of social behavior yielded high or moderate relationships to 5 of 10 variables. Strong associations occurred with the member level characteristics of general abilities (131) and social position in the group (151), and with general structural properties of the group as a whole (240). Other variables with which this class was highly associated were stimulus properties of the task (321) and member task performance in experimental settings (621).

There were no relationships or only slight relationships between member perceptions of social behavior and two operating conditions imposed upon the group: induced social conditions (312) and influence and conformity pressures (311). Interestingly, "perceptions of social behavior of self and others" was not highly related to several objective measures of member and group performance (622) (632) (633).

No cases of tested relationship occurred in the review sample between this variable class and a number of member level characteristics—personality characteristics (120), biographical characteristics (110), and member attitudes (141) (142) (143) (144). In addition, group capabilities (221) (222) and interpersonal relationships in the group (230) were not tested against member perceptions of social behavior. Of task and operating conditions imposed upon the group, feedback and reinforcement (322) and induced task conditions (323) were also not tested for relationship to the variable class under consideration. Moreover, the whole series of interaction process measures (410) (420) (430) was not tested. Finally, there was an absence of tested relationships with the series of subjective measures of member and group performances (510) (520), leadership performance (610), and certain objective measures of member and group task performance (623) (631).

Index of Relationships

130) Abilities of members as related to perceptions of social behavior of self and others

131. General abilities of members. Moderately related (2/4)

Members who behaved impulsively were rated by peers as being more independent from adults but not different in amount of group power they held, as compared with less-impulsive members.

150) Positions of members in the group as related to perceptions of social behavior of self and others

151. Social position in the group. Highly related (20/32)

The higher a member's status in an crew, the more he reported attempting to influence others (5/5). The higher a member's rank in the group, the more others indicated they worked with him (10/16), although there was some ambiguity of results because of between-group variations. Perception of social behavior of other members was only slightly related to social position in the group (2/8).

240) General structural properties of the group as related to perceptions of social behavior of self and others. Highly related (3/4)

Homogeneity of member characteristics: Members of dyads using projection as a common defense mechanism attempted to influence each other more than did dissimilar dyads or dyads using other defenses in common. (2/2).

Other structural properties: Organized groups exhibited more fear in a threatening situation than did unorganized groups (1/1).

310) Social conditions as related to perceptions of social behavior of self and others

311. Influence and conformity pressures. Slightly related (1/6)

Perceptions of own social behavior, such as attempted influence, were only slightly related to group pressure (1/4).

312. Induced social conditions. Not related (1/7)

For example, degree of threat was not related to reports of own aggressive behavior.

320) Task and operating conditions as related to perceptions of social behavior of self and others

321. Stimulus properties of the task. Highly related (4/4)

There were more reported transmissions of rumors in an ambiguous situation than in a clearly defined situation.

620) Task performance of members as related to perceptions of social behavior of self and others

621. Member task performance in experimental settings. Highly related (3/3)

The greater was the degree of own perceived influence and disagreement with others, the more was the change toward the majority opinion and the greater was the actual number of times in agreement with the majority.

622. Member task performance in operational settings: global measures. Not related (2/23)

For example, supervisor's perception of own independence was not related to his over-all performance (2/10). Subordinate ratings of leader human relations behavior were not related to technical competence of military officers (0/13).

630) Task performance of groups as related to perceptions of social behavior of self and others

632. Group task performance in operational settings: global measures. Not related (1/18)

For example, military group members' attitudes and behavior toward group problems were not related to their task performance.

633. Group task performance in operational settings: specific measures. Slightly related (7/31)

There was no clear-cut pattern of results.

610. LEADERSHIP PERFORMANCE

Definition

"Leadership performance" includes observer or superior ratings of such characteristics as permissiveness, leader job performance, administrative ability, and combat performance. In some instances this variable class derives from experimental settings and in others from operational settings.

References

Variables of this class were used in a total of 25 studies in the sample and were tested for relationships to 10 variable classes, in a total of 275 associations, of which 128 (47%) were significant. Reference numbers of studies are 95, 103, 125, 128, 132, 133, 136, 252, 254, 361, 362, 462, 728, 806, 811, 856, 941, 972, 1054, 1129, 1266, 1471, 1979, 2004, 2054.

Summary of Major Relationships

This variable class was highly or moderately related to 7 of the 10 variable classes with which it was associated. These strong relationships included a number of member level properties—personality characteristics (120), general abilities (131), task abilities (132), and social position in the group (151). There were also strong relationships with content of interaction (410) and outcomes of interaction (430). Further, measures of leadership performance were moderately related to one another (610).

There were only slight or no relationships between leadership performance and member's task or physical position in the group (152) and group training and experience (222).

There were no cases of tested relationships between leadership performance and a host of member attitudinal measures (141) (142) (143) (144) and certain group properties—general structural properties of the group (240) and interpersonal relationships in the group (230). Interestingly, there were no tested relationships between this variable class and the operating conditions imposed upon the group (311) (312) (321) (322) (323). Further, leadership performance was not tested for relationship with subjective measures of member and group performance (510) (520) nor with most of the objective measures of individual and group performance (621) (622) (623) (631) (632) (633).

Index of Relationships

110) Biographical characteristics of members as related to leadership performance. Somewhat related (8/23)

> Those with higher education had higher leaderless group discussion scores (6/6), but age and leadership in leaderless group discussions were not related (0/9). Biographical characteristics were only slightly related to leadership in operational settings (2/8).

120) Personality characteristics of members as related to leadership performance. Moderately related (12/24)

> Leaderless group discussion performance was positively and highly related to ratings on personality traits such as extroversion, assertiveness, and social maturity (10/14). However, other traits such as seriousness and general activity were but slightly related to leaderless group discussion performance (2/10)

130) Abilities of members as related to leadership performance

131. General abilities of members. Highly related (30/50)

> Group members with high general intelligence exhibited high emergent-leader behavior in leaderless group discussions (6/7). Peer ratings of a number of general abilities were related to leaderless group discussion behavior, but such ratings for a number of similar abilities were not (16/26). In an operational setting, the higher a leader's problem-solving ability and word fluency, the higher he was rated on leadership abilities by supervisors; however, this relationship held for some departments but not others (8/17).

132. Task abilities of members. Moderately related (23/47)

> Leadership nominations by friends were highly related to observed measures of leadership behavior (5/7). There was a generally high and positive relationship between ratings of supervisory or leadership potential and performance in leaderless group discussions (11/18), but the relationship was only moderate between the same variables in an Army setting (6/15).

150) Positions of members in the group as related to leadership performance

151. Social position in the group. Highly related (6/6)

Members with higher group rank exhibited more leadership behavior in leaderless group discussions.

152. Task or physical position in the group. Not related (3/23)

For example, leaderless group discussion behavior was not related to seating positions in the group.

220) Group capabilities as related to leadership performance

222. Group training and experience. Slightly related (4/18)

Leaders with training in leader techniques were rated higher on permissiveness, frankness, regulation of discussion participation, and effective resolution of conflicts than were leaders without such training. However, trained and untrained leaders did not differ on several similar measures.

410) Content of interaction as related to leadership performance. Moderately related (8/15)

Emergent leaders were higher on problem proposing, information seeking, and ego involvement and lower on development giving than were other members (4/4). Leaders did not differ from other members on goal setting, information giving, opposing, supporting, and other categories (0/7).

430) Outcomes of interaction as related to leadership performance. Highly related (5/5)

Crew leaders rated high on combat performance by superiors had crews rated high on work relationships with other crews, care of aircraft, military bearing, and so on.

610) Leadership performance as related to leadership performance. Moderately related within variable class (29/64)

Measures of leaderless group discussion performance were highly interrelated (12/12). Measures of leadership performance were more highly interrelated in four-man groups (9/14) than in two-man groups (7/17). However, measures of leaderless group discussion performance were not related to supervisory ratings in an operational setting (1/21).

621. MEMBER TASK PERFORMANCE IN EXPERIMENTAL SETTINGS

Definition

"Member task performance in experimental settings" includes experimenter or observer ratings of individual performance on motor, symbolic, and symbolic–motor tasks within experimental settings—for example, number-copying speed, arithmetic accuracy, accuracy of judgments of line length; quantity or speed of production, and maze accuracy and speed.

References

Variables of this class were used in a total of 56 studies in the sample and were tested for relationships to 21 variable classes, in a total of 473 associations, of which 214 (45%) were significant. Reference numbers of studies are 1, 1a, 53, 111, 122, 133, 144, 171, 315, 344, 351, 384, 429, 430, 464, 484, 512, 526, 621, 756, 757, 794, 807, 862, 904, 909, 1046, 1075, 1085, 1098, 1099, 1129, 1139, 1199, 1236, 1242, 1315, 1354, 1401, 1450, 1451, 1486, 1585, 1586, 1602, 1607, 1641, 1650, 1760, 1761, 1926, 1933, 1963, 1979, 1996, 2008.

Summary of Major Relationships

"Member task performance in experimental settings" was highly or moderately related to 14 of 21 variable classes. At the member property level this variable class was strongly related to abilities (131) (132) and attitudes toward issues, concepts, ideologies (144). There was also a strong association with one group level variable, group training and experience (222). Furthermore, there were strong relationships with various operating conditions imposed upon the group such as influence and conformity pressures (311), stimulus properties of the task (321), induced task conditions (323), and feedback and reinforcement conditions (322). There were also strong relationships with member perceptions of task performance and social behavior (510) (520). In addition, member performance was highly or moderately related to other measures of member task performance in experimental settings (621) and group task performance in experimental sittings (631).

It is interesting to note that there was no relationship or only a slight relationship with a number of member properties such as personality characteristics (120), biographical characteristics (110), attitudes toward the situation (142), and task or physical position in the group (152). There was also little or no relationship between member task performance in experimental settings and induced social position (312) or interaction process variable classes (420) (430).

There were no instances in the review sample of tests for relationship of member task performance in experimental settings with certain attitudinal measures (141) (143) or with interpersonal relations in the group (230). In addition, there were no cases of examined relationships with other measures of member task performance including leadership (610) (622) (623) and with two classes of group performance variables (632) (633).

Index of Relationships

110) Biographical characteristics of members as related to member task performance in experimental settings. Slightly related (13/51)

> In one study, men performed consistently better than did women (9/10). Other results did not provide a clear-cut pattern.

120) Personality characteristics of members as related to member task performance in experimental settings. Not related (2/14)

130) Abilities of members as related to member task performance in experimental settings

131. General abilities of members. Highly related (28/46)

The higher members' school grades and intelligence, the better members performed on maze-learning tasks (15/15). Intelligence was also highly and positively related to performance on two types of intellectual problems, especially for older members (11/16). However, there was no relation between intelligence and skill in perceptual tasks such as estimating number of objects (0/4). Human relations role-playing performance was moderately related to athletic ability (2/4).

132. Task abilities of members. Highly related (4/5)

Over-all grades in Air Force ground school were positively related to grades on a specific written examination.

140) Attitudes of members as related to member task performance in experimental settings

142. Attitudes toward the situation. Slightly related (2/8)

Problem-solving performance tended not to be consistently related to variables such as attitudes toward problem solving.

144. Attitudes toward issues, concepts, ideologies. Highly related (4/6)

Members with low authoritarian attitudes performed better on a maze task.

150) Positions of members in the group as related to member task performance in experimental settings

152. Task or physical position in the group. Not related (0/13)

Performance measures such as symbol identification were not related to centrality of position in the communication net.

220) Group capabilities as related to member task performance in experimental settings

222. Group training and experience. Highly related (33/46)

Members exposed to direct training had higher performance ratings than did those trained by a more-passive method (3/3). In another setting, there was slight relationship between performance improvement and experience (1/4). However, the greater the training on maze, switch adjustment, and similar motor tasks, or the later the period of testing, the better was the performance (28/35).

240) General structural properties of the group as related to member task performance in experimental settings. Somewhat related (27/68)

Group size: Statistically derived measures of "group" judgment were more accurate than were "individual" judgments, especially for unfamiliar materials (3/3). Working alone, as contrasted with working in the presence of others, was but slightly related to motor performance (2/11). Arithmetic performance did not differ for individuals working alone or in groups. There were significant differences due to age, sex, and race of members, although in an unclear pattern. The over-all relationship was moderate (15/27).

Other structural properties: Performance did not differ for various communication nets, except that **Y** nets were better than circle nets (4/4).

310) Social conditions as related to member task performance in experimental settings

311. Influence and conformity pressures. Highly related (2/2)

Members working under continuous influence pressures showed more conformity than did members working under no such pressures.

312. Induced social conditions. Not related (3/31)

Members of democratically led groups made more correct responses and fewer errors early in performance on a maze task than did members of authoritarian-led groups, but did not differ in performance later in the task series (3/7).

In other settings, conditions such as cooperation–competition did not relate to differences in performance, knowledge of audience did not aid recall, and so on (0/24).

320) Task and operating conditions as related to member task performance in experimental settings

321. Stimulus properties of the task. Moderately related (15/28)

Group problem solving was more effective if preceded by a discussion (2/4). In another setting, the greater the clarity of the stimulus, the more accurate and less variable were member judgments (6/6). In another setting, however, there was only a moderate relationship between accuracy and differences in materials (e.g., familiar vs. unfamiliar, social science vs. natural science, and so on) (7/17).

322. Feedback and reinforcement conditions. Moderately related (5/12)

Members working under positive reinforcement made fewer yielding (conforming) errors than did members working under negative reinforcement (2/2). In another setting, members performed better when feedback was their own error data (3/4), but in another study there was no relationship between performance and whether feedback was own or a combination of own and partner data (0/6).

323. Induced task conditions. Moderately related (3/5)

Problem-solving performance was more effective if groups were required to reach a decision than if they were not (1/2).

410) Content of interaction as related to member task performance in experimental settings. Moderately related (4/8)

There was no clear-cut pattern of results.

420) Patterns of interaction as related to member task performance in experimental settings. Not related (0/5)

For example, various measures of speech quality, articulation, and so on were not related to rate of verbal participation.

430) Outcomes of interaction as related to member task performance in experimental settings. Somewhat related (4/12)

There was a high and positive relationship between degree of disclosure of personal identity and yielding to group judgment (2/3). In
another setting, members shifted more toward a correct majority
opinion than toward an incorrect one and showed more opinion shift
when initial opinions were split than when they were either unanimously correct or incorrect (2/2). In a third setting, there was no
relationship between positiveness of group leader behavior and
quality of group member's speech behavior (0/6).

510) Perceptions of task performance of self and others as related to member
task performance in experimental settings. Highly related (18/29)

The higher the rating of own performance, the better was the actual
performance (3/3). There was a less clear pattern for relationships
between estimates of own performance and yielding to an incorrect
majority (5/8) and between level of aspiration and actual performance
(10/18), although the latter tended to be highly related early and late
in the task series if not in intermediate stages.

520) Perceptions of social behavior of self and others as related to member task
performance in experimental settings. Highly related (3/3)

The greater was the degree of own perceived influence and disagreement with others, the more was the change toward the majority
opinion and the greater the actual number of times in agreement with
the majority.

620) Task performance of members as related to member task performance in
experimental settings

621. Member task performance in experimental settings. Moderately
related within variable class (36/62)

Direct reliability measures of performance were highly related for
symbolic tasks (10/15), whereas performance on tasks such as maze
learning was not related to the same performance measure at a later
time (0/4).
In other settings, the less conformity there was toward an incorrect
response, the better was the performance on a variety of tasks (12/18).
There was a high relationship between accuracy of predicting a
social event and accuracy of predicting various other general and
specific measures (7/7).

630) Task performance of groups as related to member task performance in
experimental settings

631. Group task performance in experimental settings. Moderately
related (8/19)

Group maze-learning scores were highly related to individual member
maze-learning scores (6/7) but not to leader scores (0/5). In another
setting, group and member scores were highly and positively related

when the entire group was rewarded for good performance (2/3) but not when only the leader was rewarded for good group performance (0/2).

622. MEMBER TASK PERFORMANCE IN OPERATIONAL SETTINGS: GLOBAL MEASURES

Definition

"Member task performance in operational settings: global measures" is similar to the previous class, but it deals with data derived from operational settings and with global measures only. Examples are ratings of combat performance, success on a strategy task, over-all job competence, and ability to meet job demands.

References

Variables of this class were used in a total of six studies in the sample and were tested for relationships to eight variable classes, in a total of 183 associations, of which 39 (21%) were significant. Reference numbers of studies are 184, 450, 642, 678, 887, 1564.

Summary of Major Relationships

Of the eight variable classes for which this variable was tested for association, it was highly or moderately related to only one, personality characteristics of members (120).

Only slight or no relationship occurred with several member level variable classes, such as task abilities (132), certain attitudes (142) (144), and social position in the group (151). In addition, the variable class was not strongly related to perceptions of social behavior of self and others (520) or to certain objective measures of member and group performance (622) (633).

There were no tests for relationships in the review sample between this measure of member performance and member biographical characteristics (110), general abilities (131), and certain attitudes (141) (143). In addition, there were no cases of tested relationships with a number of group properties such as structure (240), group abilities (221) (222), and interpersonal relations in the group (230). Furthermore, there were no tests of relationship with the operating conditions imposed upon the group—both social conditions (311) (312) and task and operating conditions (321) (322) (323). In addition, a series of subjective performance measures (510) (520) and objective measures of member and group performance, including leadership, were not tested for relation to this variable class (610) (621) (623) (631) (632).

Index of Relationships

120) Personality characteristics of members as related to member task performance in operational settings: global measures. Moderately related (4/8)

Better over-all personal ratings were highly related to ratings of leadership in industrial work situations (3/3) but only slightly related to ratings of leadership performance in military field situations (1/5).

130) Abilities of members as related to member task performance in operational settings: global measures

132. Task abilities of members. Slightly related (17/74)

There was a high and positive relationship between an Army squad leader's knowledge of military problems and his rated performance on an actual field task (3/3) but slight relationship between Air Force ground school grades and superiors' ratings of combat performance (2/8). Perceived task abilities of self and others were only slightly related to measures such as flight proficiency (12/63).

140) Attitudes of members as related to member task performance in operational settings: global measures

142. Attitudes toward the situation. Slightly related (4/16)

Members with feelings of well-being in the Air Force and a sense of safety in flying were rated higher by superiors on combat performance. No other results were clear-cut.

144. Attitudes toward issues, concepts, ideologies. Not related (1/12)

For example, authoritarian attitudes were not related to job performance.

150. Positions of members in the group as related to member task performance in operational settings: global measures

151. Social position in the group. Slightly related (1/4)

For example, time spent in the Army tended not to be related to over-all member performance.

520) Perceptions of social behavior of self and others as related to member task performance in operational settings: global measures. Not related (2/23)

Own social behavior: For example, supervisor's perception of own independence was not related to his over-all performance (2/10).

Other-member social behavior: Subordinate ratings of leader human relations behavior were not related to technical competence of military officers (0/13).

620) Task performance of members as related to member task performance in operational settings: global measures

622. Member task performance in operational settings: global measures. Slightly related within variable class (4/19)

Rated performance in training missions and schools was only slightly related to performance in combat (3/16).

630) Task performance of groups as related to member task performance in operational settings: global measures

633. Group task performance in operational settings: specific measures. Slightly related (6/27)

For example, measures of group performance on simulated air crew tasks tended not to be consistently related to ratings of crew member performance in combat.

623. MEMBER TASK PERFORMANCE IN OPERATIONAL SETTINGS: SPECIFIC MEASURES

Definition

"Member task performance in operational settings: specific measures" is similar to the previous class, but it includes specific rather than global measures. Examples are bombing accuracy, switch adjustment speed and accuracy, errors, correct responses, time to complete task, clerical costs, piecework rates.

References

Variables of this class were used in a total of eight studies in the sample and were tested for relationships to nine variable classes, in a total of 115 associations, of which 49 (43%) were significant. Reference numbers of studies are 40, 101, 201, 470, 678, 1294, 1382, 1574.

Summary of Major Relationships

This variable class was highly or moderately related to five of nine variable classes. Strong relationships were found for general abilities of members (131), member attitudes toward issues, concepts, ideologies (144), task conditions imposed upon the group (323), structural properties of the group (240), and other measures of member task performance in operational settings: specific measures (623).

There were only slight or no relationships with certain member properties such as biographical characteristics (110), task abilities (132), and social position in the group (151). There was also no relationship with outcomes of interaction (430).

There were no cases in the review sample of tested relationships between the variable under consideration and member properties such as personality characteristics (120), certain attitudes (141) (142) (143), and task position in the group (152), or between the group level variable classes such as group capabilities (221) (222) and interpersonal relations in the group (230). With one exception, there were no tests for relationship to the various operating conditions imposed upon the group; social conditions (311) (312) and two of the task conditions (321) (322) were not tested. In addition, there was an absence of tests for relationship with two of the three interaction process measures (410) (420) and both subjective measures of member and group performance (510) (520). Finally, there were few cases of investigated relationships with other objective measures of performance; omitted were leadership (610), two classes of member task performance (621) (622), and all classes of group task performance (631) (632) (633).

Index of Relationships

110) Biographical characteristics of members as related to member task performance in operational settings: specific measures. Not related (0/7)

130) Abilities of members as related to member task performance in operational settings: specific measures

  131. General abilities of members. Moderately related (12/29)
       Air Force officer role-playing competence was highly and positively related to member ratings of intelligence, energy, and so on (8/8), but was not related to such similar peer ratings as adaptability and orderliness (0/12).

  132. Task abilities of members. Slightly related (2/8)

140) Attitudes of members as related to member task performance in operational settings: specific measures

  144. Attitudes toward issues, concepts, ideologies. Moderately related (3/5)
       There was no clear-cut pattern of results.

150) Positions of members in the group as related to member task performance in operational settings: specific measures

  151. Social position in the group. Not related (0/7)

240) General structural properties of the group as related to member task performance in operational settings: specific measures. Highly related (16/26)
     There was a high negative relationship between group size (ranging from 10 to 50 members) and performance effectiveness in one situation (8/9) but only a slight negative relationship in a different situation (1/5).

320) Task and operating conditions as related to member task performance in operational settings: specific measures

  323. Induced task conditions. Highly related (7/7)
       Employees operating under general conditions of decision autonomy had better job performance than did those working under a more hierarchal arrangement.

430) Outcomes of interaction as related to member task performance in operational settings: specific measures. Not related (1/14)
     For example, factory production was not related to absenteeism.

620) Task performance of members as related to member task performance in operational settings: specific measures

  623. Member task performance in operational settings: specific measures. Highly related within variable class (8/9)
       For example, measures of supervisor knowledge of the job, administration, and human relations performance were highly interrelated.

631. GROUP TASK PERFORMANCE
IN EXPERIMENTAL SETTINGS

Definition

"Group task performance in experimental settings" includes experimenter or observer measures of quality and quantity or speed of group performance on experimental tasks requiring both motor and intellectual performances. Such measures as speed, errors, and correct responses in maze performance, assembly tasks, verbal problem-solving tasks, perceptual estimation tasks, and puzzle tasks are included.

References

Variables of this class were used in a total of 38 studies in the sample and were tested for relationships to nine variable classes, in a total of 255 associations, of which 131 (51%) were significant. Reference numbers of studies are 53, 111, 182, 315, 384, 429, 430, 484, 512, 576, 698, 789, 867, 868, 919, 968, 1059, 1097, 1139, 1210, 1243, 1266, 1467, 1471, 1557, 1572, 1575, 1585, 1586, 1704, 1705, 1764, 1781, 1920, 1930, 1939, 1940, 2101.

Summary of Major Relationships

"Group task performance in experimental settings" was highly or moderately related to seven of nine variable classes. Strong relationships included the group level properties of general structure of the group (240) and group training and experience (222). In addition, this variable was strongly related to a number of situational conditions imposed on the group—induced social conditions (312), stimulus properties of the task (321), and induced task conditions (323). There were also high or moderate relationships with objective measures of member and group task performance in experimental settings (621) (631).

Group task performance in experimental settings showed only a slight relationship with influence and conformity pressures (311), and with content of interaction (410).

It is interesting that there were no cases of tested relationships between group task performance in experimental settings and *all* member properties: personality characteristics (120), biographical characteristics (110), member abilities (131) (132), member attitudes (141) (142) (143) (144), and positions of members in the group (151) (152). In addition, there were no tests for relationship to group abilities (221) and interpersonal relations in the group (230). Further, there were no instances of tested relationship with two interaction process measures (410) (430) or with subjective measures of member and group performance (510) (520). Finally, there were no tests for relationship with objective measures of task performance such as leadership (610), two classes of member performance (622) (623), and two classes of group performance (632) (633).

Index of Relationships

220) Group capabilities as related to group task performance in experimental settings

    222. Group training and experience. Moderately related (15/26)

        Group performance improved over successive stages of practice in symbolic-motor tasks (8/8). With symbolic tasks, all groups showed learning and greater performance proficiency over time (4/4). Sequence of experimental conditions was only slightly related to performance (3/14).

240) General structural properties of the group as related to group task performance in experimental settings. Moderately related (25/62)

        Group size: Members working alone performed better on a maze task than did those working in groups (3/3). Similar results held for "extreme errors" in another situation (2/2), although there were generally no differences between individual and group performance (1/3). On symbolic tasks, members in groups performed better than did members working alone, although less so on arithmetic and verbal problems (8/14).

        Other structural properties: In another setting, differences in performance were slightly related to differences in types of communication nets (9/35), with circle nets better than wheel nets on complex symbolic problems (5/5) but not on simple problems (0/5).

310) Social conditions as related to group task performance in experimental settings

    311. Influence and conformity pressures. Slightly related (4/15)

        Groups exposed to a unanimous, incorrect majority more often erred in their performance in the direction of the majority than did groups not exposed to such pressures (3/3); the generality of this finding was shown by the fact that it was not related to differences between several types of groups (0/9).

    312. Induced social conditions. Highly related (23/31)

        Leaders instructed to behave in an authoritarian fashion had groups who performed better than nonauthoritarian-led groups (9/9). However, in another setting, variations by a confederate in social reinforcement of others or in authoritarian–democratic behavior were only somewhat related to group performance effectiveness (4/11). Cooperative groups performed more adequately than did competitive groups (7/8).

320) Task and operating conditions as related to group task performance in experimental settings

    321. Stimulus properties of the task. Moderately related (7/13)

        The greater the discrepancy between the standard stimulus and the stimulus being judged, the greater was the performance error (7/9). However, time and phase aspects of the task were not related to group performance (0/4).

323. Induced task conditions. Highly related (9/13)

Groups receiving confirmation of expected actions by the experimenter were better performers than were those whose expectations about procedures were contradicted (5/6).

A systematic distribution of information in communication nets, rather than a random distribution among members, aided effectiveness especially for the comcon (each communicating to each) net (3/4). There was no such difference for degree of knowledge about the information distribution (0/2).

410) Content of interaction as related to group task performance in experimental settings. Somewhat related (11/29)

There was no clear-cut pattern of results. Successfully performing groups seemed to exhibit fewer disagreements, less hostility, and more support among members than did less-successful groups. Also, when more-successful groups produced stories about hypothetical groups, the stories contained more satisfactory outcomes, orderliness, harmony, and so on.

620) Task performance of members as related to group task performance in experimental settings

621. Member task performance in experimental settings. Moderately related (8/19)

Group maze-learning scores were highly related to individual member maze-learning scores (6/7) but not to leader scores (0/5). In another setting, group and member scores were highly and positively related when the entire group was rewarded for good performance (2/3) but not when only the leader was rewarded for good group performance (0/2).

630) Task performance of groups as related to group task performance in experimental settings

631. Group task performance in experimental settings. Highly related within variable class (29/47)

Group performance on a model railroad task yielded a series of measures that did not show any clear pattern of intercorrelations; e.g.; errors, correct responses, and so on.

632. GROUP TASK PERFORMANCE IN OPERATIONAL SETTINGS: GLOBAL MEASURES

Definition

"Group task performance in operational settings: global measures" includes observer or superior ratings of over-all group performance on real or simulated military and industrial tasks.

References

Variables of this class were used in a total of 13 studies in the sample and were tested for relationships to 10 other variable classes, in a total of 286 associations, of which 103 (36%) were significant. Reference numbers of studies are 83, 184, 433, 450, 606, 758, 766, 806, 941, 972, 1564, 1603, 1939.

Summary of Major Relationships

This variable class was highly or moderately related to only 3 of the 11 other variables with which it was tested for relationship in the review sample. These strongly related variables were group training and experience (222), member perceptions of task performance of self and others (510), and group task performance in operational settings: specific measures (633).

There were only slight or no relationships between this variable class and member abilities (131) (132), group abilities (221), and member perceptions of the social behavior of self and others (520). There were only equivocal relationships between "group task performance in operational settings: global measures" and personality characteristics (120), attitudes toward nongroup persons and other groups (143), and content of interaction (410).

In the studies reviewed, there were no instances of tests for relationship between this variable class and a number of member properties such as biographical characteristics (110) and several types of member attitudes (141) (142) (144). There were also no tests of relationship with general structural properties of the group (240) or interpersonal relations in the group (230). In addition, there were no tests of relationship with most operating conditions imposed upon the group (311) (312) (321) (323). It is interesting that analyses were lacking for the relationship between the variable under consideration and measures of leadership performance (610), member task performance (621) (622) (623), and other measures of group task performance (631) (632).

Index of Relationships

120) Personality characteristics of members as related to group task performance in operational settings: global measures. Somewhat related (12/38)

In a moderate relationship, the less members exhibited extreme personality characteristics, the more effective was their group performance (7/12). Members who rated themselves high on physical prowess and self-reliance belonged to groups rated high on over-all military field problem effectiveness (5/8).

130) Abilities of members as related to group task performance in operational settings: global measures

131. General abilities of members. Not related (1/10)

For example, member intelligence was not related to group performance on air crew tasks and Army field problems.

132. Task abilities of members. Slightly related (4/21)

For example, satisfaction with leader tended not to be related to such measures as production rate, simulated air crew task performance, and so on.

140) Attitudes of members as related to group task performance in operational settings: global measures

    143. Attitudes toward nongroup persons and other groups. Somewhat related (3/8)

    Army squad members who exhibited favorable attitudes and adjustment to the Army were members of squads rated high on over-all performance (3/4). However, there was no relationship between satisfaction with the Air Force or with an industrial organization and ratings of crew or group performance (0/4).

220) Group capabilities as related to group task performance in operational settings: global measures

    221. Group abilities. Slightly related (1/5)

    Air crew problem-solving test performance was not related to ratings of over-all group training performance adequacy.

    222. Group training and experience. Highly related (9/11)

    Length of time in job was highly related to group effectiveness (4/5). Crews with more flying experience were rated by supervisors as being more proficient (5/6).

320) Task and operating conditions as related to group task performance in operational settings: global measures

    322. Feedback and reinforcement conditions. Somewhat related (2/6)

    The more personal criticism instructors gave crews about performance and the more they praised their crews, the better was the group performance (2/2), although frequency of explanations, illustrations, and so on did not relate to crew performance (0/4).

410) Content of interaction as related to group task performance in operational settings: global measures. Somewhat related (32/106)

    When crews rated as more effective in combat produced stories about hypothetical groups, the stories contained more perceptions of satisfactory outcomes, orderly functioning, friendship, productivity, agreement, and so on.

510) Perceptions of task performance of self and others as related to group task performance in operational settings: global measures. Moderately related (16/36)

    Perceptions of own task performance were highly related to group performance measures, such as forestry management effectiveness (3/3). However, perceptions of performance effectiveness of other members were only slightly related to effectiveness of air crews and forestry management groups (3/12).

    Air crew members' agreement on certain task procedures was positively associated with crew proficiency ranking, but this finding did not hold with respect to other procedures (10/21).

520) Perceptions of social behavior of self and others as related to group task performance in operational settings: global measures. Not related (1/18)

>For example, military group members' attitudes and behavior toward group problems were not related to their task performance.

630) Task performance of groups as related to group task performance in operational settings: global measures

>633. Group task performance in operational settings: specific measures. Highly related (23/37)

>>The more effective were air crews on simulated air tasks, the higher they were rated by superiors on global measures of performance effectiveness in combat and training.

633. GROUP TASK PERFORMANCE IN OPERATIONAL SETTINGS: SPECIFIC MEASURES

Definition

"Group task performance in operational settings: specific measures" is similar to variable 632, but it includes specific group performance measures rather than ratings of over-all group performance. For the most part, the measures here considered are observer's or superior's formal records of "scores" of group performances for specific criteria such as speed, accuracy, and production levels in bombing, gunnery, and navigation during real or simulated military missions, clerical or surveying tasks, manufacture of a given quantity of a product, and so on.

References

Variables of this class were used in a total of 24 studies in the sample and were tested for relationships to 22 variable classes, in a total of 987 associations, of which 230 (23%) were significant. Reference numbers of studies are 201, 411, 438, 439, 450, 606a, 608, 608a, 642, 766, 767, 806, 856, 874, 941, 1564, 1567, 1701, 1707, 1782, 1832, 1999, 2000, 2058.

Summary of Major Relationships

Of the 22 variable classes to which group task performance in operational settings was tested for relationships it showed high to moderate associations with 9. Only one of these was a property of group members, namely, personality characteristics (120). Certain group properties such as group abilities (221), group structure (240), and group training and experience (222) were also strongly related to this variable class, as were feedback and reinforcement conditions (322) and induced task conditions (323). In addition, both other measures of group task performance were highly related (632) (633). The only interaction process measure showing strong association was outcomes of interaction (430).

A number of member level properties showed little or no association with group task performance in operational settings. These were biographical characteristics (110), member abilities (131) (132), and the series of member attitudes (141) (142) (143) (144). A measure of interaction process (420), one class of operating conditions imposed on the group (312), interpersonal relations in the group (320), and member perceptions of performance and social behavior (510) (520) also showed weak association. It is interesting that one measure of member task performance (622) showed slight relationship.

Although most measures of individual characteristics were tested against this variable, it is interesting that "positions of members in the group" (151) (152) was not studied vis-à-vis "group task performance in operational settings: specific measures" in the review sample. In addition, measures of leadership performance (610), two measures of member task performance (621) (623) and one measure of group task performance (631) were not studied with respect to this variable class.

Index of Relationships

110) Biographical characteristics of members as related to group task performance in operational settings: specific measures. Not related (0/7)

> Measures such as age and education were not related to performance of industrial work groups or military squads.

120) Personality characteristics of members as related to group task performance in operational settings: specific measures. Moderately related (3/7)

> Supervisors rated high in interviews on traits such as reasonableness and democratic behavior had high-producing work sections (3/3), but no such relationship was found for ratings of other, similar characteristics (0/4).

130) Abilities of members as related to group task performance in operational settings: specific measures

> 131. General abilities of members. Not related (1/10)
>
> > For example, member intelligence was not related to group performance on air crew tasks and Army field problems.
>
> 132. Task abilities of members. Not related (31/410)
>
> > For example, measures of production line effectiveness and performance on simulated air crew tasks were only slightly related to member judgments of competence and confidence in superiors (7/37). Moreover, such objective measures of task ability as ground school grades were not related to measures of performance on simulated air crew tasks (24/373).

140) Attitudes of members as related to group task performance in operational settings: specific measures

> 141. Attitudes toward the task. Not related (1/22)
>
> 142. Attitudes toward the situation. Slightly related (1/6)
>
> > Such measures as perceived social distance between self and subordinates tended not to be related to group production time.

143. Attitudes toward nongroup persons and other groups. Slightly related (19/68)

The less similarity of traits that the leader attributed to a hypothetical most- and least-preferred co-worker, the more effective was team performance for basketball teams, surveying teams, air crews (on simulated air crew tasks), tank teams (on tank training problems). However, these variables interacted with sociometric patterns: namely, the relationship described above held only when the leader had positive sociometric relationships with others in the crew (9/12). In another study, attraction toward an industrial company or the Navy was not related to factory production work time or military task proficiency (1/10).

144. Attitudes toward issues, concepts, ideologies. Not related (0/6)

For example, authoritarian attitudes were not related to drill proficiency and cleanliness.

220) Group capabilities as related to group task performance in operational settings: specific measures

221) Group abilities. Moderately related (8/14)

The higher air crews were rated on over-all value to their squadron (by superiors), the greater the number of missions they completed and the greater their performance effectiveness on a series of simulated air crew tasks (7/8). However, perceptions of task-related abilities of groups were only slightly related to group performance on aircraft manufacturing tasks, surveying tasks, and so on (1/6).

222. Group training and experience. Highly related (14/23)

Group performance improved over successive stages of practice (9/13). Crew aircraft-flying experience was positively related to performance on simulated air crew tasks, but not on other tasks (5/10).

230) Interpersonal relations in the group as related to group task performance in operational settings: specific measures. Somewhat related (10/34)

Attitude toward other members: On a factory production task, group members who were more personally attracted to one another performed more effectively (4/4), but this finding did not hold for members of military task groups (3/19).

Attitude toward the group: Group attraction was only slightly related to clerical or manufacturing productivity (2/9).

240) General structural properties of the group as related to group task performance in operational settings: specific measures. Highly related (25/39)

Group size: Small groups were more efficient than were larger groups when groups ranged in size from 10 to 50 members (5/5).

Unspecified differences among groups: Individual differences among air crews and training classes, as well as mission differences, were moderately related to differences in group performance (20/34).

310) Social conditions as related to group task performance in operational settings: specific measures

312. Induced social conditions. Not related (1/14)

Authoritarian vs. democratic leadership style was not related to performance on a simulated military task.

320) Task and operating conditions as related to group task performance in operational settings: specific measures

322. Feedback and reinforcement conditions. Moderately related (10/17)

Different critique methods produced some differences in performance of groups on later tasks. For example, expert critiques were better than unstructured crew-centered critiques and self-critiques, but were not better than structured methods (3/4). Self-critique procedures were less effective than were expert critiques but were not different from any of the other methods (1/3). An unstructured technique was poorer than an expert or structured procedure but was not different from self- and noncritique methods (2/4). Structured methods were better than unstructured ones, but no different from other procedures (1/4).

323. Induced task conditions. Highly related (5/7)

Groups with immediate access to relevant information performed better than did those with difficult access to task-related information (2/2). In another study, however, dispersion and directness of information availability was only moderately related to group performance (2/4).

420) Pattern of interaction as related to group task performance in operational settings: specific measures. Not related (0/4)

430) Outcomes of interaction as related to group task performance in operational settings: specific measures. Moderately related (14/25)

For example, crew performance in training and in combat tended to be related to crew performance in discussion tasks on use of manpower for such measures as effective coordination, control flexibility, and so on.

510) Perceptions of task performance of self and others as related to group task performance in operational settings: specific measures. Slightly related (20/120)

Own task performance: Reports of own work procedures were not related to group production work time (1/13).

Other member task performance: Member ratings of leaders on ability to make judgments, on ability to organize and enforce safety rules, on general organizing ability, on maintenance of adequate communication channels, and on conference practice and behavior consistency were positively related to group performance on air crew tasks and factory production tasks. However, other similar measures related to group performance (11/29). Perceptions of other members' performances were not related to performance on military tasks (1/48) and were only somewhat related to work group productivity in industrial tasks (7/20).

520) Perceptions of social behavior of self and others as related to group task performance in operational settings: specific measures. Slightly related (7/31)

There was no clear-cut pattern of results.

620) Task performance of members as related to group task performance in operational settings: specific measures

622. Member task performance in operational settings: global measures. Slightly related (6/27)

For example, measures of group performance on simulated air crew tasks tended not to be consistently related to ratings of crew member performance in combat.

630) Task performance of groups as related to group task performance in operational settings: specific measures

632. Group task performance in operational settings: global measures. Highly related (23/37)

The more effective were air crews on simulated air tasks, the higher they were rated by superiors on global measures of performance effectiveness in combat and training.

633. Group task performance in operational settings: specific measures. Moderately related within variable class (31/69)

When direct reliability measures were considered, relationship was high (18/25). The remaining results showed that measures from a series of simulated air crew and tank crew tasks were only somewhat interrelated. (13/43).

SECTION B
Study Annotations

INTRODUCTION

Following are annotations of the small group research studies reviewed as part of this research program. The studies appear alphabetically by author. The annotation for each study contains five parts:

1. *Bibliographical reference.* (Reference numbers refer to the general bibliography, Section C.)
2. *Purpose.* A brief statement of the central problem of the study.
3. *Procedure.* A digest of study methodology.
4. *Results.* A review of major findings.
5. *Study variables.* A list of the major classes of variables used in the study. (Variable class numbers and names are those used in Section A and discussed in earlier parts of the book.)

The studies are a composite of two samples which differ in important ways; there are a general sample of nearly 200 studies (all studies with reference numbers not followed by an asterisk) and a special sample of about 50 studies (those studies with reference numbers followed by an asterisk).

Studies in the general sample represent a selection of every seventh entry in the general bibliography, allowing for the following constraints:

1. If a bibliographic item did not contain research data (e.g., if the reference was a wholly theoretical paper), it was passed over.
2. If a single bibliographic item contained data from two independent studies (i.e., if it reported two distinct but related experiments), both of the studies were separately included in the sample, with the bibliographical reference appearing twice but that of the second part followed by an italic *a*.
3. If a bibliographic item was a study employing factor analysis, it was passed over. Although our method of classification could readily handle zero order correlations as any other correlation, we did not feel that it could handle the higher order concepts of factor analysis without doing violence to those concepts. Hence, we decided to omit factor analytic studies; three such studies appeared by random selection and were passed over.

For studies in the general sample, all relationships in the study (including those implied but not explicitly tested) were coded as "data" from the study.

The special sample was an attempt to maximize coverage in one special substantive area, task performance effectiveness. In the special sample, we attempted to include studies that focused on measures of member or group task performance. For these studies, however, only those relationships that dealt with task performance effectiveness were coded. Hence, the results and the listing of variables in the annotations of these studies are incomplete. An estimate of the amount of material omitted from each study is given in the last sentence of the results part of each study annotation. As has been noted, the asterisked studies comprise this special sample.

It is possible to cross-reference between the catalogue of relationships (Section A) and these annotations by means of the listing of study variables in each annotation and the listing of study reference numbers for each variable in the catalogue. Thus, it is possible to track down either (a) more detail about the *studies* in which a given relationship was tested, by working from the catalogue of relationships to the study annotations, or (b) more detail about a given relationship found in a particular study, by working from the annotations to the catalogue of variables.

1. Abel, Theodora M. The influence of social facilitation on motor performance at different levels of intelligence. *Amer. J. Psychol.*, 1938, *51*, 379–389.

Purpose

This study investigated the effects of social facilitation and intelligence on motor performance.

Procedure

Girls were given the task of learning a paper-and-pencil maze while working either alone or in the presence of another *S*. Performance was measured in terms of errors and time required to complete the maze.

Results

Both high- and low-intelligence *S*s performed better when working in the presence of others than when working alone (2/2). There was an improvement in performance for all *S*s in successive blocks of trials (16/17). An examination of this data showed that differences were larger when the later trials had paired *S*s. Finally, girls of high intelligence performed better than did girls of low intelligence regardless of social facilitation conditions (12/12).

Study Variables

131) General abilities of members
  Intelligence: *S* score on IQ test.
240) General structural properties of the group
  Social facilitation: *E* assignment of *S*s to work either alone or in the presence of another *S*.

621) Member task performance in experimental settings
       Performance effectiveness: S performance on a paper-and-pencil maze (number of errors, time required).

1a. Abel, Theodora M. The influence of social facilitation on motor performance at different levels of intelligence. *Amer. J. Psychol.*, 1938, *51*, 379–389.

Purpose

This study investigated the effects of social facilitation and intelligence on motor performance. The study was an extension of the immediately preceding study.

Procedure

The general procedure was identical to that reported in the preceding study. The present experiment took place two months later and used the same Ss as did the earlier study. In this later case, Ss were assigned to one of two types of conditions, regardless of their experiences in the first experiment. Ss in one condition worked alone on a paper-and-pencil maze for two periods and then worked in pairs. Ss in the other condition worked in pairs for two periods and then worked alone. Records were kept of errors and time to complete the maze.

Results

Girls working in the presence of another person in the final period generally performed better throughout the series than did those who worked alone in the final period (6/6), but all Ss tended to make fewer errors during later trials regardless of whether they worked in pairs or alone (3/4).

Generally, there was only a moderate relationship between intelligence and the amount of pencil pressure exerted on the maze or type of social facilitation and the amount of pencil pressure exerted (3/6).

Study Variables

131) General abilities of members
       Intelligence: S score on IQ test.
222) Group training and experience
       Phase of training: Ss work in different series of trials.
240) General structural properties of the group
       Social facilitation: E assignment of Ss to work either alone or in the presence of another S.
621) Member task performance in experimental settings
       Pressure exerted during maze performance: S performance on a paper-and-pencil maze.
       Member motor performance: S performance on a paper-and-pencil maze (number of errors, time required).

11. Alfert, Elizabeth. Two components of assumed similarity. *J. abnorm. soc. Psychol.*, 1958, *56*, 125–138.

Purpose

This investigation explored factors associated with the attribution of one's own personality characteristics to others.

Procedure

College students responded to a list of personality traits from several different points of view: as they felt each item applied personally to them, as they would ideally have liked to be, and as they predicted other specific group members would respond. In some groups, Ss also responded to the items as Ss thought these items actually characterized other persons in the group. From the raw data, some traits were described as being *ideal-congruent* (showing a high similarity of ideal and actual self-ratings), whereas others were identified as *ideal-discrepant*. Separate measures of assumed similarity (the similarity in assignment of traits to oneself and prediction of responses of others) were computed for total, ideal-congruent and ideal-discrepant items. Differences and relationships between the assumed similarity measures were computed.

Results

Desirable and neutral traits that Ss most frequently rated as typifying their ideal and real selves (ideal-congruent) were more frequently attributed to others than were ideal-discrepant traits (5/5). This relationship did not hold for extreme traits (0/2).

Study Variables

120) Personality characteristics of members

Degree of ideal self-congruency: S ratings of himself as he was, compared with ratings of himself as he would have liked to be.
Assumed similarity: S ratings of himself on a trait list compared with S ratings of others on a trait list.

32. Anikeeff, A. M. Sociometric empathy. *J. soc. Psychol.*, 1957, *45*, 283–287.

Purpose

This study analyzed the congruency of group members' personal sociometric choices and their estimates of the group's sociometric choice.

Procedure

Each subject was required to rank members of the class as his first, second, and third choices for classmate, social-evening companion, and group representative. Later, he repeated this ranking as he thought the group would. The two sets of preferences were compared by rank-difference correlation to determine the similarity of members' personal and perceived group preferences.

Results

Group members' predictions of their classmates' preferences did not always correspond to their own personal choices (4/7). For example, high agreement was found between members' personal and predicted group choices of social-evening companions and group representatives, but not of classmates (2/3). Also, there was a moderate relationship between personal and perceived over-all sociometric status for Ss who were first on all three criteria, but not for those Ss second or third on the combined criteria (2/4).

Study Variables

151) Social position in the group

Perceived group sociometric choice: S ranking of members as he thought the group would rank its choices of classmates, social-evening companions, and representatives.

230) Interpersonal relations in the group

Sociometric choice: S ranking of members as preferred social-evening companion, etc.

40.* Argyle, M., et al. Supervisory methods related to productivity, absenteeism, and labour turnover. *Hum. Relat.*, 1958, *11*, 23–42.

Purpose

This study investigated the relationship between industrial productivity and supervisory practices, work group size, and work group composition.

Procedure

Data on foreman supervisory practices, size of work group, worker absenteeism, labor turnover, work group sex composition, and foreman training were related to measures of worker productivity (ratio of time taken to time allowed). Data were obtained from previous studies, and comparisons were made between matched departments as identified by their wage payment system—e.g., incentive and lieu rate (individual merit rating)—and type of production control—e.g., assembly (output dependent on individual worker) and machine (output determined by machine pace).

Results

The type of supervision most strongly related to increased productivity was nonpunitive supervision (3/5). Democratic supervision was only slightly related (1/5) except in lieu-rate departments (1/1). General, low-pressure, and employee-centered supervision did not differentiate high- and low-producing sections in any of the departments (0/15).

Size of work group made no significant differences in work output (1/5) except in the lieu-rate departments (1/1), and employee turnover was associated with lowered productivity only in assembly departments (1/1).

No differences in productivity were found between sections composed primarily of men or of women, or with high or low absenteeism (0/10).

This study contained a total of 92 relationships.

Study Variables

240) General structural properties of the group

Individual work department: E designation of two matched departments.

Size of work group: E designation of smaller or larger work groups.

Sex of department workers: departments composed primarily of men or of women.

420) Patterns of interaction

Foreman work practices: E rating of foreman during interview, manager rating, and foreman score on questionnaire.

430) Outcomes of interaction

Member absenteeism: E description of section employees' absences.

Labor turnover: E count of voluntary leavers.

623) Member task performance in operational settings: specific measures

Member productivity (work output): ratio of time taken to time allowed for completion of task.

53.* **Asch, S. E.** Studies of independence and conformity: I. A minority of one against a unanimous majority. *Psychol. Monogr.*, 1956, *70*, No. 9 (Whole No. 416).

Purpose

This experiment investigated the influence of group pressures for conformity and certain stimulus characteristics on group and individual judgments.

Procedure

Groups composed of several experimenter-confederates and a single naïve S were given the task of judging line lengths. On critical trials, the confederate majority was instructed to unanimously make erroneous judgments, individually and publicly, prior to the naïve S's response. The conformity of the naïve S was measured in terms of the degree to which he erred in the direction advocated by the majority. Following the influence situation, individual interviews were conducted to determine reactions to the experimental situation.

Results

Ss exposed to a unanimous, incorrect majority judgment erred in their performance in the direction of the majority more frequently than did Ss not exposed to such pressures (3/3). This phenomenon was general, in that there were no differences in the yielding behavior of several different groups exposed to social pressures of the same type (0/9). There was little variation of the majority effect over time; only limited shifts in errors occurred over successive stages of the experiment (3/10).

Several additional analyses revealed definite relationships between conformity and a variety of stimulus characteristics—e.g., line length, size of discrepancy, stimulus modality.

Analysis of interview responses showed that the more Ss felt themselves disagreeing with the group, the more they felt they yielded and the more they actually did yield to the incorrect majority (2/2).

This study contained a total of 40 relationships.

Study Variables

311) Influence and conformity pressures
>   Characteristics of confederate response: E record of confederate responses as moderate or extreme.

321) Stimulus properties of the task
>   Stimulus characteristics: degree of discrepancy between standard and comparison lines.
>   Stimulus characteristics: S assignment to differentiate between thick and thin lines.
>   Sequence of trials: group assignment to work within different parts of experiment.
>   Origin of S sample: S selection from different populations.

430) Outcomes of interaction
>   Actual disagreement with majority: E record of number of times Ss disagreed with majority.

510) Perceptions of task performance of self and others
>   Personal disagreement with majority: S statement of number of times he disagreed with majority.
>   Estimated conformity: S statement of number of times he yielded to majority responses.
>   Estimated performance: S statement of number of errors he made.

621) Member task performance in experimental settings
>   Member performance: E record of number of errors Ss made.

631) Group task performance in experimental settings
>   Quality of group performance: E record of type of errors—moderate or extreme.
>   Group performance: E record of number and type of errors within the group.

81. Bales, R. F., et al. Channels of communication in small groups. *Amer. sociol. Rev.*, 1951, *16*, 461–468.

Purpose

This study analyzed regularity in initiation, receipt, frequency, and direction of communications among members of face-to-face groups.

Procedure

Data for this study were derived from many different studies conducted in experimental settings, natural settings, therapy groups, and case-discussion meetings of diagnostic councils. The method of observation was uniform for all, with Os recording all nonverbal and verbal communication acts and designating the originator and recipient of the act. A basic matrix was formed, with originators ranked for number of initiations across the rows, and the recipients ranked for frequency of receipt down the columns. A number of hypotheses were tested relating initiating rank to own recipient rank, others' recipient ranks, and group recipient rank. Two tests were made for each size of group—one for individual sessions and one for aggregates of individual sessions.

Results

Participants in a small face-to-face group ranked according to the number of communication acts they initiated were similarly ranked on the number of acts they received in general and from specific individuals and on the number of acts they directed to other individuals and to the group as a whole (61/64). The number of communication acts received by individuals ranked according to the frequency of their receipt of acts was parallel to the initiating rank of the originator of these acts (16/16).

In all cases where no significant relationship was found between initiating rank and recipient and number of directed acts, the measures were based on aggregates of individual sessions for three-person groups.

Study Variables

420) Patterns of interaction

Discussion initiation and receipt: O record of member participation in discussion (giving and receiving verbal and nonverbal communicative acts).

83. Balma, M. J., et al. The role of the foreman in modern industry: II. Foreman identification with management, work group productivity, and employee attitude toward the foreman. *Personnel Psychol.*, 1958, *11*, 367–378.

Purpose

This investigation studied relationships between foreman identification with management, work group productivity, and employee attitudes toward the foreman.

Procedure

An attitude measure of identification with management was administered to foremen of different industrial plants. Several management people from each plant rated the productivity of the foremen's work groups. Then a short questionnaire was given to employees in order to tap attitudes toward their foremen.

Results

Foremen of highly productive groups identified themselves more frequently with management than did foremen of less-productive groups (2/2). However, this relationship was not a simple one, because identification was different for different plants (2/2) and the interaction of plants and productivity was significant (2/2).

Employee attitudes toward foremen and foremen's age, education, and tenure did not relate to foremen's identification of themselves with management (0/8).

Neither group productivity nor type of plant (nor the interaction of these variables) related to employee attitudes toward foremen (0/6).

Study Variables

143) Attitudes toward nongroup persons and other groups
     Foreman identification with management: S responses on foreman identification-with-management measure.

230) Interpersonal relations in the group
     Employee attitude toward foreman: S questionnaire responses.

249) General structural properties of the group
     Type of industrial plant: different industrial plants chosen in the study.

632) Group task performance in operational settings: global measures
     Group productivity: management ratings of various groups on performance.

95.* **Barnlund, D. C.** Experiments in leadership training for decision-making groups. *Speech Monogr.*, 1955, *22*, 1–14.

Purpose

This experiment studied the effect of leadership training on performance of leadership functions in discussion groups.

Procedure

Students rated by peers as being ineffective leaders were assigned either to groups that met for several sessions for specific training in discussion leadership or to control groups without training. Os evaluating leadership exhibited in pretraining and posttraining discussions used a set of rating scales measuring leadership functions such as skill at initiation of discussion, stimulation of groups, and resolution of group conflicts. The effectiveness of the training program was evaluated by comparison of before-and-after ratings.

Results

Before the training courses, there were no differences in the leadership behavior exhibited by Ss in each group (1/9). Later evaluations showed that those who had been given training in leadership functions exhibited better leadership quality in discussions, regulated participation more, and showed a better ability to resolve conflicts during the group discussion period (3/3).

Degree of training did not relate to any other leader effectiveness measures (0/6). This study contained a total of 21 relationships.

Study Variables

222) Group training and experience

Group training in leadership: E division of Ss into groups receiving or not receiving training in leadership behavior.

610) Leadership performance

Performance as a leader: O rating of leader behavior on quality of remarks, permissiveness, control skill, and other rating procedures.

101. Barton, W. A., Jr. The effect of group activity and individual effort in developing ability to solve problems in first year algebra. *Educ. Admin. Superv.*, 1926, *12*, 512–518.

Purpose

The study compared the effectiveness of two methods of instruction—individual guidance and group discussion—on problem-solving performance of students.

Procedure

Pairs of Ss, matched on the basis of age and IQ, were compared. The members of one group were instructed individually in algebra and the members of the other group by group discussion. After four days of instruction, both classes were tested and compared in terms of number of correct solutions for problems of different degrees of difficulty.

Results

Students instructed by the group discussion method were significantly superior to students of equal ability receiving individual preparation (1/1).

Study Variables

240) General structural properties of the group

Method of instruction (group or individual): E assignment of Ss to individual or group discussion preparation in algebra.

623) Member task performance in operational settings: specific measures

Member performance: E scoring of Ss on number of correct answers to problems.

103. Bass, B. M. Situational tests: I. Individual interviews compared with leaderless group discussions. *Educ. psychol. Measmt*, 1951, *11*, 67–75.

Purpose

This study compared the reliability of leadership ratings of individuals in private interviews and in group discussions.

Procedure

College students were personally interviewed by two company represent-atives and were observed in a leaderless group discussion. Ratings of leadership behavior were obtained and intercorrelations of observers and situations computed.

Results

The inter-rater reliability of Leaderless Group Discussion (LGD) behavior observations and of individual interview behavior ratings, taken separately, was significant only at the .10 level for major subgroups of Ss and also for Ss in general (0/6) but was not reported for individual cases. There were no differences in reliability coefficients within major groups or among groups (0/6).

Study Variables

610) Leadership performance
    Leadership performance: O rating of behavior in leaderless group discussion.

111. Bass, B. M. *Increased attraction to the group as a function of individual and group goal attainment.* Baton Rouge, La.: Louisiana State University, 1955. (Tech. Rep. No. 2, Contract N7 ONR 35609)

Purpose

This study investigated whether performance and group effectiveness related to attraction to the group.

Procedure

Students privately ranked a set of five words according to judged familiarity. Next there was a discussion followed by a group decision. Then Ss privately ranked the words again. Various measures were obtained of accuracy, stability, and agreement among member and group judgments. In addition, each S indicated his attraction to the group before the first and after the last trial.

Results

1. Performance effectiveness measures
    a. Individual performance
        (1) Accuracy of initial and final private judgments: not related to change in attraction to the group (0/2)
        (2) Change in accuracy of private judgments: positively related to change in attraction to the group (1/1)
    b. Group performance: not related to change in attraction to the group (0/1)

2. Agreement of judgments among members and group
    a. Individual agreement among members, initially and finally, and changes in agreement: not related to change in attraction to the group (0/4)

b. Member judgment compared with group judgment: not related to change in attraction to the group (0/2)

c. Public coalescence: agreement of member's final, private decision with group decision, compared with initial agreement between individuals: not related to change in attraction to the group (0/1)

Study Variables

144) Attitudes toward issues, concepts, ideologies
   Stability of private opinion: comparison of individual member judgments.

230) Interpersonal relations in the group
   Increase in attraction to group: difference between S pre- and post-experimental ratings of the group.

240) General structural properties of the group
   Individual groups: groups selected for the experiment.

430) Outcomes of interaction
   Agreement among members: change in S judgment.
   Private coalescence: increase in private agreement among members on word judgment.
   Agreement between member and group judgment: average differences between individual and group judgments.
   Public coalescence: agreement of member final, private decision with group decision, compared with initial agreement among individuals.

621) Member task performance in experimental settings
   Private accuracy of judgment and increase in accuracy: E record of number of problems solved correctly.

621) Member task performance in experimental settings

631) Group task performance in experimental settings
   Increase in public accuracy: extent to which group decision was more accurate than was average accuracy of initial judgments of members.

631) Group task performance in experimental settings
   Accuracy of group decisions: E rating of group judgment.

122. Bass, B. M. Effects of motivation on consistency of performance in groups. *Educ. psychol. Measmt*, 1959, *19*, 247–252.

Purpose

This study investigated performance effectiveness and agreement between member and group judgments as a function of task-related motivation.

Procedure

Cadets were administered a self-rating scale indicating their degree of motivation to enter advanced ROTC. On the basis of ratings they were divided into high-, medium-, and low-level motivation groups. Each group member was asked to rank privately a set of five words according to its judged familiarity.

A discussion took place, followed by a group decision. Then, Ss privately ranked the words again. Various measures of accuracy, stability, and agreement among member and group judgments were obtained and split-half reliability correlations computed.

Results

1. Performance effectiveness measures
   a. Accuracy of initial private judgments: reliable for all levels of motivation (3/3)
   b. Accuracy of final private judgments:
      (1) reliable for medium- and low-motivation Ss (2/2),
      (2) negatively related for high-motivation Ss (1/1)

2. Agreement of judgments among members and group
   a. Individual judgments: reliable for initial and final judgments for all levels of motivation (10/10), except that initial agreement for high-motivation Ss was negative (1/1) and final agreement for low-motivation Ss was insignificant (0/1)
   b. Member and group judgments: reliable for all levels of motivation (6/6)

3. Leadership measures
   a. Private successful leadership: the extent to which Ss agreed more with a member finally than initially, and to which others changed their rankings more, was reliable for all levels of motivation (3/3)
   b. Public successful leadership: the extent to which group decision correlated with initial judgments, and to which S agreed more with group decision than with others, was reliable for all levels of motivation (3/3)
   c. Attempted leadership: the number of seconds Ss spent talking during each discussion period was reliable for all levels of motivation (3/3)

Study Variables

144) Attitudes toward issues, concepts, ideologies
   Agreement among members: S judgments of problems. Stability of private opinion: S change in judgments.

420) Patterns of interaction
   Attempted leadership: number of seconds spent talking during discussion.

430) Outcomes of interaction
   Successful private leadership: the extent other Ss agreed more with a member finally than initially and others changed their rankings more than he did.
   Agreement between member and group judgment: difference between individual and group judgments.
   Successful public leadership: extent group decision correlated with Ss' initial judgments and the extent S agreed more with group decision rather than with decisions of other Ss.
   Successful leadership: the extent Ss agreed more with a member finally than initially and others changed their rankings more.

621) Member task performance in experimental settings
         Member performance accuracy: E record of number of problems Ss
         solved correctly.

125. Bass, B. M., & Coates, C. H. Forecasting officer potential using the leaderless group discussion. *J. abnorm. soc. Psychol.*, 1952, 47, 321–325.

Purpose

This study analyzed the association between leadership ratings of ROTC cadets in a leaderless group discussion and standardized military ratings of their officer potential.

Procedure

Third-year ROTC cadets drawn from 11 classes at a semimilitary college participated in 1 of 35 initially leaderless discussions of six to eight men in which they solved a problem in military tactics. Os rated each S on a nine-item scale on leadership behavior displayed during the discussion. Standardized officer potential ratings by Army and Air Force cadet and tactical officers during the ROTC program and summer camp session were correlated with cadets' Leaderless Group Discussion (LGD) ratings.

Results

The leaderless group discussion appeared to have limited value in predicting officer potential as assessed by military personnel. Os' rating of leadership exhibited during a short leaderless discussion situation correlated with standardized military ratings based on long-term observation in approximately one half of the relationships (11/21). Of these, Air Force ratings that employed a forced-distribution technique were highly related to LGD ratings (5/6).

Study Variables

131) General abilities of members
         Officer potential: military (Army or Air Force) ratings of leader potential.
610) Leadership performance
         Leadership behavior: O rating during leaderless group discussion.

128.* Bass, B. M., & Klubeck, S. Effects of seating arrangement on leaderless group discussions. *J. abnorm. soc. Psychol.*, 1952, 47, 724–727.

Purpose

This experiment studied the effect of seating arrangements on individual performance in leaderless group discussions.

Procedure

Students in groups were seated in two different ways: a **V**-shaped arrangement and a rectangular arrangement. A leaderless group discussion period followed, during which Os rated the behavior of Ss in each arrangement.

Results

In general, differential leadership behavior within groups was not exhibited for groups operating under the two types of seating arrangements (3/23).

This study contained a total of 23 relationships.

Study Variables

152) Task or physical position in the group

Member seating arrangement: seating of Ss in rectangular or **V**-shaped arrangement during discussion.

610) Leadership performance

Leadership performance: O rating of S performance in leaderless group discussion.

132. Bass, B. M., & Wurster, C. R. Effects of company rank on LGD performance of oil refinery supervisors. *J. appl. Psychol.*, 1953, *37*, 100–104.

Purpose

This study investigated the extent to which a person's performance in a leaderless group discussion situation was influenced by his intelligence, job performance, and sociobiographical characteristics.

Procedure

About 20 supervisors at a time met for a week-long supervisory-training program. On the fourth day, they were subdivided into small groups to participate in leaderless group discussions with Os rating their leadership behavior. Also available for Ss were intelligence test scores and two criteria of on-the-job success as supervisors—forced choice and graphic ratings by their supervisors. In addition, personal data, such as rank in company, age, and similar background information, were available.

Results

The higher a person's LGD score, the more education, intelligence, and company rank he had (3/3), although LGD scores and S's age were not related (0/4).

Combined scores of Ss' success as supervisors did not relate to Ss' supervisory aptitude, intelligence, education, rank in company, LGD scores, and separate success measures (1/24).

When data about Ss' backgrounds (age, education, etc.) had been pooled to yield a single score, the new score likewise did not relate to education, age, rank in company, intelligence, supervisory aptitude, success as supervisors, and LGD scores (0/8).

Study Variables

110) Biographical characteristics of members
    Biographical characteristics: S education, age, position in company.
110) Biographical characteristics of members
131) General abilities of members
132) Task abilities of members
610) Leadership performance
    Combined biographical data, supervisory aptitude, intelligence, and leadership scores: S age, years of education, scores on intelligence test, supervisory aptitude battery, and LGD behavior.
131) General abilities of members
    Intelligence: S score on intelligence test.
132) Task abilities of members
    Supervisory aptitude: S scores on test battery.
430) Outcomes of interaction
    Discussion leadership: supervisor ratings
610) Leadership performance
    Leader job performance: O ratings of leadership exhibited in discussion.

133.* Bass, B. M., & Wurster, C. R. Effects of the nature of the problem on LGD performance. *J. appl. Psychol.*, 1953, *37*, 96–99.

Purpose

This study investigated how intelligence, supervisory aptitude, and background influenced leadership behavior in a leaderless group discussion setting. In addition, the consistency of leadership behavior in different situations was observed.

Procedure

Student LGD behavior was observed in various discussion situations, with individuals appearing in several conditions. In addition, individual oil refinery supervisors were exposed to one of four LGD situations. Os rated behavior of both types of Ss in terms of degree of leadership exhibited. Furthermore, information about supervisor's age, intelligence, rank in company, ratings of job success, and supervisory aptitude was obtained.

Results

For oil refinery supervisors, more-intelligent Ss exhibited leadership behavior more often during all types of discussions than did less-intelligent Ss (5/5). Moreover, Ss with higher rank and education exhibited more leadership behavior (10/10), although age related only slightly to leadership performance (1/5). Generally, *S*s rated as having more aptitude for supervision showed more leadership (3/5), although ratings of job success did not relate to leadership behavior (1/10).

For students, the data showed high consistency of leadership performance across several types of discussion situations (6/6).

This study contained a total of 48 relationships.

Study Variables

110) Biographical characteristics of members
> Biographical characteristics (rank, education, age): *S* statement of position in company, years of education, age.

131) General abilities of members
> Intellectual ability: *S* scores on IQ test.

132) Task abilities of members
> Supervisory aptitude: *S* performance in supervisory activities.

610) Leadership performance
> Leadership behavior: *O* rating of *S* leadership during leaderless group discussion.

621) Member task performance in experimental settings
> Member job performance: *O* ratings of supervisors.

136. Bass, B. M., et al. Personality variables related to leaderless group discussion behavior. *J. abnorm. soc. Psychol.*, 1953, *48*, 120–128.

Purpose

This investigation was designed to study the association of leaderless group discussion behavior with various personality characteristics.

Procedure

Groups of college girls conducted a leaderless discussion. *O*s used a checklist to rate each girl on exhibited leadership behavior. Following the discussion, *S*s with high and low leadership scores were interviewed or administered the Rorschach test. Interviews were recorded and responses analyzed in such terms as satisfaction with the discussion and attitudes toward own and others' behavior and characteristics. Prior to the study, *S*s were administered a battery of psychological tests including personality and attitude measures. Personality, attitude, and interview measures were related to leadership scores.

Results

Leadership exhibited during leaderless group discussion was positively related to the number of Rorschach test responses, number of responses during the interview, favorableness of attitude exhibited during the interview, and expert ratings of leadership, ascendance, and social interests. There was a negative relationship to authoritarianism (6/6). Other personality characteristics were not related (0/8).

In addition, responses to the Rorschach test were positively related to attitudes expressed during the interview (2/3).

Study Variables

110) Biographical characteristics of members
> Source of *S* sample: selection of *S*s either from students or from the California sample on whom F-scale was standardized.

120) Personality characteristics of members
> Personality characteristics: *S* responses on the Guilford-Zimmerman Temperament Survey.
> General personality adjustment: *E* evaluation of *S* scores on Rorschach test.
> Number responses on Rorschach test: *O* count of the total responses on Rorschach test.
> Frequency of responses during interview: *O* count of the total responses during interview.
> Interview behavior: *O* categorization of *S* responses during interview.

132) Task abilities of members
> *S* leadership: expert evaluations of *S*s' responses on Rorschach test in regard to their leadership status.

142) Attitudes toward the situation
> Attitude expressed during interview: *O* rating of *S* attitude during interview.

144) Attitudes toward issues, concepts, ideologies
> Authoritarianism: *S* scores on California F-scale.

610) Leadership performance
> Leadership exhibited: *O* rating of *S* behavior during a leaderless group discussion period.

144. Bass, B. M., et al. Interacting effects of control, motivation, group practice, and problem difficulty on attempted leadership. *J. abnorm. soc. Psychol.*, 1958, *56*, 352–358.

Purpose

This study examined attempts at leadership as a function of differences in member control of others, member motivation, and task difficulty.

Procedure

College sophomores were administered a questionnaire to ascertain their motivation to enter advanced ROTC. On the basis of their responses, *S*s were assembled into five-man problem-solving groups that were high, medium, or low with respect to member motivation. Within each type of group, *S*s were arbitrarily differentiated in the amount of control over others they would have—i.e., how much weight each *S* would have in evaluating other *S*s' performances. In addition, groups varied in the relative balance of control among members of a group; for example, some groups had members with equal control, whereas others had one member with a great deal of control over others. Members first privately ranked a series of words (varying in difficulty) with respect to familiarity, then carried on a group discussion and ranked the words as a group, and then again ranked them privately. Attempted leadership was measured by the amount of time that each S spent talking.

Results

Members of highly motivated groups displayed more attempts at leadership than did members of less-motivated groups (1/1), as did those Ss who were assigned more control over others (2/3). No such differences in attempted leadership occurred as a function of problem difficulty, amount of practice, or relative balance of control among group members (0/5).

In general there was only slight interaction of the main study variables (4/19), except as follows:

1. Highly motivated Ss attempted more leadership with continued group experience, whereas low-motivated Ss declined in leadership attempts (1/1).

2. Ss with more control showed more leadership attempts if they were highly motivated but only in groups where there was a disproportionate distribution of member control (1/1). No such difference occurred in more-balanced control conditions (0/1).

Study Variables

142) Attitudes toward the situation

Motivation: S questionnaire responses on desire to enter advanced ROTC.

Complaints about testing procedure: S posttest questionnaire responses.

152) Task or physical position in the group

Power of Ss: E assignment of varying power to Ss.

222) Group training and experience

Degree of practice: Ss work in different phases and with different problems.

240) General structural properties of the group

Individual groups: S division into different groups.

312) Induced social conditions

Distribution of power among group members: E manipulation of relative balance of power among group members.

321) Stimulus properties of the task

Problem difficulty: problems of varying difficulty level.

420) Patterns of interaction

Attempted leadership: total amount of time S spent talking.

510) Perceptions of task performance of self and others

Own behavior: S self-report of attempt to do a good job on test.

621) Member task performance in experimental settings
  Degree to which Ss returned questionnaires: E recording of Ss who returned questionnaires.

171. Bennett, Edith B. Discussion, decision, commitment, and consensus in "group decision." *Hum. Relat.*, 1955, *8*, 251–274.

Purpose

This study investigated the contributions of group discussion, requirement to reach a decision vs. no requirement, public commitment vs. anonymity, and group consensus on course of action in making a decision.

Procedure

Members of thirty-six groups were given a questionnaire regarding their reactions to a possible request to volunteer for an experiment. Then some groups discussed a topic, whereas others were only lectured on it. Some Ss in each type of group were then asked for an anonymous indication of their willingness to volunteer for a topic-related experiment, others for a show of hands, and others not at all. Coupled with the discussion and commitment variables was a request to certain groups to reach a definite decision. Groups were rated on their consensus or agreement statements and on general participation in the discussion. A few days later, letters were sent to all Ss asking them to appear for a special meeting, and a record was kept of their attendance. A week after the volunteering period, another questionnaire was given in order to determine the final, private reactions about willingness to volunteer.

Results

Degree of participation in discussion vs. lecture was not related either to the total number of Ss who came to the special meeting or to the number who reported positive decisions about participating in the experiment (0/6).

Degree of publicness of commitment and requirement to make a decision were only slightly related to favorable questionnaire responses or to actual appearance at the volunteering situation (2/8).

Degree of observer-rated group consensus in reaching decisions was positively related to the total number of Ss who came to the experiment (2/3) but not to the number of Ss who reported favorable decisions on the questionnaire items (1/7).

Study Variables

323) Induced task conditions.
  Publicity of the decision: E requirement for public, private, or no decision.
  Degree to which Ss were asked to make a decision: E requirement for a volunteer decision from Ss according to experiment.

420) Patterns of interaction

Discussion participation: *S* participation in discussion according to experimental instructions.

510) Perceptions of task performance of self and others

Self-reports of volunteering behavior: *S* postexperimental questionnaire responses.

621) Member task performance in experimental settings

Volunteering behavior: number of people who volunteered for the experiment, who gave positive responses, and so on.

182. Berkowitz, L. Sharing leadership in small, decision-making groups. *J. abnorm. soc. Psychol.*, 1953, *48*, 231–238.

Purpose

This study investigated the influence of individual behavior on cohesiveness, group productivity, and member satisfaction.

Procedure

Groups were observed during a problem-solving period and individual participations were categorized (for example, percentage of goal-setting or of solution-proposing remarks). Group productivity ratings were also obtained from observer ratings, along with judgments of group cohesion in terms of attractiveness of group situation, pleasantness of group atmosphere, and so on. On completion of the discussion, each member responded to a questionnaire indicating his satisfaction with the meeting. Then, Os filled out a postmeeting rating sheet about the behavior of leaders—e.g., leader control of process, permissiveness, etc. Individual behavior ratings were correlated with meeting satisfaction, group productivity, and cohesion scores.

Results

Generally, groups with more-permissive leaders were more cohesive (4/6), although no other type of leader or group member behavior related to group cohesiveness and productivity (11/118).

The more group members participated during the problem-solving discussion period, the less satisfied they were with the meeting (6/8). Other individual behavior ratings were only slightly related to member satisfaction with the conference (15/54).

Study Variables

141) Attitudes toward the task

Problem urgency: member ratings of problem urgency.

230) Interpersonal relations in the group

Cohesiveness: *O* ratings of the group.

410) Content of interaction

Discussion behavior (leader and member): *O* rating of control of procedure and permissiveness.

510) Perceptions of task performance of self and others
> Satisfaction with conference: participant ratings of leader and group after the meeting.

631) Group task performance in experimental setting
> Group productivity: O ratings of the group.

184.* Berkowitz, L. *Studies in group norms: the perception of group attitudes as related to criteria of group effectiveness.* San Antonio, Tex.: Lackland Air Force Base, Air Force Personnel and Training Research Center, November, 1954. *Res. Bull.* AFPTRC-TR-54–62.

Purpose

This study examined the influence of own and perceived task-oriented motivation of others on individual and crew performance.

Procedure

Members of bomber crews were administered a measure of their perception of the task-oriented motivation of their fellow crew members together with a scale tapping their own motivation for having an effective crew and their liking of their crew. Accuracy of perception of motivation was based upon the discrepancy between estimated and actual responses on the attitude scale. Measures of crew performance effectiveness were obtained either from instructor ratings or from the incidence of task-avoidance behavior (sick calls, failure to complete missions, and so on).

Results

Individual motivation to have an effective crew was not related to any of the measures of individual or crew performance effectiveness (0/18). In addition, there was only a slight relationship between perceptions of the crew's task motivation and individual and group performance (10/54). Finally, there was slight association of accuracy of perception of crew motivation and the various performance measures (6/38).

This study contained a total of 121 relationships.

Study Variables

141) Attitudes toward the task
> Member attitude (motivation to have effective crew): S responses to an attitude scale.
> Perceived member attitude (motivation to have an effective crew): S responses to an attitude scale estimating others' responses.
> Accuracy of social perception (task motivation): the difference between actual crew member attitudes and perceived member attitude scores.

622) Member task performance in operational settings: global measures
> Member performance: superior ratings of crew during training period

632) Group task performance in operational settings: global measures
Crew effectiveness in training: ratings of crews during training period on coordination, failure to complete mission, and so on.

189. Berkowitz, L. Liking for the group and the perceived merit of the group's behavior. *J. abnorm. soc. Psychol.*, 1957, *54*, 353–357.

Purpose

This study compared conformity and ratings of partner task skill in terms of perceived accuracy and congeniality of the partners.

Procedure

Volunteer pairs were assigned to one of four conditions of congeniality and proficiency. *S*s' task was to estimate targets for artillery fire, with one member of the pair acting as observer and the other as commander. *S*s were informed that they had been paired on the basis of personal compatibility. Unknown to *S*s, each member acted only as commander; a tape recorder provided observer communications. When the "commander" received the "observer's" estimate, he verified it by reference to a map and marked down the correct distance. During preliminary trials, *E* varied perceived partner proficiency by verifying or failing to verify the observer estimate. After each block of trials, *S* wrote the percentage of observer correct estimates. At the end, *S*s also completed a questionnaire describing their liking for the observer. *S*'s conformity score was the discrepancy between his and the observer's target estimates.

Results

Although perceived partner congeniality and proficiency were not related to conformity (0/2), compatible *S*s conditioned to perceive their partners as proficient conformed more than did incompatible *S*s (3/3), with no differences noted in the low-proficiency condition (0/2). *S*s with proficient partners conformed more than did *S*s with low-proficiency partners in the high-congeniality condition but not in the low-congeniality condition (1/2).

High-compatible *S*s rated their partners as more accurate than did low-compatible *S*s (3/3), and *S*s in high-proficiency pairs rated their partners as more accurate than did *S*s in low-proficiency pairs (2/3).

Study Variables

312) Induced social conditions
Perceived congeniality between members: *E* instructions to *S*s concerning compatibility with partner.
Perceived partner proficiency: *E* "input" faking correctness–incorrectness of partner.

430) Outcomes of interaction
Conformity: member decision relative to correct estimate in relation to partner's estimate.

510) Perceptions of task performance of self and others

Estimate of accuracy of partner: member estimate of correctness of partner's judgment.

201. Berrien, F. K., & Angoff, W. H. *Homeostasis theory of small groups.* New Brunswick, N.J.: Rutgers University, December, 1957. (Tech. Rep., Contract Nonr 404(10))

Purpose

This study examined work group productivity as a function of various factors including member judgments of supervisor and task involvement.

Procedure

Questionnaire responses were obtained from drivers employed by a company that delivered merchandise to homes. Several measures of performance were derived and related to a series of predictor variables. The performance measures were driver productivity, based on company performance records; group effectiveness, based on supervisor ratings; and member ratings of the general effectiveness of their own group. A measure of adaptability to changes in work schedules was also obtained. These criterion measures were then related to a series of predictor variables such as satisfaction with supervisor's competence, supervisory procedures, the company, and the job.

Results

There was no relationship between individual driver job productivity and feelings of task involvement, satisfaction with supervisor competence or leadership, and differences in supervisor and member perceptions (0/10). Groups that were less adaptable to such matters as changes in schedules showed a higher relationship between productivity and feelings of group competence than did groups more flexible about work schedules (1/2).

There was no relationship between measures of group performance and the various predictor variables (1/14), nor was there a relationship between member judgments of group productivity and predictor variables (2/17).

Study Variables

141) Attitudes toward the task

Task involvement: S questionnaire responses.

142) Attitudes toward the situation

Satisfaction with company: S questionnaire responses.

Group adjustment to changes in work schedule: S questionnaire responses.

Satisfaction with company: S questionnaire responses.

510) Perceptions of task performance of self and others

Discrepancy between perceptions of group by supervisors and by members: questionnaire scores.

Group performance: S rating of adequacy of group performance.
Discipline imposed by supervisor: S questionnaire responses.
Satisfaction with leadership: S questionnaire responses.
Communication between superior and group: S questionnaire responses.

623) Member task performance in operational settings: specific measures
Driver productivity: company ratings of driver productivity based on work standards.

633) Group task performance in operational settings: specific measures
Group effectiveness: supervisor ratings of groups.

212. Bieri, J. Changes in interpersonal perceptions following social interaction. *J. abnorm. soc. Psychol.*, 1953, *48*, 61–66.

Purpose

This study investigated the effects of interaction on the similarity with which members of pairs perceived each other.

Procedure

Twenty-six pairs of subjects met separately and each S completed the Rosenzweig Picture-Frustration Study as he himself would answer and as he thought his partner would probably answer. Pairs were assigned to experimental or control conditions. The experimental Ss engaged in two short discussions, whereas the controls merely wrote individual compositions without discussion. Then each S again completed the Rosenzweig instrument as he thought his partner would. Congruency of response scores on both occasions was compared, as well as behaviors observed during the experimental discussions.

Results

Unequivocally, interaction led to a higher perceived similarity between partners. Although Ss in the control condition, with no discussion of the topics on which they wrote, did not significantly differ in their projected responses to the initial and later Rosenzweig instruments (0/1), experimental S's predictions of their partner's responses following the discussion were significantly more like their own responses than were the same predictions made prior to interaction (1/1). In addition, experimental Ss had a greater increase in perceived similarity than did the controls (2/2). No discussion behavior differences were noted (0/3).

Study Variables

240) General structural properties of the group
Degree of member interaction in discussion: E assignment of Ss to discussion or no-discussion conditions.

410) Content of interaction
Discussion behavior: E record of member behavior according to Bales categories.

520) Perceptions of social behavior of self and others

> Congruency of self-response and predicted other-member responses: discrepancy between own and projected responses.

252. Borg, W. R. The behavior of emergent and designated leaders in situational tests. *Sociometry*, 1957, *20*, 95–104.

Purpose

This study compared the behavior of group members and leaders in problem-solving groups, with and without designated and emergent leaders.

Procedure

Six-man groups were given 12 problems to solve. During the first six problems, a leader was not designated, whereas one member was appointed as group leader for the last series of problems. Os rated group members on 11 categories of leadership behavior exhibited during discussions. Emergent leaders were identified as those having high leader behavior scores on the first six problems. Comparisons were made between designated leader, emergent leader, and group member discussion behavior.

Results

While non-emergent leaders behaved no differently after being designated as leaders, emergent leaders were significantly less effective when another team member was designated as leader (1/2). However, emergent leaders still continued to exhibit more leadership than did other members, even when another member of the group was designated as leader (1/1).

In addition, groups in which emergent leadership occurred had a higher average member leadership score than did those in which no emergent leadership occurred (3/3).

Study Variables

152) Task or physical position in the group

> Leadership position: *E* assignment of member as designated leader, *E* assignment of emergent leader as designated leader, and so on. Group leadership: *E* designation of leader and absence of such designation.

410) Content of interaction

> Leadership behavior: *O* rating of members' behavior in discussion behavior categories—e.g., initiating discussion, action, and so on.

610) Leadership performance

> Degree of occurrence of emergent leadership in groups: *E* designation of whether groups had none, one, or two leaders.

254. Borg, W. R., & Tupes, E.C. Personality characteristics related to leadership behavior in two types of small group situational problems. *J. appl. Psychol.*, 1958, *42*, 252–256.

Purpose

This study investigated the relationship between personality characteristics and leadership performance in different task situations.

Procedure

OCS candidates were assigned to two tasks in which leadership performance was observed. One task required solution of a simulated military problem, and the other was a leaderless group discussion. In both situations, raters judged the adequacy of leadership behavior exhibited by *S*s. Several sets of personality measures were obtained, based on judgments by upperclassmen after a short period of observation and by members of various peer groups on two occasions. Personality characteristics that were tested for relationship to leadership scores included such categories as extroversion, assertiveness, social maturity, and neuroticism.

Results

1. Short-term observer personality trait ratings
   a. Military problem leadership score
      (1) Assertiveness, orderliness, and energy: highly and positively related to score (3/3)
      (2) Other traits: not related to score (0/10)
   b. Leaderless group discussion score
      (1) Extroversion, intelligence, assertiveness, social maturity, attentiveness, orderliness, adaptability, energy, and over-all ratings: highly positively related to score (9/9)
      (2) Other traits: not related to score (0/4)
2. Short-term peer personality trait ratings,
   a. Military problem leadership score
      (1) Extroversion, assertiveness, conventionality, energy, neuroticism, social maturity, determination, and over-all ratings: highly and positively related to score (8/8)
      (2) Other traits: not related to score (0/5)
   b. Leaderless group discussion score
      (1) Extroversion, intelligence, assertiveness, social maturity, attentiveness, energy, and over-all ratings: highly and positively related to score (7/7)
      (2) Other traits: not related to score (0/6)
3. Long-term peer personality ratings
   a. Military problem leadership score
      (1) Extroversion, assertiveness, conventionality, and energy: highly and positively related to score (4/4)

    (2) Adjustment: high and negative relationship to score (1/1)

    (3) Other ratings: not related to score (0/8)

  b. Leaderless group discussion score

    (1) Extroversion, intelligence, determination, assertiveness, social maturity, neuroticism, adaptability, energy, and over-all ratings: highly and positively related to score (9/9)

    (2) Other traits: not related to score (0/4)

Furthermore, combined leadership scores on both tasks were highly and positively related to ratings of extroversion, intelligence, assertiveness, social maturity, and energy (6/6), but not to any other personality traits (0/7).

Study Variables

120) Personality characteristics of members

        Combined ratings of personality traits: O and co-worker ratings of S personality traits—e.g., extroversion, assertiveness.

        Type of personality traits rated: traits (orderliness, for example) of Ss rated on personality test.

        Personality traits: flight mates' ratings of S personality traits after six-months observation.

        Personality traits: flight mates' ratings of S personality traits.

        Personality traits: upperclassman's ratings of S traits based on one-hour observations.

321) Stimulus properties of the task

        Type of group problem situation: assignment of groups to solve either leaderless group discussion problem or small group leadership test.

        Type of rating procedure: E use of hourly, daily, or monthly rating procedures.

610) Leadership performance

        Leadership performance: O rating of S leadership during leaderless group discussion.

        Combined leadership score: officers' and upperclassmen's ratings of S leadership in general and in group problem-solving situation.

        Leadership performance: O ratings of leadership in leaderless group discussion and in group problem-solving situation.

        Homogeneity of personality and leadership ratings: similarity of personality and leadership ratings.

272. Borgatta, E. F., et al. Some findings relevant to the great man theory of leadership. *Amer. sociol. Rev.*, 1954, *19*, 755–759.

Purpose

This experiment studied the consistency of leadership behavior over several types of discussion situations.

Procedure

Three Ss worked together as a group and were rated on three leadership criteria: *task ability*, or peer ratings and IQ scores; *individual assertiveness*, or total activity rate of individual rated on Bales Interaction Process Analysis; and *social acceptability*, or sociometric popularity rated by other group members. Then, each S met with new group members. Discussion behavior was coded on Bales categories in terms of suggestions, agreement, tension release, solidarity, and tension. Results of groups with men with high leadership scores were compared with results from other groups according to Bales categories over the course of several sessions.

Results

The stability with which good leaders retained top positions in discussion behavior in subsequent groups was shown by the data. Ss in groups having leaders always gave more suggestions, showed more agreement, tension release, solidarity, and less tension than did Ss in groups without such leaders (5/5).

Furthermore, the reliability of the leadership measures was high (1/1).

Study Variables

131) General abilities of members

151) Social position in the group

Leadership: combined S and E ratings of group member on intellectual ability, discussion behavior, and sociometric popularity.

410) Content of interaction

Discussion behavior: O ratings of S behavior according to Bales categories.

285. Bovard, E. W., Jr. Conformity to social norms and attraction to the group. *Science*, 1953, *118*, 598–599.

Purpose

This study examined conformity to the group's judgment as a function of members' attraction to the group.

Procedure

College students were divided into 23 groups of from 5 to 13 members each. Group members were asked to estimate anonymously the number of dots in a square containing 500 dots within a 30-second time limit. After the Ss had read out their estimates, a group average was computed and announced by E. Ss were then asked to re-estimate privately the number of dots. The extent to which Ss estimates changed in the direction of group average was used as a conformity measure. Ss were also asked to rate their group, on an 11-point scale, to indicate their attraction to the group.

Results

According to the results, attraction for the group was not a determinant of S conformity to group judgment (0/1).

Study Variables

230) Interpersonal relations in the group

Attraction to the group: S responses to rating scale.

430) Outcomes of interaction

Conformity: difference between initial private judgment of stimulus and judgment after exposure to group average.

298. Brodbeck, May. The role of small groups in mediating the effects of propaganda. *J. abnorm. soc. Psychol.*, 1956, *52*, 166–170.

Purpose

This study investigated the extent to which social support in free group discussion counteracted the effects of adverse propaganda.

Procedure

Volunteer students filled out questionnaires to show their opinions and levels of confidence on the issue of wire tapping. They then listened to a taped speech supporting the side of the question opposed to the majority opinion of the 12 to 15 Ss comprising each group. Next, they repeated the questionnaire and filled out another indicating those in the group (whose views had been made public) to whom they would like to listen or with whom they would like to speak on the issue. Free discussion of the issue by the entire group followed. Ss again filled out the attitude questionnaire at the end of the session.

Results

Social support in free discussion was found to strengthen the confidence of Ss holding an opinion contrary to the view presented in a propaganda message: Ss with propaganda-opposed views who selected partners with similar viewpoints recovered significantly more of their initial confidence after the discussion than did those Ss choosing partners with different viewpoints (1/1). The former Ss also showed a higher confidence recovery after discussion than did those Ss in agreement with the propaganda message (1/1).

No differential preferences for a supportive partner were noted for Ss agreeing or disagreeing with the communication (0/4).

Study Variables

144) Attitudes toward issues, concepts, ideologies

Opinion on issue: S questionnaire responses giving own opinion on wire tapping.

230) Interpersonal relations in the group
Preference for supportive communication partner: *S* questionnaire rating of choice of listening and speaking partners from the group.

430) Outcomes of interaction
Recovery of initial confidence in opinion after discussion: *S* rating of own confidence in opinion before and after discussion.

308. Browne, C. G. A study of executive leadership in business: I. The R, A, and D scales. *J. appl. Psychol.*, 1949, *33*, 521–526.

Purpose

This study interrelated executives' perceived self-authority, self-responsibility, and degree of delegation of authority to assistants.

Procedure

Scales measuring responsibility, authority, and delegation of authority of executives were administered to a group of 24 executives in a tire-and-rubber manufacturing company. Data were obtained during a moderately structured interview, although some of the scales were completed at another time. In addition, data were collected concerning such factors as salary and length of time spent working with others.

Results

Executives who felt they had more responsibility and who delegated more authority had higher feelings of authority (2/2). On the other hand, delegation of authority was not related to perception of self-responsibility (0/1).

The higher the salary that *S*s had, the more they delegated authority to assistants and the higher were their feelings of authority and responsibility (3/3). In addition, men chosen as the ones with whom *S*s worked together most of the time were the ones who delegated the authority to others (1/1). There was no such association with the measure of self-responsibility and self-authority (0/2).

Length of time *S*s reported they spent in supervision was not related to their perception of authority or responsibility, or to the degree to which they delegated authority to their assistants (0/3).

Study Variables

110) Biographical characteristics of members
Background characteristics: executive salary echelon.

230) Interpersonal relations in the group
Sociometric choice: *S* listing of those with whom they worked most of the time.

510) Perceptions of task performance of self and others
Own job habits (perceived self-authority, delegation of authority, and so on): questionnaire responses.

315. Bryant, H. A., et al. *Group effectiveness, coercion, change, and coalescence among delinquents compared to non-delinquents.* Baton Rouge, La.: Louisiana State University, 1958. (Tech. Rep. No. 15, Contract N7 ONR 35609)

Purpose

This study investigated the performance effectiveness and judgmental agreement of members of delinquent and nondelinquent groups.

Procedure

*S*s were groups of delinquent and nondelinquent boys matched for age and intelligence. Each group member privately ranked five cities according to size. Afterwards, there was a discussion followed by a group decision. Then, a final private decision was obtained from each individual. Measures of agreement and accuracy of judgment within and between members and groups were derived and compared for delinquent and nondelinquent groups and for different age groups.

Results

1. Performance effectiveness measures
    a. Individual performance
        (1) Accuracy of individual and final private judgments: highly and positively related to age (3/3); initial accuracy highly related to nondelinquency (3/3), final accuracy not related to measures of delinquency (0/2)
        (2) Change in accuracy of private judgments: not related to measures of age, delinquency, or their interaction (0/3)
    b. Accuracy of group performance: not related to measures of age, delinquency, or their interaction (0/3)
    c. Accuracy of composite individual and group performance (accuracy of group decision as compared with that of average initial private judgment): not related to measures of age, delinquency, or their interaction (0/3)

2. Agreement of judgments among members and group
    a. Individual agreement
        (1) Agreement of initial and final private judgments: highly and positively related to age and nondelinquency (4/4)
        (2) Private coalescence (increase in agreement from initial to final judgments): not related to measures of age, delinquency, or their interaction (0/3)
        (3) Stability (average correlation between initial and final judgments): not related to measures of age, delinquency, or their interaction (0/3)
    b. Member judgments compared with group judgments
        (1) Agreement of initial private judgments with group judgments: highly and positively related to age and nondelinquency (2/2); not related to interaction of measures of age and delinquency (0/1)

(2) Agreement of final private judgments: highly related to age and nondelinquency (2/2); not related to interaction of measures of age and delinquency (0/1)

c. Comparison of differences between member and group judgments, and member judgments

    (1) Public coalescence (agreement of member final private decision with group decision compared with initial agreement between individuals): not related to measures of age, delinquency, or their interaction (0/3)

Study Variables

110) Biographical characteristics of members

    Biographical characteristic: age.

    Degree of delinquency: Ss selected from public schools or delinquent homes.

430) Outcomes of interaction

    Increase in private judgment accuracy: difference between final private accuracy and initial private accuracy of members in judging problems.

    Stability of private opinion: change in member judgments.

    Agreement among members: similarity of member judgments.

    Private coalescence: increase in agreement of member judgments.

    Agreement between member and group judgment: differences between individual and group judgments.

    Public coalescence: agreement of S final private judgment with group decision compared with initial agreement among members.

621) Member task performance in experimental settings

    Private accuracy in judgment: E record of number of problems members solved correctly.

631) Group task performance in experimental settings

    Accuracy of group performance: E rating of group judgment accuracy.

    Increase in public accuracy: the extent to which group decision was more accurate than average accuracy of initial judgments of members.

319. Bugental, Daphne E., & Lehner, G. F. J. Accuracy of self-perception and group-perception as related to two leadership roles. *J. abnorm. soc. Psychol.*, 1958, *56*, 396–398.

Purpose

This study investigated whether the popular group member was generally more "insightful" or if his accuracy of perception was related specifically to his role within the group.

Procedure

Students were randomly divided into five groups with from 8 to 11 Ss each. Each person rated all members of his group on leadership and popularity variables on an 18-item description questionnaire, his own group on the

Hemphill Group Dimensions Description Questionnaire, and himself on the Guilford-Zimmerman Temperament Survey and on a self-rating test.

Results

Popular group members had more accurate perception of others on popularity variables and of the group as a whole than did the group leaders (2/2).

No significant differences were found between popular members and leaders in accuracy of self-perception or in perception of others on leadership variables (0/2).

Study Variables

120) Personality characteristics of members

Accuracy of perception on personality variables: similarity of S ratings of themselves on the Guilford-Zimmerman Temperament Survey and on a self-rating test.

151) Social position in the group

Status in the group (popularity): S ratings of other members on popularity.

510) Perceptions of task performance of self and others

Status in the group (leadership): S ratings of other members on leadership.

Accuracy in perception (leadership): average difference between member ratings and the average of group ratings of leadership status of a member.

520) Perceptions of social behavior of self and others

Accuracy of perception (popularity): difference between S judgment and average of member judgments of popularity of other members.

Accuracy in perception (group characteristics): comparison of S ratings of his own group with average of member responses to a questionnaire.

344. Canning, R. R., & Baker, J. M. Effect of the group on authoritarian and non-authoritarian persons. *Amer. J. Sociol.*, 1959, *64*, 579–581. (Abstract)

Purpose

This study measured differential effects of group pressure upon Ss with authoritarian personalities and Ss with nonauthoritarian personalities.

Procedure

Authoritarian–nonauthoritarian personality scales were given to 234 introductory sociology students, and Ss with extreme scores were selected. Each S was tested in three situations requiring judgments of the movement of a light source (autokinetic phenomena): an initial individual test; a group test, in which confederates were instructed to give extreme judgments; and a second individual test.

Results

*S*s working in groups and exposed to group pressures perceived more movement of the light stimulus than did *S*s working individually. These results obtained for both authoritarian and nonauthoritarian personalities (3/3).

There was no relationship between sex or age and reactions to group pressure (0/2).

Study Variables

110) Biographical characteristics of members
     Biographical characteristics: sex, age.

240) General structural properties of the group
     Social facilitation: *S*s making judgments alone or in groups.

621) Member task performance in experimental settings
     Perceived movement of light stimulus: *S* judgment on autokinetic tests.

351. Carey, Gloria L. Sex differences in problem-solving performance as a function of attitude differences. *J. abnorm. soc. Psychol.*, 1958, *56*, 256–260.

Purpose

This study investigated how sex differences related to differences in problem-solving attitudes and performance. The study also examined changes in performance as a function of changes in attitudes.

Procedure

A scale designed to measure attitude toward problem solving and a series of problems were administered to groups of mixed sex. Group discussion followed for some groups. During a postdiscussion session, *S*s were administered an alternate form of the original attitude scale and a second set of problems.

Results

Men had more positive attitudes toward problem solving than did women (4/4), but there was only a slight relationship between attitude toward problem solving and performance (2/8).

On the other hand, women improved more in problem-solving performance, particularly when working in discussion groups (2/3).

Study Variables

110) Biographical characteristics of members
     Sex: *S* self-report of sex.

144) Attitudes toward issues, concepts, ideologies
     Attitude toward problem solving: *S* responses to attitude scale.

222) Group training and experience
     Degree of practice: *S*s work during different sessions.

240) General structural properties of the group
     Degree of discussion: *S* assignment to discussion and nondiscussion groups.

321) Stimulus properties of the task
     Sex of *E: E* statement of sex.

621) Member task performance in experimental settings
     Level of performance: *S* performance on problem-solving task.

361. Carter, L. F., et al. A further investigation of the criteria of leadership. *J. abnorm. soc. Psychol.*, 1950, *45*, 350–358.

Purpose

This study examined the intercorrelations of several measures of leadership in different task situations.

Procedure

Student groups worked on six different types of problems. *O*s recorded activities and conversations during work periods and at the end of each task rated every *S* on a leadership scale. Furthermore, leadership ratings were obtained from group members, friends, and faculty members.

Results

About half of the associations testing the reliability of the observer judgments of leadership across tasks were significant (16/31). Observer judgments of leadership were also highly related to group member leader nomination scores (5/7) but were not related either to friend or faculty-member leadership ratings or to participation in extracurricular activities (0/6).

In general, leader nomination ratings made by others in the group were reliable in half the cases (9/17) and were not related to either faculty-member ratings or extracurricular activity scores (0/4).

Leadership ratings by friends were not reliable (0/3), nor did such ratings relate to faculty-member ratings or to participation in extracurricular activities (0/4). Faculty-member ratings were also unreliable and unrelated to extracurricular activities (0/5). Extracurricular activity records, however, proved to be highly reliable measures of leadership (1/1).

Study Variables

132) Task abilities of members
     Faculty ratings of leadership: faculty members' scoring of *S*s for leadership.

151) Social position in the group
     Leadership nomination: members' and friends' scoring of others.

510) Perceptions of task performance of self and others
     Outside activities: extracurricular activities in school and social organizations.

610) Leadership performance
     Effective leadership performance: *O* rating of leadership performance.

362. Carter, L. F., et al. The behavior of leaders and other group members. *J. abnorm. soc. Psychol.*, 1951, 46, 589–595.

Purpose

This study contrasted the discussion behavior of appointed and emergent leaders with that of other group members on three types of tasks: a reasoning problem, a mechanical assembly task, and a discussion task.

Procedure

NROTC students were given pretest sociometric measures on friendship and leadership and divided into groups having Ss with nearly equal leadership and low friendship scores. These groups met in a leaderless discussion situation, and each S was rated by Os on leadership. From these ratings, Ss were further subdivided into groups of equal leadership and required to work on three tasks: a reasoning problem, a mechanical assembly task, and a discussion problem. After one meeting during which these tasks were performed, one member was replaced by an S with equal leadership ability from another group, and the new S was designated leader. Groups then performed the same three types of tasks and were rated by Os on a 53-item coding system. At the end of each task, Os also rated Ss on a scale measuring a number of characteristics, including leadership.

Results

Although appointed and emergent leaders displayed equal over-all leadership ability (0/3), they were differentiated by specific behaviors. Appointed leaders more frequently asked for opinions and desired and initiated action than did other group members (6/7), whereas emergent leaders proposed more courses of action and were more active in general than were other members (6/6). Both appointed and emergent leaders were differentiated from the other Ss by more frequently diagnosing the situation and giving action information to groups (6/6). These distinctions held for all three types of tasks.

Slight differences were noted between appointed and emergent leaders and other group members in calling for attention, asking for information, supporting own proposals, agreeing and approving, giving information, showing insight, expressing opinion, disagreeing, arguing, integrating group behavior, offering to help, performing work units, and doing nothing (17/74).

Study Variables

151) Social position in the group
   Leadership position: E appointment of S as leader or nonleader.

410) Content of interaction
   Discussion behavior: O rating of behavior according to Bales categories.

610) Leadership performance
   Leadership ability: O over-all rating of S on leadership during meetings.
   Occurrence of emergent leadership: O rating of S on leadership.

384. Cervin, V. Experimental investigation of behavior in social situations: II. Individual behavioral effects of change in group attitude from opposition to cooperation. *Canad. J. Psychol.*, 1955, *9*, 155–160.

Purpose

In this study, discussion behavior was related to variations in personality characteristics and the type of social support received from other group members.

Procedure

Three student groups created stories after viewing TAT pictures. Three of the group members were experimenter-confederates who were instructed to be supportive of suggestions made by naïve *S*s. Each naïve *S* had also been previously exposed to a situation in which his ideas were vigorously opposed by the same confederates. *S*s varied in personality characteristics, some having low and others high emotional instability scores on a personality questionnaire. Behavior was measured in terms of response latency, length of speeches (time speaking–time silent), and total group time needed to create a story.

Results

In general, those receiving support for their behavior from confederate members had lower latencies of response and less variability in response times than did those whose ideas were negated by others (4/4). Furthermore, those who were given positive support and who had more-stable personalities spoke at greater length and needed less time to complete the task (2/2). No such results occurred for those with less-stable personalities (0/2).

There was a slight relationship between the degree of stability of personality and response latency or length of time needed to complete the task (2/12).

Study Variables

120) Personality characteristics of members

Personality stability: *S* responses to a personality questionnaire.

323) Induced task conditions

Support received from another *S:* confederate support of or opposition to *S*.

621) Member task performance in experimental settings

Response characteristics: *E* record of *S* verbal responses (latency, length).

631) Group task performance in experimental settings

Task completion time: *E* record of time the group needed to complete the task.

Task completion time: tape recording to indicate time needed to complete the task.

398. Child, I. L., & Whiting, J. W. M. Determinants of level of aspiration: evidence from everyday life. *J. abnorm. soc. Psychol.*, 1949, *44*, 303–314.

Purpose

This study investigated the effects of goal success, goal importance, and confidence on level of aspiration for similar future goals.

Procedure

Psychology students were required to write a description of three incidents in their lives: complete frustration with no goal attainment; initial frustration followed by goal attainment; and simple goal attainment with no appreciable frustration. Ss checked one of several items describing the effect of each incident on hopes for achieving a similar future goal (level of aspiration). They also rated whether personal confidence increased or decreased afterwards and the strength of their reaction to complete frustration.

Results

In general, success led to a raising of level of aspiration and failure to a lowering (4/5). Also, Ss were more inclined to set a definite level of aspiration for incidents of simple success or failure than for incidents of frustration followed by goal attainment (1/1). In the latter case they frequently rated the concept as meaningless in connection with the particular incident. Greater change in general occurred with successful goal attainment (1/1).

Highly important goals more frequently led to a raising of level of aspiration than did those of less consequence (2/3). Ss who greatly increased or decreased in confidence as a result of simple success or failure also set differential levels of aspiration—an increased level of aspiration with increased confidence, a decreased level of aspiration with decreased confidence (2/2).

Study Variables

141) Attitudes toward the task

Extent to which level of aspiration to a future similar goal was raised: S rating of incident as lowering, raising, or not affecting future level of aspiration.

142) Attitudes toward the situation

Importance of goal attainment (reaction to complete frustration, feeling of ability to attain similar goal): S ratings of past incidents in terms of importance; S reaction to complete frustration incidents.

510) Perceptions of task performance of self and others

Success in goal attainment: S report of past incidents meeting with each degree of success (complete frustration, frustration followed by goal attainment, simple goal attainment).

404. Christner, C. A., & Hemphill, J. K. Leader behavior of B-29 comman
ders and changes in crew members' attitudes toward the crew. *Sociometry*, 1955, *18*, 82–87.

Purpose

This study investigated how leader behavior affected changes in air crew member attitudes toward their crew and toward other crew members.

Procedure

Members of B-29 crews were given a questionnaire measuring their leader's consideration or human relations behavior and his supervisory ability. In addition, members responded to a sociometric instrument tapping their feelings of attraction toward individual group members and toward the crew as a whole. These latter instruments were administered before and after a training period.

Results

Leader consideration of crew members was associated with a significant increase in member feelings of friendship with each other, willingness to go to combat with one another, confidence in other crew members, and communication with each other while on duty (4/4). There was no relationship to any other measures (0/6).

Leader organizing and supervisory abilities did not relate to positive changes in crew member attitudes (0/8) except to friendship and confidence among members (2/2).

Furthermore, communication off and on duty, friendliness, proficiency, and confidence of members in each other were greater after training (5/5).

Study Variables

222) Group training and experience
> Time when test was administered: S test before or after training.

230) Interpersonal relations in the group
> Sociometric choice of crew members: S ratings of friendliness, willingness to go to combat, and so on.
> Member friendship: S friendliness, willingness to go to combat, and so on.

510) Perceptions of task performance of self and others
> Supervisory structuring and organizing by leader: S ratings of leader.

520) Perceptions of social behavior of self and others
> Communication with crew members on and off duty: S ratings of communication with others.
> Degree of individual morale: S ratings of crew member morale.
> Consideration shown by leader: S ratings of leader.
> Desirability of crew: S ratings of crew morale, crew cooperation, and so on.

411.* **Cleven, W. A., & Fiedler, F. E.** *The relations of open hearth foreman's interpersonal perceptions to steel production.* Urbana, Ill.: University of Illinois, Department of Psychology, October 1955. (Tech. Rep. No. 11, Contract N6 ORI 07135)

Purpose

This study was concerned with how differences in perception of co-workers relate to industrial work group productivity.

Procedure

Steelworker hearth foremen responded to a personality questionnaire from different points of view: as they felt the man with whom they worked best would respond and as they felt the man with whom they worked least effectively would respond. On the basis of these data, a measure of assumed similarity of opposites was derived to reflect the "distance" between predictions of the positive and negative co-workers. The assumed similarity score was related to an on-the-job measure of performance based on work output.

Results

In general, supervisors of more-effective shops differentiated significantly more sharply between their best and worst co-workers than did supervisors of less-effective shops (1/1). Separate analyses of four types of supervisors revealed this tendency among pit foremen and senior melters, however, but not among general foremen and stock foremen (2/4).

This study contained a total of seven relationships.

Study Variables

240) General structural properties of the group
   Individual groups: E selection of different shops in a steel company.

520) Perceptions of social behavior of self and others
   Assumed similarity of opposites: discrepancy between Ss' predicted self-trait ratings of best and worst co-workers.

633) Group task performance in operational settings: specific measures
   Group productivity: time required to complete task by steelworkers' group.

417. **Cohen, A. R.** Experimental effects of ego-defense preference on interpersonal relations. *J. abnorm. soc. Psychol.*, 1956, *52*, 19–27.

Purpose

This study investigated the effects of psychosexual disturbance, intensity of disturbance, and personality defense preference on reactions to discussions of projective group-story pictures.

Procedure

On the basis of Blacky Pictures Test scores, *S*s were paired for common psychosexual disturbance: oral sadism, anal expulsiveness, oedipal intensity, castration anxiety, or sibling rivalry. Pairs further varied from other pairs in terms of intensity of the disturbance and in terms of defense preference—projection, avoidance, regression, reaction formation, or intellectualization. Individual *S*s completed an "individual motive interpretation" blank on a series of stories—about home, school, social group—calculated to tap their disturbance and then discussed the same material in pairs for 15 minutes to reach interpretations agreeable to both. Next, *S*s completed a questionnaire individually, rating items designed to tap their negativism toward the session they had just completed.

Results

Projectors were significantly more negative toward the discussion situation and their partners than were *S*s with other defense tendencies, particularly when both members of the pair were projectors (25/32).

Compared with other defense pairs, whose members were either similar or dissimilar, projector pairs were higher in negativism toward the interpersonal situation, the quality of the group, their partners, and their impression of the group's success. In addition, they perceived their partners as hostile, self-interested, nonsupportive, unsuccessful, and trying to influence them. Projector pairs also reported a feeling of insecurity in the relationship, a lack of motivation, and attempts to influence their partners (24/24). Similar and dissimilar defense pairs (excluding projectors) were undifferentiated on all measures (0/16).

Results were not reported for comparisons between groups differing in psychosexual disturbance, disturbance intensity, and personality defense, and for groups of mixed projectors and nonprojectors. The author's ranking of groups in terms of negative reaction, however, was as follows: (1) sibling rivalry, (2) castration anxiety, (3) oral sadism, (4) anal expulsiveness, and (5) oedipal intensity.

Study Variables

120) Personality characteristics of members

> Personally defined states: insecurity in relationship, intensity of disturbance.

141) Attitudes toward the task

> Own achievement motivation: *S* questionnaire response following discussion with partner.
>
> Negativism toward task: *S* questionnaire response following discussion with partner.

230) Interpersonal relations in the group

> Negativism toward partner: *S* questionnaire response following discussion with partner.
>
> Negativism toward group: *S* questionnaire response following discussion with partner.

240) General structural properties of the group

      Group homogeneity with respect to projection personality-defense mechanism: *S*s paired on basis of responses to Blacky Pictures Test. Type of group members: personality defense.

510) Perceptions of task performance of self and others

      Impression of group success: *S* questionnaire response following discussion with partner.

      Attempt to influence partner: *S* questionnaire response following discussion with partner.

      Perception of own success: *S* questionnaire response following discussion with partner.

      Perception of partner as trying to influence: *S* questionnaire response following discussion with partner.

      Perception of partner's support and success: *S* questionnaire response following discussion with partner.

418. Cohen, A. R. Upward communication in experimentally created hierarchies. *Hum. Relat.*, 1958, *11*, 41–54.

Purpose

This study compared communication of persons in a low status as a function of their potentiality for moving to a higher status.

Procedure

*S*s were administered the Blacky Pictures Test of psychosexual adjustment and assigned to low-status groups on the basis of messages supposedly coming from a higher-status group. Groups differed in the low-status condition in terms of perceived mobility or chance to move upward to the high-status group. *E* induced mobile–non-mobile conditions by instruction. After the task, *S*s completed a questionnaire to state whether they wanted to continue the same job, move upward to a higher status job, or be eliminated altogether from a second task. Next, they were told that the second task was eliminated and they were to fill out a longer questionnaire about the attractiveness of the group, perceptions of the social structure, and so on. *S*s were compared in terms of mobility, psychosexual dimensions, communication patterns as analyzed by message content, and reactions to the group.

Results

Mobile and nonmobile low-status *S*s were differentiated in their communication behavior. Specifically, mobile *S*s sent shorter messages to their own group and longer ones to the high-status group (2/2), were less cohesive in their in-group communication (1/1), sent fewer irrelevant messages in general (3/3), conjectured more about the job in the upper group (1/1), and tended to criticize the upper group less (2/2).

Personality differences were also noted. In the mobile condition, high-conflict *S*s asked more questions about the job and high-regression *S*s sent more communications expressing a desire for support than did low-conflict and low-regression Ss (2/2). Low-conflict Ss in the nonmobile condition sent more communications indicating confusion (0/1).

   Ss were relatively undifferentiated in their reactions to the group. Mobile and nonmobile Ss reported equal attraction to the group and equal motivation to perform, and both types perceived support given their ideas from both status levels (0/3).

Study Variables

120) Personality characteristics of members

> Personal motivation, perception of own potential mobility: S postexperimental questionnaire responses.
> Personality adjustment: E description of low–high conflict Ss according to scores on Blacky Pictures Test.
> Regression behavior: S responses to items on Blacky Pictures Test.

141) Attitudes toward the task

> Importance of job: S postexperimental questionnaire responses.

142) Attitudes toward the situation

> Flexibility of social structure: S responses regarding possible alternatives in social situation.

151) Social position in the group

> Social status: E assignment of Ss to high- and low-status conditions.

323) Induced task conditions

> Perceived chance for mobility by low-status Ss: E's instructions to Ss on possibility of moving up with good performance.

410) Content of interaction
420) Patterns of interaction

> Communication activity: number of words sent to upper group and own group, types of messages sent to upper and own group, and so on.

510) Perceptions of task performance of self and others

> Perceived group support of own ideas: member questionnaire responses following experiment.

424. Cohen, J. D., & McKelvey, R. K. *The behavior of individuals and personnel systems in the surveillance functions of an Air Defense Direction Center: III. Distribution of responses with respect to job functions.* San Antonio, Tex.: Lackland Air Force Base, June, 1955. (Res. Rep. AFPTRC-TN-55-11)

Purpose

   This report described the job activities of aircraft control and warning operators in terms of three types of behavior.

Procedure

Six Ss were selected from several teams and rotated systematically through each job position: scope operator, plotter, and teller-recorder. Each team was observed for two 24-minute periods on three successive days. Trained Es coded performance, communication, and similar activities in terms of three categories: basic job-related activities, support activities, and nonessential activities.

Results

Examination of the data revealed a considerable difference in distribution of activities within behavior categories for the three positions, although directionality of the relationship was not reported (1/1).

The authors explained these differences as follows: "Responses by the teller-recorder position were confined almost exclusively to the basic tasks of the job, logging and telling. This was not the case at the scope and plotter positions, where a considerable portion of the behavior involved elaboration and clarification of information already in the system. While the incidence of nonfunctional motor and social responses appears in general to have been relatively low, a higher proportion of this type of behavior was exhibited at the scope position than in the others."

Study Variables

152) Task or physical position in the group
    Task position: S assignment to each job position via rotation.

410) Content of interaction
    Job behavior: O record of S performance in terms of job-related activities, support activities, and nonessential activities.

428.* Coleman, J. F., et al. Task difficulty and conformity pressures. *J. abnorm. soc. Psychol.*, 1958, 57, 120–122.

Purpose

This study investigated how task difficulty affected conformity to group judgment.

Procedure

In order to create an influence situation, students were led to believe they would be working in four-man groups. The task involved a factual-knowledge questionnaire with items varying in level of difficulty. Ss responded to each critical item after hearing the incorrect reports of the simulated group members. E scored the answers in terms of how frequently Ss yielded to the group judgment.

Results

The more difficult the problem, the greater was the conformity to group judgment (2/2). The results occurred for both male and female Ss.

This study contained a total of two relationships.

Study Variables

321) Stimulus properties of the task

> Test item difficulty: E presentation of items of varying difficulty level.

430) Outcomes of interaction

> Conformity: E score of frequency with which S yielded to incorrect group judgments.

429. Comrey, A. L. Group performance in a manual dexterity task. *J. appl. Psychol.*, 1953, *37*, 207–210.

Purpose

This study investigated the relationship between the motor performance of individuals and groups.

Procedure

Volunteer students individually tested on the Purdue Pegboard Test were paired on the basis of their individual performances and retested on a second series of trials as a pair. Three combinations of Ss were used: two high scorers, two low scorers, and one high and one low scorer. Performance during the second session was recorded as a group score.

Results

No data on statistical significance of relationships were reported. The author stated, "The results showed that less than half the group performance variance could be predicted from a knowledge of the individual performances, even with the effect of errors removed. The level of group performance was only slightly more dependent on the 'low' individual performances. For all practical purposes equal weights could be used for 'high' and 'low' scores in predicting 'group' performance."

Study Variables

621) Member task performance in experimental settings

> Accuracy of individual performance: S score on Purdue Pegboard Test.

631) Group task performance in experimental settings

> Accuracy of group performance: group (pair) score on Purdue Pegboard Test.

430. Comrey, A. L., & Deskin, G. Further results on group manual dexterity in men. *J. appl. Psychol.*, 1954, *38*, 116–118.

Purpose

This experiment determined the extent to which group performance could be predicted from the performance of individuals comprising the group.

Procedure

Members of student pairs were administered the Purdue Pegboard Test assembly task individually and then together. An attempt was made to make the group and individual task as comparable as possible. On the basis of scores, pairs were divided into "high" and "low" Ss. Intercorrelations were computed between individual and group scores.

Results

A previously reported experiment was repeated with an altered design to test the former results and the hypothesis offered to account for the fact that group performance scores on a manual dexterity task could only be predicted imperfectly from knowledge of individual scores on a similar task. The hypothesis that had been offered was that the prediction might be substantially improved by a change in design to make the group and individual tasks more comparable in the character of the operations involved. Despite these changes in procedure, the amount of improvement in prediction was so slight in the new experiment that the hypothesis was rejected.

Study Variables

621) Member task performance in experimental settings
        Accuracy of individual performance: S performance on Purdue Pegboard Test assembly task.

631) Group task performance in experimental settings
        Accuracy of group performance: group performance on Purdue Pegboard Test assembly task.

433.* **Comrey, A. L., et al.** Factors influencing organizational effectiveness: I. The U.S. forest survey. *Personnel Psychol.*, 1952, 5, 307–328.

Purpose

This study compared forestry management work group effectiveness as a function of group and leader characteristics.

Procedure

Questionnaires were administered to measure attitudes toward methods of supervision, administrative practices, and interpersonal relations to forestry management personnel varying in supervisory responsibility. In addition, experts ranked groups on how well various forests were managed. Questionnaire responses were related to expert rankings of forest management effectiveness.

Results

1. Member self-judgments
   a. Biographical characteristics (number of years spent in forestry): positively related to forestry management effectiveness (2/2)
   b. Judgments about own job relations (e.g., social distance, etc): highly related to forestry management effectiveness (3/3)

2. Member judgments of supervisor

    a. Supervisor activities (e.g., conveying information, etc.): moderately related to forestry management effectiveness (1/2)

    b. Effectiveness of supervisor activities (e.g., participation in activities, etc.): positively related to forestry management effectiveness (1/1)

    c. Supervisor personal interest in subordinates: positively related to forestry management effectiveness (1/1)

3. Member judgments of over-all group management

    a. Experience of management: positively related to forestry management effectiveness (1/1)

    b. Critical attitude toward management: negatively related to forestry management effectiveness (1/1)

    This study contained a total of 128 relationships.

Study Variables

143) Attitudes toward nongroup persons and other groups

    Criticism of management: S questionnaire rating of management.

222) Group training and experience

    Length of time with forestry group: S questionnaire response.

510) Perceptions of task performance of self and others

    Own job behavior: S questionnaire responses, on social distance between self and subordinates, formality of supervision, etc.

    Supervisor work characteristics: subordinate questionnaire rating of supervisor on interest in subordinates, etc.

    Others' job behavior: subordinate questionnaire rating of supervisor on information conveyed, etc.

    Others' job performance: S questionnaire rating, on supervisor interest in subordinates, worker cooperation, etc.

632) Group task performance in operational settings: global measures

    Group performance effectiveness: rangers' questionnaire rating of forest.

    Group management effectiveness: experts' ranking of forest districts on how well they functioned.

438.* Comrey, A. L., et al. Factors influencing organizational effectiveness: VI. A survey of aircraft workers. *Personnel Psychol.*, 1955, *8*, 79–99.

Purpose

This study compared industrial group performance effectiveness as a function of group and leader characteristics.

Procedure

Questionnaires measuring different characteristics of an industrial organization—its personnel and supervisory practices, and worker attitudes toward each other, their work, and the company—were administered to workers, supervisors, and foremen of an aircraft corporation. In addition, department performance effectiveness was measured in terms of production efficiency (the number of hours spent on reworking items), production quality (the number of incomplete jobs returned for corrections), production time (the number of hours required for job completion), and over-all efficiency. Questionnaire responses were then tested for relationships to the four performance criteria.

Results

1. Production efficiency (established by the number of hours spent reworking items)
   a. Characteristics and activities of supervisors
      (1) Supervisor dependability, knowledge of the job, judgment, organizing ability, helpfulness, and enforcement of safety rules: highly and positively related to efficiency (6/6)
      (2) Other measures: not related to efficiency (0/8)
   b. Characteristics of groups
      (1) Conflicts with authorities and attraction to group: high negative relationship to efficiency (2/2)
      (2) Other measures: not related to efficiency (0/3)

2. Production quality (established by the number of incomplete jobs returned for corrections)
   a. Characteristics and activities of supervisors
      (1) Knowledge about job and ability to organize: highly and positively related to quality (2/2)
      (2) Other measures: not related to quality (0/12)
   b. Characteristics of groups: not related to any measures of quality (0/5)

3. Production speed (established by the number of hours spent on completion of job)
   a. Characteristics and activities of supervisors
      (1) Arbitrariness, social distance, communication between superiors and subordinates, ability to make judgments, and enforcement of safety rules: highly and positively related to speed (5/5)
      (2) Other measures: not related to speed (0/9)
   b. Characteristics of groups: not related to speed (0/5)

4. Over-all efficiency
   a. Characteristics and activities of supervisors: not related to over-all efficiency (0/14)
   b. Characteristics of groups: not related to over-all efficiency (0/5)

Study Variables

132) Task abilities of members
     Supervisor job characteristics: subordinate ratings of superiors on knowledge about job, arbitrariness.

230) Interpersonal relations in the group
     Group characteristics: group member rating of own departments on discord, attraction to the group, and so on.

430) Outcomes of interaction

> Group job behavior: group member rating of own group—for example, on source of leadership.

510) Perceptions of task performance of self and others

> Supervisor job behavior: subordinate rating of superiors on formality of structuring.
> Supervisor performance: subordinate rating of superiors on discipline, ability to make judgments, and so on.

520) Perceptions of social behavior of self and others

> Group performance: group member rating of degree to which members stick together.

633) Group task performance in operational settings: specific measures

> Group performance: E record of number of hours for completion and reworking, number of items completed, and so on, and staff executive ranking of aircraft departments on over-all efficiency.

439. Comrey, A. L., et al. Factors influencing organizational effectiveness: VII. A survey of aircraft supervisors. *Personnel Psychol.*, 1955, 8, 245–257.

Purpose

This study measured supervisors' self-ratings and ratings of others on management practices as related to group productivity.

Procedure

Executives rated aircraft departments in terms of time spent on reworking rejected items, number of items produced that passed the inspection, ratio of allowed to actual time spent on a task, and general productivity. In addition, a questionnaire of 24 different dimensions was given to all supervisors to obtain their self-ratings on authority, attitudes, and so on; their ratings of foremen and subordinates on communication, decision-making ability, and similar factors; and their general ratings of departments. The supervisor questionnaire responses were analyzed in relation to the various productivity measures.

Results

In general, there was little relationship between department productivity and supervisor questionnaire responses. Specifically:

1. Performance effectiveness of departments (executive rankings of the departments)

    a. Supervisor self-ratings: slightly related to department effectiveness (2/9)

    b. Supervisor ratings of other department members: slightly related to department effectiveness (2/13)

    c. Supervisor ratings of departments: highly related to department effectiveness (1/1)

2. Acceptance rate of inspected items (number of items that passed inspection)

   a. Supervisor self-ratings: not related to acceptance rate (1/9)

   b. Supervisor ratings of other department members: slightly related to acceptance rate (2/13)

   c. Supervisor ratings of the department: not related to acceptance rate (0/1)

3. Production rate of the department (ratio of allowed to actual hours spent on a job)

   a. Supervisor self-ratings: not related to production rate (0/9)

   b. Supervisor ratings of other department members: not related to production rate (0/8), except that there were high and positive relationships to foremen's conference practice (1/1), confidence in superiors (1/1), influence with superiors (1/1), job helpfulness (1/1), acceptance of employee suggestions (1/1), and non-favoritism of subordinates (1/1)

   c. Supervisors' rating of the department: not related to production rate (0/1)

4. Ratio of production time to time spent on rejected items (executive calculation of department time spent on various phases of the job)

   a. Supervisor self-ratings: not related to production–reject ratio (1/9)

   b. Supervisor ratings of other department members: not related to production–reject ratio (1/14)

   c. Supervisor ratings of the department: not related to production–reject ratio (0/1)

Study Variables

132) Task abilities of members
    Foreman job skills: supervisor questionnaire responses.

141) Attitudes toward the task
    Job related feelings (such as preferred distance between self and subordinates, satisfaction from doing job quickly): supervisor questionnaire responses.
    Superior–subordinate job characteristics: supervisor questionnaire responses.
    Attitude toward paper work: supervisor questionnaire responses.

142) Attitudes toward the situation
    Adequacy of own authority over subordinates: supervisor questionnaire responses.

143) Attitudes toward nongroup persons and other groups
    Company attitude toward human relations problems: supervisor questionnaire responses.

221) Group abilities
    Performance effectiveness of departments: executive rankings of departments.

230) Interpersonal relations in the group
    Interpersonal relations of foreman: supervisor questionnaire responses.
    Pride in work group: supervisor questionnaire responses.

510) Perceptions of task performance of self and others
      Foreman job habits: supervisor questionnaire responses.
      Own personal work habits: supervisor questionnaire responses.

633) Group task performance in operational settings: specific measures
      Ratio of production time to time spent on rejected items: time spent
      on various phases of the job.
      Performance effectiveness (acceptance rate and production rate):
      number of items that passed the inspection and allowed-vs.-actual
      hours spent on a job.

450. Courtney, D., et al. *Naval, neighborhood, and national leadership.* Philadelphia: Institute for Research in Human Relations, 1953. (Annu. tech. Rep., Contract N8 ONR 69401)

Purpose

This study investigated relationships between authoritarianism and group homogeneity with respect to authoritarianism, and company morale, job proficiency, general intelligence and achievement, and sociometric status.

Procedure

The total study population was comprised of 2139 men drawn from recruit classes at a naval training center. Every man completed a scale measuring authoritarianism, a sociometric choice questionnaire in which he named men in his company whom he preferred for various social and company activities, and an attitude scale giving his opinion of the Navy. Scores on the Navy General Classification Test and a Recruit Final Achievement Test were also used, as well as information about company proficiency awards, sick bay attendance, and demerits.

Results

Certain characteristics differentiated high and low authoritarians. Specifically, low authoritarians scored higher on achievement and intelligence tests (2/2) and received more nominations by peers to be recruit officers (2/2).

High and low authoritarians and groups varying in homogeneity of authoritarian attitudes were fairly equivalent in other respects, however—for example, in number of sociometric choices made and received from own crew as friend to take home on leave, combat leader, best athlete, and best liked (5/16); attitude toward the Navy (0/6); sick bay visits (1/8); demerits (2/4); and company performance awards (0/4).

Ss were further differentiated in terms of sociometric choices given and received. Those giving more sociometric choices among the crew also received more choices for liking others, being best athlete, being combat leader, being best liked, and being recruit chief petty officer (5/5). Ss most frequently estimated by others as "liking them best" received more votes in all sociometric choice categories (5/5). Choices received in all categories were highly intercorrelated (10/10). Recruit status was also highly and positively associated with number of choices received in all categories (14/15). Intelligence and achievement test scores correlated highly with choices given and received (13/14).

Number of demerits, sick bay visits, and morale were not strongly related to choices given (2/5) and received (6/18). Significant relationships noted were as follows: Ss most frequently chosen as combat leader, best liked, and recruit chief petty officer were lower in demerits (3/3), and those voted recruit chief petty officer reported a higher attraction to the Navy (1/1).

No significant relationships were found between morale and competitive performance awards, number of sick bay visits, number of demerits, and intelligence and achievement test scores (1/8), or between number of sick bay visits and competitive performance awards, demerits, and achievement test scores (1/5).

Study Variables

131) General abilities of members
   Intelligence: S score on intelligence test.

132) Task abilities of members
   Acquired knowledge of Navy: S achievement test score.

143) Attitudes toward nongroup persons and other groups
   Attraction to Navy: S score on attitude scale.

144) Attitudes toward issues, concepts, ideologies
   Authoritarianism: S questionnaire responses.

151) Social position in the group
   Projected sociometric choice: estimate of others' sociometric choices.
   Sociometric choices received: number of times S chosen by other recruits as best athlete, combat leader, friend, and so on.

152) Task or physical position in the group
   Member status position: recruit position as recruit petty officer or not.

230) Interpersonal relations in the group
   Sociometric choices given: number of times S chose other recruits as liked best.

622) Member task performance in operational settings: global measures
   Sick bay visits: record of hospital appearances.
   Member performance demerits: record of demerits received by S.

632) Group task performance in operational settings: global measures
   Group competitive performance awards: judge rating of company's performance on cleanliness and drill proficiency.

633) Group task performance in operational settings: specific measures
   Group performance (barracks cleanliness rating): judge rating of company.

462. Crockett, W. H. Emergent leadership in small, decision-making groups. *J. abnorm. soc. Psychol.*, 1955, *51*, 378–383.

Purpose

This study compared the behavior and characteristics of group members who exhibited different degrees of leadership in group discussions.

Procedure

Seventy-two business, industrial, and government groups, composed of from 5 to 17 members, discussed actual problems associated with their organizations. Observers rated members on several instruments, including the Bales discussion behavior category system, and on leadership exhibited during the discussion. Group members and observers also completed rating scales that measured various aspects of the discussion at the close of the meeting.

Results

Ss rated as emergent leaders were differentiated from others in the groups in that they proposed more problems, sought more information, were more ego-involved in the discussion, and gave less development in their discussion behavior (4/4). They were not different from others in the extent to which they set goals, proposed solutions, sought development, gave information, opposed, supported, or summarized (0/7).

In addition, emergent leaders were rated by the designated leader of the group as having more experience with group problems, being more important to the group, and having a higher status in the organization than were other group members (3/3).

Study Variables

141) Attitudes toward the task

      Personal stake in meeting outcome: member rating.

152) Task or physical position in the group

      Leadership assignment: E assignment of leadership roles in conference.

      Importance of members: designated leader's ranking of members on job importance.

      Member importance to group: group member's rating of other members on importance in conference.

222) Group training and experience

      Other member capability: designated leader's rating of group members on their experience with problems.

240) General structured properties of the group

      Congruency of member motivation: O postconference rating of group.

410) Content of interaction

      Discussion behavior: O rating of Ss on Bales categories.

430) Outcomes of interaction

Presence of cliques in group: postconference rating by O of presence of subgroups consistently supporting themselves and opposing others.

610) Leadership performance

Occurrence of emergent leadership: O rating of member leadership.

464. Crockett, W. H., & Meidinger, T. Authoritarianism and interpersonal perception. *J. abnorm. soc. Psychol.*, 1956, *53*, 378–382.

Purpose

This study examined authoritarianism as related to accuracy of interpersonal perception.

Procedure

Pairs of Ss were administered the California F-scale on authoritarianism. In some pairs, both members scored above the median and in others both were below the median. Other pairs were mixed, with one S above and the other below in their F-scale scores. Each pair discussed a topic and then filled out the F-scale again, this time as they felt their partners in the discussion would respond to it.

Results

Ss with low F-scale scores tended to overestimate the authoritarianism scores of other Ss, regardless of their actual scores on the F-scale (2/2). On the other hand, high-authoritarian Ss underestimated scores of other high Ss (1/1) but were quite accurate in their judgments of low authoritarians (0/1).

An examination of the differences in the patterns of over- and underestimation by high and low scorers showed no consistency (0/2).

Study Variables

240) General structural properties of the group

Composition of group (authoritarianism): judgment of Ss with high and low F-scale scores on partners' responses to the F-scale.

621) Member task performance in experimental settings

Accuracy of estimating partner's F-scale score: S estimate of partner's score as compared with actual score of partner.

470. Crow, W. J. The effect of training upon accuracy and variability in interpersonal perception. *J. abnorm. soc. Psychol.*, 1957, *55*, 355–359.

Purpose

This study investigated how training in physician–patient relationships affected ability to judge personality characteristics.

Procedure

Senior medical students were divided into an experimental group that received training in physician–patient relationships and a control group that did not receive such training. At the beginning, during, and at the end of the senior year, Ss estimated the self-ratings of patients on several personality scales and also judged the "true" status of patients on the same items. Responses by patients on the personality scales were also obtained.

Results

In some respects the results showed that students who were trained in physician–patient relationships were less perceptive of the personality characteristics of patients than were those who had no such training. Specifically, there was no relationship between training and accuracy of judgment ("true" status of patient on scale vs. patient's actual response) late in training, and a negative relationship early in training (1/2). In addition there was no difference between trained and untrained groups on a measure comparing patient responses and the judge's estimate of the patient's response (0/2). On the other hand, the results showed that groups with training had higher variability in scores than did untrained groups (4/4).

Other study results showed a high negative association of accuracy scores and variance of accuracy scores (5/5) and of scores comparing estimated patient responses and actual patient responses with the variance of these scores (3/5). Moreover, there was a high positive relationship between accuracy scores and scores comparing the true location of the patient vs. an estimate of how the patient would respond (5/7).

Study Variables

222) Group training and experience
> Training in social interactions: group training or lack of training or in physician–patient relationships.

623) Member task performance in operational settings: specific measures
> Accuracy in social perception: judgment of others' personality traits compared with actual responses of others.
> Accuracy of social perception projection: estimated self-ratings of others compared with actual ratings by others.
> Own judgment of others' personality vs. estimated self-judgment: similarity of estimated self-perception of others and own judgment of others.

473. Crowell, Laura, et al.   Self-concepts of communication skill and performance in small group discussions. *Speech Monogr.*, 1955, *22*, 20–27.

Purpose

This study examined how a person's self-evaluation as a communicator related to his performance in a group discussion.

Procedure

Two questionnaires dealing with a person's skill as a communicator and communicant, in addition to some biographical characteristics, were administered to students. Then the students were divided into three discussion groups. After completion of the discussion, ratings of performance—for example, contributions leading others, and dominance—were obtained in which every member was rated by himself and by others.

Results

Students with high self-ratings as communicators were more contributory to group decisions and understanding, more interested, more dominant, more able to keep the group's attention, more interested in doing a good job and leading, but less yielding and agreeable than were Ss with low self-ratings of communicative abilities (9/9).

On the other hand, Ss' perception of themselves as good listeners did not relate to any of the foregoing discussion behaviors (1/12).

Study Variables

132) Task abilities of members

Perceived skill as communicator and listener: S self-ratings.

510) Perceptions of task performance of self and others

Discussion performance: S rating of every group member on contribution to group decisions, leadership, and so on.

484. Danzig, E. R., & Galanter, E. H. *The dynamics and structure of small industrial work groups.* Philadelphia: Institute for Research in Human Relations, 1955. (Contract Nonr 1229(00)).

Purpose

This study examined relationships between group productivity and group sociometric structure, job satisfaction, and certain personality characteristics of the members.

Procedure

Six-man work units were assigned a task of cooperatively assembling factory products. Completion time constituted the measure of productivity. A sociometric scale was also used to measure social distance within the unit. In addition, self-estimates and peer estimates of job satisfaction were obtained. Interviews followed the work sessions in which Ss listed, among other things, the names of their preferred co-workers. After all units had finished the assembly task and interviews, a battery of paper-and-pencil tests was administered, including a measure of the discrepancy between self-perception and peer perception of preferences, a short-form Sanford Authoritarianism scale, and a measure of level of aspiration.

Results

In general, social distance within a group related highly to group performance; groups with close sociometric linkages of various types performed better than did groups with fewer such ties between members (4/4).

Group performance did not relate, however, to any creativeness exhibited during the interview (as measured by word association and other tasks) (0/4), nor to S leisure activities, satisfaction with the job, authoritarianism scores, or perceptions of other group members' satisfaction with group or job (0/9).

Study Variables

144) Attitudes toward issues, concepts, ideologies
> Authoritarianism: S responses to Sanford Authoritarianism Scale. Satisfaction with different situations and objects: S responses to a 20-item list.

230) Interpersonal relations in the group
> Sociometric linkages among members: S responses to sociometric instrument.

420) Patterns of interaction
> Member creative behavior: number of responses, number of word associations produced by S.

510) Perceptions of task performance of self and others
> Satisfaction with the job: S questionnaire responses.
> Perceived satisfaction of other members with job: S questionnaire responses.
> Discrepancy between own satisfaction and perceived satisfaction of other group members: average discrepancy between self-estimates and estimates of peer ratings of job satisfaction.

520) Perceptions of social behavior of self and others
> Discrepancy between self-preference and perceived group preference for leisure activities: average discrepancy between self-preference and perceived group preference of leisure activities, as measured by questionnaire responses.

621) Member task performance in experimental settings
> Discrepancy between perceived and actual rate of speed: average discrepancy between perceived and actual speed measures of behavior.

631) Group task performance in experimental settings
> Group performance: time needed to solve problem.

496. Davitz, J. Social perception and sociometric choice of children. *J. abnorm. soc. Psychol.*, 1955, *50*, 173–176.

Purpose

This study analyzed the tendency for children to perceive similarity between themselves and those they chose sociometrically.

Procedure

*S*s were children in a summer camp living in groups of from four to six. Sociometric choices were obtained by asking each *S* to rank his cabinmates in the order that he would like them as cabinmates and for inviting to a party. *S* also stated his own preferences in an activity inventory, plus those preferences he thought his highest and lowest sociometric choices would have. *Perceived similarity* was derived from the correspondence between *S*'s own activity preferences and his projected responses. *Actual similarity* was the true correspondence between activity preferences.

Results

Children with a high degree of liking for each other perceived each other as highly similar whether this similarity was actually the case or not. Although no differences were found in actual similarity between *S*'s highest and lowest choices and himself (0/1), he perceived his most-preferred cabinmate as choosing the same activities as himself more than would his least-preferred cabinmate, and more than his most-preferred cabinmate actually did (2/2). *S*'s predictions of his least-preferred cabinmate's choice of activities, on the other hand, closely corresponded to the least-preferred's actual choices (0/1).

Study Variables

230) Interpersonal relations in the group
   Sociometric choice: *S* ranking of other *S*s in terms of preference as cabinmates and inviting to a party.

240) General structural properties of the group
   Actual similarity of *S*s: discrepancy between *S*'s preferences for activities and his highest and lowest choices' preferences for activities.

520) Perceptions of social behavior of self and others
   Perceived similarity of *S*s: discrepancy between *S* preferences for activities and his projected estimates of the preferences of his highest and lowest sociometric choices.

512. Deutsch, M. An experimental study of the effects of cooperation and competition upon group process. *Hum. Relat.*, 1949, *2*, 199–231.

Purpose

This study compared the behavior and characteristics of groups motivated to perform cooperatively with the behavior and characteristics of groups motivated to perform competitively on human relations and problem-solving tasks.

Procedure

Volunteers were assigned to five-man groups and given the tasks of solving human relations and puzzle problems at each of several meetings. Groups were assigned either to cooperative or competitive conditions. *E* instructed cooperative groups that the group turning in the best solution would be rewarded.

Individuals were to be rewarded in the competitive groups. Os rated both individuals and groups on behavior and characteristics during the discussions. Members completed a short questionnaire after each meeting and another more comprehensive one a week after concluding the experiment.

Results

Although discussion processes were generally more group- and goal-oriented in cooperative as compared with competitive groups, the differences were even more marked in the human relations task.

Cooperative groups in both tasks were better oriented, more coordinated, orderly, group-centered, ready to accept each others' ideas, and friendly (12/12). Also, they paid more attention to each other, worked together more frequently, and exhibited greater discussion insight and productivity (8/8). Members in the cooperative groups reported more of a feeling for the group and less desire to excel others in the group (4/4).

Although cooperative Ss behaved so as to facilitate group goal attainment rather than to satisfy individual needs in the human relations task, no such differences were noted in puzzle solving. Specifically, cooperative Ss more frequently adopted follower roles (1/1), whereas competitive Ss were observed satisfying individual needs, defending their own positions, acting as evaluator-critics and blockers, and behaving aggressively (5/5). More-competitive Ss also wrote individual solutions to the human relations problem rather than conferring on a joint solution (5/5).

Moreover, members in the cooperative condition agreed with their fellow members more often and perceived them as cooperating more, giving greater assistance, and contributing more to the discussion (4/4). Conversely, competitive Ss reported difficulties in communicating with and understanding others in the group (2/2). Whereas cooperative Ss felt an obligation to the group and were more motivated to achieve and excel, competitive members were more conscious of pleasing the experimenter (5/5). No similar differences were found in the puzzle-solving task.

There were no observed differences between groups working on either task in respect to group involvement (0/2) or individual member productivity (0/2). Also, Ss did not differ in perceptions of their own interest, attentiveness, competitiveness, discussion, learning, member agreement with them, and over-all group effectiveness (0/7).

Study Variables

120) Personality characteristics of members
> Member personal feelings: member questionnaire responses on desire to excel, attentiveness, etc.
> Personal evaluative feelings: member questionnaire responses on desire for respect, motivation to please, etc.

132) Task abilities of members
> Academic grade: instructor grading of S.

230) Interpersonal relations in the group
> Feeling for group: member questionnaire responses.

323) Induced task conditions
    Cooperativeness of groups: E instructions to work either cooperatively for group rewards or competitively for individual rewards.

410) Content of interaction
    Participation behavior: O rating of group members' discussion behavior.

430) Outcomes of interaction
    Group discussion behavior: rating of group behavior.
    Group performance effectiveness: O rating of group discussion process regarding quality, productivity, etc.
    Group orientation toward problem: O rating of group.
    Group characteristics: O rating of group on group involvement, friendliness between members, etc.

510) Perceptions of task performance of self and others
    Member judgment of others' performance: member questionnaire responses.
    Own competitiveness: member questionnaire responses.
    Own performance judgment: member questionnaire responses on difficulty in communicating with and understanding others.
    Member perception of others' judgments of him: member questionnaire responses.

510) Perceptions of task performance of self and others
520) Perceptions of social behavior of self and others
    Perceived group cooperation, quality of product, group effectiveness: member questionnaire responses.

520) Perceptions of social behavior of self and others
    Frequency of others' reactions: member questionnaire responses.

621) Member task performance in experimental settings
    Member discussion productivity: O rating of member behavior.

631) Group task performance in experimental settings
    Discussion product rating: judge rating of group solution.

526. Dittes, F. E., & Kelley, H. H. Effects of different conditions of acceptance upon conformity to group norms. *J. abnorm. soc. Psychol.*, 1956, *53*, 100–107.

Purpose

This study investigated conformity of group members as a function of perceived acceptance by the group.

Procedure

Volunteers assigned to groups were instructed that a prize would be awarded for effective group performance. Unanimous decisions were highly desirable and members had the option of voting to eliminate those interfering with success. Two tasks were used: rating the worthiness of juvenile gangs on the basis of simulated records and estimating which of two blocks had more dots. The gang ratings were done publicly (with discussion) and privately. During discussion, groups were rated by Os on their agreement and participation. Variables introduced during the session were faked acceptance ratings of members by the group and new information on the worthiness of the juvenile gangs. Ss' ratings following introduction of the variables were analyzed for conformity changes. During the dot judgment task, faked group messages were used to indicate that the wrong block had more dots. Private and public responses were analyzed for conformity. At the end of the trials, Ss reported feelings of acceptance by the group and attraction to the group.

Results

Perceived acceptance by the group was related to various conformity scores with certain qualifications: high-acceptance Ss were slower in completing the gang judgment task than were average-acceptance Ss (1/1); average-acceptance Ss conformed more to group opinion in dot judgment than did low-acceptance Ss (2/2). No strong differences were found among Ss in a group-member gang evaluation discrepancy measure of conformity (1/3). Also, Ss were not differentiated on *change* in amount of conforming comments made after the introduction of new information on gangs (0/7).

More complex indexes of conformity, combining some of the above measures, indicated that high-acceptance Ss scored lower on group member similarity in gang evaluations than did others (1/1) but were not clearly differentiated on group-member similarity on *both* gang and dot judgment tasks (1/2).

Ss' perceived acceptance accounted for some other differences. Although Ss in general were similar in anticipated rejection by the group (0/3), very low-acceptance Ss anticipated rejection significantly more than did all others (3/3). Low-acceptance Ss also markedly decreased in over-all participation after hearing their acceptance ratings (1/1). Perceived acceptance was also highly related to member valuation of group membership (6/7).

Study Variables

142) Attitudes toward the situation
Feelings of freedom to express contrary opinion: S report of freedom he felt in expressing opinion.

144) Attitudes toward issues, concepts, ideologies
Conformity: member private rating of desirability of gang in case history.

230) Interpersonal relations in the group
Valuation of group membership: S questionnaire evaluation of group.

312) Induced social conditions
Perceived acceptance by others: E false report to Ss of their acceptance by group.

410) Content of interaction
Conforming comments after introduction of new information: O tally of Ss' conforming remarks compared with previous comments.

420) Patterns of interaction

Amount of participation in discussion: O record of number of S participations.

Conformity: O record of S speed in finishing task.

520) Perceptions of social behavior of self and others

Recall of presumed group acceptance ratings: S recall of rating received from group.

Anticipated rejection by group: S responses describing whether they would be rejected by group.

621) Member task performance in experimental settings

Conformity (perception task): S public and private judgment of number of dots on blocks.

Conformity (gang problem): S evaluation of case history of gang compared with group evaluation of gang.

Over-all conformity: S judgment of gang compared with group judgment and S judgment of number of dots on two blocks compared with group judgment.

542. Downing, J. Cohesiveness, perception, and values. *Hum. Relat.*, 1958, *11*, 157–166.

Purpose

This study examined experimentally induced cohesiveness and influence on conformity to group judgment.

Procedure

Each S was asked to estimate autokinetic movement in two situations; in the first, Ss worked individually and in the other they worked in groups in which the other members were experimenter-confederates. E manipulated group cohesion by telling Ss either that they would like and be liked by other members or that they would not. In addition, two types of induced pressure were employed: *positive*, used to increase Ss' estimations by announcing group estimates as being about 50 percent higher than Ss' initial ones while working individually; and *negative*, group estimates about 50 percent lower than Ss' initial individual estimates. After the group session, Ss were administered a questionnaire item asking whether they would like to be better acquainted with the other group members.

Results

Degree of induced cohesion was not related to Ss' conformity to the group judgment (0/3), although Ss in high-cohesion groups desired to know their group members better than did Ss in low-cohesion groups (1/1).

In all instances, the pressure exerted by confederates resulted in increased conformity by Ss'—whether the pressure was in the direction to increase or decrease their initial judgments (2/2).

Study Variables

230) Interpersonal relations in the group

> Desire to know members better: S responses on sociometric choice items.

240) General structural properties of the group

> Degree of presence of others: E assignment of Ss to work either individually or in presence of others.

312) Induced social conditions

> Degree of cohesion: E assignment of Ss to groups of perceived low or high cohesion.

430) Outcomes of intention

> Conformity: change in perceived autokinetic movement in the direction of group norm.

566. Exline, R. V. Group climate as a factor in the relevance and accuracy of social perception. *J. abnorm. soc. Psychol.*, 1957, 55, 382–388.

Purpose

This study examined congeniality of groups as a factor affecting the accuracy of estimates of other group members' characteristics and feelings.

Procedure

Students were assigned to "congenial" or "noncongenial" groups as created by instructions. Each group worked on a discussion task, after which Ss responded to rating scales designed to measure the accuracy of their perception of task-oriented behavior in others and ego-oriented behavior of others (i.e., sociometric choices of other group members), satisfaction with group progress, and willingness to continue to work in the same group. Accuracy of perception was measured by comparing estimated responses of another person with the person's actual response to the rating scales.

Results

Ss from congenial groups were more willing to work with others, were more satisfied with group progress, liked their co-workers better, and were more accurate in perceiving task-oriented behavior of others (5/5). Congeniality, however, did not relate to accuracy of perception of interpersonal relations in groups (0/2).

Men were less accurate in estimating interpersonal relations than were women (1/1), but sex did not relate either to satisfaction with group progress or to accuracy in perceiving task-oriented behavior (0/5).

Group members who were willing to continue working with the same group were more accurate in estimating task-related behavior but less accurate in estimating interpersonal relations in the group (2/2).

Study Variables

110) Biographical characteristics of members
Biographical characteristics: sex.

230) Interpersonal relations in the group
Sociometric choice of co-workers: S scores on sociometric questionnaire.
Degree of willingness to work with group: S scoring the group on sociometric questionnaire.

312) Induced social conditions
Perceived group congeniality: S motivation according to experimental instructions regarding group compatibility.

510) Perceptions of task performance of self and others
Satisfaction with group progress: S ratings of group progress.

520) Perceptions of social behavior of self and others
Accuracy of interpersonal perception: discrepancy between S estimates of others and actual self-judgments by others.

576.* **Faust, W. L.** Group versus individual problem-solving. *J. abnorm. soc. Psychol.*, 1959, *59*, 68–72.

Purpose

This study compared individual and group problem-solving performance.

Procedure

Students were assigned to work either in groups or alone on spatial and anagram problems. Performance was scored in terms of the number of problems solved correctly, and group and individual performance were compared. "Nominal groups" were also formed by random grouping of data from individual Ss. This "nominal group" performance was compared with real group performance.

Results

Groups performed definitely better than individuals on both types of problems (4/4), but there was only a slight difference in the performance of real and "nominal" groups on either spatial or verbal problems (1/4).

This study contained a total of eight relationships.

Study Variables

240) General structural properties of the group
Occurrence of group: E assignment of Ss to work alone or in groups.

631) Group task performance in experimental settings
Group performance on spatial and verbal problems: number of spatial and anagram problems Ss solved correctly.

593. Festinger, L., & Hutte, H. A. An experimental investigation of the effect of unstable interpersonal relations in a group. *J. abnorm. soc. Psychol.*, 1954, 49, 513–522.

Purpose

This experiment studied the effect of stability of interpersonal relations within a group on the accuracy of perception of social preference and communication behavior.

Procedure

Strangers in groups introduced themselves and later completed individual questionnaires rating the others sociometrically and estimating what the others thought of themselves. *S*s were then given false information on how the two persons they liked best felt about each other, and placed in either *compatible* groups (*S*s liking each other) or *incompatible* groups (*S*s not liking each other). During a discussion period, observations were made of who talked to whom and for how long. After the discussion, *S*s were readministered the sociometric preference scale along with a questionnaire obtaining their feelings about various aspects of the discussion. This experiment was conducted with the same procedures in Holland and in the U.S.

Results

In both countries, those *S*s who perceived their sociometric choices to be incompatible tended to change their choices more frequently than did those in the compatible situations (2/2).

*S*s in both countries and in perceived compatible and incompatible conditions communicated more frequently with those they sociometrically liked or disliked and less with those to whom they were indifferent, and more to liked *S*s than to disliked *S*s (8/8). Similarily, they were communicated with more frequently by those they saw as either liking or disliking them than by those they perceived as neutral to them (8/8). The data did not show any consistent pattern of differences in communication between the compatible and incompatible groups in either country (2/6).

Study Variables

222) Group training and experience
       Stage of experiment: *S* working early or late in experiment.

230) Interpersonal relations in the group
       Sociometric choice: *S* questionnaire responses.

312) Induced social conditions
       Perceived compatibility among group members: *E* providing of false information about member personal compatibility.

420) Patterns of interaction
       Discussion behavior: frequency of *S* communication with one another.

510) Perceptions of task performance of self and others

Perceived frequency of communication received from others: S questionnaire ratings.

Perceived frequency of communication given to other members: S questionnaire ratings.

520) Perceptions of social behavior of self and others

Perceived sociometric choice of self: S estimates of others' choice of self.

Perceived sociometric choice: S estimates of other Ss' liking of other members.

Accuracy of perceived-self sociometric preferences: S estimate of others' liking of self compared with actual rating by others.

606. Fiedler, F. E. Assumed similarity measures as predictors of team effectiveness. *J. abnorm. soc. Psychol.*, 1954, *49*, 381–388.

Purpose

This study was concerned with how differences in the way in which team members saw themselves and their co-workers related to team performance effectiveness.

Procedure

High-school basketball team members responded to a personality questionnaire from three different points of view: as the items described the Ss themselves, as the Ss thought the person with whom they worked best would respond, and as they thought the person with whom they worked least well would respond. From these data, a measure of assumed similarity was derived to reflect the similarity of self-descriptions with the prediction of the positive-choice responses. A measure of assumed similarity of opposites was also generated to indicate the congruency of predicted responses of best and worst co-workers. These measures were tested for relationship to team performance effectiveness, as measured by number of games won.

Results

To an extent, differentiation of personalities was found to be associated with performance effectiveness. Members of good teams showed greater discrepancies in their ratings of best and worst co-workers (1/1), and players voted as "best co-worker" on the more-effective teams showed significantly less similarity in their ratings of themselves and their positive choices and their positive and negative choices than did "best co-worker" on less-effective teams (2/2).

Other associations between member perceptions and team effectiveness were not significant (0/2).

Study Variables

520) Perceptions of social behavior of self and others

> Assumed similarity of opposites: similarity of estimates of co-workers' responses.

> Assumed similarity of member with self: difference between self-rating and estimated rating of other team members.

632) Group task performance in operational settings: global measures

> Group effectiveness: E record of number of basketball games won during the season.

606a. Fiedler, F. E. Assumed similarity measures as predictors of team effectiveness. *J. abnorm. soc. Psychol.*, 1954, *49*, 381–388.

Purpose

This investigation was concerned with how differences in the way members saw themselves and their co-workers related to team performance effectiveness. The study was an extension of the immediately preceding study.

Procedure

Student surveying teams responded to a personality questionnaire from different points of view: as the items described the *S*s themselves, as the *S*s thought the person with whom they worked best would respond, and as they thought the person with whom they worked least well would respond. From these data, a measure of assumed similarity was derived to reflect the similarity of self-descriptions with predictions of the positive-choice responses. A measure of assumed similarity of opposites was also generated to indicate the congruency of predicted responses of best and worst co-workers. These measures were related to several indexes of surveying proficiency, such as accuracy, speed, and smoothness of team operation.

Results

Most-preferred co-workers from high-accuracy surveying teams differentiated significantly more between their positive and negative choices in their predicted ratings than did those on low-accuracy teams (1/1). No difference was noted, however, in the discrepancy between self-ratings and predicted best co-worker's ratings (0/1). Also, no assumed similarity differences were noted with respect to the extent *S*s made sociometric choices from their own vs. other teams (0/1).

Performance criteria of accuracy and speed were positively related (1/1). Greater conflict was observed in high-speed groups than in low-speed groups (1/1), but no such relationship occurred with respect to the criterion accuracy (0/1). Neither speed nor accuracy was related to member ratings of their own group's quality (0/2)

Study Variables

221) Group abilities

Over-all quality of group: S ranking of groups in terms of quality.

230) Interpersonal relations in the group

Intrateam sociometric attraction: discrepancy between number of times Ss chose members of own or other teams.

430) Outcomes of interaction

Conflict in groups: E ranking of groups on conflict exhibited.

520) Perceptions of social behavior of self and others

Assumed similarity of opposites: discrepancy between S predictions of his best and worst co-workers' self-ratings.

Assumed similarity with positive choice: discrepancy between S rating of self and projected ratings of best co-worker's self-ratings.

633) Group task performance in operational settings: specific measures

Speed of group performance: E record of group speed in surveying task.

Group performance accuracy: E rating of group performance.

608. Fiedler, F. E. The influence of leader-keyman relations on combat crew effectiveness. *J. abnorm. soc. Psychol.*, 1955, *51*, 227–235.

Purpose

This study investigated how differences in the way in which aircraft crew commanders saw themselves and their crews affected crew task performance.

Procedure

Air crews in training were administered a personality questionnaire to which they responded from different points of view: as they thought the man with whom they worked best would respond and as they thought the man with whom they worked worst would respond. From these data, a measure of assumed similarity of opposites for crew commanders was derived to reflect the similarity of predicted responses of best and worst co-worker. This assumed similarity measure was related to indexes of crew performance effectiveness, simulated bombing accuracy, and navigational competence. The association of these variables was investigated for various levels of crew members on the basis of responses to a sociometric instrument.

Results

Similarity of ratings of most- and least-preferred co-workers did not differentiate commanders of crews varying in performance effectiveness (0/3). However, when sociometric preferences indicated by and for the aircraft commander were taken into account, similarity of ratings was significantly associated with performance. For example, the less similarity between opposites reported by aircraft commanders who had high sociometric choices for keymen (or high sociometric choice for and from keymen), the better was the crew bombing performance (4/4). Conversely, the greater the similarity reported by aircraft commanders who were most preferred by their crew, the greater was the navigational accuracy (1/1). Aircraft commanders were undifferentiated in terms of the camera bombing performance criterion (0/6).

Other relationships dealing with perceived similarity of opposites and performance, when considered in light of less-positive sociometric associates, were not significant (1/18).

Study Variables

151) Social position in the group

> Aircraft commander preference status: crew member ranking of aircraft commander on sociometric choice items.

520) Perceptions of social behavior of self and others

> Assumed similarity of opposites: S's responses to personality questionnaire items as he expected his most- and least-preferred work companions would respond.

> Sociometric choice: member rating of others regarding selection for activities such as going on leave or sharing military tasks.

633) Group task performance in operational settings: specific measures

> Group performance accuracy: crew performance on simulated navigational task.

> Group performance accuracy: crew performance on simulated air crew tasks measuring radar bombing accuracy.

608a. Fiedler, F. E. The influence of leader-keyman relations on combat crew effectiveness. *J. abnorm. soc. Psychol.*, 1955, *51*, 227–235.

Purpose

This study investigated how differences in the way in which tank crew commanders saw themselves and their crews affected crew task performance. The study was an extension of the immediately preceding study.

Procedure

Army tank crews were administered a personality questionnaire to which they responded from different points of view: as they thought the man with whom they worked best would respond and as they thought the man with whom they worked worst would respond. From these data, a measure of assumed similarity of opposites for crew commanders was computed to reflect the similarity of predicted responses of best and worst co-workers. This assumed similarity score was related to various measures of tank crew performance— time to hit a target, time to travel from target to target, and a complex score of probability of winning an engagement. The association of these variables was studied for various levels of crew member attraction, based on responses to a sociometric instrument.

Results

No clear-cut relationship was noted between similarity of ratings of best- and least-preferred co-workers by aircraft commanders and over-all performance level of their crews (6/19).

Significant trends were noted, however, in that the less similarity there was in ratings of best and least liked co-workers by a commander who was most-preferred member of the crew and who endorsed the gunner as his sociometric choice, the less time was required by the crew to hit a target (2/3). Likewise, the less the similarity seen by a commander who endorsed and was endorsed by the gunner, the higher was the crew score on probability of winning an engagement (2/3).

Degree of discrepancy between ratings of best- and least-liked co-workers by tank commanders at other levels of preference status failed to differentiate crews in terms of time to hit target (1/7). Crews were also undifferentiated with respect to their performance on travel time from target to target (0/7).

Study Variables

151) Social position in the group
> Sociometric choice: member ratings of other group members as most-preferred and least-preferred co-workers.

520) Perceptions of social behavior of self and others
> Assumed similarity: S estimate of responses of most- and least-preferred co-worker on personality traits.

633) Group task performance in operational settings: specific measures
> Crew performance: rater description of time to hit the target and time to travel from target to target.

621. Fisher, S., & Lubin, A. Distance as a determinant of influence in a two-person social interaction situation. *J. abnorm. soc. Psychol.*, 1958, *56*, 230–238.

Purpose

This study investigated changes in judgments as a function of perceived discrepancy between one's own judgments and those of another team member.

Procedure

Pairs were placed in a social influence situation requiring judgments of the number of paratroopers seen in briefly exposed photographs. Distance—the size of the discrepancy between S's judgment and his partner's—was systematically varied by intercepting written estimates and replacing them with bogus estimates at a predetermined distance. Influence effects were determined by computing changes in judgments from trial to trial.

264 CATALOGUE

Results

Statistical results were not reported. There seemed to be a positive trend, however, between the discrepancy of S's and partner's presumed judgments and susceptibility to influence.

Study Variables

430) Outcome of interaction
Susceptibility to influence: change in judgment of a stimulus.
621) Member task performance in experimental settings
Discrepancy between S and E judgments: S judgment and E-set stimulus judgments on a trial.

642. Forgays, D. G., & Irwin, I. A. *Measures of combat performance used in B-29 training.* San Antonio, Tex.: Lackland Air Force Base, Human Resources Research Center, December, 1952. (Tech. Rep. 52–14)

Purpose

This study determined the reliability and interrelationships of several measures of air crew effectiveness.

Procedure

Several measures were obtained of performance effectiveness of air crews in combat-training courses. These measures included simulated radar-bombing accuracy, visual-bombing accuracy, and navigation accuracy (control time). In addition, flight instructor ratings of crew performance and training school grades were obtained.

Results

In general, measures of crew performance on simulated radar-bombing accuracy, visual-bombing accuracy, and measures of navigation accuracy were reliable (5/5). With respect to the radar-bombing accuracy measure, more specific results indicated that reliability was higher with crew instructors present (2/4) than with instructors absent (0/4).

There was no interrelationship of the various objective measures of crew performance (1/9). In addition, ground school grades and flight instructor ratings were only somewhat related to measures of crew performance (2/6).

Study Variables

132) Task abilities of members
Member school grades: crew members' grades in ground school. Performance in ground school: S performance on a written examination.
School performance: S performance on a written examination.
222) Group training and experience
Degree of crew experience: E selection of crews with varying amounts of experience.

240) General structural properties of the group
   Type of training sections: crew assignment to different training sections.

622) Member task performance in operational settings: global measures
   Member performance in practice: instructor rating of students after the mission.

633) Group task performance in operational settings: specific measures
   Crew performance: crew score on simulated bomb runs, visual bomb attacks, and so on.

660. French, Elizabeth G. Motivation as a variable in work-partner selection. *J. abnorm. soc. Psychol.*, 1956, *53*, 96–99.

Purpose

This study investigated how work-partner choices of a competent non-friend and a less-competent friend were affected by a person's personal achievement or affiliation motives.

Procedure

Friendship ratings and achievement and affiliation motivation scores were obtained by means of a questionnaire from 137 airmen. *S*s were divided into groups on the basis of their friendship ratings. Each group was made up of three mutual friends and one *S* not considered a friend by the others. *S*s worked on a task individually, with the nonfriend permitted to succeed and the friends made to fail. After the test, the results of which were made public, *S*s were told that they were to work on a similar test in pairs and asked to write down their choice of a work partner.

Results

In general, there was an over-all association of affiliation and achievement motivation and selection of work partners (2/2). More specifically, *S*s with high motivation for achievement chose working partners more often from the successful *S*s (5/8), whereas *S*s with high affiliation motivation selected friends more often (5/8).

However, *S*s *low* in both achievement and personal affiliation motivation tended to select friends as working partners more often than they selected successful *S*s (1/1), whereas *S*s *high* in both achievement and personal affiliation motivation chose both friends and successful *S*s (3/3).

Study Variables

120) Personality characteristics of members
   Personal motivation: *S* scores on an achievement and affiliation motivation test.

230) Interpersonal relations in the group
   Partner choice: *S* choice of partners after completion of first problem.

663. French, J. R. P., Jr. Organized and unorganized groups under fear and frustration. *Univ. of Iowa Stud. Child Welf.*, 1944, *20*, No. 409, 231–308.

Purpose

This study examined the behavior of organized and unorganized groups in realistically frustrating and fear-producing situations.

Procedure

Organized groups, where Ss were teammates and clubmates, and unorganized groups, where Ss did not know one another, were frustrated by requiring them to solve insoluble problems and by exposing them to a fear situation simulating a fire. During problem solving, Os rated group behavior in such terms as frustration and interdependence and wrote a description of group behavior. In addition, phonographic recordings of behavior were made and questionnaires were distributed to Ss to investigate their personal feelings. During the fear situation, the same types of data were collected.

Results

Organized groups exhibited more fear and frustration but showed more equality of member participation, more "we feeling," more interdependence, and more aggression than did unorganized groups (5/5). Groups were not differentiated, however, in motivation, escape responses, or other behaviors (1/8).

Study Variables

120) Personality characteristics of members
> Personal fear exhibited: S self-description.

142) Attitudes toward the situation
> Personal feelings about situation—for example, motivation: S questionnaire responses.

240) General structural properties of the group
> Organization in groups: S membership on either organized or unorganized groups.

430) Outcomes of interaction
> Member behavior in frustration or fear situations: O ratings of group members' behavior as friendly, aggressive, and so on.
> Group behavior in frustrating and fear situations: O ratings of group behavior, for "we feeling," interdependence, and so on.

430) Outcomes of interaction
520) Perceptions of social behavior of self and others
> Self-perceived and group-observed fear: S and O ratings of groups' activities.

678. French, R. L., et al. *Measures of attitude and performance during early training as predictors of B-29 crew performance in Korean combat.* San Antonio, Tex.: Lackland Air Force Base, Crew Research Laboratory, March, 1956. (Lab. Note CRL-LN-56-4)

Purpose

This study investigated the usefulness of measures of attitudes toward the group and performance in training as predictors of air crew combat proficiency.

Procedure

Ratings on several dimensions of crew performance in combat were obtained from superior officers for a number of bomber crews. These performance criteria were correlated with training performance data that included ground school grades, instructor ratings of individuals and crews, and performance on a series of tasks—for example, simulated bomb run accuracy, navigational competence, and visual target identification. In addition. these performance measures were tested for relationship to member ratings of liking for own crew, confidence in Air Force management, sense of safety in flying, and so on.

Results

None of the questionnaire measures, ground school grades, or instructor and superior ratings of individual and crew performance in training was more than slightly related to combat proficiency (18/88).

Further analysis of the data indicated that crew navigational competence in training was related to ratings of combat skill for pilots, navigators, and radar observers.

Study Variables

132) Task abilities of members
  Grades in ground school: records from ground school.

142) Attitudes toward the situation
  Personal feelings of well-being in Air Force and safety while flying: *S* questionnaire responses.

143) Attitudes toward nongroup persons and other groups
  Confidence in Air Force management: *S* questionnaire responses.

151) Social position in the group
  Perceived liking by crew: *S* estimate of crew liking for him on a sociometric test.

230) Interpersonal relations in the group
  Liking of own crew: *S* questionnaire responses.

622) Member task performance in operational settings: global measures
  Member combat performance: superior rating of crew members during combat missions.
  Member training performance: instructor rating of crew members during training session .

623) Member task performance in operational settings: specific measures
      Crew problem-solving performance: crew performance during train-
      ing on simulated bombing task, navigational task, and so on.

693. Gerard, H. B. The effect of different dimensions of disagreement
on the communication process in small groups. *Hum. Relat.*, 1953, 6,
249–271.

Purpose

This study was concerned with the effects of variations in perceived group
homogeneity with respect to task ability and pressures to help achieve a group
solution on influence processes.

Procedure

College students expressed their opinions about a hypothetical legislative
problem, discussed their opinions with others in a group by means of written
notes, and then indicated their final vote privately. In order to contrast homogeneity with heterogeneity, members of some groups were instructed that all
members had equal task skills and members of other groups that there were
marked differences in member skills. Within each of these conditions, high and
low pressures toward uniformity were supplied by informing some but not
other groups that they would later have to defend their group opinions.
Groups were compared in terms of opinion changes and patterns of communication. For analysis purposes, Ss were identified as in the minority or majority
on the basis of their judgments of issue importance.

Results

With respect to number of communications and number of "influence"
communications, the data showed little consistent evidence of differences between groups varying in perceived homogeneity of abilities and pressures
toward uniformity (2/6), with the exception that minority Ss wrote more
influence notes and less notes in general (in the high-pressure condition) than
did majority Ss.

Other discussion data showed that communication was greater on the
issue judged important, particularly for minority Ss (2/2), with no differences
among the various experimental conditions (0/1).

Opinion change was greater in the high-pressure conditions (1/1), and
majority Ss changed their opinions more than did minority Ss in the homogeneous conditions (1/1), although the situation was reversed with respect to
issue importance (1/1). There was slight relationship between change in opinion
and degree of opinion deviation or indexes of change toward opinion uniformity
(2/8).

Study Variables

144) Attitudes toward issues, concepts, ideologies
      Opinion change: *S* responses on issue.
      Importance of issue: *S* responses to rating item.

152) Task or physical position in the group

Majority position in the group: Ss position in majority or minority of the group.

240) General structural properties of the group

Homogeneity of groups regarding member skills: group instruction as to homogeneity or heterogeneity of skills by E.

311) Influence and conformity pressures

Degree of pressure on groups: E exertion of low or high pressure toward uniformity of group opinion.

410) Content of interaction

Degree of changes in opinion: S responses on the notes.
Degree of deviation of opinion: S ratings on the notes.

420) Patterns of interaction

Direction of communication: number of notes sent by Ss to other members.
Amount of communication: total number of notes written by members.
Attempted influence: number of notes written by Ss.

430) Outcomes of interaction

Change in opinion: difference in opinion between first and second session.

510) Perceptions of task performance of self and others

Attempted influence on others: S questionnaire responses.
Perceived disagreement within the group: S questionnaire responses.
Perception of qualifications of other group members: group members' perceptions of others as more or less qualified than themselves.
Perceived influence by group: S questionnaire responses.

695. Gerard, H. B. Some factors affecting an individual's estimate of his probable success in a group situation. *J. abnorm. soc. Psychol.*, 1956, *52*, 235–239.

Purpose

This study examined previous success experience and knowledge of group membership as determinants of estimated future group success.

Procedure

Ss were given a prior experience of either success or failure in group action. They also received either *equivocal information* (by which they knew they would be in a group with two of four possible people) or *nonequivocal information* (by which they knew the composition of the future group). Then they were asked to estimate the probable odds of success for the future group on a task. Es recorded these choices of odds. Afterward, a questionnaire was administered to provide another measure of subjective likelihood of success.

Results

The more successful was an individual's past experience in a group, the more favorable was his estimate of future group success (2/2).

Knowledge of membership composition of a group resulted in more consistent and more favorable predictions of success (2/2) but did not relate to Ss' confidence in their own opinions (0/1).

Study Variables

120) Personality characteristics of members
     Confidence in own opinion: S questionnaire responses.

142) Attitudes toward the situation
     Consistency of estimates: E record of S choice of odds for group success.
     Expected group performance: E record of S choice of odds for group success.

312) Induced social conditions
     Knowledge about composition of future groups: E manipulation of information to give either equivocal or unequivocal information about group composition.

323) Induced task conditions
     Degree of success experienced: E exposure of Ss to previous failure or success.

697. Gerard, H. B. Some effects of involvement upon evaluation. *J. abnorm. soc. Psychol.*, 1958, 57, 118–120.

Purpose

This study analyzed the effect of motivation to perform well on individuals' evaluations of their own and others' contributions to a group discussion.

Procedure

Students were assigned to four-member groups to discuss and formulate questions from a chapter in their textbook. One member from each group was assigned the role of recorder, and as such did not participate in the discussion. High-motivation groups were told that their discussion performance woud be observed and graded, whereas low-motivation groups received no such instructions. After the discussion, Ss ranked each other and themselves on discussion performance and estimated the rankings of each of the other group members.

Results

There was a tendency for highly motivated group members to overestimate their value to the group. In both self-performance rankings and projected rankings by the group, high-motivation Ss ranked themselves significantly higher in performance than they were ranked by other group members (2/2). The self-rankings by low-motivated Ss were not significantly different from their rankings by other group members (0/2). Also, in the high-motivation groups the recorder was more accurate than were discussants in predicting rankings assigned by the group (1/1), whereas no such differences occurred for the low-motivation groups (1/2).

Study Variables

141) Attitudes toward the task

Motivation: E instructions to S concerning importance of discussion.

152) Task or physical position in the group

Participation in discussion: E assignment of S to role of recorder or discussant.

510) Perceptions of task performance of self and others

Member performance: S ranking of each S in group on knowing most, explaining best, and contributing most in discussion.

Prediction of member performance: S prediction of ranking each member would receive from others.

S self-performance rank relative to others' ranking of him (overestimation): discrepancy between rank of S by others and S self-ranking.

Accuracy of prediction of others' ranking of S on performance: discrepancy between rankings by others and projected rankings.

698. Ghiselli, E. E., & Lodahl, T. M. Patterns of managerial traits and group effectiveness. *J. abnorm. soc. Psychol.*, 1958, 57, 61–66.

Purpose

In this study the association of member personal traits and group performance was investigated.

Procedure

Questionnaires measuring supervisory ability and decision-making ability were administered to college students who were then organized into task groups with from two to four members. Groups were given a task—operating a complicated model railroad set—that required intellectual and motor skills and the cooperation of all group members. Performance measures of two basic types were employed—number of correct responses (trips completed around the tracks) and number of errors (train wrecks)—and various combinations and ratios of these two basic measures.

Results

On the basis of intercorrelations of the various performance measures, two clusters were identified and then related to member personal characteristics.

Productivity measures of correct responses (trips completed) were related to some measures of member supervisory ability and decision-making ability but not to others (4/8). For example, there was no relation between performance and average group scores or highest individual scores on both traits (0/4), but there was a high relationship between performance and measures of skewness and range of scores (4/4).

Carefulness measures of incorrect responses (train wrecks) were not related to measures of supervisory and decision-making ability (1/8).

Analysis also showed that the more-productive groups on both criterion measures made fewer changes in team organization and problem-solving approach than the less-productive groups (2/2).

Study Variables

132) Task abilities of members
Supervisory ability: S responses on a self-description inventory.
Decision-making ability: S responses on a self-description inventory.

631) Group task performance in experimental settings
Group problem-solving behavior: E record of organizational changes made by group, changing methods of solving a problem, and so on.
Group performance: ratings of degree of carefulness.
Group performance effectiveness: number of correct responses and errors.

715. Gibb, Lorraine M., & Gibb, J. R. *Effects of the use of "participative action" groups in a course in general psychology.* Boulder, Colo.: University of Colorado September, 1952.

Purpose

This study tested the effectiveness of different teaching methods in a classroom situation.

Procedure

Control groups were taught by a traditional lecture–discussion method with occasional demonstrations or movies, whereas experimental groups were taught by a "participative action" method that maximized student participation by allowing group goal setting, problem formulation, decision making, and so on. Os rated performance and participation during several discussion periods. In addition, multiple-choice and essay tests were given, together with other measures that tapped satisfaction with the course, likableness of others, etc.

Results

Teaching method did not relate to performance on any type of written test, although students from experimental groups were rated as exhibiting more ability to think during the discussion, as having more knowledge about psychological terms, and as being more effective group members (3/3).

Type of training did not relate, however, to participation in discussion (0/2) or satisfaction with the course (0/1).

Study Variables

131) General abilities of members
Member performance: S performance on achievement test.

132) Task abilities of members
Leadership ability: Ss ranking of their fellow group members on leadership ability.
Discussion performance: S performance in discussion as ranked by graduate students in terms of ability to think during discussions and effectiveness as group members.

141) Attitudes toward the task
Satisfaction with the training course: S rating of the course.

151) Social position in the group
Likability: Ss ranking their fellow group members on likability.

222) Group training and experience
Type of training: S instruction by direct participation method or more passive procedure.
Type of group-teaching method: E assignment of groups to training conditions of high or low direct participation.

420) Patterns of interaction
Participation in discussion: O record of each S's participation in discussion.

430) Outcomes of interaction
Choice of further courses: S choice of additional psychological courses.

520) Perceptions of social behavior of self and others
Social perceptiveness: deviation of S ranking of group from the median group rating.
Self-insight: difference between S self-ranking and ranking given him by others.

728. Gleason, W. J. Predicting army leadership ability by modified leaderless group discussion. *J. appl. Psychol.*, 1957, *41*, 231–235.

Purpose

This study analyzed the association between peer rankings of leadership following leaderless group discussion and intelligence and leadership in a training school.

Procedure

Basic-training graduates assigned to a military leadership course comprised the subjects of this study. On the first day of the course, Ss were assigned to seven- to nine-man leaderless groups to discuss the problem of training leaders. Following the discussion, group members ranked each other on leadership displayed. At the end of the course, group members were given a final leadership score based on the following: personality and over-all leadership ability ratings by faculty, personality and leadership ratings by Os during training and during performance on an OSS-type situational test, and peer ratings by fellow students.

Results

Group member rankings of leadership displayed during a leaderless group session were predictive of leadership scores received in training (20/27). Peer rankings were also correlated with the other criteria used in the final leadership grade: faculty ratings of personality traits and over-all leadership abilities and O ratings of traits and leadership during training and on an OSS-type situational test (3/3).

The relationship between peer leadership rankings and intelligence was unclear, with a positive relation for pooled classes (1/1) and an ambiguous relationship for individual classes (6/10). A similar trend was noted between intelligence test scores and final leadership scores (4/11).

Study Variables

120) Personality characteristics of members

Personality ability: faculty ratings of S on personality traits and leadership.

131) General abilities of members

Intelligence: S score on Area Aptitude Intelligence Test.

132) Task abilities of members

Peer rating of leadership: S rating of other members on leadership. Peer ranking of leadership: S ranking of other members in terms of leadership.

610) Leadership performance

Leadership performance: O rating of S during situational test. Personality and leadership performance: O rating of S during training period.

740. Goldman-Eisler, Frieda. The measurement of time sequences in conversational behavior. *Brit. J. Psychol.*, 1951, *42*, 355–362.

Purpose

This study examined the hypothesis that certain relations between time sequences in conversation were constant, within limits, for individuals, regardless of situation, topics, or partners.

Procedure

Series of conversations of the same speakers with different people were recorded on a chronograph tape with respect to the durations of actions (talk and gestures) and silences. Measures were determined for long and short actions and silences, and various ratios of these measures were computed. Scores were derived for the same individual over several sessions ("individual" scores) and for different individuals ("groups"). These individual and group scores were compared with respect to their stability.

Results

For the ratio of long actions to long silences, group scores (from different Ss) showed a greater skewness than did those scores based on a single person (1/1). Moreover, kurtosis of the group scores indicated "peakedness" of the distribution (1/1).

For the ratio of short silences to long silences, skewness and kurtosis results were identical to those described in the preceding paragraph (2/2).

In connection with these results, the author stated, "The frequency of long silences thus shows a higher degree of reliability than any of the other ratio-components used in this investigation. A capacity for maintaining long periods of silence, or holding up action, or, viewed differently, an inhibition of expression in social interaction, seems to constitute a relatively permanent feature in an individual's conversational behaviour."

Study Variables

240) General structural properties of the group
Occurrence of group: statistical derivation of scores of Ss alone or in group.

420) Patterns of interaction
Discussion behavior (ratios of action and silence, short and long silence periods, and so on): E record of S actions.

756. Grace, H. A. The effects of different degrees of knowledge about an audience on the content of communication: the comparison of male and female audiences. *J. soc. Psychol.*, 1952, *36*, 89–96.

Purpose

This study investigated the effects of different degrees of knowledge about an audience on immediate recall.

Procedure

College students of each sex were individually instructed on procedure in one of three ways:

1. Some students were told that two minutes would be allowed to study objects on the table, after which S was to report these items to a person in an adjoining part of the room.

2. In addition to the foregoing, some Ss were told the sex of the person to whom they would report.

3. In addition to the foregoing, some Ss were briefed very carefully about the sex of their audience and told to keep that sex in mind while studying the items.

About half the Ss reported to female audiences and half to male audiences. Of the 45 life-sized, randomized objects, 15 were female-linked, 15 male-linked, and 15 neuter-linked.

Results

There was no relationship between sex of the audience and *S*s' recall of any type of items (3/39). Also, no relationships were found for sex and recall of any items (0/9) or knowledge about the sex of the audience and recall (0/18).

In addition, different interactions of sex of the audience, sex of *S*s, and knowledge about audience sex were not related to recall for any type of item (15/161).

Study Variables

110) Biographical characteristics of members

Substitute: Biographical characteristic: *S* sex.

312) Induced social conditions

Degree of knowledge about audience: *S*s' knowledge of sex of *E* to whom they would have to report.

Sex of experimenter: receipt by either man or woman of *S* reports.

621) Member task performance in experimental settings

Individual performance: accuracy of recall of items.

757. Grace, H. A. The effects of different degrees of knowledge about an audience on the content of communication: the male audience. *J. soc. Psychol.*, 1952, *36*, 83–88.

Purpose

This study compared the recall of sex-linked items for persons given different degrees of information about the sex of an audience to whom they were reporting.

Procedure

Individual *S*s were required to study 45 objects that were classified as male sex-linked, female sex-linked, or neuter-linked. After study, they reported as many objects as remembered to a recorder. The amount of information given *S*s about the sex of the audience to which they were to report was varied: some *S*s were not told the recorder's sex, others were told the sex of the recorder, and still others were impressed with the sex of the recorder by *E*.

Results

No differences in recall were found between males and females with different degrees of information about the sex of the audience (2/54).

With respect to the recall of sex-linkage characteristics, however, both sexes recalled sex-linked items more frequently than neutral items (6/8) but did not differentially recall specific types of sex-linked items (1/4). These results occured only in cases where sex of audience was *not known*; a slight relationship was found between item characteristics and recall for conditions where the audience was known (6/24).

Study Variables

110) Biographical characteristics of members
Biographical characteristic: S sex.

312) Induced social conditions
Knowledge about audience: E instructions to Ss regarding sex of recorder to whom they would report.
Stimulus characteristics: E designation of sex linkage of items S required to remember and report.

621) Member task performance in experimental settings
Recall: E record of number of stimulus items Ss correctly reported.

758.* **Grace, H. A.** Conformance and performance. *J. soc. Psychol.*, 1954, *40*, 333–335.

Purpose

This study investigated whether group performance was a function of the similarity of member attitudes and the degree of cooperation among members.

Procedure

The performance of high school basketball teams was determined on the basis of their percentage of wins during a basketball season. Then, two measures were administered: a sociometric preference inventory, in which each player chose team members he considered most and least cooperative, and a scale in which Ss selected statements as most and least descriptive of themselves. Several measures derived from these instruments were tested for relationship to team performance.

Results

Results of statistical tests of significance were not presented. However, the author stated that the sociometric measures of cooperation and the method of scoring a self-attitude inventory yielded an attitude similarity score suggesting that good group performance was a function of the similarity of the members of the group to each other and to the general sample of which they were a part.

This study contained a total of 20 relationships.

Study Variables

240) General structural properties of the group
Conformity: similarity of S responses on a self-description test.

510) Perceptions of task performance of self and others
Perceived team cooperation: S responses on a sociometric choice instrument.

632) Group task performance in operational settings: global measures
Team performance: E rating of team according to percentage of games won.

766. Greer, F. L. *Small group effectiveness.* Philadelphia,Pa.: Institute for Research in Human Relations, 1955. (Inst. Rep. No. 6, Contract No. Nonr-1229(00))

Purpose

This study investigated how personality variables and group cohesion influenced Army squad effectiveness.

Procedure

Infantrymen were administered questionnaires measuring adjustment to the Army, paranoid tendencies, social activities, equalitarianism, physical prowess, group cohesion, and helpfulness of leaders. In addition, *S*s participated in an individual interview. Furthermore, information was obtained about position in the squad and the length of time *S*s had spent in the squad. Group effectiveness measures were based upon ratings of infantry rifle squads during a six-hour blank-firing simulated tactical problem. According to their performance, squads were divided into low- and high-performance groups. Questionnaire responses were related to performance scores.

Results

The higher members scored on measures of physical prowess, self-reliance, social activeness, and general adjustment to the Army and the lower they scored on paranoid tendencies and nervousness, the better was squad performance (15/24). Other personality variables were only slightly related to squad effectiveness (4/20).

There was a slight relationship between sociometric choices or group cohesiveness and squad effectiveness in performance (17/68), except that sociometric choices for squad leaders and ratings of their helpfulness related positively to group effectiveness (15/25).

Study Variables

110) Biographical characteristics of members

Biographical characteristics (length of time spent in the squad): *S* report of length of time served in squad.

120) Personality characteristics of members

Perceived personality characteristics of self: *S* scores on questionnaire tapping paranoid tendencies, nervousness, and so on.

Perceived physical prowess of self: *S* answers to an attitude questionnaire.

Perceived self-reliance: *S* scores on an attitude questionnaire.

Personal equalitarianism: *S* scores on questionnaire.

Level of aspiration: *S* scores on questionnaire.

132) Task abilities of members

Helpfulness with problems: *S* ranking of leaders.

Discrepancy between ideal and actual leader: *S* ranking of leaders.

143) Attitudes toward nongroup persons and other groups
    General adjustment to Army: *S* questionnaire response.
151) Social position in the group
    Group status: *S* position in the squad.
230) Interpersonal relations in the group
    Sociometric choice and rejection: *S* scores on sociometric test.
    Sociometric choices given and received by squads and squad leader:
    scores on sociometric test.
632) Group task performance in operational settings: global measures
    Type of squad: effective or ineffective.
633) Group task performance in operational settings: specific measures
    Squad effectiveness: *O* rating of squad performance in military field
    problem.

767.* Greer, F. L., et al. Interpersonal knowledge and individual and group effectiveness. *J. abnorm. soc. Psychol.*, 1954, *49*, 411–414.

Purpose

This experiment studied the association between knowledge of interpersonal relationships and group performance effectiveness.

Procedure

Two measures of group-related attitudes and perceptions were obtained during individual interviews with Army infantry squad members: sociometric rankings of other squad members and rankings of popularity of others and himself as he estimated the squad would respond. Accuracy of perception of interpersonal relationships in squads was measured by comparing estimated and actual judgments for each person. In addition, personal background information and intelligence test data were obtained. Furthermore, *O*s rated each squad on its performance effectiveness while carrying out assigned missions.

Results

The more accurate were squad members in perceiving sociometric relationships within their squads and the more intelligent were the squad leaders, the more effective were the squads in carrying out their tasks (3/3). Age, rank, and other biographical characteristics were not related to squad effectiveness (0/5).

In addition, *S*s with greater popularity were also more accurate in perceiving the interpersonal structure of their squads (3/3).

This study contained a total of 15 relationships.

Study Variables

110) Biographical characteristics of members
    Biographical characteristics: *S* self-report during interview on age,
    education, military rank, and so on.

131) General abilities of members

> Intelligence: *S* scores on intelligence test.

151) Social position in the group

> Popularity: *S* ranking of other group members on liking.
>
> Accuracy of social perception: squad members' ranking of other group members on liking compared with estimate of squad judgment of liking.

152) Task or physical position in the group

> Rank of member in the squad: *S* selection for the experiment— leaders and squad members.

230) Interpersonal relations in the group

> Sociometric choice of *S* for a particular activity: *S* score on 10-item sociometric test.

633) Group task performance in operational settings: specific measures

> Squad effectiveness: *O* rating of squads on their specific actions in mission.

777. Gross, E. Primary functions of the small group. *Amer. J. Sociol.*, 1954, *60*, 24–30.

Purpose

This study measured group morale as related to group cohesion.

Procedure

Enlisted officers and men attached to an Air Force base were used as *S*s. Three indexes of group cohesion were obtained from responses to rating scales: *integration*, or *S*'s activity preference and history of interaction with others; *correspondence plurel*, or *S*'s preferences regarding with whom to correspond after leaving Air Force; and *frequency of interaction*, or *O*'s rating of frequency that *S*s attended informal gatherings together. Morale was measured by responses to several rating scales: satisfaction with Air Force, satisfaction with air site, satisfaction with job, personal commitment to group goals, and personal *esprit*.

Results

*S*s of more-integrated groups were less satisfied with the air site and their jobs than were *S*s of less-integrated groups (2/2), but integration was not related to satisfaction with Air Force, personal commitment to group goals, or *esprit* (0/3).

*S*s more willing to correspond with other group members had a higher personal *esprit* and also liked the Air Force better than did those who did not want to correspond with others (2/2). However, there was no relationship between the desire to correspond with others and satisfaction with air site, job, or personal commitment to group goals (0/3).

The more frequently Ss interacted with other group members, the more they were commited to group goals—and the more frequently they showed less personal *esprit* (2/2). However, frequency of interaction did not relate to Ss' satisfaction with the Air Force, the air site, or their jobs (0/3).

Study Variables

141) Attitudes toward the task

Feelings of personal commitment to group goals and *esprit:* S self-rating

Job satisfaction: S rating of job.

143) Attitudes toward nongroup persons and other groups

Satisfaction with Air Force and air site: S score on rating scale.

230) Interpersonal relations in the group

Liking of others: S ratings of people with whom they spent time and with whom they would like to correspond.

420) Patterns of interaction

Group interaction: E rating of frequency of informal group interaction.

778. Gross, E. Symbiosis and consensus as integrative factors in small groups. *Amer. sociol. Rev.*, 1956, *21*, 174–179.

Purpose

This study compared the attraction between members of groups of different size and composition (according to biographical characteristics).

Procedure

Questionnaire responses of Air Force personnel to questions about the identity of their companions during their free hours were compared, and groups varying in size from two to four were identified. A measure of mutual attraction was obtained by S's ratings of those they most enjoyed being with and those they "would rather not have around." Average attraction scores were obtained for groups of each size and each degree of homogeneity with respect to age, marital status, siblings, and other biographical characteristics.

Results

Similarity of biographical traits of group members appeared to play a part in member attraction to each other, particularly for pairs. For example, members of pairs *similar* in marital status, birthplace of parents, other source of income, and college attendance reported significantly *lower* attraction to one another than did unlike pairs (7/8). On the other hand, similarity in terms of Air Force career intention, length of time in service, background in other branches of service, present career intention, and high school graduation was *positively* related to mutual attraction (6/10).

Groups of three reported higher attraction when they were dissimilar in technical training in the Air Force and marital status, groups of four when they were dissimilar in religion and Air Force career intention (4/4).

Traits that failed to differentiate groups of all sizes were age, siblings, overseas service, time in present specialty, preservice occupation, and work section (0/24). Dyads were further undifferentiated with respect to technical training in the Air Force and religion (0/4); triads were further undifferentiated on birthplace of parents, other source of income, length of time in service, background in other branches of service, present career intention, college attendance, high school graduation, technical training in Air Force, and marital status (0/18).

Study Variables

230) Interpersonal relations in the group

Member mutual attraction: S rating of others on sociometric instrument.

240) General structural properties of the group

Group homogeneity in biographical characteristics: E description of whether Ss were similar in age, religion, time in service, and so on.

789.* Guetzkow, H., & Dill, W. R. Factors in the organizational development of task-oriented groups. *Sociometry*, 1957, *20*, 175–204.

Purpose

This study examined how communication restrictions and occasional removal of such restrictions affected group performance.

Procedure

Groups solved problems under one of three types of communication nets: *all-channel* (having no restrictions upon communication), *wheel*, and *circle*. However, in some circle groups (circle A–C), there was an intertrial period in which all channels were open for member communications. On task trials, the appropriate channels were closed. Performance level was measured in terms of the length of time the groups required to solve a problem. Observations were also made of various types of communications among members.

Results

Circle-net groups allowed completely open channels (circle A–C) between task trials performed no better than did circle groups without such intertrial communication (0/2) and performed worse than all-channel groups (2/2). No differences occurred between circle A–C and wheel groups (0/2).

This study contained a total of 162 relationships.

Study Variables

240) General structural properties of the group

Type of communication nets: E assignment of groups to all-channel, wheel, or circle nets.

631) Group task performance in experimental settings
     Group performance: *E* record of time needed by groups to finish
     the task.

790.* Guetzkow, H., & Gyr, J. An analysis of conflict in decision-making groups. *Hum. Relat.*, 1954, 7, 367–382.

Purpose

This study explored discussion factors associated with group consensus
in groups differing with respect to degree of discussion conflict.

Procedure

Use was made of data collected from business and governmental conferences. High- and low-consensus groups were designated from *S*s' responses
during a postconference interview on the discrepancy between their own and
group final opinions on the question discussed.

*O*s kept accounts of the direction of participations, the nature of each
contribution in terms of its problem-solving characteristics (whether it gave
information, requested opinions, clarified, and so on), and comments relating
to personal and interpersonal aspects of discussions. In addition, some *S*s
were interviewed to provide supplementary information. On the basis of discussion behavior, analyses were conducted to compare groups who exhibited
high and low substantive conflict (disagreements about the issues) and high
and low affective conflict (group "frustrations").

Groups high and low in consensus were subdivided according to degree
and kind of conflict and then compared with respect to various aspects of
discussion and interview behavior.

Results

In general groups terminating their discussion with high consensus of
individual members were rated as more orderly than were groups with low
consensus (3/4). This finding held for all groups except those with low affective
conflict.

High-consensus groups also showed greater understanding of each other
in the high-conflict conditions, both affective and substantive (2/2), but not
in the low-conflict conditions (0/2). In addition, consensus groups were differentiated on problem-solving efficiency in the substantive conflict groups (2/2)
and not in the affective conflict groups (0/2).

This study contained a total of 89 relationships.

Study Variables

430) Outcomes of interaction
        Group discussion performance: *O* postconference rating on order-
        liness, efficiency of problem-solving process in group.

510) Perceptions of task performance of self and others
        Perceived group consensus: *S* report in interview on similarity of
        own and group opinions.

794. Gurnee, H. Maze learning in the collective situation. *J. Psychol.*, 1937, *3*, 437–443.

Purpose

This study compared the learning rate of a group proceeding through the steps of a maze by plurality votes with the learning rate of individuals working alone.

Procedure

Forty-two individuals and 12 groups were required to learn the correct pathway of an electric-contact maze. The groups proceeded by plurality votes, voting by acclamation, with a show of hands in case of a tie. *E* asked for the decision each time, stated the vote, and recorded the errors. *S*s' scores on the Bernreuter Personality Inventory, their college grades, and their scores on a general aptitude test for chemistry were also obtained.

Results

Groups made fewer errors in maze learning than did *S*s working alone (3/3). Also, the higher were *S*s' college grades and chemistry aptitude scores, the fewer errors *S*s made in maze learning (2/2).

There was no significant relationship between the number of errors and any of the tested personality characteristics: self-sufficiency, introversion, dominance, confidence, and sociability (0/5).

Study Variables

120) Personality characteristics of members
       Personality characteristics (self-sufficiency, introversion, and so on): scores on Bernreuter Personality Inventory.
131) General abilities of members
       College grades: grades in college.
       Intellectual ability: scores on aptitude test.
240) General structural properties of the group
       Social facilitation: *S* assignment to work alone or in groups.
       Sex homogeneity of groups: *S* assignment to homogeneous or mixed-sex groups.
621) Member task performance in experimental settings
       Performance in maze learning: number of *S* errors.

806. Hall, R. L. *Predicting bomber crew performance from the aircraft commander's role.* San Antonio, Tex.: Lackland Air Force Base, Crew Research Laboratory, 1956. (Res. Rep. AFPTRC-TN-56-28)

Purpose

This study examined relationships between several aspects of aircraft commander behavior and crew performance effectiveness and attitudes.

Procedure

Aircraft crews completed a questionnaire dealing with three aspects of their commander's behavior: nurturance-supportiveness, intimacy with crew members, and militariness. Crews also expressed their opinions on what an "ideal" leader should be like in these respects. In addition, crews were administered an attitude scale measuring aspects of their attitudes toward the Air Force. Several measures of performance in combat and training missions were obtained by peer and superior ratings.

Results

There were four main predictor variables: actual behavior of commander, ideal behavior of commander, agreement among crew members on ideal commander behavior, and discrepancy between ideal and actual behavior of the commander. Each of these measures was obtained for nurturance, intimacy, and militariness items of the questionnaire.

There were also two major resultant variable classes, each consisting of several subtypes:

1. Performance measures, which included crew compatibility in combat performance, quality of crew, over-all effectiveness of combat performance, technical proficiency of crew in combat, lack of crew adjustment in combat tasks, peer ratings of technical proficiency of fellow members, and over-all effectiveness of commander's combat performance

2. Attitude measures, which included degree of safety in flying, satisfaction with job assignment, liking for own crew, sense of personal well-being in Air Force, confidence in superior officers, peer choices of crew members for friends, motivation to have an effective crew, and attitude toward importance of Korean conflict

These variables were tested for relationships to each other with the following results:

1. Ideal aircraft commander role behavior

   a. Nurturance (the extent to which commander was concerned with crew member personal welfare and comfort)

     (1) Performance measures: highly and positively related to crew compatibility, quality, and technical proficiency (3/3), not related to other measures (0/4)

     (2) Attitude measures: positively and highly related to member liking of their own crew and job assignment, safety in flying, and peer ratings of fellow members (4/4), not related to other measures (0/4)

   b. Intimacy (the extent to which commander established personal ties and engaged in social activities with crew)

     (1) Performance measures: highly and positively related to crew compatibility (1/1), not related to other measures (0/6)

     (2) Attitude measures: highly and positively related to peer ratings of fellow members and friends, safety in flying, satisfaction with job assignment, liking of own crew and Air Force, and motivation to have effective crew (7/7), not related to remaining measures (0/1)

   c. Militariness (the extent to which commander enforced military standards and procedures)
- (1) Performance measures: not related to militariness (0/7)
- (2) Attitude measures: not related to militariness (0/8)

2. Agreement among crew members on ideal commander's behavior

   a. Nurturance
- (1) Performance measures: not related to nurturance (0/7)
- (2) Attitude measures: not related to nurturance (0/8)

   b. Intimacy
- (1) Performance measures: high negative relationship to crew compatibility and peer ratings of technical proficiency of fellow members (2/2); not related to other measures (0/5)
- (2) Attitude measures: high negative relationship to safety in flying, satisfaction with job assignment, liking of own crew, personal well-being, and opinions of Korean conflict (5/5); not related to other measures (0/3)

   c. Militariness
- (1) Performance measures: not related to militariness (0/7)
- (2) Attitude measures: not related to militariness (0/8)

3. Actual role behavior of commanders

   a. Nurturance
- (1) Performance measures: highly and positively related to crew compatibility, quality, and technical proficiency in combat (3/3), not related to other measures (0/4)
- (2) Attitude measures: highly and positively related to safety in flying, satisfaction with job assignment, and liking of own crew (3/3), not related to other measures (0/5)

   b. Intimacy
- (1) Performance measures: not related to intimacy (0/7)
- (2) Attitude measures: highly and positively related to liking of own crew, satisfaction with job assignment, and personal well-being (3/3), not related to other measures (0/5)

   c. Militariness
- (1) Performance measures: not related to militariness (0/7)
- (2) Attitude measures: not related to militariness (0/8)

4. Discrepancy between ideal and actual behavior ratings of commander

   a. Nurturance
- (1) Performance measures: high negative relationship to compatibility and peer ratings of technical proficiency of fellow members (2/2); not related to other measures (0/5)
- (2) Attitude measures: high negative relationship to motivation for effective crew (1/1); not related to other measures (0/7)

   b. Intimacy
- (1) Performance measures: high negative relationship to crew compatibility and technical proficiency and to member technical proficiency (3/3); not related to other measures (0/4)

(2) Attitude measures: high negative relationship to liking of own crew and satisfaction with job assignment (2/2); not related to others measures (0/6)

c. Militariness

(1) Performance measures: highly related to lack of adjustment in combat tasks (1/1), not related to other measures (0/6)

(2) Attitude measures: high negative relationship to confidence in superior officers (1/1); not related to other measures (0/7)

Study Variables

141) Attitudes toward the task

Motivation to have effective crew: crew member responses to attitude scale.

142) Attitudes toward the situation

Sense of safety in flying: crew member responses to attitude scale.
Satisfaction with assignment: crew member responses to attitude scale.
Personal well-being in Air Force: crew member responses to attitude scale.

143) Attitudes toward nongroup persons and other groups

Confidence in superiors: crew member responses to attitude scale.

144) Attitudes toward issues, concepts, ideologies

Ideal leader behavior: crew member questionnaire responses regarding militariness, nurturance, intimacy with crew.
Attitude toward importance of Korean conflict: crew member responses to attitude scale.

230) Interpersonal relations in the group

Choice of others for friends and combat: crew member questionnaire responses.
Liking for own crew: crew member responses to attitude scale.

240) General structural properties of the group

Type of crews in experiment: selection of individual crews for the study.

430) Outcomes of interaction

Crew compatibility in combat: staff officer rating of crew compatibility.
Quality of crew coordination, teamwork, motivation, ability to stand up to stress: crew qualifications based on rating by staff officers.

510) Perceptions of task performance of self and others

Technical proficiency and compatibility of crew members: crew member rating of fellow members on questionnaire.

520) Perceptions of social behavior of self and others

Leader behavior: crew member rating of commander on militariness, nurturance, and intimacy with crew.
Discrepancy between ideal and actual leader behavior: discrepancy between ideal and actual behavior rating of aircraft commander on militariness, nurturance, and intimacy with crew.

610) Leadership performance
    Crew leader combat effectiveness: staff officer rating of commander performance.

632) Group task performance in operational settings: global measures
    Crew combat performance: staff officer rating of crew performance. Crew adjustment in combat: staff officer rating of crew on discipline, aborted missions, and so on.

633) Group task performance in operational settings: specific measures
    Technical proficiency of crew in combat: staff officer rating of crew technical proficiency.

807.* Hall, R. L. Group performance under feedback that confounds responses of group members. *Sociometry*, 1957, *20*, 297–305.

Purpose

This study investigated performance effectiveness as a function of practice and the type of feedback information received about earlier performance.

Procedure

Air Force trainees were assigned to work in pairs on a perceptual motor task. Each S performed alone and after each trial was given a team score that was a weighted average of his own and his partner's score. This "socially confounded feedback" was based either on an equal weighting of both S's scores, or on a disproportionate weighting of the score of one of the partners. Pretraining also varied, in that one group of Ss were given accurate feedback about their own performance whereas others were pretrained under confounded conditions identical to those to which they would be exposed during the experimental sessions. Team performance was based on the combined scores of both Ss.

Results

Ss were undifferentiated in actual performance whatever the nature of the pretraining feedback (0/2). Also, equal or disproportionate weighting of member scores did not yield performance differences (0/2).

There was a trend of increasing accuracy for all teams over 10 trials (2/2) but not over 25 trials (1/2). Teams with team-feedback pretraining, however, improved at a faster rate over 25 trials than did teams with individual pretraining (2/2). This difference was not significant over a 10-trial period (0/2).

All other first- and second-order interactions between type of pretraining, equality of weighting member scores, and stage of practice were not related to team accuracy (0/6).

This study contained a total of 40 relationships.

Study Variables

222) Group training and experience
    Stage of practice: E count of each trial in sequence.

322) Feedback and reinforcement conditions

Type of pretraining feedback: *E* manipulation of feedback as team or individual.

Equality of weight of team member participations: *E* manipulation of relative weight of member's accuracy to total accuracy score for team at 3:1 or 2:2 ratio.

621) Member task performance in experimental settings

Accuracy of member performance: *E* record of distance of switch adjustments where a predetermined distance was correct response.

811.* **Halpin, A. W.** *Studies in aircrew composition: III. The combat leader behavior of B-29 aircraft commanders.* Washington, D.C.: Bolling Air Force Base, Human Factors Operations Research Laboratory, September, 1953. (HFORL Memorandum No. TN-54-7)

Purpose

This study evaluated the relationship between group member ratings of leader behavior and leader combat performance.

Procedure

A questionnaire administered to air crew members required ratings of crew commanders in terms of consideration, human relations behavior, and supervisory behavior. Also, squadron and wing superiors rated crew commanders, during an interview, on technical competence, motivation, over-all effectiveness, and similar measures. In addition, crew members rated commanders on confidence, friendship, proficiency, morale, and cooperation. Correlations were computed for the two leader behavior dimensions and the sets of ratings by superiors and crew members.

Results

Generally, crew member judgments of leader supervisory behavior were highly and positively related to leader effectiveness as measured by superior ratings (8/10), although consideration–human relations behavior was not (0/13).

There was a slight relationship between crew member ratings of leader friendship, cooperation, and member satisfaction with the leader and his performance effectiveness (1/6).

This study contained a total of 32 relationships.

Study Variables

230) Interpersonal relations in the group

Satisfaction, friendship with leader: crew member responses to rating form.

610) Leadership performance

Leader supervisory behavior: crew member questionnaire responses. Leader human relations behavior: crew member questionnaire responses.

Supervisor effectiveness performance: staff officer rating of supervisors during an interview.

Commander supervisory and human relations behavior: crew member questionnaire responses.

814. Halpin, A. W. The leadership ideology of aircraft commanders. *J. appl. Psychol.*, 1955, *39*, 82–84.

Purpose

This study compared actual with ideal behavior and characteristics of air crew leaders.

Procedure

Air Force air crews—both commander and crew members—completed an 80-item leader behavior questionnaire. In responding, the crew commander indicated his feelings about the ideal crew leader's behavior, and the crew members rated the actual behavior of their aircraft commander on the same items. The questionnaire covered two areas, supervisory ability and human relations behavior.

Results

The aircraft commander's opinion and knowledge about how he should behave as a leader did not coincide in all cases with the way he actually behaved as perceived by his crew.

Aircraft commanders' opinions about how a leader should supervise group operations did not relate to actual supervisory behavior (0/1). Moreover, the correlation between commanders' awareness of the human relations aspect of leadership and ratings received from their crew members barely reached significance (1/1). Leader ideal supervisory behavior was highly related to ideal leader human relations behavior (1/1). Similarly, crew ratings of their leader on supervision were related to ratings on human relations behavior (1/1).

Study Variables

144) Attitudes toward issues, concepts, ideologies

Ideal leader supervisory behavior: aircraft commander questionnaire responses on ideal supervisory methods.

Ideal leader human relations behavior: leader questionnaire responses on personal relations with crew.

240) General structural properties of the group

Individual crews: E designation of each crew used in study.

510) Perceptions of task performance of self and others

Leader actual supervisory behavior: crew member questionnaire responses about leader supervisor.

520) Perceptions of social behavior of self and others

Leader actual human relations behavior: crew member questionnaire responses.

837. Harris, E. F., & Fleishman, E. A. Human relations training and the stability of leadership patterns. *J. appl. Psychol.*, 1955, *39*, 20–25.

Purpose

This study evaluated a human relations training program in terms of changes in leadership behavior and attitudes of workers toward their leader.

Procedure

Members of factory work groups were administered questionnaires requiring judgments of the supervisory behavior and human relations–consideration behavior of their foremen. Foremen also completed the questionnaire from the point of view of how the "ideal supervisor" should behave. One group of foremen then attended a refresher training course in human relations, whereas other foremen did not. Still other foremen had neither initial nor refresher training. Both questionnaires were then readministered to all groups and scores were compared to see whether changes had occurred as a function of the refresher training course.

Results

This experiment demonstrated the general effect of human relations training on attitudes of workers toward their supervisors.

Foremen who had had no training whatsoever in human relations (initial or refresher) showed a high consistency of pre- and posttraining supervisory and consideration scores received from subordinates (2/2). Contrariwise, those who had had some initial training showed less correlation of the pre- and posttraining scores (1/2).

Of those who had received the initial training, some were exposed to a refresher course and some were not. There were slight changes in ratings of leaders on their supervisory consideration behavior for either type of group (1/6), and no differences in foremen's ratings of ideal supervisor's behavior (0/6).

However, for those who took the refresher course, there was little relationship between pre- and postrefresher test scores (1/2), as compared with the scores of those who had not taken the course (2/2).

In addition, foremen's ratings of what they considered to be ideal behavior were consistently related, regardless of training conditions (4/4).

Study Variables

144) Attitudes toward issues, concepts, ideologies

Leader ideal behavior: leader questionnaire responses on what an ideal leader should do.

222) Group training and experience

Leader training in human relations: E selection of leaders with or without training in human relations.

510) Perceptions of task performance of self and others

> Leader behavior-initiating structure: group member ratings of supervisors.
>
> Leader behavior effectiveness: group member ratings of their supervisors.

849. Harvey, O. J., & Consalve, C. *Status and conformity to pressures of informal groups.* Nashville, Tenn.: Vanderbilt University, 1958. (Tech. Rep. No. 6, Contract Nonr-214902)

Purpose

This study examined the conformity of individuals of various sociometric status when the individuals were under pressure from other group members.

Procedure

Twenty-seven sociometrically selected cliques of delinquent boys from a training school were used, with each clique made up of four to five Ss. Members of each group were asked to judge the distance between two simultaneous flashes of light in a dark room. The top-ranking, second-ranking, and lowest-ranking members estimated the distance between one set of flashes while the rest of the group members judged another set of flashes. Ss were under the impression that they all saw the same lights. Judgments were made under public and private conditions.

Results

In general, the sociometric status of a group member was found to be a rather important determinant of conformity behavior.

Group members ranked second in sociometric status conformed more to group judgments of others than did either the highest- or lowest-ranking members during the public judgment period (2/2). No differences occurred under private judgment conditions for any Ss (0/3).

Top- and second-ranked members exerted a greater influence on public judgments than did the lowest-ranked persons (2/2). The magnitude of this influence by the highest-ranked person was also pronounced under private judgment conditions (2/2).

Study Variables

230) Interpersonal relations in the group

> Sociometric status: S choice of group members on sociometric test.

430) Outcomes of interaction

> Conformity and influence on others: change in initial judgment, change in other members' judgment, and so on.
>
> Member influence on group: difference between group and individual judgment of stimulus.

856.* Havron, M. D., et al.   *The effectiveness of small military units.* Washington, D.C.: The Adjutant General's Office, Personnel Research Section, 1952. (PRS Rep. 980)

Purpose

This study investigated how job knowledge, biographical information, attitudes, and similar variables influenced performance of Army squads and squad leaders.

Procedure

Members of Army rifle squads were administered paper-and-pencil tests measuring attitudes and personality characteristics, military job knowledge, biographical information, squad friendship choices, and so on. Squads were assigned to different courses of training, and umpires rated squad and squad leader performance on various field problems. Questionnaire scores were related to performance scores in order to predict squad performance in field problems.

Results

In respect to leader performance, results showed that the better the leader's military knowledge and the more generally effective the squads, the better was the leader's performance in field problems (5/5). However, leader personal history, personality characteristics, and internal squad sociometric patterns were only slightly related to leader performance (3/18).

In respect to squad performance, results showed that general ratings of squad over-all effectiveness did not relate to performance (0/3).

In respect to combined leader and squad performance, results showed that leader military knowledge, physical prowess, and adjustment to the Army were highly related to combined performance scores (10/10), whereas other attitudes, type of regiment from which squads came, sociometric choice patterns within squads, squad members' personal history characteristics, and type of field problem were only slightly related to performance (11/71).

This study contained a total of 217 relationships.

Study Variables

110) Biographical characteristics of members
   Biographical characteristics: age, education, time in Army and combat, etc.

120) Personality characteristics of members
   Personality characteristics: squad member questionnaire responses on authoritarianism, nonconformism, self-reliance, etc.

131) General abilities of members
   Perceived physical skills: squad member questionnaire responses.

132) Task abilities of members
   Leader military knowledge: S responses to NCO military knowledge test.

230) Interpersonal relations in the group
      Sociometric choices: squad member sociometric choices.

240) General structural properties of the group
      Type of regiment from which squads were selected: E selection of squads.

321) Stimulus properties of the task
      Type of task courses: E assignment of Ss to different courses of equal difficulty.
      Type of subtask: E assignment of the order of phases within the field problem.

610) Leadership performance
      Leader performance: umpire rating of leaders on field problems.
      Over-all leader effectiveness: platoon leader rating of squad leaders.

633) Group task performance in operational settings: specific measures
      Over-all effectiveness of squads: platoon leader rating of squads on field problems.
      Combined squad and member performance: umpire rating of leaders and squads on military field problem.

862.* Haythorn, W. W. The influence of individual members on the characteristics of small groups. *J. abnorm. soc. Psychol.*, 1953, *48*, 276–284.

Purpose

This study examined how individual performance behavior and personality characteristics related to group characteristics and performance.

Procedure

College student groups worked on reasoning, mechanical assembly, and discussion tasks. Os rated individuals in terms of categories such as efficiency and insight exhibited while working on all three tasks. After the session, Ss and Os rated the group on characteristics such as morale, competition exhibited, and so on. In addition, Ss selected the best and poorest leaders, chose group members they liked best, and responded to a personality inventory.

Results

In general, there was no relationship between observations of individual performance effectiveness and member ratings of group performance effectiveness (0/27), except that member efficiency was positively related to cooperation, morale, occurrence of social interactions, and motivation (3/3) and negatively related to talkativeness (4/4). Member insight related negatively to talkativeness (3/3) but was unrelated to other characteristics (1/30).

Sociometric choice patterns within groups related only slightly to objective group performance measures (2/11).

There was also no relationship between personality traits and group performance (0/30), except that suspiciousness related negatively to cohesiveness and friendliness (2/2), as did practicality and productivity (1/1) and moodiness–depression and morale (1/1). On the other hand, liking of people in general related positively to social interaction, as did emotional stability and morale (2/2).

This study contained a total of 453 relationships.

Study Variables

120) Personality characteristics of members
Personality characteristics: S responses on Cattell Personality Factor Questionnaire.

230) Interpersonal relations in the group
Sociometric choice: S selection of co-workers and leaders.

430) Outcomes of interaction
Group performance on talkativeness, productivity, and so on: O rating of groups during the meeting.

510) Perceptions of task performance of self and others
Perceived group performance: group member ratings of their groups on productivity, morale, cooperativeness, and similar considerations, after the meeting.

621) Member task performance in experimental settings
Member performance efficiency: O rating of S performance on reasoning, assembly, and discussion tasks.

867. Haythorn, W. W., et al. The behavior of authoritarian and equalitarian personalities in groups. *Hum. Relat.*, 1956, *9*, 57–74.

Purpose

This study investigated the discussion behavior manifested in groups composed of high- and low-authoritarian individuals.

Procedure

Ss homogeneous in respect to authoritarianism scores on the California F-scale and Cattell's Q_1 scale were placed in four-man groups and given the task of composing a script for a movie scene. Os observed and rated Ss independently during the task performance through a one-way mirror. Immediately after the session, each O rated Ss on 16 behavioral traits: friendliness, submissiveness, and so on. At the end of each session, four Os, E, and Ss filled out a postmeeting questionnaire that tapped various aspects of the discussion. In addition, Ss indicated preferences for various group members and their satisfaction with the group, and rated the group's productivity.

Results

According to Os' ratings, Ss who were emergent leaders and who had high F-scores were less equalitarian, secure, submissive, sensitive, and satisfied with the meeting; they made fewer sanction-seeking proposals, initial and positive acts, diagnoses of situations, and successful attempts at leadership, but strove for group goals and commanded others more often than did leaders with low F-scores (13/13).

Furthermore, all Ss with high F-scores were less agreeable and attentive, less prone to ask for expressions of opinion, less apt to diagnose and clarify acts and situations, less satisfied and positive about their actions, and more withdrawn and concerned with out-of-field activities than were Ss with low F-scores (9/9). Ss and emergent leaders with high F-scores were less intelligent than Ss with low F-scores (2/2).

In addition, groups composed of Ss with high F-scores had less motivation toward the group goal, strove for it less, and were more dissatisfied with goal progress than were groups of Ss with low F-scores (3/3). No other traits or types of behavior were related either to leadership or to Ss' authoritarianism (0/128).

According to Ss' ratings, groups with high F-scores were less competitive, more cooperative, and had fewer differences in opinion than did groups with low F-scores (3/3), but no other type of behavior was related to authoritarianism (0/13).

Study Variables

144) Attitudes towards issues, concepts, ideologies
    Authoritarianism: S responses on California F-scale.
430) Outcomes of interaction
    Discussion behavior and characteristics: O ratings of S behavior and traits exhibited during meeting.
    Individual performance effectiveness: O ratings of S behavior, during the meeting, in terms of intelligence, adaptability, etc.
    Group discussion behavior: O responses to a postmeeting rating scale testing dissatisfaction with goal, equal participation, etc.
510) Perceptions of task performance of self and others
    Member rating of group performance effectiveness: S responses to a postmeeting rating scale.
631) Group task performance in experimental settings
    Group performance effectiveness: O responses to a postmeeting rating scale testing competence of members, productivity, etc.

868.* Haythorn, W. W., et al. The effects of varying combinations of authoritarian and equalitarian leaders and followers. *J. abnorm. soc. Psychol.*, 1956, *53*, 210–219.

Purpose

This study investigated the influence of authoritarian attitudes on discussion behavior.

Procedure

The California F-scale was administered to Ss, and four-man groups were assembled. Groups with high or low F-scores were assigned leaders with either high or low F-scores, so that there was a total of four leader-member combinations. The groups discussed a human relations problem presented by a film. Individual and group behavior was observed and recorded by Os during the meeting and by Os and Ss on a postmeeting questionnaire.

Results

There were very few differences in the general performance effectiveness of authoritarian and nonauthoritarian leaders, followers, or groups. Specifically, nonauthoritarian leaders were no more adaptive or sensitive to their groups than were authoritarian leaders (0/4), although the nonauthoritarians did exhibit more intelligent discussion behavior (3/4). No comparable differences occurred for group members (2/8). Moreover, ratings of such factors as group competence, productivity, and communication effectiveness had slight relationship to authoritarian attitudes (3/16).

With respect to similarity of leader and member F-scores, groups homogeneous in member and leader authoritarian scores were not differentiated on measures of member performance effectiveness from heterogeneous groups (2/8). No clear-cut group performance differences appeared for homogeneous and heterogeneous groups (4/8).

This study contained a total of 558 relationships.

Study Variables

144) Attitudes toward issues, concepts, ideologies
      Leader authoritarianism: S responses on California F-scale.

240) General structural properties of the group
      Degree of leader and follower authoritarian attitude homogeneity: groups formed according to F-scale scores, with varying combinations of high and low leader and follower authoritarianism.

430) Outcomes of interaction
      Member discussion performance: O rating of S on intelligence, adaptability, etc.

631) Group task performance in experimental settings
      Group discussion performance: O rating of groups on productivity, communication effectiveness, etc.

869. Hearn, G. Leadership and the spatial factor in small groups. *J. abnorm. soc. Psychol.*, 1957, *54*, 269–272.

Purpose

This study examined the effect of different types of leadership on discussion communication patterns.

Procedure

Groups of students were assigned to two types of training: a *self-motivated method*, in which a leader did not impose himself on the group but was available for aid; and a *trainer-induced method*, in which a leader played a very strong and active role in the discussion, criticizing and coaching as appropriate. Members and leader of each type of group occupied the same positions in a U-type arrangement for several sessions. Their task was to solve a different problem during each discussion period. O coded Ss' interactions during discussions to indicate to whom a comment was directed.

Results

The character of leadership significantly influenced communication patterns among group members during the group discussion. In the self-motivated groups, Ss tended to interact more with persons opposite them (1/1), whereas Ss in the trainer-induced groups communicated more frequently with group members sitting on either side of them (1/1).

Study Variables

152) Task or physical position in the group
Seating position of recipient with respect to communicator: arrangement of Ss in different positions.

420) Patterns of interaction
Number of communications directed to recipient: O count of the number of messages received by each S.

874.* Heise, G. A., & Miller, G. A. Problem solving by small groups using various communication nets. J. abnorm. soc. Psychol., 1951, 46, 327–337.

Purpose

This study investigated the effect of different communication nets and task characteristics on group problem-solving performance.

Procedure

The performance of a single three-man group was studied under different communication nets, different signal-to-noise ratios, and different tasks (assembling a list of words, completing sentences, and working anagrams). E recorded performance in terms of time required to complete the task, accuracy, and number of words spoken by each S.

Results

Statistical results were not reported. The authors summarized as follows: While solving the list-assembly problem, Ss showed that a closed chain with only one-way communication was the least efficient, an open chain that allowed two-way communication between adjacent members was intermediately efficient, and a closed chain where all members talked and listened to all other members was most efficient. Results for the sentence-completion problem were somewhat similar, except that an open chain where one man coordinated communication was most efficient.

Lowering the signal-to-noise ratio reduced performance efficiency in general and emphasized the inefficiency of the one-way closed chain.

This study contained a total of 20 relationships.

Study Variables

240) General structural properties of the group

Type of communication nets: E assignment of communication nets in which Ss worked (chain net with varying types of communication).

633) Group task performance in operational settings: specific measures

Group performance: E record of the time needed to complete the problems and the number of correct responses.

877. Hemphill, J. K. Relations between the size of the group and the behavior of "superior" leaders. *J. soc. Psychol.*, 1950, *32*, 11–22.

Purpose

This study compared the behavior and characteristics of superior leaders in different-sized groups.

Procedure

Five hundred Ss completed a questionnaire about any group in which they had participated within the past two or three years, describing the group size, quality of leadership, and specific details of the behavior and characteristics of their leaders. Ss rated their leaders as "always," "frequently," "occasionally," "seldom," or "never" exhibiting these specific behaviors (or answered "don't know" or "does not apply" when appropriate). Questionnaires in which Ss had rated their leaders as "good" or "excellent" were analyzed to determine what differentiated the leaders of the large groups (31 or more members) from the leaders of the small groups (30 or less members).

Results

Some differences were apparent between leaders of large and small groups. Specifically, leaders of large groups were rated as "always" or "frequently" (14/14) showing the following:

1. Leader evaluative actions: coordinating activities, clearly informing members of rules and regulations, trying hard to achieve, displaying physical and moral courage, delegating authority wisely, making subordinates feel inferior

2. Leader evaluative characteristics: having more technical and job knowledge, being less approachable

3. Leader descriptive characteristics: enjoying the role of "ruling the roost"

4. Leader descriptive actions: working harder and longer than others' informing members of things concerning them, making decisions for the group rather than individuals

Leaders of large groups also "occasionally," "seldom," or "never" were thought to relax group discipline, criticize with tact, listen to others, explain actions, arouse enthusiasm in members, treat members as individuals, treat rules with flexibility, show fickleness in decisions, and treat members equally (9/9). On many of the foregoing, members of small groups checked "don't know" or "does not apply" about their leaders (13/23).

No differences were found (0/56) between leaders of large and small groups on most of the behavior items:

1. Leader evaluative actions: "passing the buck," ability to express expectations of others, good decision making, lack of control of group and individual members, ability to instill desire to work in members, fulfillment of promises, "ruling with an iron hand," "sticking his neck out" for the group, inconsistency in enforcing rules for self and others, persuasive ability, planning, overseriousness, boastfulness, pleasant manner of speaking and commanding, attention to dress, knowing what to expect of members

2. Leader evaluative characteristics: dependability, respect of superiors, thinking only of self, realization of own abilities and limitations, lack of foresight, friendliness, haughtiness, standoffishness, endurance, objectivity, cooperativeness, exemplary member of group, task know-how

3. Leader descriptive characteristics: interest in group success, concern with own record only, "couldn't be told anything," confidence in decisions, time for group, pride in group, appreciation of people, appreciation of good joke on self, belief in group's purpose, preference for associating with superiors

4. Leader descriptive actions: remembering good work of members, quick decision making, losing temper, putting group activities first, "making the group laugh," identifying with members' complaints

Study Variables

510) Perceptions of task performance of self and others

Leader behavior (working harder and longer than others): S rating of leader on behavior.

520) Perceptions of social behavior of self and others

Leader characteristics (high interest in group): S rating of leaders on characteristics.

Evaluations of leader characteristics: S rating of leaders on characteristics.

Leader behavior (informing members of things concerning themselves, treating all members equally, remembering good work of members, and so on): S rating of leaders on behavior.

Leader performance effectiveness: S rating of leader on performance.

887. Hemphill, J. K., & Sechrest, L. B. A comparison of three criteria of aircrew effectiveness in combat over Korea. *J. appl. Psychol.*, 1952, *36*, 323–327.

Purpose

This study interrelated three classes of criteria of air crew effectiveness: superior ratings of performance, records of bombing accuracy, and sociometric nominations.

Procedure

Air crews were rated as units by squadron or wing staff officers in terms of their bombing accuracy, performance in carrying out combat missions, skill as technicians, ability to work with other crews and superiors, over-all crew value as part of combat unit, and similar measures. A sociometric nomination form was also given to crew members requiring them to choose airmen for forming another crew. An objective measure of accuracy of bombing performance (circular error) was obtained from photographs of where bombs actually hit.

Results

Ratings by superiors of crew performance variables (successful completion of missions, technical skills, accuracy in bombing targets, leadership effectiveness, and so on) and crew's characteristics (for example, consideration among crew members and crew's over-all value to squadron) were all positively related to each other (54/54). There was also a strong relationship between these superior ratings and the objective measure of crew performance (10/11).

With respect to sociometric choices, results showed that more effective crews, rated by superiors as taking better care of the aircraft and a having better military bearing, more often chose members of their own crews (3/3). However, no other rated crew performance measure, crew characteristic, or the objective performance measure was related to sociometric choice (0/9).

Study Variables

221) Group abilities

  Consideration among members: crew rating by officers.
  Crew value to squadron: crew rating by staff officers.

230) Interpersonal relations in the group

  Sociometric choice: *S* choice of their own crew members on sociometric nomination form.

240) General structural properties of the group

  Type of crew: individual crews.

622) Member task performance in operational settings: global measures

  Effectiveness of crew leadership: crew member rating by staff officers on combat performance.

904.* Heyns, R. W., & Miller, E. *Communication*. Ann Arbor, Mich.: University of Michigan, 1949. (Contract No. NR 172–301)

Purpose

This study investigated the effect of variations in leadership on conference performance behavior.

Procedure

Discussion groups were organized under two different types of leadership: *positive*, in which the chairman was an active leader who attempted to increase understanding, unify the group, and so on; and *negative*, in which the chairman's behavior was calculated to have a negative effect on the problem-solving process. Four types of member communication measures were used: measures of verbal characteristics such as audibility and quality of speaking, measures of physical behavior such as gestures, measures of difficulty participants had in understanding what was said, and measures of the understandability of participants by others. The first two measures were derived from O judgments and the second two from group member postexperimental questionnaire responses.

Results

The communication process was very similar in all groups under both leadership conditions. There were no differences in member over-all quality of speaking, articulation, pronunciation, vocal variety, voice quality, and intelligibility (0/5).

In addition, verbal characteristics such as rate and quality of speech were not related to intelligibility to others, to the number of times members were requested to clarify statements, or to the quality of the solutions members proposed (0/4). All intercorrelations of performance measures failed to reach significance (0/11).

This study contained a total of 160 relationships.

Study Variables

312) Induced social conditions

Leader behavior: E instructions to chairman to behave in positive or negative manner during conference.

420) Patterns of interaction

Discussion behavior: E count of number of words per minute spoken by each S during discussion, number of times each S requested other members to clarify statements, etc.

Discussion behavior (rate of speaking): E count of number of words per minute spoken by each S during discussion.

Member performance: O record of number of times O did not understand discussion contributions by each S.

Member performance: expert rating of S discussion contributions in terms of quality of speech, articulation, etc.

510) Perceptions of task performance of self and others

Intelligibility of discussion behavior: number of times S was designated by other group members as difficult to understand.

Others' performance: S estimate of others' statements that he had trouble understanding and number of Ss he found difficult to understand.

621) Member task performance in experimental settings

Member performance: O rating of problem solution quality.

909. Hilgard, E. R., et al. Level of aspiration as affected by relative standing in an experimental social group. *J. exp. Psychol.*, 1940, 27, 411–421.

Purpose

This study investigated differences between estimated and actual performance on arithmetic problems of varied difficulty.

Procedure

College students in groups with from three to six members worked on an arithmetic task. Two series of problems were presented. Problems in one series were of medium difficulty during the first three trials; easy, medium, and hard during the following eight trials; and the same for the last trials. Problems in the second series were all of equal difficulty. Ss were unaware of the different difficulty levels. After each trial E announced the time in which students solved the problems, and Ss made private estimations of the time they would need for the next trial.

Results

Problem difficulty played some role in Ss' estimations of their own success. Students solving problems of various difficulty levels underestimated their success on easy problems during the last trial (1/2) and overestimated success on hard problems on the last trial (1/2). In addition, these Ss overestimated their success for problems of medium difficulty (3/5).

While working on problems of equal difficulty, Ss with low and medium performance scores overestimated their future success (4/6), whereas there was no strong relationship for Ss with high performance scores in regard to estimated future success (1/3).

Study Variables

321) Stimulus properties of the task

Difficulty of task material: E assignment of easy, medium, or hard problems to Ss.

510) Perceptions of task performance of self and others

Aspiration for future problem solving: S estimates of time they would need to complete the next problem.

621) Member task performance in experimental settings
> Performance effectiveness: length of time needed to complete problems.
> Rank of performance: length of time required to complete each task.

919. Hoffman, L. R. Similarity of personality: a basis for interpersonal attraction. *Sociometry*, 1958, *21*, 300–308.

Purpose

This study analyzed the mutual attraction within groups whose members differed with respect to personality characteristics, sex, and problem-solving performance.

Procedure

On the basis of scores on the Guilford-Zimmerman Temperament Scale, college student *S*s were divided into four-person groups homogeneous or heterogeneous in personality. All groups worked on an intellectual problem. During the last session, *S*s rated each other on a sociometric questionnaire.

Results

Although similarity-dissimilarity of group member personalities did not clearly account for mutual attraction between members and performance in general (1/3), the two types of groups were differentiated under certain conditions. Specifically, heterogeneous personality groups with a sex ratio of three men to one woman reported higher attraction to each other than did groups with two or more women (1/1). These results did not hold for groups homogeneous in personality (0/1).

Interpersonal attraction was moderately related to group effectiveness in the homogeneous condition only (1/2). Both homogeneous and heterogeneous personality groups in which all members participated reported higher mutual attraction than did those in which some members were inactive (1/1).

Study Variables

120) Personality characteristics of members
> Personality characteristics: *S* responses to personality items.

240) General structural properties of the group
> Group homogeneity with respect to personalities: group members' temperament test scores highly correlated or did not significantly correlate.
> Group sex composition: ratio of men to women.

420) Patterns of interaction
> Group participation: *E* record of whether or not all members in the group were present.

631) Group task performance in experimental settings
> Group performance effectiveness: group score on solution to mined road problem.

927. Hollander, E. P. The reliability of peer nominations under various conditions of administration. *J. appl. Psychol.*, 1957, *41*, 85–90.

Purpose

This study examined variables affecting peer nominations: period of time group spent together, type of nomination "set," and characteristic to be evaluated by nominator in making his judgments.

Procedure

Naval officer candidates rated their peers on enthusiasm for the Navy, leadership qualities, and probability of success as officers. Two rating "sets" were induced: a *research set* (in which the ratings, for "research" only, would not affect candidates' naval careers); and an *administrative set* (in which the ratings would be used for "administrative" purposes).

The instruments were administered several times during the training program.

Results

Under both rating sets, peer nominations of leaders and peer ratings of others' interest and enthusiasm for the Navy, leadership qualities, and probability of success as officers were highly correlated when data from different sessions were compared (30/30). Type of judgment set (administrative or research) or the trait being rated did not produce differences in the level of reliability (3/25).

Study Variables

120) Personality characteristics of members

Type of personality trait rated: *E* classification of rating items by type.

152) Task or physical position in the group

Peer characteristics: ratings of peers with respect to enthusiasm for Navy, leadership, success in OCS, etc.

323) Induced task conditions

Type of judgment set: *S* instruction according to judgment set.

941. Hood, P. D., et al. *Crew member agreement on RB-47 crew operating procedure.* San Antonio, Tex.: Lackland Air Force Base, May, 1957. (Rep. No. AFPTRC-TN-57-64)

Purpose

This study investigated crew agreement on operating procedures as related to performance, over-all proficiency, flying experience, and crew member attitudes toward their leader.

Procedure

Flight crews were administered a questionnaire pertaining to crew operating procedures (those methods of accomplishing the task that had been worked out by the individual crew for its own use) in four task areas: mission planning, high-altitude photoruns, radar bomb score, simulated photoflash bomb runs, and night celestial navigation. Agreement scores of total crew consensus on each item were obtained for each crew. Data were also obtained on flying experience as transcribed from official records, crew member reports of length of experience together in each of the task areas, superior ratings of crew proficiency and crew status, objective crew performance scores (flight line deviation, radarscope photography, radar bomb score, and simulated photoflash bomb runs), and crew attitudes toward the aircraft commander's supervisory and human relations behavior. Intercorrelations were obtained on the foregoing measures.

Results

1. Relationship of measures to crew agreement
   a. Objective performance scores: not related to crew agreement in any of the task areas (1/48)
   b. Superiors' ratings of proficiency and status: proficiency highly related to combined agreement measure (4/4), moderately related to all measures of agreement in specific task areas (3/7); crew status not related to agreement in any of the task areas (0/6)
   c. Crew members' flying experience: not related to agreement in any of the task areas (2/26)
   d. Length of flying experience together: highly related to agreement in all task areas (7/7), highly related to agreement on mission-planning operating procedure (5/5), somewhat related to agreement in other specific task areas (5/15)
   e. Member rating of aircraft commander on supervisory activity and human relations: slightly related to agreement on operating procedures (2/11)
   f. Agreement measures: highly interrelated (24/35)

2. Relationships of other measures
   a. Objective performance measures: highly related to superiors' ratings of crew proficiency and crew status (10/16) and to multijet flying experience of crew members (5/8), not related to total flying experience (0/8); these latter measures were not clearly interrelated with each other (11/27).
   b. Superior's ratings of crews: highly related to objective performance measures (10/16) (as in 2a), highly related to crew members' flying experience (5/6), highly related to crew experience together in all task areas (4/4), negatively related to extent of aircraft commander's supervisory activity but not to his human relations behavior rating (1/2)
   c. Crew members' flying experience and multijet flying experience: highly related to objective performance scores (5/8) but not to total flying experience (0/8) (as in 2a), highly related to superior's ratings of crew

proficiency and crew status (as in 2b) (5/6), highly related to crew members' experience together in all task areas (8/8), not related to crew rating of aircraft commander on supervisory and human relations behavior (0/4); *total* and *multijet flying time* highly correlated (2/2)

d. Length of crew experience together: highly related to superior's ratings of proficiency and crew status in all task areas (4/4) (as in 2b), highly related to crew members' flying experience (8/8) (as in 2c), highly and positively related to members' rating of aircraft commander's human relations behavior (3/4) but not of his supervisory behavior (0/4); crew experience together in the four major task areas highly interrelated (6/6)

e. Crew ratings and self-ratings of aircraft commander's supervisory and human relations behavior: extent of supervision negatively related to crew proficiency ratings while human relations behavior not related (1/2) (as in 2b), not related to crew members' flying experience (0/4) (as in 2c); human relations rating highly related to length of crew experience together (3/4) while supervisory activity not related (0/4) (as in 2d); aircraft commanders' ratings of themselves on supervision and human relations not related to crew members' ratings of them (0/5)—a significant lack of agreement between ratings made by the aircraft commander and ratings made by the pilot and observer in crews (4/5)

Study Variables

141) Attitudes toward the task
Crew agreement on task operation procedures: member responses to task operation procedures—planning, photorun, radar bomb, and navigation operating procedures.

152) Task or physical position in the group
Crew member status: E designation of S as observer, pilot, or aircraft commander.

222) Group training and experience
Member flying experience: flying hours recorded on official record. Crew experience together: crew member report of length of experience with each of the other crew members on tasks.

240) General structural properties of the group
Each Air Force wing: individual groups studied.

510) Perceptions of task performance of self and others
Leader supervisory behavior self-rating: self-rating of own supervisory practices.

510) Perceptions of task performance of self and others
520) Perceptions of social behavior of self and others
Self-rating of human relations behavior: commander self-rating of extent of consideration for crew.

510) Perceptions of task performance of self and others
610) Leadership performance
Similarity of commander and member descriptions: discrepancy between aircraft commander self-rating and crew rating of aircraft commander on supervisory practices.

520) Perceptions of social behavior of self and others
610) Leadership performance
>Similarity of commander and crew ratings: discrepancy between aircraft commander self-rating and crew rating of aircraft commander on consideration shown crew.
610) Leadership performance
>Leader supervisory behavior: S rating of aircraft commander supervisory practices.
>
>Leader human relations behavior: S rating of consideration shown by crew leader.
632) Group task performance in operational settings: global measures
>Crew proficiency: over-all proficiency rank of each crew by superiors.
633) Group task performance in operational settings: specific measures
>Crew performance: crew performance on simulated air combat tasks—bombing, navigational accuracy, etc.
>
>Crew task performance: photographed crew deviation from prescribed flight line on simulated air mission.

944. Horowitz, M. W., et al. Induction of forces in discussion groups. *Hum. Relat.*, 1951, *4*, 57–76.

Purpose

This study examined interpersonal relationships as determinants of others' social judgments.

Procedure

Group members completed a sociometric questionnaire ranking others in terms of personal liking. Then there was a group discussion, during which Os maintained a running account of verbal interactions. At the conclusion of the discussion, Ss were readministered the sociometric questionnaire and another instrument measuring their reactions to other Ss' discussion behavior, their own behavior and feelings, and perceptions of others' feelings about them and others in the group.

Results

There is no clearcut relationship between liking of one group member and estimates of that member's approval of the actions of a third member (6/11). Rather, one must consider such estimated judgments in light of the judging person's liking of that third member. For example, when one S had neutral or negative feelings toward the person being judged, he estimated a third member's reaction to the person's behavior as identical to his own (6/8).

No such relationship occurred in cases where the source liked the person being judged (0/3).

Study Variables

230) Interpersonal relations in the group
>Liking of other group member: S scores on sociometric questionnaire.

Estimation of member B's judgment of desirability of member C's behavior: *S* scores on a sociometric questionnaire.

Group attraction: *S* score on a sociometric questionnaire.

520) Perceptions of social behavior of self and others

Member performance: *S* scores on a sociometric questionnaire

949. Horwitz, M., & Cartwright, D. A projective method for the diagnosis of group properties. *Hum. Relat.*, 1953, *6*, 397–410.

Purpose

This experiment investigated the applicability of a modified TAT technique for the study of group properties.

Procedure

An ambiguous group picture was given to groups with instructions to create a story. The entire discussion was recorded and coded according to a system describing the referent of the comments, the type of characterization in the story, procedures, and nonstory ideas. Following the discussion, a questionnaire was given to *S*s requiring them to indicate the "most productive" individual and their preferred leisure companion.

Results

Certain results were interpreted as supporting use of a projective technique for describing group properties. For example, the more stories contained characterizations of "lack of interest," the less members indicated satisfaction with the discussion (1/1). In addition, the greater the story characterization of leader influences, the greater was the tendency of *S*s to rate their group leader as most productive (1/1). Finally, the greater the incidence of hostility in the stories, the less *S*s chose leisure companions from within their own group (1/1).

Other results indicated a negative relationship between story characterizations of nondefensiveness and hostility and a positive association of emotional responses and hostility, etc. (3/4).

Study Variables

230) Interpersonal relations in the group

Sociometric choice for leisure companion: *S* ratings on a sociometric questionnaire.

Sociometric choice for productive leaders: *S* ratings on a sociometric questionnaire.

410) Content of interaction

Discussion behavior: *E* coding of discussion-behavior content of story (story group attentiveness, leader influence, hostility, emotionality, etc.)

430) Outcomes of interaction

Satisfaction with the meeting: *S* ratings of own group.

968. Husband, R. W. Cooperative versus solitary problem solution. *J. soc. Psychol.*, 1940, *11*, 405–409.

Purpose

This study compared the time consumed in solving various problems by individuals with time consumed by pairs.

Procedure

One hundred twenty *S*s were used; 40 *S*s worked alone and 80 worked in pairs. Of the 40 pairs, some were composed of friends and others of comparative strangers. There were three types of problems to solve: a word puzzle (code solution), a jigsaw puzzle, and a number of arithmetic problems. *E* recorded the time required to solve each problem.

Results

Groups needed less time to solve word and jigsaw puzzles than did *S*s working alone (2/2), but there were no differences in performance on the arithmetic problems (0/3).

Study Variables

240) General structural properties of the group
Occurrence of group: *S* assignment to work alone or in pairs.
312) Induced social conditions
Friendship: *S* pairing with stranger or with friend.
631) Group task performance in experimental settings
Group performance: length of time required to solve problems.

972. Irwin, I. A. *A procedure for evaluating instructor technique during critiques of crew performance.* San Antonio, Tex.: Randolph Air Force Base, ARDC, Crew Research Laboratory, February, 1956. (Res. Rep. AFPTRC-TN-56-32)

Purpose

This report evaluated instructor critique techniques in terms of variations in air crew members' behavior, attitudes, and performance.

Procedure

Instructors and student crews were rated on the quality of critique session discussion behavior and several other aspects of behavior, such as giving and receiving praise and criticism. In addition, several measures of participant attitudes were obtained by means of questionnaires. Questions covered were sense of personal well-being in the Air Force, confidence in Air Force management, liking for own crew, and acceptance of Air Force goals. These scales were administered to crew members twice—once shortly after their first mission and again about seven weeks later. Instructors also rated each crew at the completion of crew training for over-all effectiveness and performance.

Results

Several major categories of data were analyzed: reliabilities of measures, interrelationships of these measures, and critique behavior scores as related to crew members' attitudes, crew members' and instructors' reactions, and crew's over-all performance and effectiveness.

1. Reliabilities of ratings of critique behavior scores
    a. Instructors' critique behavior: highly reliable (11/15)
    b. Crew members' critique behavior: less reliable (2/7)
2. Interrelationships of critique behavior scores
    a. Instructors' critique behavior scores: slightly interrelated (29/106)
    b. Crew members' critique behavior scores: somewhat interrelated (6/16)
    c. Instructors' critique behavior scores and crew members' scores: not interrelated (2/28)
3. Critique behavior scores compared with crew members' attitudes
    a. Ss' personal well-being in Air Force
        (1) Instructors' critique behavior scores: not related to S well-being (1/22)
        (2) Crew members' critique behavior scores: slightly related to S well-being (1/6)
    b. Ss' confidence in Air Force management
        (1) Instructors' critique behavior scores: not related to S confidence (0/22)
        (2) Crew members' critique behavior scores: not related to S confidence (0/7)
    c. Ss' attraction to crew
        (1) Instructors' critique behavior scores: not related to S attraction (1/22)
        (2) Crew members' critique behavior scores: not related to S attraction (0/6)
4. Critique behavior scores compared with crew members' and instructors' reactions
    a. Instructors' reactions
        (1) Instructors' critique behavior scores: slightly related to instructor reactions (5/33)
        (2) Crew members' critique behavior scores: not related to instructor reactions (0/8)
    b. Crew members' reactions
        (1) Instructors' critique behavior scores: somewhat related to crew reactions (1/3)
        (2) Crew members' critique behavior scores: somewhat related to crew reactions (1/3)
5. Critique behavior scores compared with crew performance and over-all effectiveness
    Crews' over-all effectiveness
        (1) Instructors' critique behavior scores: slightly related to over-all effectiveness (2/11)
        (2) Crew members' critique behavior scores: slightly related to over-all effectiveness (1/4)

Study Variables

143) Attitudes toward nongroup persons and other groups
      Confidence in Air Force management: crew member responses on attitude scale.
      Satisfaction with Air Force: crew member responses on attitude scale.
      Acceptance of Air Force goals: crew member responses on attitude scale.

230) Interpersonal relations in the group
      Liking of own crew: crew member responses on attitude scale.

240) General structural properties of the group
      Type of classes of student crews in experiment: classes of student crews selected for experiment.

322) Feedback and reinforcement conditions
      Types of critique measures used in experiment.

420) Patterns of interaction
      Crew discussion behavior: O record of crew multiple conversations. Indexes of member–instructor discussion behavior: O record of proportion of student-initiated topics to total number of topics, student communications to total number of communications, etc. Over-all discussion orderliness: O record of multiple conversations and rating of orderliness.

430) Outcomes of interaction
      Orderliness of crew: O rating of crew behavior.

510) Perceptions of task performance of self and others
      Student reactions to instructor behavior: instructor judgment of extent to which he directed group in desired direction.

610) Leadership performance
      Leader discussion behavior: O record of instructor in respect to such measures as proportion of specific praises to total number of praises, praises to praises and criticisms, frequency of explanations given to crews, encouragement of students' participation in discussion, etc. Instructor discussion leadership adequacy: O record of instructor in respect to such measures as proportion of time spent on more important topics to time spent in all topics together, etc.

632) Group task performance in operational settings: global measures
      Crew effectiveness compared with effectiveness of crews taught previously: instructor rating of crews on a questionnaire item.

979. Jackson, J. M. The effect of changing the leadership of small work groups. *Hum. Relat.*, 1953, *6*, 25–44.

Purpose

This study compared changes in employee self-ratings and supervisor ratings as a function of changes made in group leadership.

Procedure

Nine sections of telephone repairmen were given a pre-experimental battery of attitude tests, including a scale designed to measure attitudes toward immediate supervisors. On the basis of scores, three pairs of foremen were exchanged among six groups. The remaining foremen's group assignments were kept intact as controls. After four months of working under these arrangemets, Ss were retested with the same battery of self and supervisor attitude instruments.

Results

When supervisors were changed, groups significantly modified ratings of their immediate supervisors (5/6). Upper-level management ratings and immediate supervisor ratings in the control groups remained relatively constant (2/7).

Employee personal characteristics—feeling of belonging to work group, feeling of status both in the work situation and outside, outlook for the future, evaluation of own past successes or failures, and so on—were not related to supervisor ratings (0/15).

Certain of the foregoing personal characteristics were found to be highly associated with each other; for example, outlook for the future was highly related to evaluation of past achievements, feeling of belonging to work group, and a secure sense of status outside the work situation (3/3).

Employee ratings of immediate and upper-level management were positively correlated (2/2).

Study Variables

141) Attitudes toward the task
   Task-related personal feelings: member questionnaire responses on belongingness to group, status, future job outlook, etc.
143) Attitudes toward nongroup persons and other groups
   Attitude toward higher-level supervisors: S questionnaire responses.
230) Interpersonal relations in the group
   Attitude toward immediate leader: S questionnaire responses.
240) General structural properties of the group
   Individual groups: E designation of groups used in study.
323) Induced task conditions
   Leadership structure: E designation of new leader for group or continued assignment of old leader.
510) Perceptions of task performance of self and others
   Own performance: member questionnaire responses on own past job successes or failures.

984. Jackson, J. M., & Saltzstein, H. D. The effect of person-group relationships on conformity processes. *J. abnorm. soc. Psychol.*, 1958, *57*, 17–24.

Purpose

This study examined the effect on conformity of differences in induced group attraction, acceptance by other members, and method of reward for performance.

Procedure

Groups of students were exposed to variations in interpersonal relationships among members. Group attraction was manipulated by informing some *S*s that members were compatible and that the task was important, whereas others were informed somewhat to the contrary. Within the foregoing conditions, some *S*s were led to believe (by false information) that their group was composed of members who personally accepted one another, whereas others believed that one member was not accepted by the others. On the basis of the attraction and acceptance manipulations, four types of group members were identified: *members* (high acceptance, high attraction to group), *nonmembers* (low acceptance, low attraction), *preference S*s (low acceptance, high attraction), and *marginal S*s (high acceptance, low attraction). Some groups were told that a group score would be received, whereas others were instructed that individual scores would be determined and compared. The task assigned was a perceptual one requiring judgments about ambiguous stimuli. Individual answers were written down and collected by *E*, who then gave false information about other *S*s' responses. Conformity was measured by the proportion of judgment changes toward the presumed majority. At the completion of the task, *S*s responded to a questionnaire measuring various aspects of the situation.

Results

In general, there were only slight effects of group attractiveness, perceived acceptance by other members, or type of reward for performance on conformity (3/15). Rather, these variables interacted to affect level of conformity. For example, members and marginal members conformed more when they believed that a group score would be received than when they believed that individual scores would be received (2/2). In addition, these same *S*s had a greater subjective desire to conform under the group-scoring condition (2/2), whereas there were no differences for other *S*s (0/2).

Study Variables

132) Task abilities of members

Estimation of own ability relative to that of others: *S* questionnaire responses.

142) Attitudes toward the situation

Desire to conform: *S* questionnaire responses.

230) Interpersonal relations in the group

Attraction to the group: *S* questionnaire responses.

312) Induced social conditions

Perceived acceptance by other members: *E* assignment of *S*s to high- and low-acceptance categories by instructions.

Type of membership: *E* instruction to *S*s about compatibility of group and acceptance of themselves by others.

Attraction to the group: *E* instruction to *S* about compatibility of *S*s.

323) Induced task conditions
Performance-scoring conditions: *E* instructions on individual or group-scoring method.

420) Patterns of interaction
Number of messages received from others: *E* record of number of messages received.

430) Outcomes of interaction
Conformity: proportion of trials on which judgment was changed to that of the divergent majority

510) Perceptions of task performance of self and others
Influence exerted by others: *S* questionnaire responses.

520) Perceptions of social behavior of self and others
Personal acceptance by other members: *S* questionnaire responses.

999. James, J. Clique organization in a small industrial plant. *Res. Stud., State Coll. Wash.*, 1951, *19*, 125–130.

Purpose

This study analyzed sex, age, and work situation similarities as factors in industrial workers' mutual "friend" choices.

Procedure

Employees of a small industrial plant were required to answer the question, "Who are your friends here—the persons you like best?" From the answers given, cliques of two and three persons were identified on the basis of mutual choices, and compared in terms of clique composition in regard to sex, age similarity, and similarity in work performed, work area, and work shift.

Results

In general, women showed a stronger inclination toward clique formation, particularly within their own sex, than did males. The women workers made more over-all mutual sociometric choices (1/1) as well as more intrasex choices (2/3). Although a difference was indicated between men and women in the number of choices made by each (1/1), the report did not specify which sex chose more co-workers as friends.

Study Variables

110) Biographical characteristics of members
Biographical characteristics: *S* report of sex and age.

152) Task or physical position in the group
Work group characteristics (proximity of work areas, similarity of work shifts, etc.): *Ss*' work in same or different areas, work shifts, etc.

230) Interpersonal relations in the group
Clique membership: mutual choices (as friends) of each type made by *Ss*.

1005. Janis, I. L., & King, B. T. The influence of role playing on opinion change. *J. abnorm. soc. Psychol.*, 1954, *49*, 211–218.

Purpose

This study examined the effect on opinion change of communication content and degree of participation in discussion.

Procedure

A questionnaire was administered to male college students to determine their opinions on three topics: the meat supply, a cold cure, and movie theaters. Afterwards, some of the students were assigned to two groups: *active participants*, who were to play the role of advocate of a given point of view on one of the topics; and *passive participants*, who were first to read and then listen to the same communications on the two other topics—in other words, each active S delivered a speech arguing in favor of specific conclusions on one of the three topics and then was passively exposed to the two other topics. Opinion measures obtained at the end of the session were compared with measures obtained before the experiment. Ss also rated themselves and the performance of each speaker.

Results

In general, active participants tended to be more influenced by the communications than were passive Ss (2/3), and those exposed to the communications passively or actively changed their opinions more than did control Ss who were not exposed at all (6/6). However, relative activity of participants was not related to amount of opinion change or to shift in confidence in own opinions (1/22).

There was slight relationship between the particular topic of discussion and the self-ratings on performance given by active Ss in reference to such qualities as coherence and monotony (5/20).

Study Variables

321) Stimulus properties of the task

Time of passive exposure to communication: E designation of passive exposure either before or after S speech.

323) Induced task conditions

Degree of participation in discussion: E designation of S's roles as passive or active.

410) Content of interaction

Type of communication content: different topics of communication.

430) Outcomes of interaction

Change in confidence in own opinion: S self-ratings.

Change in opinion: S questionnaire responses.

510) Perceptions of task performance of self and others

Self-ratings of over-all performance (monotony of voice, incoherence of arguments, etc.) S rating of own behavior.

1033. Jones, E. E., & deCharms, R. Changes in social perception as a function of the personal relevance of behavior. *Sociometry*, 1957, *20*, 75–85.

Purpose

This study compared member ratings of an unsuccessfully performing confederate by group members motivated to work either as individuals or as a cooperative group.

Procedure

*S*s were assigned to problem-solving groups that had an experimenter-confederate. In some groups, *S*s were rewarded for individual success and in others for group success. On the basis of their scores on a pre-experimental need-for-achievement questionnaire, *S*s in each type of reward group were further subdivided into low- and high-achievement groups. Prior to the experiment, the confederate had acted intelligently, but he deliberately failed two tasks during the experiment. *S*s made trait ratings of the confederate and one other member before and after task performance.

Results

Unsuccessful performance by a group member affected ratings of him on traits related to successful task performance, particularly in groups where total cooperation was emphasized as being important; all groups rated an experimenter confederate lower on competence, motivation, and dependability after his unsuccessful task performance (12/12), and *S*s motivated for group success changed more in their ratings of the confederate's competence, dependability, and personality than did those motivated for individual success (3/3).

However, likability ratings were not significantly affected by the confederate's failure (0/2), and both individual reward and group-reward *S*s were undifferentiated in the degree to which they changed their ratings of his motivation and likability (0/2). No difference in likability ratings was noted in terms of *S*s' need to achieve (0/3).

Study Variables

120) Personality characteristics of members
      Achievement motivation: "need-for-achievement" scores on pre-experimental questionnaire.

222) Group training and experience
      Time of rating of confederate: *S* rating of confederate before and after tasks.

230) Interpersonal relations in the group
      Confederate competence, motivation, likability, dependability: group member rating.

322) Feedback and reinforcement conditions
      Type of reward motivation: *E* announcement of individual or group reward.

1033a. Jones, E. E., & deCharms, R. Changes in social perception as a function of the personal relevance of behavior. *Sociometry*, 1957, *20*, 75–85.

Purpose

This study compared member ratings of an unsuccessfully performing confederate in groups motivated to work cooperatively or as individuals and varying in belief about the relation of the task to intelligence. The study was an extension of the immediately preceding study.

Procedure

*S*s were assigned to problem-solving groups, each of which had an experimenter-confederate. In some groups *S*s were rewarded for individual success and in others for group success. In addition, groups in each condition were further subdivided by instructions to the effect that task performance was closely related either to intelligence or to motivation to work hard. Prior to the experiment, the confederate had acted intelligently, but he deliberately failed two tasks during the experiment. *S*s made trait ratings of the confederate and one other member before and after task performance.

Results

Analysis of ratings of the confederate revealed an almost unqualified negative shift in impressions of his competence, motivation, and dependability for all *S*s (11/12), but likability ratings remained unchanged in all conditions (0/4).

Study Variables

141) Attitudes toward the task
Task value for tapping motivation and competence: member rating of task effectiveness.

222) Group training and experience
Time of rating of confederate: *S* rating of confederate before and after tasks.

230) Interpersonal relations in the group
Confederate's likability, personality, dependability: *S* rating of confederate before and after tasks.

323) Induced task conditions
Degree of motivation or intelligence required for task success: *E* instructions to *S*s that task required motivation or intelligence.

1046. Kaplan, A., et al. The prediction of social and technological events. *Publ. Opin. Quart.*, 1950, *14*, 93–110.

Purpose

This study investigated individual and group accuracy in predicting future social and technological events.

Procedure

A group of specialists individually completed questionnaires predicting future events in social science and technology. Ss were required to rank alternatives on the probability that they would occur within 20 weeks, assigning percentages to each alternative with cumulative percentages equaling 100 percent. For each question, Ss explained the basis of their judgment. The percentage of times events ranked as most probable actually did occur within the specified time constituted the measure of accuracy of prediction. Later, half of the Ss individually completed similar probability questionnaires without discussion, as before, while the other half of the Ss were reassigned to group conditions, in which some groups had a discussion before writing individual answers and other groups followed discussion with group answers. Scores of individual and group prediction were compared for accuracy. Achievement test scores on the Cooperative General Culture Test in social science and natural science provided indexes of experiment-related knowledge that were also compared with accuracy in the two areas of prediction.

Results

Groups were more accurate than individuals in predicting events in both social science and technology (2/2). Accuracy in predicting the probability of events (precision in assignment of percentage values) was also positively related to over-all accuracy of prediction (3/3). On the other hand, definiteness of prediction (the extent to which the percentage value assigned each alternative differed from 25%) and preference rank for each alternative per question were not related to over-all accuracy (0/2).

The relationship between subject matter and accuracy of prediction was moderate (4/7). The predictor's knowledge of subject matter, however, was highly related to accurate prediction in both fields (4/4). Finally, those Ss giving "justification type" and "guess type" reasons as a basis for their judgments made more accurate predictions than did those replying with "rationalization type" and "special-comment type" statements (2/4).

Study Variables

132) Task abilities of members
Degree of knowledge of subject matter: S test score on subject matter of predicted event.

144) Attitudes toward issues, concepts, ideologies
Prediction of social events: S ranking of predicted social and technological events in terms of relative probability.

240) General structural properties of the group
Individual vs. group approach: E assignment of Ss to varying conditions (individual problem consideration and prediction, group problem consideration and individual prediction, group problem consideration and group prediction).

321) Stimulus properties of the task
Event-task characteristics: stability of event, subject matter, and so on of the social event to be predicted.

621) Member task performance in experimental settings

> Reason given by S for judgment: E classification of type of reason given by S for estimate of probability.
>
> Accuracy of prediction: E count of percentage of times events S ranked as most probable actually did occur.

1054. Katz, D., et al. *Productivity, supervision, and morale in an office situation.* Ann Arbor, Mich.: University of Michigan, Institute for Social Research, 1950.

Purpose

This study compared the behavior and characteristics of supervisors and employees in high- and low-producing offices.

Procedure

On the basis of productivity level—the ratio of actual time spent in completing a given amount of work to an "expected" base—high- and low-performing clerical groups were identified. Supervisors and employees were interviewed individually and rated both on personality characteristics, such as warmth and cooperativeness and on characteristics related to office practices and job attitudes.

Results

Certain responses and personality factors exhibited by supervisors and employees during interviews were found to differentiate high- and low-producing clerical sections. Supervisors in high-producing sections generally spent more time in supervision, identified primarily with employees rather than the company, and emphasized human relations rather than production; they were generally nonsupportive of their employees, prone to give no reasons for job or change in job methods, rated higher on reasonableness, democratic personality, and over-all judgmental ability, and most frequently moderately or highly satisfied with their positions (9/9).

Employees of high-producing sections were high in pride in their work groups (2/2) but did not participate in company recreational activities (1/1).

Most of the interview data failed to differentiate supervisors and employees of high- and low-producing clerical sections on such variables as member and rater judgments of individual and group behavior and characteristics, member reports of own behavior and characteristics, and member evaluations of official policies, procedures, and tangible aspects of job such as salary and working hours (0/73).

This study contained a total of 94 relationships.

Study Variables

110) Biographical characteristics of members

> Supervisor biographical characteristics: supervisor statements of age, marital status, education, time with company.

120) Personality characteristics of members

Supervisor personality characteristics: interviewer rating of personality traits exhibited by supervisor during interview.

131) General abilities of members

Employee comprehension of company policy: supervisor report of employees' understanding of company and employee matters.

141) Attitudes toward the task

Job and environment satisfaction: interview response.

Job satisfaction: employee responses evaluating job, type of work, feeling of accomplishment from job.

Employee satisfaction with training received for own job: employee interview responses.

Supervisor emphasis on human relations role: supervisor interview responses about job and coder analysis of interview record.

142) Attitudes toward the situation

Supervisor and employee work-related characteristics: interview responses about company identification, intention to stay with company, etc.

Employee approval of enforcement of conduct rules in his section: employee interview evaluation of section enforcement of conduct rules.

Employee satisfaction with company: employee interview responses.

Satisfaction with company activities: S interview responses evaluating company policies and practices.

Perception of employee approval of company complaint policy: supervisor's projected evaluation of company by employees during interview.

Awareness of time while working: employee interview response.

Satisfaction with working hours: employee interview evaluation of working hours.

Family and friends' approval of employment with company: employee interview responses.

Employee satisfaction with information received on company activities: employee interview responses about himself and company newspaper.

Approval of employee rating system: supervisor interview report and evaluation of system.

Satisfaction and identification with company: employee interview responses about company and coder rating of attitude toward and identification with company.

Financial and job status satisfaction: employee interview responses evaluating salary and progress, and coder rating of frustration evidenced by employee.

Group morale: employee interview responses about various employee feelings.

143) Attitudes toward nongroup persons and other groups

Supervisor sureness of management opinion of him: supervisor interview responses.

230) Interpersonal relations in the group

>Pride in work group: employee interview responses evaluating work group and coder rating of employee identification with work group. Employee opinion about supervisors: employee interview responses of his feelings toward his supervisors.

430) Outcomes of interaction

>Group activities: supervisor interview responses about section activities—for example, cooperation, use of information sources.

510) Perceptions of task performance of self and others

>Group performance: S interview responses to questions about procedures, helpfulness of discussions, etc.

>Job-related activities: S interview report of own activities, such as participation in company recreation and training courses.

>Supervisor job activities and procedures: supervisor interview responses about his own behavior—time spent in supervision, freedom of employee conduct, delegation of authority, etc.

>Supervisor performance: employee interview resposes about supervisor job behavior.

>Estimate of approval of rules governing office conduct: supervisor interview report of how employees felt about office conduct rules.

520) Perceptions of social behavior of self and others

>Group satisfaction: supervisor estimate of feelings of his employees and their attitude toward job.

>Member characteristics: supervisor interview responses about other employees—e.g., on whether they were closely supervised, friends, etc.

>Supervisor behavior: employee interview responses about supervisor job behavior.

610) Leadership performance

>Supervisor practices: ratings of close employee supervision, exerting production pressure.

1059.* Katz, I., et al. Behavior and productivity in bi-racial work groups. *Hum. Relat.*, 1958, *11*, 123–141.

Purpose

This study investigated the influence of type of reward and prestige upon group productivity.

Procedure

Students divided into groups composed of two Negroes and two whites worked on various problem-solving tasks. Some groups worked under individual-reward motivation, in which Ss were given special bonuses for individual performance, whereas other groups operated on a group-reward basis. Variations in feelings of group prestige also were experimentally induced by instructions about the caliber of member intellectual skills. Os rated the behavior of group members in terms of type, amount, and direction of communication to others. Group productivity was measured by actual performance scores and by ratings of performance by Os.

Results

During a second experimental session, groups under the group-reward condition were more productive than were groups operating on the basis of individual bonuses (1/1), although type of reward did not relate to productivity during a first session (0/1).

Neither group prestige nor the interaction of reward and prestige related to group productivity (0/4).

This study contained a total of 833 relationships.

Study Variables

151) Social position in the group
Prestige induced for Ss: E assignment of low or high prestige by instruction.

322) Feedback and reinforcement conditions
Type of group-reward motivation: E promise of individual or group rewards.

631) Group task performance in experimental settings
Group productivity: O rating of group performance.

1074. Kelley, H. H., & Lamb, T. W. Certainty of judgment and resistance to social influence. *J. abnorm. soc. Psychol.*, 1957, 55, 137–139.

Purpose

This study analyzed certainty of judgment as a factor in conformity to majority opinion.

Procedure

Ss privately tasted an ordinary gum label (label A), a pineapple-flavored label (label B), and a "tasteless or bitter" label (label C); the latter had been coated with PTU (phenyltheourea) and cherry flavoring, which together are either tasteless or bitter to most people. Ss were asked to rate the flavor desirability of the second two labels relative to that of the first and to express level of confidence in their judgments. Then Ss were classified as "tasters" or "nontasters" according to their reactions to label C. Next, Ss were divided into three-man groups, in half of which tasters were in the majority and in half of which nontasters were in the majority. These groups met publicly, retasted the labels, and publicly announced their ratings of labels B and C. Each time, the majority persons—whether tasters or nontasters—individually announced their ratings first. Initial private ratings of label C desirability were compared with public ratings of minority Ss as a measure of conformity.

Results

The effects of majority opinion on public judgments of the stimulus were markedly dependent upon Ss' taste sensitivity. Nontasters shifted significantly more toward the majority opinion in the second ratings of label C than did tasters (1/1), even though nontasters initially rated label C as more desirable than did the tasters (1/1). Moreover, tasters were consistent in their ratings whether they were in the minority or majority (0/1) and also indicated greater confidence in their initial judgments than did nontasters (2/2).

Study Variables

120) Personality characteristics of members

Confidence in initial private judgment: S rating of his confidence.

131) General abilities of members

S taste sensitivity: Ss with and without taste sensitivity for stimulus.

323) Induced task conditions

Type of group (extent to which tasters were in minority or majority): E assignment of taster Ss as one third or two thirds of group.

430) Outcomes of interaction

Public conformity: discrepancy between S initial private rating and later public rating of stimulus taste desirability.

1075. Kelley, H. H., & Shapiro, M. M. An experiment on conformity to group norms where conformity is detrimental to group achievement. *Amer. sociol. Rev.*, 1954, *19*, 667–677.

Purpose

This study compared conformity and reactions to the group of members with different perceptions of their acceptance by the group.

Procedure

Volunteers were assigned to task groups that they thought were assembled on the basis of their choice of co-workers on a pre-experimental questionnaire. On their task, Ss communicated by notes passed through E (who intercepted actual messages and substituted others recommending the wrong answer). Fake acceptability ratings were "accidentally" passed out to each S before the task to induce the impression of high or low acceptance by the group. Ss then rated their desire to remain in the group, and E informed them that the "decision" was to maintain the group. Ss were given the task of judging which of two blocks had more dots. After each trial S rated his confidence in his judgment. Conformity was measured by a composite of direction and confidence in judgment. Following the last trial, each S rated the desirability of the group and co-workers, annoyance with co-workers, liking for experiment, and how co-workers would evaluate them. Valuation of membership scores were derived from these and previous ratings. Six weeks later, Ss answered more questions on their expectations of being accepted by groups.

Results

In general, members with different perceived and actual levels of acceptance in the group were only slightly differentiated in the extent to which they conformed to the group norm (2/9). Factors other than group acceptance seemed to account for the conformity differences. For example, Ss designated low-acceptance by E conformed considerably more than did high-acceptance Ss on the last trials (1/1) although not initially (0/1). Also, both designated and actual low-acceptance Ss who gave a high valuation to the rest of the membership conformed significantly more than did the high-acceptance Ss who also assigned high ratings to the others (2/2).

In the case of Ss designated high-acceptance, the more they expected to be accepted in groups on the basis of their work, the less they showed conformity (1/1). No conformity distinctions were noted for low-acceptance Ss or for those expecting to be accepted on the basis of personality alone (0/3).

Members' attraction to the situation appeared to stem directly from their perceptions of acceptance, with high-acceptance Ss indicating a greater desire to remain in the group, a greater enjoyment of the experiment, and a higher annoyance with their co-workers (3/3).

Study Variables

142) Attitudes toward the situation
Member enjoyment of experiment: S rating of experiment.

230) Interpersonal relations in the group
Valuation of membership: S rating of group and other members in group.
Expectation of being accepted by group: S rating of acceptance on basis of personality.
Expectation of being accepted by group: S rating of acceptance on basis of work.
Acceptability of member to other members: assignment of acceptance ratings to S by others.
Satisfaction with co-workers: S rating of annoyance and acceptability of co-workers.
Member desire to remain in group: S rating after being informed of faked acceptability.

312) Induced social conditions
Member perceived acceptance by group of self: E assignment of Ss to faked high- and low-acceptance groups.

430) Outcomes of interaction
Conformity to group opinion: S rating of choice confidence—the right choice (not favored by group) or the wrong one (which group favored).

621) Member task performance in experimental settings
Perceptual judgment: S initial judgment of number of dots on block.

1077. Kelley, H. H., & Volkhart, E. H. The resistance to change of group-anchored attitudes. *Amer. sociol. Rev.*, 1952, *17*, 453–465.

Purpose

This study investigated the effect of privacy of attitude expressions and valuation of group membership on opinion change.

Procedure

A prequestionnaire to measure attraction to their troops was given to Boy Scouts. Another questionnaire in regard to attitudes toward camping, woodcraft, and similar activities was also administered. Then these activities were criticized and others were recommended in a speech, following which the attitude questionnaire was readministered. Now, however, some Ss were informed that their answers would be kept secret, whereas others were told that their answers would be made public.

Results

There was only a moderate relationship between the degree of privacy Ss believed their opinions would have and change in opinion about various camping activities (1/2).

On the other hand, Ss who highly valued group membership changed their opinion significantly less in the private condition than did those who were not as attracted to their group (4/4). Valuation of membership did not relate to opinion changes in the public condition (0/5).

Study Variables

230) Interperonal relations in the group

> Attraction to group: S scores on a questionnaire of valuation of membership.

312) Induced social conditions

> Privacy of opinion: S knowledge of whether the test results would be private or public.

430) Outcomes of interaction

> Change in opinion: S score difference from initial to postpropaganda situation.

1085. Kidd, J. S. Social influence phenomena in a task-oriented group situation. *J. abnorm. soc. Psychol.*, 1958, *56*, 13–17.

Purpose

This study compared the conformity and performance efficiency of persons with varying degrees of contact with others and of groups differing in size.

Procedure

Volunteers were assigned to two-, four-, or six-man groups who met for one, two, or three work sessions. Other volunteers performed individually. After completion of the sessions, Ss estimated individually the number of times a light flickered during a five-second period. E collected estimates and presented a fake average to those Ss in groups. Individuals were given an average estimate from a vague, anonymous source. Ss then re-estimated the number of flickers. Conformity was defined as the degree of similarity between the purported group judgment and S's second estimate of flicker.

Results

Group size and duration of contact among members as such did not account for conformity changes (0/4). However, group members who believed the popular opinion to be that of their own group conformed significantly more than did individuals who were given no specific referent for the announced opinion (2/2).

Also, although no differences in performance efficiency were noted among groups ranging in size from two to six (0/2), when individuals were included in the comparison a *decrease* in group size was found to be associated with an *increase* in efficiency (2/2).

Study Variables

240) General structural properties of the group

    Group size: E assignment of S to work as individuals or as members of two-, four-, or six-man groups.

311) Influence and conformity pressures

    Identifiability of influence source: E report to S of an average estimate —source unknown, source known.

323) Induced task conditions

    Duration of contact with other members: E assignment of Ss to a certain number of sessions (one, two, or three).

430) Outcomes of interaction

    Conformity to group: similarity between S judgment and faked average perceptual judgment given by E.

621) Member task performance in experimental settings

    Performance efficiency: time required to finish tasks correctly.

1086. Kidd, J. S., & Campbell, D. T. Conformity to groups as a function of group success. *J. abnorm. soc. Psychol.*, 1955, *51*, 390–393.

Purpose

This study compared the conformity of subjects in groups with varying amounts of perceived task success.

Procedure

Three-man groups were assigned to one of four conditions: success, partial success, failure, and control. Each group in the first three conditions was given three trials on an anagram task and their purported success as a group was reported by E after each trial. Next, all Ss were individually required to undergo two trials estimating the number of times a light flickered during a five-second period. After the first trial, a group "average estimate" was announced. Ss' second estimates were compared with their first to determine their conformity —the percentage of movement toward the announced "average."

Results

Members of successful groups unequivocally shifted their individual judgments more toward the estimate they believed to be the group's than did the other groups (6/6). This finding held only for groups consistently successful (on three out of three trials); no conformity differences were found among partially successful (two out of three trials), failure, and control groups (1/9). Also, conformity scores for the controls, who had no prior experience with a group, were significantly lower than the average score for all other Ss (1/1).

Study Variables

322) Feedback and reinforcement conditions

Degree of group success: E feedback to Ss about task success.

430) Outcomes of interaction

Conformity: average percentage of S change toward reported group average.

1097.* Klugman, S. F.   Cooperative versus individual efficiency in problem-solving. *J. educ. Psychol.*, 1944, *35*, 91–100.

Purpose

This study investigated how social facilitation influenced accuracy and speed in problem solving.

Procedure

Grade school children matched for sex, race, grade, age, and IQ responded to the Otis Arithmetic Reasoning Test either as individuals or as cooperating pairs. Records were kept of the number of correctly solved problems and solution time per problem.

Results

In general, children working in pairs solved more problems correctly but took more time to do it (2/2).

More specifically, pair accuracy was higher than individual accuracy for pairs from higher grades for both boys and girls, and for white children (4/4).

No such differences occurred as a function of age or IQ, or in lower grades, or for Negroes (0/7).

Time to solve problems, on the other hand, was longer for female pairs, Negro pairs, older pairs, and low-IQ pairs than for comparable subjects working as individuals (5/5). None of the other categories related to problem-solving speed (0/5).

This study contained a total of 104 relationships.

Study Variables

240) General structural properties of the group
    Occurrence of group: *E* assignment of *S*s to work alone or in pairs.
631) Group task performance in experimental settings
    Group performance accuracy and speed: *E* report of *S* score and length of time spent on test.

1098. Klugman, S. F. Group judgments for familiar and unfamiliar materials. *J. gen. Psychol.*, 1945, *32*, 103–110.

Purpose

This study compared the accuracy of estimation of familiar and unfamiliar objects by individuals and groups.

Procedure

Children in the sixth grade were selected on the basis of age, sex, IQ, and race to estimate individually the number of objects placed in a series of glass jars. *S*s were dichotomized as young or old, male or female, and so on, and objects were defined as familiar (marbles, jacks, etc.) and unfamiliar (dried split peas, lima beans, etc.). The relative accuracy of individual and group estimates was determined by the percentage of individuals guessing closer to the true count than the mean of the group or, conversely, the percentage of cases where the group mean was closer to the true count than individual estimates per item.

Results

The group (member average) estimate of unfamiliar objects was closer to the true count significantly more often than were individual estimates (3/3), and errors in estimating these objects were more frequently in the direction of underestimation than overestimation (2/3). With familiar objects, however, no differences were found either in accuracy of estimation or tendency toward under- or overestimation (1/3).

Individual differences in terms of age, sex, IQ, and race failed to account for differences in accuracy of estimation (0/20).

Study Variables

110) Biographical characteristics of members
    Biographical characteristics: race, age, sex.

131) General abilities of members
    Intelligence: score on IQ test.

240) General structural properties of the group
    Type of estimator: individual or statistically derived group.

321) Stimulus properties of the task
    Type of task: guessing number of unfamiliar and familiar objects.

621) Member task performance in experimental settings
    Performance accuracy: accuracy in estimating number of objects in jar.
    Performance accuracy: under- or over-estimation of number of objects in jar.

1099. Klugman, S. F. Group and individual judgments for anticipated events. *J. soc. Psychol.*, 1947, *26*, 21–28.

Purpose

This experiment investigated the difference between accuracy of group and individual judgments.

Procedure

Military men were asked to fill out a questionnaire about their age, marital status, length of service, rank, educational training, and so on. *S*s then estimated the date that Germany and Japan would sign an armistice with the Allies during World War II. After the War ended, errors in individual judgments were compared with errors of the statistically derived "group."

Results

In reference to the German armistice date, there was a significant number of individuals making greater errors than the average error ("group" score) (1/1). No greater effectiveness of the "group" occurred in estimates of the Japanese armistice date (0/1).

Personal background characteristics did not relate to accuracy of judgment (0/12).

Study Variables

110) Biographical characteristics of members
    Biographical characteristics: age, sex, education, etc.

240) General structural properties of the group
    Occurrence of group: statistically derived "group" estimates versus individual estimates.

621) Member task performance in experimental settings
    Accuracy of estimation of date of German and Japanese surrender: member questionnaire responses.

1122. Landsberger, H. A. Interaction process analysis of the mediation of labor-management disputes. *J. abnorm. soc. Psychol.*, 1955, *51*, 552–558.

Purpose

This study analyzed the success of discussion groups in the collective bargaining field in terms of specific member interactions and over-all group problem-solving patterns.

Procedure

E procured tape recordings from labor-management discussions of actual cases involving labor disputes and analyzed each in terms of specific behaviors according to Bales Interaction Process Analysis. Each case was also given a success rank based on the extent to which the problem had been solved at the end of the discussion.

Results

The nature of group interactions as coded according to the Bales system was only slightly related to problem-solving success in collective bargaining (4/16). Apparently, the most detrimental single factor was disagreement among members, particularly when it persisted at the end of the meeting (2/4). On the other hand, agreement did not contribute significantly to discussion success (0/4). Initial hostility among members also interfered with their effectiveness (1/1), whereas mutual support at the conclusion of discussion facilitated problem solving (1/1).

In line with the foregoing temporally related findings, the over-all interaction pattern was found to be associated with discussion success (1/1). According to the author, discussion behavior conforming to a hypothesized sequence allowing for the individual element in problem solving provided the most comprehensive explanation of discussion success in this study. Analysis over several groups, moreover, supported the notion that groups tended to move through phases in problem solving (1/1).

Study Variables

222) Group training and experience

Temporal phase of meeting: time periods from beginning to end of meeting.

410) Content of interaction

Discussion behavior: *E* coding of behavior according to Bales categories.

430) Outcomes of interaction

Success of group discussion outcome: *E* ranking of groups on success in settling problem.

1128. Lanzetta, J. T., et al. Some effects of situational threat on group behavior. *J. abnorm. soc. Psychol.*, 1954, *49*, 445–453.

Purpose

This study investigated effects of situational threat on the behavior of group members.

Procedure

Groups worked in a laboratory setting on a problem-solving task. General threat was imposed by instructing *S*s that their performance would become part of their ROTC records. Additional threat variables that were induced were *locus of threat* (performance ratings by *O*s or by peers) and *target of threat* (evaluations of the group or the individual). *O*s classified discussion behavior in terms of Bales Interaction Process Analysis for solidarity, agreement, and similar measures. After the experimental session, each *S* was rated on a number of traits, such as efficiency and adaptability, and both *O*s and *S*s filled out a questionnaire designed to assess various group characteristics, such as goal orientation and productivity. *S*s also responded to an adjective check list and a social-sensitivity questionnaire, rating their own anxiety, relaxation, and so on.

Results

*S*s working in nonthreat groups were more efficient and adaptive, gave more suggestions, and participated more in the discussion, but asked less for orientation, expressed less organic symptoms, and strove less for group acceptance than did *S*s in threat groups (3/3). Otherwise, variations in the source and target of threat or incidence in threat were unrelated to characteristics or behavior of groups or group members (0/121). In addition, the interaction of source and target of threat were not related either to group or individual characteristics and behavior (0/39).

Study Variables

120) Personality characteristics of members
> Personal feelings of anxiety, relaxation, etc.: *S* scores on adjective list.

312) Induced social conditions
> Degree of threat: threat conditions produced by *E* according to experimental instructions.
> Source of threat: threat source either *O* or peers—induced by *E* instructions.
> Target of threat: target of threat as either the group or the individual

410) Content of interaction
> Discussion behavior, tension release, agreement, and so on: *E* rating of discussion behavior on Bales categories, *O* rating of traits exhibited during group discussion.

430) Outcomes of interaction
> Performance efficiency, adaptability: *O* ratings of behavior exhibited during group discussion.

Group performance effectiveness: O ratings of groups on goal orientation, productivity, etc.

510) Perceptions of task performance of self and others

Member ratings of group performance effectiveness: S ratings of group on productivity, orientation, etc.

520) Perceptions of social behavior of self and others

Personal report of behavior: S self-report of aggression, dominance, etc., on adjective check list.

1129.* Lanzetta, J. T., et al. The effects of an "anxiety-reducing" medication on group behavior under threat. *J. abnorm. soc. Psychol.*, 1956, 52, 103–108.

Purpose

This study investigated the behavioral effects of groups working under different degrees of threat with or without "anxiety-reducing" medicine.

Procedure

ROTC students were assigned to three-man groups for a task requiring flexibility and interdependence of members. Groups were assigned to one of three conditions varying in experimentally induced threat instructions and "anxiety-reducing" medication as follows: no threat and no medicine; threat and anxiety-reducing medicine; threat and no anxiety-reducing medicine.

Os categorized member behavior according to the Bales system and rated Ss on several personality and performance effectiveness measures at the end of the session. Ss also reported perceptions of their group and their own motivational state on an adjective check list.

Results

In general, the less threat to which Ss were exposed, the more efficiently they performed (2/3). Specifically, groups who received no threat instructions and no drugs worked more efficiently than did groups under threat with or without "anxiety-reducing" medicine (2/2). No significant differences were observed between the threatened groups (0/1).

There was no relationship between type of group and type of leadership exhibited (0/3).

This study contained a total of 105 relationships.

Study Variables

312) Induced social conditions

Degree of induced threat and threat alleviation: E instructions to elicit threat or nonthreat conditions with or without anxiety-reducing drugs.

610) Leadership performance

Degree of leadership exhibited: O rating of leadership exhibited by Ss in group during military strategy task.

621) Member task performance in experimental settings
Member performance efficiency: O rating of efficiency exhibited by
Ss in group during military strategy task.

1134. Lawson, E. D., & Stagner, R. Group pressure, attitude change, and autonomic involvement. *J. soc. Psychol.*, 1957, *45*, 299–312.

Purpose

This study examined whether attitude changes during group discussion were accompanied by changes in a physiological indicator of anxiety.

Procedure

Two types of attitude scales measuring nationalist-internationalist opinions were administered to students. Then they were assigned as participants either to discussion groups with an instructed majority opposing their opinions or to control groups with no discussion. Self-perceived anxiety was measured by giving the Taylor scale of anxiety to Ss, and an indication of objective anxiety was obtained by measuring palmar sweat before and after the discussion period. Both attitude scales were readministered after the discussion.

Results

In general, the presence of an opposition majority did not result in more than slight attitude change as evidenced by comparisons of discussion and no-discussion groups (5/20). These results obtained for Ss whose palmar sweat level changed and fluctuated to varying degrees. Type of attitude did not relate to the amount of sweat produced (0/2), although nationalists perceived their anxiety as being higher than did internationalists according to the Taylor measure of anxiety (1/1). In addition, nationalists with high fluctuations in palmar sweat changed their attitudes significantly (2/2), whereas internationalists did not (0/2).

Study Variables

120) Personality characteristics of members
Manifest anxiety: S responses on Taylor Scale of Anxiety.
Palmar sweat: amount of sweat as measured by densitometer.

144) Attitudes toward issues, concepts, ideologies
Change in nationalist attitude: S scores on attitude scale.
Type of attitude: Ss classified as nationalists or internationalists according to attitude scores.

222) Group training and experience
Time palmar sweat test was administered: test administration before or after discussion.

430) Outcomes of interaction
Degree of participation in discussion: S assignment to discussion or no-discussion groups.

1139. Leavitt, H. J. Some effects of certain communication patterns on group performance. *J. abnorm. soc. Psychol.*, 1951, *46*, 38–50.

Purpose

This study compared the performance and behavior of groups and individuals as a function of communication net pattern and position.

Procedure

Volunteers were assigned to groups operating in one of four communication nets: circle, chain, **Y**, and wheel. All groups were given the task of identifying one symbol missing from a set of symbols on each of 15 trials. Only written communication between *S*s was allowed, and each trial lasted until all members indicated they had the solution. After the last trial, *S*s completed a questionnaire describing group activity, leadership, and perceptions of the group.

Results

In general, groups were undifferentiated with respect to performance efficiency and member accuracy under different communication net conditions. Only slight differences existed among nets in time required for fastest correct solution (2/12) and individual errors (4/24). All the observed accuracy differences derived from a comparison of circle and **Y** patterns, with *S*s in the **Y** net making significantly fewer errors than did those in the circle (4/4).

Centrality of member position in the chain, **Y**, and wheel accounted for no differences in individual accuracy (0/13). Central and intermediate *S*s, however, were more active in problem solving, sending more messages (10/10). They were also more satisfied with their jobs than were those at the ends of the chain, **Y**, and wheel nets (6/8). Central and intermediate *S*s in these nets, as well as *S*s in the circle, were not different from one another in communication activity and job satisfaction (0/8).

Study Variables

141) Attitudes toward the task

Satisfaction with job: *S* postexperimental questionnaire responses.

152) Task or physical position in the group

Perception of occurrence of a leader : *S* designation of group leader on postexperimental questionnaire.

Centrality of member communication position in group: *E* assignment of *S*s to places in communication nets.

323) Induced task conditions

Group communication pattern: *E* assignment of *S*s to circle, chain, **Y**, or wheel patterns.

420) Patterns of interaction

Participation content and frequency: *E* count of total messages and types of messages sent by members.

510) Perceptions of task performance of self and others

> Perception of communication pattern: *S* description of his group organizational structure as wheel, circle, **Y**, or chain.
>
> Group performance potentiality: *S* postexperimental questionnaire responses.
>
> Member rating of group performance: *S* rating of group following experiment.

621) Member task performance in experimental settings

> Individual performance: *E* record of each *S*'s incorrect responses.

631) Group task performance in experimental settings

> Group performance: time required for fastest correct solution.

1145. Lennard, H. et al. Lysergic acid diethylamide (LSD-25): XII. A preliminary statement of its effects upon interpersonal communication. *J. Psychol.*, 1956, *41*, 185–198.

Purpose

This study explored the effects on interpersonal communication of a drug which produces changes in intellectual and emotional functioning.

Procedure

Two *S*s were given 50 micrograms of LSD-25 orally in tap water, and two were given 100 micrograms. *S*s had not eaten or smoked since the previous night. They met for discussion of a topic and their participation was observed according to Bales Interaction Process Analysis categories. Five months later, the procedure was repeated—except that, unknown to *S*s, they were given tap water only.

Results

The findings were not reported in terms of statistical probabilities. The author merely identified some patterns of group communication under LSD-25:

1. Verbal output of members under the influence of the drug was restricted or shortened.

2. There was a tendency for those who had not received the drug to increase their communication output.

3. When all members were given LSD-25, there was a reduction in negative interpersonal responses.

4. The ratio between amounts of task activity and socioemotional activity did not differ under the drug and control conditions.

5. The ratio of questions to answers, as well as the ratio of orientation to evaluative responses, was higher in the group under the drug condition.

Study Variables

120) Personality characteristics of members
> Member physiological drug state: S condition with and without LSD-25.

410) Content of interaction
> Discussion behavior: member behavior coded according to Bales categories.

1151. Levi, M. *"Group atmosphere" and completion of survival instructor training.* Reno, Nev.: Stead Air Force Base, Crew Research Laboratory, February, 1956. (Lab. Note CRL-LN-56-205)

Purpose

This study investigated how leader training affected performance, attraction to groups, and rate of attrition from groups.

Procedure

Fifteen groups of survival instructor trainees were assigned to either experimental groups that were given a course in fostering better group atmosphere or control groups that were not given such training. Before the beginning of formal training, a questionnaire was administered to tap sociometric choices and attraction to the group. The same questionnaire was readministered after the training period, together with a scale measuring the behavior of instructors and other group members.

Results

The different methods of leader training did not produce any differential levels or changes of member feelings of attraction to their group or leader (0/6) or variations in member ratings of crew leader performance (0/2).

Neither changes in members' attraction to their group, sociometric choices, nor adequacy of leader and member behavior related to the rate of attrition from groups (1/16).

Study Variables

222) Group training and experience
> Type of leader training: leader assignment to be trained or not trained in creating a better atmosphere.

230) Interpersonal relations in the group
> Sociometric choice: member judgments of liking others.
> Member attraction to group: member questionnaire responses.

430) Outcomes of interaction
> Rate of attrition from group: O records of attrition.

520) Perceptions of social behavior of self and others
> Adequacy of leader and crew behavior: S questionnaire responses.

1195. Lippitt, R., et al. The dynamics of power: a field study of social influence in groups of children. *Hum. Relat.*, 1952, *5*, 37–64.

Purpose

This study investigated the relationship between attributed power of group members and their direct and indirect influence on the behavior of other members of the group.

Procedure

Mentally disturbed boys and girls were asked to evaluate their peers by arranging their pictures according to their social, physical, and other abilities and their influence on the group (attributed power). In addition, Os and counselors rated the behavior of the children in terms of impulsiveness, the extent to which others spontaneously imitated them without any influence attempt on their part (contagion), their direct influence on others, and so on. Furthermore, information was collected about Ss' height, weight, and age. Ratings of attributed power were compared with perception of others and behavior ratings.

Results

In general, Ss were viewed as possessing more power if they perceived themselves as being more powerful, were rated as being more skilled in camp-craft and fighting, and were best-liked by others (18/18), whereas weight, height, and impulsiveness were not related to status position (0/4).

Furthermore, Ss with more attributed power exhibited more indirect influence (contagion), were more susceptible to influence, were more successful in directly influencing others, and received more deference behavior from others (12/14). Attributed power was only slightly related to either indirect influence received or nonsocial behavior (2/8), and self-perception of power was only slightly related to frequency of attempt to influence others (2/8).

Study Variables

110) Biographical characteristics of members
  Biographical characteristics: S self-report of age.
  Physical characteristics: S weight and height.
120) Personality characteristics of members
  Personality characteristic (independence from adults): S rating by other group members.
131) General abilities of members
  Intelligence: S scores on an IQ test.
132) Task abilities of members
  Campcraft skill: counselor rating of S abilities.
  Fighting ability: counselor rating of S abilities.
151) Social position in the group
  Perception of own power: S rating of own power in group.
  Attributed power of others: S rating of power of other members.

230) Interpersonal relations in the group
    Personal liking: *S* sociometric choices of other members.

410) Content of interaction
    Direct attempt to influence others: *O* ratings of *S* influence behavior.
    Behavior impulsiveness: counselor rating of each *S* on personal impulsiveness.

420) Patterns of interaction
    Member activity level: *O* rating of each *S* on general camp activity level.

430) Outcomes of interaction
    Indirect influence (initiation and receipt): *O* record of the extent to which *S* behavior was copied by others (and vice versa) without direct attempts at influence.
    Social interactions to and from power source: *O* record of social, deference, nonsocial, and other behavior by group members.

520) Perceptions of social behavior of self and others
    Perceived campcraft skill: *S* rating of other group members.
    Perceived fighting ability: *S* rating of other group members.

1195a. Lippitt, R., et al. The dynamics of power: a field study of social influence in groups of children. *Hum. Relat.*, 1952, 5, 37–64.

Purpose

This study investigated the relationship between attributed power of group members and their direct and indirect influence on the behavior of other members of the group. The study was an extension of the immediately preceding study.

Procedure

Mentally disturbed boys and girls were asked to evaluate their peers by arranging their pictures according to their social, physical, and other abilities and their influence on the group (attributed power). In addition, *O*s and counselors rated the behavior of the children in terms of impulsiveness, the extent to which others spontaneously imitated them without any influence attempt on their part (contagion), their direct influence on others, and so on. Furthermore, information was collected about *S*s' height, weight, and age. Ratings of attributed power were compared with perception of others and behavior ratings.

Results

In general, boys with high attributed power attempted to influence others more frequently, were more successful doing it, and initiated the imitation of their behavior by others more often than did *S*s with low attributed power (6/6). Specifically, boys with high attributed power were more likely to be imitated, to exert direct influence on others, to receive deference behavior, and to attempt influence from others than were those with low attributed power (4/4). However, there was no relationship between attributed power and any of these behavior characteristics for girls (0/4).

Study Variables

151) Social position in the group
> Attributed power of others: member rating by other group members.

410) Content of interaction
> Impulsiveness exhibited: counselor rating of S abilities.

430) Outcomes of interaction
> Influence behavior exhibited: O rating of behavior of Ss regarding contagion initiated, contagion picked up, deference behavior, influence attempts, etc.

1199. Lipsitt, L. P., & Vallance, T. R. The expression of teleonomic trends in private and in group-related problem situations. *J. Pers.*, 1955, *23*, 381–390.

Purpose

This study tested the hypothesis that general personality characteristics are evoked and manifested more clearly in group situations than in private problem-solving settings.

Procedure

Fourteen undergraduate females responded to "moral dilemma" problems in the privacy of their rooms and in the presence of other Ss under the expectation that their responses would be read, discussed, and criticized in the group. Descriptions of all Ss in terms of general personality traits were obtained from acquaintances. Acquaintances were also asked to rank the characteristics in terms of the strength with which they applied to each S. A group of 12 matchers then matched the personality trait descriptions with the written responses to the moral dilemma problems.

Results

The four best over-all matchers were more successful in matching problem responses with the personality descriptions in the group situation than in the private situation (1/1). However, there was no difference in matching accuracy when data for all 12 judges were used (0/1).

Study Variables

240) General structural properties of the group
> Occurrence of group: S work alone and in groups.

621) Member task performance in experimental settings
> Outside judges' accuracy in matching personality characteristics with behavior.

1210. Lorge, I., et al. Solutions by teams and by individuals to a field problem at different levels of reality. *J. educ. Psychol.*, 1955, *46*, 17–24.

Purpose

This study compared the quality of individual and group solutions to a practical field problem in four settings differing in degree of reality.

Procedure

The problem of crossing a mined road was presented to 60 AFROTC students at four different levels of reality: verbal description only, verbal description plus a photo of the setting, verbal description plus a scale model of the setting, and verbal description plus a scale model that could be manipulated by *S*s during the task. Some *S*s were assigned as individuals to one of these conditions and others worked in teams of five men. Written solutions were submitted by individuals and by groups (as written by a team member under advisement by the others) and analyzed for over-all quality.

Results

No differences in the quality of the solutions appeared as a function of the reality of the situation (0/1). Separate analysis showed that group solutions were generally better than individual solutions (1/1).

Study Variables

240) General structural properties of the group

Group structure (individual vs. team member): *E* assignment of *S*s to individual or team conditions.

321) Stimulus properties of the task

Problem characteristic (degree to which problem approached reality): *E* assignment of *S*s to work on problem with merely verbal description, photo of problem area and verbal description, scale model with verbal description, scale model that could be manipulated by *S*s and verbal description.

631) Group task performance in experimental settings

Group problem-solving performance: *E* analysis of solution for quality.

1227. Lundy, R. M. Assimilative projection and accuracy of prediction in interpersonal perceptions. *J. abnorm. soc. Psychol.* 1956, *52*, 33-38.

Purpose

This study investigated whether the focus of attention on self or on another person and the desire of knowledge about another person influenced predictions of another's behavior.

Procedure

Fifty-two college students completed the Allport-Vernon Scale of Values. After a few weeks they met in pairs to discuss a topic. Before and after each discussion they completed the scale of values as they thought their partners would respond. Before one of the discussions, Ss were instructed to pay attention to themselves and what they were saying; before the other discussion they were asked to focus attention upon their partner's remarks.

Results

Ss who paid more attention to their own behavior showed a greater change in correspondence of their own A-V scores with predicted partner score than did those who focused on others (1/1). The Ss focusing on self also showed a greater correspondence following interaction than before interaction (1/1).

On accuracy of social predictions, results showed that Ss who focused on partner behavior showed an increase in accuracy of their judgment after interaction (1/1) and also increased more in judgment accuracy than did those who focused on themselves (1/1).

Study Variables

131) General abilities of members
      Degree of knowledge about other persons: S responses to test instruments before and after interaction with another person.
144) Attitudes toward issues, concepts, ideologies
312) Induced social conditions
      Discussion focus of attention: instructions to Ss to focus attention on their own remarks or on their partner's.
520) Perceptions of social behavior of self and others
      Social prediction (attributed similarity of partner to self): discrepancy between S scores on Allport-Vernon Scale of Values when rating self and estimating other's responses.
      Accuracy of social perception: discrepancy between estimated partner response to Allport-Vernon Scale of Values and actual partner response.

1236. Macbride, P. D. *Studies in conformity and yielding: IX. The influence of confidence upon resistance of perceptual judgments to group pressure.* Berkeley, Calif.: University of California, 1958. (Tech. Rep. No. 10, Contract NR 170-159)

Purpose

The study investigated personal confidence in judgment as a factor related to susceptibility to group influence.

Procedure

A visual maze (line-tracing task) was presented to individuals in simulated five-man groups, along with unanimous wrong answers supposedly coming from other group members. Each S was assigned to answer last in turn, after

E had supplied the other answers. In order to create different degrees of confidence, E then presented a new series of trials without group influence and gave positive and negative information about Ss' errors. Following these trials, Ss were exposed again to the simulated group pressure condition, to determine whether confidence influenced yielding. On a later questionnaire, Ss indicated their own perceived accuracy of performance, confidence in their judgment, and the degree to which they had been influenced by others.

Results

Simulated influence resulted in a significant amount of yielding as defined by erroneous judgment in the direction of the majority opinion (4/4).

The greater the experimentally induced confidence in performance, however, the less Ss yielded toward the majority opinion (2/2). Moreover, the same results held for Ss' own judgments of confidence and their yielding (2/2).

Several other relationships showed no major consistencies—for example, perception of performance and yielding (3/6), sequence of trials and yielding (4/8). Perceived influence by others was positively related to yielding (2/2).

Study Variables

311) Influence and conformity pressures

Pressure exerted on Ss: E creation of different conformity pressures on Ss by manipulating response-control lights.

322) Feedback and reinforcement conditions

Type of reinforcement: E presentation of positive and negative reinforcement to Ss.

430) Outcomes of interaction

Conformity (yielding to erroneous majority opinion): E record of S responses to a visual maze.

510) Perceptions of task performance of self and others

Degree of perceived influence: S questionnaire responses.

Confidence in own judgment: S questionnaire responses.

Perceived accuracy of own performance: S estimate of own accuracy on visual maze.

621) Member task performance in experimental settings

Accuracy of member performance: E record of S responses to a visual maze.

1242.* McCurdy, H. G., & Eber, H. W. Democratic versus authoritarian: a further investigation of group problem-solving. *J. Pers.*, 1953, *22*, 258–269.

Purpose

This study compared the performance of persons with high- and low-authoritarian attitudes working in democratic and authoritarian atmospheres.

Procedure

College student Ss scoring either high or low on a measure of authoritarianism were assembled into homogeneous groups which had either authoritarian or democratic modes of operation. By instruction, democratic groups were urged to work cooperatively, with no leader appointed and all members having an equal say in activities. An authoritarian atmosphere was created by appointing one S leader and giving him absolute command over the group. Group performance was measured by number of correct responses per unit time, time per unit of work, number of errors per unit of time and per unit of work.

Results

In general, democratic work groups made more correct responses than did authoritarian work groups (1/1). This generalization did not hold strongly, however, when performance was measured in terms of number of errors per unit of work or number of errors per unit of time (2/6). Democratic groups made fewer errors during the first and second minutes of the task but were undifferentiated from authoritarian groups in later periods.

Also, democratic work groups composed of Ss with democratic attitudes only made fewer errors per unit of time than those with authoritarian members (4/4). (In a replication experiment, the same comparison barely failed to reach significance (0/2).)

This study contained a total of 20 relationships.

Study Variables

131) General abilities of members
Academic achievement: S final grade in psychology course.

144) Attitudes toward issues, concepts, ideologies
Authoritarianism: S responses to E-scale.

323) Induced task conditions
Group organization: E assignment of Ss to leaderless or leader-directed work situation.

621) Member task performance in experimental settings
Accuracy of member performance: E record of number of correct responses.

1243. McCurdy, H. G., & Lambert, W. E. The efficiency of small human groups in the solution of problems requiring genuine co-operation. *J. Pers.*, 1952, *20*, 478–494.

Purpose

This study compared individuals and groups (who operated with and without leaders) in terms of performance on a manipulation task.

Procedure

Two samples of Ss followed identical procedures except that one sample was divided into groups that had no appointed leader and the other sample into groups that alternated between leader and leaderless conditions. In both samples

*S*s were seated either individually or in three-man groups at a table. On the table were six switches—all six in front of each *S* in the individual condition and two apiece in front of each group member. The task required *S*s to turn each switch to the right or left until the correct switch was turned and the signal lamp was lighted. Trials continued until the correct series was discovered and an errorless trial completed.

Results

Groups excelled individuals in over-all performance only where no leadership was present. No strong differences occurred for groups that alternated between the leader and leaderless conditions (1/2). Also, groups with alternating leadership conditions performed equally well with and without a leader (0/2).

Although no differences existed between individual and group *average* number of errors on the first trial (0/1), *excessive* errors on the first run were made significantly more often by groups than by individuals (2/2).

Study Variables

240) General structural properties of the group
   Occurrence of group: *E* assignment of *S*s to individual or three-man group conditions.
   Presence of designated leader: *E* designation of leader (or no designation of leader).

631) Group task performance in experimental settings
   Group performance: number of errors made by group.

1244. McDavid, J., Jr. Personality and situational determinants of conformity. *J. abnorm. soc. Psychol.*, 1959, *58*, 241–246.

Purpose

This study investigated the conformity behavior of individuals in terms of their consistent dispositional tendencies to be either task-oriented or person-oriented.

Procedure

Using a sentence-completion test, boys of a junior high school were divided into message-oriented (task-oriented) and source-oriented (person-oriented) groups. *S*s were then assigned to a simulated group with a task to count a number of sets of metronomic clicks. Each *S* was informed that his classmates were simultaneously participating in the experiment and two unidentifiable voices recorded predetermined responses into a tape in order to simulate the presence of anonymous peers. Task difficulty was manipulated by varying the number of clicks presented on a trial. Degree of discrepancy between the "majority" report and the actual number of clicks was also manipulated. Conformity was measured by the number of times *S* agreed with the false judgments, yielded to them, or compromised with them.

Results

Message-oriented Ss—those who were disposed to focus on the task—were generally less susceptible to group influence, felt less personal need to change their behavior, were less affected by manipulations of report discrepancy, were more affected by manipulations of task difficulty, and were more likely to compromise with rather than yield to discrepant group judgments (6/6) compared to Ss who were source-oriented—i.e., oriented to other persons.

Study Variables

311) Influence and conformity pressures
    Degree of discrepancy between actual stimulus and false majority report: E manipulation of degree of discrepancy of false information of "group" from true stimulus characteristics.

321) Stimulus properties of the task
    Task difficulty: E assignment of easy or difficult tasks by varying rate of sound stimuli.

410) Content of interaction
    Type of task orientation: E division of Ss, through analysis of sentence-completion test, into message-oriented and source-oriented groups.

430) Outcomes of interaction
    Conformity: number of times S agreed with group completely, yielded by agreement, or compromised on judgment of auditory stimulus.

510) Perceptions of task performance of self and others
    Self-evaluation: S rating of adequacy of own performance.

520) Perceptions of social behavior of self and others
    Perceived need for changing own behavior: S rating of desirability of changing behavior.

1249. McGinnies, E., et al. The effects of sound films on opinions about mental illness in community discussion groups. *J. appl. Psychol.*, 1958, *42*, 40–46.

Purpose

This study was concerned with group discussion and degree of exposure to communication as determinants of attitude change.

Procedure

Adult community discussion groups viewed three mental health films after responding to a questionnaire measuring their attitudes toward mental health concepts. Some groups discussed the films, whereas others did not. Following the last viewing and the discussion in which some of the groups participated, Ss were readministered the attitude questionnaire.

Results

Results showed that *S*s exposed to films alone and to films with discussion changed their attitudes more than did control groups (3/4). However, there was no difference in the attitude change of film-only and film-discussion groups (0/1).

Study Variables

222) Group training and experience
   Degree of exposure to film and discussion: *E* assignment of groups to conditions with varying degree of exposure to film and discussion of mental health concepts.

323) Induced task conditions
   Time of testing: groups' responses before and after film or film-discussion treatments.

430) Outcomes of interaction
   Attitude and change in attitude toward mental health: *S* responses to mental health opinion inventory.

1249a. McGinnies, E., et al. The effects of sound films on opinions about mental illness in community discussion groups. *J. appl. Psychol.*, 1958, *42*, 40–46.

Purpose

This study was concerned with group discussion and degree of exposure to communication as determinants of attitude change. The study was an extension of the immediately preceding study.

Procedure

Adult community discussion groups viewed a mental health film after responding to a questionnaire measuring their attitudes toward mental health concepts. Some groups discussed the film, whereas others did not. Following the viewing or the viewing plus discussion, *S*s were readministered the attitude questionnaire.

Results

Groups exposed to only one film or one film plus a discussion treating the subject of mental health (rather than a series of three as in the previous study) showed no significant differential attitude change from before to after exposure (1/7).

Study Variables

222) Group training and experience
   Time of testing: groups responses before and after film-discussion treatments.

321) Stimulus properties of the task
>   Degree of exposure to film and discussion: exposure to film or film plus discussion of mental health concepts.

430) Outcomes of interaction
>   Attitude and change in attitude toward mental health: S responses to mental health opinion inventory.

1252. Mack, R. W. The prestige system of an air base: squadron rankings and morale. *Amer. sociol. Rev.*, 1954, *19*, 281–287.

Purpose

This experiment studied factors associated with the prestige of air squadrons.

Procedure

Questionnaire responses of 6612 airmen were used to rank squadrons in a hierarchy of prestige and to relate prestige to squadron activities, biographical characteristics of the people who ranked them, the morale of the rankers, their judgments about work conditions, and so on.

Results

The higher outsiders rated working conditions in a squadron, the more prestige the squadron had among its own members (1/1). On the other hand, members' ratings of working conditions and squadron prestige were not related (0/1).

The higher the enlisted grades of Ss and the longer they had been in the Air Force the better was their morale (3/3). However, there was no relationship between the prestige of squadron among its own members and Ss' morale (0/1). No other results were reported.

Study Variables

110) Biographical characteristics of members
>   Biographical background (enlisted grade, time spent in the Air Force): S questionnaire responses.

141) Attitudes toward the task
142) Attitudes toward the situation
>   Morale: S questionnaire responses.

142) Attitudes toward the situation.
>   Future plans with Air Force: S intentions to re-enlist in Air Force.
>   Working conditions in squadron: Ss rating of working conditions.
>   Perceived evaluations of squadrons by outsiders: estimate of outsiders' rating of working conditions in the squadron.

240) General structural properties of the group
>   Prestige of squadrons in Air Force base: squadron members ranking of their own squadron.

321) Stimulus properties of the task

> Type of activity in squadrons: description of squ .drons in terms of different tasks.
>
> Relation of judge to the squadron: squadron members' and non-members' rating of the squadron.

1266.* Maier, N. R. F., & Maier, R. A. An experimental test of the effects of "developmental" vs. "free" discussion on the quality of group decisions. *J. appl. Psychol.*, 1957, *41*, 320–323.

Purpose

This study compared the effects on performance of two types of discussion methods.

Procedure

Student groups discussed and arrived at a solution to a case history problem while working under two different leadership or discussion situations. In one instance, *free discussion* was allowed, with the leader instructed to assist the group by being permissive and helpful but to avoid structuring the direction and course of the discussion.

In the other case, *developmental discussion*, the leader was not only permissive and helpful but also assisted by clearly defining the problem and the direction in which the group should progress. Following discussions and statements of group opinion, each S privately indicated his own opinion on the topic.

Results

A higher percentage of Ss in the developmental discussion groups, in which the leader played a definite role, solved the problem correctly than in the free discussion groups (2/2). Groups were undifferentiated, however, in the extent to which they achieved unanimous decisions (0/2).

This study contained a total of four relationships.

Study Variables

430) Outcomes of interaction

> Unanimity of member problem solutions: E count of groups that were split or unanimous in their answer.

610) Leadership performance

> Leader behavior discussion: group leader action either to structure group processes or not to structure them.

631) Group task performance in experimental settings

> Quality of member performance: E designation of percentage of Ss giving right or wrong answer in group.

1276. Manis, M. Social interaction and the self concept. *J. abnorm. soc. Psychol.*, 1955, *51*, 362–370.

Purpose

This investigation explored changes in the similarity of a person's self-concept and friends' impressions of him over a period of time.

Procedure

College men responded to a personality trait scale from three different points of view: the characteristics they ideally would like to have had, the characteristics they actually possessed, and their judgments of personality characteristics of other *S*s. *S*s also completed a sociometric questionnaire. Both types of instruments were administered on two occasions separated by six weeks of close contact. Relationships between the sociometric data and various indexes derived from the personality data were studied.

Results

There was no clear-cut relationship between increased familiarity of *S*s (by virtue of living closely together) and the congruency of self-descriptions and others' descriptions of *S* (4/9). These relationships, however, evidently needed to be considered in terms of friendship factors and positivity–negativity of self-descriptions. For example, congruency among friends was greater, particularly if *S*s rated themselves more positively than did their peers (2/3). Also, the second self-description was more similar to the friends' first description, especially for *S*s who rated themselves negatively (2/2), and not, when self-ratings were more positive than peer ratings (0/1).

The results also showed a greater increase in agreement of self-ratings and other's ratings for friends than for nonfriends (1/1), particularly for *S*s who rated themselves positively (1/2).

Other relationships of increased interaction, attraction, congruency of perception, and so on were not significant (1/9).

Study Variables

120) Personality characteristics of members

> Similarity of self-perception and others' perception of self: *S* responses to a personality trait scale as he saw himself and ratings of *S* by other *S*s.

230) Interpersonal relations in the group

> Attraction between group members: *S* scores on a sociometric scale.

240) General structural properties of the group

> Degree of familiarity between *S*s: time of contact—early and later.

1294. Marriott, R. Size of working group and output. *Occup. Psychol.* 1949, *23*, 47–57.

Purpose

This study investigated the performance efficiency of industrial work groups of varying sizes. Individuals and small work groups were also compared.

Procedure

Actual work groups in two automobile factories were used in the analysis. Average efficiency measures (the ratio of time allowed to time required for completion of group operation for groups in factory A and hourly average net piecework earnings per man for seven groups in factory B) were obtained for specified periods and correlated with size of the work group. Groups varied in size up to 50 members. Individual workers were also compared with groups of less than 10.

Results

Smaller groups had consistently higher production rates for all periods than did larger groups (13/13). No productivity differences existed between individuals and small groups (0/1).

Study Variables

240) General structural properties of the group
Size of group: *E* description of group size in terms of individuals (10's, 10–50+).

623) Member task performance in operational settings: specific measures
Member performance efficiency: *E* calculation of average piecework earnings per man per hour.
Group performance efficiency: *E* calculation of ratio of time allowed to time required for completion of group task.

1305. Martin, W. E., et al. Studies of group behavior: II. Methodological problems in the study of interrelationships of group members. *Educ. psychol. Measmt,* 1952, *12*, 533–553.

Purpose

The main purpose of this study was to see how mutuality of sociometric choice related to cohesiveness among college women.

Procedure

On two occasions the residents of 13 college housing units were given a sociometric inventory requiring judgments about others as roommates, co-workers, persons in whom to confide, and so on. From these data were computed indexes of sociometric mutuality (the ratio of the actual number of mutual choices in a group to the number of mutual choices that would be expected by chance) and cohesiveness of choices (the extent to which members of the group chose Ss within that group rather than outsiders).

Results

There was no relationship between Ss' sociometric mutuality and group cohesiveness (0/17).

In general, the intercorrelations of the individual cohesiveness measures were not significant (1/10). Moreover, the intercorrelations of the individual sociometric choice items were not significant (5/71).

Study Variables

230) Interpersonal relations in the group
   Mutual sociometric choice: S questionnaire responses on choice of others as roommates, persons in whom to confide, etc.
   Cohesiveness: ratio of friendship, roommate, and similar choices made within the group to those made outside the group.

1315. Mausner, B. Studies in social interaction: III. Effect of variation in one partner's prestige on the interaction of observer pairs. *J. appl. Psychol.*, 1953, *37*, 391–393.

Purpose

This study determined how variations in a partner's prestige affected conformity to that partner's influence attempts.

Procedure

Individual students were first given the Meier Art Judgment Test. A week later, the test was readministered. Ss in one group repeated the test alone; Ss in two other groups repeated it with a partner. The partner was introduced to one group as a fellow student; to the other as an "art authority." The partner in all cases made choices indicated as wrong by the scoring key. Social influence or conformity was measured in terms of the shift in frequency of wrong judgments from the "alone" situation to the "social" situation.

Results

Conformity occurred when Ss worked with a fellow student or "art authority" who stated his judgments first (2/2). Conformity responses did not occur when partners made their judgments last (0/2). There was no significant difference in conformity between the two prestige variations (0/1).

Study Variables

312) Induced social conditions
   Perceived partner status: S work under different conditions according to experimental instructions regarding status of partner.
621) Member task performance in experimental settings
   Stimulus judgment: S judgment on Meier Art Judgment Test.

1316. Mausner, B. The effect of one partner's success in a relevant task on the interaction of observer pairs. *J. abnorm. soc. Psychol.*, 1954, *49*, 557–560.

Purpose

This study compared the degree to which *S*s changed their judgments when paired with a person they perceived as either successful or unsuccessful.

Procedure

*S*s judged the length of a line at two different times, first alone and later paired with another *S* whose judgment differed from their own. Between the two judgments, the partner gave the impression of being skillful or unskilled in estimating length in a similar task in the presence of *S*. The partner was a confederate acting in accordance with *E*'s instructions.

Results

*S*s who perceived their partner as skillful were significantly influenced in their own judgments. Comparison of estimates given before and after exposure to successful or unsuccessful partners revealed that those paired with the successful partner changed more often than did the others (1/1).

Study Variables

323) Induced task conditions

Perceived success of partner: confederate judgment of length skillfully or unskillfully according to *E* instructions.

430) Outcomes of interaction

Shift in judgment: *S* judgment of length of lines—alone and in group situation.

1325. Medalia, N. Z. Authoritarianism, leader acceptance, and group cohesion. *J. abnorm. soc. Psychol.*, 1955, *51*, 207–213.

Purpose

This study investigated whether the differences among group members in authoritarianism related to differences in leader acceptance and group cohesiveness.

Procedure

A randomly selected sample of enlisted airmen completed attitude scales measuring authoritarianism, acceptance of their leader, and group cohesiveness (defined as desire to re-enlist in the Air Force). Measures were also obtained of rank and years spent in the service.

Results

*S*s with high authoritarianism and confidence in their leader accepted leaders more frequently than did those with low authoritarianism and confidence (4/4).

The higher the authoritarianism score, the more *S*s wanted to re-enlist in the Air Force (1/1), although authoritarianism did not relate to number of years served in the Air Force, rank, or type of squadron (0/3).

Study Variables

110) Biographical characteristics of members
         Biographical characteristics: years in Air Force, rank in Air Force.

142) Attitudes toward the situation
         Action intentions: *S* questionnaire responses regarding re-enlistment.

144) Attitudes toward issues, concepts, ideologies
         Authoritarianism: *S* scores on attitude scale.

230) Interpersonal relations in the group
         Confidence in leader: *S* scores on attitude scale.
         Acceptance of leader: *S* scores on attitude scale.

240) General structural properties of the group
         Type of squadron: squadron description according to functions.

1333. Meyer, H. H.   Factors related to success in the human relations aspect of work-group leadership. *Psychol. Monogr.*, 1951, *63*, No. 3.

Purpose

The purpose of this study was to identify personal characteristics related to success as a supervisor.

Procedure

Several tests were given to utility company supervisors; included were ability measures, such as the Wonderlic Personnel Test, and various social attitude measures. A personal data inventory (interests, hobbies, education, and so on) was not administered at the testing session, but each testee filled out the form on his own time and returned it by mail. An index of leadership skill was also obtained from higher-level supervisor ratings of testees on job knowledge, administration, and human relations.

Results

Highly related to good supervision were high social judgment ability, high problem-solving skill, high word fluency, and good personal background (26/34). Age, years of experience, and various personality traits and social attitudes were not found to differentiate good and poor leaders (0/29).

Study Variables

110) Biographical characteristics of members
   Biographical characteristics: age, years of experience.

120) Personality characteristics of members
   Personal background data: supervisor scores on a personal data inventory.

120) Personality characteristics of members

131) General abilities of members
   Word fluency, social judgment, background, and personal data: supervisor scores on word fluency test, difference between expert and supervisor scores on a human relations test, supervisor scores on a personal data inventory.

131) General abilities of members
   Problem-solving ability and word fluency: scores on tests.
   Social judgment (ability to predict human reactions): difference between expert and supervisor scores on a human relations test.

132) Task abilities of members
   Leadership: higher-level supervisors' ratings of Ss on job knowledge, administration, and human relations.

143) Attitudes toward nongroup persons and other groups
   Personality traits of ideal supervisor: supervisor questionnaire responses.

144) Attitudes toward issues, concepts, ideologies
   Attitude in dealing with people: supervisor questionnaire responses.

240) General structural properties of the group
   Type of work groups: supervisor work in different groups or departments.

1345. Mills, T. M. Power relations in three-person groups. *Amer. sociol. Rev.*, 1953, *18*, 351–357.

Purpose

This study investigated the development of coalitions and patterns of discussion in three-person groups.

Procedure

Student groups discussed and created a single dramatic story from TAT pictures. There was a minimum of restraint with no limit on type of story, content, or on who should play what role in telling the story. Each act of Ss was scored in sequence according to Bales Interaction Process Analysis and grouped in terms of group-contribution acts, positive support acts, and negative nonsupport acts. Various combinations of these three types of data were used to differentiate groups and to describe group members.

Results

On the basis of positive support contributions, four types of relationships between the two most active members were identified: *solidary*, in which both members were highly supportive; *conflicting*, in which both were not supportive, *dominant*, in which the most-active *S* was supportive, the other not; and *contending*, in which the less-active *S* was highly supportive, the other not.

In general, the results showed only slight relationship between type of support pattern, as evidenced by discussion remarks, and degree of support or opposition elicited or received by the least active member of the group, except in the solidary pattern (2/12). The results also indicated that activity positions were stable in the solidary, contending, and dominant patterns, but unstable in the conflicting one (3/4).

Study Variables

321) Stimulus properties of the task
    Stage of experiment: group participation in different sessions.
410) Content of interaction
    Discussion behavior: *E* record of each act of group members according to Bales categories.

1354. Mitnick, L. L., & McGinnies, E.   Influencing ethnocentrism in small discussion groups through a film communication. *J. abnorm. soc. Psychol.*, 1958, *56*, 82–90.

Purpose

This study examined the effect of film communication with and without discussion on ethnocentric attitudes.

Procedure

*S*s were tested on the California Ethnocentrism Scale and classified as low, average, or high. They were then divided into three homogeneous groups, one of which viewed a film on prejudice and later discussed it, another of which viewed the film but did not discuss it, and the last of which, the control, neither saw the film nor had a discussion. The E scale was twice readministered to the two experimental groups, once immediately after they had completed the viewing or the viewing with discussion, and again one month later. The experimental groups also took an information test on the film on both of these later occasions.

Results

Initial change in ethnocentrism was associated with an extreme initial attitude, the film communication, and discussion. *S*s exposed to both film and discussion showed greater attitude change (3/3). They were also more stable in this change as measured one month later (1/1). Initial ethnocentrism was not an unequivocal factor in attitude change (0/1). *S*s initially high in ethnocentrism changed more than did less-prejudiced *S*s from the first to second testing only in the film–no discussion condition (2/2).

Initial ethnocentrism and film-discussion exposure were not as strongly related to learning and retention of film information. Ss under different film-discussion conditions were undifferentiated with respect to film information (0/2). The more ethnocentric were Ss, however, the less film information they learned and retained (5/5). There was no relationship between amount of discussion participation and attitude change (0/3), although highly active participants learned and retained more than did less-active members (4/10).

Study Variables

131) General abilities of members
    Intelligence: S scores on California Mental Maturity Test.

144) Attitudes toward issues, concepts, ideologies
    Ethnocentric attitude and change in attitude: S attitude questionnaire responses.

222) Group training and experience
    Time of testing: administration of test immediately after film and one month later.

321) Stimulus properties of the task
    Degree of exposure to discussion and film: E assignment of Ss to conditions without film or discussion, with film but without discussion, and with film and discussion.

420) Patterns of interaction
    Participation in discussion: O record of Ss' comments during discussion.

621) Member task performance in experimental settings
    Film information (learned and retained): S scores on film information test.

1356. Moeller, G., & Applezweig, M. H. A motivational factor in conformity. J. abnorm. soc. Psychol., 1957, 55, 114–120.

Purpose

This study compared the susceptibility to group influence of those differentially motivated by needs for self-approval and social approval.

Procedure

Ss were selected on the basis of pre-tests indicating a high motivation for self-approval, social approval, or both self and social approval and a high or low need for security. Each S was assigned to a group, with from four to six members, in which the other members were confederates. Groups were required to match the length of a line on one card with the length of one of three other lines on another card. Most of the confederates gave the same wrong answer before S responded. Ss were given a short interview at the end of the experiment during which reactions to the experiment were elicited.

Results

Ss with a high need for social approval appeared to be more influenced by group opinion than were others. Although comparison across all three motivational categories barely failed to reach significance (0/2), socially motivated Ss yielded to the group more frequently than did both self-approval and self-approval-plus-social-approval Ss (2/2).

Interview results were not reported.

Study Variables

120) Personality characteristics of members
Personal need for approval motivation (self-approval and/or social approval) and security: S questionnaire responses.

311) Influence and conformity pressures
Member temptation to answer as others did and concern with what others thought: S questionnaire responses.
S concern over disagreement with group and/or doubtfulness of own accuracy: S questionnaire responses.

430) Outcomes of interaction
Susceptibility to group influence: number of times Ss yielded to group (confederate) judgments of line lengths.

510) Perceptions of task performance of self and others
Agreement with others against own choice: S questionnaire responses.
Accuracy of own judgment: S questionnaire responses.
Perception of accuracy of group judgment: S questionnaire responses.

520) Perceptions of social behavior of self and others
Estimate of others' opinion of self: S questionnaire responses to item ("Others think something's wrong with me").

1382. Morse, Nancy, & Reimer, E. The experimental change of a major organizational variable. *J. abnorm. soc. Psychol.*, 1956, *52*, 120–129.

Purpose

This study compared productivity and satisfaction under situations varying in amount of authority allowed to employees.

Procedure

Department store clerical workers performing routine work were assigned to one of two decision-making conditions: an *autonomy* condition, in which authority was given Ss to make their own decisions; and a *hierarchy* condition, in which decisions were made by executives or supervisor personnel. Supervisors were trained in such roles prior to the experiment. Measures of employee satisfaction were obtained by questionnaire before and after the experimental treatment. Productivity records were also obtained and compared.

Results

Employees allowed to make their own decisions showed higher over-all satisfaction and productivity than did those working under supervisor control of decision making.

Autonomy-condition Ss evaluated their superiors at all levels of supervision more favorably than did hierarchy-condition Ss (6/6). Change in attitude toward higher-level supervisors was particularly marked, with autonomy-condition Ss becoming more satisfied (10/12) and hierarchy-condition Ss becoming less satisfied (11/12). On the other hand, only some change occurred in attitudes toward immediate supervisors (4/12).

Employee satisfaction in other areas followed consistently. Autonomy-condition Ss perceived their jobs as offering greater opportunity for self-actualization (1/1), and their outlooks were more positive on a second testing than on the first (2/3). Although both groups were equal in over-all job satisfaction (0/1), hierarchy-condition Ss showed a marked decrease in satisfaction (2/3). Satisfaction with the company was directly affected by each condition, with autonomy-condition Ss becoming more satisfied (2/3) and hierarchy-condition Ss becoming less satisfied (3/3).

Unequivocally, autonomy-condition groups were rated higher on productivity (7/7).

Study Variables

141) Attitudes toward the task

Job satisfaction: S questionnaire evaluation of job satisfaction.

Perceived job opportunities: S questionnaire responses on opportunity for self-actualization in job.

S job satisfaction: S questionnaire ranking of his job compared with others.

142) Attitudes toward the situation

Satisfaction with company: S questionnaire responses.

143) Attitudes toward nongroup persons and other groups

Satisfaction with relationship with superiors (higher-level management): S questionnaire responses about assistant manager and manager.

Satisfaction with superiors as representatives (higher-level management): S questionnaire responses about assistant manager and manager.

230) Interpersonal relations in the group

Satisfaction with relationship with superiors (supervisors—immediate level): S questionnaire responses.

Satisfaction with superiors as representatives (immediate-level supervisor): S questionnaire response about supervisor.

323) Induced task conditions

Type of decision-making situation: E designation of autonomy and hierarchy situation.

430) Outcomes of interaction
> Degree of employee turnover: records of number of persons leaving the company (per type of group).

623) Member task performance in operational settings: specific measures
> Performance effectiveness (employee productivity): records of clerical costs.

1390. Mouton, Jane S., et al. The relationship between frequency of yielding and the disclosure of personal identity. *J. Pers.*, 1956, *24*, 339–347.

Purpose

This study examined yielding to a group's judgment as influenced by *S*'s submissiveness, anonymity of judgment, and stimulus background characteristics.

Procedure

Male students were used as *S*s on an individual basis after their personal ascendency–submissiveness had been measured by the Allport A-S Reaction Scale. The task was to count metronome clicks. Clicks were sounded at a constant of 180 per minute, and each set of three trials contained 14, 32, or 49 clicks. A simulated group technique was used, with previously recorded responses presented to *S*s. These simulated responses of other *S*s contained either uniformly incorrect responses (uniform background) or half correct and half incorrect responses (split background). *S*s operated either anonymously or publicly; in the latter case they stated their names before each response. The degree to which *S*s yielded to group judgment was indicated by the discrepancy between *S* report of stimulus characteristics and correct response in the direction of the incorrect background response.

Results

Personal anonymity and perception of how others had responded seemed to be factors affecting conformity.

Combined scores for *S*s, and submissive ones in particular, showed more yielding to the group judgment when personal identity was disclosed than when response was anonymous (2/3). Also, *S*s presented with uniformly incorrect simulated responses of other members yielded more to group judgment than did *S*s presented with split background information (3/3).

Neither the pattern of metronome clicks nor the degree of *S*'s personal submissiveness was related to yielding (0/3).

Study Variables

120) Personality characteristics of members
> Submissiveness: *S* responses on Allport A-S Reaction Scale.

311) Influence and conformity pressures
> Type of information presented: *S* manipulation by information about stimulus characteristics (simulated group uniformly incorrect or split).

312) Induced social conditions

Degree of disclosure of personal identity: S anonymous or public response.

321) Stimulus properties of the task

Stimulus input characteristics: E presention of different patterns of clicks to Ss.

430) Outcomes of interaction

Degree of yielding to group judgment: discrepancy between S report of stimulus characteristics and correct response in the direction of incorrect background response.

1401. **Nakamura, C. Y.** *The relation between conformity and problem-solving.* Stanford, Calif.: Stanford University, Department of Psychology, 1955. (Contract No. 25125)

Purpose

This experiment investigated the relationship between conformity and achievement in problem solving and intelligence.

Procedure

Groups of male and female college students were given two types of problems to solve: *straightforward* problems, which were solvable by direct methods and *restructuring* problems, which required a change in set before solution could be achieved. At a second session Ss were placed in an influence situation in which their judgments were contrary to the judgments of others—experimental Ss were exposed unknowingly to a stimulus different from that given others in the group. Conformity was measured by a calculation of the number of responses that deviated from the objectively correct response in the direction of the purported majority. Two measures of intelligence were also employed. One was a vocabulary test and the other was a test measuring word-analogy skills. The interrelations of the problem-solving scores, conformity scores, and intelligence scores were then determined.

Results

Conformity was generally related to problem-solving performance. The less Ss conformed, the better they performed on problems in general (5/7) and on the restructuring type of problems in particular (6/7). However, there was only slight relationship between conformity and performance on the straightforward type of problem (1/4).

Ss scoring high on the vocabulary intelligence measure conformed less than did low-scorers (3/4); however, only slight relationship obtained between the word-analogy measure of intelligence and conformity (1/4).

As to relationships between intelligence measures and performance, results showed that the more-intelligent Ss performed better in general on both types of problems (15/16), with the exception of the lack of relationship between the vocabulary measure and performance on straightforward problems (0/4).

Study Variables

110) Biographical characteristics of members

Biographical characteristics: sex of S.

131) General abilities of members

Intelligence: S scores on word-analogy and vocabulary tests.

321) Stimulus properties of the task

Type of problems: E presenting intellectual problems requiring either direct attacks or restructuring.

430) Outcomes of interaction

Conformity on objective items: deviation of S responses to questionnaire items from correct answers in the direction of presumed majority responses.

Attitudinal conformity: change in S responses to an attitude questionnaire in the direction of other group members.

621) Member task performance in experimental settings

Member performance: S correct performance.

1420. Northway, Mary L., & Wigdor, B. T. Rorschach patterns related to the sociometric status of school children. *Sociometry*, 1947, *10*, 186–199.

Purpose

This study attempted to study personality factors characteristic of persons with differing sociometric status.

Procedure

Eighth-grade students were divided into three sociometric status levels (of social acceptance by classmates) and compared for personality differences on the Rorschach test. On the basis of evaluations by E and teachers, Ss low in sociometric status were further categorized as recessives or aggressives and studied for differences in personality.

Results

No distinct personality profiles of persons with differing levels of social acceptance were delineated in this study (20/68). Interestingly, both high- and low-status Ss gave "human movement" responses significantly more frequently than did those in the middle status group (2/2). Also, high-acceptance Ss responded with "animal movement" descriptions and popular responses more frequently than did the others (4/4).

Analysis of the low sociometric group indicated that aggressives reacted more quickly and rejected fewer cards than did recessives (2/2). They were also more inclined to identify "bright color with indefinite form" (1/1), whereas recessives tended to see "shading as texture and achromatic surface color" (1/1).

Study Variables

120) Personality characteristics of members

Rorschach test responses: latency of S response to Rorschach cards.
Rorschach test responses: number of responses, popular responses, original responses, number of cards rejected.
Rorschach test response-poor form: E analysis of S description of ink-blot forms.
Rorschach test responses: S description of ink-blot cards (frequency of each type of response—e.g., animal and human movement, etc.).
Aggressiveness: E description of S's general mannerisms and appearance, teacher's rating of pupil's social behavior, interview report of S's usual social activities, etc.

230) Interpersonal relations in the group

Sociometric status: S responses on sociometric instrument.

1428. Olmsted, D. W., & Monachesi, E. D. *MMPI trends of small group leaders and members.* Minneapolis: University of Minnesota, 1955. (Contract No. NR-170-169)

Purpose

This report investigated how small group leaders differed from group members in personality characteristics.

Procedure

The MMPI test was administered to formal leaders and members of 39 college student groups of two functional types, task and no-task. The MMPI was also administered to the captains and men of 40 fire-fighting groups.

Results

Leaders in task groups had higher Psychasthenia, Depression, Masculinity-Femininity, and Schizophrenia scores than did group members (6/6). No such relationship occurred in the no-task groups (0/4). Hypochondriasis, Hysteria, Psychopathic Deviate, Hypomania, and Schizophrenia did not differentiate leaders in either type of group (0/10).

For the firemen groups, captains had higher Hypochondriasis, Hysteria, Depression, and Psychasthenia scores but were not differentiated from members on the other dimensions (0/6).

There was no difference between MMPI scores of members of task and no-task groups (1/10) and only slight differences between leader scores (2/10).

Study Variables

120) Personality characteristics of members

Personality characteristics: S responses on MMPI test.

151) Social position in the group

Leadership status: E report of status of Ss as either leaders or members.

1450. Patchen, M. The effect of reference group standards on job satisfactions. *Hum. Relat.*, 1958, *11*, 303–314.

Purpose

This study compared job satisfaction and performance on tasks differing in desirability.

Procedure

*S*s of both sexes rated three kinds of jobs on desirability and were then assigned to one of three conditions of task desirability in groups. Although all groups performed the same neutral-desirability task (copying numbers), *E* informed some groups of another group working on a less-desirable task and informed other groups of another group working on a more-desirable task. Control groups were told about another group performing the same task.

After finishing, *S*s filled out questionnaires reporting satisfaction with the rules, task enjoyment, and preference for their job relative to the other one. Pretest scores were also obtained on a submission subscale of the California F-scale, together with leader ratings of submissiveness.

Results

In general, relative task desirability was only slightly related to job satisfaction (1/6) and performance (1/4). As a matter of fact, control groups paired for the same task reported greater satisfaction with work conditions and accomplished more work than did groups working on a task more desirable than that of their referent group (2/2). Members who still preferred their own group after completing the task reported no higher satisfaction with conditions than did those preferring the outside group (0/1). Task enjoyment did not facilitate work output (0/1).

Submissiveness was generally unrelated to member job satisfaction and performance. Both high- and low-submissives in each task desirability condition reported equal enjoyment of the task (1/7). Submissiveness was not related to work output (0/1).

Boys and girls were differentiated in terms of satisfaction derived from the task, with girls reporting more satisfaction with conditions (5/6) and job enjoyment (1/1). In all cases reported, girls accomplished more work (2/2) but were less accurate than were boys (1/1).

Study Variables

110) Biographical characteristics of members
> Biographical characteristics: sex.

120) Personality characteristics of members
> Personality characteristics (submissiveness): teacher rating of pupil submissiveness.

141) Attitudes toward the task
> Member job satisfaction: *S* postexperimental questionnaire responses.
> Preference for own job: *S* statement of preference for own job or another job.

144) Attitudes toward issues, concepts, ideologies
Personality characteristic (authoritarian submission): S responses on subscale of F-scale.

323) Induced task conditions
Perceived task desirability: E instructions to Ss regarding another group doing less-desirable, more-desirable, or same task.

621) Member task performance in experimental settings
Amount of work accomplished: number of sets of numbers copied by S.
Individual performance: number of errors on task.

1451.* Pavlik, W. B. *Motivational factors in individual and group productivity: IV. The effects of personal and situational motivation upon individual performance in a small group setting.* Columbus, Ohio: Ohio State University Research Foundation, 1956.

Purpose

This study examined the effect of induced motivation and personal anxiety on task performance.

Procedure

Ss were administered the Taylor Scale of Manifest Anxiety (MAS) and according to the results were divided into three-man groups having one high-, one medium-, and one low-anxiety S. Each group was given the task of constructing triangular models from Tinkertoy parts. For control groups, no motivation was introduced; for the experimental groups, the first session was conducted under nonmotivation conditions and the second session under motivation conditions. Motivation was varied by the use of incentives and time signals during the work period. Performance was measured in terms of the number of operations completed by each S.

Results

Motivation and performance were only somewhat related (1/3), and there was no relationship between degree of anxiety and performance (0/3) and between degree of anxiety and motivation (0/3).

Ss under high-motivation conditions liked the task more, found working more enjoyable and interesting, showed more motivation, and felt themselves part of the group more often than did control Ss (5/5). However, motivation did not relate to perceived importance of the task or self-estimates of productivity (0/2).

This study contained a total of 17 relationships.

Study Variables

120) Personality characteristics of members
Personality characteristics: S scores on Taylor Scale of Manifest Anxiety.

141) Attitudes toward the task
Task enjoyment: *S* responses to postexperimental questionnaire.

142) Attitudes toward the situation
Own feeling states: *S* responses to a postexperimental questionnaire regarding own motivation, feelings of being pressured, etc.

322) Feedback and reinforcement conditions
Degree of work motivation: *E* use of different instructions for groups according to experimental instruction regarding incentives for good performance.

510) Perceptions of task performance of self and others
Judgment of own productivity: *S* postexperimental questionnaire responses.

621) Member task performance in experimental settings
Member performance: *E* record of number of complete operations.

1456. Pennington, D. F., et al. *Some effects of decision and discussion on coalescence, change, and effectiveness.* Baton Rouge, La.: Louisiana State University, October, 1957. (Contract N7 ONR 35609.)

Purpose

This study examined the effect of variations in amount of group discussion and requirements for reaching a group decision on member judgments and performance.

Procedure

Groups of students were randomly divided among four conditions with varying amounts of group discussion and requirements to reach a group decision. Students first privately ranked a set of five cities according to size. Next they worked under one of the following conditions: discussion-decision, no discussion–decision, discussion–no decision, and no discussion–no decision. *S*s then privately ranked cities again. Measures were obtained for agreement among members and the group and accuracy of judgments.

Results

1. Performance effectiveness measure
   a. Change in accuracy of private judgments
      (1) Performance effectiveness (two-tailed analyses): not related to discussion, decisions, or their interaction (0/3)
      (2) Performance effectiveness (one-tailed analyses): all groups with any combination of discussion and decision exhibited more effective performance than groups with no intervening discussion or decisions (3/3)
2. Agreement of judgments among members
   a. Private coalescence (increase in agreement from initial to final judgment): highly and positively related to discussion and decision (4/4), not related to their interaction (0/2)

b. Stability (average correlation between member initial and final private judgments) negatively related to discussion and decision (2/2), not related to their interaction (0/1)

Study Variables

321) Stimulus properties of the task
  Occurrence of discussions: exposure or nonexposure of Ss to group discussions.

323) Induced task conditions
  Requirements to reach a decision: E instruction to groups to reach decision or not.

430) Outcomes of interaction
  Increase in private judgment accuracy: differences between final private performance accuracy and initial private accuracy.
  Private coalescence (increase in agreement among members): change in S judgment (increase in agreement among themselves).
  Stability of private opinion: change in S judgment.

1467.* Pepinsky, H. B., et al. Team productivity and contradiction of management policy commitments. *J. appl. Psychol.*, 1959, *43*, 264–268.

Purpose

This study examined the effect of contradictions in expected "management policy" on group performance.

Procedure

Groups of college student Ss worked on a toy-manufacturing task in a simulated industrial work situation. A set of operating rules or "management policies" were presented as the basis for team operation. For some teams these policies were upheld, but for other teams, "upper management" (the E) contradicted team members' expectations with respect to operating procedures. Team productivity was measured by net profit—an index based on number of items completed relative to cost of materials and so on.

Results

Teams whose expectations about "management" behavior were confirmed performed more adequately than did those whose expectations were not confirmed (5/5). These results occurred for over-all measures of task success and for measures of success per unit time.

This study contained a total of 23 relationships.

Study Variables

222) Group training and experience
  Time when teams were rated: E rating of teams in different stages of the study.

312) Induced social conditions

Fulfillment of expectations: *E* assignment of groups to conditions where their expectations about others' behavior were either confirmed or contradicted.

631) Group task performance in experimental settings

Group productivity: *E* record of net profit earned by groups on "toy-manufacturing" task.

1471. Pepinsky, Pauline N., et al. Attempts to lead, group productivity, and morale under conditions of acceptance and rejection. *J. abnorm. soc. Psychol.*, 1958, 57, 47–54.

Purpose

The purpose of this study was to examine how differences in personal needs for achievement or affiliation and degree of support received from others affected performance, morale, and leadership behavior.

Procedure

Students who had either a high need for achievement or a high need for affiliation were selected on the basis of responses to a questionnaire and an interview. *S*s were assigned to four-man task groups in which two of the members were experimenter-confederates who either rejected or vigorously supported the naïve *S*s when they attempted to lead. Leadership attempts based on *O*'s tallies, measures of productivity derived from the number of task units completed, and responses to a postexperimental questionnaire concerning feelings about the group and allied attitudes constituted the resultant variables.

Results

Those who were supported by confederates exhibited more leadership attempts during discussions than did those who were personally rejected (2/3). Only slight differences occurred in leadership behavior as a function of stage of the experiment, sequence of experimental conditions, personal achievement vs. affiliation needs, or the interaction of these variables (4/25).

The relationship of rejection–support conditions and group performance was not clear-cut. *S*s who were supported by confederates were rated by *O*s as exhibiting a lower number of high-quality task decisions (1/1), but they were not differentiated from rejected *S*s on a measure based on completed task units (0/1).

Finally, *S*s operating under support conditions had higher morale or attraction to their groups than did those who were rejected by confederates (2/2).

Study Variables

120) Personality characteristics of members

Need for affiliation or achievement: *O* rating of *S*s during an interview.

151) Social position in the group

Membership status: confederates and naïve group member *S*s.

222) Group training and experience

Sequence of presentation of experimental conditions: *E* presentation of experimental conditions either to first or second half of groups.

230) Interpersonal relations in the group

Sociometric choice: *S* sociometric questionnaire responses.

Orientation toward group: *S* questionnaire responses.

312) Induced social conditions

Acceptance of naïve *S*s: confederate behavior of approval or disapproval during the discussion.

420) Patterns of interaction

Group behavior: *O* recording of group actions during the discussion period (in terms of number of requests for materials related to task).

510) Perceptions of task performance of self and others

Validity of group judgments: *S* questionnaire responses.

520) Perceptions of social behavior of self and others

Perceived acceptance by others: *S* estimates of others' acceptance of him.

610) Leadership performance

Leadership: *O* rating of *S* behavior during the discussion.

631) Group task performance in experimental settings

Group task success: *O* rating of group "profits" on toy-manufacturing task.

Group decision quality: *O* rating of group responses.

1472. Pepitone, A. Motivational effects in social perception. *Hum. Relat.*, 1950, *3*, 57–76.

Purpose

This study examined the effects of induced motivation and variations in power and expressed approval, by those critical to achieving a goal, on member perceptions of power and approval.

Procedure

Students were differentially motivated to win a free ticket to a basketball game. Each *S* then faced a three-man board whose function was to ask questions about sports, comment on *S*'s answers, and decide whether he would receive the ticket. Behavior of board members systematically varied with respect to the amount of approval or support they showed *S* and the amount of power or authority they exhibited. An interview followed during which *S*s rated board members on the degree of power they possessed and the approval they showed toward him.

Results

In general there was slight relationship between variations in member motivation to achieve the reward and perceptions of approval and power (or distortions of such perceptions) of those who had control over the reward (6/36). However, significant relationships did indicate the following:

1. The greater the motivation, the greater was the perception of approval shown by friendly and neutral board members in groups containing friendly, neutral, and hostile members (2/2).

2. The greater the motivation, the greater was the perception of power held by friendly board members in groups containing friendly, neutral, and hostile members, and by neutral board members in groups containing friendly and neutral members (2/2).

On the other hand, there were very distinct and positive relationships between exhibitions of power and approval and member perceptions of such power and approval (9/9). In addition, the more that board members were positive and approving, the more they were seen as having power (5/6); and the more that they exhibited power or authority, the more they were seen as approving (3/3).

Study Variables

120) Personality characteristics of members
   Ratings of member motivation: O ratings of S motivation.

312) Induced social conditions
   Power exhibited: E confederate assumption of various degrees of power.
   Approval exhibited: confederate assumption of various degrees of approval of S.

322) Feedback and reinforcement conditions
   Degree of motivation: E introduction of high or low motivation by instructions about potential reward.

520) Perceptions of social behavior of self and others
   Perception of approval by others: S estimate of others' approval.
   Perception of power of others: S rating of power of others.
   Distortion of perception of approval: O ratings of member approval compared with actual approval elicited.
   Distortion of perception of power: O ratings of member power compared with actual power elicited.

1486. Pessin, J., & Husband, R. W. Effects of social stimulation on human maze learning. *J. abnorm. soc. Psychol.*, 1933, *28*, 148–154.

Purpose

This study examined the influence of spectators on individual learning behavior.

Procedure

Individual students learned a finger maze under varying social facilitation conditions: blindfolded with an E present, blindfolded with spectators present who were known to Ss, and not blindfolded and with spectators present and in view. *E* measured performance in terms of errors and number of trials needed to learn the maze.

Results

Type of social facilitation did not relate to performance errors or length of time needed to learn the maze (0/9).

Study Variables

240) General structural properties of the group
    Social facilitation: *S* work with either *E* or spectators present.
621) Member task performance in experimental settings
    Member performance on maze: errors, time.

1505. Precker, J. A. Similarity of values as a factor in selection of peers and near-authority figures. *J. abnorm. soc. Psychol.*, 1952, 47, 406–414.

Purpose

This study analyzed the relationship between similarity of student personal values and sociometric choice patterns.

Procedure

College students and faculty completed an open-ended questionnaire describing characteristics they felt to be important as criteria in educational evaluation. Their free responses were then classified into 39 categories and *S*s were asked to rank them in terms of importance. *S*s also responded to sociometric choice items indicating their choice of a faculty adviser and of three students with whom they wished to retain contact after graduation. Two weeks later a retest of both instruments was administered.

Results

Students reciprocating sociometric choices showed a higher similarity in values than did those making no choice at all (1/1). Reciprocating *S*s were not differentiated, however, from other pairs when a one-way choice was given. Also, where any degree of mutual choice existed between two students, they showed higher agreement than did the group in general (2/2).

Similarity of values also appeared to have some effect on choice of a faculty adviser; a higher similarity in values was noted between students and faculty advisers when the faculty member was the student's choice (1/1). Analysis in terms of lenth of the working relationship, however, showed that seniors agreed with their advisers, whether they were the students' choices or not, more than did freshmen (2/2).

Study Variables

110) Biographical characteristics of members
    Year in school: student status as freshman or senior.

144) Attitudes toward issues, concepts, ideologies

Agreement of personal values: S ranking of importance of educational values.

230) Interpersonal relations in the group

Sociometric attraction: student ratings of each other.

1522. Rasmussen, G., & Zander, A. Group membership and self-evaluation. *Hum. Relat.*, 1954, 7, 239–251.

Purpose

This study examined the interrelationships of attraction to the group, feelings of job proficiency, and degree of adherence to group standards.

Procedure

High school teachers completed a questionnaire containing several types of items: attraction to a small group of faculty in the school, predictions of group opinions on teaching procedures (and predictions of the opinions of another group of which S was not a member), and ideal and actual level of S's performance as a teacher. Intercorrelations of these measures and indexes derived from them were determined.

Results

Those who saw themselves as failures as teachers (in other words, saw a large difference between their ideal self and actual self) perceived a greater discrepancy between their actual performance and their estimates of the group's standards for teacher performance (5/7). This relationship was only slight for Ss with low attraction to their group (2/7).

Similarly, those who perceived themselves as failures were less positive in perception of their own teaching abilities, attraction to the teaching profession, and desire to work as teachers again (4/4).

There was a negative relationship between attraction to own group and discrepancy between individual and estimated own-group standard and no relationship in the case of outside groups (1/2).

Teachers' own statements of ideal teacher performance were very similar to estimates of their own group standard (2/3) but not to an outside group's standards (0/1).

Study Variables

131) General abilities of members

Perceived teaching ability: S questionnaire responses.

131) General abilities of members
143) Attitudes toward nongroup persons and other groups

Perceived failure as teacher: discrepancy between S's ideal teacher performance and his actual performance.

Correlation between perceived failure and difference between individual performance and other-group standards: S questionnaire responses.

131) General abilities of members
143) Attitudes toward nongroup persons and other groups
510) Perceptions of task performance of self and others

Correlation between perceived failure and difference between individual performance and group standards: S questionnaire responses.

131) General abilities of members
510) Perceptions of task performance of self and others

Deviation in performance from group standards: discrepancy between S's own rated actual performance as a teacher and his estimate of his own group's ideal teacher performance—questionnaire responses.

141) Attitudes toward the task

Attractiveness of teaching profession: S questionnaire responses.

143) Attitudes toward nongroup persons and other groups

Ideal teacher performance: S questionnaire responses.

Perceived other-group standards of adequate teacher performance: S questionnaire responses.

Discrepancy between ideal individual performance and estimate of other-group standards of teacher performance: S questionnaire responses.

143) Attitudes toward nongroup persons and other groups
230) Interpersonal relations in the group

Attraction to own and other groups: S questionnaire responses.

143) Attitudes toward nongroup persons and other groups
510) Perceptions of task performance of self and others

Discrepancy between individual ideal performance and estimate of own-group and other-group standards of teacher performance: S questionnaire responses.

Discrepancy between ideal individual performance and estimate of own-group standard of teacher performance: S questionnaire responses.

230) Interpersonal relations in the group

Attraction to group: S questionnaire responses.

510) Perceptions of task performance of self and others

Perceived own-group standards of adequate teacher performance: S questionnaire responses.

1528. Raven, B. H., & French, J. R. P., Jr. Legitimate power, coercive power, and observability in social influence. *Sociometry*, 1958, *21*, 83–97.

Purpose

This study examined the effects of perceived "legitimate" or "coercive" leader with respect to group member conformity.

Procedure

Two student work group situations were experimentally created: in one, a leader was represented as having group support through election; in the other, a leader was represented as having authority by appointment. Within each condition, half the groups were penalized by the leader for "nonconformity," whereas the other half were not, thus manipulating the coercive power of the leader. During the task of cutting cardboard for puzzles, Os rated conformity in terms of whether Ss speeded or slowed their cutting rate in response to leader instructions. After the work session, Ss were administered a questionnaire in which they rated themselves and their leaders in terms of the justification of leader actions, liking of leader, and so on.

Results

Perceived group support alone or variations in leader coercive power alone did not always yield clear differences in conformity, feelings of attraction to the leader, and so on (18/33). Rather these two variables interacted to produce differential member behavior. More specifically:

1. Conformity behavior
   a. Changes in public behavior
      (1) Conformity and perceived support given leader: not related except where Ss indicated liking of the leader (1/4)
      (2) Conformity and leader-exerted coercive power: highly and positively related in the no-support condition, not related when leader was perceived as having support of others (1/2)
   b. Self-ratings
      (1) Conformity and perceived support: highly and positively related in coercion condition, not related when leader did not coerce members (2/3).
      (2) Conformity and leader coercion: positively related in the no-support condition, not related over all (1/2)

2. Member judgments of leader
   a. Justification of leader behavior
      (1) Leader support and justification: moderately related in no-coercion groups only (1/2)
      (2) Leader coercion and rated justification: not related (0/1)
   b. Estimate of group approval of leader
      (1) Leader support by group and noncoercion of Ss: highly related to group approval as estimated by Ss (2/2)
   c. Acceptance of leader
      (1) Perceived leader support: highly related to leader acceptance (4/6)
      (2) Coercive behavior: somewhat related to acceptance, except on ratings of attraction (3/7)

Study Variables

230) Interpersonal relations in the group
Support supervisor will receive: S questionnaire responses.

Leader characteristics: *S* questionnaire responses regarding leader attraction, legitimacy.

312) Induced social conditions

Degree of perceived support received by appointed leader: *E* manipulation of degree of support given to leaders.

322) Feedback and reinforcement conditions

Coercive power held by leader: *E* instructions to leaders to penalize or not penalize the group.

430) Outcomes of interaction

Conformity: *E* scoring of changed task behavior in terms of production.

510) Perceptions of task performance of self and others

Conformity: *S* rating of own conformity in terms of speed and accuracy.

Leader behavior (justified in prescribing behavior of others): *S* questionnaire responses.

520) Perceptions of social behavior of self and others

Perceived acceptance of leader: *S* questionnaire responses from the group viewpoint.

1552. Riley, Matilda W., & Cohn, R. Control networks in informal groups. *Sociometry*, 1958, *21*, 30–49.

Purpose

This study examined the relationship between sociometric choice and the attribution to others of personal traits related to conformity.

Procedure

A list of personal traits and behavior was classified as indicating conformity or deviancy according to children's responses. An abbreviated list was then submitted to school children, who selected the traits and behavior that described classmates whom they liked best and liked least. Sociometric choice patterns were related to attribution of traits and behavior.

Results

*S*s liked by others in the group were assigned "conformist" traits and behaviors by the group, whereas *S*s who were disliked were assigned "deviancy" traits and behaviors (17/18).

Other results were not reported. However, the author concluded that the following hypotheses were confirmed:

1. When some *S*s like and others dislike the same person, the likers will assign conformist characteristics, and the dislikers will assign deviancy characteristics.

2. The more widely a person is liked, the more he will be described by all *S*s as having conformist characteristics.

Study Variables

131) General abilities of members
     Personal skill characteristics (ability to mix with people, expertness in
     music or sports, and so on): S questionnaire responses.

144) Attitudes toward issues, concepts, ideologies
     Personal interests (liking for adult company, interest in teen-age
     activities, etc.): S questionnaire responses.

230) Interpersonal relations in the group
     Sociometric choice: S sociometric questionnaire responses.

510) Perceptions of task performance of self and others
     Ratings of hard work expended by others: S questionnaire responses.

520) Perceptions of social behavior of self and others
     Perceived prestige, liking, and similar attitudes among others: S's
     estimate on a questionnaire of others' reactions to him.
     Personal effort to make good impression on others: S questionnaire
     responses.

1557. Roberts, A. H., et al. Effects of feeling-oriented classroom teaching
upon reactions to feedback. *Amer. Psychologist*, 1955, *10*, 420–421.
(Abstract)

Purpose

This study investigated the effect on group performance and member
perceptions produced by variations in group interaction training and type of
feedback provided in a task situation.

Procedure

College students were organized into five-man groups and given the task
of arranging sentences into logical sequences or stories. Half the groups were
composed of Ss who had had extensive training in group-oriented, feeling-
oriented methods of conducting discussions, whereas the remaining groups had
no such training. During the experiment proper, half of each type of group was
exposed to either "feeling-oriented" or "task-oriented" feedback by E during
work on the group task. Feeling-oriented feedback was presented by having Ss
respond to a questionnaire concerning feelings of comfort and similar sensations
and then presenting the results to the group. Task-oriented feedback was
presented by informing groups of their responses to a questionnaire containing
items related to task progress. Measures of feelings of defensiveness were also
obtained, along with performance efficiency scores.

Results

Groups who had been exposed to specific training in how to conduct discussions solved problems more efficiently, felt that their groups progressed
better, and showed less defensive feelings than did untrained groups (3/3).

Groups who were untrained in discussion procedures and who were given feeling-related feedback during the experimental sessions showed less defensiveness than did untrained groups given task-oriented feedback (1/1). No such results occurred for trained groups (0/1). Further, type of feedback was not related to actual or perceived group performance (0/2).

Study Variables

120) Personality characteristics of members
  Defensiveness: S responses to rating scale.

222) Group training and experience
  Training in feeling-oriented discussion procedures: degree to which groups had been exposed to training.

322) Feedback and reinforcement conditions
  Type of feedback reward: E distribution of feeling- or task-oriented feedback during task.

510) Perceptions of task performance of self and others
  Group progress: S questionnaire responses judging their own group.

631) Group task performance in experimental settings
  Group problem-solving efficiency: group performance in giving the right clues during the problem-solving periods.

1558. Roberts, B. H., & Strodtbeck, F. L. Interaction process differences between groups of paranoid schizophrenic and depressed patients. *Int. J. Group Psychother.*, 1953, 3, 29–41.

Purpose

This study investigated the differences in group discussion behavior of two types of mentally disturbed patients.

Procedure

During a discussion period, groups of paranoid schizophrenic and depressed patients were presented with a topic. Their interactions were recorded and categorized according to Bales Interaction Process Analysis, and the results for both types of groups were compared. Differences in behavior between leaders and group members were also observed.

Results

The statistical significance of results was not reported. However, the authors concluded that the depressed group directed a higher percentage of their acts to other patients than did the paranoid schizophrenic group. On the other hand, the paranoid schizophrenic groups exhibited a higher activity rate and also elicited a greater proportion of positive acts.

In addition, leaders seemed to act somewhat more aggressively and asked for orientation much more frequently in the paranoid schizophrenic group.

Study Variables

120) Personality characteristics of members
Type of group member: *S* being either depressed or paranoid patients
or discussion leaders (normals).

240) General structural properties of the group
Personality composition of group.

410) Content of interaction
Discussion behavior (solidarity, tension release, etc.): *O* categorization
of behavior according to Bales Process Analysis categories.

1564.* **Roby, T. B.** *Relationships between sociometric measures and performance in medium-bomber crews.* San Antonio, Tex.: Lackland Air Force Base, Human Resources Research Center, 1953. (Res. Bull. 53-18)

Purpose

In this study, group member attraction to one another and to the group was compared with several measures of air crew performance effectiveness.

Procedure

Members of combat air crews responded to a sociometric instrument toward the end of training. The questionnaire contained such items as ratings of the desirability of other crew members as co-workers and social companions. Several types of individual and crew performance measures were also available: instructor ratings of each *S* on individual missions, coordination between specific pairs of crew members (such as pilot and navigator), and over-all crew rankings, plus objective measures of crew performance (bombing accuracy, navigational competence, and target identification proficiency). These perform-ance scores were compared with sociometric measures for individuals, pairs, and crews.

Results

Sociometric status (number of choices received) of crew members at any of the flight positions was not related to instructor rating of general proficiency displayed during flight missions (0/33). Also, number of choices given between designated pairs in crews (aircraft commander to pilot, bombardier to navigator, and so on) did not correlate with coordination ratings of these pairs (0/60), nor did the number of choices made within the crew relate to over-all crew flight performance standing (0/5) or to scores on objective measures of bombing accuracy, navigational competence, or target identification proficiency (0/15).

This study contained a total of 113 relationships.

Study Variables

230) Interpersonal relations in the group
Sociometric status: crew members' choices of other members for
various task situations.

430) Outcomes of interaction
> Group performance: instructor ratings of particular pairs on over-all cooperation.

622) Member task performance in operational settings: global measures
> Member performance in flight situations: instructor rating of crew members on general proficiency displayed during flight missions.

632) Group task performance in operational settings: global measures
> Crew performance: instructor ranking of crews on over-all flight performance.

633) Group task performance in operational settings: specific measures
> Group performance: O measurement of bombing accuracy, navigation accuracy, and target identification.

1567.* Roby, T. B. *Sociometric index measures as predictors of medium-bomber crew performance.* San Antonio, Tex.: Lackland Air Force Base, Air Force Personnel and Training Research Center, 1956. (Res. Rep. AFPTRC-TN-56-46).

Purpose

This study investigated whether questionnaire responses of a sociometric type related to air crew performance.

Procedure

A sociometric-type questionnaire covering a range of topics from technical to social was administered to Air Force crew members on two occasions. Crews were also rated on four different types of performance: accuracy on a simulated bomb run using radar, promptness of arrival at various control points, accuracy in bombing with an optical bombsight, and level of instructor technical specialty ratings. Questionnaire responses were correlated with each other and with the performance scores.

Results

1. Performance in technical specialties
   a. Crew conformity, agreement, integration: technical performance highly related to conformity (1/1) and to agreement among crew members and social and technical integration (2/2)
   b. Performance restrictions, hostility, mistrust: high negative relationship of technical performance to restrictions in performance of verified role behavior (1/1) and to hostility and mistrust among crew members (1/1)
   c. Other sociometric measures: not related to technical performance (0/3)

2. Time required to arrive at control points: not related to any sociometric measures (0/8)

3. Accuracy on simulated bomb runs using radar
   a. Restrictions in performance of verified role behavior: positively related to accuracy (1/1)

b. Conformity among crew members: negatively related to accuracy (1/1)

c. Other sociometric measures: not related to accuracy (0/6)

4. Bombing accuracy with optical bombsight

a. Hostility and mistrust within crews: highly related to accuracy (2/2)

b. Other sociometric measures: not related to accuracy (2/2)

This study contained a total of 60 relationships.

Study Variables

152) Task or physical position in the group

Agreement among members on whom they work with: S questionnaire responses.

230) Interpersonal relations in the group

Hostility and mistrust within crews: S questionnaire responses.

510) Perceptions of task performance of self and others

Member performance ratings of others: S questionnaire responses on other crew members' performance in terms of social and technical integration, etc.

633) Group task performance in operational settings: specific measures

Crew performance: instructor rating of crews on radar bombing performance accuracy, navigational competence, etc.

Crew performance: instructor rating of crews on technical speciality abilities.

1572. Roby, T. B., & Lanzetta, J. T. *An investigation of task performance as a function of certain aspects of work-group structure.* San Antonio, Tex.: Lackland Air Force Base, Air Force Personnel and Training Research Center, June, 1956. (Res. Rep. AFPTRC-TN-56-74)

Purpose

This study examined whether group communication structure was related to group performance.

Procedure

Three-person airman groups performed a laboratory task that simulated an aircrew task. Teams were assigned to one of four conditions, which varied in the degree to which key members of groups had access to information necessary for the completion of the task. These conditions ranged from situations where all information had to be obtained from others in the group to situations where a major part of necessary information was available to the key member. Performance errors were compared to determine the effects of these varying conditions of communication structure.

Results

The more relevant information available to the appropriate group member, the more effective was group performance (1/1). However, this difference derived primarily from comparison of groups lacking relevant information with those possessing various degrees of critical information. The data also indicated significant learning or practice effects (4/4) and performance differences across individual positions in groups (1/1).

Study Variables

222) Group training and experience
  Stages of task performance: temporal periods of work.
321) Stimulus properties of the task
  Type of task: type of subtasks assigned to Ss.
  Task difficulty: confrontation of Ss with different control decisions— easy and difficult.
323) Induced task conditions
  Degree of information available to Ss: variation in amount and type of information available to key men.
631) Group task performance in experimental settings
  Group performance: E record of group errors.

1574.* Roby, T. B., & Lanzetta, J. T. Conflicting principles in man-machine system design. J. appl. Psychol., 1957, 41, 170–178.

Purpose

This experiment studied group performance as a function of differences in availability of relevant information and task load.

Procedure

Teams worked on a simulated air crew task requiring detection of changes in instrument readings, relay of information to others, and execution of simple switch adjustments according to relayed or directly available information. Teams varied in several respects: balance of information among team members, degree of independence of positions, and task load. The degree of balance of task information available to appropriate group members and their relative independence was varied in order to produce differential requirements for Ss to get information from others in the group. Task load was varied by experimental alteration of information inputs. Records were kept of error scores— incorrect switch adjustments—for the various groups.

Results

Groups operating under balanced information conditions performed more effectively than did those in which there was disproportionate distribution of information among members (1/1). In addition, the lower the input rate of new information, the more effective was the performance (1/1). All groups showed improvement in performance as a function of practice (1/1). For the most part, significance of the interactions of the experimental variables was not reported.

This study contained a total of 45 relationships.

Study Variables

222) Group training and experience

Stage of member training: S performance in successive sessions of the task.

240) General structural properties of the group

Individual groups: E designation of individual groups.

321) Stimulus properties of the task

Rate of change of task input information: E use of different rates of stimulus information input.

Task characteristics (switch arrangement): S work with six different switches on a simulated air crew task.

Arrangement of task controls: E arrangement of switch layout on simulated air crew task.

323) Induced task conditions

Amount of task information balancing among members: E manipulation of balance of critical information among crew members on simulated air crew task.

623) Member task performance in operational settings: specific measures

Member performance: number of errors made by Ss in simulated air crew task.

1575.* Roby, T. B., & Lanzetta, J. T. *A replication study of work group structure and task performance.* San Antonio, Tex.: Randolph Air Force Base, Operator Laboratory, June, 1957. (Rep. No. AFPTRC-TN-57-85)

Purpose

This study compared communication and performance of groups that had different amounts of relevant task information.

Procedure

Three-man groups performed under two of four communication conditions varying with respect to the amount of essential task information available to key Ss; control agent had immediate access either to none of the essential information, one fourth of the essential information, one half of the essential information, or three fourths of the essential information.

Teams worked on a simulated air crew task that required detection of changes in the instrument readings, relay of information to proper individuals, and execution of simple switch adjustments according to relayed or directly available information. Records were kept of the number and duration of outgoing calls, and accuracy scores were computed from frequency of incorrect switch adjustments.

Results

Groups with the greatest amount of immediately available, relevant information and the consequent minimum requirement for communication between members were the most accurate (1/1). In addition, all groups seemed to improve with practice; they made fewer errors on the last trial series, on the second of two communication structures, and on the later trials in each communication structure (3/3). There was an inverse relationship between the number of switch adjustments and errors (2/3). The results also showed a significant difference in the accuracy with which Ss adjusted each of the six switches (1/1).

This study contained a total of 42 relationships.

Study Variables

222) Group training and experience

Stage of practice: E designation of each series of trials.

Presentation order of communication conditions: E assignment of group to sequence of communication conditions.

321) Stimulus properties of the task

Task characteristics: E designation of each control lever to be adjusted on communication task.

323) Induced task conditions

Communication structure (degree of communication required): E assignment of Ss to experimental conditions with differing degrees of immediate access to information needed to perform task.

631) Group task performance in experimental settings

Group problem-solving behavior: E record of number of times group made switch adjustments.

Group performance accuracy: E record of number of times group did not correctly adjust switches in required time.

1585. Rohde, K. J. *Studies in aircrew composition: XVII. Individual executive ability as a factor in the performance of small groups.* Columbus, Ohio: Ohio State University, Personnel Research Board, 1954. (Tech. Rep. 17, Contracts AF 33(038)-10105 and AF 18(600)-27)

Purpose

This study examined the relationship between leader task abilities and group performance effectiveness under varying incentive conditions.

Procedure

Ss were pretested on a maze task to determine their relative proficiency. On the basis of scores, Ss were assigned to groups ranging in composition from those in which the designated leader and the other two members were highly proficient, through the intermediate combinations, and on to groups in which the leader and members were poor performers. In reworking the maze task, groups of each type were exposed to one of four motivational conditions, as follows: either the entire group was rewarded for good group performance, or only the leader was rewarded for good group performance, or the entire group was rewarded for good group performance but the two members were punished for poor group performance (by electric shock), or the entire group was rewarded for good group performance and the prestige of the leader reduced for poor group performance. Performance was measured in terms of number of errors made either by groups or by individuals on the maze task.

Results

There was no relationship between leader task abilities and group performance in any of the various motivational reward conditions (0/5), nor was there any relationship between group performance and the reward conditions (0/1). On the other hand, data pooled for all groups indicated a significant association of group scores with scores of highly proficient leaders, all individuals, and followers (3/3), but not with scores of less-proficient leaders (0/1).

Study Variables

132) Task abilities of members
      Management ability: O judgment of S ability to manage.

322) Feedback and reinforcement conditions
      Patterns of reward motivation: group instruction in four different ways regarding reward for good performance.

621) Member task performance in experimental settings
      Individual maze performance: member scores on maze learning.

631) Group task performance in experimental settings
      Group maze performance: group score on maze learning.

1586. Rhode, K. J. Theoretical and experimental analysis of leadership ability. *Psychol. Rep.*, 1958, *4*, 243–278.

Purpose

This study evaluated the general contribution of a leader to group performance effectiveness.

Procedure

College students were assigned to three-man groups, with one S arbitrarily chosen as a leader and the other members as helpers, to work on a maze task. Two sessions took place over a period of several weeks. In the second session, groups were reconstituted so that most Ss would not work with any of their former partners a second time. In addition, some Ss served as leaders on both occasions, some served as followers on both occasions, and the remainder served as leaders in one session and followers in the other session. A record of group performance errors over the two sessions was compared for each of the foregoing conditions.

Results

Groups of changing membership showed unrelated performance regardless of the consistency of individual member positions as leaders or as followers. Groups whose leaders were leaders on two occasions, groups whose followers were followers on two occasions, and groups having leaders who were followers in another group exhibited no performance consistency from session to session (0/4).

Study Variables

222) Group training and experience
Stage of participation in experiment: group participation first or last in experiment.

312) Induced social conditions
Type of groups: group leader-follower composition according to experimental instructions.

621) Member task performance in experimental settings
Individual performance: S scores on a maze learning task.

631) Group task performance in experimental settings
Group performance: group scores on a maze learning task.

1598. Rosenberg, S. *Similarity of interest and attitude measures as a predictor of interpersonal relationships in a medium-bomber crew.* San Antonio, Tex.: Randolph Air Force Base, Air Force Personnel and Training Research Center, Air Research and Development Command, Crew Research Laboratory, August, 1956.

Purpose

This study investigated sociometric choices among air crew members as a function of similarities in their attitudes.

Procedure

Air crew members were administered an attitude inventory pertaining to biographical, educational, religious, racial, and other differences, plus a sociometric measure tapping preferences for other members in various situations. In addition, information was obtained concerning position within the crew and military rank.

Results

There was slight relationship between the degree of similarity of member social attitudes and sociometric choices (9/44). However, further analysis indicated that when gunners rated officers and when officers rated other officers, sociometric choices and similarity of attitudes were positively related (7/9).

In addition, the higher the rater's rank, the greater was the association of social preferences and sociometric choices (2/3).

Study Variables

152) Task or physical position in the group
    Position in crew: S report of position in the crew.
    Military rank of Ss: S report of rank in the crew.

230) Interpersonal relations in the group
    Sociometric choice: S rating of others.

230) Interpersonal relations in the group

240) General structural properties of the group
    Correlation of social preference and sociometric choice: S scores on a
    sociometric instrument and attitude scale.

240) General structural properties of the group
    Similarity of member social attitudes: S scores on social preference
    scale.

1602.* Rosenberg, S., & Hall, R. L.   The effects of different social feedback
conditions upon performance in dyadic teams. *J. abnorm. soc. Psychol.*,
1958, *57*, 271–277.

Purpose

This study examined the effects of presentation of different information
about current performance on subsequent performance.

Procedure

Air Force trainees were assigned to one of three situations in which
various types of feedback were given regarding performance on an assigned
motor-skill task: *direct feedback*, in which S was given information about his
own performance, trial by trial; *confounded feedback*, in which S was given
information about the combined performance of his partner and himself;
and *other performance feedback*, in which S was given information only about the
performance of his partner. Performance measures of individuals, individuals
combined additively, and individuals combined in a discrepancy fashion were
computed and compared among the different feedback conditions.

Results

In general, performance was better when S received feedback about his
own performance, rather than about performance of others or information
about the performance of others combined with information about S's own
performance (3/4). This difference derived largely from the performance of
those who received information about their own performances as opposed to
information about their partners' performances.

There was a significant interaction between trials and type of information
for measures of individual performance (3/24). Analysis of the data showed that
learning rate was best when S received information only about his own performance and poorest when S was given information about his partner's
performance. No other interactions of type of feedback and stage of practice
were significant (1/27).

This study contained a total of 43 relationships.

Study Variables

222) Group training and experience
Sequence of trials: order in which groups participated.

322) Feedback and reinforcement conditions
Type of performance feedback information presented to Ss: E inform-ation to Ss either about their own errors, partners' errors, or their own and their partners' errors.

621) Member task performance in experimental settings
Member performance: E record of S task errors.

1603.* **Rosenberg, S., & Roby, T. B.** *Experimental assembly of B-29 crews by self-selection procedures: description and validation of the method.* San Antonio, Tex.: Lackland Air Force Base, Air Force Personnel and Training Research Center, 1956. (Res. Bull. AFPTRC-TN-56-104)

Purpose

This study investigated how member self-selection of air crew colleagues influenced crew performance.

Procedure

Airmen in training were administered questionnaires dealing with person-al background, general attitudes, and attitudes toward various aspects of crew function. Ss selected crew members on the basis of responses to the question-naires. In some cases, crews were assembled according to these rankings, whereas in other cases crews were randomly organized. Crews worked together during the remainder of the training period. During this time, some crews of each type were given a series of conferences or discussion periods, whereas others were not. Comparisons were made of crew performance as measured by instructor ratings and member sociometric choices.

Results

Crews assembled by means of self-selection on the basis of reactions to other members' personal backgrounds and attitude responses did not perform differentially from crews organized on a random basis (1/36). Moreover, crews were not differentiated in performance as a function of individual classes, occurrence as opposed to nonoccurrence of conferences during training, or the interaction of these variables (0/7).

This study contained a total of 1025 relationships.

Study Variables

240) General structural properties of the group
Individual crews and classes: E selection of crews for experiment. Homogeneity of crew member attitudes: S information about back-ground and attitudes as a means for assembling crews with homo-geneous or non-homogeneous attitudes.

Homogeneity of crew member activities: S information about crew function as a basis for assembling crews with homogeneous or non-homogeneous activities.

321) Stimulus properties of the task

Occurrence of discussions: E assignment of crews to conference or no-conference groups.

632) Group task performance in operational settings: global measures

Crew performance during training: instructor ranking of crews on performance during training.

1607. Rosenthal, D., & Cofer, C. N. The effect on group performance of an indifferent and neglectful attitude shown by one group member. *J. exp. Psychol.*, 1948, *38*, 568–577.

Purpose

This study analyzed the effects of negative behavior of one group member on others' attitudes toward the experiment, the group goal, each other, and future performance.

Procedure

Ss enrolled in introductory psychology courses were assigned to four- and five-man groups and given the task of dart throwing. In the experimental groups, one of the members was an experimenter-confederate who behaved in an indifferent and neglectful manner. In the control groups, Ss were naïve.

After the first trial, Ss completed a questionnaire on their attitudes toward the experiment, goal attainment, and the group. Following each of the succeeding trials (during which the confederate acted to distract the experimental groups) Ss gave an estimate of their own and the group's probable score on the next trial. Discrepancies between actual and estimated scores comprised group and individual level of aspiration scores. Ss also met after the third and seventh trials to agree on a collective estimate for the group. Following the last trial, Ss repeated the questionnaire. Comparisons were made between control and experimental groups initially and after the third and seventh trials.

Results

Indifference and neglect by one member during a group task significantly affected the over-all attitude of all the other members in the group. Whereas the total attitude score of control groups became more favorable during the experiment, that of the experimental groups decreased over trials (1/1). Attitudes toward the group's ability to achieve the standard (score of a fictitious group) and others' wholehearted participation toward the goal contributed most to this difference (2/2). No other attitude measures (the experiment's scientific value, member satisfaction, and member's own achievement effort) showed significant effects (0/3).

Groups were undifferentiated with respect to members' levels of aspiration for themselves and for the group (0/2), although E observed greater ease of agreement on a collective level of aspiration for the controls (2/2).

Groups were homogeneous in attitudes prior to experimental influence (0/6), and no differences were found for different-sized groups (0/2).

Study Variables

120) Personality characteristics of members
    Own achievement motivation: S questionnaire responses.

142) Attitudes toward the situation
    Satisfaction with experiment: S questionnaire responses.
    Rating of experiment scientific value: S questionnaire responses.

240) General structural properties of the group
    Size of group: E assignment of Ss to four-man or five-man groups.

323) Induced task conditions
    Indifference and neglect of one group member: E assignment of confederate to act in indifferent and neglectful manner.

430) Outcomes of interaction
    Ease of agreement when group set its achievement goal: E description of agreement process observed in group.

510) Perceptions of task performance of self and others
    Prediction of group member achievement effort: S questionnaire ratings of how hard other members would try to achieve standard.
    Group achievement potential: S questionnaire responses on probability that group would achieve standard.

510) Perceptions of task performance of self and others
621) Member task performance in experimental settings
    Individual level of aspiration: discrepancy between S score on completed trial and prediction of group score on next trial.
    Group level of aspiration: discrepancy between S score on completed trial and prediction of group score on next trial.

1639. Schachter, S., & Burdick, H. A field experiment on rumor transmission and distortion. *J. abnorm. soc. Psychol.*, 1955, *50*, 363–371.

Purpose

This study examined the circulation of rumors as influenced by varying degrees of situational confusion or unclarity.

Procedure

Six classes in a girls' school were used in this experiment. After two girls had been suddenly taken away from their classrooms by the school principal, three experimental conditions were created:

1. Rumor plus cognitive unclarity, in which rumors were started in two of the classrooms, and no reason was given for removal of the two girls

2. Cognitive unclarity only, in which no information was given and no rumor was introduced

3. Rumor only, in which a rumor was started in each class without the cognitive unclarity manipulations

Three types of data were collected: sociometric friendship choices, teachers' observations of comments addressed to them pertaining to manipulations, and a standardized group interview on what the girls had heard about the manipulations and rumors.

Results

Girls from classes where unclarity was introduced reported discussing and transmitting rumors more frequently than did girls from classes without the unclarity element (4/4). However, there was no relationship between the degree to which rumors were introduced and transmission or discussion of rumors (0/2).

There was also no relationship between sociometric choice patterns and rumor transmission (0/6).

Study Variables

230) Interpersonal relations in the group
Sociometric choice: S sociometric choice as work partner.

323) Induced task conditions
Degree of uncertainty: teacher introduction of uncertainty among students.
Occurrence of rumors: teacher introduction of rumors to classes through students.

410) Content of interaction
Personal report of activity: Ss' report of time spent in discussion, from whom they received and to whom they reported rumors, and conversational topics.

1641. Schachter, S., et al. An experimental study of cohesiveness and productivity. *Hum. Relat.*, 1951, *4*, 229–238.

Purpose

This study investigated experimentally induced cohesiveness and influence pressures as determinants of group production levels.

Procedure

Female students were assigned to low-cohesion groups (Ss were informed about the presumed impersonal character of their groups) and to high-cohesion groups (Ss were informed about the presumed congeniality of their groups). There were supposedly three tasks: cutting cardboard, mounting and pasting, and painting. The importance of quantity and speed was stressed. After this introduction each S was assigned to a different workroom, told to do the cutting, and given the impression that her partners were working on the other jobs. Communication was allowed via written notes delivered by messenger. Notes were intercepted and a standard prewritten set was substituted to induce either high or low production (positive and negative induction, respectively). Afterwards, Ss filled out a questionnaire about liking the group with which they had worked. Group productivity was measured in terms of cutting-output per unit time.

Results

In general, neither cohesion alone nor influence pressure alone unequivocally affected production levels (7/12); rather, the variables interacted as determinants of production levels.

Specifically, production lowered as pressures to decrease production were induced for high-cohesion groups (4/4) but not for low-cohesion groups (0/2). No such results held for the cases where pressures to *increase* production were induced (0/2), although positive pressures produced more general changes in production levels than did negative pressures (2/2).

Contrariwise, the data demonstrated a clear-cut and positive relationship between experimentally induced cohesion and member ratings of attraction to their groups (5/6).

Study Variables

222) Group training and experience
Type of influence periods: E division of experimental session into two periods.

230) Interpersonal relations in the group
Attraction to group: S questionnaire rating of team's actual characteristics.

311) Influence and conformity pressures
Type of influence exerted upon groups: messenger influence on groups by prewritten notes.

312) Induced social conditions
Group cohesion: E manipulation of instructions to produce different degrees of group attraction.

621) Member task performance in experimental settings
Group production: S rate of production in cutting cardboard.

1650. Schiff, H. Judgmental response sets in the perception of sociometric status. *Sociometry*, 1954, *17*, 207–227.

Purpose

In this study, several measures of perceptual tendencies reflected in Ss' sociometric ratings of selves and others were evolved to test their relationship to general adjustment, status within the group, feelings of anxiety, self-regard, and so on.

Procedure

High school students rated each other on sociometric scales in terms of acceptability as friends and predicted how they themselves would be rated by each of their classmates and how each classmate would be rated by the group. Analysis of rating discrepancies yielded four scores:

1. Self-direction scores, rating under- or overestimation of own status in the group

2. Other-direction scores, rating under- or overestimation of others' status in the group

3. Reciprocity scores, rating perception of self as under- or overreciprocating acceptance tendered by others

4. Acceptance scores, rating perception of self as accepting others more or less readily than did the rest of the group

Comparison of actual sociometric status of self and others with predictions yielded self- and other-accuracy scores.

Personality instruments were also administered. The Rorschach group test yielded an anxiety and an adjustment score. MMPI and Rorschach scores were combined with teachers' ratings of personal adjustment to give a composite adjustment score.

Other measures taken were *level of aspiration* and *goal tenacity scores*. Level of aspiration was determined when S predicted his score on the next trial of reading, arithmetic, and digit symbol tasks after hearing his score on the last trial. Goal tenacity score was the computed discrepancy between predicted score on the next trial minus actual score on the last trial and actual scores minus predicted scores on trials completed.

High and low groups were constituted according to the four perceptual-set score distributions and were compared in terms of perceptual accuracy, sociometric status, general adjustment, anxiety, level of aspiration, and goal tenacity.

Results

1. Self-direction measures (discrepancy between actual estimates by others and projected estimate by S)

   a. Self-direction scores: highly related to acceptance scores, level of aspiration, and composite personality scores (6/8), particularly for self-over-estimators (2/2)

   b. Self-direction; slightly related to reciprocity, other-direction, and goal tenacity scores (2/12), not related to Rorschach adjustment and anxiety scores (0/4)

2. Other-direction measures (discrepancy between actual estimates of others by the group and S's projected estimate of his popularity)

   a. Other-direction scores: highly related to acceptance scores (3/5), particularly for overestimators of others' sociometric status (1/1), highly interrelated with different other-direction scores (2/3)

b. Other-direction scores: slightly related to reciprocity scores (1/5), not related to self-direction scores (0/6) (as in 1b), personality measures (0/6), and level of aspiration and goal tenacity scores (0/2)

3. Reciprocity measures (discrepancy between S's rating of others and his projected estimate of their rating of him)

    a. Reciprocity scores: highly related to levels of aspiration and goal tenacity (2/2), highly related to composite personality adjustment scores (2/3)

    b. Reciprocity measures: slightly related to Rorschach adjustment and anxiety scores (1/4), acceptance scores, and self- and other-direction scores (as in 1b and 2b) (3/15)

4. Acceptance measures (discrepancy between S's ratings of other members and his projected estimate of their popularity in the group)

    a. Acceptance scores: highly related (as in 1a and 2a) to self- and other-direction scores (6/10), particularly for Ss perceiving themselves as accepting others more readily than did the rest of the group (2/2)

    b. Acceptance: not related to reciprocity scores (0/5) (as in 3b), personality measures (0/6), and level of aspiration and goal tenacity (0/2)

Study Variables

120) Personality characteristics of members

    Rorschach adjustment score: S responses to Rorschach test.

    Rorschach anxiety score: S responses to Rorschach test.

    Teacher ratings of personality adjustment: teacher ratings of S personality adjustment.

    Composite personality adjustment: S scores on MMPI, Rorschach, teacher's rating.

151) Social position in the group

230) Interpersonal relations in the group

    Accuracy of perception of others' status (other-direction score): S evaluation of others' popularity minus others' actual sociometric status.

    Accuracy of perception of others' status (other-accuracy score): S evaluation of others' popularity minus others' actual sociometric status (without regard to positive–negative direction of difference).

    Accuracy of perception of own status (self-direction score): S evaluation of how others would rate him minus others' actual ratings of him.

    Accuracy of perception of own status (self-underestimations and overestimations): positive or negative departure of estimate of others' ratings of self from self-ratings.

    Self-perception accuracy score: closeness of S evaluation of others' ratings of him minus their actual ratings (without regard to positive–negative direction of difference.)

    Reciprocity of sociometric choice: S evaluation of others minus own estimate of others' ratings of self.

    Perceived acceptance of others: S rating of other members minus S rating of estimated popularity of other members.

510) Perceptions of task performance of self and others
621) Member task performance in experimental settings

Level of aspiration: discrepancy between reported score on trial and S's estimate of own score on next trial.

Goal tenacity: difference of S predicted performance compared with actual performance on preceding trial and actual vs. predicted performance on previous trials.

1666. Scodel, A., & Freedman, Maria L. Additional observations on the social perceptions of authoritarians and non-authoritarians. *J. abnorm. soc. Psychol.*, 1956, *52*, 92–95.

Purpose

The purpose of this study was to investigate the effect of authoritarian attitudes on judgments of others' authoritarianism.

Procedure

Students were given the California F-scale in order to determine their authoritarianism. Pairs of Ss with high and low F-scale scores were placed in a social situation and instructed to discuss radio, television, and movie topics. After the discussion, each S was readministered the F-scale and instructed to respond to it as he felt his partner would respond. Discrepancy between estimated and actual F-scale scores indicated accuracy of estimate of partner attitudes.

Results

(The study compared its results with those of an earlier study. This annotation deals with data from the second study only.)

Ss of high authoritarianism rated their partners as more authoritarian than did Ss of low authoritarianism (1/1). Homogeneity of sex in pairs did not relate to perception of partner authoritarianism (0/2).

Study Variables

144) Attitudes toward issues, concepts, ideologies

Authoritarianism: S responses on California F-scale.

144) Attitudes toward issues, concepts, ideologies
520) Perceptions of social behavior of self and others

Accuracy of estimates of others' authoritarianism: discrepancy between actual F-scale scores and estimated F-scale scores.

240) General structural properties of the group

Homogeneity of sex in groups: E matching of Ss with respect to sex.

520) Perceptions of social behavior of self and others

Perceived authoritarianism: S estimate of other Ss' responses to California F-scale.

1684. Seidman, D., et al. Influence of a partner on tolerance for a self-administered electric shock. *J. abnorm. soc. Psychol.*, 1957, *54*, 210–212.

Purpose

This study compared the amount of electric shock *S*s could endure when they thought a partner was sharing the shock and when they were alone.

Procedure

Soldiers underwent two trials (one alone and one with a partner) testing their shock endurance. Electrodes were fastened to *S*s, who then increased the current to the highest point they could endure. In the partner condition, another *S* appeared to be connected to the same circuit but did not actually receive the shock. Tolerance levels were recorded by *E* for each condition.

Results

Perceived sharing of stress contributed significantly to stress tolerance. In instances where *S*s thought that another person was undergoing the same treatment as themselves, they withstood a significantly higher level of shock than they did alone (2/2).

Study Variables

132) Task abilities of members
Electric shock tolerance: *S* signal to *E* of highest current intensity *S* could endure.

222) Group training and experience
Week of testing: each week of experiment.
Presentation order of confederate partner condition: order of *E* assignment of partner to situation as first condition or second condition.

323) Induced task conditions
Perceived partner participation: *E* assignment of confederate partner in circuit with *S*.

1701. Shaw, M. E. Some effects of problem complexity upon problem solution efficiency in different communication nets. *J. exp. Psychol.*, 1954, *48*, 211–217.

Purpose

This study compared performance, amount of communication, and morale of groups solving problems of varying difficulty in two different types of communication nets.

Procedure

*S*s were assigned to three-man communication nets, forming either a wheel or a circle pattern, and given either simple identification problems or complex computation problems. Ss communicated by written notes only. After all problems were completed, Ss filled out a questionnaire indicating their reaction to the group, degree of cooperation among members, rating of group performance, and method used for problem solving.

Results

Group performance and communication were interactive functions of stage of practice, type of communication net, and problem complexity (2/2).

Although no performance differences were noted between nets on simple problems (0/5), circle nets solved complex problems more quickly and more accurately than did wheel nets (5/5). Also, central Ss sent more messages and had higher morale than did other members (2/2).

In general, all groups working on the simple problems reached a solution more quickly, communicated more, and had higher morale than did the groups working on the complex problems (3/3). Over-all amount of communication was equal for both nets (0/1) and decreased with practice (1/1).

Study Variables

222) Group training and experience
  Phase of experiment: group performance on first, second, third, or fourth trials.

240) General structural properties of the group
  Type of communication net: E assignment of groups to circle or wheel communication nets.

321) Stimulus properties of the task
  Problem complexity: E assignment of simple and complex problems.

323) Induced task conditions
  Independence of position in net (as relayer): S centrality in communication net.

420) Patterns of interaction
  Amount of communication: E record of number of messages sent by Ss.

520) Perceptions of social behavior of self and others
  Group morale: S postexperimental questionnaire responses.

633) Group task performance in operational settings: specific measures
  Group performance effectiveness: time required to solve problem, number of errors.

1704.* Shaw, M. E. A comparison of two types of leadership in various communication nets. *J. abnorm. soc. Psychol.*, 1955, *50*, 127–134.

Purpose

This study examined the effects of authoritarian and nonauthoritarian leadership on the performance of groups in various communication nets.

Procedure

College students were assigned to one of three types of communication nets: wheel, kite, or comcon. Some groups in each net were assigned an authoritarian leader, whereas others were assigned a nonauthoritarian leader. Authoritarian leaders were instructed to give orders, never accept criticism, and so on, whereas nonauthoritarian leaders were instructed to offer and accept suggestions, etc. The task was to solve arithmetic problems, with Ss allowed to communicate by written message only. Group performance was scored in terms of length of time to reach the correct answer and number of errors. After the problem-solving period, Ss filled out a scale that rated the leader on authoritarianism and indicated how well Ss had liked their job.

Results

Authoritarian leadership produced better time and accuracy scores than did nonauthoritarian leadership (9/9). Type of communication nets, however, did not relate either to time or to error scores (0/3).

Interactions of nets and leaders, leaders and trials, and nets and trials were not significant (0/3), although the three way interaction of leaders, nets, and trials was significantly related to time scores (1/1).

The significant interaction was explained by the author as follows: "These results are interpreted as showing that learning occurred under all conditions, that authoritarian leadership resulted in smaller time scores than did nonauthoritarian leadership but that in the later trials in the kite this difference disappeared, and that the comcon was faster than either the wheel or the kite with authoritarian leadership, while the kite and the comcon were both faster than the wheel with non-authoritarian leadership."

This study contained a total of 21 relationships.

Study Variables

222) Group training and experience
> Sequence of trials: E designation of first, second, and additional trials.

323) Induced task conditions
> Leader authoritarianism: E instruction to leaders to behave in either an authoritarian or nonauthoritarian way.
> Degree of freedom with which Ss might operate: E assignment of Ss to either low- or high-independence conditions.
> Type of communication net: E assignment of communication nets (wheel, kite, or comcon).

631) Group task performance in experimental settings
> Group performance: E record of time to compute answers and number of errors committed.

1705.* **Shaw, M. E.**   Random versus systematic distribution of information in communication nets. *J. Pers.*, 1956, *25*, 59–69.

Purpose

This study investigated how different communication nets, tasks, distributions of information, and knowledge about distributed information influenced problem-solving performance.

Procedure

Groups were assigned either to star or comcon communication nets. *E* gave information either randomly or systematically (grouped or categorized on a logical basis). In addition, some groups were given knowledge about the type of information distribution, whereas others were not. Arithmetic problems of varying difficulty were presented to each group for solution. *E* measured group performance in terms of solution time and errors. After the experimental session, *S*s rated their satisfaction with the task.

Results

Groups with systematically distributed information needed less time and made fewer errors per problem than did groups with randomly distributed information when both worked in the comcon communication net (3/3). Information distribution pattern did not relate to performance in the star net (0/1).

There were no over-all differences in performance for the two types of nets or for groups who had different amounts of knowledge about the nature of the information distribution (0/4).

Although there were no clear-cut differences in performance as a function of problem difficulty (1/2), the interaction between difficulty and information distribution was significant, showing that the effect of distribution was greater with the more difficult problems (1/1). The other interactions were slightly significant (2/9).

This study contained a total of 42 relationships.

Study Variables

321) Stimulus properties of the task
     Type of problems presented to groups: *E* presentation of different problems to groups.
322) Feedback and reinforcement conditions
     Knowledge about distribution of information: *E* giving or not giving information to groups about information distribution procedure.
323) Induced task conditions
     Type of communication nets: *E* assignment of groups to star or comcon communication nets.
     Type of information distribution: *E* distribution of information randomly or systematically.
631) Group task performance in experimental settings
     Group performance: *E* record of problem-solving time and number of errors.

1707. Shaw, M. E. Some effects of irrelevant information upon problem-solving by small groups. *J. soc. Psychol.*, 1958, *47*, 33–37.

Purpose

This study compared task performance and satisfaction of group members in different communication nets with different degrees of relevant task information.

Procedure

Volunteers were randomly assigned to groups to work under one of two types of communication net, star net (one member as communication link) or comcon net (communication links between all members). With relevancy–irrelevancy of information as an additional variable, E recorded the time required for each group to solve problems and the number of messages transmitted within groups. Following the experiment, all Ss completed a questionnaire on feelings of satisfaction.

Results

Ease of communication and relevancy of information facilitated group problem solving. Ss with direct contact with each other (comcon) transmitted a greater number of messages (1/1) and required less time to solve the problems (1/1) than did those working through an intermediary (star). Groups given only information relevant to the problem arrived at the correct solution more quickly than did other groups (1/1).

Communication (central) subjects indicated higher satisfaction with the star group than did other Ss (1/1). Satisfaction differences were also related to task information received (1/1).

Study Variables

222) Group training and experience
Group experience: sequence of trials.

230) Interpersonal relations in the group
Satisfaction with group: member rating of own satisfaction with group.

240) General structural properties of the group
Type of communication net: E placement of Ss in star or comcon communication pattern.

321) Stimulus properties of the task
Relevancy of task information: varying relevancy of information given groups.

420) Patterns of interaction
Problem-solving behavior: E record of number of message units transmitted.

633) Group task performance in operational settings: specific measures
Group performance: E record of time required for group to solve problem.

1716. Shelley, H. P. *The role of success and failure in determining attitude toward the group as a means to member goals.* Ann Arbor, Mich.: University of Michigan, Conf. Res., Project Report. 1950.

Purpose

This study compared the effects of success and failure in problem solving on various member perceptions and attitudes.

Procedure

Students were assigned to groups, one member of each of which was a confederate who ensured group success or failure. At the end of each task, E reported group success or failure. Following the third task, Ss estimated their success (level of aspiration) on subsequent tasks. At the end of the last task, Ss completed a rating instrument on their perceptions and attitudes regarding the group.

Results

Success and failure groups could not be unequivocally differentiated with respect to member perceptions and positive–negative feelings toward the group. Differences did exist, however, suggesting a somewhat more-positive outlook among Ss following successful performance than among Ss repeatedly meeting with failure. For example, successful Ss gave a higher estimate of their group's success on a future problem and perceived greater group unity (3/3). They also reported receiving more help from the group, saw it as providing more of a means, and indicated a higher preference for working with the same group again than did failure Ss (3/3).

Homogeneity measures revealed greater group consensus among Ss in the success condition in their estimates of future success and perceptions of help received from the group (3/3).

Several other measures of attitudes and perceptions—such as satisfaction, feelings of acceptance, liking for each other, and perception of group performance—failed to differentiate success and failure groups (0/21).

Study Variables

141) Attitudes toward the task
Need for other participants: member questionnaire responses.
Problem difficulty: member questionnaire responses.

152) Task or physical position in the group
Type of group member: E designation of confederate or naïve S.

222) Group training and experience
Time of rating: rating early or late in task series.

230) Interpersonal relations in the group
Group members' liking of each other: S questionnaire responses regarding liking of others in group.
Preference for working with group again: S questionnaire responses.

322) Feedback and reinforcement conditions
Group success: E assignment of groups to success or failure conditions.

510) Perceptions of task performance of self and others
Extent to which member felt group agreed with him: member questionnaire response.
Extent decision was group product: member questionnaire response.
Help received from group: member questionnaire response.
Member judgment of group performance: member questionnaire response regarding group success on future problem.

520) Perceptions of social behavior of self and others
     Feeling of acceptance by group: member questionnaire response.

1716a. Shelley, H. P. *The role of success and failure in determining attitude toward the group as a means to member goals.* Ann Arbor, Mich.: University of Michigan, Conf. Res. Project Report, 1950.

Purpose

This study compared the effects of success and failure in problem solving on group member perceptions and attitudes. The study was an extension of the immediately preceding one.

Procedure

Students were assigned to groups, one member of each of which was a confederate who ensured group success or failure. At the end of each task, E reported group success or failure. Following the third task, Ss estimated their success (level of aspiration) on subsequent tasks. At the end of the last task, Ss completed a rating instrument on their perceptions and attitudes regarding the group.

Results

Although success and failure groups were not unequivocally differentiated with respect to member perceptions and positive or negative feelings toward the group, some distinctions could be made. Specifically, success Ss reported having a more favorable attitude toward the group as a means, receiving more help from the group, feeling less discrepancy between their own and the group's decision, experiencing more problem difficulty, and liking other group members less than did failure Ss (12/12). Both success and failure Ss rated the quality of their group decision lower and were less satisfied with it after E suggested failure on the last trial (4/4).

No differences in relationship were found for ratings of quality of group decision, satisfaction with group decision and group process, effort by group, group unity, extent Ss felt agreed with, need for other participants, feeling of acceptance, decision as a group product, and preference for working again with the group (0/9).

Some intercorrelations of ratings were noted in success and failure groups. For success groups, attitude toward the group as a means was found to be associated with satisfaction with the group decision, help received from the group, and lack of need for other participants, while liking of other members was related to satisfaction with the group decision. In failure groups, however, expected group performance scores were highly related to attitudes toward the group as a means and high ratings of the group's solutions (7/7). Significant relationships were also found between ratings of satisfaction with group decision and estimated success on a future problem, and similarity between own and group decision and rating of group decisions (4/4). Other ratings were generally unrelated (0/45).

Study Variables

141) Attitudes toward the task
   Need for other participants: member questionnaire response.
   Perceived difficulty of problem: member questionnaire response.

152) Task or physical position in the group
   Type of group member: E designation of confederate or naïve S.

222) Group training and experience
   Time of rating: S rating before and after experimental condition.

230) Interpersonal relations in the area
   Personal liking of others: member questionnaire response.
   Preference for working again with group: member questionnaire response.

322) Feedback and reinforcement conditions
   Success of group: E assignment of Ss to success or failure conditions.

510) Perceptions of task performance of self and others
   Perceived discrepancy between own and group decision: member questionnaire response.
   Perception of extent decision was group product: member questionnaire response.
   Help received from group: member questionnaire response.
   Member judgment of group performance: member questionnaire response regarding group success on future problem, quality of group decision, satisfaction with process, and so on.
   Attitude toward group as a means and discrepancy between own and group decision: member questionnaire response.

520) Perceptions of social behavior of self and others
   Feeling of acceptance by others: member questionnaire response.

1742. Siegel, Alberta E., & Siegel, S. Reference groups, membership groups, and attitude change. *J. abnorm. soc. Psychol.*, 1957, *55*, 360–364.

Purpose

This study investigated attitude changes occurring over time when reference groups and membership groups were identical and when they were disparate.

Procedure

Women college students balloted each spring for choice of residence during the coming year. Those freshmen casting a ballot for a high-status rather than a low-status residence comprised the sample. They were tested for authoritarianism on the California E-F scale at the time of the first balloting and again after they had lived in their assigned residence for a year and were casting their second ballot. On the basis of their residence and choice, they were broken down into three groups: Ss having gained a high-status residence and not wishing to change, Ss not having gained a high-status residence and wishing to change, and Ss not having gained a high-status residence and not wishing to change. Changes in authoritarianism scores were compared for these three groups.

Results

The patterns of reference group choices and membership in groups appeared to have a pronounced effect on attitude change over a period of a year. Specifically, Ss who had initially balloted for a high-status residence but changed their ballots to a low-status residence the second year showed a greater reduction in authoritarianism than did those reballoting for the high-status residence (1/1). Also, those who lived in a low-status residence for a year decreased significantly more in authoritarianism than did those gaining assignment to the high-status houses (1/1). Ss living in a low-status residence and not reballoting for a high-status one showed a greater decrease in authoritarianism than did both those living in a low-status house and reballoting for a high-status house and those gaining assignment to a high-status house and choosing to remain (1/1).

Residents of high-status houses scored significantly higher on the E-F scale than did residents of low-status houses in the population from which this sample was drawn (1/1).

Study Variables

144) Attitudes toward issues, concepts, ideologies
      Authoritarianism: S responses to E-F scale for authoritarianism.
151) Social position in the group
      Attainment of desired status membership and membership in high-status group: E description of Ss who did and did not attain the high-status residence they had balloted for.

1751. Simpson, R. H. A study of those who influence and of those who are influenced in discussion. *Teach. Coll., Columbia Univer. Contr. Educ.*, 1938, No. 748.

Purpose

This study explored personality, demographic, and intellectual factors as determinants of susceptibility to influence and ability to influence others.

Procedure

Female students privately responded to a series of opinion items and later were assembled in groups for the purpose of collectively discussing the same items and arriving at a group decision. Several days after the group decision, Ss again responded privately to the opinion items. Immediate influence exerted by an individual was measured by the similarity of the group decision to his initial private opinion. Persisting influence of an individual was measured by the extent to which others' prediscussion private scores moved toward that person's judgment as evidenced by postdiscussion test scores. A series of personality, ability, sociometric, and biographical measures were tested for association to the influence indexes.

Results

*S*s high in both immediate group influence and persisting individual influence were frequently found to exhibit the same characteristics—high scholastic aptitude test scores (4/4), high scholastic grades (2/2), and high sociometric likeability (2/2); they were also Jewish, rather than Catholic, and were only children (4/4).

Characteristics associated with *S*s who exerted strong immediate influence on the group but not a persisting influence were high scores on tests of dominance and radicalism and low scores on a measure of self-consciousness (3/3), attendance at private rather than public elementary schools, progressive rather than traditionally oriented school training, and affiliation with Judaism rather than Protestantism (3/3). *S*s with high persistent individual influence were more likely to be juniors or seniors than freshmen or sophomores (1/1), but no such difference obtained for *S*s with high and low immediate group influence.

Neither immediate group influence nor persisting individual influence related to scores on Bernreuter scales of self-sufficiency, introversion, and dominance; a scale of nonsociability, intelligence, and self-evaluations of dominance feelings; Catholic or Protestant religious affiliation; or sibling status as oldest child (0/18).

The extent to which *S* was influenced by group discussion, as indicated by the discrepancy between pre- and postdiscussion judgments, was negatively correlated with sociometric status and positively correlated with a progressive rather than traditional educational background and a Catholic or Protestant rather than Jewish religious affiliation (4/4). Also, influenceability was inversely related to immediate and persisting influence on the group and individuals (2/2).

Study Variables

110) Biographical characteristics of members
Biographical characteristics: *S* school year, sibling state, elementary school educational training, religious affiliation.

120) Personality characteristics of members
Personality characteristics: *S* scores on Bernreuter scale, Flanagan Scale of Self-consciousness, etc.

131) General abilities of members
Intelligence: *S* score on intelligence test.
Scholastic aptitude: *S* score on verbal and mathematical sections of aptitude test.
Scholastic grades: teacher grading of *S*.

132) Task abilities of members
Score on McAdory Art Test: *S* pretest score.

151) Social position in the group
Sociometric choice (likability): *S* rank as choice of other classmates.

321) Stimulus properties of the task

Exposure to discussion: E assignment of Ss to discussion or no discussion conditions.

430) Outcomes of interaction

Influenceability: change in responses to McAdory Art Test after discussion.

Persisting individual influence: movement of other Ss' judgments toward S's judgment after discussion (McAdory Art Test).

Shift toward expert opinion: discrepancy between S and experts' responses on art test.

Immediate group influence: discrepancy between S and other individual judgments relative to discrepancy between prior S judgment and group judgment on McAdory Art Test.

1755. Slater, P. E. Role differentiation in small groups. *Amer. sociol. Rev.*, 1955, *20*, 300–310.

Purpose

This study was concerned with the extent to which group members were rated similarly on several discussion-related characteristics and the association of these ratings with discussion behavior.

Procedure

Groups of male students met on four occasions to discuss and reach solutions to hypothetical administrative problems. On the basis of O categorizations of discussion comments and peer ratings, Ss were classified according to the extent to which they maintained top positions on liking, quality of ideas, initiation of comments, and number of remarks received from others. In addition, those men who were rated high on liking and quality of ideas were compared with respect to discussion behavior.

Results

Although the significance of the correlations of peer ratings of liking, quality of ideas, guidance given, and participation given and received was not reported as such, other analyses led the authors to conclude that popularity was a specialized characteristic, in that there was little relationship between rank on popularity and rank on other measures. In addition, those high on initiation of comments were high on comments received, and those receiving high ratings on guidance also received high ratings on quality of ideas.

The data also indicated a trend toward increasing specialization, in that the percentage of cases in which the same person was top on ratings of liking and quality of ideas declined over successive sessions (2/2). Similar results obtained for participation and quality of ideas and guidance (1/1).

Further results showed that those ranked high on quality of ideas and popularity interacted with each other more than they interacted with others and more than others interacted with them (10/12).

Study Variables

144) Attitudes toward issues, concepts, ideologies
  Authoritarianism: S responses on California F-scale.

222) Group training and experience
  Stage of discussion: Ss participation rated individually from the first through the twentieth session.

230) Interpersonal relations in the group
  Number of Ss who liked *all* their fellow members: S responses on rating scale.
  Liking for other group members: S responses on a sociometric choice test.

230) Interpersonal relations in the group
510) Perceptions of task performance of self and others
  Percentage of Ss holding top ranks in quality of ideas and liking: summation of group members' scores (Ss' rating of other group members on ideas and liking).

321) Stimulus properties of the task
  Expected chance (interaction between Ss ranked high on ideas and being well-liked): E determination of the expected chances of interaction.

410) Content of interaction
  Discussion comments received: O rating of S behavior according to Bales categories.

420) Patterns of interaction
  Amount of participation: E measurement of discussion participation by each S.

420) Patterns of interaction
510) Perceptions of task performance of self and others
  Percentage of Ss rated high on participation and quality of ideas: O and S ratings of group members.
  Over-all participation: O and S rankings of group member participation.
  Average correlations of talking–receiving and guidance behavior: O and S ratings of group member behavior on quality of ideas, participation, etc.

510) Perceptions of task performance of self and others
  Quality of others' ideas: S responses on rating scale.
  Guidance offered during discussion: S ranking of other group members.
  Leadership displayed in discussion: S ranking of other group members.

1756. Slater, P. E. Contrasting correlates of group size. *Sociometry*, 1958, *21*, 129–139.

Purpose

This experiment studied group size as related to member satisfaction.

Procedure

Small groups (two, three, and four *S*s) and large groups (five, six, and seven *S*s) met for discussion of a human relations problem and then submitted a group solution. *O*s watched the discussion through a one-way mirror and categorized the interactions according to the Bales Interaction Process Analysis system. After each meeting, each *S* filled out a questionnaire consisting of sociometric ratings and a 60-item checklist.

Results

In general, the size of the group played a major role in satisfying group members. A five-man group appeared "optimal," in that members made fewer "group too small" or "group too large" complaints and a smaller total number of complaints than did *S*s of any other size group (4/4).

Small groups had the following positive features, according to the member ratings: more time for problem solving, greater efficiency, more concentration on the job and more accomplishment, less competition and isolation of group members from discussions, and more satisfaction with positions in the group (11/11).

On the other hand, large groups were rated as having a better arrangement, a more-definite and more-accepted leader, and more ability and competence among group members (5/5). Members of large groups also talked and participated more during the discussion (1/1).

Using the ratio of Bales-system "passive" or "safe" acts to "active" or "aggressive" acts as a measure of inhibitions, small groups tended to be more inhibited than were large groups (1/1). All groups in general and large groups in particular were more interested during the early stages of discussion (2/3).

Study Variables

141) Attitudes toward the task
Lack of need for a definite leader: *S* responses to a checklist item.
Availability of time to solve problems: *S* responses to a checklist item.

142) Attitudes toward the situation
Satisfaction with own position: *S* responses to a checklist item.

222) Group training and experience
Group adequacy for task: *S* responses to checklist statements.

231) Group abilities
Definite leadership and its acceptance within the group: *S* responses to a checklist item.
Talkativeness and participation among group members: *S* responses to checklist items.

Group need for guidance and over-all group competence: S responses to checklist items.

Group effectiveness in problem solving: S responses to checklist items.

240) General structural properties of the group

Size of group: E division of Ss into groups of different sizes.

321) Stimulus properties of the task

Time of interaction: E assignment of Ss to meet at different times.

430) Outcomes of interaction

Member isolation from discussions: S responses to a checklist item.

Inhibition exhibited: E report of S behavior according to Bales categories.

1760.* Smith, A. J., et al.   Consonance of interpersonal perception and individual effectiveness. *Hum. Relat.*, 1955, *8*, 385–397.

Purpose

This experiment studied the relationships between the congruency of member judgments of others with group judgments and performance effectiveness of the judge.

Procedure

Groups met several times a week to discuss such topics as leadership, role playing, and group organization. Periodically, members were asked to rate the other group members with respect to degree of power, benefit of the person to the rater, and vice versa. Ratings of other members on productivity were also obtained from each S. After the experimental period, ratings of effectiveness were obtained from Os. Individual and group judgment congruency measures were obtained by comparing each S's power ratings with the group average and by comparing individual "benefit" ratings. These indexes were compared with the various measures of performance effectiveness.

Results

The results indicated that the more similar was a person's judgment of the "power" of others to the average group judgment, the more that person was judged by Ss to be an effective performer (2/2).

This study contained a total of 45 relationships.

Study Variables

151) Social position in the group

Judgment of others' influence or power: Ss' ratings of each other regarding power.

430) Outcomes of interaction

Congruency of member judgments of one another and group average on ratings of power and value to group.

510) Perceptions of task performance of self and others
   Judgment of others' value to the discussion: Ss' ratings of each other regarding benefit to "me."

621) Member task performance in experimental settings
   Individual performance effectiveness: O ranking of individual Ss after group discussion period.

1761. Smith, A. J., et al. Productivity and recall in cooperative and competitive discussion groups. *J. Psychol.*, 1957, *43*, 193–204.

Purpose

This experiment investigated the effects of competition and cooperation upon the productivity and retention of discussion groups.

Procedure

Twenty-nine groups of college students of five persons each were studied. Roughly half of the groups were given instructions to cooperate, and the other half were given instructions to compete. Each group studied and then discussed a copy of a case. After an interval of several weeks, Ss were asked to recall as much as possible of the original discussion. Analyses of discussion protocols were made to determine the number of contributions made by individuals, number of statements recalled, and so on.

Results

Groups motivated to cooperate contributed more ideas to the discussion than did groups motivated to compete (1/1). Type of motivation, however, did not relate to quality of performance or to recall of discussion material (0/2).

After the six-week interval, Ss recalled their own statements more frequently than statements made by other group members (2/2).

Study Variables

312) Induced social conditions
   Degree of group cooperativeness: E instruction to groups to behave competitively or cooperatively.

420) Patterns of interaction
   Quantity of discussion contributions: O record of member participation.
   Type of material: E classification of communicators' statements or other members' statements.

621) Member task performance in experimental settings
   Member performance: S recall of original discussion material.
   Member recall performance: proportion of recalled items derived from own statements during discussion period.

1764.* Smith, E. E. *Effects of threat induced by ambiguous role expectations on defensiveness and productivity in small groups.* Boulder, Colo.: University of Colorado, Group Process Laboratory, August, 1956. (Tech. Rep. No. 1)

Purpose

This study was concerned with the effects of ambiguous relationships among group members on performance effectiveness and on member feelings of attraction toward each other and toward the group.

Procedure

Student groups varying in size from three to five members were given an intellectual task requiring identification of objects through interrogation of the experimenter. Four experimental conditions were induced by varying group composition and presenting different types of information to Ss, as follows: three naïve Ss worked with two experimenter confederates, who remained silent throughout; three naïve Ss worked with two confederates, who were silent throughout but whose probable behavior had been described in advance; three naïve Ss worked alone, as a control; and five naïve Ss worked alone, as a control. Measures compared among the four types of groups included group productivity, satisfaction with the group, measures of hostility and defensiveness, and so on.

Results

Groups with two silent confederate members whose probable behavior had been explained beforehand performed better than did groups who had received no prior information and performed no differently from groups without silent members (1/1).

No performance differences were noted as a function of the order in which groups were tested (0/4).

This study contained a total of 86 relationships.

Study Variables

312) Induced social conditions

Role ambiguity of group members: E designation of groups containing either naïve Ss and silent confederates about whose probable behavior naïve Ss were given no advance notice, naïve Ss and silent confederates about whose probable behavior naïve Ss did receive advance notice, or naïve Ss only.

321) Stimulus properties of the task

Order of group testing: E designation of groups in first or second half of testing order.

631) Group task performance in experimental settings

Group problem-solving accuracy: E record of number of correct solutions given by group to 20-questions type test.

1780. Spector, A. J. Expectations, fulfillment, and morale. *J. abnorm. soc. Psychol.*, 1956, *52*, 51–56.

Purpose

This study examined the effect of variations in expectations of success and actual success on morale.

Procedure

Groups of Army personnel were assigned the task of decoding messages. *E* experimentally induced either high or low expectations for promotion or goal achievement. Groups were further subdivided, in that some group members were actually promoted, and others were not. After decoding messages, *S*s were given a questionnaire measuring group attractiveness to members, group productivity, desire to remain a member of the group, task satisfaction, and satisfaction with the promotion system.

Results

Members of groups with higher expectations of being promoted showed lower over-all morale scores, lower evaluations of own group productivity, and less attraction to their group than did *S*s with lower expectations of being promoted (3/3). No other relationship occurred between promotion expectation and morale indexes (0/3).

On the other hand, *S*s who were actually promoted showed consistently more-favorable reactions to the group and task than did *S*s who were not promoted (6/9). The reported interactions of the two variables were of slight significance (1/4).

Study Variables

141) Attitudes toward the task
   Expected goal achievement: *S* questionnaire responses prior to introduction of the fulfillment of goal achievement.
   Satisfaction with task: *S* questionnaire responses.

141) Attitudes toward the task
142) Attitudes toward the situation
230) Interpersonal relations in the group
510) Perceptions of task performance of self and others
   Morale: *S* questionnaire responses on group attractiveness, adequacy of group performance, task desirability, satisfaction with promotion system.

142) Attitudes toward the situation
   Satisfaction with promotion system: *S* questionnaire responses.

230) Interpersonal relations in the group
   Group attractiveness: *S* questionnaire responses.

322) Feedback and reinforcement conditions
   Goal achievement: *E* promotion or nonpromotion of members.

323) Induced task conditions

> Perception of probability of goal achievement: perceived probability of goal achievement by experimental instructions.

510) Perceptions of task performance of self and others

> Group productivity: S questionnaire responses.

1781.* **Spector, P., & Suttell, Barbara J.** *Research on the specific leader behavior patterns most effective in influencing group performance.* Washington, D.C.: American Institute for Research, November, 1956. (Annu. tech. Rep., Contract Nonr 890(03), NR 171-027)

Purpose

This experiment investigated the effect of different styles of leadership on problem-solving performance.

Procedure

Navy teams were presented with a problem to solve while working under three types of leader behavior: *reinforcement* (in which the leader guided, but maximized positive reinforcement), *authoritarian* (in which the leader maximized quality of planning and decision making), and *democratic* (in which the leader maximized individual satisfaction of group members). Trials were conducted under normal and emergency conditions, including some emergencies from which the leader was absent. Performance was measured in terms of number of group errors.

Results

Neither leadership style nor leadership intelligence related to group performance in any of several problem-solving situations (1/16).

This study contained a total of 16 relationships.

Study Variables

131) General abilities of members

> Leader intelligence: S scores on Army General Classification Test.

152) Task or physical position in the group

> Military status of leaders: E choice of first petty officers or chief petty officers.

323) Induced task conditions

> Type of leader reinforcement: E assignment of Ss to groups with authoritarian or democratic leaders.

631) Group task performance in experimental settings

> Group performance: E record of errors made during the performance.

1782. Spector, P., & Suttell, Barbara J. *An experimental comparison of the effectiveness of three patterns of leadership behavior.* Washington, D.C.: American Institute for Research, September, 1957. (Tech. Rep. No. AIR-196-57-FR-164, Contract Nonr 89003)

Purpose

This study compared the over-all performance effectiveness of groups under the direction of three different patterns of leadership.

Procedure

*S*s were assigned to three-man groups according to scores on an intelligence test. High- and low-intelligence groups were exposed to three types of leadership as role-played by trained assistants: a social reinforcement–support pattern, an authoritarian pattern, and a democratic pattern. Groups worked on several tasks in the following order: a task designed to induce boredom, fatigue, and disinterest; a matching task; a cognitive information processing task; and a performance test. *E* recorded scores made on the last task as a basis for measuring team performance.

Results

Groups were only slightly differentiated for over-all performance effectiveness as a function of either intelligence level or type of leadership (3/16). Also, slight differences were found between individual leaders or phases (trials) of their experience (3/14).

Study Variables

131) General abilities of members
Intelligence: *S* score on GCT test.
222) Group training and experience
Phase of leader experience: different trials.
321) Stimulus properties of the task
Individual leader difference: *E* designation of each leader.
323) Induced task conditions
Type of leadership: confederate leader activities (social reinforcement, authoritarian, democratic).
633) Group task performance in operational settings: specific measures
Team performance effectiveness: *E* record of groups' scores on performance task.

1785. Stafford, A. R., et al. *The effects of choice of working partner on student achievement and attitudes.* San Antonio, Tex.: Lackland Air Force Base, Air Force Personnel and Training Research Center, December, 1955. (Res. Rep. AFPTRC-TN-55-61)

Purpose

This experiment tested the influence of sociometric choice of working partners upon school achievement and attitudes toward a training course.

Procedure

Sixty airmen, matched on mechanical aptitude test scores, were divided into experimental and control groups. *S*s in the experimental groups were paired according to their sociometric preferences, whereas those in the control group were not. Pairs then worked together on a set of tasks that were part of the training course. At the end of the course, *S*s were readministered an attitude questionnaire measuring feelings toward the course and the sociometric scale. Scores on an achievement measure covering course topics constituted the measure of group achievement.

Results

Pairs of *S*s who were allowed to work with their preferred classmate showed greater course achievement and chose partners more frequently from their own group than did control pairs (2/2). There were no differences in attitude toward the technical training course (0/1).

Study Variables

131) General abilities of members
     Level of achievement: *S* responses to an achievement test.

230) Interpersonal relations in the group
     Posttest sociometric choice of working partners: *S* questionnaire responses.
     Degree of sociometric attraction between *S*s: *E* division of *S*s into groups according to or regardless of personal preferences.

321) Stimulus properties of the task
     Instructor pairs: assignment of pairs of different instructors to groups.

430) Outcomes of interaction
     Change in attitudes toward technical-training courses: *S* scores on attitude questionnaire.

1793. Steiner, I. D., & Peters, S. C.   Conformity and the A-B-X model. *J. Pers.*, 1958, *26*, 243–258.

Purpose

This study compared conformer's and nonconformer's partner perceptions in a public response situation.

Procedure

Pairs (one naïve and one confederate) were required to respond to questions individually in the presence of each other. The confederate always preceded the naïve *S* and responded with a preset series of answers, half of which were "popular" and half "unpopular." Responses were recorded and a conformity score derived by comparing agreement and disagreement responses.

Prior to the experiment, *S*s rated themselves as well as good and poor co-workers on the Assumed Similarity of Opposites (ASo) Inventory, a 26-item personality scale. Following the experiment *S* rated his partner on the same scale. In addition, S's self-rating was done three times—from optimistic, pessimistic, and realistic points of view—and a self-rating range was computed.

Indexes of S's devaluation of his partner and tendency to over- or underestimate disagreements were obtained from his responses to questionnaire items concerning the "importance of making accurate judgments" and the number of disagreements remembered.

Results

In line with the authors' hypothesis concerning alternative responses to conformity, the following differences were noted between conformers and nonconformers:

Nonconformers rated their partners lower than themselves on the ASo inventory (2/2) and underestimated their disagreements over trials more than did conformers (1/1). In addition, the discrepancy between their ratings of best- and least-liked partners was greater than that of conformers (2/2).

No relationships were noted, however, in tendency to devaluate the partner (0/1) or in the discrepancy between realistic and optimistic self-ratings on the ASo attribute scale (0/2). Also, the similarity–dissimilarity of Ss' ratings of good and poor co-workers was not related to the tendency to assign lower trait ratings to the confederate partner than to themselves (0/1).

Study Variables

120) Personality characteristics of members
Similarity of realistic and optimistic ratings of own attributes: discrepancy between S self-ratings from optimistic and pessimistic points of view.
Ratio of discrepancy between optimistic and realistic ratings of own attributes to realistic and pessimistic ratings of own attributes: ratio of two discrepancies of S self-ratings.

143) Attitudes toward nongroup persons and other groups
Devaluation of dissenting partner: S true–false responses to items describing hypothetical person who completed problems successfully.

230) Interpersonal relations in the group
Rejection of dissenting partner: S self-ratings compared with S ratings of confederate partner.

311) Influence and conformity pressures
Presence of confederate dissenter in group: E use of confederate to give experimentally planned answers.

430) Outcomes of interaction
Conformity: S agreement or disagreement with partner responses to problems.
Recall of disagreements with partner: discrepancy between actual and recalled disagreements with confederate partner.

520) Perceptions of social behavior of self and others
Assumed similarity of opposites: S estimate of best- and least-effective co-worker's response to personality trait questionnaire.

1796. Steinzor, B. The spatial factor in face-to-face discussion groups. *J. abnorm. soc. Psychol.*, 1950, *45*, 552–555.

Purpose

This study compared the frequency of interaction between members of discussion groups in terms of the distance between them.

Procedure

Two groups of 10 Ss met separately for discussions and were seated by E in a circular arrangement. A leader was appointed for one group but not for the other. During the discussion, E tallied the number of contributions made by each S in terms of his position in the circle.

Results

In general, members facing each other in a small discussion group tended to interact more frequently than did those seated next to each other (2/2).

Study Variables

152) Task or physical position in the group
  Seating distance between members: responder position in terms of number of seats distant from initiator of remark.

420) Patterns of interaction
  Discussion behavior (sequential interaction between members): E tally of remarks made by Ss and pattern of initiating comments and responses.

1810. Stogdill, R. M. The sociometry of working relationships in formal organizations. *Sociometry*, 1949, *12*, 276–286.

Purpose

This study examined the influence of personal background on sociometric choices within naval organizations.

Procedure

Naval officers from administrative and training types of organizations were administered a sociometric questionnaire in which they ranked fellow members in terms of the amount of time spent together in getting the work done. From these ratings, a sociometric score was computed to reflect the frequency with which each S was mentioned as being the one with whom most time was spent. In addition, information was obtained concerning military status and rank, supervisory methods, degree of responsibility, authority, delegation, and length of time spent in various activities.

Results

Officers with a higher level in the organization received higher sociometric scores (3/4). Furthermore, the higher the military rank in the training type of organization, the higher were sociometric scores (2/2). Military rank did not relate, however, to sociometric choices in administrative organizations (0/2).

In addition, neither methods of supervision, responsibility, authority, and delegation nor length of time spent in various activities related more than slightly to sociometric choice (10/56).

Study Variables

152) Task or physical position in the group

Subjective authority and responsibility: S rating of his own responsibility and authority.

Organization position and military rank: S report of status and rank.

230) Interpersonal relations in the group

Individual with whom S spent most time working: sociometric choice made by S during interview.

510) Perceptions of task performance of self and others

Supervision method: S report of own methods of leadership.

Work activities: time spent in inspection, research, etc.

1832. Stotland, E. Determinants of attraction to groups. *J. soc. Psychol.*, 1959, *49*, 71–80.

Purpose

This study examined how personal and situational factors affected attraction to a group.

Procedure

Ss were administered a measure of self-esteem to tap the degree to which they met their own needs in ways considered to be ideal. Then, variations in group aspiration were experimentally induced to produce feelings in each person of either high or low expectations of achievement by the group. At the same time, tasks were described as being either relevant or nonrelevant to the group goal. Within each of these conditions, some Ss were given easy tasks and others were given difficult tasks. E recorded the time needed to complete the tasks. Afterwards, a questionnaire was administered to measure attraction to the group.

Results

There was no over-all relationship between expectation of achievement or task relevancy and attraction to the group (0/2), although the easier the task, the more attracted were members to their groups (2/2). However, more detailed analyses showed that this latter difference derived mainly from groups where Ss had low expectations of achievement and were working on a relevant task.

The interactions of relevancy, task difficulty, and expectation were only slightly significant (1/4).

The data also showed that Ss with high self-esteem and working on difficult tasks were more attracted to their groups than were Ss with low self-esteem (1/1). There was no such relationship for those working on easy tasks (0/1).

Study Variables

120) Personality characteristics of members
Self-esteem: S scores on a questionnaire; the difference between ideal behavior and actual behavior.

230) Interpersonal relations in the group
Group attraction: S questionnaire responses.

321) Stimulus properties of the task
Task difficulty: type of task presented to Ss.

323) Induced task conditions
Perceived proficiency of performance expected by Ss: E instruction to Ss about proficiency expected of them.
Task relevancy: E statement of the importance of tasks to Ss by experimental instructions.

633) Group task performance in operational settings: specific measures
Group performance effectiveness: speed in performing tasks.

1841. Strodtbeck, F. L., & Mann, R. D. Sex role differentiation in jury deliberations. *Sociometry*, 1956, *19*, 3–11.

Purpose

This study compared the behavior of jurors during a mock jury deliberation in terms of sex, level of activity, and member ratings.

Procedure

The data were derived from mock jury deliberations. Jurors, drawn by lot from regular jury pools, listened to a recorded trial, deliberated, and returned their verdict. Deliberations were recorded and scored in terms of Bales Interaction Process Analysis categories. Member behavior was analyzed in terms of sex of jurors, over-all activity in deliberations, and ratings by members of the value of individual contributions to the final decision.

Results

Some differences in discussion behavior during mock jury deliberations were accounted for by juror sex, level of participation, or status (in terms of value to the group in reaching a decision). Men were higher than women in giving opinions and orienting the group but lower on positive reactions such as showing solidarity, tension release, and agreement (3/3). Active participants more frequently gave orientation, asked for orientation, opinion, and suggestions and showed negative reactions such as disagreement, tension, and antagonism (3/3). Jury members voted by the others as being of the greatest assistance during the deliberation were high on giving suggestions (1/1).

No differences were found between men and women in giving suggestions, questioning others, and showing negative reactions (0/3), nor were there any differences between active and inactive members in showing positive reactions, giving suggestions, and giving opinions (0/3). In addition, no differences existed between high- and low-status Ss on number of positive reactions, opinions, orientations, questions, and negative reactions (0/5). No interactions of sex, level of activity, or choice status were significant (0/24).

Study Variables

110) Biographical characteristics of members
Biographical characteristics: sex.

410) Content of interaction
Discussion behavior: O record of S behavior according to Bales categories.

420) Patterns of interaction
Discussion activity: O record of S participation.

510) Perceptions of task performance of self and others
Sociometric choice: member selection of other members who "really helped the group to arrive at its decision."

1871. Tagiuri, R., et al. The transparency of inter-personal choice. *Sociometry*, 1955, *18*, 624–635.

Purpose

This study analyzed sociometric choice patterns associated with predictability of another person's sociometric choice.

Procedure

The members of a naval crew of 22 men who had lived and worked together for at least two months were given a sociometric questionnaire. Ss chose the members with whom they would like to spend a 72-hour liberty and guessed which Ss would choose themselves, underlining the three most preferred of their choices and guesses. Ss also guessed which three men each other crew member would choose and the members by which each of the others would feel chosen.

Results

Group members with a high reciprocation of choices were significantly more predictable in their choices than were the others (2/2). Choices given and received by a member, on the other hand, were not found to be related to the accuracy with which choices were guessed by the others (0/2). Level of confidence in being chosen by the others was also not related to choice predictability (0/1).

Study Variables

151) Social position in the group

> Member confidence in receiving others' choices: number of members by whom S predicted he would be chosen.

230) Interpersonal relations in the group

> Sociometric choice: members' friendship choice of others.
> Reciprocated sociometric choices: discrepancy between choices given by S and choices received from those chosen.
> Expansiveness of member: number of sociometric choices made by S.

230) Interpersonal relations in the group
510) Perceptions of task performance of self and others

> Transparency score of member (accuracy of others in predicting sociometric choices): discrepancy between S's actual choices and others' projected choices.

520) Perceptions of social behavior of self and others

> Member prediction of others' sociometric choices: S guesses of each other crew member's choices.

1874. Tagiuri, R., et al. Differentiation of sociometric choice and status relations in a group. *Psychol. Rep.*, 1958, *4*, 523–526.

Purpose

This study investigated various patterns of sociometric choice and perception of choice in relation to the sociometric status of the chosen and the chooser.

Procedure

The student body of a boarding school designated the students with whom they would prefer to room the following year and those whom they felt would choose them as roommates. To determine status, Ss were grouped according to the number of choices they received. Analyses were then conducted to compare status and choice patterns for the following classes of Ss: those chosen only; those chosen and perceived as reciprocating choice; and those perceived as choosing but not being chosen. Similarity of status between choosing and chosen Ss was also examined.

Results

Sociometric status or popularity was clearly related to choices made by members of the group. First, Ss tended to choose others with a status similar to their own (1/1). Second, Ss only chosen were higher in status than were those chosen and perceived as reciprocating the choice (5/5), but both of these latter were of higher status than the person merely perceived as choosing (2/2).

Study Variables

151) Social position in the group

Perception of others' sociometric choice of self: S prediction of whether others would or would not choose him as roommate.

Sociometric status: number of times Ss were chosen as roommates.

1884. Talland, G. A., & Clark, D. H. Evaluation of topics in therapy group discussion. *J. clin. Psychol.*, 1954, *10*, 131–137.

Purpose

This study analyzed patient agreement on helpfulness, disturbance, and hindrance of certain discussion topics to their own and group therapy progress.

Procedure

Patients undergoing group therapy ranked 15 topics on helpfulness, disturbance, and hindrance to their own and the group's therapy progress. Expert judges also marked items that could be discussed in an intimate setting only and ranked the 15 topics in terms of their personal intimacy.

Results

Psychiatric patients were in considerable agreement about the effect of different discussion themes on over-all therapy progress. Analysis within groups, between men and women, and between unmarried and married members showed unequivocal agreement on the helpfulness of certain topics to the group's therapy progress (9/9). Topics perceived as having a disturbing effect upon both the group and the individual were felt to be the most helpful (2/2).

In addition, topics judged by experts as very intimate in content were felt to be most helpful by individual patients (1/1).

Study Variables

141) Attitudes toward the task

Helpfulness of discussion topics: group therapy member ranking of 15 topics on helpfulness, disturbance, hindrance to group and own therapy progress.

321) Stimulus properties of the task

Intimacy of discussion topics: judges' ranking of topics.

1895. Taylor, F. Display of dyadic emotions. *Hum. Relat.*, 1957, *10*, 257–262.

Purpose

This study investigated factors related to the transparency with which members of pairs showed feelings of liking toward each other.

Procedure

Data was obtained from therapy groups and from student groups. Each S was paired with another from his group and then asked to answer questionnaire items on whether he would choose his partner for a friend and whether he thought his partner liked him. He also ranked all others in the group with respect to whether he liked them and whether he thought they liked him. An "accuracy of perception" score was derived from A's rating of B minus B's estimate of A's rating of B.

Ss ranked group members on popularity, dominance, and friendliness as they thought the group would. Finally, Ss rated the group's attraction to themselves.

Results

In general, judgments made by more-popular members of the group were estimated more accurately than were judgments made by less-popular members —in other words, more popular members showed their feelings more openly (1/1). Specifically, member estimates of moderately and highly popular members' ratings of them as friends were significantly closer to the actual ratings than were estimates of ratings by unpopular Ss (1/1). Moderately and highly popular members were undifferentiated from each other in the transparency of their feelings toward others (0/2).

Ss were undifferentiated on transparency as a function of the dominance and friendliness rank assigned them by the others (0/2).

Study Variables

110) Biographical characteristics of members

> Sex: E description of men and women.

151) Social position in the group

> Perceived self-attraction (member estimate of own appeal to group): S perception of own appeal to group.

> Perceived friendliness and popularity: member estimates of group's impression of S friendliness.

> Dominance: member estimates of group impression of S dominance.

151) Social position in the group

230) Interpersonal relations in the group

> Accuracy of social perception: discrepancy between A's actual rating of B as friend and B's projected estimate of A's rating of B.

240) General structural properties of the group

> Sex homogeneity of group: E description of group composition as same or mixed in sex.

> Type of group: E description of population from which groups were drawn (therapy group or students).

1914. Thibaut, J. W. An experimental study of the cohesiveness of under-privileged groups. *Hum. Relat.*, 1950, *3*, 251–278.

Purpose

This experiment studied the effects of group status position and changes in status on feelings of attraction to groups.

Procedure

Three types of status levels were induced upon groups of boys in a team-game situation: *unsuccessful group action* (in which *E* continuously disfavored one group), *successful group action* (in which *E* initially disfavored one group but during the last session granted the group's wishes), and *control treatment* (in which *E* accorded both teams equal fates). After each of these game sessions, a sociometric question was asked, and any shift toward increased proportion of own-group choices was taken as a measure of increased cohesiveness. After the experiment, *S*s filled out a questionnaire tapping several aspects of the experiment. *S* and group behavior were observed during the game period in such terms as aggression, attempts to leave the group, and so on.

Results

In general, group status did not relate to group cohesion as measured by changes in *S* sociometric choice (0/12). However, members of consistently high-status teams and popular members of unsuccessful low-status teams increased their selection of in-group choices (3/3).

In regard to the reported relationships of group status and observed behavior, the results for popular and unpopular *S*s of unsuccessful low-status groups showed no difference in absolute number of changes in "affect" communications compared with such changes among successful *S*s (0/4). However, the successful low-status groups in general did show a higher change and absolute level of "affect" communications (2/2).

Study Variables

142) Attitudes toward the situation
　　　Perceived frustration: *S* scores on postsession questionnaire.

143) Attitudes toward nongroup persons and other groups
　　　Estimates of outside-group feelings about own group: *S* scores on postsession questionnaire.
　　　Liking of outside-group members: *S* sociometric responses about members of the other team.

151) Social position in the group
　　　Popularity of group members: *S* ratings of other members of own group.

230) Interpersonal relations in the group
　　　Sociometric choice: *S* choice, on sociometric questionnaire, of others in own group or other groups.
　　　Desire to leave the group: *S* ratings of their group and its attractiveness.

323) Induced task conditions

Group status: E assignment of Ss to groups of different, E-contrived success or failure.

410) Content of interaction

Member behavior: E recordings of S communications in terms of playful and serious aggression, affective content, etc.

420) Patterns of interaction

Communication between teams: E record of amount of communication between groups.

520) Perceptions of social behavior of self and others

Anger at opponents: S reports of anger with others.

1919. Thibaut, J. W., & Strickland, L. H. Psychological set and social conformity. *J. Pers.*, 1956, 25, 115–129.

Purpose

This study measured conformity and personal confidence as affected by motivational set and exposure to pressures to conform.

Procedure

Students in six-person groups made judgments about presented stimuli. Each S worked privately on his own solution and also indicated on a ballot the degree of confidence he had in his answer. Original ballots were replaced by simulated ones to create various degrees of pressure on S to abandon his initial judgments. Within each pressure condition, Ss were either instructed to act as a member of a team (group set) or to focus on successful task completion (task set). Conformity was measured as the degree of change of initial private judgment.

Results

In general, students conformed more when working under group-set instructions than they did under task-set instructions (1/1). Moreover, this relationship became more apparent as pressure to conform increased (2/3). Concomitantly, as pressure to conform increased, task-set Ss became more confident about the correctness of their judgments than did group-set Ss (1/2).

Study Variables

322) Feedback and reinforcement conditions

Pressure to conform: E influence upon the group via false information

323) Induced task conditions

Type of work set: S solution of problems under either task-set or group-set instructions.

430) Outcomes of interaction

Change in confidence: S self-confidence expressed by voting.

Conformity: S change in judgment about stimulus objects.

1920. Thibaut, J. W., et al. Communication, task demands, and group effectiveness. *J. Pers.*, 1960, *28*, 156–166.

Purpose

This study analyzed the relation of group size, communication patterns, and accuracy of perceptual judgment.

Procedure

Groups consisted of one or two dyads, of which some were allowed no communication among members and others some intermember communication prior to a group response. All groups were subjected to three stimulus-presentation orders in blocks of trials of increasing instability: *perseveration*, where correct responses were identical throughout all trials of the block; *alternation*, where correct responses were identical on all odd and even trials of the block; and *random*, where correct responses formed no pattern.

Single dyads were tested first, with Ss separated by a partition. A number of dots was briefly projected on a screen and each S selected the correct answer from one of four alternatives. An accurate response was a correct total from both Ss. After 30 trials, varied as described in the preceding paragraph, a dyad was substituted for each of the single persons behind the partition, and the procedure was repeated.

Results

Over-all performance was better during the block of trials in which the correct responses formed a stable pattern; groups generally decreased in accuracy over the experiment as they went from the uniform order of stimulus presentation to the random order (1/1).

Double dyads performed better than did single dyads, particularly under the stable conditions (2/2). Groups permitted communication before responding were also more accurate than were those with no communication (1/1). This difference was even more marked when task demands were unstable (1/1).

No significant differences in relationship occurred for the interaction of group size and communication or for the interaction of group size, communication, and response stability (0/2).

Study Variables

240) General structural properties of the group

Social facilitation: E assignment of Ss to one-man or two-men sub-units of group.

321) Stimulus properties of the task

Stability of sequence of stimulus presentation: E presentation of stimulus in three orders—random with correct responses forming no pattern, alternating with correct responses identical on odd and even trials, uniform with correct responses identical throughout all trials.

323) Induced task conditions

Degree of member communication: E assignment of subunits to communication or no-communication conditions.

631) Group task performance in experimental settings
>
> Group problem-solving accuracy: E record of number of times group selected correct response.

1926.* Thomas, E. J. Effects of facilitative role interdependence on group functioning. *Hum. Relat.*, 1957, *10*, 347–366.

Purpose

This study investigated the effects of various degrees of member task interdependence on performance.

Procedure

Female utility company workers were assigned to five-person groups, seated at a circular table, and given the task of building miniature houses of cardboard. Ss were instructed that there would be either a division of labor method of production or that each would work completely independently, and either to work for a common team goal or to work for an individual goal. Four experimental conditions were thus introduced: high task interdependence (division of labor) and common team goal; high task interdependence and individual goals; low task interdependence (working independently) and common team goal; and low task interdependence and individual goals.

S voted for rest periods periodically during the task session, at which time E recorded votes and the number of units produced by each S. Ss also completed a postexperimental questionnaire concerning various aspects of the task situation.

Results

High task-interdependence (division of labor) groups were more productive than were low task-interdependence (individual production) groups (1/1). However, groups with a common goal and groups with individual member goals were equal in productivity (0/1)—except when both types of groups were working on an individual production basis. When this was the case, common-goal groups produced more units than did individual-goal groups (1/1).

In addition, the higher the attraction to the group, the more productive were the members (1/1). Perceived hindrance from others was not related to productivity (0/1).

This study contained a total of 40 relationships.

Study Variables

120) Personality characteristics of members
>
> Emotional tension exhibited: E record of number of times Ss requested rest period during task.

230) Interpersonal relations in the group
>
> Attraction to work group: S postexperimental questionnaire responses describing self and the group.

323) Induced task conditions

Task linkage: E instructions to group members (high or low task interdependence).

Goal cooperation of members: E instructions to work for common goal or for individual goals.

510) Perceptions of task performance of self and others

Other member performance: S postexperimental questionnaire responses on amount group members hindered her in her job.

621) Member task performance in experimental settings

Member performance: E count of number of units produced by members.

1930.* **Thorndike, R. L.** The effect of discussion upon the correctness of group decisions, when the factor of majority influence is allowed for. *J. soc. Psychol.*, 1938, 9, 343–362.

Purpose

This study investigated the effects of group discussion and majority influence on the accuracy of member judgments.

Procedure

Students made stimulus value judgments for pictures, poems, and so on, in problems for which they selected the better of two alternatives. Ss also indicated their confidence in each judgment. After completing private judgments, Ss discussed each problem in groups of four, five, or six and attempted to reach consensus. If consensus was not obtained, a vote was recorded.

Results

Group discussion and majority opinion were found to be highly related to shifts in individual member judgments and the accuracy of these judgments. Ss shifted postdiscussion judgment toward a correct majority judgment more frequently than they did toward an incorrect majority judgment (1/1), and groups with the highest percentage of members highly confident of their answers shifted more toward the right answer than did other groups (1/1). However, groups equally divided in the proportion of right and wrong answers on initial judgments shifted more toward the right answer after discussion than did groups with an initially correct or incorrect majority (1/1). Level of confidence and individual accuracy were positively associated (1/1).

In general, the proportion of right answers in groups after discussion was significantly greater than that proportion before discussion (1/1). Also, judgments of a statistically derived group (using judgments of the majority only) were more accurate than the average judgments of all members of groups (1/1).

This study contained a total of seven relationships.

Study Variables

120) Personality characteristics of members

Confidence in opinion: S rating of own confidence level.

240) General structural properties of the group

    Degree of groupness (statistically derived): E designation of the majority opinion of a group compared with the average member opinion.

311) Influence and conformity pressures

    Division of initial opinion: E description of proportion of members in group giving same or different answers—group majority wrong, majority right, or group equally divided right and wrong.

321) Stimulus properties of the task

    Exposure to group discussion: E assignment of groups to discussion situation (prediscussion and postdiscussion).

430) Outcomes of interaction

    Member shift to initial majority decision: E count of percentage of members shifting decisions after discussion to initial majority opinion. Shift of judgment: E count of discrepancy between number of correct judgments before and after discussion.

631) Group task performance in experimental settings

    Performance accuracy: E count of number of correct judgments by group members.

1933.* **Thrasher, J. D.** Interpersonal relations and gradations of stimulus structure as factors in judgmental variation: an experimental approach. *Sociometry*, 1954, *17*, 228–241.

Purpose

    This experiment studied the effect on performance of degree of stimulus field structure and degree of friendship among group members.

Procedure

    Students working alone, students paired with strangers, and students paired with friends were assigned to one of three judgment situations varying in the degree to which a stimulus was structured. Ss instructed to describe the location and size of luminous circles were presented with stimuli containing three points of light, five points of light, or a complete circle.

Results

    There were fewer errors and less variability of performance as the stimulus situation became more structured when Ss worked alone (6/6).

    When the stimulus was highly or moderately unstructured, students working with friends performed better than did students working with strangers (2/2). However, when the stimulus was completely structured, strange pairs performed as well as friend pairs (0/1).

    This study contained a total of nine relationships.

Study Variables

230) Interpersonal relations in the group
240) General structural properties of the group
   Friendship composition of group: *S* work in pairs with strangers or friends.
321) Stimulus properties of the task
   Degree of stimulus structure: *E* presentation of complete circle of lucite, three points of glowing lucite, and five points of glowing lucite.
621) Member task performance in experimental settings
   Member performance: *E* record of *S* errors in reports of stimulus light.

1939. Torrance, E. P. *Crew performance in a test situation, as a predictor of field and combat performance.* Washington, D.C.: ARDC, Bolling Air Force Base, 1953. (HFORL Rep. No. 33)

Purpose

   Good and poor crews in training, and effective and ineffective combat crews were compared with respect to problem-solving performance and perceptions of group interaction in projective sketches.

Procedure

   Air crews at the SAC Advanced Survival School were given crew performance tests which consisted of measures of intellectual and problem-solving ability. In addition, crews were asked to respond to two group interaction picture stories from the Michigan Group Projection Sketches. This test required *S*s individually and collectively to make up stories about pictures presented to them. The pictures depicted various groups in activities of several types. *O*s rated crews and individuals on what they said they saw in the picture —for example, harmony of interaction, members leaving group, productivity, and so on.

   While in school, all crews were also rated by superiors as good and poor. After several months of actual combat, these crews were again rated on effectiveness by two criteria: percentage of successful combat missions and superior officers' judgments of better, poorer, and drop-out crews. Comparisons were made between the various measures of crew effectiveness, problem-solving performance, and perceptions of group interactions in the projective sketches.

Results

1. Crew effectiveness in survival school (instructor ratings)
   a. Problem-solving test and survival school effectiveness: highly related *in all respects*—utilization of manpower, participation, coordination, control, flexibility, and over-all performance score (6/6)

  b. Perceptions of group-interaction sketches and survival school effectiveness: not related to members' perceptions of group disagreement, neutrality, type of group (such as family, friendship, and so on) (0/10)

2. Crew effectiveness in bombing missions (number of missions successfully completed)

  a. Crew problem-solving performances: somewhat related to bombing effectiveness (2/6)

  b. Perceptions of group-interaction sketches: not related to bombing effectiveness (3/24)

3. Crew combat effectiveness (superior ratings)

  a. Problem-solving performance: moderately related to combat effectiveness (7/15), but with better crews scoring significantly higher than did drop-outs on all observer measures (5/5)

  b. Perceptions of group-interaction sketches: somewhat related to combat effectiveness (26/72), but with 22 of the 26 significant comparisons involving comparison of better crews with poorer crews or drop-outs.

Study Variables

120) Personality characteristics of members
     Individual behavior on projective sketches: O rating of individual perceptions of content in Michigan Group Projection Sketches.

120) Personality characteristics of members
410) Content of interaction
     Similarity between member and crew perceptions of story in projective sketches: O analysis of difference between member and crew perceptions of content in Michigan Group Projection Sketches.

221) Group abilities
     Crew performance: score on problem-solving test.

410) Content of interaction
     Crew behavior on projective sketches: O rating of crew perception of content in Michigan Group Projection Sketches.

631) Group task performance in experimental settings
     Crew performance effectiveness (problem-solving): O rating of crew's behavior in problem-solving task.

632) Group task performance in operational settings: global measures
     Crew performance effectiveness: O rating of crews in survival school and in combat, successful combat missions.

1940. Torrance, E. P. Methods of conducting critiques of group problem-solving performance. *J. appl. Psychol.*, 1953, *37*, 394–398.

Purpose

   This study evaluated the effectiveness of four alternative methods for conducting critiques of group problem-solving performance.

Procedure

Fifty-seven combat air crews were divided randomly into four experimental and one control group. Each experimental group was given a problem-solving test and then a critique of one of four types: directive or expert, structured and unstructured, democratic or crew-centered, and private or self-administered. After critiques a second test was given. The control group was not critiqued between the two tests. Crews were given their test scores and were rated on manner of performance during both tests by Os.

Results

Over-all, the four critique methods resulted in no different problem-solving scores (0/1) but did lead to different ratings by Os (1/1). Also, the structured critique methods (crew-centered, expert) yielded different levels of performance than did unstructured techniques (crew-centered, self-critique) (2/2).

More specifically:

1. The expert critique resulted in greater improvement in performance than did unstructured crew-centered critique groups, self-critique groups, and control groups (3/3), but was not different from structured method (0/1).

2. The self-critique resulted in lower improvement in performance than did the expert critique (1/1) and was no different from other procedures (1/3).

3. The unstructured crew-centered critique resulted in less improvement in performance than did the structured method and expert critique method (2/2), and was no different from the self-critique and control groups (0/2).

4. The structured crew-centered critique resulted in greater increase in performance than did the unstructured method (1/1), and was no different from other critique procedures.

Study Variables

321) Stimulus properties of the task
Individual Os: E rating of crews.

322) Feedback and reinforcement conditions
Structure displayed in criticism of crew's performance: E conduct of criticisms in either an unstructured or structured way.
Methods of conducting critiques: E conduct of criticism of crews in different ways.

631) Group task performance in experimental settings
Crew performance: E rating of crews on organization, use of personnel, etc., and crew scores on problem solving.
Improvement in crew performance: E ranking of crews on improvement in performance.

1945. Torrance, E. P. *Some consequences of power differences on decisions in B-26 crews.* San Antonio, Tex.: Lackland Air Force Base, Air Force Personnel and Training Research Center, 1954. (Res. Bull. AFPTRC-TR-54-128)

Purpose

This study examined how permanency of groups and member status position within groups related to group problem-solving, discussion behavior, and perceptions.

Procedure

Permanent and rearranged combat crews consisting of a pilot, a navigator, and a gunner were administered decision-making problems of varying nature and difficulty: an arithmetic problem, a perceptual judgment task, a discussion of a picture, and a crew survival problem. Both individual and group decisions were elicited. Measures were obtained of such individual and crew behavior as influence attempts (similarity of answers) and agreement with crew decisions, along with behavior observations recorded according to Bales Interaction Process Analysis. After the last problem-solving period, a questionnaire was given to crew members to determine their perceived influence upon the crew and attraction to the group.

Results

Members of permanent groups showed a greater concern for keeping together in the survival problem, but had less influence on the crew discussion story and felt less need for revisions of it (3/3). Permanency of groups did not otherwise relate to problem-solving measures of any type or to crew member or crew behavior ratings by Os (3/43).

In general, pilots' perceived and actual influence over crew decisions was greatest (6/6). On the other hand, navigators participated in and disagreed with crew decisions more, exerted greater effort to influence crew decisions, and were more attracted to the group than were either pilots or gunners (9/9). In addition, pilots and navigators were more in agreement with crew decisions than were gunners (4/4). Status position within the group did not relate to any other type of behavior or individual judgments (0/43).

Study Variables

152) Task or physical position in the group

Member status in the group: Ss either navigators, pilots, or gunners in the crew.

230) Interpersonal relations in the group

Attraction to group: S questionnaire responses.

240) General structural properties of the group

Permanency of group: groups either temporary or permanent.

410) Content of interaction

> Member discussion behavior: O categorization of member content and process in story.
>
> Discussion behavior of group: O categorization of content and process of crew story.

420) Patterns of interaction

> Degree of individual influence on crew decisions: number of times each S influenced and failed to influence crew decisions.

510) Perceptions of task performance of self and others

> Influence on crew: S questionnaire responses.
>
> Agreement, satisfaction with crew decision: S questionnaire responses.

1961. Trapp, E. P. Leadership and popularity as a function of behavioral predictions. *J. abnorm. soc. Psychol.*, 1955, *51*, 452–457.

Purpose

This study compared leaders and nonleaders in accuracy of prediction of others' behavior and popular and nonpopular leaders in accuracy of estimate of others' predictions of their behavior.

Procedure

Members of a sorority ranked each other on leadership and liking. They also responded to five social prediction items adapted from the Rosenzweig Picture Frustration Test from three points of view: as they themselves would behave, as others in the group would behave, and as others would estimate their (the respondent's) behavior. Two leaders, one high in popularity and one low in popularity, were designated from the groups' rankings, and discrepancy scores were obtained for actual and projected responses.

Results

The two leaders were significantly more accurate in predicting others' responses to social situations than was the rest of the group, and the more popular of the leaders was more accurate in estimating others' predictions of his own responses than was the less popular of the leaders (2/2).

Leaders and nonleaders were undifferentiated in their actual responses to the test (0/1).

Study Variables

151) Social position in the group

> Popularity of leader: S ranking of members as persons worth being with.

152) Task or physical position in the group

> Leadership: S ranking of other group members on leadership.

240) General structural properties of the group

> Similarity of member and group responses to social situations: average member deviation from average member responses.

510) Perceptions of task performance of self and others

> Accuracy of perception of others' responses to social situation: discrepancy between others' actual responses to test and S estimate of their responses.
>
> Accuracy of perception of others' projected estimates of own responses to social situation: discrepancy between others' projected estimates of self and S's perception of others' projected estimates of self.
>
> Desirability of others' projected estimates of leaders' responses to social situations: discrepancy between outside-group statement of ideal responses to test and other S's estimates of leaders' responses to test.

1963. Travers, R. M. W. The general ability to judge group knowledge. *Amer. J. Psychol.*, 1943, 57, 95–99.

Purpose

The purpose of this study was to investigate whether an individual could judge with equal accuracy the knowledge of his own social group and a group composed of people unknown to him.

Procedure

Students in introductory psychology classes were asked to state the percentage of their class that they believed knew the correct meaning of each of a number of words on vocabulary-synonym word comprehension, and contemporary affairs tests, and then to make similar judgments for the adult population of the United States. Actual data against which to evaluate the accuracy of Ss judgments was collected for the class and available for the country.

Results

The more errors Ss made in judging adult population on word knowledge, the higher Ss estimated the number of errors of their own group in word knowledge (2/2).

As to personality factors, results showed that the better the total score and emotional adjustment score on the Bell Personality Scale, the fewer were the errors made in judging the adult population (2/2).

Number of errors made in judging population word knowledge was not related to home, health, and social adjustment scales or to intelligence (0/6).

There was a definite positive relationship between ability to judge one's own group's performance and the performance of the population at large for combined scores on vocabulary-synonym tasks, word comprehension, and contemporary affairs (2/2). However, no such relationship obtained when the vocabulary-synonym task measure was used alone (0/2).

Study Variables

120) Personality characteristics of members

> Personality characteristics: S responses to Bell Adjustment Inventory.

131) General abilities of members
    Intelligence: *S* scores on Ohio State Psychological Examination.

621) Member task performance in experimental settings
    Individual performance effectiveness: *S* errors in judgment task.

1968. Trow, D. B. Autonomy and job satisfaction in task-oriented groups. *J. abnorm. soc. Psychol.*, 1957, *54*, 204–209.

Purpose

This study compared job satisfaction and status perception for members differing in relative autonomy and in centrality in the group.

Procedure

On the basis of their answers to a "need-for-autonomy" pretest, volunteer *S*s were placed in three-person communication nets varying in terms of position autonomy (independence of action) and centrality (access to communication channels). Four conditions of autonomy–centrality were induced by prewritten notes, circulated by *E*, which *S*s believed had come from the other two members. *S*s completed a postexperimental questionnaire on the satisfaction they had derived from their job and the importance of their job relative to the jobs of others in the group.

Results

Job autonomy and communication centrality appeared to influence the job satisfaction and status perceptions of members of task-oriented groups, especially when satisfaction and status were considered in light of *S*s need for autonomy. Although experimentally defined autonomous *S*s generally reported a higher level of job satisfaction than did dependent *S*s (1/1), this difference stemmed primarily from *S*s with a high personal need for autonomy (1/1); there was no relationship between autonomy and satisfaction among *S*s with a low personal need for autonomy (0/1). Central and peripheral *S*s reported no differences in job satisfaction (0/1).

In addition, although peripheral *S*s perceived their jobs as more important than did central *S*s in general and those central *S*s with low personal needs for autonomy in particular (2/2), no differences were found among *S*s with a high need for autonomy (0/1). Autonomy-dependence was not related to status impression (0/3).

Study Variables

120) Personality characteristics of members
    Need for independence of action: member ranking of importance of need for independence as a life principle.

141) Attitudes toward the task
    Job satisfaction: *S* postexperimental questionnaire responses.

152) Task or physical position in the group
   Centrality position in communication net: E assignment of Ss to positions in net.
   Perception of position status: S ranking of importance of his job.

323) Induced task conditions
   Independence of action: E placement of S in communication net position where independent or dependent action was possible.

1976. Tuddenham, R. D., & MacBride, P. D. *Studies in conformity and yielding. The yielding experiment from the point of view of the subject.* Berkeley, Calif.: University of California, 1958. (Tech. Rep. No. 9, Contract NR 170-159)

Purpose

This experiment studied the relationship between the way a person perceives various features of a task and his group and his tendency to yield.

Procedure

Individual students were placed in simulated groups and asked to make a series of judgments about the characteristics of visual stimuli, information-type questionnaire items, and personal opinion items. For critical items of each type, Ss were given incorrect information about the supposed responses of others in their group prior to their own response. Yielding or conformity was measured as the extent to which Ss responses were in the direction of the supposed group majority. Following the experimental sessions, Ss completed a questionnaire measuring their reactions to aspects of the experimental procedure, their own performances and attitudes, and the performance of others.

Results

Conformity to group judgment was not related to any type of questionnaire response: descriptions of personal states (social isolation, tension, etc.) (0/20), description of personal actions (attention to experimental instructions, consistency in work, etc.) (0/30), evaluations of personal characteristics (adequacy of background, etc.) (0/8), evaluations of personal performance (performance on test, satisfaction with performance, etc.) (0/9), description of other group member characteristics (belongingness to group, etc.) (0/3), and evaluation of the task (test attractiveness, etc.) (0/22).

In addition, sex did not relate to these variables (0/31) except in the following cases: men perceived their performance level to be higher; had greater confidence in their own accuracy and greater satisfaction in their performance, and had less knowledge of others' performance, than did women (4/4).

Study Variables

110) Biographical characteristics of members
   Sex: S report of own sex.
   Personal background of adequacy: S questionnaire responses.

131) General abilities of members
    Other members' abilities: *S* questionnaire responses on items concerning intelligence, knowledge, and so on.

142) Attitudes toward the situation
    Personal feeling about situation: *S* questionnaire responses on items concerning tension, concern about behavior, etc.
    Feelings of adequacy of time to answer: *S* questionnaire responses.
    Task-situation adequacy: *S* questionnaire responses on adequacy of lighting, ventilation, etc.

230) Interpersonal relations in the group
    Belongingness to the group: *S* questionnaire responses.

430) Outcomes of interaction
    Conformity: similarity of *S* responses to stimulus and personal items of purported group.

510) Perceptions of task performance of self and others
    Behavior in situation: *S* questionnaire responses on following instructions, working hard, etc.
    Own performance adequacy: *S* questionnaire responses.
    Reliability of other members' judgment in answering questions: *S* questionnaire responses.

1979.* Tupes, E. C., et al. Performance in role-playing situations as related to leadership and personality measures. *Sociometry*, 1958, *21*, 165–179.

Purpose

This investigation studied the association of performance in role-playing situations with personality characteristics, discussion behavior, and academic proficiency.

Procedure

Air Force officer candidates were assigned to role-playing situations in which they assumed various military positions and worked through problems with upperclassmen serving as actor-participants. Superiors observed each *S*'s performance and used a checklist to describe his behavior. In addition, *O*s rated each *S* on a series of personality and other traits, such as athletic ability and assertiveness, at the completion of six role-playing situations. Role-playing scores were related to OCS grades and performance, physical proficiency measures, personality trait scores, and performance in a leaderless group discussion in which *O*s rated each *S*'s leadership effectiveness.

Results

1. The following measures of role playing behavior were highly related to other variables:

    a. Human relations problems role-playing behavior measures were highly and positively related to LGD performance, effectiveness of impromptu speech preparation, effectiveness in situational problems, competence in role-playing trait rating, OCS grades, distinguished graduate status, simulated effectiveness report score, peer ratings of personality adjustment, effectiveness of intelligence, determination, and energy high negative relationship to role-playing assertiveness (21/21)

b. Competence in human relations role-playing behavior: high positive relationship to LGD performance and to effectiveness of speech (2/2)

c. Role-playing athletic ability rating: high positive relationship to effectiveness in situational problem solution and physical proficiency (2/2)

d. Role-playing assertiveness rating: high negative relationship to human relations problems role-playing behavior and high positive relationship to LGD performance and effectiveness in situational problem solution (5/5)

2. The following measures of role-playing behavior were unrelated to other variables:

a. Officer human relations problems role-playing behavior was slightly related to role-playing athletic ability ratings and physical proficiency, trait ratings of neuroticism, conscientiousness, attentiveness to people, extroversion, assertiveness, conventionality, emotionality, insistent orderliness, and adaptability (5/24).

b. General competency in human relations role-playing behavior was not related to effectiveness in situational problems or physical proficiency (0/2)

c. Role-playing athletic ability rating was not related to LGD performance or to effectiveness of impromptu speech (0/2)

d. Role-playing assertiveness rating was not related to effectiveness of impromptu speech or to degree of physical proficiency (0/2)

This study contained a total of 665 relationships.

Study Variables

120) Personality characteristics of members
General personality adjustment: peer ratings of S on personality traits such as extroversion and assertiveness.
Assertiveness: O rating of S assertiveness as inferred from human relations situation.

120) Personality characteristics of members
132) Task abilities of members
610) Leadership performance
Officer effectiveness report score: tactical officers' and supervisors' ratings of S on exhibited officer potential during OCS, peer rating of S on several personality traits, and average score of S on objective OCS course exams.

132) Task abilities of members
General performance competency: O ratings of S competency in handling Air Force officer problem situations.
Athletic ability: O rating of athletic ability inferred from human relations role playing.

132) Task abilities of members

610) Leadership performance

> Distinguished OCS graduate status: tactical officers' and supervisors' ratings of S on exhibited officer potential during OCS, fellow flight members' ratings of S on exhibited officer potential during OCS, and peer average score of S on objective OCS course exams.

610) Leadership performance

> Leadership behavior: O rating of Ss on LGD behavior.
>
> OCS military grade: tactical officers', supervisors', and fellow flight members' ratings of Ss' officer potential.

621) Member task performance in experimental settings

> Role-playing effectiveness: O ratings of S competency in handling Air Force officer problem situations.
>
> Speech preparation effectiveness: O ratings of S on speech behavior items.
>
> Problem-solving effectiveness: O ratings of S in situational construction problem.
>
> Physical proficiency: O ratings of S behavior in physical proficiency and gymnastic tests on behavioral checklist items.

1996. Vinacke, W. E. Some variables in buzz sessions. *J. soc. Psychol.*, 1957, *45*, 25–33.

Purpose

This study compared performance and attitudes before and after discussion for groups differing in size.

Procedure

Ss completed two different tasks: ranking important minority groups in the continental United States and evaluating racial prejudice in Hawaii. Ss worked under three different conditions—alone and in groups of two or three. They completed identical questionnaires on the issues before and after discussions, giving their answers and opinions about the assigned questions and also about the discussion and experiment. Changes in answers and attitudes before and after discussion were analyzed with respect to task and group size.

Results

The most significant problem-solving changes occurred among persons working in groups as compared with persons working as individuals. In all cases where single and discussion Ss were compared for changes in answers before and after buzz sessions, groups showed the largest differences on both tasks, specifically expressing a greater number of ideas and making more over-all response changes (4/4). Comparison of all three sizes of groups, however, failed to reveal any differences (0/6).

Size of group and type of task in general did not appear to significantly affect Ss' attitudes toward the task; although groups of three indicated a greater positive change in over-all attitude toward the task and the experiment following discussion (2/2), only slight additional differences were noted in terms of group size (2/10), and none for type of task (0/1).

Study Variables

240) General structural properties of the group
   Size of discussion group: E assignment of Ss to one-, two-, or three-person groups.

321) Stimulus properties of the task
   Type of question: E assignment to S of ranking on evaluation tasks.

430) Outcomes of interaction
   Attitude change: S change in estimate of importance of question, attitude toward experiment, etc.

621) Member task performance in experimental settings
   Problem-solving behavior: increase in number, kind, length, etc., of solutions listed.

1998. Vinacke, W. E., & Arkoff, A. An experimental study of coalitions in the triad. *Amer. sociol. Rev.*, 1957, *22*, 406–414.

Purpose

This study investigated the formation of coalitions in groups as a function of the power given to each group member.

Procedure

Students assigned to three-man groups played a series of problem-solving games. E assigned power (import of player's moves to game outcome) of various degrees to Ss in each triad according to a prearranged plan. At any time during a game each S could ally with another group member, in return for a guarantee of some part of the prize. Any player could also concede defeat when his position seemed hopeless. E recorded the types of coalitions formed, the initiator in forming each coalition, and the division of prizes.

Results

In general, Ss with equal power tended to form coalitions more frequently against a more- or less-powerful third member (2/3). Coalitions were not formed in groups where *all* members had equal power (0/1), and in only one type of group where all members had differentiated power (1/2).

Ss with less power initiated the formation of coalitions more often (4/6); and the more power an individual S had, the more disproportionate were the agreements on division of the prizes (4/6).

Furthermore, degree of exposure to the task situation did not relate to the frequency of types of coalitions formed among different groups (0/22).

Study Variables

222) Group training and experience
  Period of training: group participation in a series of games.
323) Induced task conditions
  Distribution of power among members: *E* distribution of different amounts of power to group members by instructions.
430) Outcomes of interaction
  Member formation of coalitions: *O* record of extent to which different coalitions were formed, initiation of coalitions by different members, etc.

1999. Voiers, W. D. *A comparison of the components of simulated radar bombing error in terms of reliability and sensitivity to practice.* San Antonio, Tex.: Lackland Air Force Base, Air Force Personnel and Training Research Center, December, 1954. (Res. Bull. AFPTRC-TR-54-74)

Purpose

This study compared various components of simulated radar bombing performance error in terms of average error, reliability, and sensitivity to practice.

Procedure

Bombing accuracy scores were obtained for 213 crews over several months of simulated radar photoflash bomb runs. Circular, range, and deflection error scores (distances from target zero as shown on radar tracings) were analyzed for differences among crews, training classes, bomb drop order (practice effect), and missions. First-order interactions were also tested for performance effects.

Results

Circular and range errors were both found to decrease with practice (6/7), with range error showing the greatest practice effect (4/4). No changes were noted in deflection error scores over sessions (0/3).

Crews and training classes were strongly differentiated on circular errors and range errors (9/9) but only somewhat differentiated on deflection errors (2/6). There were no differences between missions (0/3). No first-order interactions were significant (0/9).

The descending order of reliability for the measures, over eight missions, was circular error, range error, and deflection error. The first two measures were highly reliable (6/6), and the last was significantly less reliable (1/4).

Study Variables

222) Group training and experience
  Order of bomb drop: *E* description of bomb-drop order (first to eighth).

240) General structural properties of the group
      Individual bombing crews and training classes.

633) Group task performance in operational settings: specific measures
      Accuracy of group performance: crews' circular error on radar tracings, range error, deflection error.

2000. Voiers, W. D. *Bombing accuracy as a function of the ground school proficiency structure of the B-29 bomb team.* San Antonio, Tex.: Lackland Air Force Base, Air Force Personnel and Training Research Center, 1956. (Res. Rep. AFPTRC-TN-56-4)

Purpose

This study investigated the relationship between crew member grades in ground training school, and crew performance on simulated bomb run error tests.

Procedure

The proficiency of air crew bomb team members was evaluated by means of ground school grades on objective tests. Team performance was measured during eight simulated radar bombing runs in terms of three types of error scores indicating distance of crew "bomb drop" from the target. These three measures were circular error, deflection error, and range error.

Results

Team members' grades in the ground training school did not relate in any consistent pattern to crew circular, range, or deflection error scores during the simulated bombing runs (23/369). There was one exception, however. Radar observer school proficiency scores, correlated consistently with crew performance when aircraft commanders had high training school grades (6/6).

Study Variables

132) Task abilities of members
      School grades: *S* grades in ground school.

633) Group task performance in operational settings: specific measures
      Crew performance (circular error, range error, deflection error): accuracy of crew performance.

2004.* Vroom, V. H. Some personality determinants of the effects of participation. *J. abnorm. soc. Psychol.*, 1959, *59*, 322–327.

Purpose

This study investigated relationships between participation in decision-making activities, personality characteristics, and job performance.

Procedure

Supervisors were administered questionnaires measuring perception of participation in decision making, job attitudes, needs for independence, and authoritarianism. In addition, their performance was rated by Os acquainted with their work. Two performance scores were obtained: an over-all performance rating based on a modified forced-choice merit-rating technique and a summary appraisal, based on graphic-type ratings, of ability to meet job demands. Questionnaire scores were compared with job performance scores.

Results

Generally, supervisor feelings of participation in decision making related only slightly to over-all performance (2/11) and not at all to ability to meet the demands of the job (0/8) when these elements were analyzed separately for each degree of authoritarianism and independence needs, but these variables were related highly when data from pooled Ss were examined (6/6). An exception, occurred for Ss who felt they participated more in activities and who also had moderate and high independence scores; these Ss were rated as being more able to meet the demands of the job (3/3).

Generally, neither need for independence nor degree of authoritarianism, considered alone, related to job performance (3/22).

This study contained a total of 78 relationships.

Study Variables

120) Personality characteristics of members
  Need for independence: S questionnaire responses.

141) Attitudes toward the task
  Psychological participation in activities: S questionnaire responses.

144) Attitudes toward issues, concepts, ideologies
  Authoritarianism: S responses on California F-scale.

610) Leadership performance
  Supervisor performance: superiors' ratings of general performance and ability to meet job demands.

2008. Wapner, S., & Alper, Thelma G. The effect of an audience on behavior in a choice situation. *J. abnorm. soc. Psychol.*, 1952, 47, 222–229.

Purpose

This study examined the effect of an audience on choice behavior under different instructional sets and task materials.

Procedure

The experiment was conducted in a one-way vision observation room with three audience situations: no audience, unseen audience known to be present, and seen audience. Ss of both sexes were given two types of instructions: *task-oriented* (with emphasis on the material as the subject of study) and *ego-oriented* (with emphasis on S's personality as the object of study). The task was

to choose words best fitted for a given phrase. An equal number of personality-
and neutral-oriented items, emphasizing traits of people and qualities of things
respectively, were used. Items varied in difficulty. As soon as S had read the
phrase he was instructed to signal by raising his hand, while E, either male or
female, recorded the length of time S took to make the decision.

Results

In general, Ss took more time to make a decision when the choice items
were difficult (7/7).

During the first half of the session, Ss took more time for making decisions
on difficult personality items when the audience was unseen than when there
was no audience or a visible one (3/4). Such a relationship held only slightly
for easy personality choices (1/5), and only moderately for easy or difficult
neutral choices (4/7). Ss generally needed less time to decide during the
second half of the session (1/1), but audience characteristics did not relate to
decision time or changes in the decision time (0/5).

Neither sex of E or Ss, instructional sets (task- or ego-oriented), nor any
of the interactions of these variables related to the length of time Ss spent
making decisions (7/102).

Stupy Variables

110) Biographical characteristics of members
     Sex of subjects: Ss report of sex.
222) Group training and experience
     Phase of experiment: S choices during first or second half of session.
312) Induced social conditions
     Type of audience: S work under different conditions (seen, unseen,
     and no audience).
321) Stimulus properties of the task
     Type of question material: E selection of different choice questions
     for Ss.
     Individual experimenters.
323) Induced task conditions
     Type of task instructions: E use of task-oriented or ego-oriented
     instructions.
621) Member task performance in experimental settings
     Time required to make decisions: E record of length of time S took
     to make decisions.

2029. White, Martha S. *Attitude change as related to perceived majority opinion.* San Antonio, Tex.: Lackland Air Force Base, Air Force Personnel and Training Research Center, 1957. (Rep. No. AFPTRC-TN-57-79, Contract No. AF 33(038)-26646)

Purpose

This study analyzed member change in opinion and conformity to the
majority as a function of shifts in perception of group opinion, perception
of group pressures, and attraction to the group.

Procedure

College students completed a questionnaire asking for the following information: their own opinion on several educational issues, their estimates of the group's opinion, their ranking of the importance of the issues taken individually, their level of certainty and intensity of feeling about the issues, and their attraction to their own group and to other reference groups. During the following week their classes position on three critical issues was reported as well as the positions of other reference groups. At this time subjects also repeated the questionnaire.

Discrepancy scores from time 1 to time 2 were obtained yielding the following measures for each S: change in perception of the group opinion, change in own opinion, and change toward conformity with the group opinion. Scores were also derived for tolerance of noncomformity (discrepancy between initial personal opinion and estimate of group opinion) and perceived group pressures (discrepancy between announced opinion for own group and estimated reference group opinion).

Results

1. Change in perceived group opinion was highly related to change in S's own opinion and to change toward conformity with the group's opinion (4/4)

2. Tolerance for nonconformity (discrepancy between initial personal opinion and estimate of group opinion) was highly related to member change in opinion and conformity with some qualifications

   a. Attitude item: evaluation issue
      The smaller the difference between initial opinion and perceived group opinions the greater the change in opinions and the greater the conformity. This relationship holds only for Ss who perceived a large change in group opinions (2/2) but not for Ss in general (0/2)

   b. Attitude item: statement of ideal
      Generally no relationship (2/8)

3. Perceived group pressures: the less the discrepancy between own group perceived opinion and outside reference the greater the conformity to own group's position (2/2)

4. Identification with own group (S's report of importance to him of agreement with the group), was not related to conformity (0/3)

5. Subjects' certainty and ratings of importance of issue were highly and inversely related to conformity when *item* differences were tested (2/2), but not when *subjects* were compared (0/6)

6. Subjects intensity of feeling about the issue were somewhat related to conformity (1/3)

Study Variables

141) Attitudes toward the task
   Intensity of feeling about item: S rating of intensity of his agreement or disagreement.

Certainty in own opinion: S questionnaire responses.

Importance of item: S rating of important and unimportant items.

311) Influence and conformity pressures

Discrepancy perceived between reference group opinion and announced own group opinion: discrepancy between opinions reported for S's group and the group for which S indicated a preference.

Similarity of initial opinion and estimated group opinion: discrepancy between S opinion and estimate of group opinion.

321) Stimulus properties of the task

Individual items: E designation of each critical item in questionnaire.

430) Outcomes of interaction

Change in own opinion of ideal question: S opinions at time one and at time two.

Change in estimate of group opinion: S estimates of group feeling on questionnaire item at time one and at time two.

Convergence toward estimated group opinion: S opinions and estimates of group opinion at time one and at time two.

Convergence toward estimated group opinion: S change in opinion on questionnaire from time one to time two toward group opinion.

Convergence of own opinion toward estimated group opinion: S questionnaire responses on all items at time one and time two and discrepancy between these responses and estimated group opinions.

510) Perception of task performance of self and others

Identification with group: S questionnaire response indicating how important agreement with students was to him.

Change in own opinion: S questionnaire response on attitude at time one and at time two.

2046. Willerman, B. The relation of motivation and skill to active and passive participation in the group. *J. appl. Psychol.*, 1953, *37*, 387–390.

Purpose

This study investigated how participation within a group was related to motivation, general abilities, and personality characteristics.

Procedure

A questionnaire containing items related to satisfaction with their group was given to members of high-school academic sororities. Five-point rating scales elicited self-estimates of amount of participation in activities, importance of self to the group, feelings of belongingness, and satisfaction with and acceptance of group decisions. Friendship choices, extrasorority activities, and some background data were also obtained, together with scores on the MMPI and ACE Psychological Examination. In addition, group members rated each other on participation within the group, thus indicating active and passive members.

Results

*S*s rated as more active in the group felt more important and more closely related to their group, agreed with group actions, accepted its decisions, and liked compulsory functions and the atmosphere within the group more than did passive *S*s (6/6). Active *S*s also perceived activities in the sorority to be more important than did others and disliked lack of interest and cooperation in other group members (2/2). In addition, girls rated as more valuable to the group had more friends outside the group, belonged more often to other groups, had higher ACE scores and high-school academic rank, and were more confident (5/5).

Level of activity in the group did not relate, however, to complaints about amount of time spent in various functions or to masculinity–femininity and psychopathic deviation scores (MMPI) (0/4).

Study Variables

110) Biographical characteristics of members
Membership in extrasorority groups: *S* report of membership in other groups.

120) Personality characteristics of members
Personality characteristics (self-confidence, psychopathic deviation, etc.): *S* scores on MMPI test.

131) General abilities of members
Intellectual ability: scores on ACE Psychological Examination.
Academic proficiency: high-school academic rank.

151) Social position in the group
Perceived importance of self and belonging to the group: *S* self-ratings.
Degree of *S* value to group: *S* questionnaire responses.

230) Interpersonal relations in the group
Sociometric choice: *S* identification of friends.

510) Perceptions of task performance of self and others
Effectiveness of own participation in group: *S* self-ratings.
Effectiveness of participation of others: *S* responses on rating scale.
Personal evaluation of group performance: *S* ratings of group behavior.

520) Perceptions of social behavior of self and others
Pleasantness of group atmosphere: *S* responses on rating scale.

2054. Williams, S. B., & Leavitt, H. J. Group opinion as a predictor of military leadership. *J. consult. Psychol.*, 1947, *11*, 283–291.

Purpose

This study evaluated the usefulness of measures of sociometric choice, personality characteristics, and ability as predictors of success in OCS and military combat.

Procedure

OCS candidates were given a series of tests and rating instruments during training. These included a questionnaire in which classmates rated each other on desirability as roommates, ability as combat officers, ability as leaders, and so on. In addition, Ss responded to scales tapping biographical and personality characteristics. Scores on these measures were compared with indexes of performance effectiveness based on follow-up ratings by superiors of combat proficiency and on success in OCS.

Results

Group member evaluations of other members' characteristics (such as leadership, desirability as a roommate) were highly intercorrelated with each other and with indexes of combat proficiency and success in OCS (12/14).

Interestingly, all other ratings of individual member characteristics—for example, ratings by instructor and platoon officer, ratings by self, and ratings on objective measures of general intelligence, mechanical ability, and so on— were not related to each other or to the final criteria, combat proficiency and success in OCS (0/13).

Study Variables

120) Personality characteristics of members
   Personality characteristics: S questionnaire responses on personality and biographical characteristics.

131) General abilities of members
   Self-rating as combat officer: S self-rating.
   Task and intellectual skills: OCS final grade, Army general classification test scores, instructor ratings of leadership, etc.

132) Task abilities of members
   Task ability: platoon sergeant's and lieutenant's rating of S.

510) Perceptions of task performance of self and others
   Discrepancy between group and projected estimate of group's rating.

610) Leadership performance
   Sociometric ratings of leadership, friendship, etc.: member rating of S as leader.

2058.* **Wilson, R. C., et al.** Factors influencing organizational effectiveness: III. A survey of skilled tradesmen. *Personnel Psychol.*, 1953, 6, 313– 325.

Purpose

This study compared high- and low-producing groups in terms of workers' attitudes toward their supervisors, their co-workers, themselves, and their jobs.

Procedure

Teams of aircraft repairmen were divided into high-, medium-, and low-production groups according to the amount of time each team needed to complete a job. *S*s in each group completed a questionnaire measuring attitudes toward their immediate supervisor, their own job-related characteristics, characteristics of their work group, and various aspects of the work situation. Responses to the attitude items were compared among the various production groups.

Results

Supervisors of high- and low-production shops were differentiated from heads of medium-production shops by the attitudes they displayed to their subordinates. Employees in high- and low-production groups perceived their supervisors as being more helpful, sympathetic, nonhypercritical, self-reliant, as having better judgment, and as being more consistent in behavior, than did employees from medium-production groups (6/6). Reports of supervisor looseness of supervision or lack of favoritism were not related to group production (0/2).

In addition, there was no relation between production level and reports of employee behavior, employee characteristics, and work conditions—for example, employee ambition, employee participation in self-improvement activities, employee pressure to restrict production, informal leadership within the group, formalized work procedures of production (0/5).

This study contained a total of 31 relationships.

Study Variables

141) Attitudes toward the task
Employee job rating: employee questionnaire responses indicating desire to get to higher job.

510) Perceptions of task performance of self and others
Employee behavior: employee questionnaire responses on participation in self-improvement activities.
Supervisor characteristic: employee questionnaire responses on looseness of supervision and helpfulness of supervision.
Supervisor performance: employee questionnaire responses on good judgment and consistency of behavior exhibited by supervisor.
Work group characteristics: employee questionnaire responses on employee pressure to restrict production, formalized work procedures.
Supervisor behavior and characteristic: employee questionnaire responses on nonhypercritical attitude of supervisor toward subordinates.

520) Perceptions of social behavior of self and others
Supervisor characteristics: employee questionnaire responses on supervisor sympathy, self-reliance, etc.

633) Group task performance in operational settings: specific measures
Work group productivity: foreman (management) evaluation of work groups in terms of work time required per job relative to standards.

2076. Wright, M. E. The influence of frustration upon social relations of young children. *Charact. & Pers.*, 1943, *12*, 111–122.

Purpose

This study examined the effect of experimentally induced frustration on the play and social relations of children in a small group.

Procedure

Thirty-nine pairs of children from three to six years old were selected as *S*s on the basis of the degree of friendship existing between pair members. Each pair of strong and weak friends played together in a control session, during which they had access to very desirable and less-desirable toys and later in a frustrating session during which the desirable toys were present but not accessible. Behavior was rated during both play situations in terms of cooperation, social contacts, impersonal and conflicting actions, and so on.

Results

The frustration condition led to more cooperation and less conflict for strong friends when compared with control conditions (4/4) but yielded no differences for weak friends (0/2). Frustration did not relate to sociable, social parallel, or matter-of-fact behavior for either type of friendship (0/9). Furthermore, *S*s in the highly frustrating situation exhibited more destructive behavior than did *S*s in control conditions (1/1).

Strong friends were more cooperative and less in conflict in frustrating situations than were weak friends (2/2), with no friendship differences in the control situation (0/2). Degree of friendship did not relate, however, to sociable, social parallel, and matter-of-fact behavior (0/6). Both weak and strong friends showed more negative and less positive reactions during the frustrating session (9/9).

In addition, the more cooperative *S*s were, the less conflict they had (1/1). Emotionality was not related to destructive behavior (0/1), nor was *S*'s age related to sociable behavior in either type of play condition (0/2).

Study Variables

110) Biographical characteristics of members
     Age of subjects.

230) Interpersonal relations in the group
     Degree of friendship: *E* report about children in preschool situation.

323) Induced task conditions
     Type of play conditions, in terms of degree of frustration: *S* exposure to frustrating or nonfrustrating play conditions.

430) Outcomes of interaction
     Group behavior: *E* report of children's behavior during the experiment, in such terms as cooperative, sociable, social parallel, etc.

2091. Zander, A. F., & Cohen, A. R. Attributed social power and group acceptance: a classroom experimental demonstration. *J. abnorm. soc. Psychol.*, 1955, *51*, 490–492.

Purpose

This study compared the reactions of *S*s to their group as a function of their status in the group.

Procedure

College *S*s were assigned to seven-person groups each of which played the role of a committee formed to recommend ways to spend a donation received by the school. Groups were told to assume that they had met before and that additional members were needed. Two members from each group were sent out of the room and instructed to return on signal to different groups with a different partner. The remaining members were told that the two newcomers would be a "dean" and a "freshman" according to which of the seats they selected on entering the room, but that the newcomers were not to be informed of their positions. All *S*s gave their reactions to the meeting in questionnaires completed afterward.

Results

Although members in the group were not specifically instructed to behave differently toward the "dean" and the "freshman," they spontaneously accorded deference to the dean and were relatively inattentive to the freshman. Accordingly, though unaware of their official status in the group, the deans registered a generally more positive reaction to the meeting (4/5): they reported a higher attraction to the group, saw the group as being in agreement with them more often, and perceived themselves as making a greater impression on the group and being more influential during the process of the meeting than did the freshman. However, freshmen and deans felt equally at ease in the new group (0/1).

Study Variables

142) Attitudes toward the situation
   Feeling of ease in discussion: member responses to rating scale.

151) Social position in the group
   Status position in group: *E* instruction to other group members.

230) Interpersonal relations in the group
   Attraction to group: member response to rating scale.

510) Perceptions of task performance of self and others
   Perceived impression made on group: member response to rating scale.
   Perceived influence on group: member response to rating scale.
   Perceived agreement of group with ideas: member response to rating scale.

2101.* **Ziller, R. C.** Scales of judgment: a determinant of the accuracy of group decisions. *Hum. Relat.*, 1955, *8*, 153–164.

Purpose

This study investigated the effect of group power structure, heterogeneity of group judgments, and other factors on accuracy of performance.

Procedure

Air crews discussed and arrived at a group judgment on a perceptual task (estimating the number of dots in an area) while operating in one of three conditions: preceding the discussion, individuals made public judgments in the ascending order of their military rank; preceding the discussion, individuals made public judgments in the reverse order of rank; preceding the discussion, individuals made no statements. *O*s recorded participation behavior and accuracy of group judgments. After group decision, individual *S*s submitted private judgments and completed a questionnaire measuring reactions to aspects of the discussion.

Results

Groups whose members initially made judgments in ascending order of military rank performed no better than did groups whose members initially made judgments in an order counter to military rank (0/4).

The data also indicated that the more heterogeneous were the initial judgments of members, the more effective was the group performance. In addition, more-effective performance was associated with more-conforming behavior (yielding to group judgment when individual judgment conflicted) (2/3).

This study contained a total of seven relationships.

Study Variables

312) Induced social conditions
> Order in which prediscussion judgments were submitted: *S* submission of prediscussion judgments in ascending or descending order of military rank.

420) Patterns of interaction
> Spread of member participation: *O* rating of *S* participation.

430) Outcomes of interaction
> Homogeneity of member judgments: similarity of *S* judgments of the number of dots within a given area.
> Conformity: discrepancy between individual estimates and crew estimates.

520) Perceptions of social behavior of self and others
> Perceived consideration exhibited by group: *S* questionnaire responses.

631) Group task performance in experimental settings
> Crew performance: *E* record of group accuracy in estimates of number of dots in a given area.
> Crew performance accuracy: *E* score of correctness of crew estimates of number of dots in a given area.

2104. Ziller, R. C. Leader acceptance of responsibility for group action under conditions of uncertainty and risk. *J. Psychol.*, 1959, *47*, 57–66.

Purpose

This study related leader's acceptance of responsibility for actions to various personal and social characteristics.

Procedure

Men in air crews were given a series of questionnaires measuring social conformity and group attraction, plus the California F-scale measuring their authoritarianism. Several other measures tapping various aspects of "motivational" tendencies were evolved from S's ratings of himself as he was and as he would have liked to be on physical, social, intellectual, and artistic abilities. The following measures were derived:

1. Self-concept ratings of self as S thought he was
2. Goal aspiration ratings of the ideal that S would have liked to achieve
3. Discrepancy difference between actual and ideal self

E described situations during individual interviews with the group leaders, inducing them to make decisions about a military problem and allowing alternatives that indicated degrees of willingness to accept responsibility for their decisions. Scores on the several questionnaire measures were related to decision characteristics.

Results

Leader acceptance of responsibility for actions did not relate to their self-ratings on group attraction, social conformity, authoritarianism, or the various measures of motivation (0/5).

As to interrelationships of the predictor variables, results showed that Ss who were more authoritarian had higher goal aspiration scores and greater discrepancies between actual and ideal self-ratings (2/2). Furthermore, the higher Ss' goal aspiration, the higher was their self-rated motivation and the greater was the difference between self-ratings and ideal ratings (2/2). None of the other intercorrelations was significant (0/11).

Study Variables

120) Personality characteristics of members
    Self-motivation: S responses to rating scale.
    Degree of motivation (difference between self-ratings and goal aspiration): S responses to rating scale.

141) Attitudes toward the task
    Motivation (level of goal aspiration): S responses to rating scale.

144) Attitudes toward issues, concepts, ideologies
    Authoritarianism: S responses to California F-scale test.

230) Interpersonal relations in the group
    Degree of attraction for group: S questionnaire responses.

510) Perception of task performance of self and others
> Member estimate of own conformity: S questionnaire responses.
> Leader acceptance of responsibility for action: S self-rating in decision making.

2108. Ziller, R. C., et al. The newcomer in open and closed groups. Paper read at East. psychol. Ass., Atlantic City, N.J., April, 1959.

Purpose

This study investigated the relative power of a newcomer and a regular group member on member judgments.

Procedure

Two naïve Ss and a supposedly naïve confederate were grouped together to work on a set of judgment tasks requiring an estimate of the number of dots on a card. Half of the Ss were told about changes that would be made in group membership, whereas the others were not. Ss worked on tasks individually, after which a group decision was made. Next, individual members were asked to submit a second private judgment. Then, a new member (also a confederate) was added to the group and the procedure was repeated with another problem. One of the confederates always knew the correct answer. Several questionnaire-type measures of the influence of and member satisfaction with the confederate were obtained, along with differences between the group answer and the correct answer, member decisions and correct answers, and so on.

Results

Groups anticipating membership changes liked the newcomer and his ideas better than did groups that did not foresee the changes; otherwise the entrance of a new member did not relate to the influence of the new member, amount of communication among Ss, discrepancy between private and group agreement, group's consideration for individual opinion, or Ss satisfaction with participation and his respect for his group (1/16).

Members of groups in which core members possessed the correct solution reported less change in estimated judgment than did those groups in which the newcomer was correct (2/2); but no major differences occurred on the other variables discussed for cases where either the core confederate or newcomer confederate held the correct answer (3/26).

Study Variables

230) Interpersonal relations in the group
> Increased respect for group's methods: S ratings.
> Satisfaction with composition of group: S ratings.

312) Induced social conditions
> Knowledge of change in group membership: E giving or not giving information to group about future membership changes.

420) Patterns of interaction
Communication among group members: number of notes sent to confederate by naïve members.

430) Outcomes of interaction
Discrepancy between private decision and group agreement on the problem.

510) Perceptions of task performance of self and others
Satisfaction with own participation: S ratings.
Change in own judgment: S report of own judgment change in problem solving.
Discussion influence of member: S judgment of newcomer.
Newcomer's pleasantness and quality of group ideas: S judgment of newcomer.
Group consideration of individual opinions: S ratings of group.

SECTION C
Bibliography of Small Group Research

INTRODUCTION

Several bibliographies dealing with the small group field have already been published. In spite of some overlap, each has made a distinctive contribution by focusing on a particular aspect of the field, as follows:

1. Bass, B. M. *Leadership, psychology, and organizational behavior.* New York: Harper & Row, 1960.

This book contained a 1155-item bibliography covering areas related to leadership. As one feature, the bibliography included a number of articles taken from foreign journals to give the reader some information on research outside the United States in the field of leadership and in related areas of the small group field.

2. Hare, A. P., et al. (Eds) *Small groups: studies in social interaction.* New York: Knopf, 1955.

The authors listed 594 articles, generally taken from Strodtbeck and Hare (see following), which dealt most specifically with small groups. Each article was abstracted to give the reader a concise review of the content.

3. Hare, A. P. *Handbook of small group research.* New York: Free Press, 1962.

This bibliography was an updated and enlarged version of the preceding one.

4. Raven, B. H. *A bibliography of publications relating to the small group.* Los Angeles: University of California, Department of Psychology, November, 1959. (Techn. Rep. No. 1. Contract Nonr 253(54) (NR 171–350)

The materials for this bibliography were taken from a card system designed for the author's use. A major portion of the items came directly from Hare, A. P., et al. (see 2, above.) Additional journal articles were added as received. The criterion for including items was the apparent relevancy to the small group area as indicated by the study title. All items were cross-referenced according to a coding system based on the content of the article.

5. Stogdill, R. M. *Individual behavior and group achievement.* New York: Oxford, 1959.

This bibliography dealt mostly with studies of organizations, achievement in groups, leadership, and group and individual performance effectiveness. It consisted of 794 items.

6. Strodtbeck, F. L., & Hare, A. P. Bibliography of small group research: from 1900 through 1953. *Sociometry,* 1954, *17,* 107–178.

The authors included 1407 research reports that placed central emphasis on the nature and consequences of face-to-face interaction in small groups. Research dealing with direct observation of natural or artificial groups or analysis of the effects of small group participation on the individual was considered of major importance. Dissertations, unpublished materials, and research on nonhuman groups were not cited. The bibliography covered the period from 1900 to 1953 but included a few pre-1900 articles.

7. Thibaut, J. W., & Kelley, H. H. *The social psychology of groups.* New York: Wiley, 1959.

This book contained 314 items from the general small group field. The items were used as supplementary sources of information in the preparation of the present publication.

8. Other available bibliographies include lists of Air Force Personnel and Training Research Center research reports, Human Resources Research Institute indexes of publications, and Office of Naval Research bibliographies of unclassified research reports.

CHARACTERISTICS OF THE BIBLIOGRAPHY

In compiling research titles in the small group area, the authors attempted to enlarge upon existing bibliographies, rather than duplicate them. The research appearing in professional journals and books was here supplemented, in particular, by a concentration on publications of research sponsored by Army, Navy, Air Force, and other government agencies. A large number of such studies, not having been published in a form other than technical reports, are not widely known, although they are readily available through the generating agencies and the Armed Services Technical Information Agency.

The main sources of cited research reports were as follows:

1. Psychological and sociological professional journals
2. Bibliographies and lists of reports of research by a number of government agencies
3. Psychological Abstracts and Armed Services Technical Information Agency abstracts
4. Abstracts of papers presented at professional society meetings, symposia, and so on
5. Correspondence with many authors engaged in sponsored research in the small group area

Some general features of the bibliography should be noted. Only selected group psychotherapy studies were included–namely, those dealing directly with small group methods and concepts. Masters and doctoral theses were omitted because of their relative unavailability to most researchers. Furthermore, only studies written in the English language were included because access to foreign journals is limited.

It should be pointed out that there are several duplications in the bibliography, because some reports completed under government support have also appeared as journal articles. We have deliberately duplicated such items because initial technical reports usually contain more detailed information than do articles published in journals and may therefore be of use to the reader who wishes to obtain further information about a study.

The main bibliography is most comprehensive for the period 1950–1959. The Addenda at the end of the main listing includes additional studies for this period and more recent studies appearing in professional journals from 1960 through the last part of 1962, as well as a large number of technical reports issued by government, private agency, and university research laboratories. Because we were unable to screen these latter sources comprehensively, not all such studies during the period from 1959 through 1962 have been included.

The articles are alphabetized according to the system of the American Psychological Association. Each study is given a consecutive number. The asterisk preceding certain numbers indicates studies in the review sample. The supplement of recent studies appears at the end of the bibliography.

LIST OF JOURNALS WHICH WERE SYSTEMATICALLY REVIEWED FOR ARTICLES DEALING WITH SMALL GROUPS

Acta Psychologica
American Journal of Psychology
American Journal of Sociology
American Psychologist
American Sociological Review
Annual Review of Psychology
Behavioral Science
British Journal of Psychology
Contemporary Psychology
Educational and Psychological Measurement
Human Organization
Human Relations
Journal of Abnormal and Social Psychology
Journal of Applied Psychology
Journal of Consulting Psychology
Journal of Experimental Psychology
Journal of General Psychology
Journal of Personality
Journal of Psychology
Journal of Social Issues
Journal of Social Psychology
Personnel
Psychological Abstracts
Psychological Bulletin
Psychological Monographs: General and Applied
Psychological Reports
Psychological Review
Psychometrika
Social Forces
Sociological Review
Sociometry

*1) Abel, Theodora M. The influence of social facilitation on motor perform-ance at different levels of intelligence. *Amer. J. Psychol.*, 1938, *51*, 379–389.

2) Adams, J. S., & Romney, A. K. A functional analysis of authority. Paper prepared at Air Force Office of Scientific Res. Behav. Sci. Conf., Albuquerque, N.M., 1958, [Contract AF 49-(638)-33].

3) Adams, S. Effect of equalitarian atmospheres upon the performance of bomber crews. *Amer. Psychologist*, 1952, *7*, 398. (Abstract)

4) Adams, S. Status congruency as a variable in small group performance. *Soc. Forces*, 1953, *32*, 16–22.

5) Adams, S. Social climate and productivity in small military groups. *Amer. sociol. Rev.*, 1954, *19*, 421–425.

6) Adams, S. N., & Sammons, H. W., Jr. *An analysis of the combat performance of Air Force reserves. Part I–special combat crew studies.* Washington, D.C.: Bolling Air Force Base, Human Resources Research Labora-tories, May, 1952. (HRRL Memorandum Rep. No. 21)

7) Aikman, L., et al. Differences in the quality of the solution to a practical field problem at various degrees of remoteness from reality. *Amer. Psychologist*, 1953, *8*, 311. (Abstract)

8) Air Force Personnel and Training Research Center. *Index to 1954 technical documentary reports.* Lackland Air Force Base, Tex.: Author, Decem-ber, 1954. (Res. Bull. AFPTRC-TR-54-132)

9) Air Force Personnel and Training Research Center. *Index to 1955 technical documentary reports.* Lackland Air Force Base, Tex.: Author, December, 1955. (Res. Rep. AFPTRC-TN-55-84)

10) Albert, R. S. Comments on the scientific function of the concept of cohesiveness. *Amer. J. Sociol.*, 1953, *59*, 231–234.

*11) Alfert, Elizabeth. Two components of assumed similarity. *J. abnorm. soc. Psychol.*, 1958, *56*, 125–138.

12) Allport, F. H. The influence of the group upon association and thought. *J. exp. Psychol.*, 1920, *3*, 159–182.

13. Allport, F. H. *Social psychology.* Boston: Houghton Mifflin, 1924.

14) Allport, F. H. Methods in the study of collective action phenomena. *J. soc. Psychol.*, 1942, *15*, 165–185.

15) Allport, G. W. The psychology of participation. *Psychol. Rev.*, 1945, *52*, 117–132.

16) Allport, G. W. The historical background of modern social psychology. In G. Lindzey (Ed.), *Handbook of social psychology.* Reading, Mass.: Addison-Wesley, 1954. Pp. 3–56.

17) Alpert, B., & Smith, Patricia A. How participation works. *J. soc. Issues*, 1949, *5* (1), 3–13.

18) Altman, I. *The distribution of verbal output and number of participations among members of community discussion groups.* Bethesda, Md.: National Institute of Mental Health, March, 1955. (Spec. Grant 3M-9064)

19) Altman, I. *Spontaneity in community discussion groups.* Bethesda, Md.: National Institute of Mental Health, May, 1955. (Spec. Grant 3M-9064)

20) Altman, I., & McGinnies, E. Interpersonal perception and communication in discussion groups of varied attitudinal composition. *J. abnorm. soc. Psychol.*, 1960, *60*, 390–395.

21) Altman, I., & McGrath, J. E. *A conceptual framework for the integration of small group research information.* Arlington, Va.: Human Sciences Research, Inc., February, 1959. [Tech. Note, Contract No. AF 49(638)-256].

22) Altman, I., et al. *The translation of small group research information for computer analysis.* Arlington, Va.: Human Sciences Research, Inc., October, 1959. [Tech. Note, Contract No. AF 49(638)-256].

23) American Institute for Research. *The development of performance flight checks for B-29 combat crews.* Washington, D.C.: Bolling Air Force Base, Human Factors Operations Research Laboratories, February, 1952. (HFORL memorandum Rep. No. 19)

24) Ames, R. Leaderless group discussion and experience in group leadership. *Calif. J. educ. Res.*, 1955, *6*, 166–169.

25) Anderson, A., & Moore, O. K. The formal analysis of normative concepts. *Amer. sociol. Rev.*, 1957, *22*, 9–17.

26) Anderson, A. R. *The formal analysis of normative systems.* New Haven, Conn.: Yale University, Interaction Laboratory, November, 1956. [Tech. Rep. No. 2, Contract Nonr-609(16)]

27) Anderson, C. A. An experimental study of "social facilitation" as affected by intelligence. *Amer. J. Sociol.*, 1929, *34*, 874–881.

28) Anderson, H. H. Domination and integration in the social behavior of young children in an experimental play situation. *Genet. psychol. Monogr.*, 1937, *19*, 341–408.

29) Anderson, H. H. Experimental study of dominative and integrative behavior in children of pre-school age. *J. soc. Psychol.*, 1937, *8*, 335-345.

30) Anderson, H. H. Domination and social integration in the behavior of kindergarten children and teachers. *Genet. psychol. Monogr.*, 1939, *21*, 287–385.

31) Andrews, R. E. *Leadership and supervision.* Washington, D. C.GPO: 1955. (U.S. Civil Serv. Commission Personnel Mgmt Ser. No. 9).

*32) Anikeeff, A. M. Sociometric empathy. *J. soc. Psychol.*, 1957, *45*, 283–287.

33) Ansbacher, H. L. The history of the leaderless group discussion technique. *Psychol. Bull.*, 1951, *48*, 383–391.

34) Arensberg, C. H. Behavior and organization: industrial studies. In J. H. Rohrer and M. Sherif (Eds.), *Social psychology at the crossroads.* New York: Harper & Row, 1951.

35) Argyle, M. Concepts of role and status. *Sociol. Rev.*, 1952, *44* (3), 39–52.

36) Argyle, M. Methods of studying small social groups. *Brit. J. Psychol.*, 1952, *43*, 269–279.

37) Argyle, M. The study of social behavior. In B. A. Farrell (Ed.), *Experimental psychology.* New York: Philosophical Library, 1955.

38) Argyle, M. *The scientific study of social behavior.* New York: Philosophical Library, 1957.

39) Argyle, M. Social pressure in public and private situation. *J. abnorm. soc. Psychol.*, 1957, *54*, 172–175.

*40) Argyle, M., et al. Supervisory methods related to productivity, absenteeism, and labor turnover. *Hum. Relat.*, 1958, *11*, 23–42.

41) Argyris, C. *Personality and organization.* New York: Harper & Row, 1957.

42) Argyris, C. Organizational leadership. Paper read at Sympos. Leadership interpers. Behav. Baton Rouge, La.: Louisiana State University, 1959.

43. Aronson, E., & Mills, J. The effect of severity of initiation on liking for a group. *J. abnorm. soc. Psychol.*, 1959, *59*, 177–181.

44) Arrington, Ruth E. Interrelations in the behavior of young children. Child Develpm. Monogr., 1932, No. 8.

45) Arrington, Ruth E. Time-sampling studies of child behavior. *Psychol. Monogr.*, 1939, *51*, No. 2.

46) Arrington, Ruth E. Time sampling in studies of social behavior: a critical review of techniques and results with research suggestions. *Psychol. Bull.*, 1943, *40*, 81–124.

47) Arsenian, Jean M. Young children in an insecure situation. *J. abnorm. soc. Psychol.*, 1943, *38*, 225–249.

48) Asch, M. J. Nondirective teaching in psychology: an experimental study. *Psychol. Monogr.*, 1951, *65*, No. 4 (Whole No. 321).

49) Asch, S. E. Studies in the principles of judgments and attitudes. II. Determination of judgments by group and by ego-standards. *J. soc. Psychol.*, 1940, *12*, 433–465.

50) Asch, S. E. Effects of group pressure upon the modification and distortion of jugments. In H. Guetzkow (Ed.), *Groups, leadership, and men.* Pittsburgh, Pa.: Carnegie Press, 1951. Pp. 171–190.

51) Asch, S. E. *Social psychology.* Englewood Cliffs, N.J.: Prentice-Hall, 1952.

52) Asch, S. E. Opinions and social pressure. *Sci. Amer.*, 1955, *193* (5), 31–35.

*53) Asch, S. E. Studies of independence and conformity: I. A minority of one against a unanimous majority. *Psychol. Monogr.*, 1956, *70*, No. 9 (Whole No. 416).

54) Atthowe, J. M., Jr. The process of interpersonal influence: influence transmission and development. *Amer. Psychologist*, 1959, *14*, 382. (Abstract)

55) Ausubel, D. F., et al. A preliminary study of developmental trends in socio-empathy: accuracy of perception of own and others' sociometric status. *Child Develpm.*, 1952, *23*, 111–128.

56) Avery, R., & Bachelis, W. Reliability of scoring in interaction process analysis. Paper read at Amer. sociol. Soc., Detroit, 1956.

57) Azrin, N. H., & Lindsley, O. R. The reinforcement of cooperation between children. *J. abnorm. soc. Psychol.*, 1956, *52*, 100–102.

58) Babchuk, N., & Goode, W. F. Work incentives in a self-determined group *Amer. sociol. Rev.*, 1951, *16*, 679–687.

59) Back, K. W. Interpersonal relations in a discussion group. *J. soc. Issues*, 1948, *4*, 61–65.

60) Back, K. W. Influence through social communication. *J. abnorm. soc Psychol.*, 1951, *46*, 9–23.

61) Back, K. W. Power, influence and pattern of communication. In L. Petrullo and B. M. Bass (Eds.), *Leadership and interpersonal behavior.* New York: Holt, Rinehart and Winston, 1961. Pp. 137–164.

62) Back, K. W., & Strickland, L. H. Group formation, communication and influence. Paper read at Sympos. Leadership interpers. Behav. Baton Rouge, La.: Louisiana State University, 1959.

63) Baker, B. O., & Sarbin, T. R. Differential mediation of social perception as a correlate of social adjustment. *Sociometry*, 1956, *19*, 69–83.

64) Bakke, E. W. *The fusion process. A map for the exploration of the relationship of people and organizations.* New Haven, Conn.: Yale University, Labor and Management Center, 1953.

65) Baldwin, A., et al. Patterns of parent behavior. *Psychol. Monogr.*, 1945, *58*, No. 268.

66) Bales, R. F. *Interaction process analysis: a method for the study of small groups.* Reading, Mass.: Addison-Wesley, 1950.

67) Bales, R. F. A set of categories for the analysis of small group interaction. *Amer. sociol. Rev.*, 1950, *15*, 257–263.

68) Bales, R. F. Reply to Keller's comment. *Amer. sociol. Rev.*, 1951, *16*, 843.

69) Bales, R. F. Some statistical problems in small group research. *J. Amer. Statist. Ass.*, 1951, *46*, 311, 322.

70) Bales, R. F. The equilibrium problem in small groups. In T. Parsons, et al. (Eds). *Working papers in the theory of action.* New York: Free Press, 1953. Pp. 111–161.

71) Bales, R. F. In conference. *Harvard Bus. Rev.*, 1954, *32*, 44–50.

72) Bales, R. F. How people interact in conferences. *Sci. Amer.*, 1955, *192* (3), 31–35.

73) Bales, R. F. Task status and likeability as a function of talking and listening in decision-making groups. In L. D. White (Ed.), *The state of the social sciences.* Chicago: University of Chicago Press, 1956. Pp. 148–161.

74) Bales, R. F. Small group theory and research. In R. K. Merton, L. Brown, and L. S. Cottrell, Jr. (Eds.), *Sociology today: problems and prospects.* New York: Basic Books, 1959. Pp. 293–305.

75) Bales, R. F., & Borgatta, E. F. Size of group as a factor in the interaction profile. In A. P. Hare et al. (Eds.), *Small groups: studies in social interaction.* New York: Knopf, 1955. Pp. 396–413.

76) Bales, R. F., & Flanders, N. A. Planning an observation room and group laboratory. *Amer. sociol. Rev.*, 1954, *19*, 771–781.

77) Bales, R. F., & Gerbrands, H. The "interaction recorder": an apparatus and check list for sequential content analysis of social interaction. *Hum. Relat.*, 1948, *1*, 456–463.

78) Bales, R. F., & Slater, P. Role differentiation in small decision-making groups. In T. Parsons et al. (Eds.), *Family, socialization, and interaction process.* New York: Free Press, 1955. Pp. 259–306.

79) Bales, R. F., & Slater, P. E. Notes on "Role differentiation in small decision-making groups." Reply to D. Wheeler. *Sociometry*, 1957, *20*, 152–155.

80) Bales, R. F., & Strodtbeck, F. L. Phrases in group problem solving. *J. abnorm. soc. Psychol.*, 1951, *46*, 485–495.

*81) Bales, R. F., et al. Channels of communication in small groups. *Amer. sociol. Rev.*, 1951, *16*, 461–468.

82) Bales, R. F., et al. Structure and dynamics of small groups: a review of four variables. In J. B. Gittler (Ed.), *Review of sociology: analysis of a decade.* New York: Wiley, 1957. Pp. 391–422.

*83) Balma, M. J., et al. The role of the foreman in modern industry: II. Foreman identification with management, work group productivity, and employee attitude toward the foreman. *Personnel Psychol.*, 1958, *11*, 367–378.

84) Bane, C. L. The lecture versus the class discussion method of college teaching. *Sch. & Soc.*, 1925, *21*, 300–302.

85) Banghart, F. W., et al. *Studies in problem solving.* Charlottesville, Va.: University of Virginia, September, 1959. (Contract Nonr-47408)

86) Banks, E. P. Methodological problems in the study of psychiatric wards. *Soc. Forces*, 1956, *34*, 277–280.

87) Barch, A. M., et al. Social setting and conformity to a legal department. *J. abnorm. soc. Psychol.*, 1957, *55*, 396–398.

88) Bare, R. H. The relation between criteria for B-29 total crew performance and criteria for the performance of the individual crew members. *Amer. Psychologist*, 1953, *8*, 316–317. (Abstract)

89) Barker, R. G. The social interrelations of strangers and acquaintances. *Sociometry*, 1942, *5*, 169–179.

90) Barker, R. G. *One boy's day.* New York: Harper & Row, 1951.

91) Barker, R. G., et al. Frustration and regession: an experiment with young children. *Univer. of Iowa Stud. Child Welf.*, 1941, *18*, No. 1.

92) Barker, R. G., et al. (Eds.), *Child behavior and development.* New York: McGraw-Hill, 1943.

93) Barnard, C. I. The nature of leadership. In H. Schuyler (Ed.), *Human factors in management.* Parkville, Mo.: Park College Press, 1946.

94) Barnett, C. D., et al. Experimental manipulation of verbal behavior in defectives. *Psychol. Rep.*, 1959, *5*, 593–596.

*95) Barnlund, D. C. Experiments in leadership training for decision-making groups. *Speech Monogr.*, 1955, *22*, 1–14.

96) Barnlund, D. C. A comparative study of individual, majority, and group judgment. *J. abnorm. soc. Psychol.*, 1959, *58*, 55–60.

97) Barr, J. A. A multi-question sociometric procedure. *Personnel Guidance*, 1955, *33*, 527–530.

98) Bartlett, C. J. Dimensions of leadership behavior in classroom discussion groups. *J. educ. Psychol.*, 1959, *50*, 280–284.

99) Bartlett, C. J. The relationship between self-ratings and peer-ratings on a leadership behavior scale. *Personnel Psychol.*, 1959, *12*, 237–246.

100) Bartlett, F. C. The social psychology of leadership. *J. nat. Inst. Indus. Psychol.*, 1926, *3*, 188–193.

*101) Barton, W. A., Jr. The effect of group activity and individual effort in developing ability to solve problems in first year algebra. *Educ. Admin. Superv.*, 1926, *12*, 512–518.

102) Bass, B. M. An analysis of the leaderless group discussion. *J. appl. Psychol.*, 1949, *33*, 527–533.

*103) Bass, B. M. Situational tests: I. Individual interviews compared with leaderless group discussions. *Educ. psychol. Measmt*, 1951, *11*, 67–75.

104) Bass, B. M. Situational tests: II. Leaderless group discussion variables. *Educ. psychol. Measmt*, 1951, *11*, 196–207.

105) Bass, B. M. The leaderless group discussion. *Psychol. Bull.*, 1954, *51*, 465–492.

106) Bass, B. M. The leaderless group discussion as a leadership evaluation instrument. *Personnel Psychol.*, 1954, 7, 470–477

107) Bass, B. M. Leadership and the psychology of learning Theories of leadership. *Amer. Psychologist*, 1954, 9, 502. (Abstract)

108) Bass, B. M. Authoritarianism or acquiescence. *J. abnorm. soc. Psychol.*, 1955, *51*, 616–623.

109) Bass, B. M. *Behavior in groups*. Baton Rouge, La.: Louisiana State University, 1955. (Contract No. NR 171-029)

110) Bass, B. M. *Consistent differences in the objectivly measured performance of members and groups*. Baton Rouge, La.: Louisiana State University, 1955. (Tech. Rep. No. 3, Contract N7 ONR 35609)

*111) Bass, B. M. *Increased attraction to the group as a function of individual and group goal attainment*. Baton Rouge, La.: Louisiana State University, 1955. (Tech. Rep. No. 2, Contract N7 ONR 35609)

112) Bass, B. M. *Interrelations among measurements of leadership and associated behavior*. Baton Rouge, La.: Louisiana State University, 1955. (Tech. Rep. No. 5, Contract N7 ONR 35609)

113) Bass, B. M. *Interrelations among measurements of member and group performance*. Baton Rouge, La.: Louisiana State University, 1955. (Tech. Rep. No. 4, Contract N7 ONR 35609)

114) Bass, B. M. *Outline of a theory of leadership and group behavior*. Baton Rouge, La.: Louisiana State University, 1955. (Tech. Rep. No. 1, Contract N7 ONR 35609)

115) Bass, B. M. *Leadership and group effectiveness*. Baton Rouge, La.: Louisiana State University, 1956. (Annu. tech. Rep. Contract No. NR 171-029)

116) Bass, B. M. Reply to Messick and Jackson's comments on authoritarianism or acquiescence. *J. abnorm. soc. Psychol.*, 1957, 54, 426–427.

117) Bass, B. M. *Test of a proposed theory of leadership*. Baton Rouge, La.: Louisiana State University, 1957. (Third Annu. Rep., Contract N7 ONR 35609)

118) Bass, B. M. *Behavior in groups: tests of a proposed theory of leadership*. Baton Rouge, La.: Louisiana State University, 1958. (Contract N7 ONR 35609)

119) Bass, B. M. *Measures of average influence and change in agreement of rankings by a group of judges*. Baton Rouge, La.: Louisiana State University, 1958. (Tech. Rep. No. 19, Contract N7 ONR 35609)

120) Bass, B. M. *Shortcuts for hand-calculating measures of agreement among members and relative successful leadership*. Baton Rouge, La.: Louisiana State University, May, 1958. (Tech. Rep. No. 19, Contract N7 ONR 35609)

121) Bass, B. M. An approach to the objective assessment of leadership. In B. M. Bass and I. A. Berg (Ed.), *Approaches to objective personality assessment*. Princeton, N. J.: Van Nostrand, 1959.

*122) Bass, B. M. Effects of motivation on consistency of performance in groups. *Educ. psychol. Measmt*, 1959, *19*, 247–252.

123) Bass, B. M. *Leadership, psychology, and organizational behavior.* New York: Harper & Row, 1960.

124) Bass, B. M. Some observations about a general theory of leadership and interpersonal behavior. In L. Petrullo and B. M. Bass (Eds.), *Leadership and interpersonal behavior.* New York: Holt, Rinehart and Winston, 1961. Pp. 3–9.

*125) Bass, B. M., & Coates, C. H. Forecasting officer potential using the leaderless group discussion *J. abnorm. soc. Psychol.*, 1952, *47*, 321–325.

126) Bass, B. M., & Gaier, E. L. *Test of a proposed theory of leadership: behavior in groups.* Baton Rouge, La.: Louisiana State University, 1955. (Contract N7 ONR 35609)

127) Bass, B. M., & Klubeck, S. Amenability to leadership training related to leadership status. *Amer. Psychologist*, 1952, *7*, 310. (Abstract)

*128) Bass, B. M., & Klubeck, S. Effects of seating arrangement on leaderless group discussions. *J. abnorm. soc. Psychol.*, 1952, *47*, 724–727.

129) Bass, B. M., & Norton, Fay-Tyler, M. Group size and leaderless discussions. *J. appl. Psychol.*, 1951, *35*, 397–400.

130) Bass, B. M., & White, D. L., Jr. Validity of leaderless group discussion observers' descriptive and evaluative ratings for the assessment of personality and leadership status. *Amer. Psychologist*, 1950, *5*, 311–312. (Abstract)

131) Bass, B. M., & White, O. L. Situational tests: III. Observers' ratings of leaderless group discussion participants as indicators of external leadership status. *Educ. psychol. Measmt*, 1951, *11*, 355–361.

*132) Bass, B. M., & Wurster, C. R. Effects of company rank on LGD performance of oil refinery supervisors. *J. appl. Psychol.*, 1953, *37*, 100–104.

*133) Bass, B. M., & Wurster, C. R. Effects of the nature of the problem on LGD performance. *J. appl. Psychol.*, 1953, *37*, 96–99.

134) Bass, B. M., & Wurster, C. R. Using "mark sense" for ratings and personal data collection. *J. appl. Psychol.*, 1956, *40*, 269–271.

135) Bass, B. M., et al. Factors influencing reliability and validity of leaderless group discussion assessment. *J. appl. Psychol.*, 1953, *37*, 26–30.

*136) Bass, B. M., et al. Personality variables related to leaderless group discussion behavior. *J. abnorm. soc. Psychol.*, 1953, *48*, 120–128.

137) Bass, B. M., et al. Situational and personality factors in leadership among sorority women. *Psychol. Monogr.*, 1953, *67*, No. 16 (Whole No. 366).

138) Bass, B. M., et al. *Attempted leadership as a function of motivation interacting with amount of control.* Baton Rouge, La.: Louisiana State University, 1956. (Contract No. NR 171-029)

139) Bass, B. M., et al. *Metagnosiometry: the study of changing behavior in groups.* Baton Rouge, La.: Louisiana State University, 1956. (Contract No. NR 171-029)

140) Bass, B. M., et al. Studying behavior in groups by digital and analog computer. *Amer. Psychologist*, 1956, *11*, 400. (Abstract)

141) Bass, B. M., et al. *Effects of status–esteem conflict on subsequent behavior in*

groups. Baton Rouge, La.: Louisiana State University, 1957. (Tech. Rep. No. 10, Contract N7 ONR 35609)

142) Bass, B. M., et al. *Group effectiveness as a function of attempted and successful leadership.* Baton Rouge, La.: Louisiana State University, 1957. (Tech. Rep. No. 12, Contract N7 ONR 35609)

143) Bass, B. M., et al. An objective method for studying behavior in groups. *Psychol. Rep.,* 1957, *3,* 265–280.

144) Bass, B. M., et al. Interacting effects of control, motivation, group practice, and problem difficulty on attempted leadership. *J. abnorm. soc. Psychol.,* 1958, *56,* 352–358.

145) Bassett, R. E. Cliques in a student body of stable membership. *Sociometry,* 1944, *7,* 290–302.

146) Bassett, R. E. Sampling problems in influence studies. *Sociometry,* 1948, *11,* 320–328.

147) Bates, A. P. Some sociometric aspects of social ranking in a small, face-to-face group. *Sociometry,* 1952, *15,* 330–341.

148) Bates, A. P., & Cloyd, J. S. Toward the development of operations for defining group norms and members' roles. *Sociometry,* 1956, *19,* 26–39.

149) Bates, F. L. A conceptual analysis of group structure. *Soc. Forces,* 1957, *36,* 103–111.

150) Baumgartel, H. Leadership, motivations, and attitudes in research laboratories. *J. soc. Issues,* 1956, *12*(2), 24–31.

151) Bavelas, A. Morale and the training of leaders. In G. Watson (Ed.), *Civilian morale.* New York: Reynal, 1942. Pp. 143–165.

152) Bavelas, A. Role playing and management training. *Sociometry,* 1947, *1,* 183–191.

153) Bavelas, A. A mathematical model for group structures. *Appl. Anthrop.,* 1948, *7,* 16–30.

154) Bavelas, A. Communication patterns in task groups. *J. acoust. Soc. Amer.,* 1950, *22,* 725–730.

155) Bavelas, A. Communication patterns in problem-solving groups. In H. vonFoerster et al. (Eds.), *Cybernetics: circular casual and feedback mechanisms in biological and social systems.* New York: Josiah Macy, Jr. Foundation, 1952.

156) Bavelas, A., & Barrett, D. An experimental approach to organizational communication. *Personnel,* 1951, *27,* 367–371.

157) Bavelas, A., & Lewin, K. Training in democratic leadership. *J. abnorm. soc. Psychol.,* 1942, *37,* 115–119.

158) Beaver, Alma P. A preliminary report on a study of a preschool "gang." In Dorothy S. Thomas (Ed.), *Some new techniques for studying social behavior.* New York: Columbia University, Teachers College, 1929. Pp. 99–117.

159) Beaver, Alma P. The initiation of social contacts by pre-school children. *Child Develpm. Monogr.,* 1932, No. 7.

160) Becker, H., & Useem, Ruth H. Sociological analysis of the dyad. *Amer. sociol. Rev.,* 1942, *7,* 13–26.

161) Beem, H. P., et al. Predicting effective organizations. *Res. Stud., State Coll. Wash.,* 1952, *20,* 58–62.

162) Beer, M., et al. Some perceived properties of the difference between leaders and non-leaders. *J. Psychol.*, 1959, *47*, 49–56.

163) Bell, G. B., & French, R. L. Consistency of individual leadership position in small groups of varying membership. *J. abnorm. soc. Psychol.*, 1950, *45*, 764–767.

164) Bell, G. B., & Hall, H. E. The relationship between leadership and empathy. *J. abnorm. soc. Psychol.*, 1954, *49*, 156–157.

165) Beloff, Halla. Two forms of social conformity: acquiescence and conventionality. *J. abnorm. soc. Psychol.*, 1958, *56*, 99–104.

166) Bender, I. E., & Hastorf, A. H. The perception of persons: forecasting another person's responses in three personality scales. *J. abnorm. soc. Psychol.*, 1950, *45*, 556–561.

167) Benne, K. D., & Levit, Grace. The nature of groups and helping groups improve their operation. *Rev. educ. Res.*, 1953, *23*, 289–308.

168) Benne, K. D., & Muntyan, B. *Human relations in curriculum change.* New York: Holt, Rinehart and Winston, 1951.

169) Benne, K. D., & Sheats, P. Functional roles of group members. *J. soc. Issues*, 1948, *4*(2), 41–49.

170) Benne, K. D., et al. *Group dynamics and social action.* Washington, D.C.: National Education Association, 1950.

*171) Bennett, Edith B. Discussion, decision, commitment, and consensus in "group decision." *Hum. Relat.*, 1955, *8*, 251–274.

172) Bennis, W. G., & Shepard, H. A. A theory of group development. *Hum. Relat.*, 1956, *9*, 415–437.

173) Ben-Zeev, S. Comparison of diagnosed behavioral tendencies with actual behavior. In Dorothy Stock and H. A. Thelen (Eds.), *Emotional dynamics and group culture.* New York: New York University Press, 1958. Pp. 26–34.

174) Ben-Zeev, S. Sociometric choice and patterns of member participation. In Dorothy Stock and H. A. Thelen (Eds.), *Emotional dynamics and group culture.* New York: New York University Press, 1958. Pp. 84–91.

175) Berelson, B. *Content analysis in communication research.* New York: Free Press, 1952.

176) Berelson, B. Content analysis. In G. Lindzey (Ed.), *Handbook of social psychology.* Reading, Mass.: Addison-Wesley, 1954. Pp. 488–522.

177) Berenda, Ruth W. *The influence of the group on the judgments of children.* New York: King's Crown, 1950.

178) Berg, J. Cooperation without communication and observation. *J. soc. Psychol.*, 1955, *41*, 287–296.

179) Berkowitz, L. *Group norms and the readiness of aircrews to complete training missions.* San Antonio, Tex.: Lackland Air Force Base, Human Resources Research Center, December, 1952. (Res. Note CCT 52-2)

180) Berkowitz, L. Informal norms and willingness to fly in combat crews. *Amer. Psychologist*, 1952, *7*, 314–315. (Abstract)

181) Berkowitz, L. *An exploratory study of the roles of aircraft commanders.* San Antonio, Tex.: Lackland Air Force Base, Human Resources Research Center, December, 1953. (Res. Bull. 53-65)

*182) Berkowitz, L. Sharing leadership in small, decision-making groups. *J. abnorm. soc. Psychol.*, 1953, *48*, 231–238.

183) Berkowitz, L. Group standards, cohesiveness, and productivity. *Hum. Relat.*, 1954, *8*, 509–519.

*184) Berkowitz, L. *Studies in group norms: the perception of group attitudes as related to criteria of group effectiveness.* San Antonio, Tex.: Lackland Air Force Base, Air Force Personnel and Training Research Center, November, 1954. (Res. Bull. AFPTRC-TR-54-62)

185) Berkowitz, L. Group norms among bomber crews: patterns of perceived crew attitudes, "actual" crew attitudes, and crew liking related to air-crew effectiveness in Far Eastern combat. *Sociometry*, 1956, *19*, 141–153.

186) Berkowitz, L. Personality and group position. *Sociometry*, 1956, *19*, 210–222.

187) Berkowitz, L. Social desirability and frequency of influence attempts as factors in leadership choice. *J. Pers.*, 1956, *24*, 424–435.

188) Berkowitz, L. Effects of perceived dependency relationships upon conformity to group expectations. *J. abnorm. soc. Psychol.*, 1957, *55*, 350–354.

*189) Berkowitz, L. Liking for the group and the perceived merit of the group's behavior. *J. abnorm. soc. Psychol.*, 1957, *54*, 353–357.

190) Berkowitz, L., & Haythorn, W. The relationship between dominance tendencies and leadership choice. *Amer. Psychologist*, 1955, *10*, 343. (Abstract)

191) Berkowitz, L., & Howard, R. C. Reactions to opinion deviates as affected by affiliation need (n) and group member interdependence. *Sociometry*, 1959, *22*, 89–91.

192) Berkowitz, L., & Levy, B. I. Pride in group performance and group task motivation. *J. abnorm. soc. Psychol.*, 1956, *53*, 300–306.

193) Berkowitz, L., & Lundy, R. M. Personality characteristics related to susceptibility to influence by peers or authority figures. *J. Pers.*, 1957, *25*, 306–316.

194) Berkowitz, L., et al. Effects of performance evaluations on group integration and motivation. *Hum. Relat.*, 1957, *10*, 195–208.

195) Berkowitz, M. I. *Group size and social organizations.* New Haven, Conn.: Yale University, Interaction Laboratory, November, 1957. (Contract Nonr-60916)

196) Berkun, M., & Meeland, T. Sociometric effects of race and of combat performance. *Sociometry*, 1958, *21*, 145–149.

197) Bernhardt, K. S., et al. An analysis of the social contacts of pre-school children with the aid of motion pictures. *Univer. Toronto Stud. Child Develpm.*, 1937, No. 10.

198) Bernstein, S. *Charting group process.* New York: Association Press, 1949.

199) Berrien, F. K. Attempts to measure attitudinal changes as a consequence of permissive discussions. *Amer. Psychologist*, 1950, *5*, 246–247. (Abstract)

200) Berrien, F. K. Leadership and the homeostasis of groups.—Implications

for leadership. In L. Petrullo and B. M. Bass (Eds.), *Leadership and interpersonal behavior*. New York: Holt, Rinehart and Winston, 1961. Pp. 82–99.

*201) Berrien, F. K., & Angoff, W. H. *Homeostasis theory of small groups*. New Brunswick, N.J.: Rutgers University, December, 1957. [Tech. Rep., Contract Nonr 404(10)]

202) Berrien, F. K., & Angoff, W. H. *Homeostasis theory of small groups II*. New Brunswick, N.J.: Rutgers University, September, 1958. [Tech. Rep. No. 3, Contract Nonr 404(10)]

203) Berrien, F. K., & Angoff, W. H. *Homeostasis theory of small groups III*. New Brunswick, N.J.: Rutgers University, March, 1959. [Tech. Rep. No. 4, Contract Nonr 404(10)]

204) Bettelheim, B., & Sylvester, Emmy. Therapeutic influence of the group on the individual. *Amer. J. Orthopsychiat.*, 1947, *27*, 684–692.

205) Beum, C. O., Jr., & Brundage, E. G. A method for analyzing the socio-matrix. *Sociometry*, 1950, *13*, 141–145.

206) Biber, Barbara, et al. *Life and ways of the seven-to-eight year old*. (2nd ed.) New York: Basic Books, 1952.

207) *A bibliography of ONR Group Psychology Branch Projects Report*. July, 1955. Also *Supplement*, May, 1956.

208) *A bibliography of research reports representing Air Force activities integrated within the crew research laboratory*. San Antonio, Tex.: Randolph Air Force Base, Air Force Personnel and Training Research Center, September, 1954.

209) *A bibliography of research reports of the crew research laboratory*. San Antonio, Tex.: Randolph Air Force Base, Air Force Personnel and Training Research Center, January, 1955.

210) *A bibliography of research reports of the crew research laboratory*. San Antonio, Tex.: Randolph Air Force Base, Air Force Personnel and Training Research Center, March, 1955.

211) *A bibliography of research reports of the crew research laboratory*. San Antonio, Tex.: Randolph Air Force Base, Air Force Personnel and Training Research Center, April, 1955–April, 1956.

*212) Bieri, J. Changes in interpersonal perceptions following social interaction. *J. abnorm. soc. Psychol.*, 1953, *48*, 61–66.

213) Bion, W. R. Experience in groups: I. *Hum. Relat.*, 1948, *1*, 314–320.

214) Bion, W. R. Experiences in groups: II. *Hum. Relat.*, 1948, *1*, 487–496.

215) Bion, W. R. Experiences in groups: III. *Hum. Relat.*, 1949, *2*, 13–22.

216) Bion, W. R. Experiences in groups: IV. *Hum. Relat.*, 1949, *2*, 295–303.

217) Bion, W. R. Experiences in groups: V. *Hum. Relat.*, 1950, *3*, 3–14.

218) Bion, W. R. Experiences in groups: VI. *Hum. Relat.*, 1950, *3*, 395–402.

219) Bion, W. R. Experiences in groups: VII. *Hum. Relat.*, 1951, *4*, 221–227.

220) Bion, W. R. Group dynamics: a review. *Int. J. Psycho-Anal.*, 1952, *33*, 235–247.

221) Bion, W. R., & Rickman, J. Intragroup tensions in therapy: their study as the task of the group. *Lancet*, 1943, *245*, 678–681.

222) Bishop, Barbara M. Mother-child interaction and the social behavior of children. *Psychol. Monogr.*, 1951, *65*, No. 11 (Whole No. 328).

223) Bjerstedt, A. A "chess-board sociogram" for sociographic representation of choice directions and for the analysis of "sociometric locomotions." *Sociometry*, 1952, *15*, 244–262.

224) Bjerstedt, A. The interpretation of sociometric status scores in the classroom. *Acta psychol.*, 1956, *12*, 1–14.

225) Bjerstedt, A. A field-force model as a basis for predictions of social behavior. *Hum. Relat.*, 1958, *11*, 331–340.

226) Blake, R. R. The interaction-feeling hypothesis applied to psychotherapy groups. *Sociometry*, 1953, *16*, 253–265.

227) Blake, R. R. Social standards and individual conduct. *Southwest. Soc. Sci. Quart.*, 1954, 11–24.

228) Blake, R. R. The other person in the situation. In R. Tagiuri, and L. Petrullo (Eds.), *Person perception and interpersonal behavior*. Stanford, Calif.: Stanford University Press, 1958. Pp. 229–242.

229) Blake, R. R., & Brehm, J. W. The use of tape recording to simulate a group atmosphere. *J. abnorm. soc. Psychol.*, 1954, *49*, 311–313.

230) Blake, R. R., & Mouton, J. S. The dynamics of influence and coercion. *Int. J. soc. Psychiat*, 1957, *2*, 263–274

231) Blake, R. R., et al. The consistency of interpersonal behavior judgments made on the basis of short-term interaction in three-man groups. *J. abnorm. soc. Psychol.*, 1954, *49*, 573–578.

232) Blake, R. R., et al. *Development of improved measures of interpersonal relationships among air crew members*. Austin, Tex.: University of Texas, November, 1954. [Final Rep., Contract AF 18(600)-602]

233) Blake, R. R., et al. Gift giving as a function of group standards. *Hum. Relat.*, 1955, *8*, 61–74.

234) Blake, R. R., et al. The generality of conformity behavior as a function of factual anchorage, difficulty of task, and amount of social pressure. *J. Pers.*, 1957, *25*, 294–305.

235) Blake, W. D., & Harriman, A. E. The selection and training of executives. *J. soc. Psychol.*, 1949, *29*, 29–36.

236) Blau, P. M. Cooperation and competition in a bureaucracy. *Amer. J. Sociol.*, 1954, *59*, 530–535.

237) Blau, P. M. Patterns of interaction among a group of officials in a government agency. *Hum. Relat.*, 1954, *7*, 337–348.

238) Block, J. The assessment of communication: role variations as a function of interactional context. *J. Pers.*, 1952, *21*, 272–286.

239) Block, J., & Bennett, Lillian. The assessment of communication. *Hum. Relat.*, 1955, *8*, 317–325.

240) Block, J., & Block, Jeanne. An interpersonal experiment on reactions to authority. *Hum. Relat.*, 1952, *5*, 91–98.

241) Blood, R. O., & Livant, W. P. The use of space within the cabin group. *J. soc. Issues*, 1957, *13*(1), 47–53.

242) Blumer, H. Psychological import of the human group. In M. Sherif, and M. O. Wilson (Eds.), *Group relations at the crossroads*. New York: Harper & Row, 1953. Pp. 185–202.

243) Bogardus, E. S. Measurement of person-group relations. *Sociometry*, 1947, *10*, 306–311.

244) Bogardus, E. S. Group behavior and groupality. *Sociol. soc. Res.*, 1954, *38*, 401–403.

245) Bonner, H. *Group dynamics*. New York: Ronald Press, 1959.

246) Bonney, M. E. The constancy of sociometric scores and their relationships to teacher judgments of social success and to personnality self-ratings. *Sociometry*, 1943, *6*, 409–424.

247) Bonney, M. E. A sociometric study of the relationship of some factors to mutual friendships on the elementary, secondary, and college levels. *Sociometry*, 1946, *9*, 21–47.

248) Bonney, M. E. Sociometric study of agreement between teachers' judgments and student choices. *Sociometry*, 1947, *10*, 133–146.

249) Bonney, M. E., & Powell, J. Differences in social behavior between sociometrically high and sociometrically low children. *J. educ. Res.*, 1953, *46*, 481–495.

250) Bonney, M. E., et al. A study of some factors related to sociometric status in a men's dormitory. *Sociometry*, 1953, *16*, 287–301.

251) Borg, W. R. Leadership reactions in situational tests. *Amer. Psychologist*, 1956, *11*, 379. (Abstract)

*252) Borg, W. R. The behavior of emergent and designated leaders in situational tests. *Sociometry*, 1957, *20*, 95–104.

253) Borg, W. R. Prediction of roles in small group activity. *Amer. Psychologist*, 1957, *12*, 378-379. (Abstract)

*254) Borg, W. R., & Tupes, E. C. Personality characteristics related to leadership behavior in two types of small group situational problems. *J. appl. Psychol.*, 1958, *42*, 252–256.

255) Borgatta, E. F. The use of psychodrama, sociodrama, and related techniques in social psychological research. *Sociometry*, 1950, *13*, 244–258.

256) Borgatta, E. F. An analysis of three levels of response: an approach to some relationships among dimensions of personality. *Sociometry*, 1951, *14*, 267–316.

257) Borgatta, E. F. A diagnostic note on the construction of sociograms and action diagrams. *Group Psychother.*, 1951, *3*, 300–308.

258) Borgatta, E. F. Analysis of social interaction and sociometric perception. *Sociometry*, 1954, *17*, 7–31.

259) Borgatta, E. F. Analysis of social interaction: actual, role playing, and projective. *J. abnorm. soc. Psychol.*, 1955, *51*, 394–405.

260) Borgatta, E. F. Research pure and applied. *Group Psychother.*, 1955, *8*, 263–277.

261) Borgatta, E. F. A commentary on small group research. Paper prepared at Air Force Office of Scientific Res. Behav. Sci. Conf. Albuquerque, N.M., 1957. [Contract AF 49(638)-33]

262) Borgatta, E. F., & Bales, R. F. The consistency of subject behavior and the reliability of scoring in interaction process analysis. *Amer. sociol. Rev.*, 1953, *18*, 566–569.

263) Borgatta, E. F., & Bales, R. F. Interaction of individuals in reconstituted groups. *Sociometry*, 1953, *16*, 302–320.

264) Borgatta, E. F., & Bales, R. F. Task and accumulation of experience as

factors in the interaction of small groups. *Sociometry*, 1953, *16*, 239–252.

265) Borgatta, E. F., & Bales, R. F. Sociometric status patterns and characteristics of interaction. *J. soc. Psychol.*, 1956, *43*, 289–297.

266) Borgatta, E. F., & Cottrell, L. S. On the classification of groups. *Sociometry*, 1955, *18*, 665–678.

267) Borgatta, E. F., & Cottrell, L. S. Directions for research on group behavior. *Amer. J. Sociol.*, 1957, *63*(1), 42–48.

268) Borgatta, E. F., & Eschenbach, A. E. Factor analysis of Rorschach variables and behavior observation. *Psychol. Rep.*, 1955, *3*, 129–136.

269) Borgatta, E. F., & Mann, J. H. Personality and behavior correlates of changes produced by role playing experience. *Psychol. Rep.*, 1959, 505–526.

270) Borgatta, E. F., & Moreno, J. L. An experiment with sociodrama and sociometry in industry. *Sociometry*, 1951, *14*, 71–104.

271) Borgatta, E. F., et al. *Staff command conflicts and other sources of tension in relation to officer leadership and organizational effectiveness.* 1953. [Final Rep., Contract No. AF 33(038)-12782]

*272) Borgatta, E. F., et al. Some findings relevant to the great man theory of leadership. *Amer. sociol. Rev.*, 1954, *19*, 755–759.

273) Borgatta, E. F., et al. On the dimensions of group behavior. *Sociometry*, 1956, *19*, 223–240.

274) Borgatta, E. F., et al. The spectrum of individual characteristics. *Psychol. Rep.*, 1958, *4*, 279–319.

275) Borgatta, E. F., et al. Structure and dynamics of small groups. In J. Gittler (Ed.), *Review of sociology*. New York: Wiley, 1958.

276) Borgatta, E. F., et al. Initial expectation, group climate, and the assessments of leaders and members. *J. soc. Psychol.*, 1959, *49*, 285–296.

277) Bos, Maria C. Experimental study of productive collaboration. *Acta psychol.*, 1937, *3*, 315–426.

278) Bossard, J. H. S. Law of family interaction. *Amer. J. Sociol.*, 1945, *50*, 292–294.

279) Bott, Helen McM. *Method in social studies of young children.* Toronto: University of Toronto Press, 1933.

280) Bovard, E. W., Jr. Social norms and the individual. *J. abnorm. soc. Psychol.*, 1948, *43*, 62–69.

281) Bovard, E. W., Jr. *Change in frame of reference for satisfaction with group estimates following presentation of an objective criterion.* Ann Arbor, Mich.: University of Michigan, 1950. (Contract No. NR. 172-301)

282) Bovard, E. W., Jr. The experimental production of interpersonal affect. *J. abnorm. soc. Psychol.*, 1951, *46*, 521–528.

283) Bovard, E. W., Jr. Group structure and perception. *J. abnorm. soc. Psychol.*, 1951, *46*, 398–405.

284) Bovard, E. W., Jr. Clinical insight as a function of group process. *J. abnorm. soc. Psychol.*, 1952, *47*, 534–539.

*285) Bovard, E. W., Jr. Conformity to social norms and attraction to the group. *Science*, 1953, *118*, 598–599.

286) Bovard, E. W., Jr. Grouping error and interpersonal affect: a correction. *J. abnorm. soc. Psychol.*, 1956, *52*, 283–284.

287) Bovard, E. W., Jr. Interaction and attraction to the group. *Hum. Relat.*, 1956, *9*, 481–489.

288) Bovard, E. W., Jr., & Guetzkow, H. *A validity study of rating scales as a device to distinguish participants in stable and temporary groups.* Ann Arbor, Mich.: University of Michigan, 1950. (Conf. Res. Project Rep.)

289) Boyd, R. W., & DiMascio, A. Social behavior and autonomic physiology: a sociophysiologic study. *J. nerv. men. Dis.*, 1954, *120*, 3–4.

290) Bradford, L. P. *Exploration in human relations training–an assessment of experience,* 1947–1953. Washington, D.C.: National Education Association, National Training Laboratory, 1954

291) Bradford, L. P., & French, J. R. P., Jr. (Eds.) The dynamics of the discussion group. *J. soc. Issues*, 1948, *4*(2).

292) Bradford, L. P., & Lippitt, R. Role-playing in supervisory training. *Personnel*, 1946, *22*, 358–369.

293) Brandenburg, E. Problems in measuring the results of discussion. *J. Communication*, 1953, *3*, 28–33.

294) Brandenburg, E., & Neal, P. A. Graphic techniques for evaluating discussion and conference procedures. *Quart. J. Speech*, 1953, *39*, 201–208.

295) Bray, C. W. *Psychology and military proficiency.* Princeton, N.J.: Princeton University Press, 1948.

296) Brehm, J., & Festinger, L. Pressures toward uniformity of performance in groups. *Hum. Relat.*, 1957, *10*, 85–91.

297) Bristow, W. B. A group discussion approach in training courses for nurses and religious counselors. In Helen I. Driver (Ed.), *Counseling and learning through small-group discussion.* Madison, Wis.: Monona Publications, 1958. Pp. 355–357.

*298) Brodbeck, May. The role of small groups in mediating the effects of propaganda. *J. abnorm. soc. Psychol.*, 1956, *52*, 166–170.

299) Brody, W. Judging candidates by observing them in unsupervised group discussion. *Personnel J.*, 1947, *26*, 170–173.

300) Bronfenbrenner, U. A constant frame of reference for sociometric research. *Sociometry*, 1943, *6*, 363–397.

301) Bronfenbrenner, U. A constant frame of reference for sociometric research: Part II. Experiment and inference. *Sociometry*, 1944, *7*, 40–75.

302) Bronfenbrenner, U. The influence of parental roles on adolescent behavior. In L. Petrullo and B. M. Bass (Eds.), *Leadership and interpersonal behavior.* New York: Holt, Rinehart and Winston, 1961, 239–971.

303) Bronfenbrenner, U., & Newcomb, T. M. Improvisations– an application of psychodrama in personality diagnosis. *Sociatry*, 1948, *1*, 367–382.

304) Brown, J. C. An experiment in role-taking. *Amer. sociol. Rev.*, 1952, *17*, 587–597.

305) Brown, P. *Bureaucracy in a government laboratory.* Los Angeles: University of California, 1954. (Contract No. NR 171-056)

306) Brown, Paula, & Brown, R. A note on hypotheses in Homan's "The human group." *Amer. sociol. Rev.*, 1955, *20*, 83–85.

307) Brown, W. H. An instrument for studying viscidity within small groups. *Educ. psychol. Measmt*, 1953, *13*, 402-417.

*308) Browne, C. G. A study of executive leadership in business: I. The R, A, and D scales. *J. appl. Psychol.*, 1949, *33*, 521-526.

309) Browne, C. G. Study of executive leadership in business: II. Social group patterns. *J. appl. Psychol.*, 1950, *34*, 12-15.

310) Browne, C. G. Study of executive leadership in business: III. Goal and achievement index. *J. appl. Psychol.*, 1950, *34*, 82-87.

311) Browne, C. G., & Cohn, T. S. (Eds.) *The study of leadership*. Danville, Ill.: Interstate Printers and Publishers, 1958.

312) Bruner, J. S. Social psychology and group processes. *Annu. Rev. Psychol.*, 1950, *1*, 119-150.

313) Bruner, J. S., & Tagiuri, R. The perception of people. In G. Lindzey (Ed.), *Handbook of social psychology*. Reading, Mass.: Addison-Wesley, 1954. Pp. 634-654.

314) Bruner, J. S., et al. The meaning of traits in isolation and in combination. In R. Tagiuri and L. Petrullo (Eds.), *Person perception and interpersonal behavior*. Stanford, Calif.: Stanford University Press, 1958. Pp. 277-288.

*315) Bryant, H. A., et al. *Group effectiveness, coercion, change, and coalescence among delinquents compared to non-delinquents*. Baton Rouge, La.: Louisiana State University, 1958. (Tech. Rep. No. 15, Contract N7 ONR 35609)

316) Buchheimer, A., & Pendleton, P. The reliability and validity of the group participation scale. *Educ. psychol. Measmt*, 1954, *14*, 566-569.

317) Buck, R. C. Acquaintance positions in the group. *Sociol. soc. Res.*, 1952, *37*, 33-36.

318) Buehler, R. E. An investigation of relationship between motivation and interaction behavior in small groups. *Amer. Psychologist*, 1952, *7*, 314. (Abstract)

*319) Bugental, Daphne E., & Lehner, G. F. J. Accuracy of self-perception, and group-perception as related to two leadership roles. *J. abnorm. soc. Psychol.*, 1958, *56*, 396-398.

320) Buhler, Charlotte. Social behavior of the child. In C. A. Murchison (Ed.), *A handbook of child psychology*. Worcester, Mass.: Clark University Press, 1931. Pp. 392-431.

321) Burchard, E. M. L., et al. Criteria for the evaluation of group therapy. *Psychosom. Med.*, 1948, *10*, 257-274.

322) Burdick, H. A. Three experiments in conformity. *Amer. Psychologist*, 1959, *14*, 334. (Abstract)

323) Burgess, E. W., & Cottrell, L. S. *Predicting success or failure in marriage*. Englewood Cliffs, N.J.: Prentice-Hall, 1939.

324) Burke, H. R. A training course for leaders in the mental health association. In Helen I. Driver (Ed.), *Counseling and learning through small-group discussion*. Madison, Wis.: Monona Publications, 1958. Pp. 372-376.

325) Burke, H. R. Training program on conference leadership in industry. In Helen I. Driver (Ed.), *Counseling and learning through small-group discussion*. Madison, Wis.: Monona Publications, 1958. Pp. 368-390.

326) Burnham, W. H. The hygiene of home study. *Pedag. Sem.*, 1905, *12*, 213–230.

327) Burnham, W. H. The group as a stimulus to mental activity. *Science*, 1910, *31*, 761–767.

328) Burns, T. The reference of conduct in small groups: cliques and cabals in occupational milieux. *Hum. Relat.*, 1955, *8*, 467–486.

329) Burrow, T. The group method of analysis. *Psychoanal. Rev.*, 1927, *14*, 268–280.

330) Burton, A. The influence of social factors upon the persistence of satiation in pre-school children. *Child Develpm.*, 1941, *12*, 121–129

331) Burtt, H. E. Sex differences in the effect of discussion. *J. exp. Psychol.*, 1920, *3*, 390–395.

332) Byrd, E. A study of validity and constancy of choices in a sociometric test. *Sociometry*, 1951, *14*, 175–181.

333) Byrne, D., & Buehler, J. A. A note on the influence of propinquity upon acquaintanceships. *J. abnorm. soc. Psychol.*, 1955, *51*, 147–148.

334) Calhoon, R. P. *The competitive factor in employee performance* Chapel Hill, N.C.: University of North Carolina, School of Business Administration, April, 1959. (Res. Paper 1)

335) Calia, V. F. A junior college guidance program with a team approach In Helen I. Driver (Ed.), *Counseling and learning through small-group discussion*. Madison, Wis.: Monona Publications, 1958. Pp. 318–321.

336) Calvin, A. D., et al. The effect of intelligence and social atmosphere on group problem solving behavior. *J. soc. Psychol.*, 1957, *45*, 61–74.

337) Campbell, D. T. An error in some demonstrations of the superior social perceptiveness of leaders. *J. abnorm. soc. Psychol.*, 1955, *51*, 694.

338) Campbell, D. T. Factors relevant to the validity of experiments in social settings. *Psychol. Bull.*, 1955, *54*, 297–312.

339) Campbell, D. T. *Leadership and its effects upon the group*. Columbus, Ohio: Ohio State University, Bureau of Business Research, 1956. (Res. Monogr. No. 83)

340) Campbell, D. T., & Mehra, K. Individual differences in evaluations of group discussions as a projective measure of attitudes toward leadership. *J. soc. Psychol.*, 1958, *47*, 101–106.

341) Campbell, D. T., & Tyler, Bonnie B. The construct validity of work-group morale measures. *J. appl. Psychol.*, 1957, *41*, 91–92.

342) Campbell, J. D., & Yarrow, M. R. Personal and situational variables in adaptation to change. *J. soc. Issues.*, 1958, *14*(1), 29-46.

343) Campbell, J. D., et al. A study of adaptation to a new social situation. *J. soc. Issues*, 1958, *14*(1), 3–7.

*344) Canning, R. R., & Baker, J. M. Effect of the group on authoritarian and non-authoritarian persons. *Amer. J. Sociol.*, 1959, *64*, 579–581. (Abstract)

345) Canter, N. Focus and function in group discussion. *Teach. Coll. Rec.*, 1952, *53*, 375–382.

346) Caplow, T. The criteria of organizational success. *Soc. Forces*, 1953, *32*, 1–9.

347) Caplow, T. A theory of coalitions in the triad. *Amer. sociol. Rev.*, 1956, *21*, 489–493.

348) Caplow, T. Further development of a theory of coalitions in the triad. *Amer. J. Sociol.*, 1959, *64*, 488–493. (Abstract)

349) Caplow, T., & Forman, R. Neighborhood interaction. *Amer. sociol. Rev.*, 1950, *15*, 357–366.

350) Carey, Gloria L. *Reduction of sex differences in problem-solving by improvement of attitude through group discussion.* Stanford, Calif.: Stanford University, March, 1955. (Techn. Rep. No. 9, Contract N6 ONR-25125)

*351) Carey, Gloria L. Sex differences in problem-solving performance as a function of attitude differences. *J. abnorm. soc. Psychol.*, 1958, *56*, 256–260.

352) Carr, L. J. Experimental sociology: a preliminary note on theory and method. *Soc. Forces*, 1929, *8*, 63–74.

353) Carr, L. J. Experimentation in face-to-face interaction. *Amer. Sociol. Soc. Papers*, 1930, *24*, 174–176.

354) Carter, L. F. *The consistency of leadership behavior.* Rochester, N.Y.: University of Rochester, 1949. (Contract No. NR 171–342)

355) Carter, L. F. *Group structures and interaction as a function of task, personality, and goal.* Rochester, N.Y.: University of Rochester, 1950. (Contract No. NR 171-342)

356) Carter, L. F. Leadership in small groups. Washington, D.C.: *ONR Research Reviews*, February, 1951.

357) Carter, L. F. Some research on leadership in small groups. In H. Guetzkow (Ed.), *Groups, leadership and men: research in human relations.* Pittsburgh, Pa.: Carnegie Press, 1951. Pp. 146–157.

358) Carter, L. F. Leadership and small-group behavior. In M. Sherif and M. O. Wilson (Eds.), *Group relations at the crossroads.* New York: Harper & Row, 1953. Pp. 257–284.

359) Carter, L. F. Recording and evaluating the performance of individuals as members of small groups. *Personnel Psychol.*, 1954, *7*, 477–484.

360) Carter, L. F., & Nixon, Mary. Ability, perceptual, personality, and interest factors associated with different criteria of leadership. *J. Psychol.*, 1949, *27*, 377–388.

*361) Carter, L. F., et al. A further investigation of the criteria of leadership. *J. abnorm. soc. Psychol.*, 1950, *45*, 350–358.

*362) Carter, L. F., et al. The behavior of leaders and other group members. *J. abnorm. soc. Psychol.*, 1951, *46*, 589–595.

363) Carter, L. F., et al. A note on a new technique of interaction recording. *J. abnorm. soc. Psychol.*, 1951, *46*, 258–260.

364) Carter, L. F., et al. The relation of categorizations and ratings in the observation of group behavior. *Hum. Relat.*, 1951, *4*, 239–254.

365) Cartwright, D. Social psychology in the United States during the Second World War. *Hum. Relat.*, 1948, *1*, 333–352.

366) Cartwright, D. Achieving change in people: some applications of group dynamics theory. *Hum. Relat.*, 1951, *4*, 381–392.

367) Cartwright, D. Emotional dimensions of group life. In M. L. Reymert (Ed.), *Feelings and emotions*. New York: McGraw-Hill, 1952. Pp. 439–447.

368) Cartwright, D. Social psychology. *Annu. Rev. Psychol.*, 1957, *8*, 211–236.

369) Cartwright, D. (Ed.) *Studies in social power*. Ann Arbor, Mich.: Institute for Social Research, 1959. (RCGD Monogr. Ser. No. 6)

370) Cartwright, D., & Harary, F. Structural balance: a generalization of Heider's theory. *Psychol. Rev.*, 1956, *63*, 277–293.

371) Cartwright, D., & Lippitt, R. Group dynamics and the individual. *Int. J. Group Psychother.*, 1957, 7(1), 86–102.

372) Cartwright, D., & Zander, A.F. (Eds.), *Group dynamics: research and theory*. New York: Harper & Row, 1953 (2nd edition 1960)

373) Cartwright, Rosalind D., et al. Patterns of perceived interpersonal relations. *Sociometry*, 1956, *19*, 166–177.

374) Castore, G. F., et al. Measurements of a therapeutic group by a scale of communication complexity in interpersonal interactions: a study of interjudge reliability. *Provo Papers*, 1959, *3*(1), 1–20.

375) Cattell, R. B. Concepts and methods in the measurement of group syntality. *Psychol. Rev.*, 1948, *55*, 48–63.

376) Cattell, R. B. Determining syntality dimension as a basis for morale and leadership measurement. In H. Guetzkow (Ed.), *Groups, leadership and men: research in human relations*. Pittsburgh, Pa: Carnegie Press, 1951. Pp. 16–27.

377) Cattell, R. B. New concepts for measuring leadership in terms of group syntality. *Hum. Relat.*, 1951, *4*, 161–184.

378) Cattell, R. B. An attempt at more refined definition of the cultural dimensions of syntality in modern nations. *Amer. sociol. Rev.*, 1952, *17*, 408–421.

379) Cattell, R. B. On the theory of group learning. *J. soc. Psychol.*, 1953, 37, 27–52.

380) Cattell, R. B., & Stice, G. F. Four formulae for selecting leaders on the basis of personality. *Hum. Relat.*, 1944, *7*, 493–507.

381) Cattell, R. B., & Wispe, L. G. The dimensions of syntality in small groups. *J. soc. Psychol.*, 1948, *28*, 57–78.

382) Cattell, R. B., et al. The dimensions of syntality in small groups. *Hum. Relat.*, 1953, *6*, 331–356.

383) Cervin, V. Experimental investigation of behavior in social situations: I. Behavior under opposition. *Canad. J. Psychol.*, 1955, *9*, 107–116.

*384) Cervin, V. Experimental investigation of behavior in social situations: II. Individual behavioral effects of change in group attitude from opposition to cooperation. *Canad. J. Psychol.*, 1955, *9*, 155–160.

385) Cervin, V. Individual behavior in social situations: its relation to anxiety, neuroticism, and group solidarity. *J. exp. Psychol.*, 1956, *51*, 161–168.

386) Cervin, V. Relationship of ascendant-submissive behavior in dyadic groups of human subjects to their emotional responsiveness. *J. abnorm. soc. Psychol.*, 1957, *54*, 241–249.

387) Cervin, V. A centroid method for estimating cohesiveness in small groups. *Amer. Psychologist*, 1959, *14*, 381. (Abstract)

388) Cervin, V., & Ketchum, J. D. Experimental investigation of behavior in social situations: III. Behavior under frustration. *Canad. J. Psychol.*, 1956, *10*, 23–30.

389) Cervinka, V. A dimensional theory of groups. *Sociometry*, 1948, *11*, 100–107.

390) Champney, H. The variables of parent behavior. *J. abnorm. soc. Psychol.*, 1941, *36*, 525–542.

391) Chapin. F. S. A three-dimensional model for visual analysis of group structure. *Soc. Forces*, 1952, *31*, 20–25.

392) Chapman, L. J., & Campbell, D. T. *An attempt to predict the performance of three-man teams from attitude measures.* Chicago: University of Chicago, 1954. [Res. Rep. No. 14, Contract AF 18(600)-170]

393) Chapple, E. D. Measuring human relations: An introduction to the study of interaction of individuals. *Genet. Psychol. Monogr.*, 1940, *22*, 3–147.

394) Chapple, E. D. The measurement of interpersonal behavior. *Trans. N. Y. Acad. Sci.*, 1942, *4*, 222–233.

395) Chapple, E. D. The standard interview as used in interaction chronograph investigations. *Hum. Organization*, 1953, *12*, 23–32.

396) Chapple, E. D., & Lindemann, E. Clinical implications of measurements on interaction rates in psychiatric interviews. *Appl. Anthrop.*, 1942, *1*, 1–11.

397) Chesler, D. J., et al. Effect on morale of infantry team replacement and individual replacement systems. *Sociometry*, 1955, *18*, 587–597.

*398) Child, I. L., & Whiting, J. W. M. Determinants of level of aspiration: evidence from everyday life. *J. abnorm. soc. Psychol.*, 1949, *44*, 303–314.

399) Chittenden, Gertrude E. An experimental study in measuring and modifying assertive behavior in young children. *Soc. Res. Child Develpm. Monogr.*, 1942, *7*, No. 1.

400) Chowdhry, Kamla, & Newcomb, T. M. The relative abilities of leaders and non-leaders to estimate opinions of their own groups. *J. abnorm. soc. Psychol.*, 1952, *47*, 51–57.

401) Christensen, H. T., & Philbrick, R. E. Family size as a factor in the marital adjustments of college couples. *Amer. sociol. Rev.*, 1952, *17*, 306–312.

402) Christie, L. S., et al. *Communications and learning in task-oriented groups.* Cambridge, Mass.: Research Laboratory of Electronics, 1952.

403) Christie, L. S., et al. Information handling in organized groups. In J. F. McCloskey and J. M. Coppinger (Eds.), *Operations research for management.* Vol. 2. Baltimore: The Johns Hopkins Press, 1956.

*404) Christner, C. A., & Hemphill, J. K. Leader behavior of B-29 commanders and changes in crew members' attitudes toward the crew. *Sociometry*, 1955, *18*, 82–87.

405) Clampitt, R. R., & Charles, D. C. Sociometric status and supervisory evaluation of institutionalized mentally deficient children. *J. soc. Psychol.*, 1956, *44*, 223–231.

406) Clark, R. A. Analyzing the group structure of combat rifle squads. *Amer. Psychologist*, 1953, *8*, 333. (Abstract)

407) Clark, R. A. *A study of the personal interactions which are related to the differences between effective and ineffective rifle squads.* Washington, D.C.: Human Resources Research Office, December, 1953. (Project No. 095 50 000)

408) Clark, R. A. *Leadership in rifle squads on the Korean front line.* Washington, D. C.: Human Resources Research Office, September, 1955. (Tech. Rep. No. 21)

409) Clark, R. A., & McGuire, C. Sociographic analysis of sociometric valuations. *Child Develpm.*, 1952, *23*, 129–140.

410) Cleveland, S. E., & Fisher, S. Prediction of small group behavior from a body image schema. *Hum. Relat.*, 1957, *10*, 223–233.

*411) Cleven, W. A., & Fiedler, F. E. *The relations of open hearth foreman's interpersonal perceptions to steel production.* Urbana, Ill.: University of Illinois, Department of Psychology, October, 1955. (Tech. Rep. No. 11, Contract N6 ORI 07135)

412) Cloonan, T. F., et al. Group effectiveness in bomber crews: analysis of in-flight procedures as a criterion source. *Amer. Psychologist*, 1953, *8*, 333–334. (Abstract)

413) Coch, L., & French, J. R. P., Jr. Overcoming resistance to change. *Hum. Relat.*, 1948, *1*, 512–532.

414) Cocherell, D. L. A study of the play of children of pre-school age by an unobserved observer. *Genet. Psychol. Monogr.*, 1935, *17*, 377–469.

415) Coffey, H. S. Socio and psyche group process: integrative concepts. *J. soc. Issues*, 1952. *8*(2), 65–74.

416) Cogan, E. A., & Shapiro, D. Object choice and group development. *Amer. Psychologist*, 1958, *13*, 349. (Abstract)

*417) Cohen, A. R. Experimental effects of ego-defense preference on interpersonal relations. *J. abnorm. soc. Psychol.*, 1956, *52*, 19–27.

*418) Cohen, A. R. Upward communication in experimentally created hierarchies. *Hum. Relat.*, 1958, *11*, 41–54.

419) Cohen, A. R. Situational structure, self esteem, and threat-oriented reactions to power. In D. Cartwright (Ed.), *Studies in social power.* Ann Arbor, Mich.: Institute for Social Research, 1959.

420) Cohen, B. P. A probability model for conformity. *Sociometry*, 1958, *21*, 69–81.

421) Cohen, D., et al. Effect of group cohesiveness and training upon creative thinking. *Amer. Psychologist*, 1959, *14*, 410–411. (Abstract)

422) Cohen, E. The effect of members' use of a formal group as a reference group upon group effectiveness. *J. soc. Psychol.*, 1957, *46*, 307–309.

423) Cohen, I. K., et al. *Developing a ground training course in aircrew operations procedure.* Washington, D. C.: Bolling Air Force Base, Human Factors Operations Research Laboratory, August 1953. (HFORL Memorandum 37)

*424) Cohen, J. D., & McKelvey, R. K. *The behavior of individuals and personnel systems in the surveillance functions of an Air Defense Direction Center: III. Distribution of responses with respect to job functions.* San Antonio, Tex.: Lackland Air Force Base, June, 1955. (Res. Rep. AFPTRC-TN-55-11)

425) Cohen, J. D., & McKelvey, R. K. *The behavior of individuals and personnel systems in the surveillance functions of an Air Defense Direction Center: IV. Operational performance criteria.* San Antonio, Tex.: Lackland Air Force Base, September, 1956. (Res. Rep. AFPTRC-TN-56-117)

426) Cohen, M., & Murray, E. J. Sociometric choice patterns and degree of maladjustment. *Amer. Psychologist*, 1957, *12*, 371. (Abstract)

427) Cole, D. "Rational argument" and "prestige suggestion" as factors influencing judgement. *Sociometry*, 1954, *17*, 350–354.

*428) Coleman, J. F., et al. Task difficulty and conformity pressures. *J. abnorm. soc. Psychol.*, 1958, *57*, 120–122.

*429) Comrey, A. L. Group performance in a manual dexterity task. *J. appl. Psychol.*, 1953, *37*, 207–210.

*430) Comrey, A. L., & Deskin, G. Further results on group manual dexterity in men. *J. appl. Psychol.*, 1954, *38*, 116–118.

431) Comrey, A. L., & Deskin, G. Group manual dexterity in women. *J. appl. Psychol.*, 1954, *38*, 178–180.

432) Comrey, A. L., & Staats, C. K. Group performance in a cognitive task. *J. appl. Psychol.*, 1955, *30*, 354–356.

*433) Comrey, A. L., et al. Factors influencing organizational effectiveness: I. The U.S. forest survey. *Personnel Psychol.*, 1952, *5*, 307–328.

434) Comrey, A. L., et al. Factors influencing organizational effectiveness: II. The department of employment survey. *Personnel Psychol.*, 1953, *6*, 65–79.

435) Comrey, A. L., et al. Factors influencing organizational effectiveness: V. A survey of district rangers. *Personnel Psychol.*, 1954, *7*, 533–547.

436) Comrey, A. L., et al. *Factors influencing organizational effectiveness: a final report.* Los Angeles: University of Southern California, 1954. (Final Rep., Contract N6 ONR 23815)

437) Comrey, A. L., et al. Factored dimensions of organizational behavior: I. Field service workers. *Educ. Psychol. Measmt*, 1955, *15*, 225–235.

*438) Comrey, A. L., et al. Factors influencing organizational effectiveness: VI. A survey of aircraft workers. *Personnel Psychol.*, 1955, *8*, 79–99.

*439) Comrey, A. L., et al. Factors influencing organizational effectiveness: VII. A survey of aircraft supervisors. *Personnel Psychol.*, 1955, *8*, 245–257.

440) Conrad, Dorothy C., & Conrad, R. The use of personal pronouns as categories for studying small group interaction. *J. abnorm. soc. Psychol.*, 1956, *52*, 277–278.

441) Cooley, C. H. *Human nature and the social order.* New York: Scribner, 1902.

442) Cooley, C. H. *Social organization.* New York: Scribner, 1909.

443) Coon, C. S. The universality of natural groups in human societies. *J. educ. Sociol.*, 1946, *20*, 163–168.

444) Cooper, H. C. Perception of subgroup power and intensity of identification with a reference group. *Amer. Psychologist*, 1958, *13*, 349. (Abstract)

445) Corsini, R., & Rosenberg, Bina. Mechanisms of group psychotherapy. *J. abnorm. soc. Psychol.*, 1955, *51*, 406–411.

446) Coser, L. A. The functions of small group research. *Soc. Probl.*, 1955, *3*, 1–6.

447) Cottrell, L. S., Jr. The analysis of situational fields in social psychology. *Amer. sociol. Rev.*, 1942, 7, 370–382.

448) Cottrell, L. S., Jr., & Gallagher, Ruth. Developments in social psychology 1930–1940. *Sociometry Monogr.*, 1941, No. I.

449) Courtney, D., et al. *Leadership identification and acceptance.* Philadelphia: Institute for Research in Human Relations, February, 1952. (Annu. tech. Rep., Contract N8 ONR 69401)

*450) Courtney, D., et al. *Naval, neighborhood, and national leadership.* Philadelphia: Institute for Research in Human Relations, 1953. (Annu. tech. Rep., Contract N8 ONR 69401)

451) Courtney, D., et al. *Leadership: a review and summary with an article on sociometric choice.* Philadelphia: Institute for Research in Human Relations, 1954. [Tech. Rep., Contract Nonr-1229(00)]

452) Coyle, Grace L. *Social process in organized groups.* New York: Richard Smith, 1930.

453) Coyle, Grace L. (Ed.), *Studies in group behavior.* New York: Harper & Row, 1937.

454) Crannell, C. W., & Mollenkopf, W. G. Combat leadership. In *Psychological research on problems of redistribution.* Washington, D. C.: GPO, 1947. (AAF Aviation Psychol. Program, Rep. No. 14)

455) Creelman, J. A. The relative effectiveness of three methods of teaching landing approaches. *Amer. Psychologist*, 1956, *11*, 417. (Abstract)

456) Criswell, Joan H. Social structure revealed in a sociometric retest. *Sociometry*, 1939, *2*, 69–75.

457) Criswell, Joan H. Sociometric methods of measuring group preferences. *Sociometry*, 1943, *6*, 398–408.

458) Criswell, Joan H. Sociometric concepts in personnel administration. *Sociometry*, 1949, *12*, 287–300.

459) Criswell, Joan H. The sociometric study of leadership. In L. Petrullo and B. M. Bass (Eds.), *Leadership and interpersonal behavior.* New York: Holt, Rinehart and Winston, 1961. Pp. 10–29.

460) Criswell, Joan H., & Petrullo, L. *Bibliography of unclassified research reports in group psychology.* Washington, D. C.: Office of Naval Research, 1957. (ONR Rep. ACR-22)

461) Crockett, E. P. *Authoritarianism and leader acceptance.* Washington. D.C.: Office of Naval Research, Group Psychology Branch, 1958. [Tech. Rep. No. 5, Contract Nonr 2149(02)]

*462) Crockett, W. H. Emergent leadership in small, decision-making groups. *J. abnorm. soc. Psychol.*, 1955, *51*, 378–383.

463) Crockett, W. H., & Meidinger, T. The effects of F-scale score, similarity, and relevance of information upon accuracy of interpersonal perception. *Amer. Psychologist*, 1955, *10*, 341. (Abstract)

*464) Crockett, W. H., & Meidinger, T. Authoritarianism and interpersonal perception. *J. abnorm. soc. Psychol.*, 1956, *53*, 378–382.

465) Croft, I. J., & Grygier, T. G. Social relationships of truants and juvenile delinquents. *Hum. Relat.*, 1956, *9*, 439–465.

466) Cronbach, L. J. Processes affecting scores on "understanding of others" and "assumed similarity." *Psychol. Bull.*, 1955, *52*, 177–193.

467) Cronbach, L. J. Proposals leading to analytic treatment of social perception scores. In R. Tagiuri, and L. Petrullo (Eds.), *Person perception and interpersonal behavior*. Stanford, Calif.: Stanford University Press, 1958. Pp. 353–379.

468) Cronbach, L. J., & Fiedler, F. E. *Social perception and group effectiveness*. Urbana, Ill.: University of Illinois, February, 1953. (Annu. Status Rep., Contract N6 ORI-07135)

469) Cronbach, L. J., et al. *Investigation of the character and properties of assumed similarity measures*. Urbana, Ill.: University of Illinois, Bureau of Research and Service, 1953. (Tech. Rep. No. 7, Contract N6 ORI-07135)

*470) Crow, W. J. The effect of training upon accuracy and variability in interpersonal perception. *J. abnorm. soc. Psychol.*, 1957, *55*, 355–359.

471) Crow, W. J., & Hammand, K. R. The generality of accuracy and response sets in interpersonal perception. *J. abnorm. soc. Psychol.*, 1957, *54*, 384–390.

472) Crowell, Laura. Problems in measuring participation in discussion. *J. Communication*, 1953, *3*, 17–20.

*473) Crowell, Laura, et al. Self-concepts of communication skill and performance in small group discussions. *Speech Monogr.*, 1955, *22*, 20–27.

474) Crum, Elba. A training project for lady leaders of children's play groups. In Helen I. Driver (Ed.), *Counseling and learning through small-group discussion*. Madison, Wis.: Monona Publications, 1958. Pp. 376–379.

475) Crutchfield, R. S. Assessment of persons through a quasi group-interaction technique. *J. abnorm. soc. Psychol.*, 1951, *46*, 577–588.

476) Crutchfield, R. S. Correlates of individual behavior in a controlled group situation. *Amer. Psychologist*, 1953, *8*, 338. (Abstract)

477) Crutchfield, R. S. Social psychology and group processes. *Annu. Rev. Psychol.*, 1954, *5*, 171–202.

478) Crutchfield, R. S. Conformity and character. *Amer. Psychologist*, 1955, *10*, 191–198.

479) Cunningham, Ruth, et al. *Understanding group behavior of boys and girls*. New York: Columbia University, Teachers College, Bureau of Publications, 1951.

480) Curran, C. A. *Personality factors in counseling*. New York: Grune & Stratton, 1945.

481) Curtis, Q. F., & Gibbard, H. A. *The acquiring of membership in established groups*. Morgantown, W. Va.: West Virginia University, February, 1955. [Annu. Tech. Rep. Nonr-1365(01)]

482) Dahlke, H. O. Determinants of sociometric relations among children in the elementary school. *Sociometry*, 1953, *16*, 327–338.

483) Daniels, H. W. The development of criteria of safe operation for groups. *Amer. Psychologist*, 1953, *8*, 338. (Abstract)

*484) Danzig, E. R., & Galanter, E. H. *The dynamics and structure of small industrial work groups*. Philadelphia: Institute for Research in Human Relations, 1955. [Contract Nonr 1229(00)]

485) Darley, J. G., et al. Studies of group behavior: the stability, change, and interrelations of psychometric and sociometric variables. *J. abnorm. soc. Psychol.*, 1951, *46*, 565–576.

486) Darley, J. G., et al. Studies in group behavior: factors associated with the productivity of groups. *J. appl. Psychol.*, 1952, *36*, 396–403.

487) Dashiell, J. F. An experimental analysis of some group effects. *J. abnorm. soc. Psychol.*, 1930, *25*, 190–199.

488) Dashiell, J. F. Experimental studies of the influence of social situations on the behavior of individual human adults. In C. Murchison (Ed.), *A handbook of social psychology*. Worcester, Mass.: Clark University Press, 1935. Pp. 1097–1158.

489) Davis, A. The motivation of the underprivileged worker. In W. F. Whyte (Ed.), *Industry and society*. New York: McGraw-Hill, 1946. Pp. 84–106.

490) Davis, F. J. Conceptions of official leader roles in the Air Force. *Soc. Forces*, 1954, *32*, 253–258.

491) Davis, J. A. Correlates of sociometric status among peers. *J. educ. Res.*, 1957, *50*, 561–569.

492) Davis, J. A. A formal interpretation of the theory of relative deprivation. *Sociometry*, 1959, *22*, 280–296.

493) Davis, J. A., & Warnath, C. F. Reliability, validity, and stability of a sociometric rating scale. *J. soc. Psychol.*, 1957, *45*, 111–121.

494) Davis, R. Group factors related to scientific performance. Paper read at Amer. sociol. Soc., Urbana, Ill., 1954.

495) Davis, R. L. Structures of dominance relations. *Bull. math. Biophysics*, 1954, *16*, 131–140.

*496) Davitz, J. Social perception and sociometric choice of children. *J. abnorm. soc. Psychol.*, 1955, *50*, 173–176.

497) Davitz, J., et al. The evaluation of group versus individual decisions. *Amer. Psychologist*, 1952, *7*, 313. (Abstract)

498) Davol, S. H. The effect of personality upon extreme mutual choice and rejection in domiciliary living groups. *Amer. Psychologist*, 1958, *13*, 329. (Abstract)

499) Davol, S. H. An empirical test of structural balance in sociometric triads. *J. abnorm. soc. Psychol.*, 1959, *59*, 393–398.

500) Dawe, Helen C. The influence of the size of kindergarten group upon performance. *Child Develpm.*, 1934, *5*, 295–303.

501) Dean, J. P., & Rosen, A. *A manual of intergroup relations*. Chicago: University of Chicago Press, 1955.

502) deCharms, R. *Social conformity and achievement motivation*. Chapel Hill, N.C.: University of North Carolina, 1956. (Contract No. NR 170–046)

503) deCharms, R. Affiliation motivation and productivity in small groups. *J. abnorm. soc. Psychol.*, 1957, *55*, 222–226.

504) deCharms, R., & Rosenbaum, M. E. The effects of verbal expression of hostility. Paper prepared at Air Force Office of Scientific Res. Behav. Sci. Conf., Albuquerque, N. M., 1958. (Contract AF 49(638)-33)

505) deCharms, R., & Rosenbaum, M. E. Report of the project investigating vicarious satisfaction. Paper prepared at Air Force Office of Scientific

Res. Behav. Sci. Conf., Albuquerque, N. M., 1958. [Contract AF 49(638)33]

506) DeFleur, M. L. The emergence and functioning of opinion leadership: some conditions of informal influence transmission. Paper prepared at Air Force Office Scientific Res. Beh. Sci. Conf., Albuquerque, N. M., 1958. [Contract AF 49(638)-33]

507) De Gaugh, R. A. The relationship between attitudes and combat performance of B-29 crews in the Far East. *Amer. Psychologist*, 1953, *8*, 340. (Abstract)

508) De Gaugh, R. A., & Knoell, Dorothy M. *Attitudes relevant to bomber crew performance in combat.* San Antonio, Tex.: Lackland Air Force Base, Air Force Personnel and Training Research Center, 1954. (Res. Bull., AFPTRC-TR-54-18)

509) DeGre, G. Outlines for a systematic classification of social groups. *Amer. sociol. Rev.*, 1949, *14*, 145–148.

510) De Monchaux, Cecily, & Shimmin, Sylvia. Some problems in experimental group psychology: considerations arising from crosscultural experiments on threat and rejection. *Hum. Relat.*, 1955, *8*, 53–60.

511) De Montmollin, Germaine. Group effects on perceptive structuration. *Année psychol.*, 1957, *57*, 51–72.

*512) Deutsch, M. An experimental study of the effects of cooperation and competition upon group process. *Hum. Relat.*, 1949, *2*, 199–231.

513) Deutsch, M. A theory of cooperation and competition. *Hum. Relat.*, 1949, *2*, 129–152.

514) Deutsch, M. The effects of past experience of success or failure, the perceived attitudes of other members, and the probability of goal attainment and group performance. *Amer. Psychologist*, 1954, *9*, 355. (Abstract)

515) Deutsch, M. Field theory in social psychology. In G. Lindzey (Ed.), *Handbook of social psychology.* Reading, Mass.: Addison-Wesley, 1954. Pp. 181–222.

516) Deutsch, M. Experimental studies of trust and suspicion. The effect of motivational orientation. *Amer. Psychologist*, 1955, *10*, 377. (Abstract)

517) Deutsch, M. Trust and suspicion. *Conflict Resolution*, 1958, *2*(4), 265–279.

518) Deutsch, M. Some factors affecting membership motivation and achievement motivation in a group. *Hum. Relat.*, 1959, *12*, 81–95.

519) Deutsch, M., & Gerard, H. B. A study of normative and informational social influences upon individual judgement. *J. abnorm. soc. Psychol.*, 1955, *51*, 629–636.

520) Deutsch, M., & Solomon, L. Reactions to evaluations by others as influenced by self-evaluations. *Sociometry*, 1959, *22*, 93–112.

521) Deutsch, M., et al. Leadership in the small group. *J. soc. Issues*, 1948, *4*(2), 31–40.

522) Deutschberger, P. The tele-factor: horizon and awareness. *Sociometry*, 1947, *10*, 242–249.

523) Deutscher, Verda, & Deutscher, I. Cohesion in a small group: a case study. *Soc. Forces*, 1955, *33*, 336–341.

524) Dickens, M. A statistical formula to quantify the "spread of participation" in group discussion. *Speech Monogr.*, 1955, *22*, 28–30.

525) DiMascio, A., et al. Physiological correlates of tension and antagonism during psychotherapy: a study of interpersonal physiology. *Psychosom. Med.*, 1957, *19*(2), 99–104.

*526) Dittes, F. E., & Kelley, H. H. Effects of different conditions of acceptance upon conformity to group norms. *J. abnorm. soc. Psychol.*, 1956, *53*, 100–107.

527) Dittes, J. E. Attractiveness of group as function of self-esteem and acceptance by group. *J. abnorm. soc. Psychol.*, 1959, *59*, 77–82.

528) Dittman, A. T. The interpersonal process in psychotherapy: development of a research method. *J. abnorm. soc. Psychol.*, 1952, *47*, 236–244.

529) Di Vesta, F. J. Instructor-centered and student-centered approaches in teaching a human relations course. *J. appl. Psychol.*, 1954, *38*, 329–335.

530) Di Vesta, F. J. *Studies in conformity behavior.* Syracuse, N. Y.: Syracuse University, February, 1957. (Rep. No. AFOSR TN-57-138, ASTIA Document No. 120 495)

531) Di Vesta, F. J. *Susceptibility to pressures toward uniformity of behavior in social situations: a study of task, motivational and personal factors in conformity behavior.* Syracuse, N.Y.: Syracuse University, June, 1958. [Contract No. AF 18(603)-20]

532) Di Vesta, F. J. Effects of confidence and motivation on susceptibility to informational social influence. *J. abnorm. soc. Psychol.*, 1959, *59*, 204–209.

533) Di Vesta, F. J., & Blake, Kathryn. The effects of instructional "sets" on learning and transfer. *Amer. J. Psychol.*, 1959, *72*, 57–67.

534) Di Vesta, F. J., & Merwin, J. C. *The effect of need-oriented communications on attitude structure and change.* Syracuse, N.Y.: Syracuse University, June, 1958. [WADC tech. Rep. No. 58–93, Contract AF 41(657)-73]

535) Di Vesta, F. J., et al. Rating conference participation in a human relations training program. *J. appl. Psychol.*, 1951, *35*, 386–391.

536) Dodd, S. C. A social distance test in the Near East. *Amer. J. Sociol.*, 1935, *41*, 194–204.

537) Dodd, S. C. The transact model. *Sociometry*, 1955, *18*, 688–703.

538) Dodd, S. C., & Garabedian, P. G. *The logistic law in interaction in different sized cliques.* Seattle: University of Washington, Washington Public Opinion Laboratory, May, 1957.

539) Dodd, S. C., & Garabedian, P. G. *The logistic law of interaction when people pair off "at will."* Seattle: University of Washington, Washington Public Opinion Laboratory, May, 1957.

540) Douglas, Ann G. *The mediation of labor-management disputes.* Buffalo, N.Y.: University of Buffalo, 1954. (Contract No. NR 170–012)

541) Douglas, Ann G. The peaceful settlement of industrial and intergroup disputes. *Conflict Resolution*, 1957, *1*, 69–81.

*542) Downing, J. Cohesiveness, perception, and values. *Hum. Relat.*, 1958, *11*, 157–166.

543) Driver, Helen I. (Ed.) *Counseling and learning through small group discussion.* Madison, Wis.: Monona Publications, 1958.

544) Driver, Helen I. Organizing a large meeting for individual participation. In Helen I. Driver (Ed.), *Counseling and learning through small group discussion*. Madison, Wis.: Monona Publications, 1958. Pp. 387–390.

545) Driver, Helen I. The T-group: a learning laboratory for leadership skills. In Helen I. Driver (Ed.), *Counseling and learning through small group discussion*. Madison, Wis.: Monona Publications, 1958. Pp. 342–345.

546) Dugan, R. D. Comparison of evaluation of B-29 crews in training and in combat. *Amer. Psychologist*, 1953, *8*, 343. (Abstract)

547) Dunkerly, M. D. A statistical study of leadership among college women. *Stud. in Psychol. Psychiat.*, 1940, *4*, 1–65.

548) Dunn, T. F., et al. The application of measurement techniques to the evaluation of military group effectiveness. *Amer. Psychologist*, 1952, *7*, 390. (Abstract)

549) Dupuis, A. M. Group dynamics: philosophical presuppositions. *J. soc. Psychol.*, 1959, *50*, 247–260.

550) Durkheim, E. *Division of labor*. New York: Free Press, 1947.

551) Dwyer, P. S. *Development of generalized mathematical procedures for optimal assembly of potentially effective crews*. San Antonio, Tex.: Lackland Air Force Base, Air Force Personnel and Training Research Center, December, 1956. (Res. Rep. AFPTRC-TN-56-139)

552) Dwyer, P. S. *Mathematical procedures and multiple criteria for assembly of large work groups*. San Antonio, Tex.: Lackland Air Force Base, 1957. [Project No. 7713, Contract No. AF 41(657)-9]

553) Eber, H. W. Problem solving by small groups under varying conditions of personality and organization. *Amer. Psychologist*, 1952, *7*, 306. (Abstract)

554) Edwards, A. L. Experiments: their planning and execution. In G. Lindzey (Ed.), *Handbook of social psychology*. Reading, Mass.: Addison-Wesley, 1954. Pp. 259–288.

555) Eisman, Bernice. Some operational measures of cohesiveness and their interrelations. *Hum. Relat.*, 1959, *12*, 183–189.

556) Eister, A. W. Basic continuities in the study of small groups. In H. Becker and A. Boskoff (Eds.), *Modern sociological theory*. New York: Holt, Rinehart and Winston, 1957. Pp. 305–339.

557) Ekman, Gosta. The four effects of cooperation. *J. soc. Psychol.*, 1955, *41*, 149–162.

558) Elkes, Regina. Group casework experiment with mothers of children with cerebral palsy. *J. soc. Casewk*, 1947, *28*, 95–101.

559) Elliott, H. S. *The process of group thinking*. New York: Association Press, 1928.

560) Ellis, A. Questionnaire vs. interview methods in the study of human love relationships. *Amer. sociol. Rev.*, 1947, *12*, 541–553.

561) Emerson, R. M. Deviation and rejection: an experimental replication. *Amer. sociol. Rev.*, 1954., *19*, 688–693.

562) Eng, E. W. An approach to the prediction of sociometric choice. *Sociometry*, 1954, *17*, 329–339.

563) Epstein, H. L., & Slavin, S. Common elements in group influence attempts. *J. soc. Issues*, 1952, *8*(2), 45–53.

564) Ericksen, C. W., et al. Research on interpersonal communication processes. Paper prepared at Air Force Office of Scientific Res. Behav. Sci. Conf., Albuquerque, N.M., 1957. [Contract AF 49(638)-33]

565) Ex, J. The nature of contact between cooperating partners and their expectation concerning the level of their common achievement. *Acta psychol.*, 1959, *16*, 99–107.

*566) Exline, R. V. Group climate as a factor in the relevance and accuracy of social perception. *J. abnorm. soc. Psychol.*, 1957, *55*, 382–388.

567) Exline, R. V., & Ziller, R. C. Status congruency and interpersonal conflict in decision-making groups. *Hum. Relat.*, 1959, *12*, 147–162.

568) Faget, R. *A model of riskless choice.* Stanford, Calif.: Stanford University, 1956. (Contract No. NR 171-034)

569) Faris, R. E. L. Development of small-group research movement. In M. Sherif and M. O. Wilson (Eds.), *Group relations at the crossroads.* New York: Harper & Row, 1953, Pp. 155–184.

570) Farmer, R. A. A group discussion approach in freshman orientation. In Helen I. Driver (Ed.), *Counseling and learning through small group discussion.* Madison, Wis.: Monona Publications, 1958 Pp. 321–325.

571) Farnsworth, P. R. Concerning so-called group effects. *J. genet. Psychol.*, 1928, *35*, 587–594.

572) Farnsworth, P. R., & Behner, Alice. A note on the attitude of social conformity. *J. soc. Psychol.*, 1931, *2*, 126–128.

573) Farnsworth, P. R., & Williams, M. F. The accuracy of the median and mean of a group of judgments. *J. soc. Psychol.*, 1936, *7*, 237–239.

574) Farr, J. N. *Some effects of the presence of a disliked third person on two-party trust.* New York: New York University, 1957. (Contract No. NR 170-130)

575) Faunce, D., & Beegle, J. A. Cleavages in a relatively homogeneous group of rural youth: an experiment in the use of sociometry in attaining and measuring integration. *Sociometry*, 1948, *11*, 207–216.

*576) Faust, W. L. Group versus individual problem-solving. *J. abnorm. soc. Psychol.*, 1959, *59*, 68–72.

577) Feather, N. T. Success probability and choice behavior. *J. exp. Psychol.*, 1959, *58*, 257–266.

578) Feldman, M. J., & Bierman, R. The effect of reward on conforming and independent behavior. *Amer. Psychologist*, 1959, *14*, 334. (Abstract)

579) Feldman, M. J., & Goldfried, M. Independence and conformity as a function of the validity of group judgment. *Amer. Psychologist*, 1958, *13*, 355. (Abstract)

580) Fessenden, S. A. An index of cohesiveness-morale based on the analysis of sociometric choice distribution. *Sociometry*, 1953, *16*, 321–326.

581) Festinger, L. Wish, expectation, and group standards as factors influencing level of aspiration. *J. abnorm. soc. Psychol.*, 1942, *37*, 184–200.

582) Festinger, L. The role of group belongingness in a voting situation. *Hum. Relat.*, 1947, *1*, 154–180.

583) Festinger, L. The analysis of sociograms using matrix algebra. *Hum. Relat.*, 1949, *2*, 153–158.

584) Festinger, L. Informal social communication. *Psychol. Rev.*, 1950, *57*, 271–292.

585) Festinger, L. Laboratory experiments: the role of group belongingness. In J. G. Miller (Ed.), *Experiments in social process.* New York: McGraw-Hill, 1950. Pp. 31–46.

586) Festinger, L. Architecture and group membership. *J. soc. Issues*, 1951, *7*(2), 152–163.

587) Festinger, L. Informal communications in small groups. In H. Guetzkow (Ed.), *Groups, leadership and men: research in human relations.* Pittsburgh, Pa Carnegie Press, 1951. Pp. 28–43.

588) Festinger, L. An analysis of compliant behavior. In M. Sherif and M. O. Wilson (Eds.), *Group relations at the crossroads.* New York: Harper & Row, 1953. Pp. 232–256.

589) Festinger, L. Group attraction and membership. In D. Cartwright and A. F. Zander (Eds.), *Group dynamics: research and theory.* New York: Harper & Row, 1953 Pp 92–101

590) Festinger, L. Laboratory experiments. In L. Festinger and D. Katz (Eds.), *Research methods in the behavioral sciences.* New York: Holt, Rinehart and Winston, 1953. Pp. 136–172.

591) Festinger, L. Theory of social comparison processes. *Hum. Relat.*, 1954 *7*, 117–140.

592) Festinger, L. Social psychology and group processes. *Annu. Rev. Psychol.*, 1955, *6*, 187–216.

*593) Festinger, L., & Hutte, H. A. An experimental investigation of the effect of unstable interpersonal relations in a group. *J. abnorm. soc. Psychol.*, 1954, *49*, 513–522.

594) Festinger, L., & Katz, D. (Eds) *Research methods in the behavioral sciences.* New York: Holt, Rinehart and Winston, 1953.

595) Festinger, L., & Thibaut, J. Interpersonal communication in small groups. *J. abnorm. soc. Psychol.*, 1951, *46*, 92–99.

596) Festinger, L., et al. A study of rumor: its origin and spread. *Hum. Relat.*, 1948, *1*, 464–486.

597) Festinger, L., et al. *Social pressures in informal groups: a study of human factors in housing.* New York: Harper & Row, 1950.

598) Festinger, L., et al. *Theory and experiment in social communication.* Ann Arbor, Mich.: Edwards Bros., 1950.

599) Festinger, L., et al. The influence process in the presence of extreme deviates. *Hum. Relat.*, 1952, *5*, 327–346.

600) Festinger, L., et al. Some consequences of de-individuation in a group. *J. abnorm. soc. Psychol.*, 1952, *47*, 382–389.

601) Festinger, L., et al. Self-evaluation as a function of attraction to the group. *Hum. Relat.*, 1954, *7*, 161–174.

602) Festinger, L., et al. *Basic studies on individual and group behavior.* Minneapolis: University of Minnesota, February, 1955. (Annu. tech. Rep., Contract N8 ONR 66216)

603) Festinger, L., et al. *When prophecy fails.* Minneapolis, University of Minnesota Press, 1956.

604) Fiedler, F. E. *Assumed similarity measures as predictors of team effectiveness*

in surveying. Urbana, Ill.: University of Illinois, 1953. (Tech. Rep. 1–20, Contract N6 ORI 07135)

605) Fiedler, F. E. Psychological-distance dimension in interpersonal relations. *J. Pers.*, 1953, *22*, 146–150.

*606) Fiedler, F. E. Assumed similarity measures as predictors of team effectiveness. *J. abnorm soc. Psychol.*, 1954, *49*, 381–388.

607) Fiedler, F. E. *Social perception and group effectiveness.* Urbana, Ill.: University of Illinois, February, 1954. (Annu. Status Rep., Contract N6 ORI 07135)

*608) Fiedler, F. E. The influence of leader-keyman relations on combat crew effectiveness. *J. abnorm. soc. Psychol.*, 1955, *51*, 227–235.

609) Fiedler, F. E. A note on leadership theory: the effect of social barriers between leaders and followers. *Sociometry*, 1957, *20*, 87–94.

610) Fiedler, F. E. Interpersonal perception and group effectiveness. In R. Tagiuri and L. Petrullo (Eds.), *Person perception and interpersonal behavior.* Stanford, Calif.: Stanford University Press, 1958. Pp. 243–257.

611) Fiedler, F. E. *Leader attitudes and group effectiveness.* Urbana, Ill.: University of Illinois Press, 1958.

612) Fiedler, F. E. *The effect of informal organizational structure on the leader's influence.* Amsterdam, Netherlands: University of Amsterdam, undated. (Contract NR 170–106, N6 ORI 07135)

613) Fiedler, F. E., & Bass, A. R. *Delinquency, confinement and interpersonal perception.* Urbana, Ill.: University of Illinois, Department of Psychology, Group Effectiveness Research Laboratory, December, 1959. (Tech. Rep. No. 6)

614) Fiedler, F. E., & Jones, R. E. Quasi-therapeutic and maladjustive interpersonal attitudes among members of small face-to-face groups. *Amer. Psychologist*, 1955, *10*, 345–346. (Abstract)

615) Fiedler, F. E., et al. Unconscious attitudes as correlates of sociometric choice in social group. *J. abnorm. soc. Psychol.*, 1952, *47*, 790–796.

616) Fiedler, F. E., et al. *The relationship of interpersonal perception to effectiveness in basketball teams.* Urbana, Ill.: University of Illinois, College of Education, Bureau of Research and Service, February, 1953. (Tech. Rep. No. 3, Contract N6 ORI 07135)

617) Fiedler, F. E., et al. *The measurement of personality adjustment and personality change in non-clinical populations.* Urbana, Ill.: University of Illinois, May, 1957. (Interim tech. Rep. No. 5, Contract DA 49 007 MD 569)

618) Fiedler, F. E., et al. Quasi-therapeutic relations in small college and military groups. *Psychol. Monogr.*, 1959, *73*, No. 473.

619) Findley, W. G. A statistical index of participation in discussion. *J. educ. Psychol.*, 1948, *39*, 47–51.

620) Fischer, P. H. An analysis of the primary group. *Sociometry*, 1953, *16*, 272–276.

*621) Fisher, S., & Lubin, A. Distance as a determinant of influence in a two-person social interaction situation. *J. abnorm. soc. Psychol.*, 1958, *56*, 230–238.

622) Fisher, S., et al. Intertrial effects of immediate self-commital in a continuous social influence situation. *J. abnorm. soc. Psychol.*, 1956, *52*,
200–207.

623) Flanagan, J. C. *Leadership skills: their identification, development and
evaluation.* Pittsburgh, Pa.: American Institute for Research, 1959.

624) Flanders, N. A. Personal-social anxiety as a factor in experimental learning
situations. *J. educ. Res.*, 1951, *45*, 100–110.

625) Fleishman, E. A. Leadership climate and supervisory behavior: a study
of the leadership role of the foreman in an industrial situation.
Personnel Res. Bd Monogr., Ohio State University, Columbus, 1951.

626) Fleishman, E. A. The leadership role of the foreman in industry. *Engng.
exp. Sta. News*, 1952, *24*, 27–35.

627) Fleishman, E. A. The measurement of leadership attitudes in industry.
J. appl. Psychol., 1953, *37*(3), 153–158.

628) Flint, A. W., & Bass, B. M. *Comparison of the construct validities of three
objective measures of successful leadership.* Baton Rouge, La.: Louisiana
State University, 1958. (Tech. Rep. 17, Contract N7 ONR 35609)

629) Flint, A. W., et al. *Esteem and successful leadership.* Baton Rouge, La.:
Louisiana State University, 1957. (Tech. Rep. No. 11, Contract N7
ONR 35609)

630) Flint, A. W., et al. *Esteem, status, motivation, and attraction to the group.*
Baton Rouge, La.: Louisiana State University, 1957. (Tech. Rep.
No. 9, Contract N7 ONR 35609)

631) Florence, E. deC. *Motivational factors in individual and group productivity:
II. Validation and standardization of the student behavior description.*
Columbus, Ohio: Ohio State University Research Foundation, 1956.

632) Foa, U. G. The foreman-worker interaction: a research design. *Sociometry*,
1955, *18*, 226–244.

633) Foa, U. G. Relation of workers' expectation to satisfaction with supervisor.
Personnel Psychol., 1957, *10*, 161–168.

634) Foa, U. G. Behavior, norms, and social rewards in a dyad. *Behav. Sci.*,
1958, *3*, 323.

635) Foa, U. G. The contiguity principle in the structure of interpersonal
relations. *Hum. Relat.*, 1958, *11*, 229.

636) Foa, U. G. Empathy or behavioral transparency? *J. abnorm. soc. Psychol.*,
1958, *51*, 62–64.

637) Foa, U.G., & Zacks, S. *A stochastic facet theory of social interaction in the
dyad.* Jerusalem, Israel: Israel Institute of Applied Social Research,
April, 1959. [Tech. Note No.1, Contract AF 61(052)-121]

638) Fogleman, C. W., & Parenton, V. J. Disaster and aftermath: selected aspects of individual and group behavior in critical situations. *Soc. Forces*, 1959, *38*, 129–135.

639) Ford, C. S. *A pilot study in the systematic organization of empirical data
on interpersonal phenomena.* New Haven, Conn.: Yale University,
Human Relations Area Files, Inc., 1953. (Final Project Rep., Contract
NR-176-Op7)

640) Forgays, D. G. *Prediction of bomber crew performance in combat from
measures of performance in training.* San Antonio, Tex.: Lackland Air

Force Base, Air Force Personnel and Training Research Center, Undated Res. Rep.

641) Forgays, D. G., & Clogston, J. I. *Criteria of B-29 crew performance in Far Eastern combat: III.* San Antonio, Tex.: Lackland Air Force Base, Air Force Personnel and Training Research Center, 1953. (Res. Rep.)

*642) Forgays, D. G., & Irwin, I. A. *Measures of combat crew performance used in B-29 training.* San Antonio, Tex.: Lackland Air Force Base, Human Resources Research Center, December, 1952. (Tech. Rep. 52–14)

643) Forgays, D. G., & Levy, B. I. *Combat performances characteristics associated with changes in the membership of medium bomber crews.* San Antonio, Tex.: Lackland Air Force Base, Air Force Personnel and Training Research Center, Undated Res. Rep.

644) Forgays, D. G., & Roby, T. B. Group effectiveness in bomber crews: analysis of in-flight communications in the study of coordination. *Amer. Psychologist,* 1953, *8,* 351. (Abstract)

645) Forgays, D. G., & Roby, T. B. *A problem-solving model for analysis of communication in B-29 crews.* San Antonio, Tex.: Lackland Air Force Base, Human Resources Research Center, August, 1953. (Res. Bull. 53–30)

646) Forsyth, Elaine, & Katz, L. A matrix approach to the analysis of socio-metric data: preliminary report. *Sociometry,* 1946, *9,* 340–347.

647) Foulkes, R. G Resolving the resistance of intellectualization in seminary students. In Helen I. Driver (Ed.), *Counseling and learning through small group discussion.* Madison, Wis.: Monona Publications, 1958. Pp. 350–352.

648) Foulkes, S. H. Group therapy: a short survey and orientation with particular reference to group analysis. *Brit. J. Med. Psychol.,* 1950, *25,* 199–205.

649) Fouriezos, N. T., et al. Measurement of self-oriented needs in discussion groups. *J. abnorm. soc. Psychol.,* 1950, *45,* 682–690.

650) Fox, D. J., & Lorge, I. The effect of increasing the available time for problem solving on the relative quality of decisions written by individuals and by groups. *Amer. Psychologist,* 1957, *12,* 382–383. (Abstract)

651) Fox, D., et al. Comparison of decisions written by large and small groups. *Amer. Psychologist,* 1953, *8,* 351. (Abstract)

652) Fox, H. G., et al. *Selected annotated bibliography on leadership and executive development.* San Antonio, Tex.: Lackland Air Force Base, Air Force Personnel and Training Research Center, December, 1955. (Res. Rep. AFPTRC-TN-55-67)

653) Fox, J. B., & Scott, J. F. *Absenteeism: management's problem.* Boston: Harvard University, Graduate School of Business Administration, 1943.

654) Fox, W. F. Group reaction to two types of conference leadership. *Hum. Relat.,* 1957, *10,* 279–289.

655) Frank, J. D. Experimental studies of personal pressure and resistance: I. Experimental production of resistance. *J. gen. Psychol.,* 1944, *30,* 23–64.

656) Frank, J. D., et al. Two behavior patterns in therapeutic groups and their apparent motivation. *Hum. Relat.*, 1952, *5*, 289–317.

657) Freedman, M. A mental health association lay discussion program. In Helen I. Driver (Ed.), *Counseling and learning through small-group discussion.* Madison, Wis.: Monona Publications, 1958. Pp. 384–387.

658) Freedman, M. B., et al. The interpersonal dimension of personality. *J. Pers.*, 1951, *20*, 143–161.

659) French, Elizabeth G. Effects of the interaction of feedback and motivation on task performance. *Amer. Psychologist*, 1956, *11*, 395. (Abstract)

*660) French, Elizabeth G. Motivation as a variable in work-partner selection. *J. abnorm. soc. Psychol.*, 1956, *53*, 96–99.

661) French, Elizabeth G., & Chadwick, Irene. *Some characteristics of affiliation motivation.* San Antonio, Tex.: Lackland Air Force Base, November, 1956. (Res. Rep. AFPTRC-TN-56-126)

662) French, J. R. P., Jr. The disruption and cohesion of groups. *J. abnorm. soc. Psychol.*, 1941, *36*, 361–377.

*663) French, J. R. P. Jr. Organized and unorganized groups under fear and frustration. *Univer. of Iowa Stud. Child Welf.*, 1944, *20*, No. 409, 231–308.

664) French, J. R. P., Jr. The dynamics of the discussion group. *J. soc. Issues*, 1948, *4*(2), 8–9.

665) French, J. R. P., Jr. Field experiments: changing group productivity. In J. G. Miller (Ed.), *Experiments in social process:* New York: McGraw-Hill, 1950. Pp. 79–96.

666) French, J. R. P., Jr. Group productivity. In H. Guetzkow (Ed.), *Groups, leadership and men: research in human relations.* Pittsburgh, Pa.: Carnegie Press, 1951. Pp. 44–45.

667) French, J. R. P., Jr. Experiments in field settings. In L. Festinger and D. Katz (Eds.), *Research methods in the behavioral sciences.* New York: Holt, Rinehart and Winston, 1953. Pp. 98–135.

668) French, J. R. P., Jr. A formal theory of social power. *Psychol. Rev.*, 1956, *63*, 181–194.

669) French, J. R. P., Jr., & Raven, B. H. Legitimate power, coercive power, and observability in social influence. *Sociometry*, 1958, *21*, 83–97.

670) French, J. R. P., Jr., & Zajonc, R. B. An experimental study of cross-cultural norm conflict. *J. abnorm. soc. Psychol.*, 1957, *54*, 218–224.

671) French, J. R. P., Jr., & Zander, A. The group dynamics approach. In A. Kornhauser (Ed.), *Psychology of labor-management relations.* New York: Amer. Book, 1949. Pp. 71–80.

672) French, J. R. P., Jr., et al. Conflict and cooperation in industry. *J. soc. Issues*, 1946, *2*, 2–55.

673) French, R. L. Morale and leadership. In Panel on Psychology and Physiology (Eds.), *Human factors in undersea warfare.* Washington, D.C.: National Academy of Sciences–National Research Council, 1949.

674) French, R. L. Verbal output and leadership status in initially leaderless discussion groups. *Amer. Psychologist*, 1950, *5*, 310–311. (Abstract)

675) French, R. L. Sociometric status and individual adjustment among naval recruits. *J. abnorm. soc. Psychol.*, 1951, *46*, 64–72.

676) French, R. L. Social psychology and group processes. *Annu. Rev. Psychol.*, 1955, 7, 63–94.

677) French, R. L., & Mensh, I. N. Some relationships between interpersonal judgments and sociometric status in a college group. *Sociometry*, 1948, *11*, 335–345.

*678) French, R. L., et al. *Measures of attitude and performance during early training as predictors of B-29 crew performance in Korean combat.* San Antonio, Texas: Lackland Air Force Base, Crew Research Laboratory, March, 1956. (Lab. Note CRL-LN-56-4)

679) Frue, R. L., & Adams, H. E. Effect of the volunteer variable on leaderless group discussion experiments. *Psychol. Rep.*, 1959, 5, 184.

680) Fulton, Ruth E. Relationship between teammate status and measures of skill in volleyball. *Res. Quart. Amer. Ass. Hlth*, 1950, *21*, 274–275.

681) Furfey, P. H. Some factors influencing the selection of boys' chums. *J. appl. Psychol.*, 1927, *11*, 47–51.

682) Gage, N. L., & Cronbach, L. Conceptual and methodological problems in interpersonal perception. *Psychol. Rev.*, 1955, *62*, 411–422.

683) Gage, N. L., & Exline, R. L. Social perception and effectiveness in discussion groups. *Hum. Relat.*, 1953, 6, 381–396.

684) Gage, N. L., et al. Teachers' understanding of their pupils and pupils' ratings of their teachers. *Psychol. Monogr.*, 1955, 69, No. 21 (Whole No. 206).

685) Gage, N. L., et al. The intermediary key in the analysis of interpersonal perception. *Psychol. Bull.*, 1956, *53*, 258–266.

686) Gaier, E. L., & Bass, B. M. *Effects of city familiarity on size estimation.* Baton Rouge, La.: Louisiana State University, 1955. (Tech. Note No. 1, Contract N7 ONR 35609)

687) Gardner, E. F., & Thompson, G. G. *Social relations and morale in small groups.* New York: Appleton, 1956.

688) Gardner, G. Functional leadership and popularity in small groups. *Hum. Relat.*, 1956, 9, 491–509.

689) Gates, Georgina S. The effect of an audience upon performance. *J. abnorm. soc. Psychol.*, 1924, *18*, 334–342.

690) Gebel, A. S. Self-perception and leaderless group discussion status. *J. soc. Psychol.*, 1954, *40*, 309–318.

691) Gekoski, N. Predicting group productivity. *Personnel Psychol.*, 1952, 5, 281–292.

692) General Assembly's Training School. Informal discussion groups for graduate students in Christian education. In Helen I. Driver (Ed.), *Counseling and learning through small group discussion.* Madison, Wis.: Monona Publications, 1958. Pp. 358–360.

*693) Gerard, H. B. The effect of different dimensions of disagreement on the communication process in small groups. *Hum. Relat.*, 1953, 6, 249–271.

694) Gerard, H. B. The anchorage of opinions in face-to-face groups. *Hum. Relat.*, 1954, 7, 313–326.

*695) Gerard, H. B. Some factors affecting an individual's estimate of his probable success in a group situation *J. abnorm. soc. Psychol.*, 1956, *52*, 235–239.

696) Gerard, H. B. Some effects of status, role clarity, and group goal clarity upon the individual's relations to group process. *J. Pers.*, 1957, *25*, 475–488.

*697) Gerard, H. B. Some effects of involvement upon evaluation. *J. abnorm. soc. Psychol.*, 1958, *57*, 118–120.

*698) Ghiselli, E. E., & Lodahl, T. M. Patterns of managerial traits and group effectiveness. *J. abnorm. soc. Psychol.*, 1958, *57*, 61–66.

699) Gibb, C. A. The principles and traits of leadership. *J. abnorm. soc. Psychol.*, 1947, *42*, 267–284.

700) Gibb, C. A. The research background of an interactional theory of leadership. *Aust. J. Psychol.*, 1950, *1*, 19–41.

701) Gibb, C. A. The sociometry of leadership in temporary groups. *Sociometry*, 1950, *13*, 226–243.

702) Gibb, C. A. An experimental approach to the study of leadership. *Occup. Psychol.*, 1951, *25*, 233–248.

703) Gibb, C. A. Leadership. In G. Lindzey (Ed.), *Handbook of social psychology*. Reading, Mass.: Addison-Wesley, 1954. Pp. 877–920.

704) Gibb, J. R. The effects of group size and of threat reduction upon creativity in a problem-solving situation. *Amer. Psychologist*, 1951, *6*, 324. (Abstract)

705) Gibb, J. R. *Factors producing defensive behavior within groups*. Boulder, Colo.: Office of Naval Research, February, 1954. [Quart. Status Rep. Contract Nonr 1147(03), NR 170 226]

706) Gibb, J. R. *Factors producing defensive behavior within groups*. Boulder, Colo.: University of Colorado, February, 1955. [Contract Nonr-1147 (03) NR 170-226]

707) Gibb, J. R. *Factors producing defensive behavior within groups* Boulder, Colo.: University of Colorado, November, 1955. [Contract Nonr-1147 (03) NR 170-226]

708) Gibb, J. R. Socio-psychological process of the instructional group. In G. E. Jensen et al. (Eds.), *The dynamics of instructional groups*. Yearb. Nat. Soc. Stud. Educ., 1959.

709) Gibb, J. R. Defense level and influence potential in small groups. In L. Petrullo and B. M. Bass (Eds.), *Leadership and interpersonal behavior*. New York: Holt, Rinehart and Winston, 1961. Pp. 66–81.

710) Gibb, J. R. *A norm-centered framework for research on change induction*. Newark, Del.: University of Delaware, Fels Group Dynamic Center, undated.

711) Gibb, J. R., & Gorman, A. W. Effects of induced polarization in small groups upon accuracy of perception. *Amer. Psychologist*, 1954, *9*. (Abstract)

712) Gibb, J. R., & Platts, G. *The effects of special training and of knowledge of results upon self-insight*. Boulder, Colo.: University of Colorado, September, 1950.

713) Gibb, J. R., et al. *Dynamics of participative groups*. Washington, D. C.: National Education Association, 1951.

714) Gibb, J. R., et al. Effects of positive and negative feedback upon defensive behavior in small problem-solving groups. *Amer. Psychologist*, 1955, *10*, 335. (Abstract)

*715) Gibb, Lorraine M., & Gibb, J. R. *Effects of the use of "participative action" groups in a course in general psychology*. Boulder, Colo.: University of Colorado, September, 1952.

716) Gilchrist, J. C. The formation of social groups under conditions of success and failure *J. abnorm. soc. Psychol.*, 1952, *47*, 174–187.

717) Gilchrist, J. C., et al. Some effects of unequal distribution of information in a wheel group structure. *J. abnorm. soc. Psychol.*, 1954, *49*, 544–556.

718) Gillespie, J. J. Free discussion groups in work. *Hlth. Educ. J.*, 1953, *11*, 139–150.

719) Glanzer, M., & Glaser, R. *A review of team training problems*. Pittsburgh, Pa.: American Institute for Research, September, 1955. (Tech. Rep., Contract N7 ONR 37008, NR 154-079)

720) Glanzer, M., & Glaser, R. *Performance characteristics of three types of Navy teams*. Pittsburgh, Pa.: American Institute for Research, May, 1957. (Tech. Rep. No. AIR-26-57-FR-152, Contract N7 ONR 37008)

721) Glanzer, M., & Glaser, R. *Techniques for the study of team structure and behavior. Part II: empirical studies of the effects of structure*. Pittsburgh, Pa.: American Institute for Research, 1957. (ONR Tech. Rep. No. AIR-26-57-FR-154)

722) Glanzer, M., & Glaser, R. Techniques for the study of group structure and behavior: I. Analysis of structure. *Psychol. Bull.*, 1959, *56*, 317–332.

723) Glanzer, M., et al. *The team performance record: an aid for team analysis and team training*, Pittsburgh, Pa.: American Institute for Research, December, 1956. (Contract N7 ONR-37008, NR-154-079)

724) Glaser, R. *Descriptive variables for the study of task-oriented groups*. Pittsburgh, Pa.: American Institute for Research, June, 1956. [Contract N7 ONR-37008, NR-154-079)

725) Glaser, R., & Glanzer, M. *Team behavior—studies in search of a theory*. Pittsburgh, Pa.: American Institute for Research, May, 1959. [Contract Nonr-2551(00)]

726) Glaser, R., et al. *Description and analysis of team activity*. Pittsburgh, Pa.: American Institute for Research, December, 1954. (Contract Nonr-37008, NR-154-079)

727) Glaser, R., et al. *A study of some dimensions of team performance*. Pittsburgh, Pa.: American Institute for Research, September, 1955. (Tech. Rep., Contract N7 ONR-37008, NR-154-079)

*728) Gleason, W. J. Predicting army leadership ability by modified leaderless group discussion. *J. appl. Psychol.*, 1957, *41*, 231–235.

729) Glidewell, J. C. Work-emotionality characteristics of the total group and their relation to group problem solving. In Dorothy Stock and H. A. Thelen (Eds.), *Emotional dynamics and group culture*. New York: New York University Press, 1958. Pp. 122–126.

730) Godfrey, Eleanor P., et al. The effect of interpersonal relations on the success of consumer cooperatives. Paper read at Amer. sociol. Soc., Washington, D.C., September, 1955.

731) Godfrey, Eleanor P., et al. *Boards, management, and company success.* Danville, Ill.: University of Illinois, Group Effectiveness Research Laboratory, November, 1957. (Tech. Rep. No. 13, Contract N6-ORI-07135)

732) Goffman, I. Alienation from interaction. *Hum. Relat.,* 1957, *10,* 47–60.

733) Golb, Eileen F., & Fiedler, F. E. *A note on psychological attributes related to the score assumed similarity between opposites.* Urbana, Ill.: University of Illinois, Bureau of Research and Service, October, 1955. (Tech. Rep. No. 12, Contract N6-ORI-07135)

734) Gold, M. Power in the classroom. *Sociometry,* 1958, *21,* 50–60.

735) Goldberg, S. C. Three situational determinants of conformity to social norms. *J. abnorm. soc. Psychol.,* 1954, *49,* 325–329.

736) Goldberg, S. C. Influence and leadership as a function of group structure. *J. abnorm. soc. Psychol.,* 1955, *51,* 119–122.

737) Goldberg, S. C., & Lubin, A. Influence as a function of perceived judgment error. *Hum. Relat.,* 1958, *11,* 275.

738) Goldman, M., et al. The effect of group structure on the performance of groups engaged in a problem-solving task. *Amer. Psychologist,* 1958, *13,* 353. (Abstract)

739) Goldman, R. M. Conflict, co-operation, and choice: notes for an exploration of conceptual relationships. Paper prepared at Air Force Office of Scientific Res. Behav. Sci. Conf. Albuquerque, N.M., 1958. [Contract AF 49(638)-33]

*740) Goldman-Eisler, Frieda. The measurement of time sequences in conversational behaviour. *Brit. J. Psychol.,* 1951, *42,* 355–362.

741) Goodacre, D. M. The use of a sociometric test as a predictor of combat unit effectiveness. *Sociometry,* 1951, *14,* 148–152.

742) Goodacre, D. M. Group characteristics of good and poor performing combat units. *Sociometry,* 1953, *16,* 168–178.

743) Goodchilds, J. D. Effects of being witty on position in the social structure of a small group. *Sociometry,* 1959, *22,* 261–272.

744) Goodenough, Florence L. Measuring behavior traits by means of repeated short samples. *J. juv. Res.,* 1928, *12,* 230–235.

745) Goodenough, Florence L. Interrelationships in the behavior of young children. *Child Develpm.,* 1930, *1,* 29–48.

746) Goodenough, Florence L., & Anderson, J. E. *Experimental child study.* New York: Appleton, 1931.

747) Goodnow, R. E., & Tagiuri, R. Religious ethnocentricism and its recognition among adolescent boys. *J. abnorm. soc. Psychol.,* 1952, *47,* 316–320.

748) Gordon, J. E. Interpersonal predictions of repressors and sensitizers. *J. Pers.,* 1957, *25,* 686–698.

749) Gordon, Kate. Group judgments in the field of lifted weights. *J. exp. Psychol.,* 1924, *3,* 398–400.

750) Gordon, R. L. Interaction between attitude and the definition of the situation in the expression of opinion. In D. Cartwright and A. F. Zanders (Eds.), *Group dynamics: research and theory.* New York: Harper & Row, 1953. Pp. 163–176.

751) Gordon, T. *Group-centered leadership: a way of releasing the creative power of groups.* Boston: Houghton Mifflin, 1955.

752) Gorlow, L., et al. *The nature of nondirective group psychotherapy.* New York: Colombia University, Teachers College, 1952.

753) Gottheil, E. Changes in social perceptions contingent upon competing or cooperating. *Sociometry*, 1955, *18*, 132–137.

754) Gouldner, A. W. (Ed.) *Studies in leadership.* New York: Harper & Row, 1950.

755) Grace, H. A. The effects of different degrees of knowledge about an audience on the content of communication. *J. soc. Psychol.*, 1951, *34*, 31–40.

*756) Grace, H. A. The effects of different degrees of knowledge about an audience on the content of communication: the comparison of male and female audiences. *J. soc. Psychol.*, 1952, *36*, 89–96.

*757) Grace, H. A. The effects of different degrees of knowledge about an audience on the content of communication: the male audience. *J. soc. Psychol.*, 1952, *36*, 83–88.

*758) Grace, H. A. Conformance and performance. *J. soc. Psychol.*, 1954, *40*, 333–335.

759) Grace, H. A. Leadership: the educator's challenge. *Educ. Adm. Superv.*, 1955, *41*, 416–430.

760) Grace, H. A., & Tandy, M. J. Delegate communication as an index of group tension. *J. soc. Psychol.*, 1957, *45*, 93–97.

761) Gradolph, I. The task approach of groups of single-type and mixed-type valency compositions. In Dorothy Stock and H. A. Thelen (Eds.), *Emotional dynamics and group culture.* New York: New York University Press, 1958. Pp. 127–130.

762) Green, Elise H. Friendship and quarrels among preschool children. *Child Develpm.*, 1933, *4*, 237–252.

763) Green, Elise H. Group play and quarreling among preschool children. *Child Develpm.*, 1933, *4*, 302–307.

764) Green, N. E. Verbal intelligence and effectiveness of participation in group discussion. *J. educ. Psychol.*, 1950, *41*, 440–445.

765) Greenberg, Pearl J. Competition in children: an experimental study. *Amer. J. Psychol.*, 1932, *44*, 221–248.

*766) Greer, F. L. *Small group effectiveness.* Philadelphia, Pa.: Institute for Research in Human Relations, 1955. [Inst. Rep. No. 6, Contract No. Nonr-1229(00)]

*767) Greer, F. L., et al. Interpersonal knowledge and individual and group effectiveness. *J. abnorm. soc. Psychol.*, 1954, *49*, 411–414.

768) Greer, F. L., et al. *Evasion and survival problems and the prediction of crew performance.* Arlington, Va.: Psychological Research Associates, July, 1957. (PRA Rep. 57–15)

769) Grinker, R. R., & Spiegel, J. P. *Men under stress.* New York: McGraw-Hill-Blakiston, 1945.

770) Gronlund, N. E. The accuracy of teachers' judgments concerning the sociometric status of sixth-grade pupils. *Sociometry Monogr.*, 1951, No. 25.

771) Gronlund, N. E. The relative ability of home-room teachers and special-

subject teachers to judge the social acceptability of pre-adolescent pupils. *J. educ. Res.*, 1955, *48*, 381–391.

772) Gronlund, N. E. The relative stability of classroom social status with unweighted and weighted sociometric choices. *J. educ. Psychol.*, 1955, *46*, 345–354.

773) Gronlund, N. E. Sociometric status and sociometric perception *Sociometry*, 1955, *18*, 122–128.

774) Gronlund, N. E. The general ability to judge sociometric status: elementary student teachers' sociometric perceptions of classmates and pupils. *J. educ. Psychol.*, 1956, *47*, 147–157.

775) Gronlund, N. E. Generality of teachers' sociometric perceptions: relative judgment accuracy on several sociometric criteria. *J. educ. Psychol.*, 1956, *47*, 25–31.

776) Gross, E. Some functional consequences of primary controls in formal work organizations. *Amer. sociol. Rev.*, 1953, *18*, 368–373.

*777) Gross, E. Primary functions of the small group. *Amer. J. Sociol.*, 1954, *60*, 24–30.

*778) Gross, E. Symbiosis and consensus as integrative factors in small groups. *Amer. sociol. Rev.*, 1956, *21*, 174–179.

779) Gross, E. Characteristics of cliques in office organizations. *Res. Stud.*, State Coll. Wash., 1951, *19*.

780) Gross, N., & Martin, W. E. On group cohesiveness. *Amer. J. Sociol.*, 1952, *57*, 546–554.

781) Gross, N., et al. Studies of group behavior: leadership structures in small organized groups. *J. abnorm. soc. Psychol.*, 1953, *48*, 429–432.

782) Grossack, M. Controlling interaction in small group research. *J. Psychol.*, 1953, *35*, 241–244.

783) Grossack, M. M. Some effects of cooperation and competition upon small group behavior. *J. abnorm. soc. Psychol.*, 1954, *49*, 341–348.

784) Grosser, D., et al. A laboratory study of behavioral contagion. *Hum. Relat.*, 1951, *4*, 115–142.

785) Grusky, O. A case for the theory of familial role differentiation in small groups. *Soc. Forces*, 1957, *35*, 209–217.

786) Guetzkow, H. (Ed) *Groups, leadership and men: research in human relations.* Pittsburgh, Pa.: Carnegie Press, 1951.

787) Guetzkow, H. Effects of communication restriction upon the development and functioning of small problem-solving groups. *Amer. Psychologist*, 1953, *8*, 359. (Abstract)

788) Guetzkow, H. Organizational leadership in task-oriented groups. In L. Petrullo and B. M. Bass (Eds.), *Leadership and interpersonal behavior.* New York: Holt, Rinehart and Winston, 1961. Pp. 187–200.

*789) Guetzkow, H., & Dill, W. R. Factors in the organizational development of task-oriented groups. *Sociometry*, 1957, *20*, 175–204.

*790) Guetzkow, H., & Gyr, J. An analysis of conflict in decision-making groups. *Hum. Relat.*, 1954, *7*, 367–382.

791) Guetzkow, H., & Simon, H. A. The impact of certain communication nets upon organization and performance in task-oriented groups. *Mgmt Sci.*, 1955, *1*, 233–250.

792) Gunderson, E. K., et al. Interpersonal maturity and changes in non-conformist attitudes induced by closed living groups. *Amer. Psychologist*, 1956, *11*, 424. (Abstract)

793) Gurnee, H. A comparison of collective and individual judgments of facts. *J. exp. Psychol.*, 1937, *21*, 106–112.

*794) Gurnee, H. Maze learning in the collective situation. *J. Psychol.*, 1937, *3*, 437–443.

795) Gurnee, H. Group interaction in a learning situation. *Amer. Psychologist*, 1948, *3*, 270. (Abstract)

796) Gurvitch, G. Microsociology and sociometry. *Sociometry*, 1949, *12*, 1–31.

797) Gynther, Ruth A. The effects of anxiety and of situational stress on communicative efficiency. *J. abnorm. soc. Psychol.*, 1957, *54*, 274–276.

798) Gyr, J. Analysis of committee member behavior in four cultures. *Hum. Relat.*, 1951, *4*, 193–202.

799) Hagman, Elizabeth P. The companionships of preschool children. *Univer. of Iowa Stud. Child Welf.*, 1933, *7*, No. 4.

800) Hahn, C. P. *The development and validation of situational problems for training in those leadership behaviors essential for effective performance as a junior officer*. Washington, D.C.: American Institute for Research, October, 1956. [Final Rep., Contract Nonr 890(04)]

801) Haigh, G. V., & Schmidt, W. The learning of subject matter in teacher-centered and group-centered classes. *J. educ. Psychol.*, 1956, *47*, 295–301.

802) Haiman, F. S. *Group leadership and democratic action*. Boston: Houghton Mifflin, 1951.

803) Hall, C. E., et al. Small group leadership. *Amer. Psychologist*, 1958, *13*, 402. (Abstract)

804) Hall, D. M. *Dynamics of group action*. Danville, Ill.: Interstate Printers and Publishers, 1957.

805) Hall, R. L. Social influence on the aircraft commander's role. *Amer. sociol. Rev.*, 1955, *20*, 292–299.

*806) Hall, R. L. *Predicting bomber crew performance from the aircraft commander's role*. San Antonio, Tex.: Lackland Air Force Base, Crew Research Laboratory, 1956. (Res. Rep. AFPTRC-TN-56-28)

*807) Hall, R. L. Group performance under feedback that confounds responses of group members. *Sociometry*, 1957, *20*, 297–305.

808) Hall, R. L., & Rosenberg, S. An S-R analysis of social interaction. *Amer. Psychologist*, 1957, *12*, 370–371. (Abstract)

809) Halpin, A. W. Current conceptual trends in small group study: social psychology. *Autonomous Groups Bull.*, 1952, *7*, 4–17.

810) Halpin, A. W. The relation between the crew's perception of the leadership behavior of airplane commanders and superiors' ratings of their combat performance. *Amer. Psychologist*, 1952, *7*, 309–310. (Abstract)

*811) Halpin, A. W. *Studies in aircrew composition. III. The combat leader behavior of B-29 aircraft commanders*. Washington, D.C.: Bolling Air Force Base, Human Factors Operations Research Laboratory, September, 1953. (HFORL Memorandum No. TN-54-7)

812) Halpin, A. W. The leadership behavior and combat performance of airplane commanders. *J. abnorm. soc. Psychol.*, 1954, *49*, 19–22.

813) Halpin, A. W. The leader behavior and leadership ideology of educational administrators and aircraft commanders. *Harv. educ. Rev.*, 1955, *25*, 18–32.

*814) Halpin, A. W. The leadership ideology of aircraft commanders. *J. appl. Psychol.*, 1955, *39*, 82–84.

815) Halpin, A. W., & Winer, B. J. *The leadership behavior of the airplane commander.* Columbus, Ohio: Ohio State University Research Foundation, 1952.

816) Hamblin, R. L. Group integration during a crisis. *Hum. Relat.*, 1958, *11*, 67–76.

817) Hamblin, R. L. Leadership and crisis. *Sociometry*, 1958, *21*, 322–335.

818) Handlon, B. J., & Gross, Patricia. The development of sharing behavior. *J. abnorm. soc. Psychol.*, 1959, *59*, 425–428.

819) Hanfmann, Eugenia P. Social structure of a group of kindergarten children. *Amer. J. Orthopsychiat.*, 1935, *5*, 407-410.

820) Hansche, J., & Gilchrist, J. C. Three determinants of the level of aspiration. *J. abnorm. soc. Psychol.*, 1956, *53*, 136–137.

821) Harary, F. Status and contrastatus. *Sociometry*, 1959, *22*, 23–43.

822) Harary, F., & Ross, I. C. The number of complete cycles in a communication network. *J. soc. Psychol.*, 1954, *40*, 329–332.

823) Harary, F., & Ross, I. C. A procedure for clique detection using the group matrix. *Sociometry*, 1957, *20*, 205–215.

824) Hardee, M. D., & Bernauer, Margaret. A method of evaluating group discussion. *Occupations*, 1948, *27*, 90–94.

825) Hardy, K. R. Determinants of conformity and attitude change. *J. abnorm. soc. Psychol.*, 1957, *54*, 289–294.

826) Hardy, M. C. Social recognition at the elementary school age. *J. soc. Psychol.*, 1937, *8*, 365–384.

827) Hare, A. P. A study of interaction and consensus in different sized groups. *Amer. sociol. Rev.*, 1952, *17*, 261–267.

828) Hare, A. P. Small group discussions with participatory and supervisory leadership. *J. abnorm. soc. Psychol.*, 1953, *48*, 273–275.

829) Hare, A. P. Situational differences in leader behavior. *J. abnorm. soc. Psychol.*, 1957, *55*, 132–135.

830) Hare, A. P. Areas for research in small groups. *Sociol. soc. Res.*, 1958, *42*, 430–435.

831) Hare, A. P. Group dynamics as a technique for reducing intergroup tensions. In J. B. Gittler (Ed.), *Reducing intergroup tensions.* New York: Wiley, 1958.

832) Hare, A. P., & Hare, Rachel T. Family friendship within the community. *Sociometry*, 1948, *11*, 329–334.

833) Hare, A. P., et al. (Eds.) *Small groups: studies in social interaction.* New York: Knopf, 1955.

834) Harleston, B. W., et al. Organization and group vigilance. *Amer. Psychologist*, 1959, *14*, 381–382. (Abstract)

835) Harnack, R. V. Problems in measuring discussion process. *J. Communication*, 1953, *3*, 13–16.

836) Harnack, R. V. An experimental study of the effects of training in the recognition and formulation of goals upon intra-group cooperation. *Speech Monogr.*, 1955, *22*, 31–38.

*837) Harris, E. F., & Fleishman, E. A. Human relations training and the stability of leadership patterns. *J. appl. Psychol.*, 1955, *39*, 20–25.

838) Harris, H. *The group approach to leadership-testing.* London: Routledge, 1949.

839) Horrocks, J. E., & Buker, Mae E. A study of the friendship fluctuations of pre-adolescents. *J. genet. Psychol.*, 1951, *78*, 131–144.

840) Horrocks, J. E., & Thompson, G. G. A study of the friendship fluctuations of rural boys and girls. *J. genet. Psychol.*, 1946, *69*, 189–198.

841) Harter, G. A., & Fitts, P. M. *The functional simulation of complex systems by means of an analog computer, with the F-86D, E-4 System as a specific example.* San Antonio, Tex.: Lackland Air Force Base, December, 1956. (Res. Rep. AFPTRC-TN-56-133)

842) Hartley, Ruth E. *Relationships between perceived values and acceptance of a new reference group.* New York: City College, March, 1958. (Tech. Rep. No. 8, Contract Nonr-159701)

843) Hartley, Ruth E., et al. *Understanding children's play.* New York: Columbia University Press, 1952.

844) Harvey, O. J. An experimental approach to the study of status reactions in informal groups. *Amer. sociol. Rev.*, 1953, *18*, 357–367.

845) Harvey, O. J. An experimental investigation of negative and positive relations between small groups through judgmental indices. *Sociometry*, 1956, *19*, 201–209.

846) Harvey, O. J. *Reactions to negative information about the self as a function of the unfavorableness of the information, source of the evaluations and personality characteristics of the recipient.* Nashville, Tenn.: Vanderbilt University, 1958. [Tech. Rep. No 8, Contract Nonr-2149(02)]

847) Harvey, O. J. *Reciprocal influence of group and three types of leaders in an unstructured situation.* Nashville, Tenn.: Vanderbilt University, 1958. (Tech. Rep. No. 4, Contract Nonr-214902)

848) Harvey, O. J. *Social and personality factors in attitude change.* Nashville, Tenn.: Vanderbilt University, November, 1958. (Annu. tech. Rep., Contract Nonr-214902)

*849) Harvey, O. J., & Consalvi, C. *Status and conformity to pressures of informal groups.* Nashville, Tenn.: Vanderbilt University, 1958. (Tech. Rep. No. 6, Contract Nonr-214902)

850) Harvey, O. J., & Rutherford, Jeanne. *Relationship of status in the informal group to influence and influencibility at differing age levels.* Nashville, Tenn.: Vanderbilt University, 1957. (Tech. Rep. No. 3, Contract Nonr-214902)

851) Harvey, O. J., & Rutherford, Jeanne. Gradual and absolute approaches to attitude change. *Sociometry*, 1958, *21*, 61–68.

852) Harvey, O. J., et al. Reactions to unfavorable evaluations of the self made by other persons. *J. Pers.*, 1957, *25*, 393–411.

853) Hastorf, A. H. *A preliminary study of the perception of the group and the relation to behavior in the group.* Cambridge, Mass.: Harvard University, Laboratory of Social Relations, August, 1957. (Contract N5 ORI-07670)

854) Havron, M. D., & McGrath, J. E. Contribution of the leader to the effectiveness of small military groups. In L. Petrullo and B. M. Bass (Eds.), *Leadership and interpersonal behavior.* New York: Holt, Rinehart and Winston, 1961. Pp. 167–178.

855) Havron, M. D., et al. *Research on the effectiveness of small military units.* Washington, D.C.: The Adjutant General's Office, Personnel Research Section, 1951. (PRS Rep. No. 885)

*856) Havron, M. D., et al. *The effectiveness of small military units.* Washington, D.C.: The Adjutant General's Office, Personnel Research Section, 1952. (PRS Rep. 980)

857) Havron, M. D., et al. *An interview study of human relations in effective infantry squads.* Washington, D.C.: The Adjutant General's Office, Personnel Research Section, December, 1952. (PRS Rep. No. 983)

858) Havron, M. D., et al. *The assessment and prediction of rifle squad effectiveness.* Washington, D.C.: The Adjutant General's Office, Personnel Research Branch, November, 1954. (Tech. Res. Note 31)

859) Havron, M. D., et al. *A research study of the tactical training of the infantry rifle squad.* Arlington, Va.: Psychological Research Associates, August, 1954. (PRA Rep. 54-10)

860) Hawkes, R. Communication as a variable intervening between reward structure and group behavior. *Amer. Psychologist*, 1956, *11*, 360. (Abstract)

861) Hays, D. G., & Bush, R. R. A study of group action. *Amer. sociol. Rev.*, 1954, *19*, 693–701.

*862) Haythorn, W. W. The influence of individual members on the characteristics of small groups. *J. abnorm. soc. Psychol.*, 1953, *48*, 276–284.

863) Haythorn, W. W. A study of the distribution of informal group roles on medium bomber crews. *Amer. Psychologist*, 1953, *8*, 364. (Abstract)

864) Haythorn, W. W. *An analysis of role distribution in B-29 crews.* San Antonio, Tex.: Lackland Air Force Base, December, 1954. (Res. Bull. AFPTRC-TN-56-104)

865) Haythorn, W. W. *Relationships between sociometric measures and performance in medium-bomber crews in combat.* San Antonio, Tex : Lackland Air Force Base, December, 1954. (Res. Bull. AFPTRC-TN-54-101)

866) Haythorn, W. W. *A review of research on group assembly.* San Antonio, Tex : Lackland Air Force Base, May, 1957. (Res. Rep. AFPTRC-TN-57-62)

*867) Haythorn, W. W, et al. The behavior of authoritarian and equalitarian personalities in groups. *Hum. Relat.*, 1956, *9*, 57–74.

*868) Haythorn, W. W., et al. The effects of varying combinations of authoritarian and equalitarian leaders and followers. *J. abnorm. soc. Psychol.*, 1956, *53*, 210–219.

*869) Hearn, G. Leadership and the spatial factor in small groups. *J. abnorm. soc. Psychol.*, 1957, *54*, 269–272.

870) Heber, R. F., & Heber, Mary E. The effect of group failure and success on social status. *J. educ. Psychol.*, 1957, *48*, 129–134.

871) Hedberg, R. D. A study of leadership as a function of communication channels. *Amer. Psychologist*, 1959, *14*, 353. (Abstract)

872) Heider, F. Attitudes and cognitive organization. *J. Psychol.*, 1946, *21*, 107–112.

873) Heinicke, C., & Bales, R. F. Developmental trends in the structure of small groups. *Sociometry*, 1953, *16*, 7–38.

*874) Heise, G. A., & Miller, G. A. Problem solving by small groups using various communication nets. *J. abnorm. soc. Psychol.*, 1951, *46*, 327–337.

875) Helson, H., et al. Petition-signing as adjustment to situational and personal factors. *J. soc. Psychol.*, 1958, *48*, 3–10.

876) Hemphill, J. K. Situational factors in leadership. *Ohio Sate Univer. Educ. Res. Monogr.*, 1949, No. 32.

*877) Hemphill, J. K. Relations between the size of the group and the behavior of "superior" leaders. *J. soc. Psychol.*, 1950, *32*, 11–22

878) Hemphill, J K. Aircrew composition research. *Engng Exp. Sta. News*, Ohio State University 1952, *24*, 21–23.

879) Hemphill, J. K. *Aircrew composition research at the Personnel Research Board Laboratory, Ohio State University.* Columbus, Ohio: Ohio State University, Personnel Research Board, February, 1954. [Final Rep., Contracts AF 33(038)-10105 & AF 18(600)-27]

880) Hemphill, J. K. A proposed theory of leadership in small groups. In J. K. Hemphill et al. (Eds.), *Leadership acts: I. An investigation of the relation between possession of task relevant information and attempts to lead.* Columbus, Ohio: Ohio State University, 1954.

881) Hemphill, J. K. Effectiveness of work teams. *Acta psychol.*, 1955, *11*, 174–175. (Abstract)

882) Hemphill, J. K. Leadership behavior associated with the administrative reputation of college departments. *J. educ. Psychol.*, 1955, *46*, 385–401.

883) Hemphill, J. K. *Group dimensions: a manual for their measurement.* Columbus, Ohio: Ohio State University (Bureau of Business Res. Monogr. No. 87), 1956.

884) Hemphill, J. K. Why people attempt to lead. In L. Petrullo and B. M. Bass (Eds.), *Leadership and interpersonal behavior.* New York: Holt, Rinehart and Winston, 1961. Pp. 201–215.

885) Hemphill, J. K., & Coons, A. E. Leader behavior description. In R. M. Stogdill and A. E. Coons (Eds.), *Leader behavior: its description and measurement.* Columbus Ohio: Ohio State University (Bureau Business Res., Monogr. No. 88), 1957.

886) Hemphilll, J. K., & Pepinsky, Pauline N. *Leadership acts: II.* Columbus, Ohio: Ohio State University Research Foundation, February, 1954. (Rep. No. 2, Contract N6 ORI-17 T. C. III NR 171 123)

*887) Hemphill, J. K., & Sechrest, L. B. A comparison of three criteria of aircrew effectiveness in combat over Korea. *J. appl. Psychol.*, 1952, *36*, 323–327.

888) Hemphill, J. K., & Westie, C. M. The measurement of group dimensions. *J. Psychol.*, 1950, *29*, 325–342.

889) Hemphill, J. K., et al. (Eds) *Leadership acts: I. An investigation of the relation between possession of task relevant information and attempts to lead.* Columbus, Ohio: Ohio State University, 1954

890) Hemphill, J. K., et al. *Leadership acts: III. The effects upon attempts to lead of task motivation and the expectancy of accomplishment of the task.* Columbus, Ohio: Ohio State University Research Foundation, 1955. [Contract ONR (NR 171-123)]

891) Hemphill, J. K., et al. The relation between possession of task relevant information and attempts to lead. *Psychol. Monogr.,* 1956, *70,* No. 7.

892) Hemphill, J. K., et al. Effects of task motivation and expectancy of accomplishment upon attempts to lead. *Psychol. Monogr.,* 1957,*71,* No. 22.

893) Henry, W. E., & Guetzkow, H. Group projection sketches for the study of small groups. *J. soc. Psychol.,* 1951, *33,* 77–102.

894) Herbert, Eleonore L., & Trist, E. L. The institution of an absent leader by a students' discussion group. *Hum. Relat.,* 1953, *6,* 215–248.

895) Herbst, P. G. The measurement of family relationships. *Hum. Relat.,* 1952, *5,* 3–35.

896) Herbst, P. G. Analysis and measurement of a situation: the child in the family. *Hum. Relat.,* 1953, *6,* 113–140.

897) Herbst, P. G. Situation dynamics and the theory of behavior systems. *Behav. Sci.,* 1957, *2,* 13–29.

898) Herrold, K. F. Evaluation and research in group dynamics. *Educ. psychol. Measmt,* 1950, *10,* 492–504.

899) Herrold, K. F., et al. Difficulties encountered in group decision-making. *Personnel Guid. J.,* 1953, *31,* 516–523.

900) Hersko, M., & Winder, A. E. Changes in patient's attitude toward self and others during group therapy. *Amer. Psychologist,* 1956, *11,* 408. (Abstract)

901) Heyns, R. W. *Functional analysis of group problem-solving behavior.* Ann Arbor, Mich.: University of Michigan, Conference Research Project Report. October, 1948.

902) Heyns, R. W. Social psychology and group processes. *Annu. Rev. Psychol.,* 1958, *9,* 419–452.

903) Heyns, R. W., & Lippitt, R. Systematic observational techniques. In G. Lindzey (Ed.), *Handbook of social psychology.* Reading, Mass.: Addison-Wesley, 1954. Pp. 370–404.

*904) Heyns, R. W., & Miller, E. *Communication.* Ann Arbor, Mich.: University of Michigan, 1949. (Contract No. NR 172–301)

905) Heyns, R. W., & Zander, A. F. Observation of group behavior. In L. Festinger and D. Katz (Eds.), *Research methods in the behavioral sciences.* New York: Holt, Rinehart and Winston, 1953. Pp. 381–417.

906) High, W. S., et al. Factored dimensions of organizational behavior: II. Aircraft workers. *Educ. psychol. Measmt,* 1955, *15,* 371–382.

907) High, W. S., et al. Factors influencing organizational effectiveness: VIII. A survey of aircraft foremen. *Personnel Psychol.,*1955,*8,*355–368.

908) High, W. S., et al. Factored dimensions of organizational behavior: III. Aircraft supervisors. *Educ. psychol. Measmt,* 1956, *16,* 38–53.

*909) Hilgard, E. R., et al. Level of aspiration as affected by relative standing in an experimental social group. *J. exp. Psychol.*, 1940, *27*, 411–421.

910) Hilkevitch, Rhea R. Social interactional processes: a quantitative study. *Amer. Psychologist*, 1956, *11*, 400. (Abstract)

911) Hill, E.'S., & Hill, W. F. *Interaction matrix for group psychotherapy.* Provo, Utah: Utah State Hospital, April, 1957.

912) Hill, E. S., & Hill, W. F. Learning and teaching through discussion. *Notes and Essays on Education for Adults*, 1958, *22*.

913) Hill, R. Review of current research on marriage and the family. *Amer. sociol. Rev.*, 1951, *16*, 694–701.

914) Hill, W. F. Study of subgrouping as a dynamic of groups. *Amer. Psychologist*, 1955, *10*, 379. (Abstract)

915) Hill, W. F. The need characteristics of subtypes and their relation to behavior. In Dorothy Stock and H. A. Thelen (Eds.), *Emotional dynamics and group culture.* New York: New York University Press, 1958. Pp. 102–113.

916) Hites, R. W., & Campbell, D. T. A test of the ability of fraternity leaders to estimate group opinion. *J. soc. Psychol.*, 1950, *32*, 95–100.

917) Hochbaum, G. M. The relation between group members' self-confidence and their reactions to group pressures to uniformity. *Amer. sociol. Rev.*, 1954, *19*, 678–687.

918) Hoffman, P., & Maier, N. R. F. The use of group decision to resolve a problem of fairness. *Personnel Psychol.*, 1959, *12*, 545–560.

*919) Hoffman, L. R. Similarity of personality: a basis for interpersonal attraction. *Sociometry*, 1958, *21*, 300–308.

920) Hoffman, L. R. Homogeneity of member personality and its effect on group problem-solving. *J. abnorm. soc. Psychol.*, 1959, *58*, 27–32.

921) Hoffman, M. L. Conformity as a defense mechanism and a form of resistance to genuine group influence. *J. Pers.*, 1957, *25*, 412–424.

922) Hoffman, P. J., et al. Tendencies toward group comparability in competitive bargaining. *Hum. Relat.*, 1954, *7*, 141–159.

923) Hohn, F. E. *Some methods of comparing sociometric matrices.* Urbana, Ill.: University of Illinois, College of Education, Bureau of Research and Service, January, 1953. (Contract No. 07135)

924) Hollander, E. P. Authoritarianism and leadership choice in a military setting. *J. abnorm. soc. Psychol.*, 1954, *49*, 365–370.

925) Hollander, E. P. The friendship factor in peer nominations. *Personnel Psychol.*, 1956, *9*, 435–447.

926) Hollander, E. P. Interpersonal exposure time as a determinant of the predictive utility of peer ratings. *Psychol. Rep.*, 1956, *2*, 445–448.

*927) Hollander, E. P. The reliability of peer nominations under various conditions of administration. *J. appl. Psychol.*, 1957, *41*, 85–90.

928) Hollander, E. P. Conformity, status, and idiosyncrasy credit. *Psychol. Rev.*, 1958, *65*, 117–127.

929) Hollander, E. P. Some points of reinterpretation regarding social conformity. *Sociol. Rev.*, 1959, *7*, 159–168.

930) Hollander, E. P. Emergent leadership and social influence. In L. Petrullo and B. M. Bass (Eds.), *Leadership and interpersonal behavior*. New York: Holt, Rinehart and Winston, 1961. Pp. 30–47.

931) Hollander, E. P., & Webb, W. B. Leadership, followership, and friendship: an analysis of peer nominations. *J. abnorm. soc. Psychol.*, 1955, *50*, 163–167.

932) Holt, R. T. *An analysis of the problem of stability and cohesive membership in coalitions*. Minneapolis: University of Minnesota, 1954. (Tech. Rep. No. 3, Contract N8 ONR 66216)

933) Homans, G. C. The Western Electric researches. In National Research Council (Eds.), *Fatigue of workers: its relation to industrial production*. New York: Reinhold, 1941.

934) Homans, G. C. The Western Electric researches. In S. D. Hoslett (Ed.), *Human factors in management*. Parkville, Mo.: Park College Press, 1946. Pp. 152–185.

935) Homans, G. C. A conceptual scheme for the study of social organization. *Amer. sociol. Rev.*, 1947, *12*, 13–26.

936) Homans, G. C. *The human group*. New York: Harcourt, 1950.

937) Homans, G. C. Status among clerical workers. *Hum. Organization*, 1953, *12*, 5–10.

938) Homans, G. C. The cash posters: a study of a group of working girls. *Amer. sociol. Rev.*, 1954, *19*, 724–733.

939) Homans, G. C. Social behavior as exchange. *Amer. J. Sociol.*, 1958, *63*, 597–606.

940) Hood, P. D. *Crew agreement on RB-47 crew operating procedures as a function of experience with the aircraft and with the crew*. Merced, Calif.: Castle Air Force Base, Air Force Personnel and Training Research Center, Field Unit #1, Air Research and Development Command, April, 1956. (Lab. Note AORL-LN-56-2)

*941) Hood, P. D., et al. *Crew member agreement on RB-47 crew operating procedure*. San Antonio, Tex.: Lackland Air Force Base, May, 1957. (Rep. No. AFPTRC-TN-57-64)

942) Horowitz, M. W., & Perlmutter, H. V. The concept of the social group. *J. soc. Psychol.*, 1953, *37*, 69–95.

943) Horowitz, M.W., & Perlmutter, H. V. The discussion group and democratic behavior. *J. soc. Psychol.*, 1955, *41*, 231–246.

*944) Horowitz, M. W., et al. Induction of forces in discussion groups. *Hum. Relat.*, 1951, *4*, 57–76.

945) Horsfall, A. B., & Arensberg, C. M. Teamwork and productivity in a shoe factory. *Hum. Organization*, 1949, *8*, 13–25.

946) Horwitz, M. The conceptual status of group dynamics. *Rev. educ. Res.*, 1953, *23*, 309–328.

947) Horwitz, M. The recall of interrupted group tasks: an experimental study of individual motivation in relation to group goals. *Hum. Relat.*, 1954, *7*, 3–38.

948) Horwitz, M. *Group effects on tension patterns and motivation*. New York: New York University, Research Center for Human Relations, 1959. [Tech. Rep. No. 1, Contract Nonr-285(28)]

*949) Horwitz, M., & Cartwright, D. A projective method for the diagnosis of group properties. *Hum. Relat.*, 1953, *6*, 397–410.

950) Horwitz, M., & Lee, F. J. Effects of decision-making on motivational processes in group members. *Amer. Psychologist*, 1952, *7*, 312. (Abstract)

951) Horwitz, M., & Lee, F. J. Effects of decision making by group members on recall of finished and unfinished tasks. *J. abnorm. soc. Psychol.*, 1954, *49*, 201–210.

952) Horwitz, M., et al. *Motivational effects of alterative decision-making processes in groups.* Urbana, Ill.: Bureau of Educational Research, University of Illinois, 1953.

953) Horwitz, M., et al. Veridicality of attitudes toward authority and effects on learning. *Amer. Psychologist*, 1955, *10*, 336. (Abstract)

954) Horwitz, M., et al. *Effects of two methods of changing a frustrating agent on reduction of hostility.* Urbana, Ill.: University of Illinois, Bureau of Educational Research. (Contract NR. 171-201), 1955.

955) Horwitz, M., et al. *A further study of the effects of power reduction on arousal of hostility.* Urbana, Ill.: University of Illinois, College of Education, Bureau of Education Research. (Contract NR. 171-201) Undated.

956) Hovland, C. I., et al. (Eds.) *Communication and persuasion.* New Haven, Conn.: Yale University Press, 1953.

957) Hovland, C. I., et al. Assimilation and contrast effects in reactions to communication and attitude change. *J. abnorm. soc. Psychol.*, 1957, *55*, 244–252.

958) Howard, R. C., & Berkowitz, L. Reactions to the evaluators of one's performance. *J. Pers.*, 1958, *26*, 494–507.

959) Howell, C. E. Measurement of leadership. *Sociometry*, 1942, *5*, 163–168.

960) Hoyt, D. P. An evaluation of group and individual programs in vocational guidance. *J. appl. Psychol.*, 1955, *39*, 26–30.

961) Hubbard, Ruth M. A method of studying spontaneous group formation. In Dorothy S. Thomas (Ed.), *Some new techniques for studying social behavior.* New York: Columbia University, Teachers College, 1929. Pp. 76–85.

962) Hughes, E. C. The knitting of racial groups in industry. *Amer. sociol. Rev.*, 1946, *11*, 512–519.

963) Human Resources Research Center, Air Research and Development Command. *Index to quarterly research reports (personnel), January 1947–September 1949.* San Antonio, Tex.: Lackland Air Force Base, June, 1953. (Res. Bull. 53–14)

964) Human Resources Research Institute, Air Research and Development Command. *Index to HRRI 1953 publications.* Maxwell Air Force Base, Ala.: Author, January, 1954. (Res. Memorandum No. 9)

965) Hunt, J. McV., & Solomon, R. L. The stability and some correlates of group status in a summer camp group of young boys. *Amer. J. Psychol.*, 1942, *55*, 33–45.

966) Hurlock, Elizabeth B. The use of group rivalry as an incentive. *J. abnorm. soc. Psychol.*, 1927, *22*, 278–290.

967. Hurwitz, J. I., et al. Some effects of power on the relations among group

members. In D. Cartwright and A. F. Zander (Eds.), *Group dynamics: research and theory*. New York: Harper & Row, 1953. Pp. 483–492.

*968) Husband, R. W. Cooperative versus solitary problem solution. *J. soc. Psychol.*, 1940, *11*, 405–409.

969) Husband, R. W. A statistical comparison of the efficacy of large lecture versus smaller recitation sections upon achievement in general psychology. *Amer. Psychologist*, 1949, *4*, 216. (Abstract)

970) Hyman, H. H. The psychology of status. *Arch. Psychol.*, 1942, No. 269.

971) Irwin, I. A. *A preliminary study of methods for conducting the post-mission critique in a combat crew training situation*. San Antonio, Tex.: Lackland Air Force Base, Human Resources Research Center, June, 1953. (Res. Bull. TN-53-16)

*972) Irwin, I. A. *A procedure for evaluating instructor technique during critiques of crew performance*. San Antonio, Tex.: Randolph Air Force Base, ARDC, Crew Research Laboratory, February, 1956. (Res. Rep. AFPTRC-TN-56-32)

973) Israel, J. *Self-evaluation and rejection in groups*. Stockholm: Almqvist & Wiksell, 1956.

974) Israel, J. A note on measurement of cross-pressures in groups. *Acta psychol.*, 1958, *14* (5), 353–358.

975) Izard, C. E. Personality correlates of sociometric status. *J. appl. Psychol.*, 1959, *43*, 89–93.

976) Izard, C. E. Personality similarity and friendship. *Amer. Psychologist*, 1959, *14*, 366. (Abstract)

977) Jackson, J. *Group membership and conformity processes*. Ann Arbor, Mich.: University of Michigan, Research Center for Group Dynamics, 1956. (Contract No. NR 171–272)

978) Jackson, J., & Snoek, J. D. Effect of invidious exclusion from a group on feelings toward self, others, and on tendencies to conform. *Amer. Psychologist*, 1959, *14*, 335. (Abstract)

*979) Jackson, J. M. The effect of changing the leadership of small work groups. *Hum. Relat.*, 1953, *6*, 25–44.

980) Jackson, J. M. A review of "Group dimensions," by Hemphill. *Personnel Psychol.*, 1957, *10*, 383–385.

981) Jackson, J. M. Reference group processes in a formal organization. *Sociometry*, 1959, *22*, 307–327.

982) Jackson, J. M. A space for conceptualizing person-group relationships. *Hum. Relat.*, 1959, *12*, 3–16.

983) Jackson, J. M., & Saltzstein, H. D. *Group membership and conformity processes*. Ann Arbor, Mich.: University of Michigan, Research Center for Group Dynamics, Institute for Social Research, August, 1956. [ONR Contract Nonr 1224(11)]

*984) Jackson, J. M., & Saltzstein, H. D. The effect of person–group relationships on conformity processes. *J. abnorm. soc. Psychol.*, 1958, *57*, 17–24.

985) Jackson, W. M. Interaction in a college fraternity. *Appl. Anthrop.*, 1944, *3*, 16–21.

986) Jacobs, J. H. The application of sociometry to industry. *Sociometry*, 1945, *8*, 181–198.

987) Jacobson, E. *An analysis of foreman–steward power relationships.* Ann Arbor, Mich.: University of Michigan, 1949. (Contract No. NR 170–272)

988) Jacobson, E. *Communication structure and attitudes in large organizations.* Ann Arbor, Mich.: University of Michigan, 1951. (Contract No. NR 170–272)

989) Jacobson, E. *A method for studying the relationship between communications structure and attitudes in complex organizations.* Ann Arbor, Mich.: University of Michigan, 1952. (Contract No. NR 170-272)

990) Jacobson, E. *Morale and motivation in a changing economy.* Ann Arbor, Mich.: University of Michigan, 1952. (Contract No. NR 170-272)

991) Jacobson, E. The growth of groups in a voluntary organization. *J. soc. Issues,* 1956, *12* (2), 18–23.

992) Jacobson, E. *The effect of changing industrial methods and automation on personnel.* Washington, D. C.: Walter Reed Medical Center, Walter Reed Army Institute of Research, April, 1957.

993) Jacobson, E., & Seashore, S. E. Communication practices in complex organizations. *J. soc. Issues,* 1951, *7*(3), 28–40.

994) Jacobson, E., et al. Research in functioning organizations. *J. soc. Issues,* 1951, *7*(3), 64–71.

995) Jacobson, E., et al. The use of the role concept in the study of complex organizations. *J. soc. Issues,* 1951, *7*(3), 18–27.

996) Jahoda, Marie, et al. *Research methods in social relations.* New York: Holt, Rinehart and Winston, 1951.

997) James, B. J. Methodological problems in the application of sociometry under "uncontrolled" conditions. *Sociometry,* 1955, *18*, 111–121.

998) James, J. Some elements in a theory of small groups. *Res. Stud., State Coll. Wash.,* 1950, *18*, 144–152.

*999) James, J. Clique organization in a small industrial plant. *Res. Stud., State Coll. Wash.,* 1951, *19*, 125–130.

1000) James, J. A preliminary study of the size determinant in small group interaction. *Amer. sociol. Rev.,* 1951, *16*, 474–477.

1001) James, J. The distribution of free-forming small group size. *Amer. sociol. Rev.,* 1953, *18*, 569–570.

1002) James, J. Verbal behavior in problem-solving small groups without formally designated leaders. *Res. Stud., State Coll. Wash.,* 1956, *24*, 125–133.

1003) Jameson, S. H. Principles of social interaction. *Amer. sociol. Rev.,* 1945, *10*, 6–12.

1004) Janicki, W. P., & Schroder, H. M. *A method of studying interaction under conditions of interpersonal conflict.* Washington, D.C.: Office of Naval Research, Group Psychology Branch, August, 1959. [Project No. NR 171-055, Contract Nonr 1858(12)]

*1005) Janis, I. L., & King, B. T. The influence of role playing on opinion change. *J. abnorm. soc. psychol.,* 1954, *49*, 211–218.

1006) Jansen, L. T. Measuring family solidarity. *Amer. sociol. Rev.,* 1952, *17*, 727–733.

1007) Jaques, E. Interpretive group discussion as a method of facilitating social change. *Hum. Relat.,* 1948, *1*, 533–549.

1008) Jaynes. W. E. *An analysis of differences among Navy officer specialties and among Navy organizations.* Columbus, Ohio: Ohio State University, Ohio State University Research Foundation, Personnel Research Board, 1952. (Contract No. NR 171–123)

1009) Jaynes, W. E. Differences between jobs and between organizations. In R. M. Stodgill et al. (Eds.), *Patterns of administrative performance.* Columbus, Ohio: Ohio Sate University, (Bur. Business Res. Monogr. No. 81), 1956.

1010) Jenkins, D. H. Feedback and group self-evaluation. *J. soc. Issues,* 1948, *4*(2), 50–60.

1011) Jenkins, D. H. What is group dynamics? *Adult Educ. J.,* 1950, 54–60.

1012) Jenkins, D. H., & Lippitt, R. *Interpersonal perceptions of teachers, students, and parents.* Washington, D.C.: National Education Association, 1951.

1013) Jenkins, J. G. Nominating technique as a method of evaluating air group morale. *J. Aviat. Med.,* 1948, *19*, 12–19.

1014) Jenkins, W. O. A review of leadership studies with particular reference to military problems. *Psychol. Bull.,* 1947, *44*, 54–79.

1015) Jenness, A. The role of discussion in changing opinion regarding a matter of fact. *J. abnorm. soc. Psychol.,* 1932, *27*, 279–296.

1016) Jenness, A. Social influences in the change of opinion. *J. abnorm. soc. Psychol.,* 1932, *27*, 29–34.

1017) Jennings, Helen H. Structure of leadership—development and sphere of influence. *Sociometry,* 1937, *1*, 99–143.

1018) Jennings, Helen H. Individual differences in the social atom. *Sociometry,* 1941, *4*, 269–277.

1019) Jennings, Helen H. Experimental evidence on the social atom at two time points. *Sociometry,* 1942, *5*, 135–145.

1020) Jennings, Helen H. A sociometric study of emotional and social expansiveness. In R. G. Barker, J. S. Kounin, and H. F. Wright (Eds.), *Child behavior and development.* New York: McGraw-Hill, 1943. Pp. 527–543.

1021) Jennings, Helen H. Leadership and sociometric choice. *Sociometry,* 1947, *10*, 32–49.

1022) Jennings, Helen H. Sociometric differentiation of the psychegroup and the sociogroup. *Sociometry,* 1947, *10*, 71–79.

1023) Jennings, Helen H. *Leadership and isolation.* (2nd ed.) New York: David McKay, 1950.

1024) Jennings, Helen H. Sociometric grouping in relation to child development. In Caroline Tryon (Ed.), *Fostering mental health in our schools.* Washington, D.C.: National Education Association, 1950.

1025) Jennings, Helen H. Sociometric structure in personality and group formation. In M. Sherif and M. O. Wilson (Eds.), *Group relations at the crossroads.* New York: Harper & Row, 1953. Pp. 332–365.

1026) Jersild, A. T., & Fite, Mary D. The influence of nursery school experience on children's social adjustments. *Child Develpm. Monogr.,* 1939, No. 25.

1027) Joel, W., & Shapiro, D. A. A genotypical approach to the analysis of personal interaction. *J. Psychol.,* 1949, *28*, 9–17.

1028) Johnson, E. E. *A survey of tank crew problems.* Fort Knox, Ky.: Army Medical Research Laboratory, August, 1952. (AMRL Project 6-95-20-001)

1029) Johnson, P. E. A training course in pastoral counseling. In Helen I. Driver (Ed.), *Counseling and learning through small-group discussion.* Madison, Wis.: Monona Publications, 1958. Pp. 352–355.

1030) Johnson, R. M., et al. *Differential prediction with incomplete criterion data.* Seattle, Wash.: University of Washington, August, 1959. (Contract Nonr-47708)

1031) Jolles, I. An experiment in group guidance. *J. soc. Psychol.*, 1946, *23*, 55–60.

1032) Jones, E. E., & Daugherty, B. N. Political orientation and the perceptual effects of an anticipated interaction. *J. abnorm. soc. Psychol.*, 1959, *59*, 340–349.

*1033) Jones, E. E., & deCharms, R. Changes in social perception as a function of the personal relevance of behavior. *Sociometry*, 1957, *20*, 75–85.

1034) Jones, E. E., et al. Some effects of feedback from the experimenter on conformity behavior. *J. abnorm. soc. Psychol.*, 1958, *57*, 207–213.

1035) Jones, E. E., et al. Reaction to unfavorable personal evaluation as a function of the evaluator's perceived adjustment. *J. abnorm. soc. Psychol.*, 1959, *59*, 363–370.

1036) Jones, F. D., & Peters, H. N. An experimental evaluation of group psychotherapy. *J. abnorm. soc. Psychol.*, 1952, *47*, 345–353.

1037) Julian, J. W., & Steiner, I. D. *Perceived acceptance as a determinant of conformity behavior.* Urbana, Ill.: University of Illinois, Department of Psychology, Group Effectiveness Research Laboratory, November, 1959. (Tech. Rep. No. 4)

1038) Kagan, J., & Mussen, P. H. Dependency themes on the TAT and group conformity. *J. consult. Psychol.*, 1956, *20*, 29–32.

1039) Kahn, R. L. *Twelve factors associated with productivity.* Ann Arbor, Mich.: University of Michigan, 1955. (Contract NR 170–272)

1040) Kahn, R. L. The prediction of productivity. *J. soc. Issues*, 1956, *12*(2), 41–49.

1041) Kahn, R. L., & Katz, D. *Some relationships between organizational characteristics and productivity.* Ann Arbor, Mich.: University of Michigan, 1951. (Contract No. NR 170-272)

1042) Kahn, R. L., & Katz, D. Leadership practices in relation to productivity and morale. In D. Cartwright and A. F. Zander (Eds.), *Group dynamics: research and theory.* New York: Harper & Row, 1953. Pp. 612–628.

1043) Kahn, R. L., & Morse, N. C. The relationship of productivity to morale. *J. soc. Issues*, 1951, *7*(3), 8–17.

1044) Kaiser, R. L., & Blake, R. R. Aspiration and performance in a simulated group atmosphere. *J. soc. Psychol.*, 1955, *42*, 193–202.

1045) Kallejian, V. Some aspects of the relationship between "understanding" and "acceptance" of others. *Amer. Psychologist*, 1953, *8*, 376. (Abstract)

*1046) Kaplan, A., et al. The prediction of social and technological events. *Publ. Opin. Quart.*, 1950, *14*, 93–110.

1047) Kaplan, H., & Willemin, L. P. Effect of shorter acquaintance, or of adding cadre raters, on the validity of early buddy ratings of combat aptitude. *Amer. Psychologist*, 1959, *14*, 435. (Abstract)

1048) Karcher, E. K., Jr., et al. *Unit effectiveness tests*. Washington, D.C.: Department of the Army, TAGO, Personnel Research Section, January, 1952. (Army Project No. 29565100, PRS Rep. 923.)

1049) Katz, D. Employee groups: what motivates them and how they perform. *Advanc. Mgmt*, 1949, *14* (3), 119–124.

1050) Katz, D. *Morale and motivation in industry*. Ann Arbor, Mich.: University of Michigan, 1949. (Contract NR 170–172)

1051) Katz, D. Social psychology and group processes. *Annu. Rev. Psychol.*, 1951, *2*, 137–172.

1052) Katz, D. Conditions and factors involved in attitude changes. *J. Pers.*, 1959, *27* (3).

1053) Katz, D., & Kahn, R. Some recent findings in human relations research. In G. E. Swanson et al. (Eds.), *Readings in social psychology*. (2nd. ed.) New York: Holt, Rinehart and Winston, 1952.

*1054) Katz, D., et al. *Productivity, supervision, and morale in an office situation*. Ann Arbor, Mich.: University of Michigan, Institute for Social Research, 1950.

1055) Katz. D., et al. *Productivity, supervision, and morale among railroad workers*. Ann Arbor, Mich.: University of Michigan Survey Research Center, 1951.

1056) Katz, E., et al. Leadership stability and social change: an experiment with small groups. *Sociometry*, 1957, *20*, 36–50.

1057) Katz, I. *Studies in productivity and cohesiveness of culturally mixed groups: I. Effects on behavior and productivity of variations in reward structure and attributed prestige*. New York: New York University, Research Center for Human Relations, 1957. (Contract Nonr-28524)

1058) Katz, I. *Studies in productivity and cohesiveness of culturally mixed groups: II. Effects of variations in reward structure, authoritarianism, and group prestige*. New York: New York University, Research Center for Human Relations, 1958. (Tech. Rep. No. 2, Contract Nonr-28524.)

*1059) Katz, I., et al. Behavior and productivity in bi-racial work groups. *Hum. Relat.*, 1958, *11*, 123–141.

1060) Katz, L. *An operational procedure for reduction of the choice matrix*. East Lansing, Mich.: Michigan State University, 1952. (Contract No. NR 170–115)

1061) Katz, L. *Recent advances and some unsolved problems of sociometric theory*. East Lansing, Mich.: Michigan State University, 1952. (Contract No. NR 170-115)

1062) Katz, L. *Reciprocity index*. East Lansing, Mich.: Michigan State University, 1952. (Contract No. NR 170-115)

1063) Katz, L. A new status index derived from sociometric analysis. *Psychometrika*, 1953, *18*, 39–43.

1064) Katz, L. *Mathematical models for human group organizations*. Washington, D.C.: Office of Naval Research, Department of the Navy, Group Psychology Branch, June, 1958. [Contract Nonr 785(00)]

1065) Katz, L., & Powell, J. H. A proposed index of the conformity of one sociometric measurement to another. *Psychometrika*, 1953, *18*, 249–256.

1066) Katz, L., & Powell, J. H. Measurement of the tendency toward reciprocation of choice. *Sociometry*, 1955, *18*, 659–665.

1067) Katz, L., et al. A note on estimating the statistical significance of mutuality. *J. gen. Psychol.*, 1958, *58*, 97–108.

1068) Keedy, T. C., Jr. Factors in the cohesiveness of small groups. *Sociol. soc. Res.*, 1956, *40*, 329–332.

1069) Keet, C. D. Two verbal techniques in a miniature counseling situation. *Psychol. Monogr.*, 1948, *62*, No. 294.

1070) Keller, J. B. Comment on "Channels of communications in small groups." *Amer. sociol. Rev.*, 1951, *16*, 842–843.

1071) Kelley, H. H. Communication in experimentally created hierarchies. *Hum. Relat.*, 1951, *4*, 39–56.

1072) Kelley, H. H. Group membership and resistance to influence. In C. I. Hovland et al. (Eds.), *Communication and persuasion*. New Haven, Conn.: Yale University Press, 1953. Pp. 134–173.

1073) Kelley, H. H. Salience of membership and resistance to change of group-anchored attitudes. *Hum. Relat.*, 1955, *8*, 275–290.

*1074) Kelley, H. H., & Lamb, T. W. Certainty of judgment and resistance to social influence. *J. abnorm. soc. Psychol.*, 1957, *55*, 137–139.

*1075) Kelley, H. H., & Shapiro, M. M. An experiment on conformity to group norms where conformity is detrimental to group achievement. *Amer. sociol. Rev.*, 1954, *19*, 667–677.

1076) Kelley, H. H., & Thibaut, J. W. Experimental studies of group problem solving and process. In G. Lindzey (Ed.), *Handbook of social psychology*. Reading, Mass.: Addison-Wesley, 1954. Pp. 735–785.

*1077) Kelley, H. H., & Volkhart, E. H. The resistance to change of group-anchored attitudes. *Amer. sociol. Rev.*, 1952, *17*, 453–465.

1078) Kelley, H. H., & Woodruff, C. L. Members' reactions to apparent group approval of a counternorm communication. *J. abnorm. soc. Psychol.*, 1956, *52*, 67–74.

1079) Kelly, R. W., & Ware, H. F. An experiment in group dynamics. *Advanc. Mgmt*, 1947, *12*, 116–119.

1080) Kelman, H. C. Effects of success and failure on "suggestibility" in the autokinetic situation. *J. abnorm. soc. Psychol.*, 1950, *45*, 267–285.

1081) Kelman, H. C. Attitude change as a function of response restriction. *Hum. Relat.*, 1953, *6*, 185–214.

1082) Kennedy, J. L. Learning for performance in groups. Paper read at Sympos. Psychol. Learning Basic Military Train. Problems, Panel Train. & Train. Devices Committee Hum Resources Res. & Develpm. Bd, Washington, D.C., May, 1953.

1083) Kephart, W. M. A quantitative analysis of intragroup relationships. *Amer. J. Sociol.*, 1950, *60*, 544–549.

1084) Keppers, G. L. A graduate course in group techniques in guidance. In Helen I. Driver (Ed.), *Counseling and learning through small group discussion*. Madison, Wis.: Monona Publications, 1958. Pp. 338-342.

*1085) Kidd, J. S. Social influence phenomena in a task-oriented group situation. *J. abnorm. soc. Psychol.*, 1958, *56*, 13–17.

*1086) Kidd, J. S., & Campbell, D. T. Conformity to groups as a function of group success. *J. abnorm. soc. Psychol.*, 1955, *51*, 390–393.

1087) Kimbrell, D. L., & Blake, R. R. Motivational factors in the violation of a prohibition. *J. abnorm. soc. Psychol.*. 1958, *56*, 132–133.

1088) Kinney, Elva E. A study of peer group social acceptability at the fifth grade level in a public school. *J. educ. Res.*, 1953, *47*, 57–64.

1089) Kipnis, Dorothy M. Interaction between members of bomber crews as a determinant of sociometric choice. *Hum. Relat.*, 1957, *10*, 263–270.

1090) Kipnis, Dorothy M. The effects of leadership style and leadership power upon the inducement of an attitude change. *J. abnorm. soc. Psychol.*, 1958, *57*, 173–180.

1091) Kirkpatrick, C., & Hobart, C. Disagreement, disagreement estimate, and non-empathetic imputations for intimacy groups varying from favorite date to married. *Amer. sociol. Rev.*, 1954, *19*, 10–19.

1092) Kirscht, J. P., et al. Some factors in the selection of leaders by members of small groups. *J. abnorm. soc. Psychol.*, 1959, *58*, 406–408.

1093) Klein, A., & Keill, N. The experiencing of group psychotherapy. *Sociatry*, 1953, *5*, 205–221.

1094) Klein, Josephine. *The study of groups.* London: Routledge, 1956.

1095) Klopfer, W. G. The efficacy of group therapy as indicated by group Rorschach records. *Rorschach Res. Exch.*, 1945, *9*, 207–209.

1096) Klubeck, S., & Bass, B. M. Differential effects of training on persons of different leadership status. *Hum. Relat.*, 1954, *7*, 59–72.

*1097) Klugman, S. F. Cooperative versus individual efficiency in problem-solving. *J. educ. Psychol.*, 1944, *35*, 91–100.

*1098) Klugman, S. F. Group judgments for familiar and unfamiliar materials. *J. gen. Psychol.*, 1945, *32*, 103–110.

*1099) Klugman, S. F. Group and individual judgments for anticipated events. *J. soc. Psychol.*, 1947, *26*, 21–28.

1100) Knickerbocker, I. Leadership: a conception and some implications. *J. soc. Issues*, 1948, *4*, 23–40.

1101) Knoell, Dorothy M. *Relationships between attitudes of bomber crews in training and their attitudes and performance in combat.* San Antonio, Tex.: Lackland Air Force Base, Air Force Personnel and Training Research Center, 1956. (Res. Rep. AFPTRC-TN-56-49)

1102) Knoell, Dorothy M., & DeGaugh, R. A. *A scaling technique designed to give approximation to factor scales.* San Antonio, Tex.: Lackland Air Force Base, Air Force Personnel and Training Research Center, February, 1957. (Res. Rep. AFPTRC-TN-57-21)

1103) Knoell, Dorothy M., & Forgays, D. G. *Interrelationships of combat crew performance in the B-29.* San Antonio, Tex.: Lackland Air Force Base, Human Resources Research Center, December, 1952. (Res. Note CCT 52-1)

1104) Knoell, Dorothy M., & Stice, G. *Development of attitude scales relevant to combat crew membership.* San Antonio, Tex.: Lackland Air Force

Base, Air Force Personnel and Training Research Center, November, 1954. (Res. Bull. AFPTRC-TN-54-63)

1105) Knoell, Dorothy M., et al. *Criteria of B-29 crew performance in Far Eastern combat*: *I. Ratings*. San Antonio, Tex.: Lackland Air Force Base, Human Resources Research Center, October, 1953. (Tech. Rep. 53-32)

1106) Kogan, N., & Tagiuri, R. Interpersonal preference and cognitive organization. *J. abnorm. soc. Psychol.*, 1958, *56*, 113-116.

1107) Kogan, N., & Tagiuri, R. On visibility of choice and awareness of being chosen. *Psychol. Rep.*, 1958, *4*, 83-86.

1108) Kogan, N., et al. Perception of reciprocity and the grouping principle. *J. soc. Psychol.*, 1959, *49*, 27-32.

1109) Kohn, H. B. *Susceptibility to communicative persuasion and perception of apparent movement*. Reno, Nev.: Stead Air Force Base, Crew Research Laboratory, Field Unit #2, October, 1954. (CRL intern. Memorandum 54-207)

1110) Kotkov, B. A bibliography for the student of group therapy. *J. clin. Psychol.*, 1950, *6*, 77-91.

1111) Kozman, Hilda C. *Group process in physical education*. New York: Harper & Row, 1951

1112) Krebs, A. M. Two determinants of conformity: age of independence training and achievement. *J. abnorm. soc. Psychol.*, 1958, *56*, 130-131.

1113) Krech, D., & Crutchfield, R. S. *Theory and problems of social psychology*. New York: McGraw-Hill, 1948.

1114) Kuusela, Ruth. Systematic observation methods in the study of small groups. *Acta psychol.*, 1956, *12*, 25-46.

1115) *Laboratory of social relations*. Cambridge, Mass.: Harvard University, Author, August, 1958. (Final Rep., Contract No. N5 ORI 07646)

1116) LaForge, R., & Suczek, R. F. The interpersonal dimension of personality: III. An interpersonal check list. *J. Pers.*, 1955, *24*, 94-112.

1117) Laird, D. A., & Laird, Eleanor C. *The new psychology of leadership*. New York: McGraw-Hill, 1956.

1118) Lake, R. A. Methods and techniques of group procedure. *Provo Papers*, 1959, *3*, 32-42.

1119) Lambert, W. E., & Lowy, F. H. Effects of the presence and discussion of others on expressed attitudes. *Canad. J. Psychol.*, 1957, *11*, 151-156.

1120) Landis, M. H., & Burtt, H. E. A study of conversations. *J. comp. Psychol.*, 1924, *4*, 81-89.

1121) Landsberger, H. A. Interaction process analysis of professional behavior: a study of labor mediators in twelve labor-management disputes. *Amer. sociol. Rev.*, 1955, *20*, 566-575.

*1122) Landsberger, H. A. Interaction process analysis of the mediation of labor-management disputes. *J. abnorm. soc. Psychol.*, 1955, *51*, 522-558.

1123) Lanzetta, J. T. Group behavior under stress. *Hum. Relat.*, 1955, *8*, 29-52.

1124) Lanzetta, J. T., & Kanareff, Vera T. The effects of congruent and conflicting social and task reinforcements on the acquisition of an imitative response. *Amer. Psychologist*, 1959, *14*, 382. (Abstract)

1125) Lanzetta, J. T., & Roby, T. B. Group performance as a function of work-distribution patterns and task load. *Sociometry*, 1956, *19*, 95–104.

1126) Lanzetta, J. T., & Roby, T. B. *Effects of work-group structure and certain task variables on group performance.* San Antonio, Tex.: Lackland Air Force Base, April, 1957. (Res. Rep. AFPTRC-TN-57-45)

1127) Lanzetta, J. T., & Roby, T. B. Group learning and communication as a function of task and structure "demands." *J. abnorm. soc. Psychol.*, 1957, *55*, 121–131.

*1128) Lanzetta, J. T., et al. Some effects of situational threat on group behavior. *J. abnorm. soc. Psychol.*, 1954, *49*, 445–453.

*1129) Lanzetta, J. T., et al. The effects of an "anxiety-reducing" medication on group behavior under threat. *J. abnorm. soc. Psychol.*, 1956, *52*, 103–108.

1130) Lasswell, H. D. Person, personality, group, culture. *Psychiatry*, 1939, *2*, 533–561.

1131) Lawlor, Monica. An investigation concerned with changes of preferences which are observed after group discussion. *J. soc. Psychol.*, 1955, *42*, 323–332.

1132) Lawrence, Lois C., & Smith, Patricia C. Group decision and employee participation. *J. appl. Psychol.*, 1955, *39*, 334–337.

1133) Lawshe, C. H., et al. Studies in management training evaluation: II. The effects of exposures to role playing. *J. appl. Psychol.*, 1959, *43*, 287–292.

*1134) Lawson, E. D., & Stagner, R. Group pressure, attitude change, and autonomic involvement. *J. soc. Psychol.*, 1957, *45*, 299–312.

1135) Leary, T. The theory and measurement methodology of interpersonal communication. *Psychiatry*, 1955, *18*, 147–161.

1136) Learly, T. *Interpersonal diagnosis of personality.* New York: Ronald, 1957.

1137) Leary, T., & Coffrey, H. The prediction of inter-personal behavior in group psychology. *Group Psychother.*, 1954, *7*, 7–51.

1138) Leary, T., & Coffrey, H. S. Interpersonal diagnosis: some problems of methodology and validation. *J. abnorm. soc. Psychol.*, 1955, *50*, 110–124.

*1139) Leavitt, H. J. Some effects of certain communication patterns on group performance. *J. abnorm. soc. Psychol.*, 1951, *46*, 38–50.

1140) Leavitt, H. J., & Mueller, R. A. H. Some effects of feedback on communication. *Hum. Relat.*, 1951, *4*, 401–410.

1141) Leavitt, H. J., et al. "Authoritarianism" and agreement with things authoritative. *J. Psychol.*, 1955, *40*, 215–221.

1142) Lee, F. J., et al. *Power over decision making and the response to frustration in group members.* Urbana, Ill.: University of Illinois, Bureau of Educational Research, 1954. (Contract NR 171–201)

1143) Leeman, C. P. Patterns of sociometric choice in small groups: a mathematical model and related experimentation. *Sociometry*, 1952, *15*, 220–243.

1144) Lemann, T. B., & Solomon, R. L. Group characteristics as revealed in sociometric patterns and personality ratings. *Sociometry*, 1952, *15*, 7–90.

*1145) Lennard, H., et al. Lysergic acid diethylamide (LSD-25): XII. A preliminary statement of its effects upon interpersonal communication. *J. Psychol.*, 1956, *41*, 185–198.

1146) Leuba, C. J. An experimental study of rivalry in young children. *J. comp. Psychol.*, 1933, *16*, 367–378.

1147) Leventhal, H. Cognitive processes and interpersonal predictions. *J. abnorm. soc. Psychol.*, 1957, *55*, 167–180.

1148) Levi, M. *Characteristics associated with completion of survival-instructor training.* Reno, Nev.: Stead Air Force Base, Crew Research Laboratory, Field Unit #2, June, 1955. (Lab. Note CRL-LN-55-215)

1149) Levi, M. *Group atmosphere and attrition rate among survival-instructor trainees.* Reno, Nev.: Stead Air Force Base, Crew Research Laboratory, Field Unit #2, September, 1955. (Lab. Note CRL-LN-55-218)

1150) Levi, M. *Sociometric measures and completion of survival instructor training.* Reno, Nev.: Stead Air Force Base, Crew Research Laboratory, Field Unit #2, April, 1955. (Lab. Note CRL-LN-55-209)

*1151) Levi, M. *"Group atmosphere" and completion of survival instructor training.* Reno, Nev.: Stead Air Force Base, Crew Research Laboratory, February, 1956. (Lab. Note CRL-LN-56-205)

1152) Levi, M., et al *Sociometric studies of combat aircrews in survival training.* Washington, D.C.: Human Factors Operations Research Laboratories, November, 1953. (HFORL Memorandum TN-54-5)

1153) Levine, J., & Butler, J. Lecture vs. group decision in changing behavior. *J. appl. Psychol.*, 1952, *36*, 29–33.

1154) Levine, J., et al. Conforming behavior of psychiatric and medical patients. *J. abnorm. soc. Psychol.*, 1954, *49*, 251–255.

1155) Levinger, G. K. The development of perceptions and behavior in newly-formed social power relationships. *Amer. Psychologist*, 1955, *10*, 392–393. (Abstract)

1156) Levy, B. I. *A preliminary study of informal crew conferences as a crew training adjunct.* San Antonio, Tex.: Lackland Air Force Base, December, 1954. (Res. Bull. AFPTRC-TR-54-87)

1157) Levy, S. Need hierarchies as a function of group cohesiveness and member status. *Amer. Psychologist*, 1957, *12*, 365. (Abstract)

1158) Levy, S., & Willerman, B. Act and motive-oriented perceivers in interpersonal relations. *Amer. Psychologist*, 1956, *11*, 410. (Abstract)

1159) Lewin, K. Frontiers in group dynamics: II. Channels of group life; social planning and action research. *Hum. Relat.*, 1947, *1*, 143–153.

1160) Lewin, K. Frontiers in group dynamics: concept, method and reality in social science: social equilibria and social change. *Hum. Relat.*, 1947, *1*, 5–41.

1161) Lewin, K. Group decision and social change. In T. H. Newcomb and E. L. Hartley (Eds.), *Readings in social psychology.* New York: Holt, Rinehart and Winston, 1947. Pp. 330-344.

1162) Lewin, K. *Resolving social conflicts: selected papers on group dynamics.* New York: Harper & Row, 1948.

1163) Lewin, K. *Field theory in social science*. New York: Harper & Row, 1951.

1164) Lewin, K. Studies in group decision. In D. Cartwright and A. F. Zander (Eds.), *Group dynamics:.research and theory*. New York: Harper & Row, 1953. Pp. 287–301.

1165) Lewin, K., & Lippitt, R. An experimental approach to the study of autocracy and democracy: a preliminary note. *Sociometry*, 1938, *1*, 292–300.

1166) Lewin, K., et al. Patterns of aggressive behavior in experimentally created "social climates." *J. soc. Psychol.*, 1939, *10*, 271–299.

1167) Lewis, Helen B. An experimental study of the role of the ego in work: I. The role of the ego in cooperative work. *J. exp. Psychol.*, 1944, *34*, 113–126.

1168) Lewis, Helen B., & Franklin, M. An experimental study of the role of the ego in work: II. The significance of task orientation in work. *J. exp. Psychol.*, 1944, *34*, 195–215.

1169) Libo, I. M. *Measuring group cohesiveness*. Ann Arbor, Mich.: University of Michigan, Research Center for Group Dynamics, Institute for Social Research, 1953.

1170) Lichtenberg, P. Emotional maturity as manifested in ideational interactions. *J. abnorm. soc. Psychol.*, 1955, *51*, 298–301.

1171) Lichtenberg, P. Time perspective and the initiation of cooperation. *J. soc. Psychol.*, 1956, *43*, 247–260.

1172) Lichtenberg, P. Reactions to success and failure during individual and cooperative effort. *J. soc. Psychol.*, 1957, *46*, 31–34.

1173) Lichtenberg, P., & Deutsch, M. *A descriptive review of research on the staff process of decision-making*. San Antonio, Tex.: Lackland Air Force Base, December, 1954. (Res. Bull. AFPTRC-TR-54-129)

1174) Lieberman, M. A. The relation of diagnosed behavioral tendencies to member perceptions of self and of the group. In Dorothy Stock and H. A. Thelen (Eds.), *Emotional dynamics and group culture*. New York: New York University Press, 1958. Pp. 35-49.

1175) Lieberman, M. A. Sociometric choice related to affective approach. In Dorothy Stock and H. A. Thelen (Eds.), *Emotional dynamics and group culture*. New York: New York University Press, 1958. Pp. 71-83.

1176) Lieberman, S. An analysis of role change in a factory situation. *Amer. Psychologist*, 1951, *6*, 365. (Abstract)

1177) Lieberman, S. The relationship between attitudes and roles: a natural field experiment. *Psychol. Abstr.*, 1955, *15*, 636–637.

1178) Lieberman, S. The effects of changes in roles on the attitudes of role occupants. *Hum. Relat.*, 1956, *9*, 385–402.

1179) Likert, Rensis. An emerging theory of organization, leadership, and management. In L. Petrullo and B. M. Bass (Eds.), *Leadership and interpersonal behavior*. New York: Holt, Rinehart and Winston, 1961. Pp. 290–309.

1180) Lindeman, E. C. *Social discovery*. New York: Republic, 1924.

1181) Lindemann, E. Individual hostility and group integration. *Hum. Organization*, 1949, *8*, 5–9.

1182) Lindzey, G. (Ed.) *Handbook of social psychology*. Reading, Mass.: Addison-Wesley, 1954.

1183) Lindzey, G., & Borgatta, E. F. Sociometric measurements. In G. Lindzey (Ed.), *Handbook of social psychology*. Reading, Mass.: Addison-Wesley, 1954. Pp. 405–448.

1184) Lindzey, G.,& Riecken, H. W. Inducing frustration in adult subjects. *J. consult. Psychol.*, 1951, *15*, 18–23.

1185) Lindzey, G., & Urden, J. A. Personality and social choice. *Sociometry*, 1954, *17*, 47–63.

1186) Linton, H. B. Autokinetic judgment as a measure of influence. *J. abnorm. soc. Psychol.*, 1954, *49*, 464–466.

1187) Lippitt, R. Field theory and experiment in social psychology: autocratic and democratic group atmospheres. *Amer. J. Sociol.*, 1939, *45*, 26–49.

1188) Lippitt, R. An experimental study of the effect of democratic and authoritarian group atmospheres. *Univer. of Iowa Stud. Child Welf.*, 1940, *16*, 43–195.

1189) Lippitt, R. *Training in community relations: a research exploration toward new group skills*. New York: Harper & Row, 1949.

1190) Lippitt, R. Group dynamics and personality dynamics. *Amer. J. Orthopsychiat.*, 1951, *21*, 18–31.

1191) Lippitt, R. A program of experimentation on group functioning and group productivity. In W. Dennis (Ed.), *Current trends in social psychology*. Pittsburgh, Pa.: University of Pittsburgh Press, 1951. Pp. 14–49.

1192) Lippitt, R. *Final report of analysis of productivity team program*. Ann Arbor, Mich.: University of Michigan, Institute for Social Research, undated.

1193) Lippitt, R., & Radke, M. New trends in the investigation of prejudice. *Ann. Amer. Acad. Polit. Soc. Sci.*, 1946, *244*, 167–176.

1194) Lippitt, R., & White, R. K. An experimental study of leadership and group life. In T. M. Newcomb and E. L. Hartley (Eds.), *Readings in social psychology*. New York: Holt, Rinehart and Winston, 1947.

*1195) Lippitt, R., et al. The dynamics of power: a field study of social influence in groups of children. *Hum. Relat.*, 1952, *5*, 37–64.

1196) Lippitt, R., et al. *Dynamics of planned change*. New York: Robert Brunner, 1958.

1197) Lippitt, R., et al. *The dynamics of planned change: a comparative study of principles and techniques*. New York: Harcourt, 1958.

1198) Lippitt, Rosemary. Popularity among preschool children. *Child Develpm.*, 1941, *12*, 305–332.

*1199) Lipsitt, L. P., & Vallance, T. R. The expression of teleonomic trends in private and in group-related problem situations. *J. Pers.*, 1955, *23*, 381–390.

1200) Lodahl, T. M., & Porter, L. W. Relations among psychometric score patterns, social characteristics, and effectiveness of small industrial work groups. *Amer. Psychologist*, 1959, *14*, 363. (Abstract)

1201) Loomis, C. P. Informal groupings in a Spanish-American village. *Sociometry*, 1941, *4*, 36–51.

1202) Loomis, C. P., & Beegle, J. A. A topological analysis of social systems. *Sociometry*, 1948, *11*, 147–191.

1203) Loomis, C. P., & Pepinsky, H. B. Sociometry, 1937–1947: theory and methods. *Sociometry*, 1948, *11*, 262–283.

1204) Loomis, C. P., et al. The size of the family as related to social success of children. *Sociometry*, 1949, *12*, 313–320.

1205) Lorge, I.. & Solomon, H. *Individual performance and group performance in problem solving related to group size and previous exposure to the problem.* New York: Columbia University, Bureau of Applied Social Research, April, 1958. (Tech. Rep. No. 2, Contract Nonr-26643)

1206) Lorge, I., & Solomon, H. *Group and individual performance in problem solving related to previous exposure to problem, level of aspiration, and group size.* New York: Columbia University, Bureau of Applied Social Research, December, 1958. (Tech. Rep. No. 3, Contract Nonr-26643)

1207) Lorge, I., et al. Methods for the evaluation of the quality of rational decisions. *Amer. Psychologist*, 1952, *7*, 293. (Abstract)

1208) Lorge, I., et al. Decisions written by *ad hoc* staffs and simulated commanders. *Amer. Psychologist*, 1953, *8*, 391. (Abstract)

1209) Lorge, I., et al. Problem-solving by teams and by individuals in a field setting. *J. educ. Psychol.*, 1955, *55*, 160–166.

*1210) Lorge, I., et al. Solutions by teams and by individuals to a field problem at different levels of reality. *J. educ. Psychol.*, 1955, *46*, 17–24.

1211) Lorge, I., et al. The adequacy of written reports in problem-solving by teams and by individuals. *J. soc. Psychol.*, 1956, *43*, 65–74.

1212) Lorge, I., et al. A survey of studies contrasting the quality of group performance and individual performance. *Psychol. Bull.*, 1958, *55*, 337–372.

1213) Lott, A. J., et al. The effects of feedback in group processes. *Amer. Psychologist*, 1954, *9*. (Abstract)

1214) Lott, A. J., et al. Effects of feeling-oriented and task-oriented feedback upon defensive behavior in small problem-solving groups. *Amer. Psychologist*, 1955, *10*, 335. (Abstract)

1215) Lott, Bernice E., & Lott, A. L. Group cohesiveness as a learning phenomenon: the formation of attitudes toward group members. *Amer. Psychologist*, 1959, *14*, 381. (Abstract)

1216) Luce, R. D., & Perry, A. D. A method of matrix analysis of group structure. *Psychometrika*, 1949, *14*, 95–116.

1217) Luce, R. D., et al. A statistical model for relational analysis. *Psychometrika*, 1955, *20*, 319–327.

1218) Luchins, A. S. Social influences on perception of complex drawings. *J. soc. Psychol.*, 1945, *21*, 257–273.

1219) Luchins, A. S. Group structures in group psychotherapy. *J. clin. Psychol.*, 1947, *3*, 269–273.

1220) Luchins, A. S. A variational approach to social influences on perception *J. soc. Psychol.*, 1955, *42*, 113–119.

1221) Luchins, A. S., & Luchins, Edith H. On conformity with true and false communications. *J. soc. Psychol.*, 1955, *42*, 283–303.

1222) Luchins, A. S., & Luchins, Edith H. Previous experience with ambiguous and non-ambiguous perceptual stimuli under various social influences. *J. soc. Psychol.*, 1955, *42*, 249–270.

1223) Luchins, A. S., & Luchins, Edith H. Discovering the source of contradictory communications. *J. soc. Psychol.*, 1956, *44*, 49–63.

1224) Lundberg, G. A. Some problems of group classification and measurement. *Amer. sociol. Rev.*, 1940, *5*, 351–360.

1225) Lundberg, G. A., & Steele, Mary. Social attraction-patterns in a village. *Sociometry*, 1938, *1*, 375–419.

1226) Lundberg, G. A., et al. Attraction patterns in a university. *Sociometry*, 1949, *12*, 158–169.

*1227) Lundy, R. M. Assimilative projection and accuracy of prediction in interpersonal perceptions. *J. abnorm. soc. Psychol.*, 1956, *52*, 33–38.

1228) Lundy, R. M., & Bieri, J. Changes in interpersonal perceptions associated with group interaction. *Amer. Psychologist*, 1952, *7*, 306–307. (Abstract)

1229) Lundy, R. M., et al. Self acceptability and descriptions of sociometric choices. *J. abnorm. soc. Psychol.*, 1955, *51*, 260–262.

1230) Maas, H. S. Personal and group factors in leaders' social perception. *J. abnorm. soc. Psychol.*, 1950, *45*, 54–63.

1231) Maas, H. S. Evaluating the individual member in the group. In National Conference of Social Work (Eds.), *Group work and community organization, 1953–1954*. New York: Columbia University Press, 1954. Pp. 36–44.

1232) Maas, H. S. The role of members in clubs of lower-class and middle-class adolescents. *Child Develpm.*, 1954, *25*, 241–251.

1233) Maas, H. S., et al. A technique for studying the social behavior of schizophrenics. *J. abnorm. soc. Psychol.*, 1951, *46*, 119–123.

1234) Mabee, F. C., Jr. Solving a desegregation problem through small-group activity. In Helen I. Driver (Ed.), *Counseling and learning through small-group discussion*. Madison, Wis.: Monona Publications, 1958. Pp. 363–365.

1235) McAninch, W. D., & Hemphill, J. K. *Studies in aircrew composition: VIII. The relationship among various evaluations of individual crew members and B-29 crew performance in combat*. Columbus, Ohio: Ohio State University, Personnel Research Board, February, 1954. [Tech. Rep. 8, Contracts AF 33(038)-10105 and AF 18(600)-27]

*1236) Macbride, P. D. *Studies in conformity and yielding: IX. The influence of confidence upon resistance of perceptual judgments to group pressure*. Berkeley, Calif.: University of California, 1958. (Tech. Rep. No. 10, Contract NR 170-159)

1237) McBurney, J. H., & Hance, K. G. *The principles and methods of discussion*. New York: Harper & Row, 1939.

1238) McCandless, B. R. Changing relationships between dominance and social acceptability during group democratization. *Amer. J. Orthopsychiat.*, 1942, *12*, 529–535.

1239) McCandless, B. R., & Marshall, Helen R. A picture sociometric technique for preschool children and its relation to teacher judgments of friendship. *Child Develpm.*, 1957, *28*, 139–147.

1240) Maccoby, N. *The relationship of supervisory behavior and attitudes to group productivity in two widely different industrial settings.* Ann Arbor, Mich.: University of Michigan, 1949. (Contract NR 170–272)

1241) McConnell, J. V., & Blake, R. R. A methodological study of tape-recorded synthetic group atmospheres. *Amer. Psychologist*, 1953, *8*, 395. (Abstract)

*1242) McCurdy, H. G., & Eber, H. W. Democratic versus authoritarian: a further investigation of group problem-solving. *J. Pers.*, 1953, *22*, 258–269.

*1243) McCurdy, H. G., & Lambert, W. E. The efficiency of small human groups in the solution of problems requiring genuine co-operation. *J. Pers.*, 1952, *20*, 478–494.

*1244) McDavid, J., Jr. Personality and situational determinants of conformity. *J. abnorm. soc. Psychol.*, 1959, *58*, 241–246.

1245) McGinnies, E. A method for matching anonymous questionnaire data with group discussion material. *J. abnorm. soc. Psychol.*, 1956, *52*, 139–140.

1246) McGinnies, E., & Altman, I. Discussion as a function of attitudes and content of a persuasive communication. *J. appl. Psychol.*, 1959, *43*, 53–59.

1247) McGinnies, E., & Smith, C. Communicating mental health information in community discussion groups. *Amer. Psychologist*, 1955, *10*, 358. (Abstract)

1248) McGinnies, E., & Vaughan, W. Some biographical determiners of participation in group discussion. *J. appl. Psychol.*, 1957, *41*, 179–185.

*1249) McGinnies, E., et al. The effects of sound films on opinions about mental illness in community discussion groups. *J. appl. Psychol.*, 1958, *42*, 40–46.

1250) McGrath, J. E. *A framework for integration of small group research studies: a pilot study.* Arlington, Va.: Psychological Research Associates, 1957. [PRA Rep. No. 57–20, Contract No. AF 49(638)-256]

1251) McIntyre, C. J. Acceptance by others and its relation to acceptance of self and others. *J. abnorm. soc. Psychol.*, 1952, *47*, 624–625.

*1252) Mack, R. W. The prestige system of an air base: squadron rankings and morale. *Amer. sociol. Rev.*, 1954, *19*, 281–287.

1253) McKeachie, W. J. Individual conformity to attitudes of classroom groups. *J. abnorm. soc. Psychol.*, 1954, *49*, 282–289.

1254) McKeachie, W. J. Student centered versus instructor centered instruction. *J. educ. Psychol.*, 1954, *45*, 143–150.

1255) McKelvey, R. K. *The behavior of individuals and personnel systems in the surveillance functions of au Air Defense Direction Center: II. Distribution of voice communications at four critical crew positions.* San Antonio, Tex.: Lackland Air Force Base, 1954. (Tech. Rep. AFPTRC-TR-54-99)

1256) McKelvey, R. K., & Cohen, J. D. *The behavior of individuals and personnel systems in the surveillance functions of an Air Defense Direction Center: I. Experimental method.* San Antonio, Tex.: Lackland Air Force Base, December, 1954. (Tech. Rep. AFPTRC-TR-54-98)

1257) MacKinnon, D. W., et al. *An assessment study of Air Force officers. Part I: Design of the study and description of the variables.* Berkeley, Calif.: University of California, April, 1958. [WADC tech. Rep. No. 58-91, pt. 1., Contract AF 18(600)8]

1258) McMillan, J. J., & Silverberg, J. Sociometric choice patterns in hospital ward groups with varying degrees of interpersonal disturbances. *J. abnorm. soc. Psychol.*, 1955, *50*, 168–172.

1259) McPartland, T. S., & Cumming, J. H. Self-conception, social class, and mental health. *Hum. Organization*, 1958, *17*, 24–29.

1260) McPherson, J. H. A method for describing the emotional life of a group and the emotional needs of group members. *Amer. Psychologist*, 1952, *7*, 305. (Abstract)

1261) McQuitty, L. L. *A method of pattern analysis for isolation typological and dimensional constructs.* San Antonio, Tex.: Lackland Air Force Base, December, 1955. (Res. Rep. AFPTRC-TN-55-62)

1262) Macy, J., Jr., et al. Coding noise in a task-oriented group. *J. abnorm. soc. Psychol.*, 1953, *48*, 401–409.

1263) Maier, N. R. F. The quality of group decisions as influenced by the discussion leader. *Hum. Relat.*, 1950, *3*, 155–174.

1264) Maier, N. R. F. An experimental test of the effect of training on discussion leadership. *Hum. Relat.*, 1953, *6*, 161–173.

1265) Maier, N. R. F., & Danielson, L. E. An evaluation of two approaches to discipline in industry. *J. appl. Psychol.*, 1956, *40*, 319–323.

*1266) Maier, N. R. F., & Maier, R. A. An experimental test of the effects of "developmental" vs. "free" discussion on the quality of group decisions. *J. appl. Psychol.*, 1957, *41*, 320–323.

1267) Maier, N. R. F., & Solem, A. R. The contribution of a discussion leader to the quality of group thinking: the effective use of minority opinions. *Hum. Relat.*, 1952, *5*, 277–288.

1268) Maisonneuve, J. A contribution to the sociometry of mutual choices. *Sociometry*, 1954, *17*, 33–46.

1269) Maisonneuve, J., et al. Selective choices and propinquity. *Sociometry*, 1952, *15*, 135–140.

1270) Maller, J. B. Cooperation and competition: an experimental study in motivation. *Teach. Coll., Columbia Univer. Contr. Educ.*, 1929, No. 384.

1271) Maller, J. B. Size of family and personality of offspring. *J. soc. Psychol.*, 1931, *2*, 3–27.

1272) Malmo, R. B., et al. Physiological study of personal interaction. *Psychosom. Med.*, 1957, *14*, 105–119.

1273) Malone, T. P. Analysis of the dynamics of group psychotherapy based on observation in a twelve-month experimental program. *J. Pers.*, 1948, *16*, 245–277.

1274) Maloney, R. M. Group learning through group discussion: a group discussion implementation analysis. *J. soc. Psychol.*, 1956, *43*, 3–9.

1275) Mandelbaum, D. G. *Soldier groups and Negro soldiers.* Berkeley, Calif.: University of California Press, 1952.

*1276) Manis, M. Social interaction and the self concept. *J. abnorm. soc. Psychol.*, 1955, *51*, 362–370.

1277) Mann, F. C. Changing superior-subordinate relationships. *J. soc. Issues*, 1951, 7(3), 56–63.

1278) Mann, F. C., & Dent, J. K. Appraisals of supervisors and attitudes of their employees in an electric power company. *Hum. Relat.* Ser. 1, 1954, *4*.

1279) Mann, F. C., & Pelz, D. *A comparison of high and low morale work groups.* Ann Arbor, Mich.: University of Michigan, 1948. (Contract NR 170-172)

1280) Mann, J. H. Experimental evaluation of role playing. *Psychol. Bull.*, 1956, *53*, 227–234.

1281) Mann, J. H. Radical prejudice and popularity in small interracial groups. *Amer. Psychologist*, 1957, *12*, 368. (Abstract)

1282) Mann, J. H. The influence of racial prejudice on sociometric choices and perceptions. *Sociometry*, 1958, *21*, 150–158.

1283) Mann, J. H., & Borgatta, E. F. Personality and behavior correlates of changes produced by role playing experience. *Psychol. Rep.*, 1959, *5*, 505–526.

1284) Mann, J. H., & Mann, Carola H. The effect of role-playing experience on role-playing ability. *Sociometry*, 1959, *22*, 64–74.

1285) Mann, J. H., & Mann, Carola H. The importance of a group task in producing group-member personality "behavior changes." *Hum. Relat.*, 1959, *12*, 75–80.

1286) Mann, R. D. A review of the relationships between personality and performance in small groups. *Psychol. Bull.*, 1959, *56*, 241–270.

1287) Mannheim, Betty F. *The influence of reference groups and membership groups on the self-image.* Urbana, Ill.: University of Illinois, Group Effectiveness Research Laboratory, 1957. (Interim tech. Rep. No. 3, SGO Contract MD 569)

1288) March, J. G. Group norms and active minority. *Amer. sociol. Rev.*, 1954, *19*, 733–741.

1289) March, J. G. Influence measure in experimental and semi-experimental groups. *Sociometry*, 1956, *19*, 260–271.

1290) Margolin, J. B. The use of an interaction matrix to validate patterns of group behavior. *Hum. Relat.*, 1952, *5*, 407–416.

1291) Marley, F. W. *The development of performance flight checks for B-29 combat crews.* Washington, D.C.: Bolling Air Force Base, Human Resources Research Laboratories, February, 1952. (HRRL Memorandum Rep. No. 19)

1292) Marquart, Dorothy I. Group problem solving. *J. soc. Psychol.*, 1955, *41*, 103–113.

1293) Marquis, D. G., et al. A social psychological study of the decision-making conference. In H. Guetzkow (Ed.), *Group, leadership, and men: research in human relations*. Pittsburgh, Pa.: Carnegie Press, 1951. Pp. 55–67.

*1294) Marriott, R. Size of working group and output. *Occup. Psychol.*, 1949, *23*, 47–57.

1295) Marrisett, F., Jr., & Howland, C. I. A comparison of three varieties of training in human problem solving. *J. exp. Psychol.*, 1959, *58*, 52–55.

1296) Marrow, A. J. Group dynamics in industry: implications for guidance and personnel workers. *Occupations*, 1948, *26*, 472–476.

1297) Marrow, A. J., & French, J. R. P., Jr. Changing a stereotype in industry. *J. soc. Issues*, 1945, *1*, 33–37.

1298) Marschak, J. Basic problems in the economic theory of teams. *Econometrica*, 1953, *21*(3).

1299) Marschak, J. *Towards an economic theory of organization and information*. Chicago, Ill.: University of Chicago, Cowles Commission for Research in Economics, 1954. (Cowles Commission Papers, New Ser. No. 95)

1300) Marschak, J. Elements for a theory of teams. *Mgmt Sci.*, 1955, *2* (1).

1301) Marschak, J. *Theory of teams: introduction*. Chicago, Ill.: University of Chicago, Cowles Commission for Research in Economics, May, 1957. [Cowles Found. Discussion Paper No. 31, Contract Nonr-358(01), NR 047-006]

1302) Marschak, J., & Radner, R. The firm as a team. *Econometrica*, 1954, *22* (4).

1303) Martin, E. A., Jr., & Hill, W. F. Toward a theory of group development: six phases of therapy group development. *Int. J. Group Psychother.*, 1957, *7*, 20–30.

1304) Martin, W. E., et al. Studies of group behavior: leaders, followers, and isolates in small organized groups. *J. abnorm. soc. Psychol.*, 1952, *47*, 838–842.

*1305) Martin, W. E., et al. Studies of group behavior: II. Methodological problems in the study of interrelationships of group members. *Educ. psychol. Measmt*, 1952, *12*, 533–553.

1306) Masling, J., et al. Status, authoritarianism, and sociometric choice. *J. soc. Psychol.*, 1955, *41*, 297–310.

1307) Mason, D. J. Judgements of leaderships based upon physiognomic cues. *J. abnorm. soc. Psychol.*, 1957, *54*, 273–274.

1308) Mason, R. *Psychological and training factors affecting survival ration acceptability*. San Antonio, Tex.: Randolph Air Force Base, Air Force Personnel and Training Research Center, Crew Research Laboratory, 1957.

1309) Massarik, F., et al. Sociometric choice and organizational effectiveness: a multi-relational approach. *Sociometry*, 1953, *16*, 211–238.

1310) Matarazzo, J. D., et al. The interaction chronograph as an instrument for objective measurement of interaction patterns during interviews. *J. Psychol.*, 1956, *41*, 347–367.

1311) Matarazzo, J. D., et al. Stability of interaction patterns during interviews: a replication. *J. consult. Psychol.*, 1956, *20*, 267–274.

1312) Matarazzo, J. D., et al. Stability and modifiability of personality patterns during a standardized interview. In P. A. Hoch and J. Zubin (Eds.), *Psychopathology of communication*. New York: Grune & Stratton, 1958. Pp. 98–125.

1313) Matthews, J., & Bendig, A. W. The index of agreement: a possible criterion for measuring the outcome of group discussion. *Speech Monogr.*, 1955, *22*, 39–42.

1314) Maucorps, P. H. A sociometric inquiry in the French army. *Sociometry*, 1949, *12*, 46–80.

*1315) Mausner, B. Studies in social interaction: III. Effect of variation in one partner's prestige on the interaction of observer pairs. *J. appl. Psychol.*, 1953, *37*, 391–393.

*1316) Mausner, B. The effect of one partner's success in a relevant task on the interaction of observer pairs. *J. abnorm. soc. Psychol.*, 1954, *49*, 557–560.

1317) Mausner, B. The effect of prior reinforcement on the interaction of observer pairs. *J. abnorm. soc. Psychol.*, 1954, *49*, 65–68.

1318) Mausner, B. Studies in social interaction: I. A conceptual scheme. *J. soc. Psychol.*, 1955, *41*, 259–270.

1319) Mausner, B., & Bloch, Barbara. A study of the additivity of variables affecting social interaction. *J. abnorm. soc. Psychol.*, 1957, *54*, 250–256.

1320) May, M. A., & Doob, L. W. Competition and cooperation. *Soc. Sci. Res. Council Bull.*, 1937, No. 25.

1321) Mayo, E. *The human problems of an industrial civilization.* New York: Macmillan, 1933.

1322) Mayo, E., & Lombard, G. F. F. *Teamwork and labor turnover in the aircraft industry of Southern California.* Boston: Harvard University, Graduate School of Business Administration, 1944.

1323) Mead, G. H. *Mind, self, and society from the standpoint of a social behaviorist.* Chicago: University of Chicago Press, 1950.

1324) Medalia, N. Z. Unit size and leadership perception. *Sociometry*, 1954, *17*, 64–67.

*1325) Medalia, N. Z. Authoritarianism, leader acceptance, and group cohesion. *J. abnorm. soc. Psychol.*, 1955, *51*, 207–213.

1326) Medalia, N. Z., & Miller, D. C. Human relations leadership and the association of morale and efficiency in work groups: a controlled study with small military units. *Soc. Forces*, 1955, *33*, 348–352.

1327) Melbin, M. Field methods and techniques: the action-interaction chart. *Hum. Organization*, 1953, *12* (1), 34–35.

1328) Mellinger, G. D. Interpersonal trust as a factor in communication. *J. abnorm. soc. Psychol.*, 1956, *52*, 304–309.

1329) Mengert, Ida G. A preliminary study of the reactions of two-year-old children to each other when paired in a semi-controlled situation. *J. genet. Psychol.*, 1931, *39*, 393–398.

1330) Menzel, H. Public and private conformity under different conditions of acceptance in the group. *J. abnorm. soc. Psychol.*, 1957, *55*, 398–402.

1331) Merei, F. Group leadership and institutionalization. *Hum. Relat.*, 1949, *2*, 23–39.

1332) Merrill, Barbara. A measurement of mother-child interaction. *J. abnorm. soc. Psychol.*, 1946, *41*, 37–49.

*1333) Meyer, H. H. Factors related to success in the human relations aspect of work-group leadership. *Psychol. Monogr.*, 1951, *63*, No. 3.

1334) Meyers, C. E. The effect of conflicting authority on the child. *Univer. of Iowa Stud. Child Welf.*, 1944, *20*, 31–98.

1335) Michael, D. M., & Maccoby, N. Factors influencing verbal learning from films under varying conditions of audience participation. *J. exp. Psychol.*, 1953, *46*, 411–418.

1336) Middleton, T. H. Some observations on leadership in military and educational organizations. Paper read at Sympos. Leadership interpers. Behav. Baton Rouge, La., 1959.

1337) Miller, D. C. An experiment in the measurement of social interaction in group discussion. *Amer. sociol. Rev.*, 1939, *4*, 341–351.

1338) Miller, D. C. The shaping of research design in large scale group research. *Soc. Forces,* 1955, *33,* 383–390.

1339) Miller, D. C., & Medalia, N. Z. Efficiency, leadership, and morale in small military organizations. *Sociol. Rev.*, 1955, *3*, 93–107.

1340) Miller, D. C., & Philbrick, W. W. The measurement of group learning process by use of the interactional telemeter. *Amer. sociol. Rev.*, 1953, *18*, 184–189.

1341) Miller, E. *Survey of literature on communication in group discussions.* Ann Arbor, Mich.: University of Michigan, 1948. (Contract No. NR 172–301)

1342) Miller, G. A. *Communication and information as limiting factors in group formation.* Cambridge, Mass.: Harvard University Press, March, 1957.

1343) Miller, J. G. (Ed.) *Experiments in social process.* New York: McGraw-Hill, 1950.

1344) Miller, J. G. Toward a general theory for the behavioral sciences. *Amer. Psychologist*, 1955, *10*, 513–531. (Abstract)

*1345) Mills, T. M. Power relations in three-person groups. *Amer. sociol. Rev.*, 1953, *18*, 351–357.

1346) Mills, T. M. The coalition pattern in three-person groups. *Amer. sociol. Rev.*, 1954, *19*, 657–667.

1347) Mills, T. M. Developmental process in three-person groups. *Hum. Relat.*, 1956, *9*, 343–354.

1348) Mills, T. M., et al. *Group structure and the newcomer.* Oslo, Norway: Oslo University Press, 1957.

1349) Mintz, A. Non-adaptive group behavior. *J. abnorm. soc. Psychol.*, 1951, *46*, 150–159.

1350) Mischel, W. The effect of the commitment situation on the generalization of expectancies. *J. Pers.*, 1958, *26*, 508–516.

1351) Mishler, E. *Ascendant and submissive members and leaders: their interaction in group discussion.* Ann Arbor, Mich.: University of Michigan, Conference Research Project Report, 1950.

1352) Misumi, J. Research into buzz-group method with in-service classes for teachers. In Helen I. Driver (Ed.), *Counseling and learning through small-group discussion.* Madison, Wis.: Monona Publications, 1958. Pp. 365–367.

1353) Mitchell, J. V., Jr. The factor analysis of a "guess-who" questionnaire designed to identify significant behavior patterns in children. *J. Pers.*, 1956, *24*, 376–386.

*1354) Mitnick, L. L., & McGinnies, E. Influencing ethnocentrism in small discussion groups through a film communication. *J. abnorm. soc. Psychol.*, 1958, *56*, 82–90.

1355) Miyamoto, S. F., & Dornbush, S. M. A test of interactionist hypotheses of self-conception. *Amer. J. Sociol.*, 1956, *61*, 399–403.

*1356) Moeller, G., & Applezweig, M. H. A motivational factor in conformity. *J. abnorm. soc. Psychol.*, 1957, *55*, 114–120.

1357) Moldawsky, S. An empirical validation of a rigidity scale against a criterion of rigidity in an interpersonal situation. *Sociometry*, 1951, *14*, 153–174.

1358) Moon, C. G., & Hariton, T. Evaluating an appraisal and feedback training program. *Personnel*, 1958, *35*, 36–42.

1359) Moore, H. T. The comparative influence of majority and expert opinion. *Amer. J. Psychol.*, 1921, *32*, 16–20.

1360) Moore, H. T. Further data concerning sex differences. *J. abnorm. soc. Psychol.*, 1922, *17*, 210–214.

1361) Moore, J. V., et al. The effects of choice of working partner on student achievement and attitudes. *Amer. Psychologist*, 1955, *10*, 328. (Abstract)

1362) Moore, O. K. Problem solving and the perception of persons. In R. Tagiuri and L. Petrullo (Eds.), *Person perception and interpersonal behavior*. Stanford, Calif.: Stanford University Press, 1958. Pp. 131–150.

1363) Moore, O. K., & Anderson, S. B. Search behavior in individual and group problem solving. *Amer. sociol. Rev.*, 1954, *19*, 702–714.

1364) Moore, O. K., & Berkowitz, M. I. *Game theory and interaction analysis.* New Haven, Conn.: Yale University, 1956. (Contract No. NR 170-044).

1365) Moreno, Florence B. Sociometric status of children in a nursery school group. *Sociometry*, 1942, *5*, 395–411.

1366) Moreno, J. L. Foundations of sociometry: an introduction. *Sociometry*, 1941, *4*, 15–35.

1367) Moreno, J. L. Sociometry in action. *Sociometry*, 1942, *5*, 298–315.

1368) Moreno, J. L. Sociometry and the cultural order. *Sociometry*, 1943, *6*, 299–344.

1369) Moreno, J. L. (Ed.) *Group psychotherapy.* Beacon, N.Y.: Beacon House, 1945.

1370) Moreno, J. L. Contributions of sociometry to research methodology in sociology. *Amer. sociol. Rev.*, 1947, *12*, 287–292.

1371) Moreno, J. L. *The theatre of spontaneity.* Beacon, N. Y.: Beacon House, 1947.

1372) Moreno, J. L. *Sociometry, experimental method and the science of society.* Beacon, N.Y.: Beacon House, 1951.

1373) Moreno, J. L. *Who shall survive?* (2nd ed.) Beacon, N.Y.: Beacon House, 1953.

1374) Moreno, J. L. Old and new trends in sociometry: turning points in small group research. *Sociometry*, 1954, *17*, 179–193.

1375) Moreno, J. L., & Jennings, Helen H. Statistics of social configurations. *Sociometry*, 1938, *1*, 342–374.

1376) Moreno, J. L., & Jennings, Helen H. Sociometric methods of grouping and regrouping: with reference to authoritative and democratic methods of grouping. *Sociometry*, 1944, *7*, 397–414.

1377) Moreno, J. L., et al. Time as a qualitative index to interpersonal relations. *Sociometry*, 1940, *3*, 62–80.

1378) Morris, R. T., & Seeman, M. The problem of leadership: an interdisciplinary approach. *Amer. J. Sociol.*, 1950, *56*, 149–155.

1379) Morrison, H. W., et al. *Attitude change project.* Ann Arbor, Mich.: University of Michigan, January, 1958. (Contract Nonr-122410)

1380) Morissette, J. O. An experimental study of the theory of structural balance. *Hum. Relat.*, 1958, *11*, 239.

1381) Morse, Nancy. *Satisfaction in the white-collar job.* Ann Arbor, Mich.: University of Michigan, Institute for Social Research, 1953. (Contract NR 170–172)

*1382) Morse, Nancy, & Reimer, E. The experimental change of a major organizational variable. *J. abnorm. soc. Psychol.*, 1956, *52*, 120–129.

1383) Morse, Nancy, et al. Regulation and control in hierarchical organizations. *J. soc. Issues*, 1951, *7*, 41–48.

1384) Morton, A. S. *Similarity as a determinant of friendship: a multidimensional study.* Princeton, N.J.: Princeton University, April, 1959. (Contract Nonr-185815)

1385) Morton, Mary. A training program for junior student counselors. In Helen I. Driver (Ed.), *Counseling and learning through small group discussion.* Madison, Wis.: Monona Publications, 1958. Pp. 326–328.

1386) Moss, H. Standards of conduct for students, teachers, and parents. *J. couns. Psychol.*, 1955, *2*, 39–42.

1387) Motz, Annabelle B. The role conception inventory: a tool for research in social psychology. *Amer. sociol. Rev.*, 1952, *17*, 465–471.

1388) Mouton, Jane S., et al. The reliability of sociometric measures. *Sociometry*, 1955, *18*, 7–48.

1389) Mouton, Jane S., et al. The validity of sociometric responses. *Sociometry*, 1955, *18*, 181–206.

*1390) Mouton, Jane S., et al. The relationship between frequency of yielding and the disclosure of personal identity. *J. Pers.*, 1956, *24*, 339–347.

1391) Mukerji, N. P. An investigation of ability in work in groups and in isolation. *Brit. J. Psychol.*, 1940, *30*, 352–356.

1392) Mulder, M. Group structure and group performance. *Acta psychol.*, 1959, *16*, 356–402.

1393) Mumford, E. M. Social behavior in small work groups. *Sociol. Rev.*, 1959, *7*, 137–157.

1394) Murphy, G., et al. *Experimental social psychology.* New York: Harper & Row, 1937.

1395) Murphy, Lois B. *Social behavior and child personality: an exploratory study of some roots of sympathy.* New York: Columbia University Press, 1937.

1396) Murphy, Lois B., & Murphy, G. The influence of social situations upon the behavior of children. In C. Murchison (Ed.), *A handbook of social psychology.* Worcester, Mass.: Clark University Press, 1935. Pp. 1034–1096.

1397) Murstein, B. I. Some comments on the measurement of projection and empathy. *J. consult. Psychol.*, 1957, *21*, 81–82.

1398) Mussen, P. H., & Porter, L. W. Personal motivations and self-conceptions associated with effectiveness and ineffectiveness in emergent groups. *J. abnorm. soc. Psychol.*, 1959, *59*, 23–27.

1399) Myers, T. I., & Palmer, F. H. Crew description dimensions and radar crew effectiveness. *Amer. Psychologist*, 1955, *10*, 442. (Abstract)

1400) Nadler, E. B. Yielding, authoritarianism, and authoritarian ideology regarding groups. *J. abnorm. soc. Psychol.*, 1959, *58*, 408–410.

*1401) Nakamura, C. Y. *The relation between conformity and problem-solving*. Stanford, Calif.: Stanford University, Department of Psychology, 1955. (Contract No. 25125)

1402) Nakamura, C. Y. Conformity and problem-solving. *J. abnorm. soc. Psychol.*, 1958, *56*, 315–320.

1403) Neel, R. Factors related to productivity. Ann Arbor, Mich.: University of Michigan, 1951. (Contract NR 170-172)

1404) Nehnevajsa, J. Chance expectancy and intergroup choice. *Sociometry*, 1955, *18*, 153–163.

1405) Nehnevajsa, J. Probability in sociometric analysis. *Sociometry*, 1955, *18*, 678–688.

1406) Nelson, P. D. *A note on factors related to group status*. Pensacola, Fla.: Naval School of Aviation Medicine, July, 1957. (Project No. NM 16 01 11, Sub. 4, No. 3)

1407) Newcomb, T. M. *Personality and social change*. New York: Holt, Rinehart and Winston, 1943.

1408) Newcomb, T. M. Autistic hostility and social reality. *Hum. Relat.*, 1947, *1*, 69–86.

1409) Newcomb, T. M. Role behaviors in the study of individual personality and of groups. *J. Pers.*, 1950, *18*, 273–289.

1410) Newcomb, T. M. An approach to the study of communicative acts. *Psychol. Rev.*, 1953, *60*, 393–404.

1411) Newcomb, T. M. Social psychology and group processes. *Annu. Rev. Psychol.*, 1953, *4*, 183–214.

1412) Newcomb, T. M. *Interpersonal perception among group members*. Stanford, Calif.: Center for Advanced Study in the Behavioral Sciences, November, 1956. (Contract Nonr-452)

1413) Newcomb, T. M. The prediction of interpersonal attraction. *Amer. Psychologist*, 1956, *12*, 575–586. (Abstract)

1414) Newcomb, T. M. The cognition of persons as cognizers. In R. Tagiuri and L. Petrullo (Eds.), *Person perception and interpersonal behavior*. Stanford, Calif.: Stanford University Press, 1958. Pp. 179–190.

1415) Newstetter, W. I. An experiment in the defining and measuring of group adjustment. *Amer. sociol. Rev.*, 1937, *2*, 230–236.

1416) Newstetter, W. I., & Feldstein, M. J. *Wawokiye Camp: a research project in group work*. Cleveland, Ohio: Western Reserve University, School of Applied Social Sciences, 1930.

1417) Newstetter, W. I., et al. *Group adjustment: a study in experimental sociology*. Cleveland, Ohio: Western Reserve University, School of Applied Social Sciences, 1938.

1418) Norfleet, Bobbie. Interpersonal relations and group productivity. *J. soc. Issues*, 1948, *4* (2), 66–69.

1419) Northway, Mary L. *A primer of sociometry*. Toronto: University of Toronto Press, 1952.

*1420) Northway, Mary L., & Wigdor, B. T. Rorschach patterns related to the sociometric status of school children. *Sociometry*, 1947, *10*, 186–199.

1421) Norton, E. J. The disproportionate effect of "disintegrators." *J. Communication*, 1954, *4*, 140–141.

1422) Office of Special Services. Assessment Staff. *Assessment of men*. New York: Holt, Rinehart and Winston, 1948.

1423) Olmstead, J. A., & Blake, R. R. The use of simulated groups to produce modifications in judgment. *J. Pers.*, 1955, *23*, 335–345.

1424) Olmstead, M. S. Orientation and role in the small group. *Amer. sociol. Rev.*, 1954, *19*, 741–751.

1425) Olmsted, D. W. Organizational leadership and social structure in a small city. *Amer. sociol. Rev.*, 1945, *19*, 273–281.

1426) Olmsted, D. W. *Assessment of leader adequacy from structured questionnaire responses of voluntary group members: research on group structure and function as related to the personality characteristics and interests of group members*. Minneapolis: University of Minnesota, March, 1955. (Tech. Rep. No. 6, Contract N8 ONR 66216)

1427) Olmsted, D. W. Inter-group similarities of role correlates. *Sociometry*, 1957, *20*, 8–20.

*1428) Olmsted, D. W., & Monachesi, E. D. *MMPI trends of small group leaders and members*. Minneapolis: University of Minnesota, 1955. (Contract No. NR-170-169)

1429) Olmsted, D. W., & Monachesi, E. D. *Research on group structure and function as related to the personality characteristics and interests of group members*. Minneapolis: University of Minnesota, 1955. (Contract No. N8 ONR 66216)

1430) Olmsted, D. W., & Sagi, P. C. *Groups as process: a simulation of the longitudinal study of small voluntary groups by multivariate analysis*. Minneapolis: University of Minnesota, 1954. (Contract NR 170-169)

1431) Olmsted, D. W., & Sagi, P. C. *Attitudinal correlates of role-selection processes in organized groups*. Minneapolis: University of Minnesota, 1955. (Contract NR 170–169)

1432) Olson, W. C., & Wilkinson, M. M. The measurement of child behavior in terms of its social stimulus value. *J. exp. Educ.*, 1932, *1*, 92–95.

1433) O'Neill, H. E., & Kubany, A. J. Observation methodology and supervisory behavior. *Personnel Psychol.*, 1959, *12*, 85–95.

1434) Oppenheim, A. N. Social status and clique formation among grammar school boys. *Brit. J. Sociol.*, 1955, *6*, 228–245.

1435) Ort, R. S. A study of role-conflicts as related to happiness in marriage. *J. abnorm. soc. Psychol.*, 1950, *45*, 691–699.

1436) Ossorio, A. G., & Leary, T. Patterns of social interaction and their relation to personality structure. *Amer. Psychologist*, 1950, *5*, 303. (Abstract)

1437) Ostlund, L. A. Group integration in a case discussion course. *J. educ. Psychol.*, 1953, *44*, 463–474.

1438) Page, R. H., & McGinnies, E. Comparison of two styles of leadership in small group discussion. *J. appl. Psychol.*, 1959, *43*, 240–245.

1439) Paivio, A., & Lambert, W. E. Measures and correlates of audience anxiety ("stage fright"). *J. Pers.*, 1959, *27*, 1–17.

1440) Palmer, F. H., & Myers, T. I. Sociometric choices and group productivity among radar crews. *Amer. Psychologist*, 1955, *10*, 441. (Abstract)

1441) Park, R. E., & Burgess, E. W. *Introduction to the science of sociology.* Chicago, Ill.: University of Chicago Press, 1924.

1442) Parker, S. Leadership patterns in a psychiatric ward. *Hum. Relat.*, 1958, *11*, 287–301.

1443) Parsons, T., et al. (Eds.) *Working papers in the theory of action.* New York: Free Press, 1953.

1444) Parsons, T., & Shils, E. A. Values, motives, and systems of action. In T. Parsons and E. A. Shils (Eds.), *Toward a general theory of action.* Cambridge, Mass.: Harvard University Press, 1951. Pp. 47–109.

1445) Parsons, T., et al. (Eds.) *Family, socialization and interaction process.* New York: Free Press, 1955.

1446) Parten, Mildred B. Social participation among preschool children. *J. abnorm. soc. Psychol.*, 1932, *27*, 243–269.

1447) Parten, Mildred B. Leadership among preschool children. *J. abnorm. soc. Psychol.*, 1933, *27*, 430–440.

1448) Parten, Mildred B. Social play among preschool children. *J. abnorm. soc. Psychol.*, 1933, *28*, 136–147.

1449) Patridge, E. D. Leadership among adolescent boys. Teach. Coll., *Columbia Univer. Contrib. Educ.*, 1934, No. 608.

*1450) Patchen, M. The effect of reference group standards on job satisfactions. *Hum. Relat.*, 1958, *11*, 303–314.

*1451) Pavlik, W. B. *Motivational factors in individual and group productivity: IV. The effects of personal and situational motivation upon individual performance in a small group setting.* Columbus, Ohio: Ohio State University Research Foundation, 1956.

1452) Pellegrin, R. J. The achievement of high status and leadership in the small group. *Soc. Forces*, 1953, *32*, 10–16.

1453) Pelz, D. C. Leadership within a hierarchal organization. *J. soc. Issues*, 1951, *7*, 49–55.

1454) Pelz, D. C. *Power and leadership in the first-line supervisor.* Ann Arbor, Mich.: University of Michigan, Institute for Social Research, 1951. (Contract No. NR 170-272)

1455) Pelz, D. C. *Influence: a key to effective leadership in the first-line supervisor.* New York: American Management Association, 1952.

*1456) Pennington, D. F., et al. *Some effects of decision and discussion on coalescence, change, and effectiveness.* Baton Rouge, La.: Louisiana State University, October, 1957. (Contract N7 ONR 35609)

1457) Pennington, D. F., et al. Some effects of decision and discussion on coalescence, change, and effectiveness. *J. appl. Psychol.*, 1958, *42*, 404–408.

1458) Pepinsky, H. B. Productive behavior. *J. counsel. Psychol.*, 1954, *1*, 57–59.

1459) Pepinsky, H. B. Research on productive behavior. *Personnel Guid. J.* 1954, *33*, 140–144.

1460) Pepinsky, H. B., et al. Individual personality and behavior in the social group, *Amer. Psychologist*, 1950, 5, 347–348. (Abstract)

1461) Pepinsky, H. B., et al. A group participation scale. *Amer. Psychologist*, 1951, 7, 379. (Abstract)

1462) Pepinsky, H. B., et al. The criterion in counseling: a group participation scale. *J. abnorm. soc. Psychol.*, 1952, 47, 415–419.

1463) Pepinsky, H. B., et al. The criterion in counseling: I. Individual personality and behavior in a social group. *Educ. psychol. Measmt*, 1952, 12, 178–193.

1464) Pepinsky, H. B., et al. *Motivational factors in individual and group productivity: I. Successful task accomplishment as related to task relevant personal beliefs.* Columbus, Ohio: Ohio State University Research Foundation, 1956. (Contract NR 171÷123)

1465) Pepinsky, H. B., et al. Successful task accomplishment as related to task-relevant personal beliefs. *Amer. Psychologist*, 1956, 11, 400 (Abstract)

1466) Pepinsky, H. B., et al. Task-relevant personal belief and task accomplishment. *J. counsel. Psychol.*, 1958, 5, 305–311.

*1467) Pepinsky, H. B., et al. Team productivity and contradiction of management policy commitments. *J. appl. Psychol.*, 1959, 43, 264–268.

1468) Pepinsky, Pauline N., & Pepinsky, H. B. *Originality in group productivity.* Columbus, Ohio: Ohio State University Research Foundation, November, 1958. (Annu. tech. Rep. No. 4, Contract Nonr 49515)

1469) Pepinsky, Pauline N., et al. *Leadership acts: II. The relation between needs for achievement and affiliation and attempts to lead under conditions of acceptance and rejection.* Columbus, Ohio: Ohio State University Research Foundation, 1955.

1470) Pepinsky, Pauline N., et al. *Motivation factors in individual and group productivity: V. The effects of induced orientation and type of task upon group performance and group member morale.* Columbus, Ohio: Ohio State University Research Foundation, 1957. [Contract No. N6 ORI 17, T. O. III (NR 171-123)]

*1471) Pepinsky, Pauline N., et al. Attempts to lead, group productivity, and morale under conditions of acceptance and rejection. *J. abnorm. soc. Psychol.*, 1958, 57, 47–54.

*1472) Pepitone, A. Motivational effects in social perception. *Hum. Relat.*, 1950, 3, 57–76.

1473) Pepitone, A. Attributions of causality, social attitudes, and cognitive matching processes. In R. Tagiuri and L. Petrullo (Eds.), *Person perception and interpersonal behavior.* Stanford, Calif.: Stanford University Press, 1958. Pp. 258–276.

1474) Pepitone, A., & Kleiner, R. Threat, frustration, and group cohesiveness. *Amer. Psychologist*, 1956, 11, 395. (Abstract)

1475) Pepitone, A., & Kleiner, R. The effects of threat and frustration on group cohesiveness. *J. abnorm. soc. Psychol.*, 1957, 54, 192–199.

1476) Pepitone, A., & Reichling, G. Group cohesiveness and the expression of hostility. *Hum. Relat.*, 1955, 8, 327–337.

1477) Pepitone, A., & Sherberg, Janet. Intentionality, responsibility, and interpersonal attraction. *J. Pers.*, 1957, 25, 757–766.

1478) Pepitone, A., & Wilpizeski, C. *The consequences of rejection—an experimental analysis.* Philadelphia: University of Pennsylvania, June, 1959. [Tech. Rep. No. 2, Contract Nonr 551-(27)]

1479) Perkins, H. V., Jr. The effects of climate and curriculum on group learning. *J. educ. Res.,* 1950, *44,* 269–286.

1480) Perkins, H. V., Jr. Climate influences group learning. *J. educ. Res.,* 1951, *45, 1–3.*

1481) Perlmutter, H. V. Group memory of meaningful material. *J. Psychol.,* 1953, *35,* 361–370.

1482) Perlmutter, H. V. Impressions of influential members of discussion groups. *J. Psychol.,* 1954, *38,* 223–234.

1483) Perlmutter, H. V., & de Montmollin, Germaine. Group learning of nonsense syllables. *J. abnorm. soc. Psychol.,* 1952, *47,* 762–769.

1484) Personnel Research Board. *The Ohio State University leadership studies: VI.* Columbus, Ohio: Author, October, 1956.

1485) Pessin, J. The comparative effects of social and mechanical stimulation on memorizing. *Amer. J. Psychol.,* 1933, *45,* 263–270.

*1486) Pessin, J., & Husband, R. W. Effects of social stimulation on human maze learning. *J. abnorm. soc. Psychol.,* 1933, *28,* 148–154.

1487) Peters, H. N., & Jones, F. D. Evaluation of group psychotherapy by means of performance tests. *J. consult. Psychol.,* 1951, *15,* 363–367.

1488) Peterson, O. F. Leadership and group behavior. *USAF ATC Instructors J.,* 1955, *6,* 48–54.

1489) Petrullo, L. Leadership and interpersonal behavior. Introduction. In L. Petrullo and B. M. Bass (Eds.), *Leadership and interpersonal behavior.* New York: Holt, Rinehart and Winston, 1961. Pp. xii–xxix.

1490) Petrullo, L., & Bass, B. M. (Eds.) *Leadership and interpersonal behavior.* New York: Holt, Rinehart and Winston, 1961.

1491) Philips, E. L., et al. The assimilation of the new child into the group. *Psychiatry,* 1951, *14,* 319–325.

1492) Philips, B. N., & D'Amico, L. A. Effects of cooperation and competition on the cohesiveness of small face-to-face groups. *J. educ. Psychol.,* 1956, *47,* 65–70.

1493) Phillips, Jeanne S., et al. Observer reliability of interaction patterns during interviews. *J. consult. Psychol.,* 1957, *21,* 269–275.

1494) Philp, Alice J. Strangers and friends as competitors and cooperators. *J. genet. Psychol.,* 1940, *57,* 249–258.

1495) Philp, H., & Dunphy, D. Developmental trends in small groups. *Sociometry,* 1959, *22,* 162–174.

1496) Plak, H. Problems of objective observation. In L. Festinger and D. Katz (Eds.), *Research methods in the behavioral sciences.* New York: Holt, Rinehart and Winston, 1953. Pp. 243–299.

1497) Plank, R. An analysis of a group therapy experiment. *Hum. Organization,* 1951, *10,* 5–21, 26–36.

1498) Polansky, N., et al. The use of near-sociometric data in research on group treatment processes. *Sociometry,* 1950, *13,* 39–62.

1499) Polansky, N. A., et al. An investigation of behavioral contagion in groups. *Hum. Relat.,* 1950, *3,* 319–348.

1500) Porter, E. H., Jr. The development and evaluation of a measure of counseling interview procedures. *Educ. psychol. Measmt*, 1943, *3*, 105–126, 215–238.

1501) Porter, L. W., & Kaufman, R. A. Relationships between a top-middle management self-description scale and behavior in a group situation. *J. appl. Psychol.*, 1959, *43*, 345–348.

1502) Potashin, Rena. A sociometric study of children's friendships. *Sociometry*, 1946, *9*, 48–70.

1503) Powell, J. W. Process analysis as content: a suggested basis for group classification. *J. soc. Issues*, 1952, *8*(2), 54–64.

1504) Powell, R. M., et al. An experimental study of role taking, group status, and group formation. *Sociol. soc. Res.*, 1956, *40*, 159–165.

*1505) Precker, J. A. Similarity of values as a factor in selection of peers and near-authority figures. *J. abnorm. soc. Psychol.*, 1952, *47*, 406–414.

1506) Precker, J. A. The automorphic process in the attribution of values. *J. Pers.*, 1953, *21*, 356–363.

1507) Preston, M. G. Note on the reliability and the validity of the group judgment. *J. exp. Psychol.*, 1938, *22*, 462–471.

1508) Preston, M. G., & Heintz, R. K. Effects of participatory versus supervisory leadership on group judgment. *J. abnorm. soc. Psychol.*, 1949, *44*, 345–355.

1509) Proctor, C. H., & Loomis, C. P. Analysis of sociometric data. In Marie Jahoda et al (Eds.), *Research methods in social relations*. New York: Holt, Rinehart and Winston, 1951. Pp. 561–585.

1510) Pryer, Margaret W., & Bass, B. M. Some effects of feedback on behavior in groups. *Sociometry*, 1959, *22*, 56–63.

1511) Pryer, Margaret W., et al. *Group effectiveness and consistency of leadership*. Baton Rouge, La.: Louisiana State University, April, 1957. (ONR Rep. No. 8)

1512) Puffer, J. A. Boys' gangs. *Pedag. Sem.*, 1905, *12*, 175–212.

1513) Puffer, J. A. *The boy and his gang*. Boston: Houghton Mifflin, 1912.

1514) Radke, M., & Klisurich, D. Experiments in changing food habits. *J. Amer. diet. Ass.*, 1947, *23*, 403–409.

1515) Rapoport, A. Mathematical theory of motivation interactions of two individuals. *Bull. Math. Biophysics*, 1947, *9*, 17–28, 41–61.

1516) Rapoport, A. Some game-theoretical aspects of parasitism and symbiosis. *Bull. Math. Biophysics*, 1956, *18*, 15–30.

1517) Rashevsky, N. Outline of a mathematical theory of human relations. *Phil. Sci.*, 1935, *2*, 413–429.

1518) Rashevsky, N. On the variation of the structure of a social group with time. *Psychometrika*, 1941, *6*, 273–277.

1519) Rashevsky, N. Contribution to the mathematical theory of human relations: VI. Periodic fluctuations in the behavior of social groups. *Psychometrika*, 1943, *8*, 81–85.

1520) Rashevsky, N. *A mathematical theory of human relations*. Bloomington, Ind.: Principia Press, 1947.

1521) Rashevsky, N., & Householder, A. S. On the mutual influence of individuals in a social group. *Psychometrika*, 1941, *6*, 317–321.

*1522) Rasmussen, G., & Zander, A. Group membership and self-evaluation. *Hum. Relat.*, 1954, *7*, 239–251.

1523) Rasmussen, G. R. An evaluation of a student-centered and instructor-centered method of conducting a graduate course in education. *J. educ. Psychol.*, 1956, *47*, 449–461.

1524) Raush, H. L., et al. The interpersonal behavior of children in residential treatment. *J. abnorm. soc. Psychol.*, 1959, *58*, 9–26.

1525) Raven, B. H. Social influence on opinions and the communication of related content. *J. abnorm. soc. Psychol.*, 1959, *58*, 119–128.

1526) Raven, B. H., & French, J. R. P., Jr. An experimental investigation of legitimate and coercive power. *Amer. Psychologist*, 1957, *12*, 393. (Abstract)

1527) Raven, B. H., & French, J. R. P., Jr. Group support, legitimate power, and social influence. *J. Pers.*, 1958, *26*, 400–409.

*1528) Raven, B. H., & French, J. R. P., Jr. Legimate power, coercive power, and observability in social influence. *Sociometry*, 1958, *21*, 83–97.

1529) Raven, B. H., & Rietsema, J. The effects of varied clarity of group goal and group path upon the individual and his relation to his group. *Hum. Relat.*, 1957, *10*, 29–45.

1530) Ray, W. S. *A laboratory manual for social psychology.* New York: American Book, 1951.

1531) Ray, W. S. Complex tasks for use in human problem-solving research. *Psychol. Bull.*, 1955, *52*, 134–149.

1532) Redl, F. Group emotion and leadership. *Psychiatry*, 1942, *5*, 573–596. Also in Dorothea F. Sullivan (Ed.), *Readings in group work.* New York: Association Press, 1952. Pp. 318–356.

1533) Redl, F. Group psychological elements in discipline problems. *Amer. J. Orthopsychiat.*, 1943, *13*, 77–81.

1534) Redl, F. Resistance in therapy groups. *Hum. Relat.*, 1948, *1*, 307–313.

1535) Rehage, K. J. A comparison of pupil-teacher planning and teacher directed procedures in eighth grade social studies classes. *J. educ. Res.*, 1951, *45*, 111–115.

1536) Reid, I. D., & Ehle, Emily L. Leadership selection in urban locality areas. *Publ. Opin. Quart.*, 1950, *14*, 262–284.

1537) Reimer, E. *Creating experimental social change in an ongoing organization.* Ann Arbor, Mich.: University of Michigan, Institute of Social Research, 1954.

1538) Rhine, R. J. The effect of peer group responses upon concept-attitude development and change. *Amer. Psychologist*, 1957, *12*, 363. (Abstract)

1539) Rice, A. K. The use of unrecognized cultural mechanisms in an expanding machine shop. *Hum. Relat.*, 1951, *4*, 143–160.

1540) Rich, J. M. Measuring supervisory training: the sociometric approach. *Personnel*, 1952, *29*, 78–84.

1541) Richardson, Helen M. Community of values as a factor in friendships of college and adult women. *J. soc. Psychol.*, 1940, *11*, 303–312.

1542) Richardson, Helen M., & Hanawalt, N. G. Leadership as related to the Bernreuter personality measures. *J. soc. Psychol.*, 1943, *17*, 237–267.

1543) Richardson, M. W. Selection of Army officers. In G. A. Kelly (Ed.),

New methods in applied psychology. College Park, Md.: University of Maryland Press, 1947.

1544) Riddle, Ethel M. Aggressive behavior in a small social group. *Arch. Psychol.*, N.Y., 1925, *12*, No. 78.

1545) Riecken, H. W. Some problems of consensus development. *Rur. Sociol.*, 1952, *17*, 245–252.

1546) Riecken, H. W. Popularity and conformity to group norms. *Amer. Psychologist*, 1953, *8*, 420–421. (Abstract)

1547) Riecken, H. W. *The effect of status on ability to influence group solutions of problems.* Minneapolis: University of Minnesota, Laboratory for Research in Social Relations, January, 1958. (Contract N8 ONR-66216)

1548) Riecken, H. W. The effect of talkativeness on ability to influence group solutions of problems. *Sociometry*, 1958, *21*, 309–321.

1549) Riecken, H. W. A program for research on experiments in social psychology. Paper prepared at Air Force Office of Scientific Res. behav. Sci. Conf., Albuquerque, N.M., 1958. [Contract AF 49(638)-33]

1550) Riecken, H. W., & Homans, G. C. Psychological aspects of social structure. In G. Lindzey (Ed.), *Handbook of social psychology.* Reading, Mass.: Addison-Wesley, 1954. Pp. 786–832.

1551) Rigby, Marilyn K., et al. Three approaches to peer evaluation. *Amer. Psychologist*, 1953, *8*, 421. (Abstract)

*1552) Riley, Matilda W., & Cohn, R. Control networks in informal groups. *Sociometry*, 1958, *21*, 30–49.

1553) Riley, Matilda W., & Flowerman, S. H. Group relations as a variable in communications research. *Amer. sociol. Rev.*, 1951, *16*, 174–180.

1554) Riley, Matilda W., et al. Interpersonal orientations in small groups: a consideration of the questionnaire approach. *Amer. sociol. Rev.*, 1954, *19*, 715–724.

1555) Robbins, Florence G. The impact of social climates upon a college class. *Sch. Rev.*, 1952, *60*, 275–284.

1556) Roberts, A. H., & Jessor, R. *Authoritarianism, punitiveness, and perceived social status.* Newark, Del.: University of Delaware, 1958. [Tech. Rep. No. 5, Contract Nonr-1147(03), NR 170 226]

*1557) Roberts, A. H., et al. Effects of feeling-oriented classroom teaching upon reactions to feedback. *Amer. Psychologist*, 1955, *10*, 420–421. (Abstract)

*1558) Roberts, B. H., & Strodtbeck, F. L. Interaction process differences between groups of paranoid schizophrenic and depressed patients. *Int. J. Group Psychother.*, 1953, *3*, 29–41.

1559) Roberts, J. M. *Three Navaho households: a comparative study in small group culture.* Cambridge, Mass.: Peabody Museum of American Archeology and Ethnology, 1951.

1560) Robinson, K. F. An experimental study of the effects of group discussion upon the social attitudes of college students. *Speech Monogr.*, 1941, *8*, 34–57.

1561) Robson, R. A. H., & Chapin, F. S. *Research on the relation of communication and morale.* Minneapolis: University of Minnesota, April, 1953. (Tech. Rep., Contract N8 ONR 66216)

1562) Roby, T. B. The influence of subgroup relationships on the performance of group and subgroup tasks. *Amer. Psychologist,* 1952, *7,* 313–314. (Abstract)

1563) Roby, T. B. *Problems of rational group assembly exemplified in the medium-bomber crew.* San Antonio, Tex.: Lackland Air Force Base, Human Resources Research Center, 1953. (Res. Bull. 53–18)

*1564) Roby, T. B. *Relationships between sociometric measures and performance in medium-bomber crews.* San Antonio, Tex.: Lackland Air Force Base, Human Resources Research Center, 1953. (Res. Bull. 53–18)

1565) Roby, T. B. *An empirical evaluation of work partner choices after limited contact.* San Antonio, Tex.: Lackland Air Force Base, Air Force Personnel and Training Research Center, December, 1954. (Res. Bull. AFPTRC-TR-54-69)

1566) Roby, T. B. *Prerequisities for pair-scores to be used for assembling small work groups.* San Antonio, Tex.: Lackland Air Force Base, Air Force Personnel and Training Research Center, 1954. (Res. Bull. AFPTRC-TN-54-13)

*1567) Roby, T. B. *Sociometric index measures as predictors of medium-bomber crew performance.* San Antonio, Tex.: Lackland Air Force Base, Air Force Personnel and Training Research Center, 1956. (Res. Rep. AFPTRC-TN-56-46)

1568) Roby, T. B. On the measurement and description of groups. *Behav. Sci.,* 1957, *2,* No. 2.

1569) Roby, T. B. The executive function in small groups. In L. Petrullo and B. M. Bass (Eds.), *Leadership and interpersonal behavior.* New York: Holt, Rinehart and Winston, 1961. Pp. 118–136.

1570) Roby, T. B. *The influence of biographical similarity on performance and interpersonal relationships in medium bomber crews.* San Antonio, Tex.: Lackland Air Force Base, Air Force Personnel and Training Research Center. (Res. Bull.) (undated)

1571) Roby, T. B., & Forgays, D. G. *A problem-solving model for analysis of communication in B-29 crews.* San Antonio, Tex.: Lackland Air Force Base, Human Resources Research Center, August, 1953. (Res. Bull. 53–30)

*1572) Roby, T. B., & Lanzetta, J. T. *An investigation of task performance as a function of certain aspects of work-group structure.* San Antonio, Tex.: Lackland Air Force Base, Air Force Personnel and Training Research Center, June, 1956. (Res. Rep. AFPTRC-TN-56-74)

1573) Roby, T. B., & Lanzetta, J. T. Work group structure, communication, and group performance. *Sociometry,* 1956, *19,* 105–113.

*1574) Roby, T. B., & Lanzetta, J. T. Conflicting principles in man-machine system design. *J. appl. Psychol.,* 1957, *41,* 170–178.

*1575) Roby, T. B., & Lanzetta, J. T. *A replication study of work group structure and task performance.* San Antonio, Tex.: Randolph Air Force Base, Operator Laboratory, June, 1957. (Rep. No. AFPTRC-TN-57-85)

1576) Roby, T. B., & Lanzetta, J. T. *A laboratory task for the study of individuals or groups.* San Antonio, Tex.: Randolph Air Force Base, Operator Laboratory, October, 1957. (Rep. No. AFPTRC-TN-57-124)

1577) Roby, T. B., & Lanzetta, J. T. Considerations in the analysis of group tasks. *Psychol. Bull.*, 1958, *55* (2), 88–101.

1578) Roby, T. B., & Rosenberg, S. *Reactions to limited interpersonal contacts: a preliminary analysis and classification.* San Antonio, Tex.: Lackland Air Force Base, Air Force Personnel and Training Research Center, December, 1954. (Res. Bull. AFPTRC-TR-54-85)

1579) Roby, T. B., et al. *Research involving communication processes in task-oriented groups.* Medford, Mass.: Tufts University, Institute for Applied Experimental Psychology, November, 1958. (Tech. Rep. No. 1, Contract Nonr-49415)

1580) Rock, M. L., & Hay, E. N. Investigation of the use of tests as a predictor of leadership and group effectiveness in a job evaluation situation. *J. soc. Psychol.*, 1953, *38*, 109–119.

1581) Roethlisberger, F. J., & Dickson, W. J. *Management and the worker.* Cambridge, Mass.: Harvard University Press, 1939.

1582) Roff, M. A study of combat leadership in the Air Force by means of a rating scale: group differences. *J. Psychol.*, 1950, *30*, 229–239.

1583) Rogers, Maria. The human group: a critical review with some suggestions for alternative hypotheses. *Sociometry*, 1951, *14*, 20–31.

1584) Rogge, Genevieve O. *Personality factors and their influence on group behavior: a questionnaire study.* Cambridge, Mass.: Massachusetts Institute of Technology, Research Laboratory of Electronics, 1954. (Tech. Rep. No. 265)

*1585) Rohde, K. J. *Studies in aircrew composition: XVII. Individual executive ability as a factor in the performance of small groups.* Columbus, Ohio: Ohio State University, Personnel Research Board, 1954. [Tech. Rep. 17, Contracts AF 33(038)-10105 and AF 18(600)-27]

*1586) Rohde, K. J. Theoretical and experimental analysis of leadership ability. *Psychol. Rep.*, 1958, *4*, 243–278.

1587) Rohrer, J. H., & Sherif, M. (Eds.) *Social psychology at the crossroads.* New York: Harper & Row, 1951.

1588) Rohrer, J. H., et al. The stability of autokinetic judgments. *J. abnorm. soc. Psychol.*, 1954, *49*, 595–597.

1589) Rommetveit, R., & Israel, J. Notes on the standardization of experimental manipulations and measurements in cross-national research. *J. soc. Issues*, 1954, *10*(4), 61–68.

1590) Rose, E. The organization of microcultures. Paper prepared at Air Force Office of Scientific Res. Behav. Sci. Conf., Albuquerque, N.M. 1957. [Contract AF 49(638)-33]

1591) Roseborough, Mary E. Experimental studies of small groups. *Psychol. Bull.*, 1953, *50*, 275–303.

1592) Rosen, B. C. Conflicting group membership: a study of parent-peer group cross-pressures. *Amer. sociol. Rev.*, 1955, *20*, 155–161.

1593) Rosen, S. Some perceptual and behavioral components of social influence in small groups, as predicted by interpersonal adjustment in previous social enviroments. *Amer. Psychologist*, 1953, *8*, 424. (Abstract)

1594) Rosenbaum, M. E. The effects of stimulus and background factors on the volunteering response. *J. abnorm. soc. Psychol.*, 1956, *53*, 118–121.

1595) Rosenbaum, M. E. Social perception and the motivational structure of interpersonal relations. *J. abnorm. soc. Psychol.*, 1959, *59*, 130–133.

1596) Rosenbaum, M. E., & deCharms, R. Direct and vicarious reduction of hostility. Paper prepared at Air Force Office of Scientific Res. Behav. Sci. Conf., Albuquerque, N.M., 1958. [Contract AF 49(638)-33]

1597) Rosenberg, M., & Guetzkow, H. *An experimental investigation of the validity of the group projection sketches test for the description and analysis of face-to-face groups.* Ann Arbor, Mich.: University of Michigan, 1950. (Contract No. NR 172-301)

*1598) Rosenberg, S. *Similarity of interest and attitude measures as a predictor of interpersonal relationships in a medium-bomber crew.* San Antonio, Tex.: Randolph Air Force Base, Air Force Personnel and Training Research Center, Air Research and Development Command, Crew Research Laboratory, August, 1956.

1599) Rosenberg, S. Methods for the rational assembly of individuals into crews. *J. Aviat. Med.*, 1957, *28*, 185–189.

1600) Rosenberg, S. The maintenance of a learned response in controlled interpersonal conditions. *Sociometry*, 1959, *22*, 124–138.

1601) Rosenberg, S., & Hall, R. L. The distribution of knowledge of results in dyadic teams. *Amer. Psychologist*, 1957, *12*, 371. (Abstract)

*1602) Rosenberg, S., & Hall, R. L. The effects of different social feedback conditions upon performance in dyadic teams. *J. abnorm. soc. Psychol.*, 1958, *57*, 271–277.

*1603) Rosenberg, S., & Roby, T. B. *Experimental assembly of B-29 crews by self-selection procedures: description and validation of the method.* San Antonio, Tex.: Lackland Air Force Base, Air Force Personnel and Training Research Center, 1956. (Res. Bull. AFPTRC-TN-56-104)

1604) Rosenberg, S., et al. Some effects of varying combinations of group members on group performance measures and leadership behaviors. *J. abnorm. soc. Psychol.*, 1955, *51*, 195–203.

1605) Rosenfeld, H., & Jackson, J. Effect of similarity of personalities on interpersonal attraction. *Amer. Psychologist*, 1959, *14*, 366. (Abstract)

1606) Rosengren, W. R. Symptom manifestations as a function of situational press: a demonstration in socialization. *Sociometry*, 1959, *22*, 113–123.

*1607) Rosenthal, D., & Cofer, C. N. The effect on group performance of an indifferent and neglectful attitude shown by one group member. *J. exp. Psychol.*, 1948, *38*, 568–577.

1608) Rosner, S. Consistency in response to group pressures. *J. abnorm. soc. Psychol.*, 1957, *55*, 146–147.

1609) Ross, I. C., & Harary, F. On the determination of redundancies in sociometric chains. *Psychometrika*, 1952, *17*, 195–208.

1610) Ross, I. C., & Harary, F. A description of strengthening and weakening members of a group. *Sociometry*, 1959, *22*, 139–147.

1611) Rowland, H. Interaction processes in the State Mental Hospital. *Psychiatry*, 1938, *1*, 323–337.

1612) Rowland, H. Friendship patterns in a mental hospital. *Psychiatry*, 1939, *2*, 363–373.

1613) Roy, I., & Cohen, N. Some psychometric variables relating to change in sociometric status. *Amer. Psychologist*, 1955, *10*, 328. (Abstract)

1614) Rubenfeld, S., & Stafford, J. W. Reference groups in a delinquent peer culture. *Amer. Psychologist*, 1958, *13*, 349. (Abstract)

1615) Rubenstein, A. H. Problems in the measurement of interpersonal communication in an ongoing situation. *Sociometry*, 1953, *16*, 78–100,

1616) Rudin, S. A., et al. *Some empirical studies of the reliability of interpersonal perception scores*. Urbana, Ill.: University of Illinois, Bureau of Research and Service, 1952. (Tech. Rep. No. 4, Contract N6 ORI 07135)

1617) Ruesch, J. Values and the process of communication. Paper read at Sympos. preventive & soc. Psychiat., Washington, D.C., April, 1957.

1618) Ruesch, J., & Prestwood, A. R. Interaction processes and personal codification. *J. Pers.*, 1950, *18*, 391–430.

1619) Ruesch, J., et al. The assessment of communication: I. A method for the analysis of social interaction. *J. Psychol.*, 1953, *35*, 59–80.

1620) Runkel, P. J. Cognitive similarity in facilitating communication. *Sociometry*, 1956, *19*, 178–191.

1621) Rush, C. H., Jr. *Group dimensions of aircrews*. Columbus, Ohio: Ohio State University Research Foundation, 1953.

1622) Sacks, Elinor L. Intelligence scores as a function of experimentally established social relationships between child and examiner. *J. abnorm. soc. Psychol.*, 1952, *47*, 354–358.

1623) Sagi, P. C., et al. Prediction maintenance of membership in small groups. *J. abnorm. soc. Psychol.*, 1955, *51*, 308–311.

1624) Salusky, A. S. Collective behavior of children at a preschool age. *J. soc. Psychol.*, 1930, *1*, 367–378.

1625) Samelson, F. Conforming behavior under two conditions of conflict in the cognitive field. *J. abnorm. soc. Psychol.*, 1957, *55*, 181–187.

1626) Sanderson, D. Group description. *Soc. Forces*, 1938, *16*, 309–319.

1627) Sanderson, D. A preliminary group classification based on structure. *Soc. Forces*, 1938, *17*, 196–201.

1628) Sanford, F. H. *Authoritarianism and leadership*. Philadelphia: Institute for Research in Human Relations, 1950.

1629) Sanford, F. H. Leadership, identification and acceptance. In H. Guetzkow (Ed.), *Groups, leadership and men: research in human relations*. Pittsburgh, Pa.: Carnegie Press, 1951.

1630) Sanford, F. H. The social impact of research on leadership. Paper read at Sympos. Leadership interpers. Behav., Baton Rouge, La., 1959.

1631) Sappenfield, B. R. The attitudes and attitude estimates of Catholic, Protestant, and Jewish students. *J. soc. Psychol.*, 1942, *16*, 173–179.

1632) Sarbin, T. R., & Jones, D. S. An experimental analysis of role behavior. *J. abnorm. soc. Psychol.*, 1955, *51*, 236–241.

1633) Saslow, G., et al. The stability of interaction chronograph patterns in psychiatric interviews. *J. consult. Psychol.*, 1955, *19*, 417–430.

1634) Saslow, G., et al. Test-retest stability of interaction patterns during interviews conducted one week apart. *J. abnorm. soc. Psychol.*, 1957, *54*, 295–302.

1635) Sayles, L. R. *Behavior of industrial work groups.* New York: Wiley, 1958.

1636) Schachter, S. Deviation, rejection, and communication. *J. abnorm. soc. Psychol.*, 1951, *46*, 190–207.

1637) Schachter, S. Comment on "On group cohesiveness." *Amer. J. Sociol.*, 1952, *57*, 554–562.

1638) Schachter, S. *The psychology of affiliation.* Stanford, Calif.: Stanford University Press, 1959.

*1639) Schachter, S., & Burdick, H. A field experiment on rumor transmission and distortion. *J. abnorm. soc. Psychol.*, 1955, *50*, 363–371.

1640) Schachter, S., & Hall, R. Group-derived restraints and audience persuasion. *Hum. Relat.*, 1952, *5*, 397–406.

*1641) Schachter, S., et al. An experimental study of cohesiveness and productivity. *Hum. Relat.*, 1951, *4*, 229–238.

1642) Schachter, S., et al. Cross-cultural experiments on threat and rejection. *Hum. Relat.*, 1954, *7*, 403–439.

1643) Schaffner, B. (Ed.) *Group processes: transactions of the third conference.* New York: Josiah Macy, Jr. Foundation, 1957.

1644) Schank, R. L. A study of a community and its groups and institutions conceived of as behavior of individuals. *Psychol. Monogr.*, 1932, *43*, No. 2 (Whole No. 195).

1645) Scheffler, I., & Winslow, C. N. Group position and attitude toward authority. *J. soc. Psychol.*, 1950, *32*, 177–190.

1646) Scheidlinger, S. *Psychoanalysis and group behavior: a study in Freudian group psychology.* New York: Norton, 1952.

1647) Schein, E. H. The effect of reward on adult imitative behavior. *J. abnorm. soc. Psychol.*, 1954, *49*, 389–395.

1648) Schein, E. H., & Donaghy, J. E. Spontaneous organization of communication in four-man problem-solving groups. *Amer. Psychologist*, 1957, *12*, 371. (Abstract)

1649) Schein, E. H., et al. The organization of communication in small problem-solving groups. *Amer. Psychologist*, 1955, *10*, 357. (Abstract)

*1650) Schiff, H. Judgmental response sets in the perception of sociometric status. *Sociometry*, 1954, *17*, 207–227.

1651) Schiller, M., & Abeles, N. The concept of ego-strength in leadership assessment. *Amer. Psychologist*, 1959, *14*, 352–353. (Abstract)

1652) Schlesinger, L., et al. The effect upon decisions of experimentally varying the degree of control exercised by chairmen of management committees. *Amer. Psychologist*, 1958, *13*, 353. (Abstract)

1653) Schonbar, Rosalea A. The interaction of observer-pairs in judging visual extent and movement: the formation of social norms in "structured" situation. *Arch. Psychol.*, 1945, No. 299.

1654) Schonbar, Rosalea A. The modification of judgments in a group situation. *J. exp. Psychol.*, 1947, *37*, 69–80.

1655) Schooler, K. *Methodology for studying the dimensions of morale.* Ann Arbor, Mich.: University of Michigan, Institute for Social Research, 1951. (Contract No. NR 170–272)

1656) Schopler, J. H., et al. The effects of congruity of expectations upon group processes. *Amer. Psychologist*, 1954, *9*. (Abstract)

1657) Schroder, H. M., & Hunt, D. E. Dispositional effects upon conformity. *J. Pers.*, 1958, *26*, 243–258.

1658) Schroder, H. M., & Hunt, D. E. *The role of three processes in determining responses to interpersonal disagreement*. Princeton, N. J.: Princeton University, 1958. (Tech. Rep. No. 5, Contract Nonr-171055)

1659) Schutz, W. C. Reliability, continuity, and content analysis. *Psychol. Rev.*, 1952, *59*, 119–127.

1660) Schutz, W. C. Some theoretical considerations for group behavior. In *Symposium on techniques for the measurement of group performance*. Washington, D.C.: U.S. Government Research and Development Board, 1952. Pp. 27–36.

1661) Schutz, W. C. *Studies in group behavior: I. Construction of high productivity groups*. Medford, Mass.: Tufts College, Systems Research Laboratory, 1953. (Rep. 1953-494-03-04)

1662) Schutz, W. C. What makes groups productive? *Hum. Relat.*, 1955, *8*, 429–465.

1663) Schutz, W. C. *A theory of interpersonal relations*. Medford, Mass Tufts University, June, 1956. (Final Rep., Contract N5 ORI 07668)

1664) Schutz, W. C. *FIRO: a three-dimensional theory of interpersonal behavior*. New York: Holt, Rinehart and Winston, 1958.

1665) Schutz, W. C. The ego, FIRO theory and the leader as completer. In L. Petrullo and B. M. Bass (Eds.), *Leadership interpersonal behavior*. New York: Holt, Rinehart and Winston, 1961.Pp. 48–65.

*1666) Scodel, A., & Freedman, Maria L. Additional observations on the social perceptions of authoritarians and non-authoritarians. *J. abnorm. soc. Psychol.*, 1956, *52*, 92–95.

1667) Scodel, A., & Mussen, P. Social perceptions of authoritarians and non-authoritarians. *J. abnorm. soc. Psychol.*, 1953, *48*, 181–184.

1668) Scott, E. L. *Perceptions of organization and leadership behavior*. Columbus, Ohio: Ohio State University Research Foundation, 1952.

1669) Scott, E. L. *Leadership and perceptions of organization*. Columbus, Ohio: Ohio State University (*Bureau of Business Res. Monogr.*, No. 82), 1956.

1670) Scott, W. A. Factors affecting the learning of personal values through social reinforcement. *Amer. Psychologist*, 1956, *11*, 407–408. (Abstract)

1671) Scott, W. A. Personal values and group interaction. Paper prepared at Air Force Office of Scientific Res. behav. Sci. Conf., Albuquerque, N. M. 1957. [Contract AF 49(638)-33]

1672) Scott, W. A. Cognitive structure and social structure: a review of relevant concepts. Paper prepared at Air Force Office of Scientific Res. behav. Sci. Conf., Albuquerque, N. M., 1958. [Contract AF 49(638)-33]

1673) Scott, W. A. Response reinforcement, value-attitude consistency, and attitude change. Paper prepared at Air Force Office of Scientific Res. behav. Sci. Res. Conf., Albuquerque, N. M., 1958. [Contract AF 49(638)-33]

1674) Scott, W. A. Attitude change by response reinforcement: replication and extension. *Sociometry*, 1959, *22*, 328–335.

1675) Scott, W. A. Cognitive consistency, response reinforcement, and attitude change. *Sociometry*, 1959, *22*, 219–229.

1676) Sears, R. Leadership among patients in group therapy. *Int. J. group Psychother.*, 1953, *3*, 191–197.

1677) Sears, R. Leadership among patients in group therapy (II). *Int. J. group Psychother.*, 1956, *6*, 374–382.

1678) Seashore, S. *A modified sociometric technique for the study of functioning organizations.* Ann Arbor, Mich.: University of Michigan, Institute for Social Research, 1951. (Contract NR 170–272)

1679) Seashore, S. Group cohesiveness as a factor in industrial morale and productivity. *Amer. Psychologist*, 1954, *9*. (Abstract)

1680) Seashore, S. *Group cohesiveness in the industrial work group.* Ann Arbor, Mich.: Univerersity of Michigan, Institute for Social Research, 1954.

1681) Seeman, M. *A status factor approach to leadership.* Columbus, Ohio: Ohio State University Personnel Research Boad, 1951.

1682) Seeman, M. Role conflict and ambivalence in leadership. *Amer. sociol Rev.*, 1953, *18*, 373–380.

1683) Seeman, M., & Morris, R. T. *A status factor approach to leadership.* Columbus, Ohio: Ohio State University Research Foundation, 1950.

*1684) Seidman, D., et al. Influence of a partner on tolerance for a self-administered electric shock. *J. abnorm. soc. Psychol.*, 1957, *54*, 210–212.

1685) Sells, S. B. *Human flight behavior in groups.* San Antonio, Tex.: Randolph Air Force Base, School of Aviation Medicine, July, 1958. (Rev. No. 6-58, ASTIA Document No. 203–599)

1686) Selltiz, Claire, et al. *Research methods in social relations.* (Rev. one-vol. ed.) New York: Holt, Rinehart and Winston, 1959.

1687) Sengupta, N. N., & Sinha, C. P. N. Mental work in isolation and in group. *Indian J. Psychol.*, 1926, *1*, 106–110.

1688) Shapiro, D., et al. Affective style and group behavior. *Amer. Psychologist*, 1959, *14*, 367. (Abstract)

1689) Shartle, C. L. Leadership and executive performance. *Personnel*, 1949, *25*, 370–380.

1690) Shartle, C. L. Organization structure. In W. Dennis et al. (Eds.), *Current trends in industrial psychology.* Pittsburgh, Pa.: University of Pittsburgh Press, 1949. Pp. 14–31.

1691) Shartle, C. L. Leadership aspects of administrative behavior. *Advanc. Mgmt*, 1950, *15*, 12–15.

1692) Shartle, C. L. Studies of leadership by interdisciplinary methods. In A. G. Grace (Ed.), *Leadership in American education.* Chicago University of Chicago Press, 1950. Pp. 27–39.

1693) Shartle, C. L. Leader behavior in jobs. *Occupations*, 1951, *30*, 164–166.

1694) Shartle, C. L. Studies in Naval leadership. In H. Guetzkow (Ed.), *Groups, leadership and men: research in human relations.* Pittsburgh, Pa.: Carnegie Press, 1951.

1695) Shartle, C. L. Ohio State leadership studies. *Engn. Exp. Sta. News*, 1952, *24*, 16–21.

1696) Shartle, C. L. Leadership and organizational behavior. Paper prepared at Air Force Office of Scientific Res. behav. Sci. Conf., Albuquerque, N. M., 1958. [Contract AF 49(638)-33]

1697) Shartle, C. L., & Hemphill, J. K. *Aircrew effectiveness criteria.* Washington, D.C.: Bolling Air Force Base, Human Resources Research Laboratories, November, 1950. (HRRL Rep. No. 19)

1698) Shartle, C. L., & Stogdill, R. M. *Studies in naval leadership: methods, results, and applications.* Columbus, Ohio: Ohio State University, Personnel Research Board, 1953. (Final tech. Rep.)

1699) Shartle, C. L., et al. *Pilot study of a B-50 air crew.* Columbus, Ohio: Ohio State University, Personnel Research Board Research Foundation, February, 1951. [Contract AF 33(038)-10105]

1700) Shaw, M. E. Group structure and the behavior of individuals in small groups. *J. abnorm. soc. Psychol.*, 1954, *38*, 139–149.

*1701) Shaw, M. E. Some effects of problem complexity upon problem solution efficiency in different communication nets. *J. exp. Psychol.*, 1954, *48*, 211–217.

1702) Shaw, M. E. Some effects of unequal distribution of information upon group performance in various communication nets. *J. abnorm. soc. Psychol.*, 1954, *49*, 547–553.

1703) Shaw, M. E. Communications patterns in small groups. ONR *Res. Rev.*, 1955, 11–12.

*1704) Shaw, M. E. A comparison of two types of leadership in various communication nets. *J. abnorm. soc. Psychol.*, 1955, *50*, 127–134.

*1705) Shaw, M. E. Random versus systematic distribution of information in communication nets. *J. Pers.*, 1956, *25*, 59–69.

1706) Shaw, M. E. Behavior in groups: the development of a scale to measure individual prominence. Paper prepared at Air Force Office of Scientific Res. behav. Sci. Conf., Albuquerque, N. M., 1957. [Contract AF 94(638)-33]

*1707) Shaw, M. E. Some effects of irrelevant information upon problem-solving by small groups. *J. soc. Psychol.*, 1958, *47*, 33–37.

1708) Shaw, M. E. Some motivational factors in cooperation and competition. *J. Pers.*, 1958, *26*, 155–169.

1709) Shaw, M. E. Acceptance of authority, group structure, and the effectiveness of small groups. *J. Pers.*, 1959, *27*, 196–210.

1710) Shaw, M. E. Some effects of individually prominent behavior upon group effectiveness and member satisfaction. *J. abnorm. soc. Psychol.*, 1959, *59*, 382–386.

1711) Shaw, M. E., & Gilchrist, J. C. Repetitive task failure and sociometric choice. *J. abnorm. soc. Psychol.*, 1955, *50*, 29–32.

1712) Shaw, M. E., & Gilchrist, J. C. Intra-group communication and leader choice. *J. soc. Psychol.*, 1956, *43*, 133–138.

1713) Shaw, M. E., & Rothschild, G. H. Some effects of prolonged experience in communication nets. *J. appl. Psychol.*, 1956, *40*, 281–286.

1714) Shaw, M. E., et al. Decision processes in communication nets. *J. abnorm. soc. Psychol.*, 1957, *54*, 323–330.

1715) Shaw, Marjorie E. A comparison of individuals and small groups in the rational solution of complex problems. *Amer. J. Psychol.*, 1932, *44*, 491–504.

*1716) Shelley, H.P. *The role of success and failure in determining attitude toward the group as a means to member goals.* Ann Arbor, Mich.: University of Michigan, Conf. Res. Project Report, 1950.

1717) Shelley, H. P. Level of aspiration phenomena in small groups. *J. soc. Psychol.*, 1954, *40*, 149–164.

1718) Shelley, H. P. Response set and the California attitude scales. *Educ. psychol. Measmt*, 1956, *16*, 63–67.

1719) Shelley, H. P. Status consensus, leadership, and group cohesiveness. *Amer. Psychologist*, 1958, *13*, 353. (Abstract)

1720) Shepard, H. A., & Bennis, W. G. A theory of training by group methods. *Hum. Relat.*, 1956, *9*, 403–413.

1721) Shepherd, C., & Weschler, I. R. The relation between three interpersonal variables and communication effectiveness: a pilot study. *Sociometry*, 1955, *18*, 103–110.

1722) Sherif, M. A study of some social factors in perception. *Arch. Psychol.*, N. Y., 1935, *27*, No. 187.

1723) Sherif, M. *The psychology of social norms.* New York: Harper & Row, 1936.

1724) Sherif, M. *An outline of social psychology.* New York: Harper & Row, 1948.

1725) Sherif, M. A preliminary experimental study of inter-group relations. In J. H. Rohrer and M. Sherif (Eds.), *Social psychology at the crossroads.* New York: Harper & Row, 1951. Pp. 388–424.

1726) Sherif, M. Integrating field work and laboratory in small group research. *Amer. sociol. Rev.*, 1954, *19*, 759–771.

1727) Sherif, M. Sociocultural influences in small group research. *Sociol. soc. Res.*, 1954, *39*, 1–10.

1728) Sherif, M. Experiments in group conflict. *Sci. Amer.*, 1956, *195*(5), 54–58.

1729) Sherif, M. Towards integrating psychological and sociological approaches in small group research. In M. Sherif and M. O. Wilson (Eds.), *Emerging problems in social psychology.* Norman Okla.: University of Oklahoma, 1957.

1730) Sherif, M. Superordinate goals in the reduction of intergroup conflict. *Amer. J. Sociol.*, 1958, *63*, 349–356.

1731) Sherif, M., & Cantril, H. *The psychology of ego-involvements.* New York: Wiley, 1947.

1732) Sherif, M., & Harvey, O. J. A study in ego functioning: elimination of stable anchorages in individual and group situations. *Sociometry*, 1952, *15*, 272–305.

1733) Sherif, M., & Sherif, Carolyn W. *Groups in harmony and tension.* New York: Harper & Row, 1953.

1734) Sherif, M., & Wilson, M. O. (Eds.), *Group relations at the cross-roads.* New York: Harper & Row, 1953.

1735) Sherif, M., et al. Status in experimentally produced groups. *Amer. J. Sociol.*, 1955, *60*, 370–379.

1736) Shevitz, R. N. *Leadership acts: IV. An investigation of the relation between exclusive possession of information and attempts to lead.* Columbus, Ohio: Ohio State University Research Foundation, 1955.

1737) Shils, E. A. *The present situation in American sociology.* New York: Free Press, 1948.

1738) Shils, E. A. Primary groups in the American army. In R. K. Merton and P. F. Lazarsfeld (Eds.), *Continuities in social research: studies in the scope and method of "The American soldier."* New York: Free Press, 1950. Pp. 16–39.

1739) Shils, E. A. The study of the primary group. In D. Lerner and H. D. Laswell (Eds.), *The policy sciences.* Stanford, Calif.: Stanford University Press, 1951. Pp. 44–69.

1740) Shils, E. A., & Janowitz, M. Cohesion and disintegration in the Wehrmacht in World War II. *Publ. Opin. Quart.*, 1948, *12*, 280–315.

1741) Shriver, Beatrice M. Stability and status in small leaderless groups. *Amer. Psychologist*, 1952, *7*, 307. (Abstract)

*1742) Siegel, Alberta E., & Siegel, S. Reference groups, membership groups, and attitude change. *J. abnorm. soc. Psychol.*, 1957, *55*, 360–364.

1743) Siegel, L., et al. Expressed standards of behavior of high school students, teachers, and parents. *Personnel Guid. J.*, 1956, *34*, 261–267.

.1744) Siegel, S., & Shepherd, Irma L. An ordered metric measure of social distance. *Sociometry*, 1959, *22*, 336–342.

1745) Silvan, M. Sex composition of the group as a factor in the modification of individual judgment of high and low authoritarian persons. *Amer. Psychologist*, 1959, *14*, 362. (Abstract)

1746) Simmel, G. The number of members as determining the sociological form of the group. *Amer. J. Sociol.*, 1902–1903, *8*, 1–46, 158–196.

1747) Simon, H. A. Comments on the theory of organizations. *Amer. pol. sci. Rev.*, 1952, *46*, 1130–1139.

1748) Simon, H. A. A formal theory of interaction of social groups. *Amer. sociol. Rev.*, 1952, *17*, 202–211.

1749) Simon, H. A., & Guetzkow, H. Mechanisms involved in group pressures on deviate-members. *Brit. J. statist. Psychol.*, 1955, *8*, 93–100.

1750) Simon, H. A., & Guetzkow, H. A model of short and long run mechanisms involved in pressures toward uniformity in groups. *Psychol. Rev.*, 1955, *62*, 56–68.

*1751) Simpson, R. H. A study of those who influence and of those who are influenced in discussion. *Teach. Coll., Columbia Univer. Contr. Educ.*, 1938, No. 748.

1752) Sims, V. M. The relative influence of two types of motivation on improvement. *J. educ. Psychol.*, 1928, *19*, 480–484.

1753) Singer, J. L., & Goldman, G. D. Experimentally contrasted social atmospheres in group psychotherapy with chronic schizophrenics. *J. soc. Psychol.*, 1954, *40*, 23–37.

1754) Sisson, E. The criterion in Army personnel research. In G. A. Kelly (Ed.), *New methods in applied psychology.* College Park, Md.: University of Maryland Press, 1947.

*1755) Slater, P. E. Role differentiation in small groups. *Amer. sociol. Rev.*, 1955, *20*, 300–310.

*1756) Slater, P. E. Contrasting correlates of group size. *Sociometry*, 1958, *21*, 129–139.

1757) Slater, P. E., et al. The effect of group administration upon symptom formation under LSD. *J. nerv. men. Dis.*, 1957, *125*, 312–315.

1758) Slavson, S. R. *Creative group education.* New York: Association Press, 1938.

1759) Slavson, S. R. (Ed.) *The practice of group therapy.* New York: International Universities, 1947.

*1760) Smith, A. J., et al. Consonance of interpersonal perception and individual effectiveness. *Hum. Relat.*, 1955, *8*, 385–397.

*1761) Smith, A. J., et al. Productivity and recall in cooperative and competitive discussion groups. *J. Psychol.*, 1957, *43*, 193–204.

1762) Smith, C. Social selection in community leadership. *Soc. For.*, 1937, *15*, 530–535.

1763) Smith, C. E. A study of autonomic excitation resulting from the interaction of individual and group opinion. *J. abnorm. soc. Psychol.*, 1936, *31*, 138–164.

*1764) Smith, E. E. *Effects of threat induced by ambiguous role expectations on defensiveness and productivity in small groups.* Boulder, Colo.: University of Colorado, Group Process Laboratory. August, 1956. (Tech. Rep. No. 1)

1765) Smith, E. E. Choice of own versus group goal attainment under threat and reduced threat and in overt and covert situations. *Amer. Psychologist*, 1957, *12*, 366. (Abstract)

1766) Smith, E. E. The effects of clear and unclear role expectations on group productivity and defensiveness. *J. abnorm. soc. Psychol.*, 1957, *55*, 213–217.

1767) Smith, E. E. Individual versus group goal conflict. *J. abnorm. soc. Psychol.*, 1959, *58*, 134–136.

1768) Smith, E. E., & Goodchilds, Jacqueline D. Characteristics of the witty group member: the wit as leader. *Amer. Psychologist*, 1959, *14*, 375–376. (Abstract)

1769) Smith, H. C. Teamwork in the college class. *J. educ. Psychol.*, 1955, *46*, 274–286.

1770) Smith, M. A method of analyzing the interaction of children. *J. juv. Res.*, 1933, *17*, 78–88.

1771) Smith, M. Some factors in friendship selections of high school students. *Sociometry*, 1944, *7*, 303–310.

1772) Smith, M. B. Social psychology and group processes. *Annu. Rev. Psychol.*, 1952, *3*, 175–204.

1773) Smucker, O. Near-sociometric analysis as a basis for guidance. *Sociometry*, 1949, *12*, 326–340.

1774) Solomon, D. N. Professional persons in bureaucratic organizations. Paper read at Sympos. preventive & soc. Psychiat., Washington, D.C., April, 1957.

1775) Sommer, R. Studies in personal space. *Sociometry*, 1959, *22*, 247–260.

1776) Sorokin, P. A., et al. An experimental study of efficiency of work under various specified conditions. *Amer. J. Sociol.*, 1930, *35*, 765–782.

1777) Souerwine, A. H., & Conway, Kathryn L. The effects of role playing upon the social atmosphere of a small group of sixth-grade children. *Amer. Psychologist*, 1953, *8*, 439. (Abstract)

1778) South, E. B. Some psychological aspects of committee work. *J. appl. Psychol.*, 1927, *11*, 437–464.

1779) Spector, A. J. Factors in morale. *Amer. Psychologist*, 1953, *8*, 439–440. (Abstract)

*1780) Spector, A. J. Expectations, fulfillment, and morale. *J. abnorm. soc. Psychol.*, 1956, *52*, 51–56.

*1781) Spector, P., & Suttell, Barbara J. *Research on the specific leader behavior patterns most effective in influencing group performance.* Washington, D.C.: American Institute for Research, November, 1956. (Annu. tech. Rep., Contract Nonr 890(03), NR 171–027)

*1782) Spector, P., & Suttell, Barbara J. *An experimental comparison of the effectiveness of three patterns of leadership behavior.* Washington, D.C.: American Institute for Research, September, 1957. (Tech. Rep. No. AIR-196-57-FR-164, Contract Nonr 89003)

1783) Spilka, B. A study of coacting group influences on individual judgment. *Psych. Newsltr*, 1952, *37*, 1–13.

1784) Spohn, H. E. The effect of group norms upon perception in chronic schizophrenic patients. *Amer. Psychologist*, 1956, *11*, 366. (Abstract)

*1785) Stafford, A. R., et al. *The effects of choice of working partner on student achievement and attitudes.* San Antonio, Tex.: Lackland Air Force Base, Air Force Personnel and Training Research Center, December, 1955. (Res. Rep. AFPTRC-TN-55-61)

1786) Staton, T. F. An analysis of the effect of individuals on seminar discussion. *Amer. Psychologist*, 1948, *3*, 267. (Abstract)

1787) Steiner, I. D. Interpersonal behavior as influenced by accuracy of social perception. *Psychol. Rev.*, 1955, *62*, 268–274.

1788) Steiner, I. D. Human interaction and interpersonal perception. *Sociometry*, 1959, *22*, 230–235.

1789) Steiner, I. D., & Dodge, Joan S. Interpersonal perception and role structure as determinants of group and individual efficiency. *Hum. Relat.*, 1956, *9*, 467–480.

1790) Steiner, I. D., & Dodge, Joan S. A comparison of two techniques employed in the study of interpersonal perception. *Sociometry*, 1957, *20*, 1–17.

1791) Steiner, I. D., & Field, W. L. *Role assignment and interpersonal influence.* Urbana, Ill.: University of Illinois, Department of Psychology, Group Effectiveness Research Laboratory, October, 1959. (Tech. Rep. No. 3)

1792) Steiner, I. D., & McDiarmid, C. G. Two kinds of assumed similarity between opposites. *J. abnorm. soc. Psychol.*, 1957, *55*, 140–142.

*1793) Steiner, H. M., & Peters, S. C. Conformity and the A-B-X model. *J. Pers.*, 1958, *26*, 243–258.

1794) Steinzor, B. The development and evaluation of a measure of social interaction. *Hum. Relat.*, 1949, *2*, 103–121.

1795) Steinzor, B. The development and evaluation of a measure of social interaction: Part II. *Hum. Relat.*, 1949, *2*, 319–347.

*1796) Steinzor, B. The spatial factor in face-to-face discussion groups. *J. abnorm. soc. Psychol.*, 1950, *45*, 552–555.

1797) Stendler, Celia, et al. Studies in cooperation and competition: I. The effects of working for group and individual rewards on the social climate of children's groups. *J. genet. Psychol.*, 1951, *79*, 173–197

1798) Stephan, F. F. The relative rate of communication between members of small groups. *Amer. sociol. Rev.* 1952, *17*, 482–486.

1799) Stephan, F. F., & Mishler, E. G. The distribution of participation in small groups: an exponential approximation. *Amer. sociol. Rev.*, 1952, *17*, 598–608.

1800) Stephenson, T. E. The leader-follower relationships. *Sociol. Rev.*, 1959, *7*, 179–195.

1801) Stice, G. F. The effect of group discussion upon the privately expressed opinion of group members. *Amer. Psychologist*, 1952, 7, 315. (Abstract)

1802) Stice, G. F. Patterns of self-perception and affective response in the area of interpersonal behavior. *Amer. Psychologist*, 1959, *14*, 348. (Abstract)

1803) Stice, G. F., & Cattell, R. B. Personality differences found in small-group leaders selected by four independent criteria of leadership. *Amer. Psychologist*, 1953, *8*, 443. (Abstract)

1804) Stice, G. F., & Knoell, D. N. *A simple mean-difference technique for obtaining scales.* San Antonio, Tex.: Randolph Air Force Base, Human Resources Research Center, Air Research and Development Command, September, 1953. (Res. Bull. 53–36)

1805) Stock, Dorothy. Components of valency (affective approach, culture preference, and areas of concern): a case study. In Dorothy Stock and H. A. Thelen (Eds.), *Emotional dynamics and group culture.* New York: New York University Press, 1958. Pp. 50–64.

1806) Stock, Dorothy. Sociometric choice and valency patterns of members In Dorothy Stock and H. A. Thelen (Eds.), *Emotional dynamics and group culture.* New York: New York University Press, 1958. Pp. 92–101.

1807) Stock, Dorothy, & Thelen, H. A. (Eds.) *Emotional dynamics and group culture.* New York: New York University Press, 1958.

1808) Stock, Dorothy, & Thelen, H. A. *Group culture and emotional dynamics.* Chicago: University of Chicago Press, 1958.

1809) Stogdill, R. M. Personal factors associated with leadership: a survey of the literature. *J. Psychol.*, 1948, *25*, 35–71.

*1810) Stogdill, R. M. The sociometry of working relationships in formal organizations. *Sociometry*, 1949, *12*, 276–286.

1811) Stogdill, R. M. Leadership, membership and organization. *Psychol. Bull.*, 1950, *47*, 1–14.

1812) Stogdill, R. M. The organization of working relationships: twenty sociometric indices. *Sociometry*, 1951, *14*, 366–374.

1813) Stogdill, R. Leadership and morale in organized groups. In J. E. Hulett, Jr., and R. Stagner (Eds.), *Problems in social psychology.* Urbana, Ill.: University of Illinois Press, 1952.

1814) Stogdill, R. M. Measures of organization structure and operations. *Engng Exp. Sta. News*, 1952, *24* (5), 20–23, 36–38.

1815) Stogdill, R. M. Studies of Naval leadership and organization. *Engng. Exp. Sta. News,* 1952, *24* (5), 24–27.

1816) Stogdill, R. M. *Aspects of leadership and organization.* Columbus, Ohio: Ohio State University, Ohio State University Research Foundation, The Personnel Research Board, 1953. (Contract No. NR 171-123)

1817) Stogdill, R. M. *Leadership and structure of personal interaction.* Columbus, Ohio: Ohio State University (Bureau Business Res. Monogr. No. 84), 1956.

1818) Stogdill, R. M. *Individual behavior and group achievement.* New York: Oxford, 1959.

1819) Stogdill, R. M., & Coons, A. E. (Eds.) *Leader behavior: its description and measurement.* Columbus, Ohio: Ohio State University, 1957. Bureau Business Res. Monogr. No. 88)

1820) Stogdill, R. M., & Goode, O. S. Effects of the interactions of superiors upon the performances and expectations of subordinates. *Int. J. Sociometry,* 1957, *1,* 133–145.

1821) Stogdill, R. M., & Goode, O. S. A study of supervision in the MNO Company. *Management,* 1958, *9* (1).

1822) Stogdill, R. M., & Koehler, K. *Measures of leadership structure and organizational change.* Columbus, Ohio: Ohio State University Personnel Research Board, 1952. (Contract No. NR 171-123)

1823) Stogdill, R. M., & Shartle, C. L. Methods for determining patterns of leadership behavior in relation to organization structure and objectives. *J. appl. Psychol.,* 1948, *32,* 286–291.

1824) Stogdill, R. M., & Shartle, C. L. Studies in naval leadership. *ONR Res. Rev.,* 1954, 16–19.

1825) Stogdill, R. M., et al. *Leadership: a study of role expectations and performance.* Columbus, Ohio: Ohio State University, Personnel Research Board, 1953.

1826) Stogdill, R. M., et al. A factorial study of administrative behavior. *Personnel Psychol.,* 1955, *8,* 165–180.

1827) Stogdill, R. M., et al. *Leadership and role expectations.* Columbus, Ohio: Ohio State University (Bureau Business Res. Monogr. No. 86) 1956.

1828) Stogdill, R. M., et al. *Patterns of administrative performance.* Columbus, Ohio: Ohio State University (Bureau Business Res. Monogr. No. 81) 1956.

1829) Stogdill, R. M., et al. *A predictive study of administrative work patterns.* Columbus, Ohio: Ohio State University (Bureau Business Res. Monogr. No. 85) 1956.

1830) Stone, Phil, & Kamiya, J. Judgments of consensus during group discussion. *J. abnorm. soc. Psychol.,* 1957, *55,* 171–175.

1831) Stotland, E. The effects of public and private failure on self-evaluation. *Amer. Psychologist,* 1956, *11,* 357. (Abstract)

*1832) Stotland, E. Determinants of attraction to groups. *J. soc. Psychol.,* 1959, *49,* 71–80.

1833) Stotland, E., et al. The effects of group expectations and self-esteem upon self-evaluation. *J. abnorm. soc. Psychol.,* 1957, *54,* 55–63.

1834) Stouffer, S. A., et al. *The American soldier*. Princeton, N.J.: Princeton University Press, 1949.

1835) Stouffer, S. A., et al. *Compatibility and productivity of groups*. Cambridge, Mass.: Harvard University, August, 1958. (Contract No. N5 ORI 07646)

1836) Strickland, L. H. Surveillance and trust. *J. Pers.*, 1958, *26*, 200–215.

1837) Strodtbeck, F. L. Husband-wife interaction over revealed differences. *Amer. sociol. Rev.*, 1951, *16*, 468–473.

1838) Strodtbeck, F. L. The case for the study of small groups. *Amer. sociol. Rev.*, 1954, *19*, 651–657.

1839) Strodtbeck, F. L. The family as a three-person group. *Amer. sociol. Rev.*, 1954, *19*, 23–29.

1840) Strodtbeck, F. L., & Hare, A. P. Bibliography of small group research: from 1900 through 1953. *Sociometry*, 1954, *17*, 107–178.

*1841) Strodtbeck, F. L., & Mann, R. D. Sex role differentiation in jury deliberations. *Sociometry*, 1956, *19*, 3–11.

1842) Strodtbeck, F. L., et al. Social status in jury deliberations. *Amer. sociol. Rev.*, 1957, *22*, 713–719.

1843) Stroop, J. R. Is the judgment of the group better than that of the average member of the group? *J. exp. Psychol.*, 1932, *15*, 550–562.

1844) Strupp, H. H., & Housman, H. J. Some correlates of group productivity. *Amer. Psychologist*, 1953, *8*, 443–444. (Abstract)

1845) Suchman, J. R. Social sensitivity in the small task-oriented group. *J. abnorm. soc. Psychol.*, 1956, *52*, 75–83.

1846) Suci, G. J., et al. A study of the effects of "likingness" and level of objectivity on peer rating reliabilities. *Educ. psychol. Measmt*, 1956, *16*, 147–152.

1847) Sullivan, H. S. Psychiatry: introduction to the study of interpersonal relations. *Psychiatry*, 1938, *1*, 121–134.

1848) *Summaries of 1953 technical reports*. San Antonio, Tex.: Lackland Air Force Base, Human Resources Research Center, December, 1953.

1849) Suppes, P., & Krasne, F. *Application of stimulus sampling theory to situations involving social pressure*. Stanford, Calif.: Stanford University, Applied Mathematics and Statistics Laboratory, September, 1959. (Tech. Rep. No. 24, Contract Nonr 22517)

1850) Suttell, Barbara J., & Haefner, D. P. *Descriptions of 12 typical Navy teams aboard destroyer-type ships*. Washington, D.C.: American Institute for Research, July, 1955.

1851) Suttel, Barbara J., & Spector, P. *Research on the specific leader behavior patterns most effective in influencing group performance*. Washington, D.C.: American Institute for Research, November, 1955. [Annu. Tech. Rep., Contract Nonr 890(03), NR 171–027)

1852) Swanson, G. E. The development of an instrument for rating child-parent relationships. *Soc. Forces*, 1950, *29*, 84–90.

1853) Swanson, G. E. Some effects of member object-relationships on small groups. *Hum. Relat.*, 1951, *4*, 355–380.

1854) Swanson, G. E. Some problems of laboratory experiments with small populations. *Amer. sociol. Rev.*, 1951, *16*, 349–358.

1855) Swanson, G. E. A preliminary laboratory study of the acting crowd. *Amer. sociol. Rev.*, 1953, *5*, 522–533.

1856) Swanson, G. E., et al. (Eds.) *Readings in social psychology.* (2nd ed.) New York: Holt, Rinehart and Winston, 1952.

1857) Symonds, P. M. Role playing as a diagnostic procedure in the selection of leaders. *Sociatry*, 1947, *1*, 43–50.

1858) Taft, R. A psychological model for the study of social assimilation. *Hum. Relat.*, 1957, *10*, 141–156.

1859) Tagiuri, R. Relational analysis: an extension of sociometric method with emphasis upon sociometric perception. *Sociometry*, 1952, *15*, 91–104.

1860) Tagiuri, R. *On the perception of interpersonal feelings and status.* Cambridge, Mass.: Harvard University, September, 1956. (Contract N5 ORI-07646, and N5 ORI-07670)

1861) Tagiuri, R. *Studies in perception of interpersonal feelings.* Washington, D.C.: Office of Naval Research, April, 1956. (Contract No. NR 170-040)

1862) Tagiuri, R. The perception of feelings among members of small groups. *J. soc. Psychol.*, 1957, *46*, 219–227.

1863) Tagiuri, R. *Social preference and its perception.* Cambridge, Mass.: Harvard University, October, 1957.

1864) Tagiuri, R. Social preference and its perception. In R. Tagiuri and L. Petrullo (Eds.), *Person perception and interpersonal behavior.* Stanford, Calif.: Stanford University Press, 1958. Pp. 316–336.

1865) Tagiuri, R., & Goodnow, R. E. Religious ethnocentrism and its recognition among adolescent boys. *J. abnorm. soc. Psychol.*, 1952, *47*, 316–320.

1866) Tagiuri, R., & Kogan, N. The visibility of interpersonal preferences. *Hum. Relat.*, 1957, *10*, 385–390.

1867) Tagiuri, R., & Petrullo, L. (Eds.) *Person perception and interpersonal behavior.* Stanford, Calif.: Stanford University Press, 1958.

1868) Tagiuri, R., et al. Some determinants of the perception of positive and negative feelings. *J. abnorm. soc. Psychol.*, 1953, *48*, 585–592.

1869) Tagiuri, R., et al. Estimating the chance expectancies of diadic relationships within a group. *Psychol. Bull.*, 1955, *52*, 122–131.

1870) Tagiuri, R., et al. A statistical model for relational analysis. *Psychometrika*, 1955, *20*, 319–327.

*1871) Tagiuri, R., et al. The transparency of inter-personal choice. *Sociometry*, 1955, *18*, 624–635.

1872) Tagiuri, R., et al. Person perception. *SSRC Items*, 1956, *10*, 2–5.

1873) Tagiuri, R., et al. *Differentiation of sociometric choice and its implications for status relations in a group.* Cambridge, Mass.: Harvard University, Laboratory of Social Relations, 1957. (Contract N5 ORI-07670)

*1874) Tagiuri, R., et al. Differentiation of sociometric choice and status relations in a group. *Psychol. Rep.*, 1958, *4*, 523–526.

1875) Tagiuri, R., et al. On the relations between feelings and perception of feelings among members of small groups. In Eleanor Maccoby, et al. (Eds.), *Reading in social psychology.* New York: Holt, Rinehart and Winston, 1958, 110–116.

1876) Talland, G. A. The assessment of group opinion by leaders, and their influence on its formation. *J. abnorm. soc. Psychol.*, 1954, *89*, 431–434.

1877) Talland, G. A. The working system of psychotherapy groups. *Group Psychother.*, 1954, 7, 67–80.

1878) Talland, G. A. Task and interaction process: some characteristics of therapeutic group discussion. *J. abnorm. soc. Psychol.*, 1955, *50*, 105–109.

1879) Talland, G. A. Cultural differences in serial reproduction. *J. soc. Psychol.*, 1956, *43*, 75–81.

1880) Talland, G. A. Do therapists and patients share norms on the content of group discussion? *Group Psychother.*, 1957, *10*, 10–21.

1881) Talland, G. A. Rate of speaking as a group norm. *Hum. Organization*, 1957, *15* (4), 8–10.

1882) Talland, G. A. Role and status structure in therapy groups. *J. clin. Psychol.*, 1957, *13*, 27–33.

1883) Talland, G. A. Sex differences in self assessment. *J. soc. Psychol.*, 1958, *48*, 25–35.

*1884) Talland, G. A., & Clark, D. H. Evaluation of topics in therapy group discussion. *J. clin. Psychol.*, 1954, *10*, 131–137.

1885) Tannenbaum, A. S. Personality change as a result of an experimental change of environmental conditions. *J. abnorm. soc. Psychol.*, 1957, *55*, 404–406.

1886) Tannenbaum, A. S., & Allport, F. H. Personality structure and group structure: an interpretative study of their relationship through an event-structure hypothesis. *J. abnorm. soc. Psychol.*, 1956, *53*, 272–280.

1887) Tannenbaum, R. *Motivational factors in productivity.* Los Angeles: University of California, 1952. (Annu. tech. Rep. No. 1, Contract No. NR 171-056)

1888) Tannenbaum, R., et al. Training managers for leadership. *Personnel*, 1954, *30*, 254–260.

1889) Tatsuoka, M. M. *Joint-probability of membership and success in a group: an index which combines the information from discriminant and regression analyses as applied to the guidance problem.* Cambridge, Mass.: Harvard University, October, 1957. (Contract Nonr-186631)

1890) Taylor, D. W. *Problem solving by groups.* Amsterdam, Holland: North Holland Publishing Co. (Reprinted from *Proc. 14th int. Congr. Psychol.*, Montreal, June, 1954.)

1891) Taylor, D. W., & Block, C. H. *Should group or individual work come first on problems requiring creative thinking when equal time is devoted to each?* New Haven, Conn.: Yale University, December, 1957. (Tech. Rep. No. 2, Contract Nonr-60920)

1892) Taylor, D. W., & Faust, W. L. Twenty questions: efficiency in problem solving as a function of size of group. *J. exp. Psychol.*, 1952, *44*, 360–368.

1893) Taylor, D. W., & McNemar, O. W. Problem solving and thinking. *Annu. Rev. Psychol.*, 1955, 6, 455–482.

1894) Taylor, D. W., et al. *Does group participation when using brainstorming facilitate or inhibit creative thinking?* New Haven, Conn.: Yale University, November, 1957. (Tech. Rep. No. 1, Contract Nonr 60920)

*1895) Taylor, F. Display of dyadic emotions. *Hum. Relat.*, 1957, *10*, 257–262.

1896) Taylor, F. K. The three-dimensional basis of emotional interactions in small groups.: I. *Hum. Relat.*, 1954, *7*, 441–471.

1897) Taylor, F. K. The three-dimensional basis of emotional interactions in small groups.: II. *Hum. Relat.*, 1955, *8*, 3–28.

1898) Taylor, F. W. Group management. *Trans. Soc. Mech. Engr*, 1903, *24*.

1899) Taylor, F. W. *The principles of scientific management*. New York: Harper & Row, 1911.

1900) Taylor, J. H., et al. The effect of conditions of work and various suggested attitudes on production and reported feelings of tiredness and boredness. *J. appl. Psychol.*, 1937, *21*, 431–450.

1901) Tear, D. G., & Guthrie, G. M. The relationship of cooperation to the sharpening-leveling continuum. *J. soc. Psychol.*, 1955, *42*, 203–208.

1902) Terman, L. M. A preliminary study of the psychology and pedagogy of leadership. *Pedag. Sem.*, 1904, *11*, 413–451.

1903) Thelen, H. A. Engineering research in curriculum building. *J. educ. Res.*, 1948, *41*, 579–596.

1904) Thelen, H. A. Group dynamics in instruction: principle of least group size. *Sch. Rev.*, 1949, *57*, 139–148.

1905) Thelen, H. A. Educational dynamics: theory and research. *J. soc. Issues*, 1950, *6*(2), 95.

1906) Thelen, H. A. *Emotionality and work as related to productivity of human relations training in small groups*. Chicago: University of Chicago, 1952. (Contract No. NR 170-176)

1907) Thelen, H. A. *Methods for research on interaction in groups*. Chicago: University of Chicago, 1952. (Contract No. NR 170–176)

1908) Thelen, H. A. *Dynamics of groups at work*. Chicago: University of Chicago Press, 1954.

1909) Thelen, H. A. Emotionality and work in groups. In L. D. White (Ed.), *The state of the social sciences*. Chicago: University of Chicago Press, 1956. Pp. 184–200.

1910) Thelen, H. A., & Whithall, J. Three frames of reference: the description of climate. *Hum. Relat.*, 1949, *2*, 159–176.

1911) Thelen, H. A., et al. *Methods for studying work and emotionality in group operation*. Chicago: University of Chicago, Human Dynamics Laboratory, 1954.

1912) Theodorson, G. A. Elements in the progressive development of small groups. *Soc. Forces*, 1953, *31*, 311–320.

1913) Theodorson, G. A. The relationship between leadership and popularity roles in small groups. *Amer. sociol. Rev.*, 1957, *22*, 58–67.

*1914) Thibaut, J. W. An experimental study of the cohesiveness of under-privileged groups. *Hum. Relat.*, 1950, *3*, 251–278.

1915) Thibaut, J. W., & Coules, J. The role of communication in the reduction of interpersonal hostility, *J. abnorm. soc. Psychol.*, 1952, *47*, 770–777.

1916) Thibaut, J. W., & Kelley, H. H. *The social psychology of groups*. New York: Wiley, 1959.

1917) Thibaut, J. W., & Riecken, H. W. Authoritarianism, status, and the communication of aggression. *Hum. Relat.*, 1955, *8*, 95–120.

1918) Thibaut, J. W., & Riecken, H. W. Some determinants and consequences of the perception of social causality. *J. Pers.*, 1955, *24*, 113–133.

*1919) Thibaut, J. W., & Strickland, L. H. Psychological set and social conformity. *J. Pers.*, 1956, *25*, 115–129.

*1920) Thibaut, J. W., et al. Communication, task demands, and group effectiveness. *J. Pers.*, 1960, *28*, 156–166.

1921) Thistlethwaite, D. L., et al. The effects of "directive" and "nondirective" communication procedures on attitudes. *J. abnorm. soc. Psychol.*, 1955, *51*, 107–113.

1922) Thomas, Dorothy S. (Ed.) *Some new techniques for studying social behavior*. New York: Columbia University, Teachers College, 1929. (Also in *Child Develpm. Monogr.*, 1929, No. 1.)

1923) Thomas, Dorothy S. A symposium on the observability of social phenomena with respect to statistical analysis: I. An attempt to develop precise measurements in the social behavior field. *Sociologus*, 1932, *8*, 436–456. II. *Sociologus*, 1933, *9*, 1–24.

1924) Thomas, Dorothy S., et al. *Observational studies of social behavior.* Vol. 1. *Social behavior patterns.* New Haven, Conn.: Yale University, Institute of Human Relations, 1933.

1925) Thomas, E. J. Effects of ego strength upon individual functioning in groups. *Amer. Psychologist*, 1956, *11*, 395. (Abstract)

*1926) Thomas, E. J. Effects of facilitative role interdependence on group functioning. *Hum. Relat.*, 1957, *10*, 347–366.

1927) Thompson, J. D., & Simpson, R. L. *Status classes, morale, and performance in the United States Air Force: an exploratory study*. Chapel Hill, N.C.: University of North Carolina, Institute for Research in Social Science, October, 1952. (Tech. Rep. No. 6)

1928) Thompson, W. R., & Nishimura, Rhoda. Some determinants of friendship. *J. Pers.*, 1952, *20*, 305–314.

1929) Thomson, R. M., et al. *Arrangement of groups of men and machines.* Washington, D.C.: Department of Navy, Office of Naval Research, December, 1958. [ONR Contract Nonr-1798(00)]

*1930) Thorndike, R. L. The effect of discussion upon the correctness of group decisions, when the factor of majority influence is allowed for. *J. soc. Psychol.*, 1938, *9*, 343–362.

1931) Thorndike, R. L. On what type of task will a group do well? *J. abnorm. soc. Psychol.*, 1938, *33*, 409–413.

1932) Thorpe, J. G. A study of some factors in friendship formation. *Sociometry*, 1955, *18*, 207–214.

*1933) Thrasher, J. D. Interpersonal relations and gradations of stimulus structure as factors in judgmental variation: an experimental approach. *Sociometry*, 1954, *17*, 228–241.

1934) Thrasher, F. *The gang.* Chicago: University of Chicago Press, 1927.

1935) Timmons, W. M. Decisions and attitudes as outcomes of the discussion of a social problem. *Teach. Coll., Columbia Univer., Contr. Educ.*, 1939, No. 777.

1936) Timmons, W. M. Sex differences in discussions. *Speech Monogr.*, 1941, *8*, 68–75.

1937) Timmons, W. M. Can the product superiority of discussors be attributed to averaging or majority influences? *J. soc. Psychol.*, 1942, *15*, 23–32.

1938) Toeman, Zerka. Role analysis and audience structure: with special emphasis on problems of military adjustment. *Sociometry*, 1944, 7, 205–221.

*1939) Torrance, E. P. *Crew performance in a test situation, as a predictor of field and combat performance.* Washington, D.C.: ARDC, Bolling Air Force Base, 1953. (HFORL Rep. No. 33)

*1940) Torrance, E. P. Methods of conducting critiques of group problem-solving performance. *J. appl. Psychol.*, 1953, *37*, 394–398.

1941) Torrance, E. P. Perception of group functioning as predictor of group performance. *Res. Stud., State Coll. Wash.*, 1953, *21*, 262–265.

1942) Torrance, E. P. The behavior of small groups under the stress of conditions of "survival." *Amer. sociol. Rev.*, 1954, *19*, 751–755.

1943) Torrance, E. P. Leadership training to improve group performance. *Instructors J.*, 1954, *5* (6), 25–35.

1944) Torrance, E. P. Some consequences of power differences on decision making in permanent and temporary three-man groups. *Res. Stud., State Coll. Wash.*, 1954, *22*, 130–140.

*1945) Torrance, E. P. *Some consequences of power differences on decisions in B-26 crews.* San Antonio, Tex.: Lackland Air Force Base, Air Force Personnel and Training Research Center, 1954. (Res. Bull. AFPTRC-TR-54-128)

1946) Torrance, E. P. *Function of expressed disagreement in small group processes.* Reno, Nev.: Stead Air Force Base, Crew Research Laboratory, Field Unit No. 2, October, 1955. (Lab. Note CRL-LN-55-220)

1947) Torrance, E. P. Sociometric techniques for diagnosing group ills. *Sociometry*, 1955, *18*, 597–612.

1948) Torrance, E. P. *Some issues regarding power roles in emergencies and extreme conditions.* Reno, Nev.: Stead Air Force Base, Crew Research Laboratory, Field Unit No. 2, April, 1955. (Lab. Note CRL-LN-55-208)

1949) Torrance, E. P. *Techniques for studying individual and group adaptation in emergencies and extreme conditions.* Reno, Nev.: Stead Air Force Base, Air Force Personnel and Training Research Center, Crew Research Laboratory, January, 1956. (Res. Rep. AFPTRC-TN-56-17)

1950) Torrance, E. P. Group decision-making and disagreement. *Soc. Forces*, 1957, *35*, 314–318.

1951) Torrance, E. P. Leadership in the survival of small isolated groups. Paper read at Sympos. preventive & soc. Psychiat., Washington, D.C., April, 1957.

1952) Torrance, E. P. What happens to the sociometric structure of small groups in emergencies and extreme conditions? *Group Psychother.*, 1957, *10*, 212–220.

1953) Torrance, E. P. The influence of experienced members of small groups on the behavior of the unexperienced. *J. soc. Psychol.*, 1959, *49*, 249–257.

1954) Torrance, E. P. A theory of leadership and interpersonal behavior under stress. In L. Petrullo and B. M. Bass (Eds.), *Leadership and interpersonal behavior*. New York: Holt, Rinehart and Winston, 1961. Pp. 100–117.

1955) Torrance, E. P., & Ziller, R. C. *Experiments on decision-making in small groups*. Reno, Nev.: Stead Air Force Base, USAF Survival Training School, Crew Research Laboratory, March, 1956. (Lab. Note CRL-LN-56-212)

1956) Torrance, E. P., & Ziller, R. C. *Negative identification in groups as a function of personality differences*. Reno, Nev.: Stead Air Force Base, USAF Survival Training School, Crew Research Laboratory, March, 1956. (Lab. Note CRL-LN-56-210)

1957) Torrance, E. P., et al. *Survival research: a report of the third year of development*. San Antonio, Tex.: Randolph Air Force Base, Air Force Personnel and Training Center, Crew Research Laboratory, November, 1954. (Tech. Memorandum CRL-TN-54-2)

1958) Torrance, E. P., et al. *List of reports prepared by Survival Research Field Unit prior to 1 June 1955*. Reno, Nev.: Stead Air Force Base, Survival Research Field Unit, Crew Research Laboratory, 1955.

1959) Torrance, E. P., et al. *Survival research: a report of the fourth year of development*. Reno, Nev.: Stead Air Force Base, Crew Research Laboratory, October, 1955. (Lab. Note CRL-LN-55-221)

1960) Torrance, E. P., et al. *Group adaptation in emergencies and extreme conditions*. San Antonio, Tex.: Randolph Air Force Base, Air Force Personnel and Training Research Center, Office for Social Science Program, December, 1956. (Tech. Memorandum OSSP-TM-56-4)

*1961) Trapp, E. P. Leadership and popularity as a function of behavioral predictions. *J. abnorm. soc. Psychol.*, 1955, *51*, 452–457.

1962) Travers, R. M. W. A study in judging the opinions of groups. *Arch. Psychol.*, 1941, *47*, No. 266.

*1963) Travers, R. M. W. The general ability to judge group-knowledge. *Amer. J. Psychol.*, 1943, *57*, 95–99.

1964) Travers, R. M. W. A study of the ability to judge group-knowledge. *Amer. J. Psychol.*, 1943, *56*, 54–65.

1965) Triplett, N. The dynamogenic factors in pace-making and competition. *Amer. J. Psychol.*, 1898, *9*, 507–533.

1966) Trist, E. L., & Bamforth, K. W. Some social and psychological consequences of the longwall method of coal-getting. *Hum. Relat.*, 1951, *4*, 3–38.

1967) Trow, D. B. An experimental study of autonomy in task-oriented groups. *Amer. Psychologist*, 1956, *11*, 360–361. (Abstract)

*1968) Trow, D. B. Autonomy and job satisfaction in task-oriented groups. *J. abnorm. soc. Psychol.*, 1957, *54*, 204–209.

1969) Trow, W. C., et al. Psychology of group behavior: the class as a group. *J. educ. Psychol.*, 1950, *41*, 322–338.

1970) Tuddenham, R. D. *The stability of personality ratings over two decades*. Berkeley, Calif.: University of California, 1957. (Tech. Rep. No. 3, Contract NR 170-159)

1971) Tuddenham, R. D. *Studies in conformity and yielding: II. The influence upon judgment of a grossly distorted norm.* Berkeley, Calif.: University of California, 1957. (Tech. Rep. No. 2, Contract NR 170-159)

1972) Tuddenham, R. D. *Studies in conformity and yielding: IV. The influence upon judgment of an avowedly distorted norm.* Berkeley, Calif.: University of California, 1958. (Tech. Rep. No. 5, Contract NR 170-159)

1973) Tuddenham, R. D. *Studies in conformity and yielding: V. The influence upon judgment of a moderately distorted norm.* Berkeley, Calif.: University of California, 1958. (Tech. Rep. No. 6, Contract NR 170-159)

1974) Tuddenham, R. D. *Studies in conformity and yielding: VI. The influence upon judgment of a genuine norm.* Berkeley, Calif.: University of California, 1958. (Tech. Rep. No. 7, Contract NR 170-159)

1975) Tuddenham, R. D. *Studies in conformity and yielding: VII. Some correlates of yielding to a distorted group norm.* Berkeley, Calif.: University of California, 1958. (Tech. Rep. No. 8, Contract NR 170-159)

*1976) Tuddenham, R. D., & MacBride, P. D. *Studies in conformity and yielding: The yielding experiment from the point of view of the subject.* Berkeley, Calif.: University of California, 1958. (Tech. Rep. No. 9, Contract NR 170-159)

1977) Tuddenham, R. D., et al. *Studies in conformity and yielding: I. Development of standard experimental series—1.* Berkeley, Calif.: University of California, 1956. (Tech. Rep. No. 1, Contract NR 170-159)

1978) Tuddenham, R. D., et al. *Studies in conformity and yielding: III. The sex composition of the group as a determinant of yielding to a distorted norm.* Berkeley, Calif.: University of California, 1958. (Tech. Rep. No. 4, Contract NR 170-159)

*1979) Tupes, E. C., et al. Performance in role-playing situations as related to leadership and personality measures. *Sociometry*, 1958, *21*, 165–179.

1980) Turk, H. Membership's internalization of task values and the popularity of nominated task leaders. *Amer. Psychologist*, 1959, *14*, 363. (Abstract)

1981) Turner, C. E. Test room studies in employee effectiveness. *Amer. J. publ. Hlth*, 1933, *23*, 577–584.

1982) Turner, R. H. Role-taking, role standpoint, and reference-group behavior. *Amer. J. Sociol.*, 1956, *61*, 316–328.

1983) Tuthill, C. E. A postulational system on social interaction. *J. Psychol.*, 1950, *29*, 355–377.

1984) Uhlmann, F. W., & Fiedler, F. E. Choices of fraternity presidents for leadership and maintenance roles. *Psychol. Rep.*, 1958, *4*, 498.

1985) Ullmann, L. P. Closure phenomena in complex social situations. *Amer. Psychologist*, 1956, *11*, 412. (Abstract)

1986) Updegraff, Ruth, & Herbst, Edithe K. An experimental study of the social behavior stimulated in young children by certain play materials. *J. genet. Psychol.*, 1933, *42*, 372–390.

1987) Van Bergen, Annie, & Koekebakker, J. Group cohesiveness in laboratory experiments. *Acta psychol.*, 1959, *16*, 81–98.

1988) Van Dusen, A. C. Measuring leadership ability. *Personnel Psychol.*, 1948, *1*, 67–79.

1989) Van Zelst, R. H. Worker popularity and job satisfaction. *Personnel Psychol.*, 1951, *4*, 405–412.

1990) Van Zelst, R. H. An interpersonal relations technique for industry. *Personnel*, 1952, *29*, 68–76.

1991) Van Zelst, R. H. Sociometrically selected work teams increase production. *Personnel Psychol.*, 1952, *5*, 175–185.

1992) Vaughan, W., & McGinnies, E. Some biographical determiners of participation in group discussion. *J. appl. Psychol.*, 1957, *41*, 179–185.

1993) Versace, J. *The effect of emergencies and communications availability with differing entry rates. A study in human engineering aspects of radar air traffic control.* Columbus: Ohio State University Research Foundation, Aviation Psychology Laboratory, December, 1956. (WADC tech. Rep. No. 56-70, ASTIA Doc. No. 118 320)

1994) Videbeck, R., & Bates, A. P. An experimental study of conformity to role expectations. *Sociometry*, 1959, *22*, 1–11.

1995) Vinacke, W. E. *The miniature social situation.* Honolulu: University of Hawaii, 1954.

*1996) Vinacke, W. E. Some variables in buzz sessions. *J. soc. Psychol.*, 1957, *45*, 25–33.

1997) Vinacke, W. E. The effect of cumulative score on coalition formation in triads with various patterns of internal power. *Amer. Psychologist*, 1959, *14*, 381. (Abstract)

*1998) Vinacke, W. E., & Arkoff, A. An experimental study of coalitions in the triad. *Amer. sociol. Rev.*, 1957, *22*, 406–414.

*1999) Voiers, W. D. *A comparison of the components of simulated radar bombing error in terms of reliability and sensitivity to practice.* San Antonio, Tex.: Lackland Air Force Base, Air Force Personnel and Training Research Center, December, 1954. (Res. Bull. AFPTRC-TR-54-74)

*2000) Voiers, W. D. *Bombing accuracy as a function of the ground school proficiency structure of the B-29 bomb team.* San Antonio, Tex.: Lackland Air Force Base, Air Force Personnel and Training Research Center, 1956. (Res. Rep. AFPTRC-TN-56-4)

2001) Von Wiese, L., & Becker, H. *Systematic sociology: on the basis of the Beziehungslehre and Gebildelehre.* New York: Wiley, 1932.

2002) Votaw, D. F., Jr. *Review and summary of research on personnel classification problems.* San Antonio, Tex.: Lackland Air Force Base, Air Force Personnel and Training Research Center, August, 1956. (Res. Rep. AFPTRC-TN-56-106)

2003) Vreeland, F. M. Social relations in the college fraternity. *Sociometry*, 1942, *5*, 151–162.

*2004) Vroom, V. H. Some personality determinants of the effects of participation. *J. abnorm. soc. Psychol.*, 1959, *59*, 322–327.

2005) Walk, R. D., & Wellin, F. A response board for group experiments in problem solving and concept formation. *Psychol. Rep.*, 1955, *1*, 335–338.

2006) Wallen, R. Individuals' estimates of group opinion. *J. soc. Psychol.*, 1943, *17*, 269–274.

2007) Walter, P. A. F. The influence of propaganda without social support. Paper prepared at Air Force Office of Scientific Research behav. Sci. Conf., Albuquerque, N. M., 1958. [Contract AF 49(638)-33]

*2008) Wapner, S., & Alper, Thelma G. The effect of an audience on behavior in a choice situation. *J. abnorm. soc. Psychol.*, 1952, *47*, 222–229.

2009) Warriner, C. K. Leadership in the small group. *Amer. J. Sociol.*, 1955, *60*, 361–369.

2010) Washburn, Ruth W. A scheme for grading the reactions of children in a new social situation. *J. genet. Psychol.*, 1932, *40*, 84–99.

2011) Watson, G. B. Do groups think more efficiently than individuals? *J. abnorm. soc. Psychol.*, 1928, *23*, 328–336.

2012) Watson, G. B. An evaluation of small group work in a large class. *J. educ. Psychol.*, 1953, *44*, 385–408.

2013) Webb, W. B. A note on responses to faces of others. *USN Sch. Aviat. Med. Res. Rep.*, 1957. (Proj. No. NM 16 01 11, Sub 2, Rep. No. 1)

2014) Weber, L. C. A study of peer acceptance among delinquent girls. *Sociometry*, 1950, *13*, 363–381.

2015) Weiner, M. G. *Observations on the growth of information-processing centers.* Santa Monica, Calif.: Rand Corp., May, 1954. (P-529)

2016) Weiss, R. *Factors determining the adoption of decision-making as a role behavior: a study of scientists in a government agency.* Ann Arbor, Mich.: University of Michigan, Institute for Social Research, 1954. (Contract No. NR 170-272)

2017) Weiss, W. *Opinion congruence with a negative source on one issue as a factor influencing agreement on another issue.* Boston: Boston University, June, 1956. [Tech. Rep. No. 4, Contract Nonr-492(04)]

2018) Weiss, W. The relationship between judgments of a communicator's position and extent of opinion change. *Amer. Psychologist*, 1957, *12*, 363. (Abstract)

2019) Weisskopf-Joelson, Edith. Some suggestions concerning Weltanschauung and psychotherapy. *J. abnorm. soc. Psychol.*, 1953, *48*, 601–604.

2020) Wells, W. D., Weinert, G., & Rubel, Marilyn. Conformity pressure and authoritarian personality. *J. Psychol.*, 1956, *42*, 133–136.

2021) Wertheimer, M. Appendix E: values in person cognition. Paper prepared at Air Force of Scientific Res. behav. Sci. Conf., Albuquerque, N.M., 1958. [Contract AF 49(638)-33]

2022) Weschler, I. R., & Brown, Paula. *Evaluating research and development.* Los Angeles: University of California, Institute of Industrial Relations, 1953. (Contract No. NR 171-056)

2023) Weschler, I. R., et al. Job satisfaction, productivity, and morale: a case study. *Occup. Psychol.*, 1952, *26*, 1–14.

2024) Weschler, I. R., et al. A new management tool: the multi-relational sociometric survey. *Personnel*, 1952, *29*, 85–94.

2025) Weschler, I. R., et al. (Eds.) *Industrial human relations: a selected bibliography.* Los Angeles, University of California, 1959.

2026) Wheeler, D. K. Notes on "Role differentiation in small decision groups." *Sociometry*, 1957, *20*, 145–151.

2027) Wheeler, D. K., & Jordan, H. Change of individual opinion to accord with group opinion. *J. abnorm. soc. Psychol.*, 1929, *24*, 203–206.

2028) Wherry, R. J., & Fryer, D. H. Buddy ratings: popularity contests or leadership criteria. *Personnel Psychol.*, 1942, *2*, 147–149.

*2029) White, Martha S. *Attitude change as related to perceived majority opinion*. San Antonio, Tex.: Lackland Air Force Base, Air Force Personnel and Training Research Center, 1957. [Rep. No. AFPTRC-TN-57-79, Contract No. AF 33(038)-26646]

2030) White, R. K., & Lippitt, R. Leader behavior and member reaction in three "social climates." In D. Cartwright and A. Zander (Eds.), *Group dynamics*. New York: Harper & Row, 1953. Pp. 585–611.

2031) Whitehead, T. N. *The industrial worker*. Cambridge, Mass.: Harvard University Press, 1938.

2032) Whitman, R. M., & Stock, D. The group focal conflict. *Psychiatry*, 1958, *21*, 269–276.

2033) Whittemore, I. C. The influence of competition on performance: an experimental study. *J. abnorm. soc. Psychol.*, 1924, *19*, 236–253.

2034) Whyte, W. F. *Street corner society: the social structure of an Italian slum*. Chicago: University of Chicago Press, 1943.

2035) Whyte, W. F. The social structure of the restaurant. *Amer. J. Sociol.*, 1949, *54*, 302–310.

2036) Whyte, W. F. Observational field-work methods. In Marie Jahoda et al., (Eds.), *Research methods in social relations*. New York: Holt, Rinehart and Winston, 1951. Pp. 493–513.

2037) Whyte, W. F. Small groups and large organizations. In J. H. Rohrer and M. Sherif (Eds.), *Social psychology at the crossroads*: New York: Harper & Row, 1951. Pp. 297–312.

2038) Whyte, W. F. *Leadership and group participation*. Ithaca, N.Y.: Cornell University, 1953. (New York State Sch. indus. & labor Relat. Bull. 24)

2039) Whyte, W. F. *Factors affecting conference agreement*. Ithaca, N.Y.: Cornell University, 1954. (Contract No. NR 172–140)

2040) Wickham, F. H. The Navy character education program: use of discussion groups. In Helen I. Driver (Ed.), *Counseling and learning through small group discussion*. Madison, Wis.: Monona Publications, 1958. Pp. 360–362.

2041) Wiener, M. Certainty of judgment as a variable in conformity behavior. *J. soc. Psychol.*, 1958, *48*, 257–263.

2042) Wiener, M., et al. Some determinants of conformity behavior. *J. soc. Psychol.*, 1957, *45*, 289–297.

2043) Wilcox, E. J., & Hill, W. F. Group process problems in a team research program. *Provo Papers*, 1957, *1*, 37–53.

2044) Willerman, B. *Group decision and request as means of changing food habits*. Washington, D.C.: National Research Council, Committee on Food Habits, April, 1943.

2045) Willerman, B. *Overlapping group identification in an industrial setting*. Ann Arbor, Mich.: University of Michigan, Institute for Social Research, 1949. (Contract No. NR 170-272)

*2046) Willerman, B. The relation of motivation and skill to active and passive participation in the group. *J. appl. Psychol.*, 1953, *37*, 387–390.

2047) Willerman, B. *The concept of effective group opinion: estimates of group opinion as related to the opinions of high influence members.* Minneapolis: University of Minnesota, 1954. (Contract No. NR 170-169)

2048) Willerman, B. *Organizational involvement as reflected in type of member complaint: an indirect method of measurement.* Minneapolis: University of Minnesota, 1954. (Tech. Rep. No. 4, Contract N8 ONR 66216)

2049) Willerman, B. *Research on cohesive and disruptive tendencies in coalition-type groups.* Minneapolis: University of Minnesota, 1957. (Contract N8 ONR-66216)

2050) Willerman, B., & Emerson, R. *Perceived control and interdependence as related to member attitudes toward a coalition-type group.* Minneapolis: University of Minnesota, 1954. (Contract No. NR 170–169)

2051) Willerman, B., & Swanson, L. An ecological determinant of differential amounts of sociometric choices within college sororities. *Sociometry*, 1952, *15*, 326–329.

2052) Willerman, B., et al. *Preferences for working individually or in groups.* Minneapolis: University of Minnesota, 1957. (Tech. Rep. No. 6, Contract N8 ONR-66216)

2053) Williams, Ruth M., & Mattson, Marion L. The effect of social groupings upon the language of pre-school children. *Child Develpm.*, 1942, *13*, 233–245.

*2054) Williams, S. B., & Leavitt, H. J. Group opinion as a predictor of military leadership. *J. consult. Psychol.*, 1947, *11*, 283–291.

2055) Williamson, E. C. Allport's experiments in "social facilitation." *Psychol. Monogr.*, 1926, *35*(163), 138–143.

2056) Wilner, D., et al. Residential proximity and intergroup relations in public housing projects. *J. soc. Issues*, 1952, *8*(1), 45–69.

2057) Wilson, L. Sociography of groups. In G. Gurvitch and W. E. Moore (Eds.), *Twentieth century sociology.* New York: Philosophical Library, 1945. Pp. 139–171.

*2058) Wilson, R. C., et al. Factors influencing organizational effectiveness: III. A survey of skilled tradesmen. *Personnel Psychol.*, 1953, *6*, 313–325.

2059) Wilson, R. C., et al. A factor-analytic study of supervisory and group behavior. *J. appl. Psychol.*, 1954, *38*, 89–92.

2060) Wilson, R. C., et al. Factors influencing organizational effectiveness: IV. A survey of supervisors and workers. *Personnel Psychol.*, 1954, *7*, 525–531.

2061) Wilson, R. C., et al. An iterative analysis of supervisory and group dimensions. *J. appl. Psychol.*, 1955, *39*, 85–91.

2062) Wirth, L. Social interaction: the problem of the individual and the group. *Amer. J. Sociol.*, 1939, *44*, 965–979.

2063) Wischmeier, R. R. Group-centered and leader-centered leadership: an experimental study. *Speech Monogr.*, 1955, *22*, 43–48.

2064) Wiseman, I. G. A study of the interpersonal and intrapersonal factors in group discussion. *Speech Monogr.*, 1954, *21*, 184–187.

2065) Wispe, L. G. Evaluating section teaching methods in the introductory course. *J. educ. Res.*, 1951, *45*, 161–186.

2066) Wispe, L. G. Teaching methods research. *Amer. Psychologist*, 1953, *8*, 147–150. (Abstract)

2067) Wispe, L. G. A sociometric analysis of conflicting role-expectations. *Amer. J. Sociol.*, 1955, *61*, 134–137.

2068) Wispe, L. G., & Lloyd, K. E. Some situational and psychological determinants of the desire for structured interpersonal relations. *J. abnorm. soc. Psychol.*, 1955, *51*, 57–60.

2069) Withall, J. The development of a technique for the measurement of social-emotional climate in classrooms. *J. exp. Educ.*, 1949, *17*, 347–361.

2070) Withall, J. The development of the climate index. *J. educ. Res.*, 1951, *45*, 93–100.

2071) Withall, J. An objective measurement of a teacher's classroom interaction. *J. educ. Psychol.*, 1956, *47*, 208–212.

2072) Wittenberg, R. M., & Berg, Janice. The stranger in the group. *Amer. J. Orthopsychiat.*, 1952, *22*, 89–97.

2073) Wolff, K. H. *The sociology of Georg Simmel.* New York: Free Press, 1950.

2074) Wolman, B. Leadership and group dynamics. *J. soc. Psychol.*, 1956, *43*, 11–25.

2075) Wright, M. E. Constructiveness of play as affected by group organization and frustration. *Charact. & Pers.*, 1942, *9*, 40–49.

*2076) Wright, M. E. The influence of frustration upon social relations of young children. *Charact. & Pers.*, 1943, *12*, 111–122.

2077) Wrightstone, J. W. An instrument for measuring group discussion and planning. *J. educ. Res.*, 1934, *27*, 641–650.

2078) Wrightstone, J. W. Measuring the social climate of a classroom. *J. educ. Res.*, 1951, *44*, 341–351.

2079) Wurster, C. R., & Bass, B. M. Situational tests: IV. Validity of leaderless group discussions among strangers. *Educ. psychol. Measmt*, 1953, *13*(1), 122–132.

2080) Yablonsky, L. A sociometric investigation into the development of an experimental model for small group analysis. *Sociometry*, 1952, *15*, 175–205.

2081) Yablonsky, L. An operational theory of roles. *Sociometry*, 1953, *16*, 349–354.

2082) Yablonsky, L. Research in sociometry–the sociometry of the dyad. *Sociometry*, 1955, *18*, 613–616.

2083) Yarrow, L. J., & Yarrow, M. R. Leadership and inter-personal change. *J. soc. Issues*, 1958, *14*(1), 47–59.

2084) Yarrow, M. R., et al. Acquisition of new norms: a study of racial desegregation. *J. soc. Issues*, 1958, *14*(1), 8–28.

2085) Yarrow, M. R., et al. Inter-personal change: process and theory. *J. soc. Issues*, 1958, *14*(1), 60–62.

2086) Yuker, H. E. Group atmosphere and memory. *J. abnorm. soc. Psychol.*, 1955, *51*, 17–23.

2087) Zajonc, R. B. Information storage in groups. Paper prepared at Air
    Force Office of Scientific Res. behav. Sci. Conf., Albuquerque, N.M.,
    1958. [Contract AF 49(638)-33]
2088) Zander, A., et al. *Determinants of motivation and performance under pres-
    sure: a report of a field study and a laboratory experiment.* Ann Arbor,
    Mich.: University of Michigan, Institute for Social Research, February,
    1957.
2089) Zander, A. F. The WP club: an objective case study of a group. *Hum.
    Relat.*, 1948, *1*, 321–332.
2090) Zander, A. F. Systematic observation of small face-to-face groups. In
    Marie Jahoda et al. (Eds.), *Research methods in social relations:*
    New York: Holt, Rinehart and Winston, 1951. Pp. 515–538.
*2091) Zander, A. F., & Cohen, A. R. Attributed social power and group
    acceptance: a classroom experimental demonstration. *J. abnorm.
    soc. Psychol.*, 1955, *51*, 490–492.
2092) Zeleny, L. D. Characteristics of group leaders. *Sociol. soc. Res.*, 1939,
    24, 140–149.
2093) Zeleny, L. D. Sociometry of morale. *Amer. sociol. Rev.*, 1939, *4*, 799–808.
2094) Zeleny, L. D. Experimental appraisal of a group learning plan. *J. educ.
    Res.*, 1940, *34*, 37–42.
2095) Zeleny, L. D. Measurement of social status. *Amer. J. Sociol.*, 1940,
    45, 576–582.
2096) Zeleny, L. D. Measurement of sociation. *Amer. sociol. Rev.*, 1941, *6*,
    173–188.
2097) Zeleny, L. D. Selection of compatible flying partners. *Amer. J. Sociol.*,
    1947, *52*, 424–431.
2098) Zentner, H. Primary group affiliation and institutional group morale.
    Sociol. soc. Res., 1955, *40*, 31–34.
2099) Ziller, R. C. Leader-group rigidity and group cohesiveness: determinants
    of group problem-solving processes and concomitant affective group
    behavior. *Amer. Psychologist*, 1953, *8*, 459. (Abstract)
2100) Ziller, R. C. Four techniques of group decision making under conditions
    of uncertainty. *Amer. Psychologist*, 1954, *9*, 498. (Abstract)
*2101) Ziller, R. C. Scales of judgment: a determinant of the accuracy of
    group decisions. *Hum. Relat.*, 1955, *8*, 153–164.
2102) Ziller, R. C. Group size: a determinant of the quality and stability of
    group decisions. *Sociometry*, 1957, *20*, 165–173.
2103) Ziller, R. C. Communication restraints, group flexibility, and group
    confidence. *J. appl. Psychol.*, 1958, *42*, 346–352.
*2104) Ziller, R. C. Leader acceptance of responsibility for group action under
    conditions of uncertainty and risk. *J. Psychol.*, 1959, *47*, 57–66.
2105) Ziller, R. C., & Behringer, R. Assimilation of a knowledgeable new-
    comer under conditions of group success and failure. *Amer. Psycholo-
    gist*, 1959, *14*, 362. (Abstract)
2106) Ziller, R. C., & Behringer, R. Group persuasion under conditions of
    incubation and varying group size. *J. appl. Psychol.*, 1959, *43*, 402–406.
2107) Ziller, R. C., & Exline, R. V. Some consequences of age heterogeneity in
    decision-making groups. *Sociometry*, 1958, *21*, 198–211.

*2108) Ziller, R. C., et al. The newcomer in open and closed groups. Paper read at East. psychol. Ass., Atlantic City, N.J., April, 1959.

2109) Zimet, C. N., & Fine, H. J. Personality changes with a group therapeutic experience in a human relations seminar. *J. abnorm. soc. Psychol.,* 1955, *51,* 68–73.

2110) Zimmer, H. Motivational factors in dyadic interaction. *J. Pers.,* 1956, *24,* 251–261.

2111) Zink, D. L. The development of role differentiation in dyads as a function of task complexity. *Amer. Psychologist,* 1957, *12,* 371. (Abstract)

2112) Znaniecki, F. Social groups as products of participating individuals. *Amer. J. Sociol.,* 1939, *44,* 799–812.

ADDENDA

2113) Altman, I., & Terauds, Anita. *Major variables of the small group field.* Arlington, Va.: Human Sciences Research, Inc., November, 1960. [HSR-RR-60/6-Gn, Contract AF 49(638)-256]

2114) Altman, I., et al. *Annotations of small group research studies.* Arlington, Va.: Human Sciences Research, Inc., October, 1960. [HSR-RR-60/5-Gn, Contract AF 49(638)-256]

2115) Anderson, H. Group performance in an anagram task. *J. soc. Psychol.,* 1961, *55,* 67–75.

2116) Andrews, F. M., & Pelz, D. C. *Dimensions of organizational atmosphere.* Ann Arbor, Mich.: University of Michigan, Institute for Social Research, February, 1961. (Interim tech. Rep., ASTIA Document No. 256 036)

2117) Antonitis, J., & Barnes, G. W. Group operant behavior: an extension of individual research methodology to a real-life situation. *J. genet. Psychol.,* 1961, *98,* 95–111.

2118) Argyris, C. *Understanding organizational behavior.* Homewood, Ill.: Dorsey Press, 1960.

2119) Arrow, K. J., et al. (Eds.) *Mathematical models in the social sciences,* Stanford, Calif.: Stanford University Press, 1960.

2120) Asch, S. E. Effects of group pressure upon the modification and distortion of judgments. In D. Cartwright and A. Zander (Eds.), *Group dynamics: research and theory.* (2nd ed.) New York: Harper & Row, 1960. Pp. 189–200.

2121) Atthowe, J. M., Jr. Interpersonal decision making: the resolution of a dyadic conflict. *J. abnorm. soc. Psychol.,* 1961, *62,* 114–119.

2122) Bachrach. A. J. (Ed.) *Experimental foundations of clinical psychology.* New York: Basic Books, 1952.

2123) Bachrach, A. J., et al. *An investigation of pre-problem set and group pressure on decision-making.* Charlottesville, Va.: University of Virginia, 1957. [Tech. Rep. Contract Nonr 474(08)]

2124) Bachrach, A. J., et al. *Group structure, anxiety, and problem-solving efficiency.* Charlottesville, Va.: University of Virginia, 1958. [Tech. Rep., Contract Nonr 474(08)]

2125) Bachrach, A. J., et al. *Interaction of group structure and anxiety*. Charlottesville, Va.: University of Virginia, 1958. [Tech. Rep., Contract Nonr 474(08)]

2126) Bachrach, A. J., et al. *Experiments in verbal behavior: I. Group reinforcement of individual response*. Charlottesville, Va.: University of Virginia, 1960. [Tech. Rep. Contract Nonr 474(08)]

2127) Banghart, F. W. *Group influence on creativity in mathematics*. Charlottesville, Va.: University of Virginia, 1960. [Tech. Rep., Contract Nonr 474(08)]

2128) Bardach, Joan L. Effects of situational anxiety at different stages of practice. *J. exp. Psychol.*, 1960, *59*, 420–424.

2129) Bass, B. M. *Behavior in groups. Test of a proposed theory of leadership*. Baton Rouge, La.: Louisiana State University, November, 1959. (Annu. Rep. No. 5, Contract N7 ONR-35609)

2130) Bass, B. M. *Conformity, deviation, and a general theory of interpersonal behavior*. Baton Rouge, La.: Louisiana State University, March, 1960. (Tech. Rep. No. 20, Contract N7 ONR-35609)

2131) Bass, B. M. *An evaluation of the use of objective social data for training problem-solving discussants*. Baton Rouge, La.: Louisiana State University, June, 1960. (Tech. Rep. No. 22, Contract N7 ONR-35609)

2132) Bass, B. M. *A generalized IBM 650 program for calculating measures of average influence and change in agreement of rankings by a group of judges*. Baton Rouge, La.: Louisiana State University, October, 1960. (Tech. Note No. 2, Contract N7 ONR-35609)

2133) Bass, B. M. The management training laboratory. *Advanc. Mgmt*, 1960, *25*, 11–15.

2134) Bass, B. M. Measures of average influence and change in agreement of rankings by a group of judges. *Sociometry*, 1960, *23*, 195–202.

2135) Bass, B. M. *Some aspects of attempted successful and effective leadership*. Baton Rouge, La.: Louisiana State University, June, 1960. (Tech. Rep. No. 21, Contract N7 ONR-35609)

2136) Bass, B. M. Some experiments on leadership, psychology, and organizational behavior. *Amer. Psychologist*, 1960, *15*, 477. (Abstract)

2137) Bass, B. M. *Behavior in groups: experimenting with simulated manufacturing organizations*. Baton Rouge, La.: Louisiana State University, March, 1961. (Tech. Rep. No. 27, Contract N7 ONR-35609)

2138) Bass, B. M. *Behavior in groups: reactions to "12 angry men" as a measure of sensitivity training*. Baton Rouge, La.: Louisiana State University, March, 1961. (Tech. Rep. No. 26, Contract N7 ONR-35609)

2139) Bass, B. M. *Comparisons of the behavior in groups of self-oriented, interaction-oriented, and task-oriented members*. Baton Rouge, La.: Louisiana State University, January, 1961. (Tech. Rep. No. 25, Contract N7 ONR-35609)

2140) Bass, B. M. Some aspects of attempted, successful, and effective leadership. *J. appl. Psychol.*, 1961, *45*, 120–122.

2141) Bass, B. M. *Test of a proposed theory of leadership*. Baton Rouge, La.: Louisiana State University, November, 1961. (Annu. Rep. No. 7, Contract N7 ONR-35609)

2142) Bass, B. M. Individual decisions, reinforcement effects, and group behavior as a function of self, interaction, and task orientation. *Amer. Psychologist*, 1962, *17*, 309. (Abstract)

2143) Bass, B. M. Mood changes during a management training laboratory. *J. appl. Psychol.*, 1962, *46*, 361–364.

2144) Baur, E. J. Public opinion and the primary group. *Amer. sociol. Rev.*, 1960, *25*, 208–219.

2145) Behringer, R. D., & Ziller, R. C. Motivational effects on memory for biographical information of a potential newcomer to the group. *Amer. Psychologist*, 1961, *16*, 389. (Abstract)

2146) Beier, E. G., et al. Similarity plus dissimilarity of personality: basis for friendship? *Psychol. Rep.*, 1961, *8*, 3–8.

2147) Belnap, N. D., Jr. *A formal analysis of entailment.* New Haven, Conn.: Yale University, Interaction Laboratory, June, 1960. (Tech. Rep, No. 7, Contract Nonr 60916)

2148) Berg, I. A., & Bass, B. M. (Eds.) *Conformity and deviation.* New York: Harper & Row, 1961.

2149) Berkowitz, L. The judgmental process in personality functioning. *Psychol. Rev.*, 1960, *67*, 130–142.

2150) Berkowitz, L. Some factors affecting the reduction of overt hostility. *J. abnorm. soc. Psychol.*, 1960, *60*, 14–20.

2151) Berrien, F. K. *Relationship between group equilibrium, production and morale in problem-solving work groups.* New Brunswick, N.J.: Rutgers University, 1959. [Annu. tech. Rep., Contract Nonr 404(10)]

2152) Berrien, F. K. *Relationship between group equilibrium, production and morale in problem-solving work groups.* New Brunswick, N.J.: Rutgers University, 1960. [Annu. tech. Rep., Contract Nonr 404(10)]

2153) Berrien, F. K. *Studies in the homeostasis of small groups.* New Brunswick, N.J.: Rutgers University, 1960. [Tech. Rep., Contract Nonr 404(10)]

2154) Berrien, F. K. *Homeostasis theory of small groups. VII: Longitudinal studies.* New Brunswick, N.J.: Rutgers University, June, 1962. [Tech. Rep. No. 10, Contract Nonr 404(10)]

2155) Berrien, F. K., & Angoff, W. H. *Homeostasis theory of small groups. IV: Light manufacturing personnel.* New Brunswick, N.J.: Rutgers University, January, 1960. [Tech. Rep. No. 6, Contract Nonr 404(10)]

2156) Berrien, F. K., & Angoff, W. H. *Homeostasis theory of small groups. V: Case study.* New Brunswick, N.J.: Rutgers University, August, 1960. [Tech. Rep. No. 7, Contract Nonr 404(10)]

2157) Berrien, F. K., & Indik, B. P. *Homeostasis theory of small groups. VI: Voluntary organizations.* New Brunswick, N.J.: Rutgers University, December, 1961. [Tech. Rep. No. 8, Contract Nonr 404(10)]

2158) Bjerstedt, A. *Interpretations of sociometric choice status.* Lund, Sweden: Gleerup, 1956.

2159) Bjerstedt, A. The five-step intersubject interview technique in psychological research. *J. Psychol.*, 1961, *51*, 273–278.

2160) Bjerstedt, A. Preparation, process, and product in small group interaction. *Hum. Relat.*, 1961, *14*, 185–189.

2161) Blake, R. R., & Mouton, Jane S. Competition, communication and conformity. In I. A. Berg and B. M. Bass (Eds.), *Conformity and deviation.* New York: Harper & Row, 1961.

2162) Blake, R. R., & Mouton, Jane S. Loyalty of representatives to ingroup positions during intergroup competition. *Sociometry,* 1961, *24,* 177–183.

2163) Blau, P. M. Patterns of deviation in work groups. *Sociometry,* 1960, *23,* 245–261.

2164) Bogdonoff, M. D., et al. *The effect of group interaction upon central nervous system arousal in man.* Durham, N.C.: Duke University, undated. [Tech. Rep. No. 1, Contract No. 1181(11)]

2165) Bond, J. R., & Vinacke, W. E. Coalitions in mixed-sex triads. *Sociometry,* 1961, *24,* 61–75.

2166) Bonney, W. C., & George, C. E. *Adaptive behavior and adaptation level theory.* College Station, Tex.: Texas A. and M. Research Foundation, September, 1959. (Tech. Rep. No. 3, Contract Nonr 211901)

2167) Bonney, W. C., & George, C. E. *Adaptation level and small group dynamics.* College Station, Tex.: Texas A. and M. College, Basic Division, 1960. (Tech. Rep., Contract Nonr 211901)

2168) Bonney, W. C., & George, C. E. *Adaptation level theory, personality, and small group dynamics.* College Station, Tex.: Texas A. and M. Research Foundation, September, 1960. (Tech. Rep. No. 4, Contract Nonr 211901)

2169) Borg, W. R. Prediction of small group role behavior from personality variables. *J. abnorm. soc. Psychol.,* 1960, *60,* 112–116.

2170) Borgatta, E. F. *The coincidence of subtests in four personality inventories.* New York: New York University, October, 1958. [AFOSR TN 58-923, Contract AF 49(638)-195]

2171) Borgatta, E. F. *Mood, personality and interaction.* New York: New York University, November, 1958. [AFOSR TN 58-978, Contract AF 49(638)-195]

2172) Borgatta, E. F. *Rankings and self-assessments: some behavioral characteristics: replication studies.* New York: New York University, 1958. [AFOSR TN 58-737, Contract AF 49(638)-195]

2173) Borgatta, E. F. *The spectrum of individual interaction characteristics: an inter-dimensional analysis.* New York: New York University, February, 1958. [AFOSR TN 58-442, Contract AF 49(638)-195]

2174) Borgatta, E. F. *Personality concomitants of extreme response set (ERS).* New York: New York University, August, 1959. [AFOSR TN 59-808, Contract AF 49(638)-195]

2175) Borgatta, E. F. *The stability of interpersonal rankings in independent situations.* New York: New York University, January, 1959. [AFOSR TN 59-42, Contract AF 49(638)-195]

2176) Borgatta, E. F. Role and reference group theory. In L. S. Kogan (Ed.), *Social science theory and social work research.* New York: National Association of Social Workers, 1960.

2177) Borgatta, E. F. Small group research. *Current Sociology* 1960, *9,* 173–200.

2178) Borgatta, E. F. The stability of interpersonal judgments in independent situations. *J. abnorm. soc. Psychol.,* 1960, *60,* 188–194.

2179) Borgatta, E. F. *The variables and conditions of small group interaction.* New York: New York University, October, 1960. [Final Rep. No. 1, Contract AF 49(638)-195]

2180) Borgatta, E. F. Role-playing specification, personality, and performance. *Sociometry,* 1961, *24,* 218–233.

2181) Borgatta, E. F. *Small group research.* Oxford: Blackwell, 1962.

2182) Borgatta, E. F., & Glass, D. C. *Personality concomitants of extreme response set (ERS).* New York: New York University, August, 1959. [AFOSR TN 59-809, Contract AF 49(638)–195]

2183) Borgatta, E. F., & Guerrin, R. F. The two-person group: some notes on theory and research. *Sociol. soc. Res.,* 1960, *45,* 3–13.

2184) Borgatta, Marie L. Power structure and coalitions in three person groups. New York: New York University, July, 1959. [AFOSR TN 59-679, Contract AF 49(638)-195]

2185) Bovard, E. W., Jr. The psychology of classroom interaction. *J. educ. Res..* 1951, *45,* 215–224.

2186) Bovard, E. W., Jr. Conformity to social norms in stable and temporary groups. *Science,* 1953, *117,* 361–363.

2187) Bovard, E. W., Jr. The effects of social stimuli on the response to stress. *Psychol. Rev.,* 1959, *66,* 267–277.

2188) Bowers, D. G. Leadership and organizational performance in an insurance company. *Amer. Psychologist,* 1962, *17,* 383. (Abstract)

2189) Bowers, R. V., et al. *Studies in organizational effectiveness.* Washington, D.C.: Air Force Office of Scientific Research, Office of Aerospace Research, 1962.

2190) Burke, C. J. Some two-person interactions. In K. J. Arrow et al. (Eds.), *Mathematical methods in the social sciences.* Stanford, Calif.: Stanford University Press, 1960. Pp. 242–253.

2191) Burke, R. L., & Bennis, W. G. Changes in perception of self and others during human relations training. *Hum. Relat.,* 1961, *14,* 165–182.

2192) Burnstein, E., & McRaie, A. V. Some effects of shared threat and prejudice in racially mixed groups. *J. abnorm. soc. Psychol.,* 1962, *64,* 257–263.

2193) Byrne, D. Interpersonal attraction and attitude similarity. *J. abnorm. soc. Psychol.,* 1961, *62,* 713–715.

2194) Byrne, D. Interpersonal attraction as a function of affiliation need and attitude similarity. *Hum. Relat.,* 1961, *14,* 283–289.

2195) Byrne, D., & Wong, T. J. Racial prejudice, interpersonal attraction, and assumed dissimilarity of attitudes. *J. abnorm. soc. Psychol.,* 1962, *65,* 246–253.

2196) Campbell, R. J. *Originality in group productivity: III. Partisan commitment and productive independence in a collective bargaining situation.* Columbus, Ohio: Ohio State University, Personnel Research Board, 1960. (Contract Nonr 49515)

2197) Campbell, R. J. *Partisan commitment and productive independence in a collective bargaining situation.* Columbus, Ohio: Ohio State University, 1961. (Tech. Rep., Contract Nonr 49515)

2198) Carlson, E. R. Clique structure and member satisfaction in groups. *Sociometry,* 1960, *23,* 327–337.

2199) Carment, D. W. Ascendant-submissive behavior in pairs of human subjects as a function of their emotional responsiveness and opinion strength. *Canad. J. Psychol.*, 1961, *15*, 45–51.

2200) Cartwright, D., & French. J. R. P. *An experiment on active and passive resistance to social power.* Ann Arbor, Mich.: University of Michigan, Research Center for Group Dynamics, August, 1959. (Contract Nonr 122411)

2201) Cartwright, D., & Robertson, R. J. Membership in cliques and achievement. *Amer. J. Psychol.*, 1961, *66*, 441–445.

2202) Cassel, R. N., & Shafer, Alice E. An experiment in leadership training. *J. Psychol.*, 1961, *51*, 299–305.

2203) Cave, R. T., & Krumm, R. L. The effectiveness of integrated air crew simulator training for B-52 transition crews. *Amer. Psychologist*, 1960, *15*, 491. (Abstract)

2204) Cervin, V. B., & Henderson, G. P. Statistical theory of persuasion. *Psychol. Rev.*, 1961, *68*, 157–166.

2205) Cervin, V. B., et al. Relationship of some personality traits to success in a transactional bargaining game: a pilot study. *Amer. Psychologist*, 1960, *15*, 397. (Abstract)

2206) Chance, June E., & Meaders, W. Needs and interpersonal perception. *J. Pers.*, 1960, *28*, 200–209.

2207) Chaney, Marilyn V., & Vinacke, W. E. Achievement and nurturance in triads varying in power distribution. *J. abnorm. soc. Psychol.*, 1960, *60*, 175–181.

2208) Chapanis, A. *First NATO symposium on defence psychology.* London: Office of Naval Research, September, 1960. (Tech. Rep. No. ONRL-C-17-60, ASTIA Document No. 244 868L)

2209) Cleveland, S. E., & Morton, R. B. Group behavior and body image: a follow-up study. *Hum. Relat.*, 1962, *15*, 77–85.

2210) Cline, V. B., & Richards, J. M., Jr. *Variables related to accuracy in interpersonal perception.* Salt Lake City, Utah: University of Utah, November, 1959. (Annu. Rep. No. 2, Contract Nonr 128804)

2211) Cline, V. B., & Richards, J. M., Jr. Accuracy of interpersonal perception—a general trait? *J. abnorm. soc. Psychol.*, 1960, *60*, 1–7.

2212) Cline, V. B., & Richards, J. M., Jr. *Variables related to accuracy in interpersonal perception.* Salt Lake City, Utah: University of Utah, 1960. (Annu. tech. Rep., Contract Nonr 128804)

2213) Cline, V. B., & Richards, J. M., Jr. A comparison of individuals versus groups in judging personality. *J. appl. Psychol.*, 1961, *45*, 150–155.

2214) Cline, V. B., & Richards, J. M., Jr. *Variables related to accuracy in interpersonal perception.* Salt Lake City, Utah: University of Utah, November, 1961. (Annu. Rep. No. 4, Contract Nonr 128804)

2215) Cohen, A. M. *Changing small group communication networks.* Boston: Boston University, 1961. [Tech. Rep. Contract Nonr 492(05)]

2216) Cohen, A. M., & Bennis, W. G. *The effects of an elective situation on continuity of leadership under conditions of change in work structure.* Boston: Boston University, 1960. [Tech. Rep., Contract Nonr 492(05)]

2217) Cohen, A. M., & Bennis, W. G. *A model predicting the influence of previous experience on the communication systems established by problem-solving groups.* Boston: Boston University, 1960. [Tech. Rep., Contract Nonr 492(05)]

2218) Cohen, A. M., & Bennis, W. G. Continuity of leadership in communication networks. *Hum. Relat.*, 1961, *14*, 351–368.

2219) Cohen, A. M., et al. *The effects of changes in communication patterns on the behaviors of problem-solving groups.* Boston: Boston University, 1960. [Tech. Rep., Contract Nonr 492(05)]

2220) Cohen, A. M., et al. *The effects of continued practice on the behaviors of problem-solving groups.* Boston: Boston University, 1960. [Tech. Rep., Contract Nonr 492(05)]

2221) Cohen, A. M., et al. *A partial test of a model predicting the influence of previous experience on the communication systems established by problem-solving groups.* Boston: Boston University, 1960. [Tech. Rep., Contract Nonr 492(05)]

2222) Cohen, A. M., et al. The effects of continued practice on the behaviors of problem-solving groups. *Sociometry*, 1961, *24*, 416–431.

2223) Cohen, D., et al. Effect of group cohesiveness and training upon creative thinking. *J. appl. Psychol.*, 1960, *44*, 319–322.

2224) Cohen, E. Stimulus conditions as factors in social change. *Sociometry*, 1957, *20*, 135–144.

2225) Cole, M., & Schneider, A. Amount of reward and knowledge of results in a two-person game. *Amer. Psychologist*, 1961, *16*, 425. (Abstract)

2226) Coleman, J. S., & James, J. The equilibrium size distribution of freely-forming groups. *Sociometry*, 1961, *24*, 36–45.

2227) Coombs, C. H., & Pruitt, D. G. *A study of decision-making under risk.* Ann Arbor, Mich.: University of Michigan, Willow Run Laboratories, April, 1960. (Rep. No. 2900-33-T, Contract DA 36-039-sc-78801)

2228) Creager, J. A., & Miller, R. E. *Summary of regression analyses in the prediction of leadership criteria, Air Force Academy classes of 1961 through 1963.* Lackland Air Force Base, Tex.: Aeronautical Systems Division, Personnel Laboratory, April, 1961. (ASD TN 61-41, ASTIA Document No. 263 979)

2229) Croner, M. D., & Willis, R. H. Asymmetry of social influence as a function of perceived differences in task competence. *Amer. Psychologist*, 1960, *15*, 419. (Abstract)

2230) Croner, M. D., & Willis, R. H. Perceived differences in task competence and asymmetry of dyadic influence. *J. abnorm. soc. Psychol.*, 1961, *62*, 705–708.

2231) Crowell, Laura, & Scheidel, T. M. Categories for analysis of idea development in discussion groups. *J. soc. Psychol.*, 1961, *54*, 155–168.

2232) Davis, J. A., et al. A technique for analyzing the effects of group composition. *Amer. sociol. Rev.*, 1961, *26*, 215–225.

2233) Day, R., & Hamblin, R. L. *Some effects of close and punitive styles of supervision.* St Louis, Mo.: Washington University, Social Sciences Institute, 1961. [Tech. Rep. No. 8, Contract Nonr 816(11)]

2234) deCharms, R., & Bridgeman, W. *Leadership compliance and group behavior.* St Louis, Mo.: Washington University, 1961. [Tech. Rep. No. 9, Contract Nonr 816(11)]

2235) deCharms, R., & Hamblin, R. L. *Structural factors and individual needs in group behavior.* St. Louis, Mo.: Washington University, Social Sciences Institute, 1960. [Annu. tech. Rep., Contract Nonr 816(11)]

2236) deCharms, R., & Rosenbaum, M. E. *Status variables and matching behavior.* St. Louis, Mo.: Washington University, May, 1960. [Tech. Rep. No. 2, Contract Nonr 816(11)]

2237) deCharms, R., & Rosenbaum, M. E. Status variables and matching behavior. *J. Pers.,* 1960, *28,* 492–502.

2238) deCharms, R., & Wilkins, E. J. *Studies in the psychology of aggression.* St. Louis, Mo.: Washington University, Social Sciences Institute, 1960. [Tech. Rep., Contract Nonr 816(11)]

2239) Department of the Navy, Office of Naval Research. *Bibliography of unclassified research reports in group psychology.* Washington, D.C.: Author, September, 1957. (ONR Rep. ACR-22)

2240) Department of the Navy, Office of Naval Research. *Bibliography of unclassified research reports in group psychology.* Washington, D.C.: Author, October, 1959. (ONR Rep. ACR-22)

2241) Department of the Navy, Office of Naval Research. *Naval research area: RR 006: psychological sciences.* Washington, D.C.: Author, 1961. (Annu. RDT & E Program Rep.)

2242) Department of the Navy, Office of Naval Research. *Naval research area: RR 006: psychological sciences.* Washington, D.C.: Author, 1962. (Annu. RDT & E Program Rep.)

2243) De Soto, C. B. Learning a social structure. *J. abnorm. soc. Psychol.,* 1960, *60,* 417–421.

2244) De Soto, C. B., et al. Social-perception and self-perception of high and low authoritarians. *J. soc. Psychol.,* 1960, *52,* 149–156.

2245) Deutsch, M. The pathetic fallacy: an observer error in social perception. *J. Pers.,* 1960, *28,* 317–332.

2246) Deutsch, M. Cooperation and trust: some theoretical notes. In M. R. Jones (Ed.), *Nebraska symposium on motivation.* Lincoln, Neb.: University of Nebraska Press, 1962.

2247) Deutsch, M., & Krauss, R. M. The effect of threat upon interpersonal bargaining. *J. abnorm. soc. Psychol.,* 1960, *61,* 181–189.

2248) Devlin, J. P., & Rooney, W. S. *Judgments of competence and friendliness in peer ratings of performance potential.* West Point, N.Y.: Military Academy, November, 1961. (Tech. Rep. No. 4)

2249) Di Vesta, F. J., & Cox, L. Some dispositional correlates of conformity behavior. *J. soc. Psychol.,* 1960, *52,* 259–268.

2250) Doby, J. T. Some effects of bias on learning. *J. soc. Psychol.,* 1960, *51,* 199–209

2251) Doll, R. E. *Peer ratings: a note on the unrated cases.* Pensacola, Fla.: Naval School of Aviation Medicine, October, 1961. (Spec. Rep. No. 61-11, ASTIA Document No. 269 490)

2252) Donahoe, J. W. The effect of variations in the form of feedback on the efficiency of problem solving. *J. exp. Psychol.,* 1960, *60,* 193–198.

2253) Donald, Marjorie N. Information exchange in large group functioning. *Amer. Psychologist*, 1960, *15*, 419. (Abstract)

2254) Dubno, P. Decision time characteristics of leaders and group problem-solving behavior. *Amer. Psychologist*, 1961, *16*, 396. (Abstract)

2255) Dunnette, M. D., et al. The effect of group participation on brainstorming effectiveness for two industrial samples. *Amer. Psychologist*, 1962, *17*, 381. (Abstract)

2256) Egerman, K., et al. *Decremental effects of reinforcement in teams with redundant members.* Pittsburgh, Pa.: American Institute for Research, September, 1961. (ASTIA Document No. 262 742)

2257) Egerman, K., et al. *Increasing team proficiency through training: III. Decremental effects of reinforcement in teams with redundant members.* Pittsburgh, Pa.: American Institute for Research, June, 1962. (Rep. No. AIR-B64-6/62-TR, Contract Nonr 255100)

2258) Eilbert, L. R. *A survey to determine indoctrination needs for personnel at isolated arctic sites.* Ladd Air Force Base, Alaska: Arctic Aeromedical Laboratory, January, 1959. (Tech. Note AAL-TN-59-2)

2259) Eilbert, L. R. *Indoctrination procedures for personnel assigned to arctic sites.* Pittsburgh, Pa.: American Institute for Research, January, 1960. [Contract No. AF 41(657)-241]

2260) Endler, N. S. Conformity analyzed and related to personality. *J. soc. Psychol.*, 1961, *53*, 271–284.

2261) Erbe, W. Gregariousness, group membership, and the flow of information. *Amer. J. Sociol.*, 1962, *67*, 502–516.

2262) Eskola, A. Social influence and power in two-person groups. In *Transactions of the Westermarck Society*, vol. VI. Munksgaard, Copenhagen, 1960.

2263) Evans, G. C. Validity of ascendance measurements in group interaction. *Psychol. Rep.*, 1960, *7*, 114.

2264) Ex, J. The nature of the relation between two persons and the degree of their influence on each other. *Acta psychol.* 1960, *17*, 39-54.

2265) Exline, R. V. Effects of sex, norms, and affiliation motivation upon accuracy of perception of interpersonal preferences. *J. Pers.*, 1960, *28*, 397–412.

2266) Exline, R. V. Interrelations among two dimensions of sociometric status, group congeniality and accuracy of social perception. *Sociometry*, 1960, *23*, 85–101.

2267) Exline, R. V. *Effects of N affiliation, sex, and the sight of others upon initial communications in problem-solving groups.* Newark, Del.: University of Delaware, 1961. [Tech. Rep. No. 4, Contract Nonr 2285(02)]

2268) Exline, R. V. *Explorations in the process of person perception: visual interaction in relation to competition, sex and N affiliation.* Newark, Del.: University of Delaware, May, 1962. [Tech. Rep. No. 8, Contract Nonr 2285(02)]

2269) Exline, R. V., & Ziller, R. C. *A longitudinal study of the assimilation of the new child in the group.* Newark, Del.: University of Delaware, August, 1961. (Tech. Rep. No. 3)

2270) Exline, R. V., & Ziller, R. C. *Need affiliation and initial communication behavior in task-oriented groups characterized by low interpersonal visibility.* Newark, Del.: University of Delaware, April, 1961. (Tech. Rep. No. 2)

2271) Farrell, F. M., et al. The effect of knowledge of partner's responses on subjects' performance in a vigilance task. *Amer. Psychologist*, 1961, *16*, 451. (Abstract)

2272) Farrell, F. M., et al. Group decision making under two types of executive structures. *Amer. Psychologist*, 1962, *17*, 396. (Abstract)

2273) Fiedler, F. E. *Interpersonal perception and psychological adjustment of group members.* Urbana, Ill.: University of Illinois, Group Effectiveness Research Laboratory, January, 1960. (Contract DA 49-007-md-2060)

2274) Fiedler, F. E. The leader's psychological distance and group effectiveness. In D. Cartwright and Z. Zander (Eds.), *Group dynamics: research and theory.* (2nd ed.) New York: Harper & Row, 1960. Pp. 586–606.

2275) Fiedler, F. E. *Leader attitudes, group climate, and group creativity.* Urbana, Ill.: University of Illinois, 1961. [Tech. Rep., Contract Nonr 1834(36)]

2276) Fiedler, F. E. Leadership and leadership effectiveness traits: a conceptualization of the leadership trait problem. In L. Petrullo and B. M. Bass (Eds.), *Leadership and interpersonal behavior.* New York: Holt, Rinehart and Winston, 1961. Pp. 179-186.

2277) Fiedler, F. E. Leader attitudes, group climate, and group creativity. *J. abnorm. soc. Psychol.*, 1962, *65*, 308–318

2278) Fiedler, F. E., & McGrath, J. E. *Interpersonal perception and the psychological adjustment of group members.* Urbana, Ill.: University of Illinois, December, 1961. (Annu. Rep., Contract DA 49-193-md-2060)

2279) Fiedler, F. E., & Meuwese, W. A. T. *The leader's contribution to performance in cohesive and uncohesive task groups.* Urbana, Ill.: University of Illinois, April, 1962. (Tech. Rep. No. 4, Contract Nonr 1834(36), NR 177-472)

2280) Fiedler, F. E., et al. *Group and organizational factors influencing creativity.* Urbana, Ill.: University of Illinois, November, 1960. [Annu. Rep., Contract Nonr 1834(36)]

2281) Fiedler, F. E., et al. *Performance on laboratory tasks requiring group creativity: an exploratory study.* Urbana, Ill.: University of Illinois, June, 1960. (Tech. Rep. No. 10)

2282) Fiedler, F. E., et al. An exploratory study of group creativity in laboratory tasks. *Acta psychol.*, 1961, *18*, 100–119.

2283) Fiedler, F. E., et al. *Hypnotically induced leader attitudes and group creativity.* Urbana, Ill.: University of Illinois, May, 1961. (Tech. Rep. No. 11, ASTIA Document No. 260 104)

2284) Fiedler, F. E., et al. *The leader's perception of co-workers, group climate, and group creativity.* Urbana, Ill.: University of Illinois, May, 1961. [Tech. Rep. No. 1, Contract Nonr 1834(36)]

2285) Fishbein, M., & Raven, B. H. *An operational distinction between belief and attitude.* Los Angeles, Calif.: University of California, December, 1959. [Tech. Rep. No. 2, Contract Nonr 233(54)(NR 171-350)]

2286) Fiske, D. W. Variability among peer ratings in different situations. *Educ. psychol. Measmt*, 1960, *20*, 283–292.

2287) Fiske, D. W., & Cox, J. A., Jr. The consistency of ratings by peers. *J. appl. Psychol.*, 1960, *44*, 11–17.

2288) Flanders, N. A., & Havumaki, S. Group compliance to dominative teacher influence. *Hum. Relat.*, 1960, *13*, 67–82.

2289) Fleishman, E. A., & Harris, E. F. Patterns of leadership behavior related to employee grievances and turnover. *Personnel Psychol.*, 1962, *15*, 43–56.

2290) Fleishman, E. A., & Peters, D. R. Interpersonal values, leadership attitudes, and managerial "success." *Personnel Psychol.*, 1962, *15*, 127–144.

2291) Foa, U. G. Higher components of dyadic relationships. In Matilda W. Riley et al. (Eds.), *Sociological studies in scale-analysis*. New Brunswick, N. J.: Rutgers University Press, 1954.

2292) Foa, U. G. Behavior, norms, and social rewards in a dyad. *Behav. Sci.*, 1958, *3*, 323–324.

2293) Foa, U. G. *Some developments of a study of industrial relations in Israel.* Jerusalem, Israel: Israel Institute of Applied Social Research, August, 1959. [Tech. Note No. 6, Contract AF 61(052)121]

2294) Foa, U. G. Some correlates of the empathy of the workers with the foreman. *J. appl. Psychol.*, 1960, *44*, 6–10.

2295) Foa, U. G. *The structure of the action: its relationship to interpersonal variables and culture.* Jerusalem, Israel: Israel Institute of Applied Social Research, February, 1960. [Contract No. AF 61(052)121]

2296) Foa, U. G. Convergences in the analysis of the structure of interpersonal behavior. *Psychol. Rev.*, 1961, *68*, 341–353.

2297) Foa, U. G. *Convergences in the analysis of the structure of interpersonal behavior.* Jerusalem, Israel: Israel Institute of Applied Social Research, undated. [Contract No. AF 61(052)121].

2298) Foa, U. G., & Guttman, L. *Facet design and analysis of data on personality and attitudes related to human organization.* Jerusalem, Israel: Israel Institute of Applied Social Research, June, 1958. [Tech. Summary Rep. No. 1, Contract AF 61(052)121]

2299) Fokkema, S. D., & Dirkzwager, A. A comparison of subjective and objective methods for observation of discussion-groups in personnel selection. *Acta psychol.* 1960, *17*, 56–79.

2300) Ford, J. D., Jr. Some factors affecting the behavior of emergent and designated leaders in small problem-solving groups. *Amer. Psychologist*, 1961, *16*, 389. (Abstract)

2301) Francesco, E. The general orientations profile (GOP). *Psychol. Rep.*, 1959, *5*, 561-569.

2302) Francesco, E. *The general orientations profile (GOP): validation study I.* New York: New York University, August, 1959. [AFOSR TN 59-809, Contract AF 49(638)-195]

2303) French, J. R. P., Jr., & Raven, B. H. The bases of social power. In D. Cartwright et al. (Eds.), *Studies in social power*. Ann Arbor, Mich.: Institute for Social Research, 1959. Pp. 150-167.

2304) Frye, R. L., & Stritch, T. M. *Effect of group size on public and private coalescence*. Baton Rouge, La.: Louisiana State University, 1960. (Tech. Rep., Contract N7 ONR-35609)

2305) Gage, N. L., & Chatterjee, B. B. The psychological meaning of acquiescence set: further evidence. *J. abnorm. soc. Psychol.*, 1960, *60*, 280–283.

2306) Gallo, P. S., & McClintock, C. G. Behavioral, attitudinal, and perceptual differences between leaders and non-leaders in situations of group support and non-support. *J. soc. Psychol.*, 1962, *56*, 121–133.

2307) Gamson, W. A. An experimental test of a theory of coalition formation. *Amer. sociol. Rev.*, 1961, *26*, 565–573.

2308) Gamson, W. A. A theory of coalition formation. *Amer. sociol. Rev.*, 1961, *26*, 373–382.

2309) Garai, J. E. Support of judgmental independence or conformity in situations of exposure to strong group pressure. *Amer. Psychologist*, 1960, *15*, 396. (Abstract)

2310) Garfein, D. Conformity behavior and the "authoritarian personality." *J. soc. Psychol.*, 1961, *53*, 121–126.

2311) George, C. E. *Some determinants of small group effectiveness*. Washington, D.C.: George Washington University, Human Resources Research Office, October, 1962.

2312) Gerard, H. B. Acts, attitudes, and conformity behavior. *Nat. Inst. soc. Behav. Sci. Sympos. Stud.*, 1960, *4*, 1–17.

2313) Giannitrapani, D. Determining factors of group structures: I. Inmates in a federal penitentiary. *Amer. Psychologist*, 1961, *16*, 346. (Abstract)

2314) Gibb, C. A. An interactional view of the emergence of leadership. *Aust. J. Psychol.*, 1958, *10* (1), 101–110.

2315) Gibb, J. R. *Defense level and influence potential in small groups*. Washington, D.C.: National Training Laboratories, March, 1960. [Tech. Rep. No. 6, Contract Nonr 3088(00)]

2316) Gibb, J. R. *The effects of group size and of threat reduction upon creativity*. Washington, D.C.: National Training Laboratories, undated. [Tech. Rep. No. 4, Contract Nonr 3088(00)]

2317) Glanzer, M. Toward the experimental study of team training and team functioning. In R. Glaser (Ed.), *Symposium on research in training*. Pittsburgh, Pa.: University of Pittsburgh Press, 1961.

2318) Glanzer, M., & Glaser, R. Techniques for the study of group structure and behavior: II. Empirical studies of the effects of structure in small groups. *Psychol. Bull.*, 1961, *58*, 1–27.

2319) Glaser, R., et al. *Increasing team proficiency through training: II. The acquisition and extinction of a team response*. Pittsburgh, Pa.: American Institute for Research, May, 1962. (Rep. No. AIR-B64-5/62-TR, Contract Nonr 255100)

2320) Goldman, M., & Hammond, L. K. Competition and non-competition and its relationship to individual and group productivity. *Sociometry*, 1961, *24*, 24–60.

2321) Goldman, M., et al. Some conditions under which groups operate and how this affects their performance. *J. soc. Psychol.*, 1961, *54*, 47–56.

2322) Golembiewski, R. T. *The small group*. Chicago: University of Chicago Press, 1962.

2323) Goodchilds, Jacqueline, et al. *Some effects on group problem solving of an enforced separation of problem-solving stages.* Washington, D.C.: National Training Laboratories, June, 1961. [Tech. Rep. No. 8, Contract Nonr 3088(00)]

2324) Goodman, B. D. *The psychological and social problems of man in space: a literature survey.* Santa Monica, Calif.: System Development Corporation, March, 1961. (SDC Field Note No. FN-5220, ASTIA Document No. 252 434)

2325) Gordon, L. V. Conformity among the non-conformists. *Psychol. Rep.*, 1961, *8*, 383.

2326) Gorfein, D. S., et al. Cognitive dissonance and yielding behavior. *J. Psychol.*, 1960, *50*, 205–208.

2327) Gruen, W. Some factors in the etiology of social interaction and group formation. *J. soc. Psychol.*, 1961, *54*, 57–73.

2328) Gruen, W., & Bierman, R. Determinants of verbal communication among strangers. *Psychol. Rep.*, 1960, *7*, 463–469.

2329) Gunderson, E. K., & Ballard, K. B. *Discriminant analysis of variables related to non-conformity in naval recruits.* San Diego, Calif.: Naval Retraining Command, August, 1959. (Tech. Rep. No. 11, Contract Nonr 153500)

2330) Gunderson, E. K., et al. *Changes in nonconformist attitudes induced by closed living groups.* San Francisco, Calif.: San Francisco Family Relations Center, July, 1959. (Contract Nonr 153500)

2331) Gurman, E. B., & Bass, B. M. *Objective compared with subjective measures of the same behavior in groups.* Baton Rouge, La.: Louisiana State University, 1960. (Tech. Rep. No. 23, Contract N7 ONR 35609)

2332) Guttman, L. A structural theory for intergroup beliefs and action. *Amer. sociol. Rev.*, 1959, *24*, 318–328.

2333) Hamblin, R. L. *On definitions as guides to measurement.* St. Louis, Mo.: Washington University, November, 1960. (Tech. Rep. No. 6, Contract Nonr 81611)

2334) Hamblin, R. L. *The elements of logic of general theory in social science.* St. Louis, Mo.: Washington University, September 1961. (Tech. Rep. No. 11, Contract Nonr 81611)

2335) Hamblin, R. L. *The frustration-aggression hypothesis: a linear, log, or power function.* St. Louis, Mo.: Washington University, October, 1961. (Tech. Rep. No. 13, Contract Nonr 81611)

2336) Hamblin, R. L., & Miller, K. *Variations in interaction profiles and group size.* St. Louis, Mo.: Washington University, May, 1960. (Tech. Rep. No. 3, Contract Nonr 81611)

2337) Hamblin, R. L., et al. *Morale and the competence of the leader in autocratic structures.* St. Louis, Mo.: Washington University, 1960. (Tech. Rep. No. 4, Contract Nonr 81611)

2338) Hamblin, R. L., et al. Group morale and competence of the leader. *Sociometry*, 1961, *24*, 295–311.

2339) Hammond, L. K., & Goldman, M. Competition and non-competition and its relationship to individual and group productivity. *Sociometry*, 1961, *24*, 46–60.

2340) Hare, A. P. The dimensions of social interaction. *Behav. Sci.*, 1960, *5*, 211–215.

2341) Hare, A. P. *Handbook of small group research.* New York: Free Press, 1962.

2342) Hartley, Ruth E. Norm compatibility, norm preference and the acceptance of new reference groups. *J. soc. Psychol.*, 1960, *52*, 87–95.

2343) Hartley, Ruth E. Personal needs and the acceptance of a new group as a reference group. *J. soc. Psychol.*, 1960, *51*, 349–358.

2344) Hartley, Ruth E. Relationships between perceived values and acceptance of a new reference group. *J. soc. Psychol.*, 1960, *51*, 181–190.

2345) Harvey, J., et al. Conformity of children's judgments induced by simulated group technique: age, sex, and other variables. *Amer. Psychologist*, 1961, *16*, 410. (Abstract)

2346) Harvey, O. J. Reciprocal influence of the group and three types of leaders in an unstructured situation. *Sociometry*, 1960, *23*, 57–68.

2347) Harvey, O. J. *Status in the informal group: influence and influencability at differing age levels.* Nashville, Tenn.: Vanderbilt University, 1960. (Contract Nonr 214902)

2348) Harvey, O. J. *Personality correlates of conceptual functioning and change across situations.* Boulder, Colo.: University of Colorado, undated. [Tech. Rep. No. 3, Contract Nonr 1148(07)]

2349) Harvey, O. J., & Consalvi, C. Status and conformity to pressures in informal groups. *J. abnorm. soc. Psychol.*, 1960, *60*, 182–187.

2350) Harvey, O. J., & Rutherford, Jeanne. Status in the informal group influence and influencability at differing age levels. *Child Develpm.*, 1960, *31*, 377–384.

2351) Harvey, O. J., et al. *Conceptual systems and personality organization.* New York: Wiley, 1961.

2352) Hemphill, J. K. *Intergroup communication under conditions of cooperation and competition.* Princeton, N.J.: Educational Testing Service, 1960. [Annu. tech. Rep., Contract Nonr 3054(00)]

2353) Hemphill, J. K. *Structure-in-interaction in the performance of group tasks.* Princeton, N.J.: Educational Testing Service, 1960. [Annu. tech. Rep., Contract Nonr 2959(00)]

2354) Hemphill, J. K. *The function of structure-in-interaction in mutual problem solving.* Princeton, N. J.: Educational Testing Service, 1961. [Tech. Rep., Contract Nonr 2959(00)]

2355) Hemphill, J. K., & McConville, Carolyn B. The effects of communication restraints upon mutual problem-solving behavior. *Amer. Psychologist*, 1962, *17*, 335. (Abstract)

2356) Herbert, Eleonore L. The use of group techniques in the training of teachers. *Hum. Relat.*, 1961, *14*, 251–264.

2357) Herner and Company. *Basic research resumés: a survey of basic research activities in the Air Research and Development Command.* Washington, D.C.: Author, December, 1959. [AFOSR TR 59-204, Contract AF 49(638)-652]

2358) Hilkevitch, Rhea R. Social interactional processes: a quantitative study. *Psychol. Rep.*, 1960, *7*, 195–201.

2359) Hoffman, L. R. A note on ratings versus choices as measures of group attraction. *Sociometry*, 1962, *25*, 313–320.

2360) Hoffman, L. R., & Smith, C. G. Some factors affecting the behaviors of members of problem-solving groups. *Sociometry*, 1960, *23*, 273–291.

2361) Hollander, E. P. *Some further findings on leadership, followership, and friendship.* Pittsburgh, Pa.: Carnegie Institute of Technology, November, 1958. (ONR tech. Rep.)

2362) Hollander, E. P. *Consideration of some variables relative to leadership.* Pittsburgh, Pa.: Carnegie Institute of Technology, March, 1959. (Contract Nonr 184900)

2363) Hollander, E. P. *Emergent leadership and social influence.* St. Louis, Mo.: Washington University, December, 1959. (Contract Nonr 81612)

2364) Hollander, E. P. *An experimental study of idiosyncratic behavior and status.* Pittsburgh, Pa.: Carnegie Institute of Technology, May, 1959. (ONR tech. Rep.)

2365) Hollander, E. P. *Group consensus and group attraction.* Pittsburgh, Pa.: Carnegie Institute of Technology, April, 1959. (Contract Nonr 184900)

2366) Hollander, E. P. *Variables underlying sociometric status.* Pittsburgh, Pa.: Carnegie Institute of Technology, June, 1959. (Final Rep., Contract Nonr 184900)

2367) Hollander, E. P. *Emergent leadership and social influence.* St. Louis, Mo.: Washington University, 1960. (Tech. Rep., Contract Nonr 81612)

2368) Hollander, E. P. *An experimental study of competence and time in group as determiners of status and group expectancies.* St. Louis, Mo.: Washington University, 1960. (Tech. Rep., Contract Nonr 81612)

2369) Hollander, E. P. Competence and conformity in the acceptance of influence. *J. abnorm. soc. Psychol.*, 1961, *61*, 365–369.

2370) Homans, G. C. *Social behavior: its elementary forms.* New York: Harcourt, 1961.

2371) Horwitz, M. *Group effects on tension patterns and motivation.* New York: New York University, Research Center for Human Relations, 1960. [Tech. Rep., Contract Nonr 285(28)]

2372) Horwitz, M. *Group effects on tension patterns and motivation.* New York: New York University, Research Center for Human Relations, 1961. [Tech. Rep., Contract Nonr 285(28)]

2373) Hudgins, B. B. Effects of group experience on individual problem solving. *J. educ. Psychol.*, 1960, *51*, 37–42.

2374) Hunt, E. B., & Rowe, R. R. Group and individual economic decision making in risk conditions. In D. W. Taylor (Ed.), *Experiments on decision making and other studies.* Arlington, Va.: Armed Services Technical Information Agency, 1960. Pp. 21–25. (Tech. Rep. No. 6, ASTIA Document No. 253 952)

2375) Hutchins, E. B., & Fiedler, F. E. Task-oriented and quasi-therapeutic role functions of the leader in small military groups. *Sociometry*, 1960, *23*, 393–406.

2376) Indik, B. P. *A technique for the longitudinal study of group stability and its application to group homeostasis.* New Brunswick, N.J.: Rutgers University, December, 1961. (Tech. Rep. No. 9, Contract Nonr 40410)

2377) Indik, B. P. Some empirical tests of a homeostasis theory of small groups. *Proc. N. Y. Acad. Sci.*, March, 1962.

2378) Indik, B. P., & Tyler, J. *Homeostasis theory of small groups: VII. Longitudinal studies.* New Brunswick, N.J.: Rutgers University, 1962. (Tech. Rep. No. 10, Contract Nonr 40410)

2379) Iscoe, I., & Hodgden, Laurel. Use of the simulated group technique with children. *Psychol. Rep.*, 1960, *6*, 175–178.

2380) Izard, C. E. Personality similarity and friendship. *J. abnorm. soc. Psychol.*, 1960, *61*, 47–51.

2381) Izard, C. E. Personality similarity, positive affect, and interpersonal attraction. *J. abnorm. soc. Psychol.*, 1960, *61*, 484–485.

2382) Izard, C. E. *Role of positive affect in individual and interpersonal effectiveness.* Nashville, Tenn.: Vanderbilt University, 1960. [Annu. tech. Rep., Contract Nonr 2149(03)]

2383) Izard, C. E. *Personality characteristics associated with resistance to change.* Boulder, Colo.: University of Colorado, undated. [Tech. Rep. No. 2, Contract Nonr 1147(07)]

2384) Jackson, D. N. Assessing conformity with desirability judgments. *Amer. Psychologist*, 1961, *16*, 446. (Abstract)

2385) Jackson, J. M. *Some notes on Kelley and Shapiro's "Conformity to group norms where conformity is detrimental to group achievement."* Ann Arbor, Mich.: University of Michigan, Research Center for Group Dynamics, 1958. [Tech. Rep., Contract Nonr 1224(11)]

2386) Janda, K. F. Towards the explication of the concept of leadership in terms of the concept of power. *Hum. Relat.*, 1960, *13*, 345–363

2387) Jennings, E. E. *An anatomy of leadership: princes, heroes, and supermen.* New York: Harper & Row, 1960.

2388) Jones, R. L. Interaction and applicational transfer following small group discussion-decision. *Amer. Psychologist*, 1961, *16*, 375. (Abstract)

2389) Kaess, W. A., et al. Reliability, sex differences, and validity in the leaderless group discussion technique. *J. appl. Psychol.*, 1961, *45*, 345–350.

2390) Kanareff, Vera T., & Lanzetta, J. T. Effects of task definition and probability of reinforcement upon the acquisition and extinction of imitative responses. *J. exp. Psychol.*, 1960, *60*, 340–348.

2391) Kanareff, Vera T., & Lanzetta, J. T. Effects of congruent social and task reinforcement upon acquisition of imitative responses. *Psychol. Rep.*, 1961, *8*, 47–57.

2392) Kaplan, H., & De Jung, J. E. Some differential effects of race of rater and ratee on early peer ratings of combat aptitude. *Amer. Psychologist*, 1960, *15*, 417. (Abstract)

2393) Kassarjian, W. M., & Kassarjian, H. H. A group approach to the study of independence and conformity. *Amer. Psychologist*, 1961, *16*, 410. (Abstract)

2394) Kassarjian, W. M., & Kassarjian, H. H. Conformity of judgment in a group situation. *Psychol. Rep.*, 1962, *10*, 491–499.

2395) Kates, S. L. First impression formation and authoritarianism. *Hum. Relat.*, 1959, *12*, 277–286.

2396) Katz, I. *Conditions affecting productivity and cohesiveness in culturally mixed groups.* New York: New York University, 1959. [Annu. tech. Rep., Contract Nonr 285(24)]

2397) Katz, I., & Cohen, M. *Effects of variations in assertiveness of Negroes on interaction with whites.* New York: New York University, 1960. [Tech. Rep. No. 3, Contract Nonr 285(24)]

2398) Katz, L., & Powell, J. H. *Probability distributions of random variables associated with a structure of the sample space of sociometric investigations.* East Lansing, Mich.: Michigan State University, May 1956. (Rep. No. RM-20, ASTIA Document No. 100 475)

2399) Katz, L., & Proctor, C. H. The concept of configuration of interpersonal relations in a group as a time-dependent stochastic process. *Psychometrika,* 1959, *24,* 317–328.

2400) Katz, L., & Wilson, T. R. The variance of the number of mutual choices in sociometry. *Psychometrika,* 1956, *21.*

2401) Kelley, H. H., & Arrowood, A. J. Coalitions in the triad: critique and experiment. *Sociometry,* 1960, *23,* 231–244.

2402) Keltner, J. W. Communication in discussion and group processes: some research trends of the decade 1950–1959. Part I. *J. Communication,* 1960, *10,* 195–204.

2403) Kenkel, W. F. Dominance, persistence, self-confidence, and spousal roles in decision making. *J. soc. Psychol.,* 1961, *54,* 349–358.

2404) Kidd, J. S. *A comparison of one-, two-, and three-man control units under various conditions of traffic input rate.* Columbus, Ohio: Ohio State University Research Foundation, June, 1959. [WADC tech. Rep. No. 59-104, Contract AF 33(616)3612]

2405) Kidd, J. S., & Boyes, F. Input distortion and observer overlap in decision making. *Mgmt Sci.,* 1959, *6,* 123–131.

2406) Kidd, J. S., & Christy, R. T. Supervisory procedures and work-team productivity. *J. appl. Psychol.,* 1961, *45,* 388–392.

2407) Kiessling, R. J., & Kalish, R. A. Correlates of success in leaderless group discussion. *J. soc. Psychol.,* 1961, *54,* 359–366.

2408) Kinkade, R. G., & Kidd, J. S. *The effect of team size and intermember communication on decision-making performance.* Columbus, Ohio: Ohio State University Research Foundation, Aviation Psychology Laboratory, April, 1959. [WADC tech. Rep. No. 58-474, Contract AF 33(616)3612 and AF 33(616)43]

2409) Kipnis, Dorothy M. *Changes in self concepts in relation to perception of others.* Urbana, Ill.: University of Illinois, Group Effectiveness Research Laboratory, April, 1961. (Tech. Rep. No. 11, Contracts DA 49-007-md-569 and DA 49-007-md-2060)

2410) Klaf, F. S. The power of the group leader: a contribution to the understanding of group psychology. *Psychoanal. Rev.,* 1961, *48* (2), 41–51.

2411) Klaus, D. J., & Glaser, R. *Studies of Navy Guided Missile Teams.* Pittsburgh, Pa.: University of Pittsburgh and American Institute for Research, December, 1958. (Final Rep., Contract N7 ONR 37008)

2412) Klaus, D. J., & Glaser, R. *Increasing team proficiency through training.* Pittsburgh, Pa.: American Institute for Research, December, 1960. (Rep. No. AIR-264-60-TR-137, Contract Nonr 255100)

2413) Kleiner, R. J. The effects of threat reduction upon interpersonal attractiveness. *J. Pers.*, 1960, *28*, 145–155.

2414) Knutson, A. L. Quiet and vocal groups. *Sociometry*, 1960, *23*, 36–49.

2415) Lambert, W. E., et al. The effect of increased salience of a membership group on pain tolerance. *J. Pers.*, 1960, *28*, 350–356.

2416) Lana, R. E., et al. Leadership and friendship status as factors in discussion group interaction. *J. soc. Psychol.*, 1960, *52*, 127–134.

2417) Lange, C. J., & Jacobs, T. O. *Leadership in Army infantry platoons: Study II.* Washington, D.C.: Human Resources Research Office, July, 1960. (Res. Rep. No. 5, Contract DA 49-106-qm-1)

2418) Lanzetta, J. T. *Perception variables and communication efficiency.* Newark, Del.: University of Delaware, 1960. [Annu. tech. Rep., Contract Nonr 2285(02)]

2419) Lanzetta, J. T. *Experimental studies of social interaction.* Newark, Del.: University of Delaware, November, 1961. [Annu. Progress Rep. No. 4, Contract Nonr 2285(002)]

2420) Lanzetta, J. T., & Kanareff, Vera T. *Some social factors affecting the choice of an "imitative" response in a probability learning situation.* Newark, Del.: University of Delaware, 1960. (USAF WADD tech. Rep., No. 60-196)

2421) Lanzetta, J. T., & Roby, T. B. The relationship between certain group process variables and group problem-solving efficiency. *J. soc. Psychol.*, 1960, *52*, 135–148.

2422) Leavitt, H. J. Task ordering and organizational development in the common target game. *Behav. Sci.*, 1960, *5*, 233–239.

2423) Levin, G., & Shapiro, D. *The operant conditioning of conversation.* Cambridge, Mass.: Harvard University, 1961. [Tech. Rep., Contract Nonr 1866(43)]

2424) Levy, L. Studies in conformity behavior: a methodological note. *J. Psychol.*, 1960, *50*, 39–41.

2425) Lewis, M. N., & Spilka, B. Sociometric choice status, empathy, assimilative and disowning projection. *Psychol. Rec.*, 1960, *10*, 95–100.

2426) Lifton, W. M. *Working with groups: group process and individual growth.* New York: Wiley, 1961.

2427) Littunen, Y., & Gaier, E. L. Occupational values and modes of conformity. *J. soc. Psychol.*, 1960, *51*, 123–133.

2428) Litwak, E. Reference group theory, bureaucratic career, and neighborhood primary group cohesion. *Sociometry*, 1960, *23*, 72–84.

2429) Liverant, S., & Scodel, A. *Internal and external control as determinates of decision-making under conditions of risk.* Columbus, Ohio: Ohio State University Research Foundation, 1960. [Contract AF 49(638)-317]

2430) Lodahl, T. M., & Porter, L. W. Psychometric score patterns, social characteristics, and productivity of small industrial work groups. *J. appl. Psychol.*, 1961, *45*, 73–79.

2431) Lonergan, B. G. *The effects of group membership upon risk taking.* Santa Barbara, Calif.: California University, December, 1960. [Tech. Note No. 1, Contract AF 49(638)-794]

2432) Lonergan, B. G., & McClintock, C. G. Effects of group membership on risk-taking behavior. *Psychol. Rep.*, 1961, *8*, 447–455.

2433) Long, Barbara H. *The reliability of coding.* Newark, Del.: University of Delaware, Center for Research on Social Behavior, May, 1962. [Tech. Rep. No. 7, Contract Nonr 2285(02)]

2434) Loree, M. R., & Koch, Margaret B. Use of verbal reinforcement in developing group discussion skills. *J. educ. Psychol.*, 1960, *51*, 164–168.

2435) Lorge, I. *Group efficiency and group process in problem solving.* New York: Columbia University, Teachers College, 1959. [Annu. tech. Rep., Contract Nonr 266(43)]

2436) Lorge, I., & Solomon, H. Group and individual performance in problem solving related to previous exposure to problem, level of aspiration, and group size. *Behav. Sci.*, 1960, *5*, 28–38.

2437) Lott, A. J., & Lott, Bernice E. Group cohesiveness, communication level, and conformity. *Amer. Psychologist*, 1960, *15*, 396. (Abstract)

2438) Lott, Bernice E., & Lott, A. J. The formation of positive attitudes toward group members. *J. abnorm. soc. Psychol.*, 1960, *61*, 297–300.

2439) Luchins, A. S., & Luchins, Edith H. On conformity with judgments of a majority or an authority. *J. soc. Psychol.*, 1961, *53*, 303–316.

2440) Luchins, A. S., & Luchins, Edith H. Social influences on impressions of personality. *J. soc. Psychol.*, 1961, *54*, 111–125.

2441) Luchins, A. S., & Luchins, Edith H. Social influences on judgment of changing evidence. *J. soc. Psychol.*, 1961, *54*, 13–36.

2442) Lyle, J. Communication, group, atmosphere, productivity, and morale in small task groups. *Hum. Relat.*, 1961, *14*, 369–380.

2443) McBrearty, J. F., et al. Conditioning a verbal operant in a group setting: direct vs. vicarious reinforcement. *Amer. Psychologist*, 1961, *16*, 425. (Abstract)

2444) McClintock, C. G., & Gallo, P. S. Behavioral, attitudinal, and perceptual differences between leaders and nonleaders in situations of group support and nonsupport. *Amer. Psychologist*, 1960, *15*, 419. (Abstract)

2445) McGrath, J. E. *Systems of information in small group research studies.* Arlington, Va.: Human Sciences Research, Inc., April, 1960. [HSR-TN-62/2-Gn, Contract AF 49(638)-256]

2446) McGrath, J. E. *A summary of small group research studies.* Arlington, Va.: Human Sciences Research, Inc., June, 1962. [HSR-TN-62/3-Gn, Contract AF 49(638)-256]

2447) McKay, J. B., et al. *Some factors which have contributed to both successful and unsuccessful American infantry small-unit actions.* Fort Benning, Ga.: Army Infantry Human Research Unit, April, 1959. (HumRRO Res. Memorandum No. 13, ASTIA Document No. 260 994)

2448) MacKinnon, W. J. Behavioral research and intergroup communication. *J. Psychol.*, 1960, *49*, 339–348.

2449) McNulty, J. A., & Walters, R. H. Emotional arousal, conflict, and susceptibility to social influence. *Canad. J. Psychol.*, 1962, *16*, 211–220.

2450) McRae, D., Jr. Direct factor analysis of sociometric data. *Sociometry*, 1960, *23*, 360–371.

2451) Madden, J. M. Personal preferences and conformity. *J. soc. Psychol.*, 1960, *52*, 269–277.

2452) Maier, N. R. F., & Hoffman, L. R. Quality of first and second solutions in group problem solving. *J. appl. Psychol.*, 1960, *44*, 278–283.

2453) Maier, N. R. F., & Hoffman, L. R. Using trained "developmental" discussion leaders to improve further the quality of group decisions. *J. appl. Psychol.*, 1960, *44*, 247–251.

2454) Maier, N. R. F., & Hoffman, L. R. Group decision in England and the United States. *Personnel Psychol.*, 1962, *15*, 75–88.

2455) Mangan, G. L., et al. Taylor MAS and group conformity pressure. *J. abnorm. soc. Psychol.*, 1960, *61*, 146–147.

2456) Manheim, H. L. Intergroup interaction as related to status and leadership differences between groups. *Sociometry*, 1960, *23*, 415–427.

2457) Mann, J. H. Studies of role performance. New York: New York University, December, 1959. [AFOSR TN 59-1296, Contract AF 49(638)-195]

2458) Mann, J. H. The relation between role-playing ability and interpersonal adjustment. *J. abnorm. soc. Psychol.*, 1960, *62*, 177–183.

2459) Mann, J. H., & Mann, Carola H. The relative effectiveness of role playing and task-oriented group experience in producing personality and behavior change. *J. soc. Psychol.*, 1960, *51*, 313–317.

2460) Mann, J. W. Group relations in hierarchies. *J. soc. Psychol.*, 1961, *54*, 283–314.

2461) Manning, W. H., & Wicker, F. W. *Approaches to the analysis of sociometric data. A survey of the literature.* Fort Wainwright, Alaska: Alaskan Air Command, Arctic Aeromedical Laboratory, August, 1961. (Tech. Rep. 61-18, ASTIA Document No. 276 827)

2462) March, J. G., & Feigenbaum, E. A. Latent motives, group discussion, and the "quality" of group decisions in a non-objective decision problem. *Sociometry*, 1960, *23*, 50–56.

2463) Marcus, P. M. Expressive and instrumental groups. Toward a theory of group structure. *Amer. J. Sociol.*, 1961, *66*, 54–59.

2464) Marlowe, D. *Personality determinants of conformity in a simulated group situation.* Columbus, Ohio: Ohio State University, June, 1959. [AFOSR TN 59-612, Contract AF 49(638)-317]

2465) Mattsson, P. O. Communicated anxiety in a two-person situation. *J. consult. Psychol.*, 1960, *24*, 488–495.

2466) Miller, L. K., & Hamblin, R. L. *An evaluation of some assumptions of the Davis-Moore theory of stratification.* St. Louis, Mo.: Washington University, September, 1961. (Tech. Rep. No. 10, Contract Nonr 81611)

2467) Milton, Helen S., & Green, Henrietta, H. *The group vs. the individual in research.* Bethesda, Md.: Johns Hopkins University, Operations Research Office, July, 1960. (Spec. Stud. T1, Tech. Paper ORO-TP-4, ASTIA Document No. 241 351L)

2468) Minas, J. S., et al. Some descriptive aspects of two-person non-zero-sum games: II. *J. Confl. Resol.*, 1960, *4*, 193–197.

2469) Mohanna, A. I., & Argyle, M. A cross-cultural study of structured groups with unpopular central members. *J. abnorm. soc. Psychol.*, 1960, *60*, 139–140.

2470) Moore, H. G. *The effects of load and accessibility of information upon performance of small teams.* Ann Arbor, Mich.: University of Michigan, October, 1961. [Rep. No. O28p4-8-T, Contract AF 49(638)-449]

2471) Moore, O. K., & Anderson, A. R. *Some puzzling aspects of social interaction.* New Haven, Conn.: Yale University, 1961. [Tech. Rep., Contract Nonr 509(16)]

2472) Moore, O. K., & Berkowitz, M. I. *Problem solving and social interaction.* New Haven, Conn.: Yale University, November, 1956. [Tech. Rep. No. 1, Contract SAR/Nonr 609(16)]

2473) Morton, R. B. Variables influencing decision making in groups. *Amer. Psychologist*, 1961, *16*, 439. (Abstract)

2474) Mulder, M. Communication structure, decision structure, and group performance. *Sociometry*, 1960, *23*, 1–14.

2475) Mulder, M. The power variable in communication experiments. *Hum. Relat.*, 1960, *13*, 241–257.

2476) Myers, A. Team competition, success, and the adjustment of group members. *J. abnorm. soc. Psychol.*, 1962, *65*, 325–332.

2477) Nelson, P. D., & Gunderson, E. K. E. Attitude changes in small groups under prolonged isolation. *Amer. Psychologist*, 1961, *16*, 451. (Abstract)

2478) Newcomb, T. M. *The acquaintance process.* New York: Holt, Rinehart and Winston, 1961.

2479) Nicol, Elizabeth H., et al. Variables influencing information exchange within groups. *Amer. Psychologist*, 1962, *17*, 397. (Abstract)

2480) Nowlis, V. *Methods for the objective study of drug effects on group functioning.* Rochester, N.Y.: University of Rochester, September, 1959. (Tech. Rep. No. 6, Contract Nonr 66812)

2481) Oakes, W. F., et al. Reinforcement effects on participation in group discussion. *Psychol. Rep.*, 1960, *7*, 503–514.

2482) O'Connor, W. F. *The interrelationships of social perception, sociometric status, personality, and the ability to judge personality traits.* Pensacola, Fla.: Naval School of Aviation Medicine, November, 1960. (Rep. No. 9, ASTIA Document No. 253 061)

2483) Olmsted, M. S. *The small group.* New York: Random House, 1959.

2484) Palmer, G. J., Jr. *A method for objective measurement of interpersonal relations and group behavior.* New Orleans, La.: Tulane University, 1960. [Tech. Rep., Contract Nonr 475(08)]

2485) Palmer, G. J., Jr. *Test of a theory of leadership and organizational behavior with management gaming.* New Orleans, La.: Tulane University, 1960. (Annu. tech. Rep., Contract Nonr 475(08))

2486) Palmer, G. J., Jr. *Tests of interpersonal knowledge. Some development considerations and specifications for a universe of items.* New Orleans, La.: Tulane University, November, 1960. [Contract Nonr 475(08)]

2487) Palmer, G. J., Jr. Task ability and effective leadership. *Psychol. Rep.*, 1962, *10*, 863–866.

2488) Palmer, G. J., Jr., & Schroeder, R. H. *Incentive conditions and behavior in 188 industrial manufacturing organizations.* New Orleans, La.: Tulane University, 1961. [Tech. Rep., Contract Nonr 1575(05)]

2489) Parloff, M. B., & Handlon, J. H. Influence of criticalness on creative problem solving in dyads. *Amer. Psychologist,* 1961, *16,* 374. (Abstract)

2490) Parnes, S. J., & Meadow, A. Evaluation of persistence of effects produced by a creative problem-solving course. *Psychol. Rep.,* 1960, *7,* 357–361.

2491) Patel, A. S., & Gordon, J. E. Some personal and situational determinants of yielding to influence. *J. abnorm. soc. Psychol.,* 1960, *61,* 411–418.

2492) Pellegrin, R. J., & Bates, F. L. Congruity and incongruity of status attributes within occupations and work positions. *Soc. Forces,* 1959, *38,* 23–28.

2493) Pelz, D. C., & Andrews, F. M. *Organizational atmosphere as related to types of motives and levels of output.* Ann Arbor, Mich.: University of Michigan, Institute for Social Research, April, 1961. (Interim tech. Rep., ASTIA Document No. 255 903)

2494) Pelz, D. C., & Andrews, F. M. *Stimulating and inhibiting factors in scientific performance: partial support.* Ann Arbor, Mich.: University of Michigan, Institute for Social Research, April, 1961. (Final Rep. ASTIA Document No. 256 037)

2495) Pepinsky, H. B., & Pepinsky, Pauline N. *Organization, management strategy, and team productivity.* Columbus, Ohio: Ohio State University, January, 1960. [AFOSR TN 60-38, Contract AF 49(638)-373]

2496) Pepinsky, Pauline N. *Originality in group productivity: I. Productive independence in three natural situations.* Columbus, Ohio: Ohio State University Research Foundation, 1959. [Contract Nonr 495(15) (NR 170-396)]

2497) Pepinsky, Pauline N. *Productive independence in three natural situations.* Columbus, Ohio: Ohio State University, 1959. [Tech. Rep., Contract Nonr 495(15)]

2498) Pepinsky, Pauline N. *Originality in group productivity: I. Productive independence in three natural situations.* Columbus, Ohio: Ohio State University, January, 1960. [Contract Nonr 495(15)]

2499) Pepinsky, Pauline N. *The social dialectic of productive nonconformity.* Columbus, Ohio: Ohio State University, 1960. [Tech. Rep., Contract Nonr 495(15)]

2500) Pepinsky, Pauline N. A study of productive nonconformity. *Gifted Child Quart.,* 1960, Winter, 81–86.

2501) Pepinsky, Pauline N., & Pepinsky, H. B. *Originality in group productivity.* Columbus, Ohio: Ohio State University, December, 1959. [Annu. Summary Rep., Contract Nonr 495(15)]

2502) Pepinsky, Pauline N., & Pepinsky, H. B. *Originality in group productivity.* Columbus, Ohio: Ohio State University, November, 1960. [Tech. Rep. No. 12, Contract Nonr 495(15)]

2503) Pepinsky, Pauline N., & Pepinsky, H. B. *Originality in group productivity.* Columbus, Ohio: Ohio State University, November, 1961. [Tech. Rep. No. 16, Contract Nonr 495(15)]

2504) Pepinsky, Pauline N., et al. The effects of task complexity and time pressure upon team productivity. *J. appl. Psychol.,* 1960, *44,* 34–38.

2505) Pepinsky, Pauline N., et al. *The effects of varied executive sanctions upon productive independence in subordinate teams.* Columbus, Ohio: Ohio State University, 1960. [Tech. Rep., Contract Nonr 495(15)]

2506) Pepinsky, Pauline N., et al. *Originality in group productivity: II. The effects of varied executive sanctions upon productive independence in subordinate teams.* Columbus, Ohio: Ohio State University, 1960. [Contract Nonr 495(15)]

2507) Pepitone, A. *Interpersonal attraction and hostility.* Philadelphia: University of Pennsylvania, 1960. [Annu. tech. Rep., Contract Nonr 551(27)]

2508) Petrullo, L. Small group research. In A. J. Bachrach (Ed.), *Experimental foundations of clinical psychology.* New York: Basic Books, 1962. Pp. 211–253.

2509) Polansky, N. A. Small group theory: implications for casework research. In L. S. Kogan (Ed.), *Social science theory and social work research.* New York: National Association of Social Workers, 1960.

2510) Psathas, G. Phase movement and equilibrium tendencies in interaction process in psychotherapy groups. *Sociometry*, 1960, *23*, 177–194.

2511) Ramuz-Nienhuis, Wilhelmina, & van Bergen, Annie. Relations between some components of attraction-to-group: a replication. *Hum. Relat.*, 1960, *13*, 271–277.

2512) Rapoport, A., et al. Three-person non-zero-sum non-negotiable games. *Behav. Sci.*, 1962, *7*, 38–58.

2513) Rausch, H. L., et al. Person, setting, and change in social interaction: II. A normal control study. *Hum. Relat.*, 1960, *13*, 305–332.

2514) Raven, B. H. *Additions to bibliography of publications relating to the small group.* Los Angeles: University of California, November, 1959. [Tech. Rep. No. 1, Suppl. No. 2, Contract Nonr 253(54) (NR 171-350)]

2515) Raven, B. H. *A bibliography of publications relating to the small group.* Los Angeles: University of California, November, 1959. [Tech. Rep. No. 1, Contract Nonr 253(54)(NR 171-350)]

2516) Raven, B. H. The dynamics of groups. *Rev. educ. Res.*, 1959, *29*, 332–343.

2517) Raven, B. H. *Dynamics of social influence.* Los Angeles. University of California, December, 1959. [Annu. Tech. Rep. No. 1, Contract Nonr 233(54) (NR 171-350)]

2518) Raven, B. H. *An index and punch card system for coding publications relating to the small group.* Los Angeles: University of California, November, 1959. [Tech. Rep. No. 1, Suppl. No. 1, Contract Nonr 253(54) (NR 171-350)]

2519) Raven, B. H. *Index to bibliography of publications relating to the small group.* Los Angeles: University of California, November, 1959. [Tech. Rep. No. 1, Suppl. No. 3, Contract Nonr 253(54) (NR 171-350)]

2520) Raven, B. H. Leadership and social influence. *Adult Leadership*, 1959, *7*, 250–253.

2521) Raven, B. H. Social influence on opinion and the communication of related content. *J. abnorm. soc. Psychol.*, 1959, *58*, 119–128.

2522) Raven, B. H. *Bases of social influence in the small group.* Los Angeles: University of California, 1960. [Tech. Rep. Contract Nonr 233(54)]

2523) Raven, B. H. *Dynamics of social influence.* Los Angeles: University of California, 1960. [Tech. Rep., Contract Nonr 233(54)]

2524) Raven, B. H. *A bibliography of publications relating to the small group.* (2nd ed.) Los Angeles: University of California, 1961. [Tech. Rep., Contract Nonr 233(54)]

2525) Raven, B. H., & Eachus, H. T. *Cooperation and competition in means-interdependent triads.* Los Angeles: University of California, June, 1962. [Tech. Rep. No. 8, Contract Nonr 233(54)]

2526) Raven, B. H., & Fishbein, M. *Acceptance of punishment and change in belief.* Los Angeles: University of California, 1960. [Tech. Rep., Contract Nonr 233(54)]

2527) Raven, B. H., & Fishbein, M. *The effects of punishment of behavior upon change in belief.* Los Angeles: University of California, 1960. [Tech. Rep., Contract Nonr 233(54)]

2528) Raven, B. H., et al. *Group norms and dissonance reduction in belief, behavior and judgment.* Los Angeles: University of California, 1960. [Tech. Rep., Contract Nonr 233(54)]

2529) Raven, B. H., et al. *The effects of attributed ability upon expert and referent influence.* Los Angeles: University of California, 1962. [Tech. Rep. No. 10, Contract Nonr 233(54) (NR 171-350)]

2530) Reilly, M. St. A., et al. The complementarity of personality needs in friendship choice. *J. abnorm. soc. Psychol.,* 1960, *61,* 292–294.

2531) Rettig, S., et al. Attitude toward status and its effect upon status judgments. *J. soc. Psychol.,* 1960, *51,* 331–341.

2532) Rhine, R. J. The effect of peer group influence upon concept-attitude development and change. *J. soc. Psychol.,* 1960, *51,* 173–179.

2533) Richards, J. M., Jr. The cue additivity principle in a restricted social interaction situation. *J. exp. Psychol.,* 1962, *63,* 452–457.

2534) Rigby, Marilyn K., & Ossorio, Elizabeth D. *Sociometric status and attitude characteristics of successful and unsuccessful WAVE recruits.* St. Louis, Mo.: St. Louis University, September, 1959. (Tech. Rep. No. 11, Contract N7 ONR 40802)

2535) Rinn, J. L. Q methodology: an application to group phenomena. *Educ. psychol. Measmt,* 1961, *21,* 315–329.

2536) Roby, T. B. *Research involving communication processes in task-oriented groups.* Medford, Mass.: Tufts University, Institute for Applied Experimental Psychology, 1959. [Annu. tech. Rep., Contract Nonr 494(15)]

2537) Roby, T. B. *Contributions to a theory of group performance.* Medford, Mass.: Tufts University, Institute for Psychological Research, 1960. [Tech. Rep., Contract Nonr 494(15)]

2538) Roby, T. B. *Research involving communication processes in task-oriented groups.* Medford, Mass.: Tufts University, Institute for Psychological Research, 1960. [Annu. tech. Rep., Contract Nonr 494(15)]

2539) Roby, T. B. *Subtask phasing in small groups.* Medford, Mass.: Tufts University, Institute for Psychological Research, 1961. [Tech. Rep., Contract Nonr 494(15)]

2540) Roby, T. B., & Lanzetta, J. T. A study of an assembly effect in small group task performance. *J. soc. Psychol.,* 1961, *53,* 53–68.

2541) Roby, T. B., et al. *Research involving communication processes in task-oriented groups.* Medford, Mass.: Tufts University, Institute for Applied Experimental Psychology, November, 1959. [Tech. Rep. No. 2, Contract Nonr 494(15)]

2542) Roby, T. B., et al. Exploratory studies on group sub-function performance. Medford, Mass.: Tufts University, Institute for Psychological Research, 1961. [Tech. Rep., Contract Nonr 494(15)]

2543) Rogers, M. S., et al. The effects of personnel replacement on an information-processing crew. *J. appl. Psychol.*, 1961, *45*, 91–96.

2544) Ronning, R. R., & Horrocks, J. E. A method for estimating effectiveness of groups in a "group" teaching situation. *Educ. psychol. Measmt*, 1961, *21*, 331–347.

2545) Rosen, S., et al. Desired change in self and others as a function of resource ownership. *Hum. Relat.*, 1960, *13*, 187–194.

2546) Rosenbaum, M. E., & deCharms, R. Direct and vicarious reduction of hostility. *J. abnorm. soc. Psychol.*, 1960, *60*, 105–111.

2547) Rosenbaum, M. E., & Franc, D. C. Opinion change as a function of external commitment and amount of discrepancy from the opinion of another. *J. abnorm. soc. Psychol.*, 1960, *61*, 15–20.

2548) Rosenbaum, M. E., et al. Level of self-esteem and the learning of imitation and nomination. *J. Pers.*, 1962, *30*, 147–156.

2549) Rosenberg, L. A. Group size, prior experience, and conformity. *J. abnorm. soc. Psychol.*, 1961, *63*, 436–437.

2550) Rosenberg, S. Cooperative behavior in dyads as a function of reinforcement parameters. *J. abnorm. soc. Psychol.*, 1960, *60*, 318–333.

2551) Rulon, P. J., & Brooks, W. D. *On statistical tests of group differences.* Port Washington, N.Y.: U.S. Naval Training Device Center, April, 1961. (Tech. Rep., Navtradevcen 294-3)

2552) Rychlak, J. F. A socio-psychological theory of performance in competitive situations. *Hum. Relat.*, 1960, *13*, 157–166.

2553) Sampson, E. E., & French, J. R. P., Jr. An experiment on active and passive resistance to social power. *Amer. Psychologist*, 1960, *15*, 396. (Abstract)

2554) Schachter, S., et al. Emotional disruption and industrial productivity. *J. appl. Psychol.*, 1961, *45*, 201–213.

2555) Schaffner, B. (Ed.) *Group processes.* New York: Josiah Macy, Jr. Foundation, 1960.

2556) Schein, E. H. Interpersonal communication, group solidarity, and social influence. *Sociometry*, 1960, *23*, 148–161.

2557) Schlesinger, L., et al. Leader-member interaction in management committees. *J. abnorm. soc. Psychol.*, 1960, *61*, 360–364.

2558) Schonfield, J. *Selection of feed-back information as a function of situational stress, need for achievement, and interpersonal awareness: factors determining defensive behavior within groups.* Washington, D.C.: National Training Laboratories, 1961. [Tech. Rep. No. 14, Contract Nonr 1147(03)]

2559) Schroder, H. M. *Group development and functioning.* Princeton, N.J.: Princeton University, July, 1960. [Tech. Rep. No. 7. Contract Nonr 1858(12)]

2560) Schutz, W. C. *FIRO: a three-dimensional theory of interpersonal behavior.* New York: Holt, Rinehart and Winston, 1958.

2561) Schwartz, W. Toward a strategy of group work practice. *Soc. serv. Rev.,* 1962, *36,* 268–279.

2562) Scodel, A., & Minas, J. S. The behavior of prisoners in a *"prisoner's dilemma"* game. Columbus, Ohio: Ohio State University Research Foundation, May, 1960. [Tech. Note No. 1, Contract AF 49(638)-317]

2563) Scodel, A., et al. *Some descriptive aspects of two-person non-zero-sum games.* Columbus, Ohio: Ohio State University, April, 1959. [AFOSR TN 59-396, Contract AF 49(638)-317]

2564) Scofield, R. W. Task productivity of groups of friends and non-friends. *Psychol. Rep.,* 1960, *6,* 459–460.

2565) Scotland, E., et al. Group interaction and perceived similarity of members. *J. abnorm. soc. Psychol.,* 1960, *60,* 335–340.

2566) Scott, Frances G. Family group structure and patterns of social interaction. *Amer. J. Sociol.,* 1962, *67,* 214–228.

2567) Seaborne, A. E. M. Group influence on the perception of ambiguous stimuli. *Brit. J. Psychol.,* 1962, *53,* 287–298.

2568) Seashore, S. E., & Bowers, D. G. *Communications and decision processes as determinants of organizational effectiveness. Report of a field experiment.* Ann Arbor, Mich.: University of Michigan, Institute for Social Research, March, 1962. [Final Rep., Contract AF 49(638)-1032]

2569) Sells, S. B. *Abstracts of literature relating to the effectiveness of isolated military groups under stress conditions.* Fort Worth, Tex.: Texas Christian University, October, 1960. (Progress Rep., Appendix No. 2)

2570) Sells, S. B. *Military small group performance under isolation and stress—an annotated bibliography: I. Basic psychology of group behavior.* Fort Wainwright, Alaska: Arctic Aeromedical Laboratory, October, 1961. [AAL TR 61-19, Project 8243-11, Contract AF 41(657)-323]

2571) Sells, S. B. *Military small group performance under isolation and stress—an annotated bibliography: IV. Organizational staffing.* Fort Wainwright, Alaska: Arctic Aeromedical Laboratory, October, 1961. (Tech. Rep. 61-22, ASTIA Document No. 276 830)

2572) Sells, S. B. *Military small group performance under isolation and stress—an annotated bibliography: V. Organizational management and leadership.* Fort Wainwright, Alaska: Arctic Aeromedical Laboratory, October, 1961. (Tech. Rep. 61-23, ASTIA Document No. 276 831)

2573) Sells, S. B. *Military small group performance under isolation and stress—an annotated bibliography: VI. Leadership in formal groups.* Fort Wainwright, Alaska: Arctic Aeromedical Laboratory, October, 1961. (Tech. Rep. 61-24, ASTIA Document No. 276 832)

2574) Sells, S. B. *Tri-service conference on research relevant to behavior problems of small military groups under isolation and stress.* Fort Worth, Tex.: Texas Christian University, 1961. [Contract AF 41(657)-323]

2575) Sells, S. B. *Military small group performance under isolation and stress. Critical review: I. Informal, natural groups: development, structure, and function.* Fort Worth, Tex.: Texas Christian University, June, 1962. [Tech. Documentary Rep. AAL-TDR-62-31, Contract AF 41(657)-323]

2576) Sells, S. B. *Military small group performance under isolation and stress. Critical review: II. Dimensions of group structure and group behavior.* Fort Worth, Tex.: Texas Christian University, June, 1962. [Tech. Documentary Rep. AAL-TDR-62-32, Contract AF 41(657)-323]

2577) Sells, S. B. *Military small group performance under isolation and stress. Critical review: IV. Selection, indoctrination, and training for arctic remote duty.* Fort Worth, Tex.: Texas Christian University, June, 1962. [Tech. Documentary Rep. AAL-TDR-62-34, Contract AF 41(657)-323]

2578) Sells, S. B. *Military small group performance under isolation and stress. Critical review: V. Psychological principles of management and leadership.* Fort Worth, Tex.: Texas Christian University, June, 1962. [Tech. Documentary Rep. AAL-TDR-62-35, Contract AF 41(657)-323]

2579) Sells, S. B. *Symposium on dimensions of stimulus situations which account for behavior variance.* Fort Worth, Tex.: Texas Christian University, April, 1962. [Tech. Rep. No. 1, Contract Nonr 3436(00)]

2580) Sells, S. B., & Braun, J. R. *Military small group performance under isolation and stress. Critical review: III. Environmental stress and behavior ecology.* Fort Worth, Tex.: Texas Christian University, June, 1962. [Tech. Documentary Rep. AAL-TDR-62-33, Contract AF AF 41(657)-323]

2581) Selznick, P. *Leadership in administration.* New York: Harper & Row, 1957.

2582) Sermat, V. Behavior in a mixed-motive game as related to the possibility of influencing the other's behavior. *Amer. Psychologist,* 1962, *17,* 297. (Abstract)

2583) Shapiro, D. *The reinforcement of disagreement in a small group.* Cambridge, Mass.: Harvard University, 1961. (Tech. Rep. No. 2, Contract Nonr 1866(43)]

2584) Shaw, D. M. Size of share in task and motivation in work groups. *Sociometry,* 1960, *23,* 203–208.

2585) Shaw, M. E. A note concerning homogeneity of membership and group problem solving. *J. abnorm. soc. Psychol.,* 1960, *60,* 448–450.

2586) Shaw, M. E. A serial position effect in social influence on group decision. *J. soc. Psychol.,* 1961, *54,* 83–91.

2587) Shaw, M. E. Some factors influencing the use of information in small groups. *Psychol. Rep.,* 1961, *8,* 187–198.

2588) Shears, Loyda M. The effect of variation in power pattern on alliance formation in male tetrads. *Amer. Psychologist,* 1962, *17,* 335. (Abstract)

2589) Shelley, H. P. Focused leadership and cohesiveness in small groups. *Sociometry,* 1960, *23,* 209–216.

2590) Shelley, H. P. Status consensus, leadership, and satisfaction with the group. *J. soc. Psychol.,* 1960, *51,* 157–164.

2591) Sherif, M. Conformity-deviation, norms, and group relations. In I. A. Berg and B. M. Bass (Eds.), *Conformity and deviation.* New York: Harper & Row, 1961. Pp, 159–198.

2592) Sherwood, C. E., & Walker, W. S. Role differentiation in real groups: an extrapolation of a laboratory small group research finding. *Sociol. soc. Res.,* 1960, *45,* 14–17.

2593) Showel, M. Interpersonal knowledge and rated leader potential. *J. abnorm. soc. Psychol.*, 1960, *61*, 87–92.

2594) Shure, G. H., et al. Group planning and task effectiveness. *Sociometry*, 1960, *25*, 263–282.

2595) Shure, G. H., et al. The development and effectiveness of group maintenance functions in the context of task performance. *Amer. Psychologist*, 1961, *16*, 390. (Abstract)

2596) Shure, G. H., et al. Group composition and communication restrictions. *Amer. Psychologist*, 1962, *17*, 335. (Abstract)

2597) Sidowski, J. B., & Smith, M. Sex and game instruction variables in a minimal social situation. *Psychol. Rep.*, 1961, *8*, 393–397.

2598) Sidowski, J. B., et al. Pretraining reinforcement schedules and learning in a two-person interaction. *Amer. Psychologist*, 1961, *16*, 425. (Abstract)

2599) Siegel, S., & Fouraker, L. E. *Bargaining and group decision making: experiments in bilateral monopoly.* New York: McGraw-Hill, 1960.

2600) Skinner, Kathryn K., & Long, R. C. A method for the sequential observation and analysis of group interaction. *Amer. Psychologist*, 1962, *17*, 339. (Abstract)

2601) Small, D. O., & Campbell, D. T. The effect of acquiescence response-set upon the relationship of the F-scale and conformity. *Sociometry*, 1960, *23*, 69–71.

2602) Smith, A. J. The attribution of similarity: the influence of success and failure. *J. abnorm. soc. Psychol.*, 1960, *61*, 419–423.

2603) Smith, A. J. A developmental study of group processes. *J. genet. Psychol.*, 1960, *97*, 29–30.

2604) Smith, W. L. *Social adjustment and interpersonal perception.* Urbana, Ill.: University of Illinois, 1960. [Tech. Rep., Contract Nonr 1834(11)]

2605) Smoke, W. H. *A model for the cost of group decisions.* Ann Arbor, Mich.: University of Michigan, Research Center for Group Dynamics, 1961. [Tech. Rep., Contract Nonr 1224(34)]

2606) Smoke, W. H., & Zajonc, R. B. *Reliable groups of unreliable people.* Ann Arbor, Mich.: University of Michigan, Research Center for Group Dynamics, 1960. [Tech. Rep., Contract Nonr 1224(34)]

2607) Snoek, J. D. Some effects of rejection upon attraction to a group. *Amer. Psychologist*, 1960, *15*, 396. (Abstract)

2608) Snyder, A., et al. Value, information, and conformity behavior. *J. Pers.*, 1960, *28*, 333–341.

2609) Solomon, H. *Group and individual behavior in free-recall verbal learning.* New York: Columbia University, Teachers College, 1961. [Tech. Rep., Contract Nonr 266(43)]

2610) Solomon, L. The influence of some types of power relationships and game strategies upon the development of interpersonal trust. *J. abnorm. soc. Psychol.*, 1960, *61*, 223–230.

2611) Sommer, R. Leadership and group geography. *Sociometry*, 1961, *24*, 99–110.

2612) Speroff, B. J. A "needs or problems" consensus with groups. *Personnel J.*, 1961, *40*, 69–71.

2613) Steiner, I. D. Sex differences in the resolution of A-B-X conflicts. *J. Pers.*, 1960, *28*, 118–128.

2614) Steiner, I. D., & Field, W. L. Role assignment and interpersonal influence. *J. abnorm. soc. Psychol.*, 1960, *61*, 239–245.

2615) Steiner, I. D., & Rajaratnam, N. A model for the comparison of individual and group performance scores. *Behav. Sci.*, 1961, *6*, 142–147.

2616) Stimson, J. Some religious-ethnic differences in interaction rates. New York: New York University, December, 1959. [AFOSR TN 59–1297, Contract AF 49(638)-195]

2617) Stock, Dorothy. Factors determining defensive behavior within groups. Washington, D.C.: National Training Laboratories, 1961. [Tech. Rep. No. 19, Contract Nonr 1147(03)]

2618) Stock, Dorothy, *Group effects on perceptual behavior.* Washington, D.C.: National Training Laboratories, July, 1961. [Tech. Rep. No. 10, Contract Nonr 3088(00)]

2612) Stotland, E., & Cottrell, N. B. Self-esteem group interaction, and group influence on performance. *J. Pers.*, 1961, *29*, 273–284.

2620) Stotland, E., et al. Group interaction and perceived similarity of members. *J. abnorm. soc. Psychol.*, 1960, *61*, 335–340.

2621) Streufert, S. *Attitude generalization in social triads as a function of personality structure and availability of social support.* Princeton, N. J.: Princeton University, undated. [Tech. Rep. No. 10, Contract Nonr 1858(12)]

2622) Strickland, L. J., et al. Effects of group support on the evaluation of an antagonist. *J. abnorm. soc. Psychol.*, 1960, *61*, 73–81.

2623) Strodtbeck, F. L., & Hook, L. H. The social dimensions of a twelve-man jury table. *Sociometry*, 1961, *24*, 397–415.

2624) Strodtbeck, F. L., et al. Phases in group problem-solving. A revision. *Amer. Psychologist*, 1962, *17*, 335. (Abstract)

2625) Stryker, S., & Psathas, G. Research on coalitions in the triad: findings, problems and strategy. *Sociometry*, 1960, *23*, 218–230.

2626) Suppes, P., & Atkinson, R. C. *Markov learning models for multiperson situations: II. Methods of analysis.* Stanford, Calif.: Stanford University, Applied Mathematics and Statistics Laboratory, December, 1959. [Tech. Rep. No. 27, Contract Nonr 225(17)]

2627) Suppes, P., & Krasne, F. Application of stimulus sampling theory to situations involving social pressure. *Psychol. Rev.*, 1961, *68*, 46–59.

2628) Tagiuri, R. *Perceptual and cognitive processes in interpersonal relations.* Cambridge, Mass.: Harvard University, Laboratory of Social Relations, June, 1959. (Contract N5 ORI 07670)

2629) Tagiuri, R., & Kogan, N. Personal preference and the attribution of influence in small groups. *J. Pers.*, 1960, *28*, 257–265.

2630) Taietz, P. Conflicting group norms and the "third" person in the interview. *Amer. J. Sociol.*, 1962, *67*, 97–104.

2631) Tannenbaum, R., et al. *Leadership and organization.* New York: McGraw-Hill, 1961.

2632) Taylor, M., et al. Assessing emerging leadership behavior in small discussion groups. *J. educ. Psychol.*, 1961, *52*, 12–18.

2633) Terauds, Anita, et al. *A bibliography of small group research.* Arlington, Va.: Human Sciences Research, Inc., April, 1960. [HSR-RR-60/2-Gn, Contract AF 49(638)-256]

2634) Thibaut, J. W. *Perceptual and structural factors in group behavior.* Chapel Hill, N.C.: University of North Carolina, Institute for Research in Social Sciences, 1959. [Annu. tech. Rep., Contract Nonr 855(04)]

2635) Thibaut, J. W., et al. *A determinant of the perception of status in small groups.* Chapel Hill, N.C.: University of North Carolina, Institute for Research in Social Sciences, 1960. [Tech. Rep., Contract Nonr 855(04)]

2636) Thomas, E. J. Theory and research on the small group: selected themes and problems. In L. S. Kogan (Ed.), *Social science theory and social work research.* New York: National Association of Social Workers, 1960.

2637) Thomas, E. J., & Fink, C. F. Models of group problem-solving. *J. abnorm. soc. Psychol.,* 1961, *63,* 53–63.

2638) Thompson, J. D., & McEwen, W. J. Organizational goals and environment: goal-setting as an interaction process. In D. Cartwright and A. Zander (Eds.), *Group dynamics: research and theory.* (2nd ed.) New York: Harper & Row, 1960. Pp. 472–483.

2639) Triandis, H. C. Cognitive similarity and communication in a dyad. *Hum. Relat.,* 1960, *13,* 175–183.

2640) Triandis, H. C. Some determinants of interpersonal communication. *Hum. Relat.,* 1960, *13,* 279–287.

2641) Trow, D. B. Membership succession and team performance. *Hum. Relat.,* 1960, *13,* 259–269.

2642) Trumbo, D. A. Individual and group correlates of attitudes toward work-related change. *J. appl. Psychol.,* 1961, *45,* 338–344.

2643) Tuckman, J., & Lorge, I. Individual ability as a determinant of group superiority. *Hum. Relat.,* 1962, *15,* 45–52.

2644) Tuddenham, R. D. Correlates of yielding to a distorted group norm. *J. Pers.,* 1959, *27,* 272–284.

2645) Tuddenham, R. D. *The influence of a distorted norm upon judgments of children and adults.* Berkeley, Calif.: University of California, 1960. [Tech. Rep., Contract Nonr 222(14)]

2646) Tuddenham, R. D. *Studies in conformity and yielding: X. The influence of a distorted norm upon judgments of children and adults.* Berkeley, Calif.: University of California, 1960. [Tech. Rep. No. 11, Contract Nonr 222(14)]

2647) Tuddenham, R. D. The influence of a distorted group norm upon judgments of adults and children. *J. Psychol.,* 1961, *52,* 231–239.

2648) Tuddenham, R. D. The influence upon judgment of the apparent discrepancy between self and others. *J. soc. Psychol.,* 1961, *53,* 69–79.

2649) Tuddenham, R. D. *Studies in conformity and yielding: a summary and interpretation.* Berkeley, Calif.: University of California, 1961. [Final tech. Rep., Contract Nonr 222(14)]

2650) Tuddenham, R. D., & MacBride, P. D. The yielding experiment from the subject's point of view. *J. Pers.,* 1959, *27,* 259–271.

2651) Turk, H. Instrumental values and the popularity of instrumental leaders. *Soc. Forces,* 1961, *39,* 252–260.

2652) Turk, Theresa, & Turk, H. Group interaction in a formal setting: the case of the triad. *Sociometry*, 1962, *25*, 48–55.

2653) Valentine, L. D., Jr. Effect of group differences on obtained validity of aircrew selection tests. *Amer. Psychologist*, 1962, *17*, 380. (Abstract)

2654) Verba, S. *Small groups and political behavior: a study of leadership*. Princeton, N.J.: Princeton University Press, 1961.

2655) Videbeck, R. Self-conception and the reactions of others. *Sociometry*, 1960, *23*, 351–359.

2656) Vinacke, W. E. Sex roles in a three-person game. *Sociometry*, 1959, *22*, 343–360.

2657) Vinacke, W. E., & Bond, J. R. Coalitions in mixed-sex triads. *Sociometry*, 1961, *24*, 61–75.

2658) Vinter, R. D. Small group theory and research: implications for group work practice theory and research. In L. S. Kogan (Ed.), *Social science theory and social work research*. New York: National Association of Social Workers, 1960.

2659) Von Cranach, M. L. Experiments towards formation of judgment in a structure group. *Z. exp. angew. Psychol.*, 1960, *7*, 427–450.

2660) Vroom, V. H. Ego involvement, job satisfaction, and job performance. *Personnel Psychol.*, 1962, *15*, 159–178.

2661) Vroom, V. H., & Mann, F. C. Leader authoritarianism and employee attitudes. *Personnel Psychol.*, 1960, *13*, 125–140.

2662) Wallach, M. A., et al. Group influence on individual risk taking. *J. abnorm. soc. Psychol.*, 1962, *65*, 75–86.

2663) Walters, R. H., & Ray, E. Anxiety, social isolation, and reinforcer effectiveness. *J. Pers.*, 1960, *28*, 358–367.

2664) Walters, R. H., et al. Anxiety, isolation, and susceptibility to social influence. *J. Pers.*, 1960, *28*, 518–529.

2665) Warner, W. S. Behavioral contagion and social power: an experimental study. *Amer. Psychologist*, 1961, *16*, 390. (Abstract)

2666) Weiss, P., & Emmerich, W. Dependency fantasy and group conformity in ulcer patients. *J. consult. Psychol.*, 1962, *26*, 61–64.

2667) Weisskopf-Joelson, Edith, & Eliseo, T. S. An experimental study of the effectiveness of brainstorming. *J. appl. Psychol.*, 1961, *45*, 45–49.

2668) White, R. K., & Lippitt, R. *Autocracy and democracy: an experimental inquiry*. New York: Harper & Row, 1960.

2669) Wiest, W. M., et al. Relationships between individual proficiency and team performance and efficiency. *J. appl. Psychol.*, 1961, *45*, 435–440.

2670) Wilk, R. E. Self-rankings of leader behaviors by peer elected adolescent leaders. *Amer. Psychologist*, 1960, *15*, 389. (Abstract)

2671) Wilkins, E. J., & deCharms, R. *Authoritarianism and power cues*. St. Louis, Mo.: Washington University, September, 1961. [Tech. Rep. No. 12, Contract Nonr 816(11)]

2672) Willingham, W. W. *Methods for deriving standard scores for peer nominations with subgroups of unequal size*. Pensacola, Fla.: Naval School of Aviation Medicine, May, 1959. (Tech. Rep. No. 27, ASTIA Document No. 230 336)

2673) Willner, Dorothy (Ed.) *Decisions, values, and groups.* New York: Pergamon, 1960.

2674) Wilson, K. V., & Bixenstine, V. E. Forms of social control in two-person, two-choice games. *Behav. Sci.*, 1962, *7*, 92–102.

2675) Wilson, R. S. Personality patterns, source attractiveness, and conformity. *J. Pers.*, 1960, *28*, 186–199.

2676) Wilson, W., & Miller, N. Shifts in evaluations of participants following intergroup competition. *J. abnorm. soc. Psychol.*, 1961, *63*, 428–431.

2677) Wolman, B. B. Impact of failure on group cohesiveness. *J. soc. Psychol.*, 1960, *51*, 409–418.

2678) Woolman, M. Group proficiency, dependency on supervisors, and morale. *Amer. Psychologist*, 1960, *15*, 419. (Abstract)

2679) Worchel, P. Self-enhancement and interpersonal attraction. *Amer. Psychologist*, 1961, *16*, 349. (Abstract)

2680) Wright, B., & Ewitts, Mary S. Direct factor analysis in sociometry. *Sociometry*, 1961, *24*, 82–98.

2681) Wrightsman, L. S., Jr. Effects of waiting with others on changes in level of felt anxiety. *J. abnorm. soc. Psychol.*, 1960, *61*, 216–222.

2682) Wurster, C. R., et al. *A test of the proposition: we want to be esteemed most by those we esteem most highly.* Baton Rouge, La.: Louisiana State University, November, 1960. (Tech. Rep. No. 28, Contract N7 ONR 35609)

2683) Zajonc, R. B. *The effects of feedback and group task. Difficulty on individual and group performance.* Ann Arbor, Mich.: University of Michigan, Research Center for Group Dynamics, November, 1961. [Tech. Rep. No. 15, Contract Nonr 1224(34)]

2684) Zajonc, R. B. *The requirements and design of a standard group task.* Ann Arbor, Mich.: University of Michigan, Research Center for Group Dynamics, 1961. [Tech. Rep. Contract Nonr 1224(34)]

2685) Zajonc, R. B. The effects of feedback and probability of group success on individual and group performance. *Hum. Relat.*, 1962, *15*, 149–162.

2686) Zajonc, R. B. A note on group judgments and group size. *Hum. Relat.*, 1962, *15*, 177–180.

2687) Zajonc, R. B., & Smoke, W. H. Redundancy in task assignments and group performance. *Psychometrika*, 1959, *24*, 361–369.

2688) Zajonc, R. B., & Taylor, J. J. *The effect of two methods of varying group task difficulty on individual and group performance.* Ann Arbor, Mich.: University of Michigan, Research Center for Group Dynamics, May, 1962. [Tech. Rep. No. 21, Contract Nonr 1224(34)]

2689) Zander, A., & Havelin, A. Social comparison and interpersonal attraction. *Hum. Relat.*, 1960, *13*, 21–32.

2690) Zander, A., et al. Personal goals and the group goals for the member. *Hum. Relat.*, 1960, *13*, 333–344.

2691) Zander, A. et al. Unity of group, identification with group, and self-esteem of members. *J. Pers.*, 1960, *28*, 463–478.

2692) Zander, A. F. *Effects of group goals upon personal goals.* Washington, D.C.: National Training Laboratories, National Education Association, 1961. [Tech. Rep., Contract Nonr 3088(00)]

2693) Ziller, R. C., & Behringer, R. D. Assimilation of the knowledgeable newcomer under conditions of group success and failure. *J. abnorm. soc. Psychol.*, 1960, *60*, 288–291.

2694) Ziller, R. C., & Behringer, R. D. A longitudinal study of the assimilation of the new child in the group. *Hum. Relat.*, 1961, *14*, 121–133.

2695) Ziller, R. C., et al. Group creativity under conditions of success-failure and variations in group stability. *Amer. Psychologist*, 1960, *15*, 429. (Abstract)

2696) Ziller, R. C., et al. The minority newcomer in open and closed groups. *J. Psychol.*, 1960, *50*, 75–84.

2697) Ziller, R. C., et al. *A longitudinal study of the assimilation of the new child in the group.* Newark, Del.: University of Delaware, August, 1961. [Tech. Rep. No. 3, Contract Nonr 2285(02)]

2698) Ziller, R. C., et al. The newcomer in open and closed groups. *J. appl. Psychol.*, 1961, *45*, 55–58.

2699) Zolman, J. F., et al. Distance and conformity in continuous social influence interactions. *J. soc. Psychol.*, 1960, *52*, 251–257.